EARLY CHRISTIAN CHAPELS IN THE WEST

Decoration, Function, and Patronage

The Mausoleum of Galla Placidia, Ravenna. View of the interior.

GILLIAN MACKIE

EARLY CHRISTIAN CHAPELS IN THE WEST:

Decoration, Function, and Patronage

UNIVERSITY OF TORONTO PRESS
Toronto Buffalo London

© University of Toronto Press Incorporated 2003
Toronto Buffalo London
Printed in Canada

ISBN 0-8020-3504-3

Printed on acid-free paper

National Library of Canada Cataloguing in Publication

Mackie, Gillian Vallance, 1931–
 Early Christian chapels in the west : decoration, function and
 patronage / Gillian Mackie.

 Includes bibliographical references and index.
 ISBN 0-8020-3504-3

 1. Chapels – Italy – History – To 1500.   2. Mausoleums – Italy –
 History – To 1500.   3. Saints – Cult – Italy – History – To 1500.
 I. Title.

 NA5613.M32 2003   726'.4   C2002-903563-5

University of Toronto Press acknowledges the financial assistance to
its publishing program of the Canada Council for the Arts and the
Ontario Arts Council.

This book has been published with the help of a grant from the Humanities and Social Sciences Federation of Canada, using funds provided by
the Social Sciences and Humanities Research Council of Canada.

University of Toronto Press acknowledges the financial support for its
publishing activities of the Government of Canada through the Book
Publishing Industry Development Program (BPIDP).

Contents

Illustrations follow page 222

Illustrations

Frontispiece. The Mausoleum of Galla Placidia, Ravenna. View of the interior.

Fig. 1 Rome, Constantinian martyr churches and cemetery basilicas (after Krautheimer, *Three Christian Capitals* © The University of California Press). A – Lateran Basilica; B – St Peter's; C – S Sebastiano; D – SS Marcellino e Pietro; E – S Lorenzo; F – S Agnese; G – St Paul's.

Fig. 2 The Shrines of Sts Peter and Marcellinus and of St Tiburtius at the Catacomb of SS Marcellino e Pietro, Rome. (Longitudinal section, courtesy of Guyon.) A – portico; B – altar-tomb of St Tiburtius; C – upper mausoleum; D – Constantinian Basilica; E – underground room containing F – altar-tomb of Sts Peter and Marcellinus.

Fig. 3 Rome, Basilica Apostolorum (now S Sebastiano) and its chapels, plan (after Deichmann and Tschira, 1957). A – apse of basilica; B – mausoleum of the Uranii; C – 'Platonia.'

Fig. 4 Rome, S Sotere in the nineteenth century (after Grabar, following De Rossi 1854).

Fig. 5 S Sinferosa, plan (after Stevenson, 1878).

Fig. 6 The Via Latina Catacomb, plan (courtesy of Tronzo and of Ferrua).

Fig. 7 Milan ca. 400. Plan showing locations of churches and chapels (after Krautheimer, *Three Christian Capitals* © The University of California Press). 1 – SS Nabore e Felice; 2 – S Valeria; 3 – S Vitale; 4 – Basilica Ambrosiana; 5 – S Vittore in Ciel d'Oro; 6 and 7 – S Simpliciano and its chapel.

Fig. 8 S Simpliciano, Milan, and its chapel. Plan (after Krautheimer, *Three Christian Capitals* [© The University of California Press]). A – chapel; B – basilica.

Fig. 9 Ravenna, plan of city, ca. AD 500 (after Testi-Rasponi).

Fig. 10 S Vitale, Ravenna, plan (after Gerola), showing location of earlier chapels. A – site of S Vitale *memoria*; B – site of St Ursicinus *memoria*; C – Sts Gervasius and Protasius; D – Sts Nazarius and Celsus.

Fig. 11 Mosaic floor of *memoria* of St Vitalis below the pavement of S Vitale, Ravenna, showing relic container beneath the altar, and the position of its four supports (after Farioli, courtesy of Longo Editore).

Fig. 12 Ravenna, Plan of S Croce with chapels, from the 1926 excavations (after Di Pietro). A – mausoleum of Galla Placidia; B – chapel, probably S Zaccaria; C – S Croce.

Fig 13 S Croce and the Mausoleum of Galla Placidia, before 1602, as reconstructed by Ricci. Courtesy of the Soprintendenza ai Beni Architettonici e Culturali di Ravenna.

Fig. 14 Milan, S Lorenzo and Chapels (after Chierici). A – S Lorenzo; B – 'Sacristy chapels'; C – S Ippolito; D – S Aquilino with E – atrium; F – S Sisto.

Fig. 15 S Lorenzo from the SE. Foreground, L, S Aquilino. Distance, R, S Ippolito.

Fig. 16 S Vittore al Corpo, Romanesque basilica: drawing by an anonymous Dutch artist (ca. 1570), Stuttgart, Staatsgalerie, Graphische Sammlung, Inv. 5781r. L to R in middle distance: Campanile and apse of S Vittore; imperial mausoleum, possibly that of Maximian,

Photos by author unless otherwise attributed.

Abbreviations

AAVV	Autori varii
AJA	*American Journal of Archaeology*
ActaSS.	Acta Sanctorum
Acta R.Norv.	*Acta ad Archaeologiam et Artium Historiam Pertinentia*
AMSI	*Atti e memorie della società istriana di archeologia e storia patria*
ArtBull.	*Art Bulletin*
Atti della pont. acc.rom.di arch.	*Atti della pontificia Accademia romana di archeologia*
Atti del R. Istituto Veneto di S.L.A.	*Atti del Reale Istituto Veneto di scienze, lettere ed arti*
BABESCH	*Bulletin Antieke Beschaving*
BAC	*Bulletin d'archéologie chrétienne = Bullettino di archeologia cristiana*
BAR	*British Archaeological Reports*
BASD	*Bulletino di archeologia e storia dalmata*
BZ	*Byzantinische Zeitschrift*
CahArch.	*Cahiers archéologiques*
CBCR	*Corpus Basilicarum Christianarum Romae*
CC	*Corpus christianorum*
Cod.Top.	*Codice topografico della città di Roma*
CorsiCRB	*Corsi di cultura sull'arte ravennate e bizantina*
CPER	*Codex Pontificalis Ecclesiae Ravennatis*
CSEL	*Corpus scriptorum ecclesiastorum latinorum*
DACL	*Dictionnaire d'archéologie chrétienne et de liturgie*
DOP	*Dumbarton Oaks Papers*
DOS	*Dumbarton Oaks Studies*
ECBA	*Early Christian and Byzantine Architecture*

FR	*Felix Ravenna*
FSI	*Fonti per la Storia d'Italia*
HLRE	*History of the Later Roman Empire*
ILCV	*Inscriptiones Latinae Christianae Veteres*
J.Eccl.Hist.	*Journal of Ecclesiastical History*
JSAH	*Journal of the Society of Architectural Historians*
JWCI	*Journal of the Warburg and Courtauld Institutes*
Lexicon	*Niermeyer, Mediae Latinitalis Lexicon Minus*
Loeb	Loeb Classical Library
LP	*Liber Pontificalis*
LPER	*Liber Pontificalis Ecclesiae Ravennatis of Agnellus*
MGH	*Monumenta Germaniae Historica*
– *AA*	*Auctores antiquissimi*
– *ScriptRerLangob*	*Scriptores rerum langobardicarum*
– *ScriptRerMerov*	*Scriptores rerum merovingicarum*
– *ScriptRerGerm*	*Scriptores rerum germanicarum*
– *SS*	*Scriptores*
N&PNF	*A Select Library of the Nicene and Post-Nicene Fathers of the Christian Church*
NBAC	*Nuovo Bullettino (Bolletino) di Archeologia Cristiana*
NOAB	*The New Oxford Annotated edition of the Bible with the Apocrypha*
ODB	*Oxford Dictionary of Byzantium*
ODCC	*Oxford Dictionary of the Christian Church,*
PBSR	*Papers of the British School at Rome*
PG	*Patrologia Graeca*
PL	*Patrologia Latina*
PLRE	*Prosopography of the Later Roman Empire*
RAC	*Rivista di archeologia cristiana*
RACAR	*Revue d'art canadienne/Canadian Art Review*
RendPontAcc	*Atti della pontificia accademia de archeologia. Rendiconti*
RevArch	*Revue Archéologique*
RIS	*Rerum italicarum scriptores*
VAHD	*Vjesnik za arheologiju i historiju dalmatinsku (formerly Bulletino di archeologia e storia dalmata: BASD)*
Zbornik Radova	Zbornik Radova Vizantoloskog Instituta
n.d.	no date
n.p.	no page numbers
n.s.	new series
n.t.	no title

Acknowledgments

I would like to express my warmest thanks to the many individuals and institutions who have made my work possible and enjoyable during my study of medieval chapels.

This book has grown out of my doctoral dissertation on early chapels, which I completed at the University of Victoria. I owe my greatest debt to John Osborne, my adviser and friend not only during the period of my studies, but subsequently as well. We have looked at many of the buildings that are discussed here together, and I greatly appreciate his encouragement and advice, generously given throughout the past two decades. I would also like to mention the friendship of Janice Helland and Lesley Jessop, once my fellow students, whose special interests in the broad field of art history have been inspirational to me.

Much of this work was done in Italy, where I was able to use the excellent facilities of the British School at Rome as my base. The help of Maria Pia Malvezzi in gaining me access to buildings and sites not normally open to the public, both in and out of Rome, gave me the chance to obtain material at first hand, rather than only out of books. The British School's library is especially rich in my area of interest: Late Antiquity and the early Middle Ages. I am indebted to the librarian, Valerie Scott, for making it such a pleasant and accessible place to work, and for making the library's rare books available to me. I have also used the facilities of several of the other outstanding libraries in Rome: the Bibliotheca Hertziana, the library of the École Française de Rome, and the Biblioteca Apostolica Vaticana. In each of these I spent many productive hours. The Warburg Library in London has also been a major resource, and in Victoria, the library staff at the University of Victoria have been extremely helpful. The writing phase of the book was made easier in the summer of 2000 by the use of a study at the University of Washington's Whiteley Center in Friday Harbor.

Among the many friends with whom I have shared travel and discussion in Italy and at home, I would like to mention fellow students and scholars in Rome, too numerous to name individually, and the members of the Medieval Art Research Group in Victoria, among them Catherine Harding, the director of Medieval Studies there.

I especially appreciate the friendly interest, patience, and support of Barbara Porter, my editor at the Press, and the meticulous care of James Leahy, who undertook the gargantuan task of copy-editing the manuscript, imposing order wherever it was lacking. The final form of the book owes a lot to their skill and attention to detail.

My work has been generously supported by the Social Sciences and Humanities Research Council of Canada at the doctoral and postdoctoral levels, and my continuing work is funded by a research grant from the same organization. The University of Victoria has generously given a grant towards the cost of the colour frontispiece.

Lastly, I very much appreciate the interest which members of my family have shown in my work. George Mackie has enhanced many of the photographs and plans which illustrate this book, with the result of greatly increased clarity and legibility. He, and our sons and daughters – Alexander, Christina, Richard, Rachel, and Quentin – have accompanied me on research trips, put me up in London, in France, and in Italy, and come up with new approaches and insights in discussion, as well as helping me acquire necessary computer skills. I owe a great deal to them all, and dedicate my book to them.

EARLY CHRISTIAN CHAPELS IN THE WEST

Origins, Semantics, and Functions of the Early Christian Chapel

The Edict of Milan of 313, which allowed Christianity legal status as a religion following the conversion of the emperor Constantine, marked the beginning of a period of remarkable change both in Roman society and in the Church. In this period the acceptance of Christianity by the imperial family, followed gradually by other powerful and wealthy Romans, was marked by a surge of patronage.[1]

The provision of splendid new cult buildings, great basilicas for liturgical celebrations, and baptisteries for initiation rites quickly followed. But other, less imposing structures were also built, the buildings which we know as chapels. The period between the fourth and the seventh centuries was marked by the rise of the cult of the saints and the resulting proliferation of memorial chapels over the graves of the martyrs. Funerary structures for Christian burial beside the saints, shrines for the commemoration of martyr remains, and multi-purpose buildings combining funerary and memorial functions soon followed. But burial structures for the cult of the dead, while of primary importance, were not the only types of chapel to be built. Many others were built in domestic settings for the private devotions of the laity and clergy, and these chapels were also often sanctified with relics of the saints. Sacristies were also built in or beside congregational churches, to serve the practical needs of the sacred mysteries.

This book brings together the scattered information about chapels in the West in the first four centuries of organized Christianity. The main focus geographically is on North and Central Italy, along with the Istrian coast, which formed an integral part of the Upper Adriatic area in Late Antiquity. The very few chapels remaining above ground will prove to be the most revealing, as their decorative schemes can be analysed for iconographic content and thus for meaning and function. Obviously, these few chapels cannot be said to represent the 'average' early medieval chapel, since they have quite fortuitously survived the hazards, among them earthquakes, fire, redecoration, rebuilding, and replacement, as well as neglect, that have decimated their fellows. For this reason the case studies of the survivors will be considered in the second half of the book, after the broader context of the many lost chapels which are known to us from documentary or archaeological sources has been laid out in the introductory chapters.

The greatest number of the lost chapels are recorded from the three imperial capitals of the fourth century in the West, consecutively Rome, Milan, and Ravenna. Chapels also occurred in smaller communities, where they were the focus of the devotion of local congregations. Those which survive in the cities around the upper Adriatic, in a broad arc between Verona and Pula, are chosen here to represent the many other provincial chapels which are scattered throughout Italy and Istria.

One question, though, must be settled before the subject of chapels in Late Antiquity and the early Middle Ages can be discussed at all. This question is one of definition: what is meant by the word 'chapel'? In twentieth-century usage a small, free-standing consecrated building which is 'too small' to be a church is a chapel, and so is a space set aside within a church by means of a full or partial interior wall. A room in a house which is set aside and furnished for private prayer also evokes the image of 'chapel.' But do these stereotypes accurately reflect the situation in Late Antiquity?

The derivation of the word chapel is at once revealing and puzzling. It comes from the medieval Latin *cappella* or *capella*, which came into use in this context only in the seventh century. Initially, the word *capella* did not refer to a building but to a specific relic, the cloak of St Martin of Tours (ca. 316–97), the *Capella Martini*, most precious possession of the Merovingian kings, which was carried in state before them when their itinerant lifestyle took them from one to another of their capitals. By extension, the word came to be used of the tent in which the relic was displayed.[2] Thus, the word *capella* was used for the very specific contents of one particular temporary building, which was built and rebuilt for the sole purpose of housing one particularly venerated relic, and it was only later, and initially in Gaul, that by extension any building containing sacred objects or relics was also called a *capella*, and that this word came to refer to a 'church that does not have the full parochial powers.'[3]

Chapels, however, had existed for centuries before Merovingian times, and a whole variety of words were used in this early period to express the different shades of meaning and function that are now covered by the single word 'chapel.' These words, which were borrowed by the Christians from everyday Latin, frequently reveal a logical relationship between their basic meaning and their sense in the Christian context. Therefore these original terms which described the Christian chapel throw light on its ancient function, about which the word *capella* remains silent. In this way, subtle nuances of meaning which were once revealed semantically can be recaptured.

The Latin language accurately distinguished one chapel function from another by use of such words as *oratorium, oraculum, cella, cubiculum, crypta, confessio,* and *memoria* or *martyrium,* with their precise shades of meaning.[4] Thus an *oratorium* or an *oraculum* was a place set aside for prayer, and a *confessio,* originally a 'confession of faith in martyrdom,' came to mean a place where relics were kept, and by the fifth century, a 'burial place of martyrs,' the tomb of a martyr under an altar. *Memoria,* a mortuary monument, tomb of a saint, or shrine containing relics of a saint, had a similar meaning, but was usually applied to the whole building, or to the altar dedicated to a saint there, rather than to the grave or relic container itself.

More general terms sometimes used for the chapel included *crypta,* a subterranean vault or cave, and *cella,* which, though originally merely a room, became a monk's cell or by extension, a minor monastery, with *cellula,* a monk's dwelling, also coming to mean chapel, or even private church. *Cubiculum,* originally a resting or sleeping chamber, a bedroom, came to mean a chapel used for rest in the auxiliary buildings of a church, its annexes or colonnades. Here also in the funerary context, the dead would sleep until the last trump: by extension, the word *cubiculum* was also used for the tomb itself that was the chapel's raison d'être.

By the ninth century, private chapels which were adjacent to churches were even described by the term *monasterium,* with a primary meaning of monastery, monastic community, abbey church, or even cathedral church. The prime user of the term is Agnellus, in his Chronicle of the Bishops of Ravenna (the *Liber Pontificalis Ecclesiae Ravennatis*) where many buildings known on other grounds to have been annexed chapels, rather than monasteries or even full-size churches, were described as *monasteria.* This is the most common word of all those that Agnellus used for chapel in the ninth century.[5] Implicit in this use is the idea that chapels were built most frequently by ecclesiastics, members of monastic communities, usually with their own burial in mind, as emerges clearly from a study of Agnellus's Chronicle. Alessandro Testi Rasponi found that, while the ninth-century usage refers above all to private structures used for private prayers and burial, the origin of the use of the term lay in the late fifth century, when groups of monks cared for the martyrs' graves. The term *monasterium*, therefore, comes within the scope of this book.

Another term which acquired the meaning 'chapel' relatively late is *altare*, the word for the altar itself, with the plural form *altaria* also often used in the singular sense.[6] In pagan times this meant a small above-ground building, which was reserved for the cult of an individual among the many gods, in whose honour sacrifices took place there.[7] An *ara* was a smaller altar that served rather for supplications and libations. The *altare* was mainly for the service of the gods, while the *ara* served the cult of the dead. The word *altare* was adopted in just the same way for the cult of the Christians' god, and became the table where the liturgy of the One God was celebrated. Perhaps it is no coincidence that the liturgy embodies a commemoration of sacrifice. The *altare* had a flat, table-like top surface, the *mensa*. The Fathers usually reserved the word *ara* for the pagan altar.[8] It is interesting that by the late ninth century, *altare* had acquired an expanded meaning: a lateral chapel of a church.[9] There is considerable evidence, however, that as early as the mid-seventh century, and perhaps much earlier, extra altars inside actual church buildings were being provided with settings and embellishments, and coming to serve as chapels, places of the private liturgy, of private prayer, and even of burial. The prime example of this sort of 'altar-chapel' is the chapel of Pope John VII (705–7) in Old St Peter's.

Despite all these opportunities for defining chapel functions through the use of semantics, it is clear that the great majority of all early medieval chapels to have survived until today are, broadly speaking, funerary in nature. They originated as *memoriae*, and while primarily concerned with the cult of a martyr or martyrs, were also almost immediately chosen as the most favoured places for burial. While there is scattered literary evidence for the existence of domestic oratories, and a unique example survives in the palace of the Archbishops of Ravenna, my main subject-matter will be funerary in nature.

In general, *memoriae* tend to have originated as free-standing chapels. In a later development, a basilica was often built beside the *memoria* in the service of the cult. The two buildings would then be joined by way of a vestibule. The *memoria* was usually chosen at a later date as a burial place by the rich and mighty, taking on a secondary role as a funerary chapel. In the city of Rome, and probably elsewhere, private chapels in the houses of the wealthy might also evolve into parish churches or *tituli* by the addition of public congregational spaces.

Detailed case studies of two important decorated chapels will follow the survey of chapels in the imperial capitals and in the north-east, in chapter 6. In the case of S Vittore in Ciel d'Oro, Milan, the documentation provided in St Ambrose's writings is crucially important to the interpretation of the iconographic program, while in the S Prisco chapel of St Matrona there is no early documentation at all, and the iconographic program and legend of the saint take the place of the lost written records.

A special category of funerary chapel, the imperial mausoleum as built by the Christian emperors, is considered in terms both of the evolution of a functionally Christian structure from the traditional pagan one, and of its further modification by the Visigothic and Ostrogothic rulers for their needs. Study of these structures also gives the context for the Mausoleum of Galla Placidia in Ravenna, which is one of the most perfectly preserved of all early Christian chapels, and yet has the hallmarks of imperial patronage. Its attribution to the empress is strengthened by the interpretation of its decorative scheme, and a purpose is suggested for its creation.

All these funerary and commemorative structures were sanctified by relics or by actual martyr graves, and so could only be built according to Roman law and custom in the cemetery areas outside the walls of cities. Later, though, this law was relaxed, and the seventh-century *martyrium* of S Venanzio, inside the walls of Rome at the Lateran Baptistery, represents the apex of the series *cella memoriae*, funerary chapel, *martyrium*. It was built to house relics that had been gathered together far from the martyrs' actual graves and long after their deaths, and epitomizes the communal martyr shrine.

The existence of shrines devoted to noncorporeal relics – that is, without martyr graves or bones – is also discussed in terms of position, use, and function. These chapels are represented by the fifth-century shrines built by Pope Hilarus at the Lateran Baptistery, as well as those built not long after by Pope Symmachus at the Vatican. These chapels may not only have doubled as domestic oratories for the use of the donor, but signified the power of the papacy and the legitimacy of its 'high priest,' the Pope.

The difficult question of the change from annexed chapels to those built within the confines of church buildings is also considered. This change appears to take place around the sixth century but is not well defined, though connected to the doctrine of the one altar. Internal chapels fall into three main categories: the early *cubicula* in auxiliary buildings, which were used both for prayer and for rest in life and in death; the internal *oratoria* and *altaria*, which are products of the later development allowing multiple altars each to act as a focus of a separate dedicated space; and *sacraria*, here loosely called sacristies, meaning chapels given over to the practical and auxiliary needs of the clergy and congregation.

Place of prayer, relic shrine, burial place, sacristy: these continued to be the main functions of the chapel throughout the Middle Ages. Their relationships, and the changing emphasis given to the functions of the chapel as place of prayer, martyr shrine, and burial place, are revealed in the decorative and architectural programs of the chapels which survive from the first four centuries of organized Christianity in Italy and Istria.

PART ONE

The Context of the Chapels in Italy and Istria: History, Archaeology, and Topography

CHAPTER ONE

Martyr Shrine to Funerary Chapel

The Imperial Capitals – Rome, Milan, Ravenna

The end of the persecution of Christians after the Edict of Milan in 313 was followed by an explosion of interest in the cult of martyrs. The saints were honoured at their grave sites and also at their places of martyrdom. The earliest shrines marking the martyrs' graves were small memorial chapels, *cellae memoriae*. The tradition of building mausolea over the tombs of wealthy or important people was not a new or even a specifically Christian idea, but had a long history in pagan Rome. Earlier generations of Christians had venerated the graves of the martyrs, despite the danger of doing so, and by these means memory of the gravesites had been maintained. For example, the site of St Peter's tomb appears to have always been remembered, and graves have been found clustering around it in the Vatican cemetery. Now, though, the cult of the important Christian dead, the martyrs, spread rapidly, and they were venerated openly as heroes by the whole Christian community.

The veneration of the martyrs' graves followed a common pattern. The first stage was the erection of small buildings to shelter the gravesites. These *cellae memoriae* then became focal points for the piety of other Christians, who wanted to be buried near the saints, and whose graves clustered around the martyrs' tombs. Sometimes the chapels had to be enlarged to accommodate the many people who wanted this privilege. Finally, it seems, burial beside the saints came to be reserved for the great: archbishops, bishops, and the most wealthy laity. By the early sixth century, it was rare for anyone except the upper echelons of the clergy and the imperial family to be buried *ad sanctos*. At this period, there was another wave of building activity and many of the smaller chapels were enlarged and redecorated with attention to the symbolic power of both architectural form and decoration in paint or mosaic. The individuals who joined the martyr at his tomb were recorded in portraits, inscriptions, or verses, and the new decorations embodied their hopes for salvation and eternal life.

During the fourth and early fifth centuries, martyr shrines had been confined to the cemeteries outside the walls of cities, according to Roman burial law.[1] In Rome, for example, memorial chapels clustered around the cemetery basilicas of the Constantinian era above the martyr tombs which lay in the catacombs below (fig. 1). Much can be learned about the building and renovation of funerary chapels and martyrs' *memoriae* by considering them in the context of the three cities which were in turn capitals of the western empire: Rome, Milan, and Ravenna.

Rome

Rome, as the traditional capital of the West throughout the times of persecutions, was rich in sites connected with the martyrs, their lives, deaths, and burials. But an understanding of the Roman situation is hampered not only by the richness of the material, but by the three-dimensional nature of the burial sites, which consist of many layers of below-ground catacomb galleries in which both ordinary Christians and the saints were buried, plus chapels at ground level above. These probably served mainly as memorials to the saints, and frequently doubled as family burial chapels. This was because there was great reluctance to raise or disturb the bodies of the martyrs in Early Christian Rome, although disturbance must sometimes have happened as we can surmise from imperial edicts which forbade it.[2] Almost all above-ground chapels have disappeared, but the scanty evidence available will be assembled here, though a study of the smaller centres, especially of Milan and Ravenna, will give a clearer picture.

Among surviving Roman chapels at the top level of patronage are the mausoleum at the left flank of the Constantinian cemetery church of S. Agnese on the Via Nomentana, where the two daughters of Constantine, Constantina and Helena, were buried; and, in ruins, a structure that was similarly attached to the narthex of the fourth-century cemetery church of SS Pietro e Marcellino on the Via Labicana, the mausoleum of Helena, mother of Constantine (location, fig. 1; plan, fig. 43). These structures, along with the other imperial mausolea in Milan and Ravenna, constitute a special category of funerary chapel, and will be discussed as a separate group.[3] On a more humble scale, however, also located beside SS Pietro e Marcellino, there is a small, rectangular, apsed chapel, now dedicated to the Roman martyr Tiburtius,[4] and in use as the chapel of the Sisters of the Holy Family (fig. 43). Its south-east corner touches the outer curve of the basilical apse, but it is off axis to it, and may antedate it. Since it rises over the tomb chapel of Peter and Marcellinus in the catacomb below, to which it is connected by a monumental staircase, it may well be their original memorial, and Guyon believes its altar held their relics (fig. 2).[5] Nothing remains of its original decoration. It is the sole survivor of a whole group of earlier chapels and mausolea on the Via Labicana, many of which were discovered in the excavations of 1896.[6] These included a circular structure five metres in diameter, with the remains of a sarcophagus, and a groin-vaulted cruciform chapel with four niches, which was seen by Antonio Bosio,[7] and was probably the two-storey structure, already in ruins before 1569, that was illustrated by P. Ligorio.[8]

The situation at SS Pietro e Marcellino is paralleled by that at S Lorenzo fuori le mura in the Campo Verano, where excavations have revealed a Constantinian funerary basilica with its annexed chapels, while two other shrines discovered in the nineteenth century and now lost revealed traces of the decoration, in one case, and of the dedication, in the other. The decorated chapel was a small, rectangular, apsed structure which retained traces of the lower part of fifth- or sixth-century decorations, evidently of standing saints.[9] The other chapel was a triconch, discovered in 1857 near the north corner of the S Lorenzo quadriporticus, and believed to date from shortly after AD 384.[10] Its function as a martyr shrine of an otherwise unknown Leo, Bishop of an unidentified diocese outside Rome, was revealed by De Rossi, who was able to match a partial inscription found at the site with another large fragment found in S Gregorio Magno, which had originated at the Campo Verano. Together, they consisted of the text of a poem engraved on the upper part of a *transenna*, the funerary inscription of the martyr. The shrine remained in use at least until the late eighth century, when it was repaired by Hadrian I (772–95); it then disappears from the records.[11]

Traces of chapels, attached along the north wall, have also been discovered at the cemetery basilica of the Campo Verano. Their ruined walls reveal nothing of their function or decoration, though their location makes it almost certain that they were funerary chapels.[12]

At the funerary basilica *ad catacumbas* on the Via Appia, originally dedicated to the Apostles, but now known as S Sebastiano, much more survives of the annexed chapels (plan, fig. 3).[13] The complex is typical of the Roman situation in this period. The earliest chapels antedated the basilica, and were either obliterated when it was built, or annexed to it as accessory structures. One small chapel on each side, slightly off axis both to the basilica and to each other, falls into the latter category. Krautheimer found that as soon as the perimeter wall of S Sebastiano had been completed, chapels sprang up along its sides, especially on the south, where a large apsed chapel was entered from the ambulatory by a surviving, but bricked-up, triple arcade. This chapel was soon replaced by two smaller apsed structures, which survive in the present-day convent, converted to secular use. Another large and slightly later chapel was reached through a narthex with apsed ends. Slightly later still, but still of early date, as evidenced by its brickwork, is the so-called Mausoleum of the Uranii. Partly rock-cut, and with lateral niches, it measures twelve metres across, and bears the same relationship to the cemetery basilica as does Constantina's mausoleum (now S Costanza), which it strongly resembles in ground plan, to S Agnese. Three more mausolea, separated by a gap and by one of the 'off-axis' chapels, were positioned near the apse. The two nearest the apse survive, but underground, and may be substructures for surface chapels now lost. A last major structure at this end of the church is the 'Platonia,' an apse-shaped structure reached through its flat side, originally by means of a trapezoidal narthex. This has nine large, rectangular niches in the thickness of its walls, and a later descending staircase at the rounded end.

The nearby cemetery of S Callisto on the Via Appia also retains an above-ground chapel, a triconch (fig. 4), dedicated to S Sotere and now re-roofed and in use as a small church.[14] It is one of two surviving in that area.[15] A similar triconch chapel is known from mile nine on the Via Tiburtina, where foundations of an early Christian basilica have been revealed lying apse to apse with the older trichoran structure, believed to be the martyrium of S Sinferosa and her seven sons (fig. 5).[16]

Stripped of decoration, or lying in ruins, these examples do little more than underline the popularity of both the centrally planned and the apsed chapel in the funerary setting. Grabar suggested that the situation at S Sinferosa proved that the triconch was an architectural form especially chosen for the *memoriae* of martyrs, since it appears to have had no communication with the exterior save through the sanctuary of the basilica. However, since the entire layout of the *memoria* is not shown in Stevenson's plan, doubt remains on this point.[17] In either case the altar of the church was sanctified by the proximity of the martyrs' remains, which were those of Sinferosa and her seven sons.[18] Choice of the triconch form, closely associated with the architecture of the dining chamber of classical times, with its multiple sigma couches placed in niches, is probably connected to the custom of the funerary banquet or *refrigerium*, which was celebrated at the graveside on the anniversary of death.[19] The basilica must have been added to house the numerous pilgrims which the martyrs' cult generated.

Another Roman martyr with seven sons who was twice celebrated in a painted chapel was St Felicitas. One, in the catacomb of Maximus (now called St Felicitas) on the Via Salaria, was built by Pope Boniface I (418–22), to mark the saint's actual grave.[20] The other was discovered in 1812 in a room of Nero's *Domus Aurea*, facing the Colosseum on the Oppian hill beside the Baths of Titus, and so inside the city walls. Its paintings, which have now disappeared, were recorded in a drawing by Giorgio Mariani,[21] and although originally thought to be from the fourth or fifth century, have more recently been assigned to the seventh century on the basis of their iconography.[22] It is believed that this chapel marked a specific site in the passion of St Felicitas, the place of her imprisonment.

These examples of early chapels associated with the cemeteries outside the walls of Rome can give only the faintest idea of the richness and variety of the funerary structures which once sprang up in all the Christian graveyards along the roads out of the city. None survives with decoration: few even retain their dedications, and little can be inferred from their architecture when so few of the chapels which survive come securely documented as to function or donor. The situation is also complicated by the presence of martyrs' burials below ground in the catacombs. In fact, perhaps the best idea of the lost architecture and decoration of the chapels on the surface can be gained from these subterranean structures. One catacomb in particular, although relatively small and simple in its layout, and not sheltering a martyr's remains, is remarkable for both its architecture, rich in chapels, and its paintings. This is the catacomb discovered in 1955 on the Via Latina. The catacomb was constructed in several stages, starting in the early fourth century, and probably completed before the turn of the fifth.[23] It consists of a set of galleries which open out at various points into small rooms with arcosolia (plan, fig. 6). These rooms also serve as ante-chambers for other small chapels, about a dozen in all. All except two are stuccoed and painted. Some retain their marble sarcophagi and are demarcated by marble transennae. Loculus burial is kept to a mini-mum, with only the entrance and one other gallery devoted to these graves. Christian and pagan burials occur in a random fashion, and it is necessary to pass through pagan areas to reach Christian chapels, and vice versa. Not surprisingly, the themes of salvation and the after-life are common to both religious groups. It is evident that the Via Lat-ina catacomb was a private cemetery for people of means. Tronzo has drawn special attention to the fourth and last construction phase, which appears to have been a commercial venture.[24] Its architecture was of an unusual type for Rome, hinting at an Eastern influence. Yet this diversity of architecture is what best reflects the little that we know of the above-ground funerary buildings and martyria of late-fourth-century Rome.

The architectural variety is also the result of the particular condi-tions in the tufa: underground there is freedom from functional con-straints which would otherwise require that columns and lintels be weight-bearing, that vaults be supported so that they could not col-lapse, and so on. When a chapel is carved out of solid tufa, the space is hollowed out and an illusion of support is created, but the pillars and capitals, the bases and lintels are all equally illusory, doing nothing structural but satisfying the eye that is accustomed to architectural spaces being composed of these standard components. Thus vaults bil-low and chapels leave the safety of square and rectangular form for the hexagon, sometimes irregular; for lobed and pleated spaces; and for arcosolia pushing out the walls of square and rectangular chambers, with the illusion of depth and space magnified by the painted decora-tion. Nevertheless, it is the use of the standard components of 'real' architecture that makes us sure that the subterranean chapel copies the surface one, and then indulges in flights of fancy, rather than the reverse.

It is not, therefore, the more creative spaces of the Via Latina cata-comb that are most relevant to our theme, but the basic shapes that relate most directly to above-ground architecture: the square, vaulted chamber with a column 'supporting' the vault in each corner (fig. 6, B and N) and the rectangular *cubiculum* with a terminal arcosolium forming a rectangular apse, framed with columns or left plain (fig. 6: E, C). Also of interest is the basic cross-shaped structure, square with an arcosolium niche pushing out each of the three walls across from the entry, which is itself positioned in a fourth (fig. 6, A). This type of structure, immensely popular in above-ground architecture, persisted through Late Antiquity and the Middle Ages, to be revived by Renaissance architects. Hybrids between these types also existed in the Via Latina catacomb, such as the terminal *cubicula* of the two galleries, which are rectangular and have a shallow, rectangular niche on each side and a deep, terminal niche with its own tiny apse.

Just as the subterranean architecture mimics that of the world above, so also the painted ornament relates to the sculptural or mosaic enrichments of the above-ground buildings. Painted imitations of real coffered ceilings occur in the Via Latina catacomb in the barrel vault of the entrance corridor to Phase IV and, from the same phase, in the large hexagonal chamber of six columns and six exits.[25] Mosaic vaults are also imitated in paint: the vault of *cubiculum* N has an interlocking pattern of crosses and large and small hexagons which is identical with that of the entrance bay at S Costanza, which also dates from around AD 350. The latter probably represents an application of mosaic floor technique to a vault, but appears not to be a true floor pattern but a reminiscence of real architectural coffering, an imitation of exactly the same sort as the Via Latina painted vaults.

It goes without saying that the third element of the decor of the chapels – the figural painting with religious content – must also have reflected the decoration of the above-ground mausolea, of which so little survives, in content and iconography. Salvation imagery, with parallels from the Old Testament, will in all probability have constituted the major theme above ground, just as it does in the catacombs.

In summary, our knowledge of the Early Christian cemetery chapel in Rome, whether martyrium or funerary chapel, can only be gleaned from the fragmentary remains of a representative few above ground, backed up by our knowledge of the subterranean *cubicula* which are closely related to them. Outside Rome, however, the situation is very different, for chapels actually survive from the cemetery areas outside the ancient walls of Milan, Ravenna, and Capua which have retained substantial amounts of their original decorations. These are S Vittore in Ciel d'Oro in Milan, the chapel of S Matrona at S Prisco, near S Maria in Capua Vetere, and the Mausoleum of Galla Placidia in Ravenna: all are here discussed as 'case studies.' These, all of which have retained a large part of their decorations, epitomize others known only from archaeological or literary evidence, or surviving with little or nothing of their decorative programs intact. Milan and Ravenna both have numerous examples of these. In addition, Early Christian chapels survive in Verona, Vicenza, and Padua, and in Istria at Poreč and Pula, and archaeological remains give us some idea of similar structures at Concordia and Grado.[26] Not far away, at Rimini, an Early Christian chapel, cruciform in shape with a narthex and two corner rooms, was excavated in 1860 and then lost. In central Italy, remains of Early Christian chapels can be found at Bologna, Ancona, and at Narni, while in the south, the church of S Maria della Croce at Casaranello, Apulia, incorporates a fifth-century chapel, complete with its mosaic decoration, in the crossing of the transept. S Leucio, Brindisi, also incorporates an early chapel, and near Siracusa, Sicily, two undecorated Early Christian chapels of Latin cross form survive, while near Noto a triconch chapel, the Trigona of Maccari, associated with the catacombs there, has been tentatively dated to the sixth century or a little later. It is clear that such chapels were once widespread in Italy and Istria, but that most of them have vanished from our knowledge.[27]

Milan

Milan became the Roman capital in the West in the mid-fourth century, a status it maintained until 402, when Honorius moved his court to the more easily defended city of Ravenna. Milan benefited during its period as imperial capital from the presence of St Ambrose as bishop, and his writings are invaluable source material for Early Christian Milan and its martyr cult. Ambrose's writings also contain valuable information about the martyr shrines and mausolea that were erected in the Christian graveyards of the city. At Milan, as at Rome, there was a cemetery on each of the major roads leading out of town (plan, fig. 7). The most important was in the *Hortus Philippi* outside the Porta Vercellina: here the Basilica Ambrosiana, originally dedicated to the martyrs, and only later to Ambrose, arose in the *Coemeterium ad martyres*. Other cemeteries were situated outside the Porta Orientale, centred on the Basilica of the Saviour, later known as S Dionigio; on the Via Romana, around the Basilica of the Apostles; and outside the Porta Comasina, around the Basilica Vergine, now S Simpliciano.

The largest Christian cemetery, and the one about which the most is known, is the *Coemeterium ad martyres*. The graves of various martyrs

were honoured there after the Peace of the Church by the erection of
cellae memoriae. All but one of these shrines have disappeared. The solitary survivor is the chapel of S Vittore in Ciel d'Oro, now incorporated
into the Romanesque basilica of S Ambrogio as a chapel to the right of
the apse, but formerly a free-standing structure. The lost chapels
included those of saints Nabor and Felix, Valeria, and Vitalis, all
known from texts and archaeological remains, and all, like S Vittore,
orientated to the street plan of Roman Mediolanum.

The chapel of S Vitale was probably built by Ambrose for the
remains of two saints, Vitalis and Agricola, which he found in Bologna
in 393 and brought back to Milan.[28] It lay about 70 metres behind the
apse of the Ambrosiana, and has been convincingly identified with
the *Basilica Faustae* to which Ambrose took the newly discovered bones
of saints Gervasius and Protasius, passing a night of vigil over them
there.[29] This structure was referred to as 'Ecclesia Fausti in Vinea, ista
ecclesia nunc dicitur S.Vitalis' in the later Middle Ages.[30]

Approximately 40 metres away beside the present Via S Valeria,
another small chapel survived until 1786: it was dedicated to Valeria,
who according to tradition was wife to Vitalis, an officer in the imperial army. Vitalis, his *Acts* tell us, died at Ravenna, buried alive at a
place known as the Palm Tree.[31] Valeria herself suffered martyrdom on
her way back to Milan after his death. However, an inscription from
this chapel, recorded but lost, mentions its occupants as Aurelius Dio-
genes and Valeria Felicissima, Confessors of the Faith,[32] casting doubt
on Valeria, the martyr, and suggesting her identity as a member of the
Valerii, a wealthy family. This would identify this structure as an aristocratic burial chapel, rather than a martyrium.[33]

Beyond this again, out to the back of the Ambrosiana apse, to the
south of the Via Vercellina, lay another martyr chapel, dedicated to
saints Nabor and Felix. This is the building mentioned by Ambrose in
his letter to his sister Marcellina, in which he describes finding the bodies of Gervasius and Protasius, the sons of Vitalis, 'before the chancel
screen of saints Felix and Nabor,' where he identified them by their
extraordinary size.[34]

This group of pre-Ambrosian and Ambrosian chapels at the *Coemeterium ad martyres* is the largest but not the only group of Milanese martyr chapels of the fourth century to survive in fact or in memory. At the
Basilica Vergine on the Como road, the cruciform structure attached to
the east side of the left transept has now been revealed as an Early
Christian chapel (fig. 8). There is little doubt that it was used by

Ambrose's successor, Simplicianus, who was bishop from 397 to 400, as a martyrium for the Trentine saints, Sisinnius, Martirius, and Alexandrus, who were martyred in Val di Non (Anaunania) on 29 May 397. The remains of these decapitated martyrs were divided between Trento and Milan, the bodies being sent by Bishop Vigilius of Trento to Simplicianus, who had educated and ordained them, while the heads remained in Anaunania.[35] The chapel was originally a detached structure, adjacent and parallel to the apse of the church.[36] It was unusual for a martyrium in that it took the form of a *croce libera*, with no atrium, and possibly took the place of an earlier and very modest building, since reused material was included in the walls.[37] Almost certainly the original chapel was pre-Ambrosian, and the basilica was built beside it in honour of the saints buried there.[38]

On the Via Romana, in the cemetery around the Basilica Apostolorum (now S Nazaro), inscriptions record various *cellae memoriae*, which probably included one now incorporated underneath the present S Calimero, marking the place of martyrdom of the fourth bishop of Milan, who died here around AD 200. Another inscription marked the place of martyrdom and burial of Nazarius and Celsus, which, according to the mid-fifth-century chronicle of St Celsus, was 'extra portam foras portam Romanum in locum qui dicitur tres moros.'[39] Whereas the body of Nazarius, his head miraculously uncorrupted, was moved to the Basilica Apostolorum by Ambrose,[40] it seems that that of Celsus was left in the *cella memoriae* which rose over the actual place of the saints' death under Nero, around AD 57. St Eustorgius (ca. 345/6–ca. 347/8) is also presumed to have been buried outside the Porta Ticinese, where the Romanesque basilica of Sant'Eustorgio probably occupies the site of his *memoria*.[41]

This sort of replacement was a normal development. *Cellae memoriae* often became the nuclei of new church buildings as the martyr cult expanded. The passionate desire of the faithful to be buried beside the martyrs caused this to become the burial of choice for both bishops and nobility. And in the Milan area in Ambrose's time it was obviously acceptable to move martyr bones in certain circumstances. These included pious reasons, such as their use in the consecration of new churches. Gervasius and Protasius, for example, were not left in peace before the chancel screen at the chapel of Nabor and Felix where Ambrose found them, but were moved to the Basilica Ambrosiana, where they still lie under the high altar beside the remains of Ambrose himself. Nevertheless, whether the martyrs' remains had been removed or not, the sites of martyrdom and of burial continued to be venerated, and the simple memorial chapels underwent transformations into the lavishly decorated shrines of which a few representative specimens survive today.

For Milan, aside from the now undecorated chapel at S Simpliciano, the type-specimen for the martyr shrine is S Vittore in Ciel d'Oro, a chapel which retains a good part of its fifth-century decorations. The simpler structure that it supplanted, dating from the time of Ambrose, consisted of an apsed trapezoidal structure, roughly five metres wide and eight long, and orientated from NE to SW, in accordance with the Roman street plan. Its low apse was supported on the outside by buttresses and was framed at one time by paired columns on the inside of the arch, of which only the bases survive.[42] The chapel was lit by three arched windows in the apse and another in each of its long sides. An upper set of three taller windows on the same axes in the apse, with two more on each of the side walls, were at a later date blocked with masonry, while the lower ones were heightened in compensation. This change was probably associated with an early change to a semi-domed from a pyramidal apse roof.[43] The original roof of the trapezoid was probably also of wood, like the first apse, and was later replaced by a small cupola made of *tubi fitilli*, hollow for lightness, and arranged in a series of circular courses. This change probably dates from the period when the chapel was vaulted so as to receive its mosaic decoration.[44] Such building campaigns were frequently undertaken and few of the martyrs' *memoriae* survived in their original states. The primary purpose of rebuilding must have been to shelter and honour the martyrs' remains. Equally important, these holy tombs were to be made safely accessible to the faithful. This was done at S Vittore by placing them in the crypt, where they became the focus of pilgrimage, and, though physically separated from the devotees, were visible to them through a grating or *fenestrella confessionis*.[45]

The chapel of S Vittore, best documented of all early Christian martyr shrines, will be discussed in detail in a later chapter: it demonstrates the sequence from the tomb of the martyr through its development as a focus of pilgrimage to its final conversion as a very grand burial site.[46] Here Satyrus, brother of Ambrose, Bishop of Milan, was to lie beside the saint and await his resurrection, in the company of the martyr who would speak for him on the last day, and ensure a favourable outcome at the threshold of Paradise.

S Vittore in Ciel d'Oro was not the only Milanese *memoria* to be converted into a funerary chapel for a Christian aristocrat. The early bishops of Milan also chose such burial as the most efficacious for their salvation. In the fourth century, Bishop Maternus,[47] for example, was buried in the chapel of Nabor and Felix, while Bishop Monas, another early-fourth-century incumbent, was buried at S Vitalis. His body remained there until the deconsecration of the chapel in 1576.[48] Bishop Simplicianus was also interred at S Vitalis, according to the Milanese itinerary of around 798,[49] and only subsequently moved to S Simpliciano, probably between 650 and 680.[50] Others of the ecclesiastical hierarchy – among them Calimerus (probably late third century),[51] Mirocles (ca. 314), Protasius, (ca. 343–4), Eustorgius (ca. 344–55), and Ambrose – also lay in the cemeteries outside the walls, though not in the *memoriae* of the martyrs. The law requiring burial outside the walls was adhered to in Milan, but it is less clear that there was any reluctance to relocate or even divide up the martyrs' bodies. Examples of both processes abound. For example, the Lodi martyrs, Nabor and Felix, were transferred to the episcopal centre, Milan, while the bodies of the Trentine martyrs were sent to S Simpliciano though their heads were kept for Trento.[52] The relics of Bishop Maternus were also divided after death, the head going to the cathedral, though the body remained at S Nazaro. Milan was rich in martyrs, thanks to the zeal with which Ambrose searched the surrounding region for them, bringing them into the city for burial and commemoration.

Ravenna

Ravenna is the third great capital which will be surveyed for evidence of the cult of martyrs and of the chapels connected with the cult, two of which – the Mausoleum of Galla Placidia and the Archbishops' Chapel, S Andrea – survive almost intact with their mosaic decorations. These chapels will be considered in detail in a later section. Although Ravenna cannot match Milan in the number of its local or regional martyrs, or in the stature of its most famous bishop, Ambrose, it has one extraordinary asset: the ninth-century cleric Andrea Agnellus, who has left in his Chronicle a rich source of information not only on the early bishops, but on their buildings and their burial places, their epitaphs, their portraiture, and the topography of their city, much of which was still visible half a millennium after the early days of Ravenna as Western capital.

One of the most interesting features of the removal of the imperial court to Ravenna in 402 was its effect upon religious life and architecture in the new location. Ravenna, a city founded by Augustus, was more easily defended and provisioned than Milan, as it commanded both the Via Emilia and the mouth of the Po river. But before 402, it had been a small city, surrounded by walls and divided by canals. Soon after the relocation of the capital, new land was added to the city. A zone outside the walls to the north-west, Regio II, the imperial quarter, was the site of a new palace and of its palace church, S Croce, as well as of many other new churches and chapels, mostly founded by the emperors, with a few built by clerics upon land which the emperors had given to the church (plan, fig. 9).[53] Regio II was probably, for a while at least, outside the walls of the city, and for the practical purposes of burial remained outside the walls of the *pomoerium*, which was defined by the walls of the original, rectangular city of the first century AD.[54] The new quarter was the region where the Honorian family built chapels to commemorate the saints whose relics and cults they had brought with them from Milan. The saints were those dear to Ambrose, who had deeply influenced the faith of the imperial family. Chapels and churches also proliferated at Classis, the nearby Adriatic naval base, home port to 250 vessels; and in Caesarea, the area between Classis and Ravenna, where the suburban cemeteries of both cities spread out along the road that joined them.

Although it is obvious that the imperial family felt a deep need for the patronage of the saints, and for their *praesentia*,[55] a need which led them both to carry their relics to Ravenna with them and to build shrines there to house them, it is not known what exact form these relics took: bodies, body parts, or contact relics. Ambrose himself, in a letter to his sister Marcellina, makes it clear that he accepted the moving of the physical remains of saints if he was persuaded that it was God's will.[56] Thus, when following a dream he found the bodies of Gervasius and Protasius before the chancel screen of the Naboriana in Milan, he had no hesitation in moving them into his new basilica, although they were already buried in consecrated ground.[57] Although in general saints' bodies were moved only to save them from danger or dishonour, it is clear that Ambrose also needed Gervasius and Protasius for his own ends: both for the dedication of his church[58] and to sanctify the space under the altar. This was the site which he had chosen for his own burial, on the grounds that a priest should be interred in the place where he had celebrated the sacred mysteries during his lifetime. Although Ambrose did give the saints the place of honour within the grave, it is clear that he was planning a burial *ad martyres* on a very grand scale for himself.[59] Nor was it even inconceivable that saints' bodies could be divided up, as the Trentine martyrs had been, their bodies translated, their heads remaining at the place of martyrdom. In this respect the practice of Milan during the lifetime of Ambrose (ca. 339–97) differs markedly from that of Rome two centuries later under Gregory the Great (ca. 540–604), if his letter to the empress Constantina represents his real views on the moving and dismemberment of martyrs' bodies.[60] But Gregory's letter should perhaps be interpreted as an attempt to protect Rome's treasured relic, the head of St Paul, from the covetousness of Constantinople, as there is no direct evidence for Roman practice in the fourth century.[61] In Milan, however, Ambrose's letter to Marcellina makes it clear that the creation of 'contact relics' was widespread, and that the manufacture of relics was seen to be central to the practice of miraculous healing.[62] Contact relics maintained their popularity and were in widespread use in Rome at the later period, as Gregory's letters attest.[63]

Although theoretically the palace in Ravenna was in an area outside the walls, where burials of human remains would have been legal, the scanty evidence seems to point to the relics having been noncorporeal. The actual relics have in all cases disappeared. However, the container in the relic altar of the shrine of Vitalis beneath S Vitale was only 15 centimetres deep, suggesting that here, at least, the relics included neither a whole body nor any of the major bones of the saint (fig. 11).[64] The implication is that the emperors did not remove the bodies of Milan's saints to Ravenna, but contented themselves with relics such as *brandea*, cloths that had been in contact with the martyrs' bodies and so acquired their merits.

Among the group of chapels with Milanese dedications in the imperial patrimonium at Ravenna, the best known lies underneath S Vitale (fig. 10, A). Its existence was probably never entirely forgotten. It could be contacted through an opening or 'well' in the floor of the sixth-century church, at a depth of 70 centimetres below the present floor, which dates to 1539.[65] The visible part consisted of the base of the altar, with reliquary box and traces of the four colonnettes that had held up the *mensa*. This was surrounded by a mosaic pavement, centred on a central panel with a large *cantharos*, surrounded by scanty vegetation and brilliantly coloured paradise birds: peacocks, parrots, pheasants, partridges, and doves (fig. 11). On either side of this panel was a tract of ornamental mosaic: one in meander design, signifying eternity; the other, a fragmentary strip only, is of woven tresses, while a twist pattern passed behind the altar. Excavations have revealed that the first chapel had been an apsed rectangular structure, 8.5 metres long, and that this was later modified into a Latin cross, probably in the third decade of the sixth century.[66] The mosaic of the original chapel has been dated to the fifth century, three centuries after the supposed date of Vitalis's death, 28 April 171, in the persecutions of Marcus Aurelius and Lucius Verus. According to tradition the chapel occupies the site of Vitalis's grave, though this is open to doubt, for Vitalis was one of two saints whose bodies were brought to Milan from Bologna in AD 393 by Ambrose, who found their burial place in the Jewish cemetery of Bologna on 4 November 392, and recognized it by the instruments of their passion which were buried with them.[67] The cult of Vitalis then made a further transition, to Ravenna, while that of his companion, Agricola, stayed in Milan.

The history of the cult of Vitalis in Ravenna helps to explain the function of the small memorial chapel during the fifth century. We learn that a fifth-century legend gave Ravenna, pitifully short of martyrs, a whole family of patron saints who supposedly suffered martyrdom there. This legend connected the saints of the imperial chapels into a family dynasty, and had them suffer death for their faith at a place called 'the Palm-Tree,' which is now covered by Justinian's church of S Vitale. The linchpin of this legendary tale, which first appeared in an anonymous letter attributed to Ambrose,[68] was Vitalis, whose martyrdom is there described. He supposedly suffered torture on the rack and death at the Palm-Tree, as a penalty for encouraging his confessor, Ursicinus, in martyrdom. Vitalis's wife Valeria has already been encountered in Milan: according to the Ravenna legend, she died for her faith on her way home from Ravenna because she refused to eat meat sacrificed to the pagan gods. Gervasius and Protasius have also already been encountered, this time in the writings of Ambrose, who described the discovery of their bodies in Milan. In the Pseudo-Ambrose text, Vitalis is their father, Valeria, their mother. Fedele Savio has deduced that the letter of Pseudo-Ambrose was written in Ravenna, away from Ambrose's home ground, Milan, where a forgery would have run greater risk of being exposed, and that its origins lay in the struggle of the Ravenna bishopric for independence from Milan in the time of Peter Chrysologus, soon after 425.[69] This sort of fabrication is evidence for the growing interest in the cult of the saints, sole source of power for good in a malevolent world.[70] Saints were believed to look after their own devotees, whether emperor or bishop, who might pray for personal salvation or for the good of the congregation or the state. Obviously it had become desirable to provide the capital of the West, seat of the Augusti, with the prestige of its own dynasty of martyrs and its own place of martyrdom to rival Rome's Colosseum. This development may well date to the time of construction of S Vitale on the 'Palm-Tree' site, in AD 526, which would have marked the location of the church as an especially holy place of martyrdom.[71] Certainly by the mid-sixth century its site was associated with the martyrdoms of both Vitalis and the other Ravenna saints. Indeed, the new church building probably supplanted not only Vitalis's original shrine, but three of the other chapels which the Honorian family had dedicated to their patron saints (fig. 10).[72]

The saints in question were Nazarius and Celsus, Gervasius and Protasius, and Ursicinus. The sixth-century domed side chambers or sacristies at S Vitale probably replaced two previous chapels on the site with the same dedications, Gervasius and Protasius on the left and Nazarius and Celsus on the right. The cult of Ursicinus, the 'martyr of Illyria,' was centred below the arcade to the left of the altar (fig. 10, B).[73] Scholars have suggested that the layout of S Vitale was deliberately orientated so as to absorb all four of the Honorian sites,[74] though this cannot be proved since the S Vitalis primitive chapel is the only one whose physical remains have been identified.

To return to the early period, we know of several other chapels of the emperors' choice clustered around the palace and its church (plan, fig. 9). Testi-Rasponi describes the chapels around S Croce as 'una corona di sacelli, che rammentavano i santuari che a Milano non erano discosti da quel palazzo imperiale.'[75] These chapels, in addition to those dedicated to the Milanese saints, now honoured others who had topical interest for the early fifth century. Among these were John the Baptist and his father Zachariah, whose relics were discovered in AD 415 at Kapper-Gamala. A chapel dedicated to Stephen the first martyr must have subsequently become the core chapel of Maximinian's Basilica of St Stephen (550).[76] The chapel attached to the narthex of S Croce, and known as the Mausoleum of Galla Placidia, was probably dedicated not to the Roman saint Lawrence as tradition declares, but to Vincent of Saragossa, an influential Spanish martyr.[77] Behind it lay a dodecahedral shrine of the Virgin, which was probably built soon after the Council of Ephesus in 431. Part of this chapel survives as the nine-sided sanctuary of the church of S Maria Maggiore. Its three missing sides were replaced by a nave in the time of Bishop Ecclesius, around 526, and the apse was decorated with a mosaic which showed the bishop presenting his model of the church to Mary.[78] The original centrally planned structure was typical of a Marian shrine since this architectural form was often chosen for its symbolic meaning in the early Middle Ages. According to Richard Krautheimer, many of the centrally planned churches which are dedicated to the Virgin have a common origin, and relate back to the circular shrine in the Valley of Josaphat in Jerusalem which had been raised over Mary's tomb.[79] This structure, and its adjacent basilica, were still extant in 870, when they were recorded by the monk Bernard in his *Itinerary*.[80] Krautheimer traces this pair of structures back to the sixth-century *Itinera Hiero-solymitana*,[81] though the date of construction is not known, and archaeological evidence has not yet been forthcoming. By crusader times, the shrine had been rebuilt as a longitudinal basilica.[82] Probably the circular shrine at the Virgin's tomb was the model for the Ravenna builders, though its form gradually came to express other layers of symbolic meaning. Thus the Temple in Jerusalem, which had been rebuilt in a circular form after its destruction by Titus in AD 70, came to symbolize many significant events in the Virgin's life: her childhood in the Holy of Holies, her presentation and her betrothal, in addition to her virginity, her pregnancy, and her symbolic identity with the Church.[83]

Krautheimer, in his 1969 postscript to the earlier paper, mentions the Ravenna apse as 'a decagon, dated 534' that would require further documentation to prove that its original dedication was to Mary. Originally an even greater polygon, a dodecahedron, it seems Bishop Ecclesius went to considerable pains to save it and incorporate it into the new church, implying that it was of unusual beauty and that its dedication as a shrine of the Virgin fitted his plans for a larger church in her honour. At any rate, it must surely have existed before the basilica, and have dated from much earlier than 534. What relic the shrine possessed is not known.

Another chapel founded by the Augusti was dedicated to Zachariah, the father of the Baptist. Agnellus, writing in the ninth century, attributes it to Singledia,[84] niece of Galla Placidia, though no such relative is known.[85] It is, however, possible that the name is a corruption of Sounigilda, wife of the Goth Odoacer, who may subsequently have been buried there: Agnellus records that this burial place of 'Singledia' was known personally to him. The chapel, literally an arrow's flight from Galla Placidia's S Croce, was probably cruciform, or at least decorated with crosses: it owned liturgical vessels given by Galla Placidia herself, which by the ninth century were stored in the treasury of the Basilica Ursiana, Ravenna's cathedral. The inscription on the chalice, 'OFFERO SANCTO ZACHARIA GALLA PLACIDIA AUGUSTA,' suggests that Placidia may herself have been the patron of the chapel, which was probably built soon after 415, when there was a resurgence of interest in the cult of Zachariah, resulting from the discovery of his tomb.[86] Galla Placidia had the opportunity to build it at that time, since she returned to Ravenna late in 416 as a young widow, and shortly afterwards married her second husband, who was raised to the purple that year as Constantius III. Surely this was a likely time to have built her church of S Croce. The excavations of Giuseppe Cortesi discovered that the narthex of S Croce was originally symmetrical, with a second cruciform chapel opening from its north end, a mirror image of the Mausoleum of Galla Placidia (figs. 12 and 13). The subject of its floor mosaic, a fight between a soldier and a mythical beast, the hydra, which can be interpreted as an allegory of the soul's fight against death, as well as its cruciform ground plan, persuaded Cortesi that this was the chapel of S Zaccaria.[87] Cortesi also suggested that the basilica, rather than being the palace church, was just another cemetery basilica outside the walls of Ravenna, an idea which fits well with its cruciform shape and its annexed mausolea. However, this solution creates more problems than it solves, since the location of Galla Placidia's palace and its church where she had passed her nights in prayer would then be unknown.[88]

Close to S Zaccaria, so close that Testi-Rasponi refers to them as 'due sacelli quasi abbinati,'[89] was the chapel of Zachariah's son John the Baptist,[90] where Galla Placidia interred her own confessor, Barbatianus.[91] This chapel survived until the early sixteenth century, under a new dedication to Barbatianus, who had now achieved sainthood through contact with the relics of John the Baptist.

One more chapel in the imperial region first appears in the historic record for the seventh century, when Agnellus mentions it in the biography of Bishop Reperatus (671–7).[92] Northernmost of the 'crown of chapels,' and located near Ravenna's western gate, it was dedicated to Apollinaris, Ravenna's only truly local saint, and was near the public mint, which gave the chapel its designation, *in Veclo*. There is some doubt whether this chapel was an Honorian foundation, especially as Cortesi, who found its presumed remains, dated it to the seventh century. It was cruciform, appropriately for a funerary chapel.[93] By the late eighth century it had become part of the monastery from which Bishop Gratiosus came to the bishopric around 785.[94]

To sum up, the imperial family's piety and devotion to the saints gave rise to an extraordinary cluster of chapels in or near their new quarter in Ravenna. They continued in their devotion to those saints whom Ambrose had discovered and made popular in Milan: Gervasius, Protasius, Nazarius, and Celsus, as well as Vitalis and Victor, whom he had brought to Milan from Bologna. The emperors also built shrines for important biblical figures whose cults were emerging in the early fifth century – Stephen the Protomartyr, the two saints John, Zachariah, father of the Baptist, and the Virgin Mary – as well as for Vincent of Saragossa, to whom Galla Placidia seems to have owed particular devotion. Almost all these buildings were outside the early-fifth-century walls of Ravenna: theoretically it is possible that all housed, and were sanctified by, corporeal relics of the saints. It seems even more likely, however, that contact relics or other items hallowed by proximity with the saints were involved, since they were believed to absorb the actual power and presence of the holy being. Several of the structures had already, in the time of the emperors, become mausolea: this may be true of S Zaccaria, with the burial of Singledia-Sounigilda, and was certainly the case at S Giovanni Battista, funerary chapel of Galla Placidia's confessor, Barbatianus. Galla Placidia was also the probable patron of the well-known chapel at S Croce that bears her name: its decoration shows it to have been designed as a mausoleum, though it is not known if anyone was ever buried there, or even precisely for whom it was destined. The evidence has been interpreted as pointing to the projected occupant being the empress herself, together with some other member of her family, perhaps her second husband, Constantius III, or the children of her marriage to him. I will suggest another solution, that she intended it for the the burial of Theodosius (b. 414 or 415, d. 415), infant son of her marriage to the Visigothic king, Ataulf.

Although the greatest number of the chapels built in Ravenna in its early days as capital were imperial benefactions, other wealthy patrons also built churches and chapels. One of the best documented was the basilica of S Lorenzo, built by Lauricius, an official at Honorius's court. This was situated just outside the city in Caesarea and survived until 1553. Agnellus describes how Lauricius misappropriated imperial funds for his building, which was equipped with chapels and luxuriously decorated. One of the chapels, which was dedicated in 435 to saints Stephen, Gervasius, and Protasius, was used for Lauricius's own burial.[95] Agnellus tells us it was marvellously decorated with golden mosaic, with different kinds of stone (perhaps marble intarsia), and with stucco reliefs. His account of the architecture is confusing, leaving it unclear whether the chapel had an anteroom or narthex before the chamber where the sarcophagus lay. The room, or perhaps the ante-chamber, had an inscription in gold letters to the right of a mosaic picture of three boys.[96] These three boys have been tentatively identified, by Testi-Rasponi for example, as the three boys in the fiery furnace; a common salvation motif in Early Christian funerary art. He suggested that the picture may have been balanced by another on the other side of the inscription: Daniel in the Lions' Den. Since the description is vague, it has also been suggested that the picture of the three boys may have been of the three dedicatory saints, who were actually named in the inscription as Gervasius, Protasius, and Stephen.[97] Gervasius and Protasius, earlier shown in Milan as of markedly different age in S Vittore in Ciel d'Oro, had by this time in Ravenna achieved iconographic stability as young men, twins.[98] Stephen was also always depicted as a young man. The coincidence of having a triple dedication to three youthful male saints, and a single picture of three young boys, might seem to favour the latter interpretation. However, there are many pre-cedents in funerary art for depiction of the boys in the fiery furnace. It seems quite possible that this was another image of deliverance, com-parable to the many pictures in the Roman catacombs where the three boys, orant figures in short tunics, stand at prayer among the flames: an eloquent symbol of deliverance through prayer and of belief in the power of God.[99]

The chapel Lauricius built was only one of a number, probably all designed for burial, which clustered around the basilica of S Lorenzo. This was a typical fifth-century funerary basilica in the cemetery out-side the walls. In Agnellus's extraordinary story of the building of the basilica by means of misappropriated imperial funds, he recounts how Lauricius tried to hide from the emperor the fact that he was building a church and not a palace. He quotes Lauricius as saying that the 'palace' he is building has, among other rooms, 'cubilia promiscua ad ipsius domus suffulta,'[100] describing his church as if it were a dwelling, but in the reference to 'cubilia promiscua' indicating that there were many chapels, comparable to bedrooms, of which his own was probably the grandest, since he was the founder.

The burial of bishops beside the saints in their *memoriae* continued, and many early chapels seem to have been ecclesiastical rather than court benefactions. Among these was the original burial place of St Severus, first bishop of Ravenna, who was present at the Council of Sardica, ca. 343. Severus's original burial was in a room of a villa in Classe, perhaps his own family dwelling. Later, an adjacent room was given to the cult of St Ruphilus, bishop of Forlimpopoli in the fourth or fifth century, giving Severus an *ad sanctos* burial. In the time of Bishop John II Romanus (578–95), a basilica was raised beside these two chapels, and Severus was re-interred in the centre of the church.[101] Another such '*monasterium*' or chapel, probably of the late fourth century, lay just outside the city, not far from the Porta Nova. It was dedicated to the Illyrian, S Pullione. It is mentioned only once, as the burial place of the late-fourth-century Bishop Liberius III.[102] Little is known of this bishop except that his portrait may have been displayed over his tomb, since Agnellus gives a physical description of him.[103] However, another source for the likenesses of the bishops existed in Agnellus's time: an altar frontal with embroidered portraits of the twenty-eight early incumbents. Given by Maximinian to his cathedral, the Basilica Ursiana, it showed all his predecessors in office, and could well have been Agnellus's source. The frontal itself, though, must have been based on its own sources: in all probability the portraits, now lost, above the burial chambers of the bishops. Such burial portraits, in mosaic, have been found in the Galleria dei Vescovi in the Catacomb of S Gennaro in Naples in the arcosolia above the gravesites of the fifth-century bishops of Naples, and of Quodvultdeus, Bishop of Carthage, who died in Naples in 454 (fig. 62).[104]

Liberius's predecessor, Florentius, was also buried in a funerary chapel which may have been situated at his patrimony, rather than in a cemetery.[105] The chapel, later dedicated to S Petronilla, was situated on the Via Caesarea. It was eventually annexed to the fifth-century Basilica Apostolorum (now S Francesco).

Outside the walls of Classis, in the cemetery area between that city and Ravenna, lay the cemetery basilicas of S Probo, a furlong from S Apollinare in Classe, and S Severo, between that church and the Ponte Nuovo, Ravenna. Both of these cemetery churches were associated with earlier chapels. Near S Probo, for example, was the '*ecclesia*' of S Eleucadius, first burial place of the saint, an early bishop of Ravenna.[106] It probably consisted of a funerary chapel, from which his body was later moved to S Probo. Bishop Severus, also, had been laid to rest in a *memoria*, that of St Ruphilus, on his death in the mid-fourth century.[107] The site was later chosen for the funerary basilica of S Severo, to which the chapel was annexed. Severus's body was placed in the new altar, and a ciborium was placed over it by Archbishop John II (578–95). In a similar fashion, the sole survivor of the many cemetery basilicas, S Apollinare in Classe, was built in the sixth century beside or perhaps above the *memoria* of Apollinaris.[108]

These cases clearly show an evolution in the burial practices of bishops in Early Christian Ravenna. The earliest bishops were buried according to the customs of their class on their family property. After the Peace of the Church, when major churches were built both in the city and at the cemeteries, these were chosen as burial sites, and the bishops lay under the pavement or in annex chapels. It was not until the late sixth century, under Archbishop John II, that an episcopal mausoleum was prepared for all (or most) of the subsequent archbishops at S Apollinare in Classe. This mausoleum does not survive. It has been variously located in the narthex tower, or, more probably, beside the basilica, where a structure lay in ruins in the early sixteenth century.[109]

The imperial period in Ravenna came to an end with the conquest of the Goths, who brought their Arian religion with them. Not surprisingly, there are few records of church building in this period,[110] and none of chapels, other than those in the Orthodox and the Arian bishops' palaces. The Arian bishops' chapel has not survived. It must remain an open question whether any of the other structures mentioned by Agnellus were Arian in origin. It seems likely that they were, in light of Theoderic's extensive building program.[111] Evidently, knowledge of their heretical beginnings had been lost before Agnellus's time.

Shortly after the Arian period, however, there was a second great surge of building activity in Ravenna. This followed Justinian's victory in 526 and the subsequent reestablishment of orthodoxy. On a smaller scale, the situation was similar in Milan.[112] Some chapels were enlarged, and others were built from new foundations. Many chapels came into being along with the great new churches of the era, which still stand or are known from archaeology. For example, side chambers and other chapels were built at the sixth-century basilicas of S Vitale and S Stefano in the imperial quarter at Ravenna, and at S Apollinare in Classe. The S Vitale and S Apollinare side chambers have been found by Janet Smith to fulfill various functions, including burial.[113]

Agnellus continues to be a rich source of information on chapel building in the Byzantine period, though its speed had slowed down after the extraordinary burst of activity that took place after the court moved to Ravenna in 402. As one might expect from a cleric, Agnellus's information is largely concerned with ecclesiastical burials. In addition, by the fifth century a layman needed the specific, and rarely given, permission of the bishop to be buried inside a Ravenna church.[114] However, the bishops had always taken advantage of their own exclusive powers to build themselves funerary chapels, in which they hoped to find 'tranquil living space' for eternity.[115] Agnellus recorded the dedicatory inscriptions of several chapels which must have functioned as mausolea. Most important, perhaps, was the joint burial place of the Ravenna archbishops, which has already been mentioned, the chapel of saints Marcus, Marcellus, and Felicula at S Apollinare in Classe.[116] It was built and decorated with mosaic by Archbishop John II, who was buried there,[117] along with many of his successors.[118] Beneath the porch was a dedicatory inscription in verse which proved the participation of the exarch Smaragdus, who left Ravenna in 590, returning in 592.[119] On the basis of this, Testi-Rasponi suggests this chapel was started before 590 and dedicated after the exarch's return in 592, being set aside for burials and also for the use of the monks serving the great basilica. This would have been a similar usage to the Roman, where both alternate and regular clergy officiated at the tombs of the martyrs. The epigraph commemorates the transfer of relics of the titular saints, which Gregory I gave to the chapel in 599.[120] The dedicatory poem, carved in marble, was last seen in the early sixteenth century, but the whole chapel had vanished by 1589.[121]

Private burial chapels for individual bishops are also recorded from Classis. Two were situated beside the baptistery of the Basilica Petriana in Classis (493–519), the early cathedral of the city, and were redecorated in the Byzantine period. At the *monasterium* of St James, Petrus II was buried beneath his portrait, which was on the wall behind the sarcophagus, with the inscription 'DOMNUS PETRUS ARCHIEPIS-COPUS.'[122] The sarcophagus was of Proconnesian marble, with a cypress wood box inside, where Agnellus actually saw the body of Petrus lying, to his great terror. Beside this chapel was the *monasterium* of St Matthew. Agnellus informs us that each of these chapels was embellished with an apse mosaic by Archbishop Agnellus (556–69).[123]

The sixth-century situation at Ravenna was echoed at Milan, where up to that time the burial of bishops in the *memoriae* of the saints seems to have been the norm. At S Lorenzo, which was almost certainly the palace church of the Theodosian family before the move to Ravenna,[124] there are three major annex chapels, to the east, north, and south (plan, fig. 14). Despite their superficial similarity as octagons, only the east and south chapels are contemporary with the late-fourth-century church, while the north chapel is a sixth-century addition. The south chapel, S Aquilino, is a typical Late Antique imperial mausoleum, taking the form of a tall, two-storeyed octagon (fig. 15), and is a close copy of an older structure which until 1576 stood at the nearby church of S Vittore al Corpo, where it served as a chapel (fig. 16).[125] This structure had started life as an imperial mausoleum, and probably served the tetrarch Maximian (283–305, 307–8), who lived in Milan for considerable periods though he died in Gaul.[126] The very similar S Aquilino probably dates to the reign of the emperor Gratian (367–83), and may well have served in the late fourth century as the mausoleum of the imperial family in the West (fig. 17).

S Lorenzo's eastern chapel (fig. 18), which lies behind the main altar and is dedicated to Hippolytus, the jailer of St Lawrence, has no early documentation, and thus presents problems similar to those of its mother church. It is not known if its original function was as a shrine for relics of St Lawrence. In fact, there is no evidence for a cult of Lawrence in Milan during the fourth or even the fifth centuries: the earliest mention of such a cult dates only to the turn of the seventh century. However, Ambrose did mention the cult of Lawrence, and those of his companions Hippolytus and Sixtus, in his writings,[127] and Picard has proposed that the chapel was constructed to shelter the remains of St Hippolytus, rather than those of Lawrence.[128] The chapel could well have been originally designed as a martyrium, separate from but attached to the basilica, and sharing its dedication, as Suzanne Lewis has convincingly argued.[129] The relics would then have sanctified the whole complex.[130] Its form, a cross inscribed within an octagon, as well as its barrel vault supported by columns of African *breccia* with Corinthian capitals, support this view. It also once possessed a gold mosaic decoration, according to medieval sources dating from the eighth to the eleventh centuries.[131] Already by the mid-fifth century it had come to be used for the burial of bishops, among them Eusebius (d. ca. 465) and Theodore (d. 489).[132] Presumably the building had become available when the court moved to Ravenna and a palace church was no longer needed in Milan.

The shift from imperial interest in this great complex of church and chapels to episcopal ownership is confirmed by the creation there, sometime between 489 and 512, of a third and smaller octagon for the common burial of Milan's bishops (fig. 19). This chapel, S Sisto, can be dated by a sixth-century epigram to the period before the death of Bishop Laurentius in 511–12.[133] Its walls are windowless and articulated with alternating rectangular and semicircular niches. Originally it had no access to the exterior but in 1626 a door was opened to the outside, immediately opposite its main door into the church itself. Nothing is known of S Sisto's original decoration, but its position as the burial place of Milan's sixth-century bishops shows that the trend here, as in Ravenna, was away from individual funeral chapels and towards collective facilities.

Thus, the combined evidence of archaeological and literary sources supports the information contained in surviving buildings and their decorations, and defines the place of the funerary chapel in the milieu of Late Antiquity, and its relationship to the martyr shrine. Perhaps the most important of all chapel types, the funerary chapel embodied the central beliefs of its era about salvation and the afterlife. The emphasis on the role of the saints in this context draws attention to an almost universal desire among Christians to find ways of ensuring a favourable personal outcome on the day of judgment, while the evolution of ecclesiastical privilege in this important area reflects the growing power and centralization of the church.

Chapels in the North-East

The main focal point of chapel building in the Early Christian period in Italy was clearly the imperial capital of the West – in turn Rome, Milan, and Ravenna – where records, archaeological remains, and scattered survivors are rich sources of information on the *cella memoriae* and its close relative, the funerary chapel. The provinces, too, are rich in examples of chapels built in response to the cult of the saints. One area where a clear pattern of chapel building in Late Antiquity emerges is the Upper Adriatic, now divided between Italy, Croatia, and Slovenia. Reaching around the north end of the Adriatic into Istria, in an arc stretching from Brescia and Verona to Pula, each city in Late Antiquity had at least one memorial chapel of a local saint, which may have doubled as a funerary chapel; one chapel that was purpose-built for burial, but sanctified with relics of the saints; or one martyrium, where the relics of saints were gathered up and venerated. The region will be considered as representative of the situation all over Italy, and will be discussed in those terms. Its centres with surviving chapels will be considered one by one, west to east, and, where decoration survives, an attempt will be made to correlate it with the function of the chapel. It will be found that an overall pattern of use emerges much more clearly in the smaller centres than in the imperial capitals, perhaps because of the more personal ties between a smaller population and its local saint. The connections between the saint and his cult, his martyrdom, his relics, and his *memoria* are more likely to be unbroken in the smaller centres than in the capitals, where we have seen that saints' relics, legends, and even bodies were quite commonly imported for political and propaganda purposes, even in the earliest period. The chapels founded by the imperial family and upper-level clerics in the capitals were rich with such imported relics. They stand outside the mainstream of devotion to local saints, not only because of their exalted ownership and private status, but also, perhaps, because the focus of devotion and the holiness they embodied held an impersonal element, being products that power and money could import from elsewhere. Local, personal involvement may be the reason for the long history of unbroken devotion to the Upper Adriatic shrines, each of which seems to embody some or all of the steps of evolution of a shrine of the funerary cult: *memoria*, funerary chapel, and martyrium. These appeared, and to varying degrees replaced one another, as the cult of the saints became codified and attained growing importance in the life of the region. Undoubtedly, one of the most important factors in the evolution of this pattern was the public nature of these shrines. Perhaps they should be recognized as local forerunners of the great medieval pilgrimage centres, in that here the devotion of the local populace was focused on their chosen protectors, the saints, who would intervene on behalf of the individual or the community.

SS Tosca e Teuteria, Verona

The ancient city of Verona retains one such chapel, much altered. This is the chapel of saints Tosca and Teuteria at the SS Apostoli, a Romanesque church occupying the site of an Early Christian cemetery church on the *decumanus* of the city outside the Porta dei Borsari.[134] The chapel's original dedication was probably to the Ravenna saint, Apollinaris, which makes a late-fifth- or sixth-century date probable: the dedication to Tosca and Teuteria, martyred in 263, dates only to

1162, when the saints' remains were discovered in the adjacent cemetery and placed in the chapel.[135]

SS Tosca e Teuteria is situated beside and ahead of the apse of its
basilica, as are many other Early Christian chapels, for example, those
at Milan, Pula, and Padua. It now lies more than two metres below the
level of the street. The chapel was originally cruciform, with a groin
vault and equal barrel-vaulted arms, but is now an apsed square so
that the only surviving walls of the first phase, those of the ends of the
cross-arms, form the middle sections of its continuous outer walls
(plan, fig. 20; exterior, fig. 21). These sections are easily distinguished
by their construction of alternating layers of brick and smooth pebbles,
laid obliquely in imitation of *opus spiccatum*. Though the alterations of
the twelfth to fourteenth centuries have transformed the chapel into a
small, three-naved basilica, it retains its original cupola, resting on the
four central piers which were its original supports, and the original
Greek cross plan is still defined by an ancient pavement of various
coloured marbles and by the clear differences in wall structure. The
pavement gives no evidence of any graves, but the chapel may have
held an above-ground sarcophagus burial. The first secure evidence
for a funerary function dates to the period after the extensive alterations of 1160, when the chapel became the mausoleum of the Bevilac-
qua family.

Although fourteenth-century documents state that the chapel's original consecration took place in 751,[136] many factors suggest an earlier
date. The details of the wall construction are typical of the turn of the
sixth century, and the original architectural form, which was similar to
fifth- and sixth-century chapels in Ravenna and Pula, would also suggest this earlier date.

S Maria Mater Domini, Vicenza

S Maria Mater Domini at SS Fortunato e Felice, Vicenza, is a vaulted
Greek cross, four metres square, with an apse, a cupola, and a barrel-
vaulted, rectangular narthex entered from either end (fig. 22).[137] It was
built beside the cemetery basilica of saints Felix and Fortunatus on the
Via Postumia (fig. 23) and probably dates from the mid-sixth century.[138] As with so many other small, vaulted chapels of the north-east,
it survived major disasters during its history, among them the attack of
the Huns in 899, during which the basilica itself was destroyed, and
the major earthquake of 1117. Its survival, as in most similar cases,

probably results from its small size and its strong, stone-built vaulted construction.

During recent renovations the Roman windows in the north and south arms were reopened; that in the south is original. The uneven octagon of the vault merges into a hemisphere containing four more small windows; two of these are original, and one more is covered with an ancient *transenna*. The lower part of the chapel is partially clad in Proconnesian marble: a remnant, with fragmentary mosaics, of a sumptuous decoration contemporary with the chapel.

The building has been identified as a typical martyrium, dedicated to the cult of relics, rather than a cemetery chapel, built over the grave of one particular martyr.[139] This was a development that came somewhat late in the evolution of the martyr shrine, and suggests that S Maria Mater Domini, at least in its present form, postdates the foundation of its church, SS Fortunato e Felice, and that the later dates proposed for the chapel (early to mid-sixth century) are probably correct. Nevertheless, even if the chapel itself is from this late a period, there is evidence that relics of Felix and Fortunatus, who died in the persecutions of Diocletian, were physically present in Vicenza soon after their deaths. A plain sarcophagus, possibly dated to the late fourth century, with an inscribed cover which reads 'BEATI MART/URES/FELIX ET/ FORTUNA/TUS,'[140] has been found in the pagan cemetery on the road to Verona. This tomb is equipped with a hole whereby the faithful could maintain contact with the relics.[141] It is not clear when the saints' remains were moved to the basilica, though the earliest, fourth-century church took the form of a hall surrounding the *memoria* of the martyrs. The bones of Felix still lie under the altar of S Maria Mater Domini. A recent 'recognition' showed that the casket contains the skeleton of a single individual, dead by decapitation.[142] This would fit the known circumstances, for although both saints were once present in Vicenza, their bones came to be divided between Vicenza and Aquileia, which received the bones of Fortunatus. By the sixth century each saint was firmly installed in his separate home, as we learn from the poems of Venantius Fortunatus.[143]

The sixth-century date for the chapel is also suggested by the dedication inscribed on its now-lost *pergula*, which was recorded by Barbarano in 1646.[144] The text read '+ HOC ORATORIUM B.M.MATRIS DOMINI GREGORIUS/SUBLIMIS VIR REFERENDARIUS A FUN-DAMEN/TIS AEDIFICAVIT, CHRISTI + NOMI/NE DICAVIT.'[145] Thus we read that Gregorius built the chapel 'from the foundations,' implying that there was no predecessor chapel on the site, despite ancient tradition that Gregorius's building replaced a previous structure. The office, *referendarius*, held by Gregorius, was that of secretary to the emperor. It was known from the reign of Julian (361–3) and continued in use until that of Justinian (527–65).[146] Thus it is possible that the chapel was built in the period of peace between 543, when Totila destroyed Vicenza, and 568, the year of the Lombard invasion.[147] However, the offices of *sublimis vir* and *referendarios* were in use throughout the period of Gothic rule under Theoderic and continued in use in the Byzantine period. Placing Gregorius into the context of Theoderic's court, which would date the chapel to around the turn of the sixth century, is preferable for two reasons: first, the complete absence from record of a *referendarios* of the name of Gregory in either East or West, and lack of reason why an imperial *referendarios* should be endowing a chapel in Vicenza;[148] and second, the close stylistic similarities of the chapel's mosaics with those of the archbishops' chapel in Ravenna, which are also dated to the time of Theoderic.

The Vicenza mosaics, preserved in fragmentary condition under a false ceiling when the chapel was transformed into a sacristy in 1754, consist of the Lion of St Mark (fig. 24) and a medallion saint (fig. 25) in the north-west squinch, with extremely fragmentary vine tendrils and pomegranates in the south-west and south-east, as also beneath the saint's medallion in the north-west.[149] The west (entry) vault of the chapel also bears some fragments of wall painting, which have been scored for overlying plaster: a series of pleated canopies between twisted ribbon borders is represented, in white and red on gold.

A second area of original, painted decoration is the painted frieze of cornucopias which extends over more than a square metre of the narthex wall, at the level of the springing of the vault. The ornaments are tied with ribbons, which support hanging crowns on a yellow background between lanceolate leaves. Vertical, spiral ribbons complete the pattern. The designs are close to those of mid-sixth-century Ravenna, resembling the ornament at both S Apollinare in Classe and S Vitale. And finally, the iconography of the evangelist symbol, the Lion, with its single wings, halo, and codex is also appropriate to the early sixth century.

What do these fragments of decoration reveal of the function of this chapel? Regrettably, few conclusions can be reached except that S Maria Mater Domini shared its basic vocabulary with other Early Christian chapels. The formula includes a vault (here sprinkled with painted stars in *intonaco*, perhaps replacements for mosaics which fell in the 1117 earthquake), supported by the evangelist symbols at the base, as at S Vittore in Ciel d'Oro in Milan. This basic formula was accompanied by the medallion portraits of saints, perhaps portraits of those whose relics rested below. Close as it is in these features to the Ravenna Archbishops' chapel, it seems certain that its primary purpose was different: the creation of a sacred space as a setting for the images and the relics of the local martyrs, in honour of their sacrifice.

San Prosdocimo, Padua

At Padua, also, an Early Christian chapel, S Prosdocimo, is associated with the ancient tradition of devotion to local saints (plan, fig. 26). It is situated at S Giustina, a fifth-century foundation rebuilt many times throughout the centuries, notably in the twelfth, and even more completely in the fifteenth and sixteenth. Like most of the other churches in this series, S Giustina originated as a funerary basilica in the cemetery outside the city walls. Its chapel, which is now dedicated to the first bishop of Padua, Prosdocimus, but may have had an original dedication to S Giustina, is situated to the right of the sanctuary (fig. 27, interior).[150] Although originally a separate building, it is now attached to the basilica by a complex of rooms and corridors. The cruciform chapel has its arms covered by tunnel vaults and its central crossing by a cupola supported on four angular squinches alternating with windows. This type of cupola was popular in the early sixth century, and the brickwork of the exterior is also typical for this date.

An inscription in its narthex records that the patrician Opilio built both the basilica and the oratory in honour of the local martyr Justina. The text occupies the central roundel of a triangular marble tympanum (fig. 28) which was originally supported on two columns, forming the lintel of the chapel's entryway in the west arm, a position it still retained in the fifteenth century.[151] The roundel is edged by a carved wreath, and the triangular slab itself, by a leafy border. Both closely resemble borders on Ravenna sarcophagi of the early sixth century.[152] The text is flanked by two Latin crosses cut into the stone: each supports a hanging *alpha* and *omega* and two smaller crosses from its horizontal beam. The text, expanded to eliminate abbreviations, reads 'OPILIO VIR CLARISSIMUS ET IN LUSTRIS PRAEFECTUS ATQUE PRETER [or *patricius*] HANC BASILICAM VEL ORATORIUM IN HONORE SANCTAE JUSTINAE MARTYRIS A FUNDAMENTIS

COEPTAM DEO IUVANTE PERFECIT.'[153] Two individuals named Opilio are known, both consuls[154] according to their surviving inscriptions of 453 and 525.[155] Although each of these has been suggested as the Opilio of the chapel, the second is more likely,[156] because other records note Opilio's gifts of lands to the monastery and church of St Justina on 23 May 523.[157] Opilio's tomb, supported on two columns, survived in the atrium of the basilica until the fifteenth century, where it was seen by Ongarello.

It is not known when Justina's remains were moved from the chapel, where they rested in Opilio's time, to the basilica, where they were discovered in the twelfth century. Perhaps the transfer happened after one of the numerous devastations in the church's history.[158] Somewhat ironically, the chapel withstood these disasters, and the saint's remains might well have remained there in safety through much of the Middle Ages. Apparently, the remains were once again returned to the chapel after their rediscovery in the basilica, for Ongarello saw them there in 1441.[159]

Both Justina and Prosdocimus are shadowy figures, whose life stories, known from late medieval texts, are full of inconsistencies.[160] Justina, a local princess, is believed to have died in the persecutions of Maximian: her existence in Padua in the early Middle Ages is documented by Opilio's inscription, and by her appearance in the poems of Venantius Fortunatus.[161] However, her life and passion cannot be verified in the written sources of the following six centuries. Her *Acts* probably date from the discovery of her remains in the high altar in 1174. This was an era rich in such discoveries at S Giustina. The relics of St Daniel the Martyr had been discovered there in 1074, while relics of the evangelists Luke and Matthew came to light in 1177. But even though Justina's legend lacks early documentation, the late medieval version must surely have incorporated local tradition and belief, and one can assume it contains a kernel of historic truth. This conclusion is also supported by the fact that Justina was the subject of an important cult in north-eastern Italy in the early Middle Ages, where she was invoked both in the Ambrosian Canon of the Mass and in the Ravenna Litany. She also appeared in mosaic in two important mid-sixth-century monuments: she was included in the procession of twenty-two virgin martyrs in the nave at S Apollinare Nuovo, Ravenna, and she appeared among the women saints decorating the sanctuary arch of the Basilica Euphrasiana at Poreč in Istria.

Tradition declares Prosdocimus to have been the first bishop of

Padua.[162] His relics have been neither found nor documented, and were perhaps hidden centuries ago during the barbarian threat, and then lost. The rediscovery in 1957 of a Early Christian sculptured plaque in the chapel is perhaps the best proof of the existence of Prosdocimus and of his connection with the chapel. The plaque features a portrait bust of the saint, between palm trees, in shallow-cut relief (fig. 29). Although the date of the inscription 'SCS PROSDOCIMUS/EPS. ET CONFESS.'[163] has sometimes been questioned, most recently the mid-sixth-century date of both image and inscription has been accepted and both are seen as by the same hand as that of the Opilio inscription.[164] The plaque should probably be seen as an idealization of the bishop, rather than a true portrait.

The small *pergula* (fig. 27) which delimits the left niche is supported by four columns with two Byzantine and two later foliate capitals.[165] The uprights are squared, and fitted for the attachment of *plutei*, which have not survived. The beam, with a central horseshoe arch, has a foliate pattern on either side of the inscription which occupies its entire length. This border matches the one on the Opilio lintel, though the inscription appears to be later. It states that the chapel contained the relics of apostles and martyrs which had been gathered together there.[166] Among these the relics of Matthew and Luke, along with a famous icon of the Virgin painted by St Luke, were said to have been brought to Padua from Constantinople in the time of iconoclasm by a priest, St Urius.[167] The *pergula* may date from that time, and perhaps also the medieval dedication to the Virgin, which may commemorate the icon's presence in the chapel.[168] At various times up to the mid-sixteenth century the many relics once kept in S Prosdocimo were transferred to individual chapels within the rebuilt and enlarged basilica.

The relics of the apostles were obviously the inspiration for the decoration which once made the interior of S Prosdocimo bright with mosaics, for the decorative scheme is known from old descriptions to have included the twelve apostles, perhaps in the cupola, as at the two Ravenna baptisteries. However, an anonymous writer of the twelfth century described the chapel as built in honour of God, the Virgin Mary, and the host of apostles, mentioning the 'almost celestial palace' and 'green fields of Paradise' that were shown there.[169] It is only in another account, that of Girolamo da Potenza, who wrote in 1619, more than a half-century after the redecoration of 1563–4, that the pictures of the apostles are mentioned. He describes how the chapel's walls had been encrusted with beautiful marbles, with mosaics above depicting the twelve apostles.[170] I can find no evidence that the apostles were shown full length as at the Ravenna baptisteries: it seems equally likely that they were shown in medallions, as at the archbishops' chapel at Ravenna. Medallions with scriptural scenes feature in the painted soffits that replaced the mosaics at S Prosdocimo. Greek key and twisted ribbon borders which resemble the motifs of Late Antiquity are also present, and are possible quotations from the original decoration. If the apostles were shown in the soffits, the twelfth-century mention of the mosaics depicting a near celestial palace among green fields is intriguing. It calls to mind the mosaics at the Great Mosque of Damascus, or those of the cupola at St George's, Salonica. Parallels may also be drawn with the architectural façades, including thrones and altars, in the vault of the Orthodox Baptistery of Ravenna.

The anonymous twelfth-century account confirms that the body of Prosdocimus lay in the chapel at that time, and indeed it was to honour this saint that in the mid-sixteenth century the ancient decoration of marble and mosaic, blackened with smoke and age, was either removed from the walls and vault, or, just possibly, covered with plaster,[171] to be replaced by the paintings which are still *in situ*. The ancient sarcophagus now in the chapel was recut, the chapel walls were hollowed into niches and filled with statues, and the original floor was replaced. This Renaissance decor remains in the cupola and soffits, but on the lower level it has recently been stripped away, and the chapel returned to its original state. Here, the sole decorations are now the *pergula* and the recut sarcophagus, which is used as an altar and bears the bas-relief of Prosdocimus as altarpiece.

In conclusion, one may surmise that the chapel of S Prosdocimo is a second-generation martyr chapel, built in the first place for the martyr Justina, and either chosen by the early bishop Prosdocimus for his burial *ad sanctos*, or provided as his funerary chapel by those who transferred his remains from the cemetery where they already lay. It was entirely rebuilt in the early sixth century by Opilio, and possibly even served in its turn for his own burial beside the saints. The remains of Justina were later moved to the high altar of the titular basilica. Other relics, among them those of the apostles Matthew and Luke and of three of the Holy Innocents, as well as of the second bishop of Padua, St Maximus, and of St Felicity and St Daniel, were also honoured in the chapel, and gave it the role of *Sancta Sanctorum* of Padua. The mosaic decorations of the vault, as well as the original marble cladding of the walls, were probably the gifts of Opilio.[172] The chapel obviously fits into the pattern *cella memoriae*/burial *ad sanctos*/ funerary chapel/shrine for relics, and in the absence of clear documentation, I would hazard the opinion that it fulfilled all these roles in turn.

Concordia

North-east of Venice near Portogruaro, the Roman city of Iulia Concordia Sagittaria, which was destroyed in the floods of 586 and devastated in the barbarian invasions, has archaeological remains of its Early Christian monuments (fig. 30).[173] Among these was a triconch chapel, with a cruciform relic container under the site of the altar. Originally a *memoria* opening from the right corner of the sanctuary of the Basilica Apostolorum in the cemetery, at a later date it was itself converted into a small basilica by the addition of a short arcade of five pairs of columns, round which a continuous narthex and twin aisles were wrapped. This renovation probably followed the destruction of the church by the Huns under Attila in 452. The new church, like its predecessor, served a formal, walled graveyard which has also been excavated. It is not known what saint or relics sanctified this place.

Aquileia and Grado

At Aquileia, no traces of martyr or funerary chapels have come to light, and the mosaic pavements that have been claimed as the remains of domestic oratories cannot be securely identified as such. The nearby city of Grado, on the contrary, is rich in Early Christian chapels of the martyr shrine and funerary type. Its cathedral, S Eufemia, has a small, heart-shaped *cella trichora* to the left of the apse (fig. 31, A). T.G. Jackson described it as having once been a detached building with three apses paved with mosaics, connected by a mosaic-paved walkway to the front of the left aisle of the church. In Jackson's time, the late nineteenth century, nothing remained above ground level of the ancient building, and much of its site was occupied by a workshop.[174] The triconch has now been reconstructed in Early Christian style, with a little cupola of *tubi fittili*, over the ancient mosaic pavements of the chapel and its connecting passage way, which probably both dated from the bishopric of Elia (571–86).[175] The pavement in the chapel and its main apse displays geometric motifs such as knots enclosed in an interlace of squares and circles, while the mosaic floors of the lateral apses are enriched with imbrication. The anteroom, like the nave of the church, has a *pelta* wave design.[176] The chapel's position and its architectural form inform us that it originated as a *cella memoriae*, and it seems that from the time of Heraclius, who gave a relic-throne to the patriarch of Grado in 630, the saint honoured was Mark.[177] Devotion to the evangelist is also recorded from Grado's pre-Venetian days in an inscription dated to 807, during the patriarchate of John *iunior*. This inscription occupies the fragments of his *pergula* which is preserved in the *trichora*.[178] However, the original dedication of the chapel may well have been to saints Ermacora and Fortunatus, the evangelists of the Veneto region, who were honoured in both Aquileia and Grado, and whose relics are still kept in the Grado cathedral treasury.[179]

At S Eufemia a second chapel, probably the original sacristy, was later converted to a funerary chapel, while new side chambers to the south took over the old functions. This chapel lies beside the altar, at the head of the right aisle, and is built in typical Upper Adriatic style with a polygonal apse, semicircular inside (fig. 31, B). The apse has a mosaic pavement with a central cantharus, which gives rise to a lively vine-scroll (fig. 32). The rectangular main floor is centred on the monogram of the donor of the floor, Bishop Elia, and is similar to the triconch chapel floor; interlaced squares and circles contain geometric motifs, all framed by a wave meander of aquatic plants. Elia's own grave was not found in the excavations of 1966, but the chapel did contain the tomb of a bishop named Marcianus in an alcove in the wall adjacent to the main apse of the basilica. It is marked by a mosaic inscription.[180] The tomb was intact, unusual for an Early Christian burial. Marcianus's body lay in an unpretentious limestone sarcophagus, the skeleton oriented to the east with arms extended and hands crossed.[181] The inscription states that he had died at Grado, probably in 578, after spending forty of the forty-four years of his bishopric in exile. The pavements of the two funerary chapels at S Eufemia, which, judging by their designs, are contemporary with one another, are rich in the symbolism of eternity in their interlace, their knot motifs, and their circles.[182] The apse of the 'sacristy' chapel has a further design where the altar once stood, a cantharus giving rise to a luxurious grapevine, which symbolizes Christ and his blood, offered at the Eucharist at the altar above.[183] This was a concept that was expounded by several of the Church fathers. The third-century Roman theologian Hippolytus (ca. 170–ca. 236), for example, saw Christ as the vine, and its shoots as the believers, with the martyrs represented as the bunches of grapes.[184]

Investigation of the site has shown that Grado's lost Early Christian church, the sixth-century Basilica of the Piazza Vittoria, had also had its 'sacristy' converted into a relic chapel,[185] a renovation which should probably also be attributed to Bishop Elia, who is known to have transferred relics to the churches of Grado.[186] At S Maria delle Grazie, also, where twin side chambers are joined behind the apse to present a flat east façade, mosaic floors were given to the chapels in the late sixth century by individually named donors, as the mosaic inscriptions record.[187]

Chapels also survive from the Early Christian period in Trieste and its region. In the city itself, a *cella memoriae* was built in the early fifth century and dedicated to S Maria del Mare: it was soon followed by a church. Examples from outside the city include chapels at Canzian and at Timavo. In the early fourth century, a shrine was raised over the graves of the three local martyrs in the cemetery at S Canzian d'Izonzo. It consisted of a small, simple building with no apse, adhering to the Aquileia tradition. At Timavo, a chapel was dedicated to the Baptist at the start of the fifth century; by the early seventh century this had become the site of a basilica and a monastery.[188]

Poreč

Poreč (Parenzo, Parentium) is the site of another typical Upper Adriatic chapel, at the Basilica Euphrasiana (539–50). This church was rebuilt on old foundations by Bishop Euphrasius, who added a *cella trichora* to the left of the apse (plan, fig. 33).[189] This chapel, now dedicated to St Andrew, was probably formerly the *memoria* of the Parentine saints Maurus and Eleutherius, who lie there in a sarcophagus dated 1247.[190] It is also likely to have been chosen for the burial of Euphrasius himself. Much restored, it consists of a triconch preceded by an oval atrium, rectangular on the outside, with a window in the polygonal south wall. There is a stubby tower over the crossing of the triconch, and its three apses are polygonal outside and round inside, each with two windows. Traces of geometric mosaic pavement have survived, but appear to be later and cruder than the chapel itself.[191] No other decoration survives, except a marble door frame, its jambs and matching lintel profiled with parallel grooves and topped by a projecting cornice.[192]

In addition to the triconch chapel, Poreč posesses one of the oldest Early Christian chapel floors to have survived anywhere: it is a pagan pavement which has been altered by the later insertion of fish into the geometric design. These inserts, filling two square fields of the mosaic, are placed on either side of the altar site, which is marked by the traces of its four supports. The symbolic fishes, and the position at the lowest level under the pavements of the church, reveal this as the floor of the earliest place of worship at the site, though the exact date is uncertain.[193]

Remains of a third group of *memoriae* in the Čimare cemetery, east of Poreč, were found at the end of the nineteenth century. All five had semicircular apses and floor mosaics. The largest measures 14 × 7 metres. Betika, between Poreč and Pula, has also revealed an Early Christian sanctuary: an early-fifth-century triconch chapel with black and white mosaics, a 'robbed altar grave,' and a dedicatory inscription in its south apse identifying it as a martyrium, with a three-aisled basilica built onto its west end.[194]

Pula

At Pula there is a chapel which, although now isolated, is the only surviving portion of the sixth-century basilica of S Maria Formosa (plan, fig. 34). This church was built by Bishop Maximinian of Ravenna, a native of Vistro (Vistrum) in Istria, who came to the Ravenna bishopric from the diaconate at Pula, and also founded a monastery dedicated to St Andrew on an islet in Pula harbour.[195] The monastic community was transferred to the city and to S Maria Formosa in the twelfth century, with the last abbot of the monastery being installed in 1258, a date which suggests that the church and community suffered severely in the Venetian sack of 1243. By the early seventeenth century the church was in ruins, its marbles, including the columns of its nave in 1547 and the alabaster columns of its ciborium in 1605, having been purloined by Venice for her own building needs.[196]

The two aisles of the church terminated in four-niched 'sacristies' beside the altar, and applied to the outer corners of these were a pair of identical chapels on the Latin cross plan, of which the one to the right of the altar survives, dedicated to the Virgin (figs. 35 and 36). The other was dedicated to St Andrew.[197] The single door of each chapel, in the centre of the long arm of the cross, opened to the exterior rather than into the church. The chapels' ground plan included a central apse, a miniature version of the main one, polygonal outside and semicircular within. The remaining chapel has rectangular transepts, ornamented with blind arcading, and articulated with vertical pilasters on the corners. The crossing is crowned with a squat central tower, each face of which is articulated by a wide arched window under a large, hemispherical relieving arch. Small single windows light the interior of the chapel's three arms, and a nonfigural mosaic floor survives. Two of the lower windows and the large upper window in the east still possess their original traceries. It served as a funerary chapel for some part of its history, housing a bishop's sarcophagus in the sixteenth century.[198]

This chapel, known since the twelfth century as S Maria del Canneto from the reed bed by the shore in which it stood, and now simply and rather confusingly, as S Maria Formosa, is little more than an intact but empty shell. It is possible, though, to recreate a considerable part of its decorative program from the fragments and records that remain.

A substantial fragment of mosaic from the conch of the apse survives in the Pula Archaeological Museum (fig. 37). Central on the gold background among clouds of glory is the head of a young, short-haired, and beardless Christ, nimbed with a jewelled and inscribed halo. His head is slightly inclined to his right, where the fragment also includes a second haloed head: that of Peter, to judge by the short, grey beard and fringed hair style. Antonio Morassi, who apparently saw the mosaic before it was removed, suggested that this is the remnant of a *traditio legis*, the giving of the law to Peter.[199] He adds the information that Christ was depicted in the centre of the conch. The relative positions and gestures of the heads suggest that Peter was in the position of *proskynesis*, possibly in the act of receiving a scroll from Christ, as Morassi suggests. There are, however, two compositions in Early Christian art that show Christ bestowing a gift on Peter: the Giving of the Law and the Giving of the Keys, the *traditio clavium*. Either would be possible, although it is more usual, especially in the Ravenna context of which S Maria Formosa forms part, for Paul to receive the Law, and Peter the keys. The *traditio clavium* would better fit the program of the chapel as a mausoleum, since Christ's gift to Peter of the keys to heaven is a clear reference to the possibility of salvation. Paul receiving the Law might seem the logical completion of the composition; and it seems that sometime before 1922 Alessandro Testi-Rasponi did see a second figure beside Christ which he interpreted as Paul, though he read the composition as the *traditio legis*.[200] This suggests that there was a symmetrical composition in the chapel's apse, with Peter and Paul on either side of Christ.

The mosaic conch was separated from a painted composition below by an 18-centimetre stucco string course, which is still in place. It bears a repeat design of paired birds, probably doves, their heads twisted back to hold garlands of flowers and fruit beak to beak with the adjacent pairs. The vault was also decorated with a small central garland in stucco, and paired bands of leaves in the corners.

The lower part of the apse was also painted, though Morassi described the paintings as already in decay in 1924. They showed the twelve apostles, six in the hemicycle and three on each side wall.[201] On the left wall, quite well preserved, was the figure of the Baptist, with a scroll reading 'ECCE AGNUS DEI,' while on the right Paul was shown with the sword that symbolized his martyrdom. The lowest register was occupied by painted draperies. Since the apostle frieze was represented within an arcade of pointed, slightly decorated arches, it seems likely that these paintings were later than the mosaics and stuccoes, and perhaps contemporary with the twelfth-century apostle friezes at Torcello and Trieste.[202]

The chapel at Pula, a documented funerary chapel from the mid-sixth century, thus displays in its cruciform shape with crossing tower a symbolism of architectural form that speaks of Christ's death and the redemption that stems from it. It employs almost exactly the same architectural vocabulary as the Mausoleum of Galla Placidia a century earlier, itself an aristocratic burial place, which will be discussed in a subsequent chapter. The points of similarity with the Ravenna mausoleum, as well as the former presence of a sarcophagus within it, identify the Pula chapel as a funerary chapel, while its decoration of birds and garlands was appropriate paradise imagery for a place of burial. This conclusion is not contradicted by the fragmentary mosaics of the conch, which also speak of the hope of salvation. We cannot tell if this chapel was a martyr shrine in origin: the building's documentation implies that it was not, since no relics are mentioned by Agnellus, despite his listing of the numerous relics which the same patron, Maximinian, placed within the church of S Stefano, Ravenna. Nor were relics mentioned in the original charter of the church of S Maria Formosa that survived in the Pula archives until 1657.[203] Probably this chapel belongs to the generation of funeral chapels which were built for burial, and sanctified as necessary with relics. As to who were the intended occupants of the burial chapels, we have no answer. Maximinian, we know, died on 22 February 553,[204] and was buried in Ravenna beside the altar of his church of St Andrew, which he had endowed with a precious relic: the beard of the apostle.[205] But there is some doubt whether he built S Maria Formosa while bishop at Ravenna, or earlier. Its foundation deed, now lost, but signed by Maximinian, read 'Servus Christi Maximinianus per gratiam Dei episcopus sanctae ecclesiae Ravennatis inclitae urbis.' The date of this document was read as 21 February 546. However, since Maximinian did not become bishop until October 546,[206] the accuracy of this reading is in doubt: probably the date of the lost document was misinterpreted. It seems possible that Maximinian, finding a great treasure as Agnellus recounts,[207] spent some of it on S Maria Formosa, planning his own tomb there, only to be elevated to the Ravenna See, where he made new arrangements for his burial.

We have seen that S Maria Formosa also possessed paired circular side chambers beside the altar, which have been described as 'sacristies' (plan, fig. 34 B). A late-sixteenth-century observer described these chambers as being clad in figural mosaics.[208] Perhaps, as at S Vitale, Ravenna, the chambers doubled as shrines dedicated to particular saints, or, as at Grado, one or both of them were later used as burial chapels. A pair of niches, stripped to the stone, together with the thick wall behind them, survives from each structure, and that on the right forms an integral part of the wall of S Maria del Canneto (fig. 35).

Poreč and Pula are by no means the only Istrian cities to have the remains of Early Christian chapels, though theirs are the best preserved. The northern Adriatic coast has all sorts of small chapels, obviously *memoriae*, in the form of the cross or the triconch. Subterranean chapels are recorded from Koper (Capodistria), Novigrad (Cittanova), and Pican (Pedena), though their dates are uncertain, and they may not be Early Christian.[209] In addition, there are the chapels of St Agnes at Betica, and the two chapels of St Peter and of St Florian, on St Florian's Island in the Bay of Pula, while further north, near Rovinj is the chapel of St Thomas.[210] These all exhibit different variants of the three-apsed structure.[211]

A sumptuous mausoleum or martyrium of the sixth century, S Caterina, was situated in Pula harbour, on an islet connected by a bridge to Maximinian's island monastery of St Andrew, the site of which now lies beneath Venetian fortifications in the harbour. S Caterina was pictured in a series of engravings by S. Dufourney for Seroux d'Agincourt's *Storia dell'Arte* of 1825: these consisted of ground plan, elevation, section, and architectural details (fig. 38, a–e).[212] However, by Kandler's time, the mid-nineteenth century, S Caterina was in ruins. Its mosaic tesserae had fallen from the walls and lay on the ground both inside and around the building. To Kandler, this was evidence there had been glass mosaics on the exterior as well as inside.[213] This would make it unique among all known Early Christian chapels. Later, the ninth-century S Zeno chapel at S Prassede, Rome, would present a mosaic façade; nearer at hand, the decoration of the mid-sixth-century Basilica Euphrasiana, in nearby Poreč, included a mosaic program on both its exterior gables. S Caterina's site was levelled in the 1850s, the upper walls being taken down and the rooms filled in. In 1910, Anton Gnirs excavated the site, which was threatened with development. He published a measured ground plan, which broadly agrees with that of Seroux d'Agincourt, and shows many features which had been described by Kandler, though there were no traces of wall mosaics (plan, fig. 39).[214] Evidently, the ruins had been thoroughly despoiled before the chapel was levelled. However, Gnirs determined that the sanctuary had been enclosed by a *pergula*, and he found an empty cavity about a metre deep and four-fifths of a metre wide beneath the site of the altar, which must once have held the relics. He also found the remains of three sarcophagi, confirming Kandler's suggestion that the chapel had been a funerary chapel.

In conclusion, it seems obvious from the surviving evidence that the Upper Adriatic area was especially rich in chapels that were founded as *memoriae* over the graves of martyrs in the heyday of the cult, the fourth to sixth centuries. These structures were often converted to funerary chapels for the use of early bishops or aristocrats. Later chapels on the same plan as the *memoriae* were built for use as funerary chapels or as homes for relics, martyria, which need not even have been built over an actual martyr grave or site. These chapels were of two predominant architectural types: those with a cruciform ground plan, and those with the related three-lobed shape of a *trichora*.[215] The popularity of both of these architectural forms is probably related to the rediscovery of the True Cross. Indeed, the cruciform chapel form with its appropriate symbolism, came to be preferred for any building that celebrated the deaths of martyrs as imitators of Christ's sacrifice on the cross.

This discussion of the chapels in the provinces has dealt with only one representative area: the Upper Adriatic and north-east Italy, contrasting it with the three successive imperial capitals. The provincial survey has revealed a rich legacy of chapels connected with the martyr and funerary cult. There is no doubt that other regions of Italy were also richly endowed with chapels, which must have been built in the service of the martyrs and their cults, and served in their turn for burial beside the saints.[216] Some of these chapels are briefly described in the Appendix.

CHAPTER TWO

The Mausolea of the Imperial Family in the West

The previous chapter has considered many chapels that were built for different aspects of the cult of the dead. Two of these funerary chapels will be singled out for special attention in a later chapter. The unusually well-documented chapel of S Vittore in Ciel D'Oro in Milan started its existence as a martyr's *memoria* and was subsequently used for the *ad sanctos* burial of Ambrose's brother Satyrus. By contrast, the S Matrona chapel at S Prisco, rich in legend but almost undocumented, reveals in its architecture and decoration that its primary purpose was Christian burial, though who was interred there, and when, is open to speculation.

Imperial mausolea are also funerary chapels by definition, and fulfill the same functions as the smaller and more modest structures built by nonimperial patrons. They are set apart from them by their size, for even in the Christian era they inherited the grandiloquent traditions of the pagan past. Nevertheless, they must be included in any discussion of funerary chapels as Christian burial places in their own right. In addition, the imperial mausolea set the context for the Mausoleum of Galla Placidia at Ravenna. This chapel has undoubted imperial connections and therefore deserves to be compared with the other mausolea built by members of the imperial family for themselves and their families. Its main difference from them is its minuscule size, which implies that it should be considered as a typical funerary chapel, but the richness of its decoration and the enigmatic but undoubtedly august level of its patronage mark it as one of the most outstanding buildings of Late Antiquity.

In this brief space the history and patronage of the numerous Late Antique mausolea can be examined only briefly. Almost all of them are in ruins or have disappeared completely and are at best known only from Renaissance drawings. This group will be briefly surveyed here.[1] Only three of the typical imperial mausolea of the Christian era in the West have retained any of their mosaic and painted decoration, and these all date from the second half of the fourth century. They are S Costanza in Rome, S Aquilino in Milan, and the probable mausoleum of Constans I at Centcelles, near Tarragona in Spain. Analysis of their decorations in a later part of this study will throw light on the purpose for which they were built and the beliefs of their patrons as well as of the deceased who lay within. Two of the burial places of the Gothic kings will also be surveyed: the long-lost La Daurade, burial chapel of the Visigothic Kings at Toulouse, and the still extant but enigmatic mausoleum of the Ostrogothic king Theoderic at Ravenna. Finally, the Mausoleum of Galla Placidia will be compared with the others and analysed in terms of its imperial and royal connections.

Imperial mausolea are chapels in the sense of private, consecrated spaces devoted to burial. Richard Krautheimer attributed their disparity in size from the *cella memoriae* and its relatives to the fact that the imperial mausoleum had fulfilled a double function in pagan antiquity.[2] It not only provided a resting place in death, but also furnished a setting for the cult of the deceased which followed. Unlike the ordinary dead, emperors and their relatives joined the gods when they died, and their apotheosis required both a cult on earth and a shrine for its recognition.

This was the tradition that the imperial family inherited even into Christian times. The emperors in Late Antiquity continued to build funerary chapels which doubled as *heroa* and took their decorative and architectural vocabulary and magnificence of scale from the great pagan structures of the past. The centrally planned form of early mausolea relates ultimately to the tombs of Augustus and Hadrian in Rome, while the typical interior derives from the Pantheon temple type, with a circular hall, articulated by niches within, clad in marble and crowned by a heavenly dome. The tombs of the tetrarchs had followed this formula, which is epitomized by Diocletian's mausoleum in Split (fig. 40).[3] Dating from around 300, just before the era of the Christian emperors, it is a tall, two-storey octagon, circular inside, domed and colonnaded, and decorated with precious marbles and sculptures. High up under the dome, one frieze remains, its pagan subject matter perhaps too high or too indistinctly seen to be removed during the mausoleum's conversion to a church in the early Middle Ages. The frieze includes medallion portraits which are probably those of the deceased emperor and his wife Prisca, set among hunting and circus scenes which have parallels in the tombs of the fourth-century Christian emperors, such as those at Centcelles and Milan. At Centcelles, the mausoleum is girdled by a great mosaic scene of emperors at the hunt (fig. 79); at Sant'Aquilino, the sculptured frame of the inner door displays relief carvings of the chariot races. Evidently these motifs formed part of the decorative vocabulary of the imperial tomb in Late Antiquity, and equally obviously, emperors did not change their secular interests when they embraced the Christian faith: they enjoyed the royal sports of hunting and chariot racing and hoped to continue to do so in the hereafter.

Members of the imperial family built numerous mausolea of the domed rotunda type for themselves and their families in and around Christian Rome and Milan in Late Antiquity. Few of these survive, even as ruins, nor are there usually any records to identify who built them, or who occupied them in death. Fewer still retain any traces of their decorative schemes. Several of the mausolea which stand in ruins on the roads leading out of Rome have lost all trace of their former decorations, which are known in some cases from Renaissance drawings that bear witness to their splendour. For example, the ruined 'Tor de' Schiavi' on the Via Prenestina can be shown from brickstamp evidence to date from Diocletian's time at the earliest and may well be Constantinian (fig. 41). Its rich vault decoration, which is entirely lost, was drawn by Pier Sante Bartoli,[4] but since Bartoli's accuracy is open to doubt, this drawing does not provide a definitive record which might have helped to identify its patron or its occupant, or their religious beliefs. However, its position beside a basilica with a wrapped-around ambulatory makes it quite possible that it was built for a Christian member of Constantine's family, by analogy with the mausolea of Helena and of the daughters of Constantine, both of which opened off the atria of similar basilicas.[5] Renaissance drawings, such as Bartoli's, though they may give general information about now-ruined structures, are often of little value as accurate records of what has disappeared. Although it is probable that most of these ruined tombs were not built for Christian rulers, they offer proof that the advent of Christianity did not immediately lead to profound changes in the architecture of the emperors' mausolea. Over time, though, both their architectural settings and their internal decorations did undergo change and came to reflect the new beliefs.

Helena's mausoleum on the Via Labicana at Rome, the burial place of the mother of Constantine, is also now in ruins, though it was drawn by Antonio Bosio in the sixteenth century (fig. 42).[6] It has always been associated with the name of Constantine himself. It was thought that he built it for his own use or that of his dynasty, and that eventually it came to Helena as a consequence of the transfer of the capital to Constantinople. It contained a porphyry sarcophagus, which is now in the Vatican Museum, and is ornamented with the military imagery in high relief that would be appropriate for an emperor, such as Constantine himself. Alternatively, it is possible that the sarcophagus was available for Helena because it had been ordered by Constantine's rival, Maxentius, for his mausoleum on the Appian Way.[7] Since Maxentius had been declared a usurper by Constantine, he would certainly have lost his right to imperial honours on his death, honours which would have included the use of porphyry.[8]

Helena's was the first imperial mausoleum to be built for a Christian occupant, and for the first time the tomb was attached to the narthex of a Christian church (fig. 43).[9] This new arrangement embodied a radical change of orientation. In the pagan system, the mausoleum was the self-contained temple of a deceased imperial personage who had now risen to the gods. It was surrounded by a *temenos* wall, and often had an attached circus at which funerary games were celebrated: such a funerary complex survives at Maxentius's mausoleum on the Via Appia. By contrast, the new belief required that the body of the deceased be protected in the precinct consecrated to the One God, in whose temple the funerary rites would be held, and in whose shadow the body would await the day of resurrection. It appears that each of the great suburban cemetery basilicas of Rome was associated with the mausoleum of a member of the imperial family. All five of the cemetery basilicas so far discovered were built to the same plan, with a wrap-around ambulatory of about the same width as the nave, and an altar above the grave of a martyr, and all but S Lorenzo had an imperial mausoleum nearby.[10] Even there, further excavation may well reveal an imperial burial place.

Although the Mausoleum of Helena is in ruins, Antonio Bosio's early-seventeenth-century *Roma sotteranea* briefly describes the interior,[11] and recent archaeological studies have added further details. The tall, single-storeyed structure had seven niches apart from the entry, and these were alternately rectangular and semicircular. The one on the main axis was larger than the others, and must have held the porphyry sarcophagus, which was present *in situ* until the mid-twelfth century, when it was taken by Pope Anastasius IV (1153–4) for his own use. As was normal for such a tomb, the inner walls were covered with marble revetments in *opus sectile*: the varicoloured marbles used included porphyry and *giallo antico*. The holes left by the metal clamps which supported them suggest a rectangular pattern.[12] Bosio presents the only evidence, apart from a few scattered tesserae, for the mosaic decoration of the upper level which clothed all the niches and the dome. He saw the figures of several 'saints,' one with flames at his feet. He thought this panel showed the martyrdom of St Tiburtius, who was commemorated in the catacomb below. Bosio shows this mosaic in the axial niche, site of the sarcophagus, but his identification of the subject may be questioned: it is likely that it illustrated the Boys in the Fiery Furnace, a salvation theme that is common in Early Christian funerary art.[13] It occurs in numerous locations in the catacombs, while fragments of the scene survive at Centcelles, the probable tomb of Constantine's youngest son, Constans I (337–50).[14] There, it was one of the scenes of salvation that were portrayed in the dome, along with several episodes from Jonah's story and Daniel in the Lions' Den.[15] The scenes were depicted behind an irregularly spaced colonnade of spirally fluted mosaic columns, in a fashion shared with other mausoleum decorations, such as those of Sant'Aquilino, Milan, and, in a rather different form, at S Costanza, Rome. Evidence that the illusionistic device of tiered images separated by columns may have been copied from a three-dimensional original comes from the lost church of La Daurade in Toulouse, where the Early Christian decorative scheme is known to have included more than sixty mosaic images arranged in three tiers of niches, which were separated from each other by colonnettes, some thirty of which survived the destruction of the building in 1764.[16] La Daurade itself had all the hallmarks of a royal mausoleum. I have proposed elsewhere that the program of the bottom register of the decoration was concerned with salvation, marking it as a burial place.[17] This idea is also supported by the fact that the building was a polygon with a crypt below, as were the mausolea of the emperors.[18] The proposed dating of the decoration to the fifth or sixth century, which is quite consistent with an iconographic program centred on salvation, makes it likely that the church was built by the Visigothic kings who held court at Toulouse from AD 418 until 507, and that they used it as their dynastic mausoleum. Finally, many iconographic details relate the mosaics at La Daurade to the programs of other imperial mausolea of Late Antiquity; I will return to these in a subsequent chapter.

Two mausolea rose beside St Peter's, Rome, in the time of Constantine (plan, fig. 44). Both of them appear to have risen on earlier foundations: the footings of the two rotundas which had been erected on the spina of the Circus of Nero after it fell into disuse, probably in the early third century.[19] This is clear from the foundations of the easterly structure, the Vatican Rotunda, which were investigated by Castagnoli in 1957. Brick-stamp evidence dated it to the reign of Caracalla (212–17).[20] The other rotunda was until recently thought to have been built on new foundations for Honorius and his family around the time of the death of his first wife Maria in 405, and thus to have been the latest built of the great Late Antique imperial mausolea.[21] Recent opinion, however, dates the second phase of both these rotundas to the era of Constantine. Great quantities of earth were piled up around the preexistent buildings during the construction of the level platform which supported the basilica of Old St Peter's: indeed the ground level at the site of the mausolea rose by almost ten metres, completely burying the cylindrical lower storeys of the earlier buildings. To remedy this, the inner cylindrical space of each structure was filled with rubble.[22] The filled structures were then used as foundations for new rotundas. These were built in the fourth-century style, articulated on the inside by seven deep rectangular niches and the entryway. Each building also had a twin-apsed vestibule; the two mausolea were almost identical in size, with the Vatican rotunda slightly the larger. Renaissance drawings show the latter's tall, windowless lower drum which supported a smaller cylindrical upper storey.[23] This in turn was articulated with alternating deep buttresses and round-headed windows, eight in all. Evidently, it shared many features with the Mausoleum of Helena.

It is not known who built either the original or the Late Antique phases of these two mausolea, nor is it known who was buried there. However, their position on imperial property at the circus suggests that they were built as imperial mausolea.[24] As a pre-Christian building, the Vatican Rotunda was ripe for conversion into a church by the turn of the fifth century, and was dedicated to St Andrew by Pope Symmachus (498–514).[25] It was rededicated as S Maria delle Febbre in the fourteenth century in honour of its miracle-working icon, and was finally demolished in 1777 to make way for the sacristy of the new basilica.[26]

Both mausolea are also known from Alfarano, who wrote sixty years after the Honorian Mausoleum was pulled down.[27] His account is important for its record of the findings of the master mason Cosimo Fiorentino, who demolished it in preparation for laying the foundations of the south side of the new St Peter's. Cosimo found that the mausoleum had as many vaulted spaces in its foundations as it had niches in the upper storey, an arrangement which was probably common to both mausolea. We do not know whether these vaults were the original burial places or whether they had served only in times of danger: imperial burials were discovered intact about two metres beneath the pavement of the Honorian mausoleum in the fifteenth and sixteenth centuries. It has recently been suggested by Nikolaus Schumacher that the Honorian Mausoleum was built by Constantine's sister Anastasia as her own tomb and that she also built the nearby basilica.[28] Schumacher cites Damasan insciptions found near the site to support this theory and suggests that Pope Damasus (366–84) converted the mausoleum's upper storey to a baptistery, the central, rubble-filled foundations acting as the support of the font. This would then be the baptistery described in Prudentius's poem 'The Passion of St Peter and St Paul.'[29] However, there are difficulties in accepting that the Church could purloin a recently built imperial mausoleum for conversion to a baptistery at this time, since many members of the family of Constantine still resided in Rome. It is more likely that Anastasia's burial place remained in use as her mausoleum and was reused for the empress Maria when she died around the year 405.[30] Subsequent use by the family of Honorius defined it as their dynastic mausoleum. Burials at the Honorian Mausoleum probably included those of Maria's husband the emperor Honorius in 423, his second wife, Maria's sister Thermantia in 415, his half-sister Galla Placidia, who died in 450, and her baby son Theodosius, who had died in Barcelona in 415, and was reburied in Rome in 450. Galla Placidia's second husband, Constantius III, who died in 421, and her younger son, Valentinian III, who died in 455, were also probably interred here.[31]

The appearance of the Honorian Mausoleum is known only from a single fifteenth-century wood engraving, which makes it clear that it was built on the same plan as the Vatican Rotunda.[32] The quality of this sketch is very poor and it is impossible to determine any details. The interior decor of the mausoleum also remains completely unknown. The building was subsequently dedicated as a church to Petronilla, the legendary daughter of St Peter, whose body was translated to the mausoleum from the catacombs by Stephen II (752–7), and his brother, later

Paul I (757–67). S Petronilla was demolished in the sixteenth century to make way for the new basilica.

In contrast to the many losses at St Peter's, a single Late Antique imperial mausoleum does survive in Rome, the mausoleum of the daughters of Constantine on the Via Nomentana, S Costanza. This building retains a substantial part of its original decoration, and was widely admired by Renaissance artists and antiquarians, who made many drawings and descriptions of the building and its decorative scheme. All these sources of information make S Costanza the best-known of all the Late Antique imperial mausolea. It dates to a pivotal period in Early Christian art, the mid-fourth century, when pagan iconography was being reinterpreted in Christian terms, and the ambiguity of the result can perhaps be best understood in terms both of the patron and of those who would occupy the mausoleum in death. S Costanza and the other well-preserved fourth-century imperial mausolea, S Aquilino at S Lorenzo in Milan and Centcelles near Tarragona in Spain, will be considered as case studies in Part Two of this book.

CHAPTER THREE

The Domestic Oratory:
A Mirage

The domestic chapels of the aristocracy, which are mentioned in the literary sources, prove to be the most elusive of all Late Antique chapels. This is because none survive with any documentation at all, and thus none can be identified with certainty as Christian chapels. In Aquileia and Rome, a few mosaic pavements decorated with symbols capable of either Christian or pagan interpretation have been claimed as the floors of chapels in Christian houses, but their very ambiguity makes it impossible to confirm the functions of the buildings they once adorned or the beliefs of those who used them.[1] One single building, the Chapel of the Monte della Giustizia in Rome, uncovered on the Esquiline Hill during the demolitions which accompanied the building of Roma Termini railway station in 1873 (and itself almost immediately demolished before it had been fully recorded) was thought to be the sole survivor of the domestic chapel type.[2] Since it was small, measuring only three metres across, and its apse was decorated with three registers of paintings, it appeared to provide important evidence for the appearance, dimensions, and decoration of such a chapel. More recently, though, it has been identified with near certainty as a tiny church, probably S Agata in Esquilino, a church documented in the Itinerary of Einsiedeln, but not hitherto identified. It was probably built for a congregation of Gothic settlers during the unsettled period after the fall of Rome in 410. Breakdown of public order could explain its minuscule size, as it had been inserted into a *vicus*, a narrow public street, which would hardly have been possible in normal times.[3]

Therefore, in the absence of any firm archeological evidence for the existence of the private chapel, the focus must be on the literary evidence, which is scattered and sparse. The uniformity of the Christian world around the Mediterranean in the fourth century makes it possible to search for references to domestic chapels in both Latin and Greek sources. A wide search is also necessitated by the scarcity of references to private chapels in both East and West. This scarcity of mention does not necessarily mean that chapels were rare in upper-class households: it could equally well mean that chapels were as commonplace in the Christian household as *lararia*, shrines to the pagan gods, had always been in the pagan home. And their failure to survive archaeologically may depend on nothing more than the fact that it had been unwise to have a room which was obviously dedicated to a proscribed religion in one's house in times of persecution, such as the early years of the fourth century.

In Rome, scattered references in saints' lives and contemporary chronicles prove that private oratories existed there as early as the turn of the fifth century. 'Permansit tota nocte vigilans in oratorio domus suae, curvans genua usque in mane ac deprecans Dominum,'[4] we read in the life of St Melania the Younger (ca. 383–439), a Roman noblewoman, daughter of one of the richest families in Rome, the Valerii. This record of her night of prayer recalls Galla Placidia's more famous night-time vigil in her palace church at Ravenna, as told by Agnellus.[5] Both cases underline the importance to pious women and girls of good family of having an oratory in or near the home, so that they could carry out their religious obligations without risk to their safety or reputation. St Ambrose, when visiting Rome, would celebrate the liturgy at the house of a friend, a noblewoman who lived in Trastevere,[6] while St Gregory of Nazianzus, in his eulogy to his sister Gorgonia, dating between 369 and 374, told of her cure when, arising from her sickbed, she prostrated herself before the altar which contained the sacraments, taking the consecrated elements in her hand and applying them to her whole body.[7] Though most records that mention chapels in homes do so in the context of the devotions of women, men too sometimes maintained private places for prayer. For example, the emperor Constantine had a portable oratory with him on the field of battle,[8] and also another in the inner part of his palace.[9] These texts make it clear that, by the early fifth century, wealthy Christians maintained oratories in their homes for individual prayer, and that they also sometimes celebrated the liturgy privately at home with family and friends.

A further suggestion has been made that in the Early Christian period the sacrament was reserved in domestic chapels. This suggestion is borne out by Gregory's account of his sister's devotions, though no evidence in the form of containers specially decorated or inscribed for reservation of the sacrament has survived to support the theory. However, the presence of an altar and the sacraments in Gorgonia's house shows that it was possible in the middle of the fourth century for household chapels to have altars where the sacraments were reserved.

This prompts an important question: what distinguished a fully equipped domestic chapel from a house-church or *titulus*? Surely the presence of the sacraments would have automatically conferred the status of church on any chapel where they were reserved. Henri Leclercq proposed that from the apostolic age to the Peace of the Church 'chapels' were indistinguishable from churches in almost all respects, since both were the sites of liturgical celebration.[10] The defining difference appears to have been the congregation. House-churches were open to the public for celebration of the liturgy; private chapels were not. But a private chapel might evolve into a house-church through the acquisition of a congregation. G.P. Kirsch has shown that the typical Roman *titulus* contained as nucleus a preexistent chapel, often a private *memoria* of some sort, which typically was incorporated into the church as a *confessio*, a martyr shrine under the altar.[11] Relics, since the *tituli* were within the walls of the city, were probably limited to contact relics such as *brandea*. An exception among these core chapels, since it is built over the gravesite of three saints, is the small structure, complete with late-fourth-century paintings and a *fenestrella* for the devotions of the faithful, which lies under the Roman church of SS Giovanni e Paolo, the *Titulus Byzantius*, and forms its *confessio*. This has been described by Kirsch as a true domestic chapel.[12] The *Titulus Aequitii*, S Martino, lies over a cult centre of St Sylvester, dating to about AD 500, and occupying a room in the south-west corner of the church's substructure, while high up in the gallery below the church of S Pudenziana, the *Titulus Pudentis*, there is a painted niche, its floor now vanished, which must once have been a centre of the cult of the saints who later came to be venerated in the church above.[13] All these chapels date from the fourth or early fifth centuries. Probably all the other *tituli* contained similar martyr shrines or chapels, sanctified, perhaps, not by physical remains but by contact relics or venerated objects connected to the saints' lives or deaths. None of these chapels has survived intact, but their possible role in the foundation of so many *tituli* gives them an important position in the study of the early parish churches of Rome.

To recapitulate, our knowledge of domestic chapels largely depends on literary references, and without these we might presume that private chapels, defined as places of individual or family prayer in private houses, had never existed, since no sure traces of any have been found. The likelihood is, however, that chapels have not been found because they have not been recognized, either because they were undecorated, or because their decorations have not survived. Architecturally, these rooms may not have been very different from other rooms, and whatever furnishings they may have had, such as altars or images, may well have been portable. Quite possibly domestic chapels were, and always had been, so normal a part of upper-class Christian life that they were rarely mentioned, except in passing as integral parts of other stories, such as those of Melania and Gorgonia. The texts do imply, however, that the uses of private chapels were varied and that the sacraments could be celebrated in them whenever a visit from a priest made this possible. Domestic celebration of the sacraments, however, was not limited to dedicated chapels in the fourth century. Although it is unclear from Paulinus's *Vita Ambrosii* whether Ambrose celebrated at Trastevere in a chapel or in an ordinary room, Tertullian tells us in *De Fuga* that in exceptional circumstances, and especially in times of persecution, Mass was celebrated wherever and whenever it was possible, even by night.[14] An example of exceptional circumstances is that of Constantine, who was able to partake of the sacraments while on campaign.[15]

In addition to the straight literary sources, which include histories, letters, and religious tracts, a second important written source of information about the private chapel exists among the regulations which governed the usages permitted to chapels. These are recorded in the canons of the early Church Councils. For although in the early period before the mid-fourth century private places of worship do not seem to have been controlled, they later became subject to discussion at the Church Councils. These discussions led to written regulations. From canons which forbade certain uses of private houses or of chapels we can deduce that abuses were occurring, which the Church wished to correct. For example, the mid-fourth-century[16] Council of Laodicea's Canon LVIII states that 'The Oblation must not be made by bishops or presbyters in any private houses.'[17] At the Council of Gangra, convened sometime between 345 and 381, Canon VI forbids the assembly of congregations privately outside the church if they perform 'ecclesiastical acts,' by which is presumably meant the celebration of Mass.[18] This Canon is believed to have been formulated to counter a heresy, perhaps that of Eustathius (ca. 300–77), who from about 357 is believed to have been bishop of Sebaste. Eustathians avoided public services, seeking an asceticism which declared itself in a choice of celibate clergy and in the shunning of the less ascetic members of the congregation.[19] Soon after, in 387 or 390, Canon VIII of the Council of Carthage forbade the celebration of Mass in private chapels without the permission of a bishop.[20]

The Council of Chalcedon of 451, in an attempt to control the heretical monasticism of Eutychius, which like Monophysitism doubted the dual nature of Christ, proclaimed in its fourth Canon that 'no-one anywhere [may] build or found a monastery or oratory contrary to the will of the bishop of the city.'[21] The restrictions on unorthodox groups obtaining the services of a priest for heretical sacraments were enhanced by Canons V and VI, which restricted the rights of itinerant bishops and priests, and made it obligatory that all priests and deacons be ordained to a particular charge, so that none should be outside the close supervision of the Church hierarchy.[22]

Thus, the repeated legislation on the dangers of private celebration in the fourth and fifth centuries reveals that there was continuous vigilance against heresy in centuries when it was particularly rife, and confirms the existence of private chapels in which the sacraments were quite frequently celebrated. Further evidence of this is found in the proceedings of the Synod of Rome of August 430.[23] Among the accusations against Nestorius heard by Pope Celestine I (422–32) was the statement by Bishop Cyril of Alexandria that Nestorius had condemned a priest, Philip, to be deposed for celebrating Mass in a private chapel: this, Cyril asserted, was improper because the practice actually was allowed when it was necessary.[24]

In summary, it appears that there was an early period when little legislation controlled the private chapel, which functioned as a small private church. This was followed by a period in the mid-fourth century when the sacraments were absolutely banned from private oratories, which were to be used for private prayer only. Following this, the practice of celebration of Mass and even baptism in chapels was left to the discretion of the bishop, as shown by Canon IX of the Council of Carthage. Bishops exercised this control by licensing priests only to stated benefices, and by banning them from travelling at large, where they might be available for unsupervised celebration of the sacraments among the unorthodox or even among heretics. This controlling supervision is defined in the thirty-first Canon of the Quinisext Council of 692: 'Clerics who in oratories which are in houses offer the Holy Mysteries or baptize, we decree ought to do this with the consent of the bishop of the place. Wherefore if any cleric shall not have done this, let him be deposed.'[25] That is, by 692 the bishops were willing to give permission for private chapels to be used for the full liturgy, including baptism, but only under licence.

A somewhat different situation arose when the private chapel in question belonged to the bishops themselves and was situated in their own clergy house. Restrictions on their own palace chapels were presumably unnecessary, and the legitimate purposes for which they might be used were more formalized and at the same time more varied. The chapels benefited from the diocesan resources rather than private funds, and if the sole surviving example is anything to go by, the decorations and architecture may have been permanent and costly, and formed part of a complex of splendid buildings devoted to the cult of which they were an integral part.

This sole survivor is the chapel of the Archbishops of Ravenna.[26] Two bishops' palace chapels were built in that city in the time of Theoderic the Great (475–526): the chapel of St Apollinaris for the Arian sect, to which the king belonged, and St Andrew's for the orthodox hierarchy.[27] The latter is the survivor. It is the only decorated chapel of the Early Christian period which is unequivocally identified as a private chapel.

Private chapels in bishops' houses were not unusual, to judge from the fragmentary literary evidence. This literary evidence suggests that a chapel was an integral part of the facilities of most episcopal palaces.[28] Outside Italy, Gregory of Tours (ca. 540–94) mentions his new private oratory at Tours, in which he placed the relics of various saints,[29] while in central Italy, the existence of an episcopal chapel in Narni is recorded by Pope Gregory I.[30] In Rome itself, we learn in passing of a chapel dedicated to St Caesarius in the imperial palace on the Palatine, which had been newly repaired under Platon, the *cura palatii urbis Romae*, father of Pope John VII (705–7), and was the scene of the election of Pope Sergius in 687.[31] In the Lateran Palace itself, the residence of the popes in their capacity as bishops of Rome, there were three chapels by the late seventh century. One was built by Pope Theodore (642–9), and dedicated to St Sebastian.[32] By the year 687, a chapel dedicated to St Sylvester was situated in the portico to the right of the great entrance.[33] A third chapel, dedicated to St Peter, was in need of redecoration by the time of Pope Gregory II (715–31), who gave it new mosaics as well as images in silver of the twelve apostles.[34] In addition, the chapels of Pope Hilarus (461–8) at the adjacent Lateran baptistery may well have been used as private papal chapels, and those erected around the year 500 at the Vatican by Pope Symmachus will also have served this purpose.

The Ravenna chapel is the sole undisputed survivor of this once numerous category. Since it is situated on the upper floor of a building inside the walls of the city, it can never have been intended for burials. Rather, it was certainly built for the private devotions of the bishops (later archbishops) of Ravenna, forming part of their Tricoli palace. The bishops could access their chapel from inside the palace, and also, probably, by means of an elevated walkway from the fortifications of the city at the Porta Salustra.[35]

But in addition to private prayer, the function which a bishops' chapel shared with all domestic chapels, an episcopal palace chapel must have fulfilled other practical functions. In the case of the Ravenna Archbishops' Chapel, these needs can be assessed with some certainty. It was incumbent upon all clerics to celebrate Mass daily, and the Archbishops' Chapel must have had an altar for this purpose. The palace was adjacent to both the cathedral and the baptistery, suggesting that the archbishop probably robed in the chapel, and that his vestments may well have been stored there, possibly in one of the closets which occupied the spaces between the arms of the cruciform structure. The chapel or its narthex may also have been the assembly point for the participating clergy, who would process with the archbishop to the cathedral or the baptistery, according to need. Liturgical books, according to season, may also have been stored in the chapel, and been carried from there to the altar.[36] These sacred, though practical, uses may account for some features of the decoration of the chapel, and these traces of function will be sought. We have no idea how this chapel was furnished, as its ancient possessions have long ago been dispersed, but judging by the gifts given by the fifth-century popes Hilarus and Symmachus to their chapels at the Lateran and the Vatican, respectively, we can presume that the interior of the Archbishops' Chapel was enriched not only by an altar, but by crosses, crowns, lamps, and pictures or statues in precious metals and jewels, emphasizing its sacred quality.[37] Curtains were also an integral part of the furnishings of such a chapel, and were made of the most rare imported silks in diapered patterns, which themselves were echoed in the mosaic patterns chosen at this period for vaults and for niches and window embrasures. These richly decorated areas are well represented in the Chapel of the Archbishops of Ravenna, and will be encountered in chapter 5.

CHAPTER FOUR

Chapels within the Confines of Churches: A Late Development

This chapter is concerned with various categories of chapel which share a single and rather artificial feature: their location within the perimeter of a church. This distinction allows us to include chapels built for a variety of liturgical purposes. To these will be added sacristies, or 'side chambers,' to use Janet Smith's neutral term. These may also be situated inside the main structure of the church, and, like oratories, could be used for prayer and occasionally for burial. However, they had additional functions peculiar to their role as sacristies. These functions were extremely varied, and were often expressed in their architecture. As to sacristy decorative programs, the scanty evidence suggests that sacristies could be just as richly decorated as other, better-known types of interior chapels.

The chapels fall into three groups: *cubicula*, chapels of mixed use situated in auxiliary buildings of churches; *oratoria*, chapels built within churches for liturgical purposes including the Eucharist, private prayer, and Christian burial and its rites; and sacristies, broadly speaking, serving all sorts of utilitarian functions in connection with the preparation of the Eucharist and the storage of the belongings of the church and clergy.

The available data in all these three areas are scanty. *Cubicula* are known from records of the building activities of early medieval popes and other patrons. They are also occasionally identified in the archaeological record. Oratories were not built inside churches for doctrinal reasons during the first three centuries of the period under consideration. However, the limited data from the seventh and early eighth centuries illuminated the beginnings of a new development: that of subdivision of the church interior to accommodate new altars, altars which might eventually become enclosed in their own rooms within the church buildings. As for sacristies, which were included in the study for the sake of completeness, as interior rooms whose functions overlapped with those of other internal chapels, surprising evidence came to light that in Italy sacristies were the exception, rather than the rule, and that their presence seems to have implied upper-level, Eastern patronage.

Cubicula

It is difficult to trace the beginnings of the internal chapel, built for liturgical purposes and occupying part of the main body of a church, for it transpires that all the earliest examples which seem to fall into this category were actually built into such auxiliary buildings of the church as its external colonnades. They are not only chronologically earlier, but seem to be fundamentally different from true chapels inside actual church buildings. The difference is highlighted by the use of the word *cubiculum* rather than *oratorium* or *altare*, a semantic distinction that implies their origin was as resting places rather than as places of prayer or the sacraments. This rest, of course, might refer to rest and meditation in life, and also to the long rest after death. This is clear from the information given by both literary and archaeological sources, which come together at Nola. There, the *cubicula* of the Basilica Apostolorum are the best understood of all the groups of chapels inserted into church buildings in the Late Antique period, on account of the writings of Paulinus of Nola. We learn of the chapels from Paulinus's letter to Sulpicius Severus, in which he not only described building them, but explained the purposes they would serve.[1] Shortly before AD 403, a set of four *cubicula* were inserted, two to a side, into the lateral colonnades of the Basilica Apostolorum, which was then under construction. The chapels' first function was for private prayer and meditation, but they were also intended for the burial of members of the religious community and their families.[2] Paulinus told Sulpicius Severus that the outer lintel of each *cubiculum* was marked with two lines of appropriate verse, though he did not record them.[3] One of Paulinus's *cubicula* has been identified in the excavations and found to be a long, narrow room, provided with an apse at each end, and communicating by a wide entry with the side aisle of the basilica:[4] it thus doubled as an annexed chapel opening from the aisle of a cemetery basilica (plan, fig. 45, A). The need for quiet places set apart from the church for private use such as prayer and meditation, as well as for the graves of the religious community, is underscored by Paulinus's description of the noisy and drunken behaviour of the devotees who came to Nola to worship at the shrine of St Felix.[5] Prudentius, too, in his *Hymn on the Passion of Hippolytus*, describes the three-aisled basilica built over that martyr's remains in these words: 'Even when it is full [it] scarcely admits the struggling waves of people and there is turmoil in the confined space at the packed doorway where she opens her motherly arms to receive and comfort her children and they pile up on her teeming bosom.'[6] We are also reminded of Jerome's description of the pandemonium at the shrines, where dramatic spiritual conflicts between the saints and the demons of possession so terrified the congregations.[7] Similar concerns must surely have operated in other locations where chapels – *cubicula* – were built as places apart in the colonnades of the great congregational churches and cemetery basilicas of Late Antiquity and provided privacy in life and death for the clerical hierarchy and the well-to-do near the sacred places which, while replete with holiness, were devoid of privacy and noisy with the uncouth habits of the lower strata of society.

Cubicula are not peculiar to the writings of Paulinus; they also abound in the text of the *Liber Pontificalis*. Sergius (687–701), for example, repaired *cubicula* around St Peter's: according to Duchesne these were in a portico attached to the outer side walls of the church, which was furnished with cells for pilgrims.[8] Sergius likewise repaired *cubicula* around S Paolo *fuori le mura*.[9] Paulinus's explanation of the uses of such structures at Nola hints that at the Roman basilicas, too, some of the chapels may have been used for burial. But Paulinus also tells us that he provided upper-storey accommodation over the cloisters for the use of pilgrims to the shrine of St Felix.[10] This suggests that such accommodation would have been provided at any great pilgrimage church, in Rome or the provinces, and that the enclosure of colonnades and cloisters may often have had the primary function of giving shelter and rest to pilgrims.

Oratoria

Oratories in the domestic setting have already been discussed in the previous chapter. Oratories were also built at basilicas and baptisteries, and are recorded in the patronage records of the popes and other ecclesiastics. The *Liber Pontificalis*, for example, abounds in references to *oratoria* created by the popes in ecclesiastical settings, though none is dated earlier than the pontificate of Hilarus (461–8), except an *oratorium* in the catacombs that was the tomb and *memoria* of a martyr, St Felicity.[11] We will discover that there were doctrinal reasons why the earliest of these chapels were not situated in the interiors of church buildings, but were either added on to the outside as annexes or inserted into subsidiary buildings nearby.

Early papal commissions of *oratoria* in Rome took place at the Lateran Baptistery in the mid-fifth century by Pope Hilarus and at both St Peter's and S Maria Maggiore at the turn of the sixth under Symmachus.[12] In the seventh century, popes built *oratoria* in the portico outside the Porta Ostiense leading to S Paolo *fuori le mura*,[13] and the San Venanzio chapel was added to the group at the Lateran Baptistery.[14] The majority of oratories mentioned in the *Liber Pontificalis*, though, were built at St Peter's, though not, it seems, inside the basilica itself. We have seen that Pope Symmachus (498–514), for example, inserted at least four, and probably six, chapels into the niches of the Vatican Rotunda, the imperial mausoleum adjacent to the basilica's left transept, dedicating the building to St Andrew.[15] This burial place of a third-century emperor had not previously been consecrated as a church. It seems likely that the dedication of these altars to various martyrs honoured the papacy's collection of relics of the saints, though this cannot be proved. If so, the building became a collective martyrium rather than a congregational church or a basilica.

Symmachus's other building project at St Peter's is of special interest as it appears to document *oratoria* in the interior of the basilica at the start of the sixth century, which would be the earliest indisputable record of such chapels. We learn from the *Liber Pontificalis* that Symmachus built three chapels in St Peter's at the Baptistery of Pope Damasus (366–84).[16] All these chapels are referred to in the *Liber Pontificalis* as *oratoria*: they bore the same dedications – to the two saints John and to the Holy Cross – as Pope Hilarus's chapels at the Lateran baptistery. Symmachus's chapels have usually been located inside the right transept of St Peter's, because the Alfarano plan shows them there, loosely arranged around a font.[17] If these chapels really were inside the church, rather than annexed, it would suggest that chapels were built inside basilicas a full hundred years before the next recorded example.[18] The problem is that the Alfarano plan was drafted about forty years after the demolition of Old St Peter's, and cannot be relied on without corroboration. Février has recently suggested an alternative solution. He proposes that in fact the original chapels were annexed structures.[19] He bases his opinion on the twelfth-century description of Petrus Mallius, who called Symmachus's chapels *ecclesiae*, a designation he always used for annexed chapels, while he called internal chapels *oratoria*.[20] If Février's theory is correct, these chapels would fit the normal pattern of the times, when regulations, now lost, appear to have favoured external chapels, by discouraging or even forbidding the subdivision of church interiors. Furthermore, if the chapels were separate structures, Damasus's baptistery was probably a free-standing building as well, and located outside the right transept of the church. A contemporary poem appears to confirm this layout, as Prudentius describes a spring outside the church which fed the font.[21] Water channels discovered under the basilica in this location may well be the remains of the plumbing of the baptistery. Février also suggests that the remains of the baptistery and its three chapels could all have been buried without trace under the massive foundations of St Peter's.[22] Thus it appears that the St Peter's baptistery with Pope Symmachus's chapels was a much closer copy of the Lateran Baptistery complex than is usually understood, with similar or identical building types in addition to identical dedications. Although the chapels were all described as *oratoria*, on the precedent of the Lateran chapels one may surmise that they also served as *memoriae* and sheltered relics of the saints, in addition to being used for private prayer. In support of this, it is recorded that Symmachus's S Croce, like its Lateran prototype, possessed a relic of ten pounds' weight of the wood of the Cross.[23] It seems probable that these three chapels were built to honour the cults of the saints John and of the Holy Cross, as well as to underline the authenticity of Symmachus's claim to the papacy. Very likely, they also served both for private prayer, and for private celebration of the Mass, in the manner of their namesakes at the Lateran Baptistery, which will be discussed in a subsequent chapter. The chapels inside the transept of St Peter's probably date from the period of rebuilding in the fifteenth century, when the Damasus Baptistery had already been pulled down, but facilities for baptism were still needed during the interim period while the new basilica was being completed.[24]

Février's work makes it difficult to accept information documenting chapels inside church buildings as early as the reign of Symmachus without serious reservations. At a later date, though, there is firmer evidence for the existence of chapels in the interiors of churches. These chapels form the subject of this section.

Why the appearance of separately dedicated chapels within churches was a relatively late development is a question worth considering, especially in view of the popularity of such internal chapels in the later Middle Ages. The impetus for their appearance appears to be linked to changing perceptions of the nature of the altar. In the early days of the church, the altar was felt to be indivisible, as were the celebrant and the Mass itself,[25] and it seems that this indivisibility extended to the church as well, in its role as setting for the altar and temple of the mysteries.

The earliest-surviving description of a Christian church, Eusebius's passage on the church of Tyre written soon after its dedication in 317, describes the early layout with a single altar:[26] 'He hath placed in the midst the holy of holies even the altar, and again surrounded this part also, that the multitude might not tread thereon, with a fence of wooden lattice work.' It is apparent that the re-creation of the Last Supper by the celebrant, in memory of Christ's sacrifice, carries with it the idea of a single table, and a single oblation offered by an individual priest. This explains the difficulty of accepting or even contemplating the multiplication of any of the essential elements. Joseph Braun has noted that in those days secondary altars did not exist inside basilicas, *memoriae*, or chapels in either the East or the West. If new altars were needed, new churches were built or chapels were added onto the outside of existing buildings. These chapels differed from internal chapels in their possession of doors, and usually also of vestibules, which allowed them to be thought of as separate structures, completely isolated from the church.[27] An example of this sort of chapel, with its original portal and bronze doors, will be encountered at the Lateran Baptistery's Chapel of the Baptist, while the Evangelist's chapel there also retains its original portal, built of spoils, though its doors are medieval replacements.

In fact, it is not until almost three centuries after Eusebius that the earliest unequivocal mention of multiple altars within a church occurs, and it refers to Gaul, not Italy.[28] It occurs in Pope Gregory's letter to Palladius, bishop of Santenis in Gaul, written in July 596, concerning the need for relics for the thirteen altars of a church under construction there.[29] It seems, in the dearth of evidence to the contrary, that between the early fourth and the late sixth centuries the single altar had been the rule.[30] The edict 'one church, one altar,' however, evidently led to problems.[31] These have been seen by Ejnar Dyggve to have been caused by the success of the cemetery churches in attracting pilgrims,

because there each grave-top could serve as an altar. This gave opportunities, which were denied to city churches, to celebrate the Eucharist
at any hour of the day, and in the presence of the martyrs' remains.[32]
The change to multiple altars has also been attributed to the greatly
increased congregations, though the extent of such increases has not
been precisely determined. According to this argument, the expansion
of the Christian community led to an increase in the numbers of clergy
relative to the number of altars, one only to a church or to an annexed
chapel, that were available for celebration of the Mass. Thus, some
priests may have been deprived of altars at which to celebrate, while
for congregations the problem was felt especially keenly at Easter,
when some Christians even found it impossible to receive the sacraments as required of them on this day.[33] A hint of the difficulties, again
referring to Gaul, is contained in the Tenth Canon of the Council of
Auxerre of 578. This laid down that any one altar could only be used
for Mass once in a day.[34] Such legislation implies that altars were of
necessity being used more than once, perhaps because individual
priests could not find a 'resting altar' to celebrate on. Since the idea of
celebration of the sacraments upon a 'resting altar' was doctrinally
important, the solution seems to have been to allow the proliferation of
altars, so as to ensure a fresh altar for each celebrant. Thus the multi-
ple-altar church came to be accepted, though scholars have failed to
find exact documentation of this vital change, despite being able to
pinpont it to the last quarter of the sixth century.

We have seen that the evidence that appears to document chapels
inside church buildings as early as the reign of Symmachus cannot be
accepted without reservation. Nevertheless, the evidence is firmer that
from the seventh century onwards chapels could be and were built
inside the interiors of churches, though we know remarkably little
about the architectural features and decoration of these internal
chapels in the earliest period, though they have various features in
common. The sources make it clear that these 'chapels' were not completely walled-off spaces, 'rooms within rooms,' but altars, placed near
or right against the walls of the church, rather than standing in the centre of the space, as had been the custom. They were set apart by a low
and partial enclosure at most, and furnished with railings and canopies, lampholders and other plate, and above all, mosaics, paintings,
and other rich items such as curtains of precious fabric, and decorative
panels made of gold and silver.[35]

The earliest chapel of this sort that survives, though it was only recently recognized as such, is the oratory of saints Primus and Felicianus at S Stefano Rotondo, Rome. It dates to the reign of Theodore I (642–9). The unusual design of the huge, circular church, where a central, cruciform core was wrapped by two columnated ambulatories, through which the higher cross-shaped element rose, in theory allowed space for a chapel in the end of each cross-arm. Only the north-east chapel site survives, though in the seventh century one of the other cross-arms probably contained an altar dedicated to the Baptist.[36] Krautheimer and his associates have suggested that originally there may have been neither a main altar and *confessio* in the church nor even a relic of St Stephen. They point out that originally there had been a radial symmetry, with multiple entries in the perimeter wall, though very soon most of the entrances were blocked up, except for those in the north-east, which became the entryway. Cecilia Davis-Weyer suggests that there was in fact a main axis to the church, running from south-west to north-east, and that the sanctuary and altar were in the south-west arm.[37] This would make the present chapel of saints Primus and Felicianus in the north-east an entryway chapel, analogous to others attached to the narthex of Early Christian churches, such as the Mausoleum of Galla Placidia at S Croce in Ravenna. These, however, were annexed chapels rather than internal ones.

Pope Theodore chose this location to re-inter the saints' remains which he brought in from their catacomb gravesite at Mile 14 of the Via Nomentana, the first recorded translation of martyrs' remains from the suburban catacombs into the city of Rome. He carried out this exhumation and reburial at least in part to provide a burial *ad sanctos* for his father, Bishop Theodore, an exile from Jerusalem after the Arab conquest.[38] The eastern origin of the pope and his father may explain the innovative nature of this break with the Roman past, which previously had forbidden the transfer of saints' bodies.

The interest to us of Pope Theodore's chapel – which, incidentally, is not named as an *oratorium* in the *Liber Pontificalis*, but only as a *confessio*, implying an altar with relics rather than a full chapel – lies in its decoration and furnishings. These are known from the gifts in gold and silver listed in the *Liber Pontificalis*, the surviving apse mosaic, and the results of archaeological exploration. This varied information makes it potentially one of the best known of early medieval chapels within a church, in addition to being the earliest-known internal liturgical chapel to survive.

Both the small apse, less than four metres wide, and its mosaic decoration date to the time of Theodore. In the mosaic, Primus and Felicianus, named '+ SCS PRIMUS + SCS FELICIANUS,' stand on either side of a large, jewelled cross which bears a roundel with a bust of Christ (fig. 46). This cross is of an Eastern type, similar to that in the courtyard of the Anastasis in Jerusalem illustrated on the pilgrim flasks at Monza and Bobbio.[39] It seems an appropriate choice, both for the burial place of a Palestinian bishop, and for the church itself, which is widely believed to be a copy of the Holy Sepulchre. The inscription below reads 'ASPICIS AURATUM CAELESTI CULMINI TECTUM/ ASTRIFERUMQUE MICANS PRAECLARO NUMINE VULTUM' ('Reader, thou lookest on a roof golden with heavenly apex and a face gleaming like a star and shining with a wondrously divine air').[40]

The altar stood in front of the chord of the apse, and the relics were found *in situ* in its *confessio* in 1736, identified as such by a silver tablet.[41] The altar appears to have been the only one in the church, and was ornamented with the silver frontal which is recorded in Theodore's *Liber Pontificalis* biography. The sacred area and, indeed, the chapel itself were bounded by a small wall, which was wider, at 6.4 metres, than it was deep: its side walls measured 4.4 metres. It was rectangular except for the curve of the apse in the rear wall. The enclosure walls were built on top of the paving, which was of large marble slabs, and the central front opening was 1.2 metres wide and still retained a sill of green serpentine. Carlo Ceschi identified the wall as the base of a low enclosure, such as could have supported plutei and a *pergula* rail. This last would have held the papal gifts, three golden lampholders, and a pair of silver arches.

Davis-Weyer's opinion that this structure was a chapel and not the main sanctuary is based on the discovery of remnants of a *schola cantorum* and, possibly, of a bishops' chair at the other end of the 'processional way.' The chapel's unique position, directly facing the altar, is made possible by the circular plan of Santo Stefano: it suggested to her that it functioned not only as a martyrium and a mausoleum, but also, possibly, as the sacristy from which the liturgical procession would emerge on its way to the altar.[42]

Two other *oratoria* which were built by the popes in the late seventh and early eighth centuries inside Roman basilicas are described in the *Liber Pontificalis* with enough detail to give us some further idea of the furnishings of such a papal chapel. At the Lateran basilica, the otherwise unknown oratory of St Peter was rebuilt by Gregory II (715–31).[43]

He decorated it with precious metals, perhaps meaning gold mosaics, and had its altar faced with silver plaques weighing 180 pounds and depicting the twelve apostles. A short while before, Sergius I (687–701), had built a chapel in the south transept of St Peter's to shelter the remains of Leo I, whose tomb had previously been situated in the communal papal cemetery in the atrium, the *paradisum*, which was now crowded with papal graves. Although this chapel was not referred to in the *Liber Pontificalis* entry for Sergius's reign as an *oratorium*, but rather as a *tumba* (tomb), it had achieved the status of *oratorium* fifty years later, when it was again mentioned in the life of Paul I (757–67).[44] Its recorded inscription dated the translation to 28 June 688,[45] and describes its decoration as of precious marble, with pictures of the prophets and saints who were buried at St Peter's.[46]

Another important example of an interior chapel dates from the very end of the period under consideration here. It was built in 732 by Pope Gregory III (731–41), who chose Old St Peter's as the site of an *oratorium* in honour of Christ, his Mother, and all saints.[47] It was situated next to the triumphal arch and would also serve for Gregory's burial. Although, like all the other chapels in Old St Peter's, it has failed to survive, this chapel is unusually well described in the *Liber Pontificalis*, where we read that it was vaulted and decorated with mosaic. Gregory gave a *pergula* for suspension of crosses, bowl-shaped lamps, and other golden vessels and lamps, while, over the altar, a golden crown with a hanging cross and pendent jewels was suspended, a type of votive gift which is known from the late-seventh-century Guarrazar treasure. This included several golden crowns with pendent jewels and crosses.[48] The altar enclosed a *confessio* with silver-covered doors: its sides bore three silver crosses each weighing 36 pounds. Above the altar was a picture of the Mother of God with her Child, wearing a golden and jewelled diadem and a golden and jewelled necklace, which in addition bore hanging gems: her earrings, also, were ornamented with jacinths. An icon of the Virgin was recorded as behind the altar in Gregory's chapel by Mallius; probably it was still in place in his time.[49] Per Jonas Nordhagen has studied an early-eighth-century painted icon of Mary in S Maria Antiqua, Rome, finding evidence that it had been embellished with jewellery and had even had cut-out lips of precious metal applied over its painted mouth.[50] Five 'clasped-garments' were also given to Gregory's chapel; presumably these were some sort of liturgical robe. The chapel also received altar cloths, while the practical needs of the liturgy were served by gifts of chalices, a silver one for daily use and another for display in the apse, and of a pair of silver hand basins, for the celebrant's ablutions. An intriguing part of the *Liber Pontificalis* entry is an account of the chapel's endowment for the daily office: the pope thus made provision for the perpetual repetition of prayers for his salvation in the place of his burial.

Our knowledge of one other early medieval chapel from Old St Peter's is gained not only from documentation, but from the descriptions and drawings made of it at the time of its demolition along with its church, and from the major fragments of its mosaic decoration that survive. The chapel was built between 705 and 707, during the short reign of John VII, and has been the subject of extensive research, particularly by P.J. Nordhagen,[51] and, recently, by William Tronzo[52] and Ann van Dijk.[53] Tronzo concentrated on a study of the mosaics through the drawings of the lost composition and the surviving mosaic fragments in Rome, Florence, and Orte.[54] Since chapels at St Peter's underwent many changes in the thousand years between their foundation and their demolition, Tronzo's analysis of the chapel of John VII is all the more welcome. He bases his research on the structure itself as revealed in the drawings of Grimaldi,[55] which show that this *oratorium* was in fact another vestigial chapel, like those we have discussed, consisting only of an altar and its furnishings. Its features included the altar, with the tomb of John VII in front of it beneath an oval slab; a ciborium supported by two columns; pilasters on the wall which probably held lamps; and the important mosaic panel above the altar in which episodes from the life of the Virgin and of Christ surrounded a large central image of Mary at prayer, in the fashion of an icon of the *vita* type.[56] By recognizing that the mosaic panel on an adjacent wall which illustrated scenes from the lives of Peter and Paul was a later addition, and not part of the original program, Tronzo was able to see the chapel for what it was, an altar on the inner entrance wall of the church, rather than a four-square space railed off in the corner of the basilica. Thus he overcame the enigmatic quality of the chapel that had previously deterred scholars from attempting a reconstruction. Tronzo's interpretation makes it plain that it fits into the normal pattern for the earliest chapels in the interior of churches, which will be designated the 'altar-chapel.' It was also clear that a primary function of the structure was the burial of the pope who built it, thus conforming to a pattern which was to become more and more common at St Peter's in the early Middle Ages. The decoration and inscriptions, together with the humble figure of John VII in the square halo of a portrait from life, kneeling at the feet of Maria Regina, make it clear that the pope gave the chapel and mosaics to the Virgin in her role as intercessor, in expectation of her help on the day of judgment.

Thus, it was only around the time of Gregory the Great that the integrity of the internal space of the church began to be breached, and individuals of the highest ecclesiastical rank could claim a private, dedicated space right inside the basilica. These chapel spaces could be used for private prayer, private liturgical celebrations, or even for burial within the actual confines of the church.[57] In cemetery churches outside the walls of cities, burial within the church building, itself a cemetery, had been possible from an early date, and every grave-top had come to be thought of and used as an altar. However, in the Early Christian period, even in the cemetery churches, individual graves do not seem to have been enclosed in separate rooms inside the basilica itself. And even in the late seventh and early eighth centuries, the funerary chapels that were built inside churches remained vestigial, furnished and decorated as altars, and lacking the full walls and vaults that would become the ninth-century norm. The next stage, the full-room internal chapel, is exemplified by the mid-eighth-century Theodotus chapel at S Maria Antiqua in the Roman Forum, a redecoration of a preexistent room, and by the vaulted funerary chapel of saints Processus and Martinianus, in the left transept of Old St Peter's, which was built and decorated with a mosaic vault by Pope Paschal I (817–24) for his own use as a burial chapel.[58] It is a short step from such structures as these to the typical chapels inside the churches of the later Middle Ages.

Sacristies

A third important category of chapel existed within the physical boundaries of some Early Christian and Byzantine churches: the sacristy. Sacristies have sometimes been known as pastophories, but this term is better reserved for the side chambers of Middle Byzantine churches, where they had precisely determined functions in the preparations for the liturgy.[59]

Sacristies have been defined as utilitarian chapels which meet the auxiliary needs of the Mass and the congregation.[60] They are often paired, and situated on either side of the altar, though before the sixth century a single structure might meet all the practical needs and be situated at the other end of the church, beside the narthex.[61] It might even be an entirely separate structure, rather than an annex. Although some exceptional cases of paired and even multiple sacristies can be documented to the fourth and fifth centuries, these were all imperial gifts, perhaps with special significance. The change to paired sacristies in nonimperial churches can be traced to the mid-sixth century and the reign of Justinian, when the three-part sanctuary became the norm in the East and in churches built under Eastern influence in the West. The paired chambers to the left and the right of the altar would later be called *prothesis* and *diaconicon*. In our period, however, these names had not yet come into use.[62] Nevertheless, even if the functions of these chambers in terms of the liturgy had not yet become formalized, many of the needs they served were not peculiar to the Middle Byzantine period, and the chapels must therefore have served the same functions as the *prothesis* and the *diaconicon*. Among these, the most important was the preparation of the sacraments. The clergy also needed a place in which to robe themselves, light the incense, and prepare the vessels and clean them after use. Places also had to be provided to store the churches' treasures: books, plate, vestments, and money. In addition, the gifts of the congregation had to be received and stored, gifts that included the bread and wine destined for the Eucharist, as well as alms for the poor.

It is striking that despite needs that must have varied little from place to place, some Early Christian churches possessed sacristies, while others lacked them. Even when we take into account the possibility that local variants in the liturgy may have imposed needs for differing architectural ground plans, we must still ask how the sacristy functions were carried out in churches which had no special sacristy chapels, the situation, we shall discover, of most early churches in the West. Some light is thrown on this problem by Paulinus of Nola, who at the turn of the fifth century not only built a church in the cemetery at Nola, the Basilica Apostolorum, but explained the use of specific parts of its sanctuary as 'sacristies' in a letter, and recorded the epigrams which he placed above these areas to explain their functions.[63] Paulinus's new church had a trichoran apse: in his own words,[64] 'an undulating apse unfolds itself with two recesses, one to the right and one to the left.'[65] The excavations of the Basilica Apostolorum made it clear that an 'undulating apse with recesses,' *conchulae*, was an apse with a wide, three-windowed, central bay and a secondary apse on either side, each of which was lit by a single window (fig. 45, B).[66] Paulinus remarked that one recess offered a place where the priest prepared the host – the 'offers of jubilation,' and the other was for the prayers of the priest and his congregation.[67] He expounds these meanings in verse: the right sacristy (*secretarium*) of his church bore the verses 'this is the place where the awesome provisions are put, and where the life-giving ceremonial procession of the sacred sacraments is sent forth.' On the left was inscribed 'If anybody has the holy wish of meditating on the law, here sitting down he can turn to the holy books.'[68] Thus, it was the side apses of Paulinus's church that were used as sacristies, the right apse being used for storage and preparation of the elements of the Eucharist, and the left for storage of the altar books, which were available there for study by the congregation. Perhaps the furnishings on this side consisted of cupboards like the one seen in the Mausoleum of Galla Placidia lunette mosaic, with shelves for the gospel books, and doors that could be closed and presumably locked on the sacred contents (fig. 96). Across the chancel, there must have been more cupboards for the vessels, and a table for the preparations.

Paulinus solved the question of where the sacristy functions were carried out for one of the several types of church without separate, purpose-built sacristies: the *trichora*. One can only speculate that in churches which lacked both sacristies and trichoran chancels, these functions were accommodated in the subsidiary apses if the sanctuary was triple, in the areas to either side of the main apse, or at the east ends of the side aisles. It is hardly surprising that no early furnishings have survived, though an idea of them can be gained from the illustrations of book cupboards in mosaic and manuscript art.

Normally in the West, the spaces dedicated to these functions were equal in size, and symmetrically arranged on either side of the sanctuary, as Paulinus describes them. In the East, however, the utility functions came to occupy separate rooms. Such profound local architectural variants in different parts of the Early Christian world are thought to reflect regional differences in the liturgy and in the needs of congregations. In Syria, for example, archaeological evidence makes it clear that there were two types of sacristy with different functions, with the inevitable outcome of a local variant, the asymmetrical sanctuary. On one side, the utility chapel would communicate openly with the altar area and the north aisle of the church by means of archways, to facilitate the processions and the transfer of the consecrated bread and wine to the altar. On the other side, by contrast, the sacristy was closed off from view by a smaller doorway, and presumably possessed narrower and less accessible windows. Here we have physical evidence that in Syria one of the main functions of the sacristy had become that of treasury, which needed the greatest possible security. This may well be a reflection of Syria's position on the frontiers of empire. The treasure of the average Syrian church included not only the communion plate and other portable objects such as censers, candelabra, and lamps,[69] but the relics of the martyrs, which occupied stone coffers within the building.[70] These were bulky, and the need for this type of storage seems to have led to an exaggerated asymmetry of the east end of many Syrian churches, in which the treasury came to project forward from the sanctuary.[71]

The region for which the congruence between architecture and liturgy is best understood is Byzantium, where the architecture has been studied in this context by Thomas Mathews,[72] and the early liturgy has been investigated in depth by Robert Taft. Taft has analysed the text of the Liturgy of St John Chrysostom, collating the ritual and ceremony with the architecture of the church buildings and their annexes.[73] Taft and Mathews have concluded that the earliest churches in Byzantium did not have clearly demarcated sacristies, and that all their functions were in fact filled by a separate building, the skeuophylakion.[74] Brick studies of the skeuophylakion at H Sophia, Constantinople, show that it antedates Justinian's church, and belongs with the earlier church built on the site by Theodosius the Great, which was consecrated in 415. It survived the church's destruction by fire in the Nika riots of 532, and consists of a dodecahedral building with interior niches. Literary evidence for its function is found in the works of Palladius (ca. 363–ca. 431), who called it a 'separate little building in which the many sacred vessels were kept.'[75] Other Constantinopolitan churches such as H Eirene and the much smaller H Theodoros Sphorakios also had separate and circular skeuophylakions.[76] Taft's and Mathews's studies have concluded that the ceremony of the Mass in H Sophia both started and ended at the skeuophylakion.[77] Before the ceremony, the clergy vested and said the *prothesis* prayer in the skeuophylakion. The gifts were offered there by the congregation and stored there also; there too the eucharistic vessels were withdrawn from storage and charged with the bread and wine. The deacons were normally in charge of the preparations. They went in procession to the altar, where they were met by the priests: in smaller churches where there were no deacons the priests made all the preparations. After the Mass, the exit procession followed the same route in reverse, and a prayer was offered on reaching the skeuophylakion, where disrobing took place, and the sacred vessels were returned to storage.

My intention in discussing the origins of the sacristy in Constantinople is to pinpoint the influence this type of structure may have had in its evolution in Italy and the Upper Adriatic. The skeuophylakion as it developed in Constantinople seems to have been one component of metropolitan church architecture, which, even if it was not exported in exactly the same form, had a profound influence on the layout of the sanctuary of some early Italian churches. This is especially true of the churches which were most closely related to the imperial, and therefore Eastern, tradition of church building.

These churches, of course, are best known from Ravenna, but there are others in outlying areas, including Rome, which were also built under Eastern influence. The influence is very obvious in the triple east ends of these churches, which usually have characteristic apses, polygonal outside and round inside. Taft has related this feature to north Syria, for pre-iconoclastic Constantinopolitan churches had no sacristies at all, but single apses flanked by multiple entrances.[78] In Italy and Istria, the Constantinopolitan influence, even where not seen in the triple apse, may be visible in the circular chambers beside the apses of several special churches. Some of these survive, while others are known from literary or archaeological evidence. The sites of these chambers, in each case paired and adjacent to the sanctuary, are the imperially connected foundations of S Lorenzo in Milan (plan, fig. 14) and S Vitale in Ravenna (plan, fig. 10). They also occur at S Maria Formosa, Pula (plan, fig. 34), which was not only an extraterritorial Ravenna possession, but was built by Archbishop Maximinian, who was closely associated with the building of S Vitale. All three pairs of chapels were centrally planned, with internal niches, and those of Ravenna and Pula are known to have been decorated with wall mosaics.

The centrally planned chambers at S Lorenzo, Milan, presumably contemporary with the church and thus dating from the late fourth century, are known only from excavation. Octagonal in form, each small chapel had eight rectangular niches, alternating deep and shallow, with one niche penetrated by the door. These rooms flanked the martyrium, S Ippolito, behind the high altar. The octagons in their turn were flanked by rectangular, apsed chapels which still survive. Chierici and his co-authors have suggested that the right-hand octagon served as 'diaconicon.'[79] Although this feature is omitted from the most frequently reproduced ground plans, such as that of Mirabella Roberti, even there the author notes the presence on either side of S Ippolito 'due aulette ottagone, usate per *prothesis* e *diaconicon* e forse per archivio.'[80]

The set of eight chambers beside the presbytery at S Vitale have also sometimes been identified as sacristies: Janet Smith has suggested functions for each according to its architectural features (fig. 10). The Sancta Sanctorum to the south (right) of the altar, with its extra door to the outside, has served as a funerary chapel for S Vitale's founding bishops since the episcopate of Victor, who died in 544.[81] The twin chapel of Gervasius and Protasius on the north (left) of the sanctuary has no door to the exterior, and may well have been used as a sacristy and treasury. Suggestive evidence for this function is provided by an event recorded in the late-sixteenth-century *Historia di Ravenna* of Tomasso Tomai.[82] He describes a find of treasure that had occurred about fifty years previously. Gold coins were found in one container and later, under a very heavy cover, a marble sarcophagus full of closed reliquary boxes of various materials, both plain and ornamental. The boxes, of silver and of alabaster, were variously sized, from six inches ('due palmi') to a cubit ('un braccio' [18–22 inches]). These relic containers were accompanied by many loose precious stones and cameos.[83] This discovery was made in the 'little church near the afore mentioned church [of S Vitale] dedicated to saints Gervasius and Protasius, martyrs and sons of St Vitalis.' Because the text continues with a description of the decoration of the chapel 'all worked in mosaic, with most beautiful figures who mysteriously look at one another beckoning with their hands,' this has been assumed to refer to the Mausoleum of Galla Placidia, with its pairs of gesturing saints on the upper walls. However, the Mausoleum has never been dedicated to the sons of Vitalis, whereas the left-hand domed chamber of S Vitale has always borne this dedication. Perhaps there is another solution: that the find was in some way connected with the domed sacristy of Protasius and Gervasius at S Vitale, perhaps originally occupying the sarcophagus-sized niche in its outer wall.[84] This treasure, consisting in large part of relics in precious containers, was an appropriate one to come from the treasury of a great imperial church. The supposition of Corrado Ricci that the treasure must have formed part of an imperial burial seems less likely, since a sarcophagus entirely full of reliquaries would be a strange accompaniment for a secular tomb.[85] Unmounted jewels, also, do not fit the pattern that we know from the burial in Rome of the empress Maria, whose grave goods, while they included hundreds of gems, had them set as rings and other jewellery.[86] The Ravenna treasure is unfortunately dispersed, and its find location cannot be precisely determined. Since the goods it contained were so appropriate to the treasury of a great church, I offer this find as extremely tentative evidence that the chapel of Gervasius and Protasius at S Vitale, about which nothing is known of function or decoration, was a sacristy and treasure store of the church and that it was once decorated with mosaics, which have since been lost.[87]

Janet Smith has recently suggested that the three-storey chambers between the domed chapels and the sanctuary fulfilled various other storage-related functions.[88] On the middle level, the low, windowless chambers were hidden from both inside and outside: she identifies these as secret treasuries. Both top chapels are furnished with slots for shelving. They occupy the driest and best-ventilated positions in the church, and were quite possibly used as libraries. On the ground level the chapels are provided with deep rectangular niches: that on the north side is grooved for shelving. These chambers, especially the north one next to the presumed sacristy, may have held the more immediate necessities of the Mass.

The architecture of the large, domed chapels can be related both to the skeuophylakion in Constantinople, and to the needs of the treasury function: their rectangular niches, sized to hold a sarcophagus, also relate them to such structures as S Sisto, the funerary chapel of the Milanese bishops at S Lorenzo (fig. 19). As at Constantinople, each of the S Vitale chambers was circular, with niches: two larger on the outer side of the church; two smaller on the apse side. Each was lit only by a small window in the east end. Each was raised by several steps above the level of the surrounding land, which then, as now, had a high water table. This may have been designed to raise the sacristy contents out of the worst of the damp at ground level. There does not seem to be a conflict with the dedications of these two chapels as martyria, especially as we know that the actual bodies of the four Milanese saints of the dedications lay in Milan.

The sacristies at S Maria Formosa, Pula, are known both from a sixteenth-century description and from the remains of the substantial common wall, complete with niches, that survives as part of the adjacent, outer chapel, which is the only part of the great basilica to survive (fig. 35).[89] Pietro Kandler, quoting an anonymous early-sixteenth-century Pula writer, described the sacristies as having 'most beautiful monumental doors' and 'a window that gave little light' – the perfect formula for a treasury – and one can presume that they were designed as strong rooms, capable of being securely locked.[90] Inside, the floor was clad in mosaic in a compartmentalized design, of which fragments were still visible in 1845.[91] The vault was described by the anonymous writer as also clad in mosaic, and the walls below as having niches that contained statues.[92] Perhaps these were reliquaries. It seems likely that both these vaulted, niched, and securely closed chapels beside the altar served for storage of the altar wares, sacred books, and church treasures, which probably included relics, as well as the offerings for the sacraments. Marzia Vidulli Torlo has also suggested that these circular chambers at S Maria Formosa served as prothesis and diaconicon.[93]

In these churches, each with its own connection with Constantinople, it seems that the very unusual circular sacristies or treasuries are direct quotations from the capital city, where early churches kept their treasures in a separate, circular skeuophylakion. Krautheimer has argued very convincingly that such 'copies' of architecture in the Middle Ages did not slavishly imitate every feature of the original, but selected key qualities for emulation. These acted as markers of the buildings' common purpose, overriding other striking differences which were less important to the medieval mind.[94] In the case under consideration, the circular form and the niches appear to have been the fundamental points of resemblance: the position, close to the altar, rather than separated, and the duplication, may have been local features, influenced by the symmetrical architecture of the earlier churches of Milan and Ravenna.

Such circular sacristies, though, are exceedingly rare and occur only at the most richly endowed churches, and only at S Lorenzo can they be assigned a date prior to the sixth century. However, multiple rectangular side chambers beside the sanctuary distinguished Galla Placidia's two Ravenna churches, S Croce and S Giovanni Evangelista, from their contemporaries. Again the clustered side chambers seem to be a hallmark of imperial patronage. These sets have also been assigned practical functions by Janet Smith: hidden chambers for treasuries, a small relic shrine that may be a copy of Golgotha at S Croce, a library heated by a subfloor hypocaust.[95] In the absence of any other early evidence for the building of separate sacristies in the West, we are probably justified in assuming that the typical nonimperial Early Christian basilica had found no cause to build formal sacristies, finding that the arrangements described by Paulinus at Nola were quite adequate.

In the sixth century the situation seems to have changed, presumably in response to the renewed Byzantine presence in Italy from 540. From this time, the east end of nonimperial churches in Ravenna and the Upper Adriatic area were frequently provided with chapels flanking the sanctuary. Even in Rome trichoran and triple-apsed eastern ends were built under Eastern influence. Pope Vigilius's SS Quirico and Giulitta (538–45), for example, had a polygonal apse, flanked by apsed side chapels facing north and south, the assemblage creating a trefoil.[96] The SS Apostoli, first dedicated by Pope Julius I (337–52), may also have had a sixth-century trefoil chancel, with an apse at each end of the transept, and a sacristy on either side between the transept and the choir. These latter, which can be seen in a fresco in the Vatican Library, may be fifteenth-century additions built on Early Christian foundations. Even so, this would prove that there had been side chambers in the Early Christian period. Krautheimer accounts for this Eastern influence by dating the church to the Byzantine occupation of Rome under Narses.[97] S Giovanni a Porta Latina also had a tripartite choir: its central apse was polygonal outside and semicircular within, in Eastern fashion.[98] The chancel probably dated to the reign of Gelasius I (492–6), and was built with side rooms that have narrow doorways into the aisles. These were all rare features for Rome, but known from Ravenna, while the polygonal apse also points to Constantinople. The Eastern influence is confirmed at S Giovanni a Porta Latina by use of the Byzantine, rather than the Roman, foot as unit of measurement.[99]

The sixth-century churches of Ravenna and the north-east, which were plainly built under Byzantine influence, were quite often endowed with chapels beside the sanctuary. Some of these must have served as sacristies, though many were used as funerary chapels. Grado is especially rich in such structures. The cathedral, S Eufemia, has already been discussed. Nearby, at the mid-sixth-century S Maria delle Grazie, the third church to occupy the site,[100] the chapels have narrow and low doorways: in order to use the space behind the straight east wall, they open into a narrow, vaulted passageway behind the apse. This space was formerly divided by a wall into two small inner rooms in the thickness of the masonry behind the curve of the apse. The whole area is provided with fine sixth-century mosaic floors: the inner area may have served for storage of treasures, as the small, low doorways and inner recesses of the rooms would suggest: these treasures may, as in Syria, have included relics such as those donated by Bishop Elia (571–86).[101] The sacristy floors are attributed to the bishopric of Elia, who also built those of S Eufemia and of the Basilica of the Piazza Vittoria at Grado. Parts of the mosaic floors were given by individual officials and soldiers, and are dated to the second half of the sixth century.

The Basilica of the Piazza Vittoria, its dedication unknown, but dating to the first half of the fifth century, like S Maria delle Grazie had a rectangular plan with the apse inscribed within the flat east wall, and a pair of trapezoidal chambers fitted into the space around and behind it. This style, possibly of Syrian inspiration, was adhered to when the basilica was expanded in the late sixth century. The renovation probably occurred in Elia's time, when a new apse, again flanked by sacristies, was built behind the primitive one, and the nave was wrapped by lateral aisles. This time, though, the flat expanse of wall behind the main apse was broken by a small, extra apse in the right chamber, which took on the function of relic-chapel, associated with the transfer of relics to the churches of Grado in the time of Elia.[102]

At Ravenna also, fifth-century churches usually had a single apse, while in the Byzantine period of the sixth century triple apses became more common, or, alternatively, the central apse was flanked by sacristies. Archaeological evidence places the Basilica Petriana (429–49), situated in the city of Classis and destroyed in an eighth-century earthquake, in the simple category, with a single, externally hexagonal apse.[103] The suburban church of S Severo, Caesarea (570–7), was also of this simple design.[104] The three-aisled Basilica Probi, however, had a triforan east end: this may possibly be an early feature comparable to that of the Basilica Apostolorum at Nola.[105]

In conclusion, the scanty evidence concerning sacristies points to the coexistence in Italy and Istria of two different traditions. Typically, in the Early Christian period in the West, the sacristy functions were not carried out in separate rooms built for the purpose within the church. Paulinus's account confirms that specific interior chapels designated for these practical functions were not a normal part of the early basilica, any more than the church interior was subdivided at this period for other purposes. Nevertheless, there was clearly a different tradition in Constantinople, which affected church design in those parts of Italy which were closest to the influence of the capital, or were provided by the individual patronage of Eastern clerics or of the imperial family.

This tradition was manifested in a variety of plans for the sanctuary area. These allowed different functions to take place in purpose-built spaces, separated off in the form of subsidiary chapels and suitably furnished. It seems likely that all the early variants of the sanctuary with side-chamber sacristies in Italy are of Eastern origin. The great majority that have survived, or that are described in literary or archaeological sources, are in the Upper Adriatic region, including Ravenna, and date from the sixth century. They mark the Byzantine period in the Exarchate and the Eastern patronage that resulted from it.

PART TWO

The Survivors:
Iconography and Meaning

The first section of this book has surveyed a wide geographical area: the whole of north and central Italy, as well as the coast of Istria, now divided between Croatia and Slovenia. It has explored a period of over four centuries that spans Late Antiquity and the start of the 'Dark Ages.' Yet even though it covers so large an area, and such a long time span, and has brought together information about numerous chapels, few of them have survived with any of their decorations in place, and of these, fewer still are in a complete enough condition to allow the whole iconographic program to be deciphered. This is hardly surprising after an interval of anywhere from twelve to sixteen hundred years.

In addition to the more complete chapels, which will be discussed in detail in the ensuing chapters, some of those which have already been encountered retain fragmentary decorations, and many more, entirely shorn of decoration, betray symbolic meaning in their architectural form. Many more chapels are known only from the archaeological record. Descriptions in medieval and later documents, while often mystifying or at best incomplete, allow some chapels which have lost their decor or even their identity to take their place in the overall picture.[1] Drawings made in the Renaissance period are also informative. The picture that emerges tells of an artistic and architectural vocabulary which is rich in symbolic content, and which can express the various ideas and articles of faith which we know from written sources to have been important to the early Church. This impression will be confirmed by the in-depth studies that follow.

Thus, it is clear that the decorations illustrated texts appropriate to the function of each individual chapel, and that these texts were drawn from the Old Testament and the Prophets, the New Testament, apocryphal writings, and, especially, the Apocalypse. The writings of the Church Fathers also provide insights into the choice of texts, and illuminate the concerns of the era. I will also suggest that the liturgy was illustrated, and that its prayers were depicted in visible form in the space where they had been spoken. This is illustrated in the mausolea of the fourth-century Christian emperors, and, nearly half a millennium later, in the S Zeno chapel at S Prassede, Rome, in all of which the intercessory prayers of the funerary Mass were illustrated in mosaic.[2] Unfortunately, none of the surviving chapel decorations from the intervening period include this theme, though it must have remained appropriate in the context of a funerary structure. The lives and deaths of the saints also provided inspiration, especially in the *memoriae* which were erected over their graves, such as S Vittore in Ciel d'Oro, Milan, and, in a funerary context, at the Mausoleum of Galla Placidia in Ravenna. And even when no exact text can be located for a given decoration, it is likely that such a text existed, perhaps in the sermons or other oral sources of the day, but has not survived.

The material that has been gathered in the survey chapters covers a wide variety of structures, from the self-contained but annexed building with or without a vestibule to the internal secondary altar with its furnishings, partly or completely railed off; from the sacristy chapel with its multifarious practical purposes to the dedicated room within a house. Above all, the survey is essentially incomplete, since the ravages of time have taken so heavy a toll on chapels and their decorations. This is particularly true of those in the houses of the wealthy laity, which have disappeared almost without a trace, although their existence is recorded in literary sources. This lost material obviously would have counterbalanced conclusions which in default are based almost entirely on evidence from funerary structures. This is the inevitable consequence of the fact that almost all the surviving decorated chapels belong to the funerary and martyr tradition. The cult of the dead was not only responsible for their existence in the first place, but was also the reason for the care and maintenance they received in succeeding centuries. The most notable exceptions are the Archbishops' Chapel in Ravenna, the palace chapel of the Ravenna episcopate, and the chapels of the two saints John at the Lateran baptistery, all of which will be discussed in more detail in this section of the book. At the Archbishops' Chapel, it seems reasonable to ask whether its storage areas contained relics of the saints which would have given some flavour of the martyr cult to this chapel too, while at the Lateran, the chapels, built as shrines, must have held relics in their *confessiones*. This would at least partly explain the convergence of their decorative programs with those of the more overtly funerary majority that form the main subject of this book.

If the survey material and the case studies are taken together, the vocabulary of chapel decoration will be found to be that of Early Christan art in general: the three persons of the Trinity, expressed literally or metaphorically; their attendant angels; and their abode, the heavens, seen as a multilayered dome sprinkled with stars, and sheltering an appropriate flora and fauna which express layers of allegorical meaning.

In these early chapels, the Father and the Holy Spirit appear only in symbolic form: the Father for dogmatic reasons,[3] and the Holy Spirit because of the inherent difficulty in representing the nonmaterial. Thus, at S Vittore in Ciel d'Oro the Father is represented by the hand that emerges from the clouds of heaven to crown Victor in his glory, while at the S Matrona chapel the Holy Spirit is shown as a dove, following the standard formula in Early Christian art. The Son, with his two natures, human and divine, appears in human form in a medallion portrait at S Matrona, as a shepherd in the Mausoleum of Galla Placidia, and as a victorious emperor at the Archbishops' Chapel. These images do not illustrate events from the Gospels and in fact Christological narrative scenes are entirely absent in the surviving chapels. Rather, they approach the task of illustrating Christ as Man through his own words as recorded in the Gospels, or those attributed to him in the apocalyptic vision of John, which was already considered canonical in the West in the Early Christian period. Christ taught about himself in metaphors, and it is these that are expressed visually in chapel programs. For example, at the S Matrona chapel, Christ's image is flanked by the alpha and omega, illustrating his words 'I am the Alpha and the Omega, the Beginning and the End' (Rev. 21.6), while the shepherd scene at the Mausoleum of Galla Placidia is dependent on 'I am the good shepherd,' and also refers in its position over the entryway to 'I am the door: if any enters by me, he will be saved, and will go in and out and find pasture'(John 10.11, and 10.9.) The preferred dress for Christ in these images is the purple imperial *chlamys*. In the vestibule of the Archbishops' Chapel at Ravenna, the choice of imperial military dress and victory iconography makes the interest in showing Christ as ruler even more explicit. Evidently the model transferred to the heavenly realm was that of God's representative on earth, the emperor. Evidently, too, the respect given to images of the emperors in the temporal realm could be transferred to those of Christ, the heavenly ruler.[4]

Just as frequently, though, the image of Christ is expressed in symbolic forms, which may coexist with his human image in the same composition, and lend it the richness of extra layers of meaning. These symbolic images, like those already discussed, may be drawn from Gospel and Apocalyptic metaphors. Two important examples are the Lamb (Rev. 5.6–9), shown in the vaults of the two chapels of the saints John at the Lateran Baptistery, and the Vine (John 15.1–8), widespread in the vaults of chapels from the Veneto to Campania. However, a second category of symbolic image, the cryptic, does not depend on Christ's own words. The cryptic images are those which Kitzinger describes as 'material props'[5] and originate in the period when the Mosaic law against graven images held sway, and when, perhaps, Christians attempted also to put distance between themselves and the practices of Greco-Roman paganism. Most obvious of these 'props' is the simple cross, as at the Mausoleum of Galla Placidia, where it blazes among the stars of the main vault and symbolizes Christ in his second coming. Equally popular are the varied monograms using the letters of Christ's name. The most widely accepted of these was the Chrismon or chi-rho symbol, which appears in the lateral vaults at both the Mausoleum of Galla Placidia and the Archbishops' chapel in Ravenna. The cross may also be combined with the monogram, most notably at S Vittore in Ciel d'Oro. There, analysis of the complex crosses portrayed beside St Victor in the vault reveals cryptic equivalents of the name of Christ, similar to those inscribed in early days in the Roman catacombs.

The heavenly city, Jerusalem, and its twin city, Bethlehem, also form part of the decoration of at least one chapel, that of S Venanzio at the Lateran Baptistery. Interestingly, this is one of the latest and by far the largest of the chapels in our series, its size raising the question of whether this building was intended more as a church than a chapel. The meaning of the decoration was symbolic. It stood for the Church, and also for the dispensations to the Jews and the Gentiles. This symbolic content may possibly identify S Venanzio as a church, in the absence of any other 'chapels' decorated with this motif, though the group sampled is far too small to be conclusive.[6]

The apostles, also, appear in the vocabulary of Christian art in both literal and allegorical forms, and are so illustrated in the decorations of chapels. Named portraits of the twelve in medallions adorn the soffits of the arches at the Archbishops' Chapel, while at S Matrona an allegorical rendering, known from a wood engraving, showed them as twelve doves beside the cross of Christ. Lost also are the bust- or full-length figures of the twelve from the vault of the S Prosdocimo chapel at Padua's S Giustina, which may once have echoed those of the baptisteries of nearby Ravenna.

The revelation of God in the Christian faith is represented by the Gospels, which are symbolized by the evangelists. These, in turn, are portrayed in human or symbolic form, or in combinations of the two, and the chapels will be found to illustrate the evolution of such imagery during the period when Christian iconography was first established. For example, the evangelists were depicted in human form, as standing figures with their symbolic creatures above their heads in the lost vault decoration of the Baptist's chapel at the Lateran baptistery in Rome. Symbols with neither evangelists nor books survive at the S Matrona chapel and at the Mausoleum of Galla Placidia, while slightly later, the symbolic creatures are seen to be holding their books at the Archbishops' Chapel, Ravenna, and at S Maria Mater Domini in Vicenza. In all these cases the imagery represents the faith as a divinely inspired revelation. However, in one location, the Mausoleum of Galla Placidia, the Gospels are also shown separately from the evangelist symbols, and appear as named volumes in a cupboard. This unique iconography spells out the role of the books as books, rather than as revelations, in an abbreviated narrative account of the passion of St Vincent of Saragossa. This panel, incidentally, antedates other surviving narrative illustrations of the lives and passions of the saints by at least two centuries.

The Virgin Mary does not occur among the holy figures illustrated in the earliest Christian art, so it should not surprise us that she is not portrayed in the decorative programs of the earliest chapels in our series. After the Council of Ephesus of 431 which named her Mother of God, her likeness may well have been placed beside those of the martyrs and confessors in the memorial chapels sanctified by their images or relics. If so, it has not survived, even at S Maria Mater Domini, Vicenza, which has probably been dedicated to Mary since the sixth century. Her first surviving chapel image is in the seventh-century apse of S Venanzio, Rome.

As far as the saints and, especially, martyrs, are concerned, it is hardly surprising to discover their images in their places of burial and commemoration. Interestingly, they are not confined to the lowest zone of the decoration, as in the hierarchical decorative schemes of the East after iconoclasm. In the West they occur both in the lower zone, along with the ecclesiastics who had promoted their cults on earth, and also in the vault, the 'heavenly' area, where they had attained glory through martyrdom. This is especially well shown at S Vittore in Ciel d'Oro.[7] Here, the important early bishops associated with the site, Maternus and Ambrose, are pictured full-length on the side walls, each between his protectors, the martyrs whose cults he had served. Overhead, in the 'golden sky' in the centre of the dome, Victor is portrayed in glory in the heavenly abode of the Father and the Son, who are represented by their symbols.

It will also be found that the most important and ubiquitous images of chapel decorations are the holy beings who inhabit the highest heaven, seen as the zone above the sky. These are displayed in chapels as statements of the faith. The images of holy beings are joined by those of saints and martyrs, and sometimes even by the portraits and inscriptions of the donors. The gallery of holy persons can be represented in various ways. Simplest, perhaps, are the lifelike images, confined like icons within the outlines of framing medallions, a format that probably depends on the imperial portrait. Full-length figures and allegorical images are also found. In addition, the early Christians delighted in plays on words and numbers, and in mystical and cryptic ideas. This allowed them the poetry of the symbolic image, which itself led to many layers of meaning and understanding, and lifted the possibilities beyond the literal into the transcendental.

The peopling of the walls of the chapels with images of saints and martyrs was counterpoised by references in inscriptions, painting, or mosaics to the individuals responsible for the planning and financing of the decorations. There is evidence in literary sources such as the Ravenna *Liber Pontificalis* of Agnellus that a donor portrait was displayed among the holy images, though none has survived. The funerary portrait had a twofold purpose. First, and most obviously, the individual and his gift of a building and a decoration were recorded for posterity. But there were important additional reasons for picturing the deceased among the saints. These reasons, although only formally drawn up after the end of iconoclasm, and in the East, were rooted in the thinking of the Early Christian period, itself a product of the Classical, and pagan, past. From these ancient sources Christianity inherited the idea that religious images contained divine power. This idea was given authority by the Church Fathers, who were strongly influenced by Neoplatonism as early as the second century.[8] According to the theory of images which developed as a result of this interest, they had a mystical correspondence with their prototypes. The holy individuals were thus present in person in the interior space of the chapel by means of their mystical identity with their images.[9] The result was that the donor felt himself to be in the actual presence of the saints as he waited for the day of judgment. This allowed him the hope of their assistance and their intercession with Christ on that day. The portraits of donors that once signed these chapels are among the earliest recorded, and join other important examples in the major churches of Ravenna, Rome, and Poreč. It is unfortunate that the chapel donor portraits are without exception lost, for they would have not only revealed the physical likenesses of the donors to us across the centuries, but illuminated the evolutionary sequence of such portraits from Late Antique coffin pictures to the well-characterized portraits that recorded the gifts of Early Medieval and Carolingian popes to the churches of Rome.

In summary, the basic decorative elements of these early chapels were those of Early Christian art in general, and could in most cases be represented either naturalistically or in symbolic form. However, a further development took place within the chapel space itself. Here, the vaulted architecture of the chapel was utilized as a three-dimensional decorative field, and images were combined to form coherent iconographic programs covering the whole interior, including the vault. Although Early Christian baptisteries also made their centrally planned internal space the site of overall decoration, few retain any part of their decorative programs, with the exception of S Giovanni in Fonte, Naples, and the Orthodox and Arian baptisteries at Ravenna. There are many similarities, probably because there is congruence of thought between baptismal and funerary programs, which both serve the rites of passage from one state of being to another. Thus, at Naples, the vault opens illusionistically onto Christ's symbol in the starry vault, while at Ravenna, processions of the twelve apostles surround the central motifs, as they may once have done at S Prosdocimo, Padua. The Naples baptistery also has a series of narrative scenes illustrating Christ's miracles, which have no parallels in surviving chapel decorations. However, too few baptistery programs survive to determine whether these similarities, and differences, are significant. It is clear, though, that these two sorts of centrally planned buildings between them have all the elements that later would be combined to decorate the typical centrally planned Middle Byzantine church. Since the earliest Christian art was not firmly divided into Eastern and Western traditions, similar decorated chapels and baptisteries must have occurred in the East, but have failed to survive. Many of the conventions of this earliest Christian art in the vaulted buildings of East and West alike were derived from the Orient, in addition to its obvious roots in Greco-Roman art.[10] Both frontality of images of holy persons, and their depiction in front of the unbroken picture plane, rather than in a perspective recession, can be attributed to this oriental influence, which came to dominate the decorative schemes of Byzantium and was also influential in the West in the later part of the period under discussion.

Most importantly, the iconographic elements were arranged, within the confined space of the chapel interior, in such a way that they represented a microcosm of the universe as it was understood in Late Antiquity.[11] Thus, the walls were clad in precious marble, stone which both came from the earth and represented it. The ground level of the chapel at its simplest was a cube, its four corners representing the world of mortal existence. Conversely, the arching vault represents the firmament, the analogy made more vivid by the colour and decoration that was chosen and that often survives. The blue of the vault mimics the colour of the sky itself, and is often sprinkled with stars, as at the Mausoleum of Galla Placidia, or glimpsed through a fruiting arbour, as at the S Matrona chapel. The blue of reality, however, may be replaced by the shimmer of gold, as at the Lateran chapels, the Archbishops' Chapel, and S Vittore. This is not merely the replacement of one precious and expensive colour by another, even more luxurious hue, but represents a means of recreating the radiance of light. The incident light is scattered from the uneven gold glass surfaces of the mosaic, lending the imitation a mystical quality which hides the subterfuge in shimmering otherworldly radiance. A feature common to most of these vault firmaments is the central opening, an oculus bordered with sculptural detail at S Matrona, wreathed at S Vittore, framed by a support structure at the Lateran, but always revealing a vision of a realm beyond, a realm where Christ dwells with his Father and where the saints and the righteous join him in glory. Christ's presence in this realm is expressed by the monograms and symbols of his name, which again tell of the mystical and magical preoccupations of Late Antiquity, so often expressed in the cryptic language of numerology and similar systems. Even in the single example of a mortal saint ascended to glory that survives in an Early Christian chapel vault, St Victor at S Vittore in Ciel d'Oro, Milan, he is depicted between two monogrammatic crosses, elegantly replete with symbolic content which probably only the erudite could understand.

The ancestry of this idea of the domed sky re-created inside the vault of a building will be found in remote antiquity, among the Romans and before them the Etruscans. Its reinterpretation in Christian terms is not surprising, but what is especially interesting is that here in Early Christian vaulted buildings it is possible to trace the beginnings of the ideas that would become important in the decoration of post-iconoclastic Byzantine churches. These were the concepts of the mystical equivalence of the inner space of the church to the boundless universe, and of the peopling of such a space with a hierarchically arranged series of holy beings. This system of decoration would become codified as the standard decorative scheme of Byzantine churches from the ninth century until the present day.

One of the most important questions that should be considered is whether chapels display iconographic programs that relate to their specific functions. In order to answer this question, the possible uses of chapels have to be specified, and distinguished from those of churches. The Canons of the Church Councils make it clear that in the earlier part of the period under consideration privately built chapels enjoyed a full range of uses, but that these uses were increasingly restricted. In fact, it was the range of litugical acts that could be celebrated inside them that came to determine whether a building was a chapel or a church. In the earliest period, the fourth century, celebration of the sacraments had been permitted in both chapels and churches. But in the interest of suppressing heresy, the uses of a chapel became more and more limited, and soon became restricted to private prayer only. Episcopal chapels, however, must have been exempt from these regulations, since they were under the direct control of the bishops themselves. And one may speculate that the church authorities would have had little control over the mausolea of the imperial family, except, perhaps, when invited to give advice in the planning stages and to bless the deceased occupants and intercede for their salvation.

We shall see that chapels were built in the cemeteries outside cities from the very earliest days of organized Christianity, where they fulfilled publicly accessible functions which contrasted with those of the private chapel. These *memoriae* were built to commemorate the heroes of the church: their graves, their places of martyrdom, their relics. The survival of martyr shrines over other sorts of chapels is explained by the high priority they must have had for maintenance and repair in a Christian society. In a natural sequence fuelled by the increasing importance of the cult of the martyrs in Late Antiquity, the *memoriae* of the saints were seen as the most powerful sites for Christian burial, and the two functions, burial and commemoration of heroes, became intertwined. Soon, those who built themselves funeral chapels took care to provide relics in order to sanctify the space as well as to invoke the power of the martyrs for their own salvation. They also installed pictures to invoke the reality of the saints and holy beings. The relics were probably noncorporeal in the earliest times, but when the translation of human remains started to be acceptable, around the seventh century, collective martyria were built. These were shrines where the bones and other relics of the martyrs were gathered together in special surroundings for veneration. Some early chapels may have fulfilled only one of these three functions; others served each function in turn, starting with that of commemoration, and evolving through a period as funerary chapel to a full-blown martyrium, serving to shelter the remains of saints gathered in from the whole region.

Who were the Christians who were buried beside the saints in their shrines, or in private or collective graves sanctified by their remains? At first, it seems that ordinary Christians could claim the privilege of burial *ad sanctos* in the shrines. By the end of the fourth century, though, such burials were reserved for rich laymen and, especially, for the clerics who controlled the rights over the martyrs' bodies and their graves. At Milan, for example, most of the *memoriae* of the martyrs in the cemeteries outside the walls were chosen by the early bishops for their own burial. This reflects the marked preoccupation with personal salvation associated with the rise of the cult of martyrs after the Peace of the Church. A private space for rest in death, and relics and pictures of a saintly companion to ease one's way on judgment day were among the ambitions of every upper churchman.[12] It was only later, in the fifth and sixth centuries, that bishops and archbishops created collective burial chapels for themselves. At Milan, for example, an episcopal burial place was built in the sixth century as an annex to S Lorenzo. And finally, with the loosening of attitudes towards the moving of relics, by the seventh century martyria were raised which focused the devotions of a whole region, and became centres of pilgrimage.

One may well ask if there is any explanation of the overriding theme of the Early Christian decorated chapel, which is the re-creation in microcosmic form of the whole glory of the universe. In the absence of texts, one is obliged to look at the buildings themselves for the answer. It seems clear that the vault or dome was seen to arch over the chapel's interior just as the sky seemed to be a dome arching over the earth. Once the idea of the magical equivalence of images and their prototypes was accepted, the next step was the provision of a suitable setting for the holy images, and what setting would have more veracity than a re-creation of their natural abode? The space of the chapel itself would then acquire a mystical identity with the universe it imitates. The setting, however, is not only planned in the comparatively trivial expectation of providing a suitable 'stage set' for the images and their originals, but to create a sacred setting for the donors' own aspirations. These aims were to channel Christ's power through *anamnesis* in the form of pictorial remembrance, thus recreating his mystical presence on earth, and that of his saints, and ensuring that the deceased enjoyed proximity to the holy while awaiting the day of resurrection.

CHAPTER FIVE

A Sole Survivor: The Chapel of the Archbishops of Ravenna

We have already seen that none of the private chapels of the laity have survived into our times, and that even their existence would be in doubt were it not for the references to them in written sources. The other category of private chapel, the clergy-house oratory, would also be poorly known from sparse written sources if there were not a single and splendid survivor of the group, the Archbishops' Chapel in Ravenna.

The chapel is situated on the second floor of the Palace of the Archbishops of Ravenna, the Episcopium, in the precinct where the Cathedral and Baptistery stand.[1] It consists of a cruciform room, preceded by a full-width, narrow narthex (plan, fig. 47). The ground-floor rooms beneath are laid out on the same plan. There is a smaller room under the chapel's narthex which is only accessible from above, by means of a trap door in its vault. It was presumably used for the storage of ecclesiastical treasures.[2] As we have seen, hidden rooms of this sort were also present in some of the mid-sixth-century churches of Ravenna, where similar, windowless chambers, designed equally to escape detection from inside and outside the building, exist at both S Vitale and S Apollinare in Classe.[3] These rooms will have served an important function in the unsettled times of the barbarian invasions. The original function of the larger, ground-floor room at the Episcopium, which, like the chapel, is cruciform and has cupboard spaces in the corners, as well as access to the garden, is not known, though Giuseppe Gerola does not believe it was a consecrated space.[4] The presence of cupboards suggests that it may once have served as a library and study area for the archbishops, or even as their dining room. Later, from the time of Archbishop Johannes VIII (777–84), it seems to have served as a *vivarium*, while the dining room was nearby, behind the Cathedral's tribune.[5] Below again, in the cellar, similar rooms with massive arches act as foundations for the floors above.[6]

The ninth-century cleric Andrea Agnellus, author of the *Codex Pontificalis Ecclesiae Ravennatis*, the chronicle of the bishops of Ravenna, was the first to record the existence of a chapel in this location, which he describes as dedicated to St Andrew.[7] The identification of this oratory as the Archbishops' Chapel depends on three pieces of evidence: the inscription which Agnellus saw in the chapel's narthex; the portrait of the donor bishop Petrus, which Agnellus saw in the west lunette; and the monogram 'PETRUS,' which can still be seen in the mosaic above the altar.

According to Agnellus, a bishop named Peter built the episcopal palace, which was known as the Tricoli, and not far away a chapel in honour of Andrew the apostle, displaying his own portrait over the door.[8] The chapel's walls were covered with Proconnesian marble, and in the entryway was a metric inscription in twenty hexameters, which Agnellus records.[9] Significantly, fragments of the last verses of the inscription, in mosaic, were found in the vestibule of the Archbisops' Chapel in the restorations of the early twentieth century, inspiring the painted replica which is now in place (fig. 48).[10]

The inscription includes the attribution to Bishop Petrus.[11] His, too, is the mosaic monogram still visible in a pair of curved panels, one over the altar, the other across from it above the entryway. Tradition, recorded by Agnellus (805–ca. 846) over 400 years after the event, identified this Petrus with the famous Ravenna bishop, Petrus Crysologus, Peter I (ca. 426–32 to ca. 450–2). However, it seems that Agnellus was confused by the existence of several bishops called Peter, and was unaware of the second Petrus (494–518/19), the patron preferred by recent scholars.[12] His patronage would date the chapel to the first decade of the sixth century.[13]

Agnellus also associated Bishop Maximinian (546–ca. 556) with the chapel, proposing that it was he who must have finished the building. His evidence was flimsy: a monogrammed *pulvino* or secondary capital which he saw in the chapel, but which could have originated elsewhere in the Tricoli, or even in the adjacent cathedral.[14] In fact, there is no reason to associate Maximinian with the original patronage of the chapel or its decorative program, but he may have been responsible for a change of dedication to St Andrew, to whom he was particularly devoted. Unfortunately, the original dedication cannot be determined from the decorative program, since critical parts of the mosaics, including those of the apse and side lunettes, are lost. Possibly an image of the patron saint was situated in one of these areas. The apostle Peter, patron of the founder, Bishop Petrus, was the most likely choice.[15] Agnellus describes Maximinian's devotion to St Andrew. The archbishop acquired a famous relic, the apostle's beard, in Constantinople,[16] and subsequently built the church of S Andrea Maggiore near Ravenna's Roman forum to house it and for his own eventual burial.[17] He also gave relics of St Andrew to his foundation S Stefano (550) in the imperial quarter.[18] It therefore seems likely that the dedication of the Archbishops' Chapel to St Andrew dates to Maximinian and the mid-sixth century.

The cruciform main chamber of the chapel contains cupboards between three of the short arms of the cross, with a passageway occupying the north-east corner (plan, fig. 47). Gerola has suggested that the cupboards contained relics: they could equally well have housed vestments, plate, or books, as I have already suggested. Corporeal relics would have been unlikely at this date for the same reason that the chapel cannot have been designed as a funerary chapel: the Tricoli Palace was situated inside the city.

Both the cruciform room and its narthex have undergone numerous alterations in the past. To summarize, the entry door of the narrow, tunnel-vaulted narthex is in the north wall, with a lunette above. Its south wall once included a window, which was blocked in the Middle Ages. The west wall was also pierced by a door, which probably gave access to the gate turret by way of a wooden walkway. This doorway has been closed, perhaps during the sixteenth-century renovations.[19] These renovations were responsible for fundamental alterations, by which the orientation of the chapel was reversed. The apse was destroyed and replaced by an entryway from the palace; the doorway between the narthex and the chapel was eliminated and replaced by a wide arch, and the altar was moved to the west wall of the narthex. In 1796, a mosaic of the Virgin, which had been removed from a lower register of the apse mosaic of the Basilica Ursiana, the Early Christian cathedral of Ravenna, when it was rebuilt in 1734, was installed above the altar. There it was flanked by portrait medallions of Peter and Paul saved from the same early-twelfth-century composition.[20]

The twentieth-century restoration has returned the chapel to its original orientation. Examination of the entryway revealed the remains of *tubi fitilli*, interlocking terracotta tubes used for lightness in the construction of domes, and the chapel was therefore restored with a hemispherical apse rather than a rectangular niche. The walls were reclad in marble with two appropriate stucco friezes.[21] The window was restored to its original shape, and the narthex once more became the main point of entry of the chapel.

Large areas of mosaic decoration remained intact throughout these extensive alterations. These mosaics covered, in the chapel itself, the vault and the soffits of the four arches of the truncated cross (fig. 49).[22] Four upper-wall areas shaped like inverted crescents also survived (fig. 50). Lost, in addition to the apse, were the lunettes in the north, west, and south arms of the cross.[23] Some traces of the mosaics' edge were found by the restorer in the north and south lunettes, but not enough to draw any conclusions except that these areas were indeed clad with mosaic in terre-verte on a gold ground.[24] The west lunette, according to Agnellus, contained the founder's portrait. The subject matter of the other two lunettes and of the apse remains a mystery.

The most spectacular part of the mosaics is the vault design, which contains two interlocking elements (fig. 49). Four angels, dressed in white, stand on tiptoe on small, grassy hillocks in the angles of the golden vault. Their brown wings are folded, and they are haloed in white. Their upraised hands grasp the edges of a frame – concentrically edged in blue, white, and red – that allows a glimpse of blue beyond: on this blue a gold *chrismon* floats, symbol of the presence of Christ. As usual with such compositions, the impression is given of an oculus, through which a glimpse is afforded of another world: the world of the highest heaven, abode of God.[25]

This composition, where the ribs of the vault bear caryatids which appear to hold it up, has its origins in the floor and vault compositions of the Romans, and before them of the Etruscans. A Roman antecedent of the Archbishops' Chapel vault existed at S Croce at the Lateran Baptistery, Rome, where a preexisting building was reused as a chapel under Pope Hilarus, and the angels of its vault were reinterpreted as cherubs in a Renaissance drawing, that of Giuliano da Sangallo (fig. 103). Later, Pope Paschal I (817–24) would adapt the composition for his mother's burial chapel at S Prassede, the S Zeno Chapel, Rome. The contents of the oculus are the main compositional variant: there was a cross (probably a fifth-century insert into an open oculus) at S Croce, where the *opus sectile* decoration of the walls was also rich in crosses; a chi-rho symbol at the Archbishops' Chapel, Ravenna; and, for the first time among surviving monuments, the anthropomorphic image of

Christ at the S Zeno Chapel. The symbol of Christ is frequently displayed framed at the top of vaults at Ravenna – for example, in the side
niches of the Mausoleum of Galla Placidia. It is held up by pairs of
angels above the presbytery arches at S Vitale, where it is also framed,
as if it were a monogrammed shield: there it also carries a connotation
of victory.

A unique feature of the composition at the Archbishops' Chapel is
the alternation of the angels with evangelist symbols, which in later
medieval art would themselves become the main subject of quadripartite vaults, as in the late-eleventh-century decorations in the chapel
behind the altar at S Pudenziana, Rome, and the painted vault of the
early-thirteenth-century crypt of Anagni Cathedral. The four beasts
of the Apocalypse came to symbolize the evangelists in the way
explained by St Jerome, based on the opening words of their respective
gospels: Matthew by a man or (as here in the east quadrant) an angel.
Mark's Lion is in the west; the north segment holds the Eagle of St
John, the south, the Ox of St Luke. They float among the wisps of red
and blue cloud in the symbolic gold of heaven on paired brown wings.
Each is nimbed and carries a jewelled book in its arms.

The iconographic details of these symbols underwent a series of
changes in the period between 375 and 500, changes which are illustrated by several of the chapels that are discussed here. At first the
symbols had six wings, three pairs each, as in the text in the fourth
chapter of the Book of Revelation. At this period the books were not
included, and the symbols represent the apocalyptic beasts of the text,
rather than the evangelists. Symbols of this type loom in the upper
apse at S Pudenziana, Rome (ca. 390), and in the side lunettes at the S
Matrona chapel at S Prisco (ca. 410–25). Their iconography will be discussed in connection with that chapel. Over time, the supernumerary
wings were lost, as at the Mausoleum of Galla Placidia, Ravenna (ca.
416–25). The symbols at the Archbishops' Chapel are typical of the
final stage, when they come to symbolize the evangelists in a formula
which was to last throughout the Middle Ages. They appear as single-
winged, nimbed beings, each holding a gospel book. The iconographic
content of the vault composition, then, expresses Christ's presence in
the realm of Heaven, his monogram both revealed and raised up by
the attending angels which link heaven and earth. The evangelist symbols, moreover, show that the message of salvation is revealed in the
gospels, and that it is through them that the soul will attain salvation.

The narthex was once the site of the paired mosaic panels, which together comprised the inscription recorded by Agnellus. These ran along the upper wall on each side. The fragments which were discovered during the early-twentieth-century restorations matched the end phrases of the last five verses of the dedicatory poem. A painted replica has been installed, based on the mosaic original and Agnellus's text, which is divided between the two long walls of the chapel (fig. 48).[26] The restored mosaic ornament also follows the original: a wide double band of ribbon motif frames cross-shaped, lily-based motifs, which run along above the dedicatory poem, which not only names Petrus as patron, but also gives his interpretation of the role of light in the space of the narthex: either actually created here or captured and imprisoned in this space, in imitation of God's creation.

Higher again, the tunnel vault of the narthex has an all-over design of birds spaced in a network made up of shaded spheres and lily flowers. This pattern is based on a textile, probably one of the diagonally diapered silks popular at that time.[27] The vault follows the diapered silk not only in its diagonal reticulum, but also in the varied birds which are diagonally disposed within it. Paired examples face alternately left and right inside the slanting net. They include parrots, guinea fowl, ducks and drakes, peacocks, partridges, doves, and cranes. This repertory of birds is typical of Late Antiquity. For example, at the fifth-century chapel of S Giovanni Evangelista at Rome's Lateran Baptistery, the choice is similar to that at the Archbishops' Chapel, and pairs of parrots, mallards, doves, and partridges occupy green platforms in the golden vault: they symbolize the four elements, fire, water, air, and earth.[28] An even richer variety of birds, still making the same allusions, is found a little later in the presbytery vault at S Vitale, Ravenna (ca. 549), this time inside a framework of acanthus, rather than a diapered net.[29]

The original decoration of the narthex is completed by a tall, narrow lunette over the entry door. It is framed by a band of twisted gold and blue ribbon on red, and outlined with white and blue on each side. The subject is Christ, carrying a red cross on his shoulder and holding an open book with the words 'Ego sum via, veritas et vita' – 'I am the way, the truth and the life' (fig. 48) – his words recorded in St John's Gospel.[30] The lower half of Christ's body is conjectural, based on traces of military dress found at the lower edge of the torso,[31] but on the authority of Ravenna precedents such as a stucco panel in the Orthodox Baptistery,[32] the panel has been completed with the trampled lion and serpent of Psalm 91: 'Thou shalt tread upon the lion and adder: the young lion and the dragon shalt thou trample under foot.'[33] This text, which foretells Christ's victory over the forces of evil, parallels late Roman imperial imagery.[34] Perhaps as early as the start of the fifth century, and certainly by the year 610, the emperors incorporated the *calcatio colli*, ritual trampling, into their triumphs.[35] In this year the usurper Phocas was ritually trampled by the emperor Heraclius before his execution. In 706, the emperor Justinian II trampled the necks of his defeated rivals while the people intoned the verses from Psalm 91 that are illustrated in the Archbishops' Chapel: 'You will tread on the lion and the adder.' The usurpers were then led away to execution.[36]

The mosaic occupied a very important position in the chapel: the lunette above the main doorway in the exit wall. Any image in this location was a powerful reminder to those who passed beneath it out of the sacred space and into the secular world. It was above the exit doorway that Last Judgment imagery, which acted as a reminder of the dire results of doing evil in the world, would find its traditional place in the later Middle Ages. And already the earliest Judgment scenes, which consisted only of the throne prepared for Christ's second coming, were starting to take this position in Early Christian times. Such an image survives on the inner entry wall of the S Matrona chapel at S Prisco, which dates in all probability to the beginning of the fifth century (fig. 58). However, by no means all early chapels had Judgment imagery over the exit door. Some depicted Paradise, symbolized by Christ as a shepherd with his sheep, the Christian souls, a clear reference to salvation, as in the Mausoleum of Galla Placidia in Ravenna (fig. 97). The image at the Archbishops' Chapel is very different from both these themes; it is related neither to death nor to the afterlife, but shows Christ's earthly struggle. What meaning would this image of Christ trampling the forces of evil have had for the archbishop who had it installed in a location where he and his successors would be sure to see it each time they left the sanctified interior of the chapel and reentered the secular world? Could it have been designed to remind them that just as Christ himself was victorious over evil, so his struggle showed the way that the Church must take if it were to overcome its enemies? The words on Christ's book indicate that Christians would win through to eternal life only by following his true path. Thus, the archbishops of Ravenna each in turn would pass beneath this lintel into the world fortified to lead the Church as commanded by Christ and inspired by his victory.

The original design of the south lunette in the narthex has been completely lost, though we know that it once contained a window. The replacement was inspired by the ancient decorations in the crescent-shaped upper walls of the chapel's central room, which all bear related designs. Above the apse the monogram of Bishop Petrus is flanked by a pair of doves, a parrot, and a pigeon, set among leafy boughs with pomegranates and apples (fig. 50, upper crescent). Similar decorations in the side crescents are centred on the Agnus Dei, flanked by large grey birds, perhaps pelicans, their wings outstretched. Here also the vegetal scroll contains stylized fruits, single 'cherries.' The west crescent, also centred on the monogram of Petrus, has paired peacocks with, on the left, a duck and apples, and on the right, a stork and pomegranates. The symbolism of these birds and fruits relates to paradise: peacocks for immortality, pelicans for Christ's sacrifice as celebrated in the Eucharist, doves for peace and for the human soul; while the pomegranate, symbol of Proserpine's return to earth at winter's end, came in Christian thought to represent the hope of immortality and the resurrection of the Christian soul. The apple, also, can have a connotation of salvation, based on the Song of Solomon 2.3: 'As an apple tree among the trees of the wood, so is my beloved among young men ... and his fruit was sweet to my taste,' which is interpreted as an allusion to Christ.[37] Christ shown as the Lamb is a reference to the apocalyptic vision of St John, and the discreet, though central, monogram of the founder marks his hope of inclusion in paradise at his time of judgment, as well as his very human desire to record his gift of the chapel and its mosaics for posterity.

The mosaic of the apse is also an early-twentieth-century replacement, based on the central vault of the Mausoleum of Galla Placidia in Ravenna. It features a cross which floats among the gold and silver stars of a blue firmament. The colour is based on the blue and silver tesserae that were found around the edge of the missing apse.

The medallion saints in the soffits include the apostles on the main axis, six by six (fig. 50). In the east, Paul takes Christ's right, along with James and John, accompanied by Peter on the left with Andrew and Philip. In Ravenna, Paul often takes precedence over Peter, in marked contrast to Roman custom.[38] By this means, the Ravenna See may have attempted to distance itself from subservience to Rome, by questioning the primacy of St Peter.

The less important apostles are relegated to the west soffit, arranged on either side of another bust of Christ. Both medallions of Christ show him in the imperial iconography typical of Ravenna: long-haired, clad in a purple robe with gold *clavi*, and nimbed with a golden halo set with a jewelled cross (fig. 50). The example at the altar end also has white rays striking inwards from the halo's rim: this use of white recalls Christ's white 'halo' in the right lunette at S Aquilino, Milan. Here, as in Ravenna, where the white nimbus distinguishes Christ in both the chapel and its narthex, it may well be a technical device to set off the golden halo from the golden background. The halo originated in the luminous circle with which pre-Christian religions invested their deities to signify their mystical powers. Thus, it seems likely that here too it represents the mystical white light, derived from the light of the sun, which marks Christ's humanity with the light of the Deity.[39] Indeed, in one of the best-known images in Early Christian art, Christ was portrayed as the Sun God himself, riding his chariot in the sky, in the tomb of the Julii in the cemetery below St Peter's in Rome.[40]

The six women martyrs in the left arch are, from left to right, Cecilia, Eugenia, Euphemia, Daria, Perpetua, and Felicitas. Cecilia and Eugenia, like Daria, were Roman, while Perpetua and Felicitas met death in Carthage. All six were later included in the procession of female martyrs at S Apollinare Nuovo, Ravenna, and, Daria excepted, among the medallions at the Basilica Euphrasiana at Poreč in Istria. Four of them (Daria and Eugenia excepted) were among the saints of the Canon of the Ambrosian Mass, as used at Ravenna. From 550 the relics of both Euphemia and Eugenia were preserved in Ravenna in bishop Maximinian's church of St Stephen.[41] A full explanation of the choice of saints is impossible, but we may surmise that all were either connected with the Ravenna liturgy, or that their relics were venerated nearby, perhaps even in the Archbishops' Chapel itself.

Each portrait, on a deep blue background, is framed concentrically in black, orange, and white; white and red; red and gold; and gold.[42] Each saint's name is written above the frame: omission of the title 'SCA, SANCTA,' suggests an early date. The outer edge of each of the four arches is delineated by a line of 'jewelled chain': alternating oblong green and oval blue jewels punctuated by pairs of pearls. The overall effect of the quadripartite decoration is of four miniature triumphal arches: medallion saints were popular around the openings of such arches, as at S Sabina, Rome (ca. 390), or under the soffit, framing the apse, as at Poreč (ca. 550), where a dozen women saints were featured. Women, also, were the subject of a similar decoration, now almost entirely lost, at the chapel of S Maria Mater Domini, Vicenza, of which the remains were discovered above a false ceiling in 1937.[43]

These fragments have already been described: the lion of St Mark is accompanied by a medallion portrait of a young, unnamed female saint (figs. 24, 25). Damage has obliterated the upper part of her face. Perhaps the image represents one of the four female saints whose relics were kept in the chapel: Cassia, Innocenza, Gaudienza, and Neofita.[44] S Maria Mater Domini has been dated to the early sixth century on grounds of the style, technique, and clothing of the medallion image, which are all remarkably similar to those in the Archbishops' Chapel. The medallion portrait, then, was not exclusive to any one type of Early Christian chapel, for rather than being a clergy-house oratory, S Maria Mater Domini was set in the Christian cemetery around the basilica of SS Felice e Fortunato, to which it is now attached. The medallion image, an idealized 'portrait,' was utilized wherever a donor wanted to invoke the presence of a particular saint, be it in a private chapel, a martyrium, a funerary chapel, or a basilica, quite apart from its use in sculpture, on such items as sarcophagi and the products of the minor arts.

The Archbishops' Chapel is unusual in its choice of six male saints for the window arch (fig. 50). Chrysanthus, Chrysologus and Cassianus, Damianus and Cosmas, and Polycarpus are arrayed on either side of Christ's symbol. Cassianus (ca. 360–435), the saint of Imola, a dependency of the Ravenna See, and Polycarpus (ca. 69–ca. 155), were also shown in the martyrs' procession in S Apollinare Nuovo; Cosmas and Damianus were not only included in the Ambrosian Canon of the Mass, but in the Roman as well. Chrysologus, the Ravenna Bishop Peter I Chrysologus (ca. 400–51), was an obvious choice as the most illustrious predecessor of the founder in the See of Ravenna, and he also had an intimate connection with Cassianus, having died in the course of feast-day celebrations at his shrine at Imola.

Analysis of the iconographic program of any chapel is made easier if the program is complete. Unfortunately, at the Archbishops' Chapel key areas of decoration are lost. Fortunately, the vault survives. It is a representation of heaven. Its layout reveals the beginnings of the hierarchical arrangement of holy images by location, which would be typical of Middle Byzantine church decoration. Christ, the holiest being, is represented by his symbol in the highest sphere of heaven. His angels span the vault of the sky, but stand upon earth's grassy meadows. Christ also occupies the crown of each tunnel vault, his human form alternating with his symbolic *chrismon*, complete with the alpha and omega, the first and the last, another reference to him.[45] The lamb is a further symbol of Christ, 'the Lamb of God, who takes away the sins of the world,' and is also central to the apocalyptic vision. The evangelists with Gospel books – gateways both to the Christian faith and to heaven and salvation – loom in the sky above each arch, where also the Lamb takes his place amidst the symbolically powerful vegetation and bird life of paradise.[46] In the soffits below are roundels with images of the apostles and martyrs, human witnesses to the faith for which they lived and died on earth. And finally, below this again, the marble revetment symbolizes the rocky material of the earth itself from which it is fashioned.

The question of how this chapel's decoration differs from that of an Early Christian funerary chapel is difficult, if not impossible, to answer, both because of its own incompleteness and because of the lack of comparative material from other nonfunerary structures. The Archbishop's Chapel, for example, shares many features with the S Matrona chapel at S Prisco, such as the paradisical vault, evangelist symbols, alpha and omega accompanying Christ, and the apostles, there symbolized by doves. It also converges with the S Maria Mater Domini fragments, as represented by the clipeate saint's image and the evangelist symbols. Two areas seem to set it apart from the average funerary chapel. One is the series of medallions of nonbiblical male saints, the personal choice of the upper-level clerics who designed the program. Saintly liturgists, scholars, and physicians can be assumed to reflect the interests of the archbishops themselves. The other is the depiction on the inner entry wall of an exhortation to follow the precepts of Christ in this life, rather than the next, by struggling against the forces of evil in this world. Christ's battle with evil thus substitutes for the paradisical or Last Judgment imagery above the exit of other Early Christian chapels. These chapels were all devoted to the funerary cult, and the paradisical or eschatological imagery suited the needs of those who awaited Christ's second coming in the calm of the earthly paradise.

In other respects, the chapel speaks the universal language of Early Christian art – the heavenly vision; the emphasis on the teachings of the gospels and on the apostles and saints as witnesses to these teachings. The chapel, interestingly enough, was not anonymous; it contained ample evidence of the donor – his monogram and his portrait – and of his ideas, as set out in the inscription in the narthex. These personal touches are interesting forerunners of the apse inscriptions in Roman churches of the early Middle Ages, such as those of

Paschal I and Gregory IV in the ninth century. They also anticipate the placing of donor portraits in churches, both for propaganda purposes and to ensure that the donors are mystically present among their chosen saints on Judgment Day.[47]

It would be impossible to generalize from a single example of the clergy-house chapel, were it not for its convergence with the main corpus of chapels that is assembled in this survey, chapels which use the same imagery and iconography and can thus throw light upon the meaning of the decoration in the Archbishops' Chapel itself.

CHAPTER SIX

Commemoration of the Dead: S Vittore in Ciel d'Oro, Milan, and the S Matrona Chapel at S Prisco

S Vittore in Ciel d'Oro

The memorial chapels which were built over the graves of the martyrs in Early Christian times have been subjected to many hazards over the intervening centuries, among them rebuilding, redecoration, and destruction by the natural elements. As a result, very few have survived in their original form, with any portion of their decoration in place. Among these, the most important is the chapel of S Vittore in Ciel d'Oro in Milan, which has retained a major part of its mosaic decoration, and so is effectively the only survivor of the myriads of decorated shrines that were built to commemorate the martyrs in the earliest years of legalized Christianity.

S Vittore in Ciel d'Oro rose in the city of St Ambrose (339–97), probably during his lifetime, and was furnished not long after his death with mosaics that inform us of its purpose. It also records a likeness of the saint himself. The chapel has another important connection with Ambrose, though, for he not only wrote about Victor, the titular saint,[1] but also explained the practices which had evolved in connection with the cult, such as burial beside the bodies of the saints, burial *ad sanctos*.[2] Ambrose's inspiration was a personal bereavement: the death of his brother Satyrus, whose burial he subsequently arranged beside St Victor in his memorial chapel, S Vittore in Ciel d'Oro. Presumably the influence of Ambrose and of his writings on the Milanese church of which he was bishop from 374 to 397 survived his death, making it likely that his ideas about the role of the martyr shrine in the cult of the saints are illustrated in the decoration of the chapel. The connection with St Ambrose, the surviving decoration, and the archaeological findings combine to reveal the purpose and the thought behind S Vittore in Ciel d'Oro, making it the best understood of all Early Christian chapels.[3]

The identity of Victor himself is known from two sources. First, there is the name 'VICTOR' inscribed upon the open book held by his portrait in the centre of the dome (fig. 51).[4] Victor is usually identified as a common soldier (*miles*) from Mauretania,[5] though the frequent occurrence of this name in the hagiographical literature raises the question of whether Victor is a personal name, or a generic title for any saint victorious in martyrdom. However, Ambrose confirms the existence in Milan of an individual soldier named Victor in his poem to the companions in arms, Victor, Nabor, and Felix.[6] These three saints from Mauretania died together for their faith at Lodi (Laus Pompeia), during the persecutions of Maximian in the early fourth century. Their cult was established quite rapidly, for Ambrose described the saints as revered not only in Milan but throughout the whole world, likening the spread of the cult to that of the Gospel itself.[7] Their bodies had been translated to Milan with full triumphal honours before Ambrose's day, probably between 313 and 343 in the time of Maternus, his predecessor in the See of Milan, to whom tradition ascribes Victor's burial.[8] Maternus probably also built the first-phase chapel of S Vittore, and interred Nabor and Felix nearby.[9] Like Ambrose, Maternus is portrayed in the mosaics of S Vittore, standing between his patrons Felix and Nabor.

S Vittore in Ciel d'Oro is now annexed to the south flank of the Romanesque basilica of S Ambrogio, at some distance from the sanctuary. It was originally raised as a separate, wooden-roofed building over the grave of St Victor. The pyramidal first roof of the apse was soon replaced by a semidome, while the main roof of the chapel was replaced by a small, elliptical cupola, measuring almost five metres on the long axis, four and a half on the transverse. The number of windows was reduced, but those that remained were enlarged. These important changes, Reggiori suggests, were made at the time that the mosaics were added.[10]

Controversy surrounds the date of these changes, largely because of shortage of comparative mosaic material from Milan, though scholars broadly agree on the Early Christian period.[11] Pietro Toesca suggested a late-fifth- or early-sixth-century date, a period also favoured by Ferdinando Reggiori, who traced stylistic parallels between these mosaics and those of Theodoric's era at S Apollinare Nuovo, Ravenna. More recently, Carlo Bertelli has also favoured the late fifth century, while Ernst Kitzinger favours the second half of that century. Joseph Wilpert, however, on the basis of the lack of nimbi and of the abbreviation of the adjective 'sanctus' to 'SCS,' as well as the shape of the two mosaic crosses in the summit of the vault, preferred the beginning of the fifth century. Certainly, the absence of haloes and of the adjective 'sanctus,' as well as the palaeography of the inscriptions,[12] seem to point to an earlier rather than a later date, and there seems to be no difficulty with assigning a date soon after the death of Ambrose in 397. In support of an early date one may cite iconographic parallels with the mosaics of the Naples Baptistery (ca. 405). These include the absence of haloes, the absence of the abbreviation 'SCS' (though at Naples inscriptions are altogether omitted), and the position and 'open-winged' composition of the evangelist symbols which occupy pendentives or equivalent spaces. Eugenio Battisti argued that the head of Ambrose was a later insertion, since it is surrounded by an area of lighter tesserae, which form a paler 'halo.' He proposed that the composition originally portrayed another great Milanese bishop, Vitalis, between his sons, Gervase and Protase, and that Ambrose's likeness was inserted in place of that of Vitalis soon after Ambrose's death. This allowed Battisti to propose a date during Ambrose's lifetime for the mosaics, the period between Satyrus's burial in the chapel in 375 or 377 and Ambrose's death in 397. A date during Ambrose's lifetime would otherwise have been unlikely.[13] Although Satyrus's burial would seem an obvious occasion for alterations and a new and sumptuous decoration, Battisti's argument is usually rejected, because Reggiori was unable to find any evidence that Ambrose's head was an intrusion: rather, he found that the area around the head was concentrically set as an aureole of lighter blue tesserae.[14] As a result, scholars have settled for a date after Ambrose's death. The first decade of the fifth century, as proposed by Achille Ratti, seems quite possible.[15]

The decoration of the renovated chapel survives only in part, though that part is substantial (plan and section, figs. 52 and 53). The marble that once sheathed the lower walls, as well as the mosaics of the apse and of the curvature at the base of the dome, have all been lost, while those of the supporting areas of the dome were replaced in the nineteenth century following earlier drawings and extremely fragmentary remains.[16] However, the mosaics of the dome and of the interfenestrations beneath it survive in near original condition, with only minor restorations. Together, they make up the only complete dome decoration of an Early Christian *cella memoriae* to survive anywhere in Italy, one which may well have been typical of the decor of Early Christian martyr chapels in general.

The most striking feature of the decoration is its unique golden dome, which reflects its symbolic meaning in the popular name, 'ciel d'oro' or golden sky. The dome is girdled at the base by a frieze with a repeated design of twenty-four oval medallions containing full-face portraits, cameo style (fig. 54). Each cameo is set on a support between opposed doves and framed by tendrils of acanthus. Above, each unit is surmounted by a shell-shaped feature that imitates a sculptured niche. This composition has been compared with the late-fifth-century decoration of the upper walls of S Apollinare Nuovo, Ravenna, where as at S Vittore each interfenestration holds a figure standing beneath a shell-shaped 'umbrella' with paired doves. The mosaics are believed to date from the late years of the reign of Theoderic (r. 476–526), whose palace chapel this was. The 'umbrella' suggested immortality or resurrection to Otto von Simson, who interpreted the paired doves at Ravenna as the apostles, a reading that seems to be belied by the considerable numbers of birds depicted (sixty-four at Ravenna, forty-eight at S Vittore in Ciel d'Oro).[17] It seems more likely that they represent saints in general, and in the Milanese chapel, more specifically, the souls of the martyrs, the many anonymous companions in martyrdom of those named in the chapel.[18] The medallions may express the same idea as a collection of ancestor masks, commemorating the heroes of the past and more specifically those 'whose names are in the book of life.'[19] Above the frieze, the laying of the gold tesserae is in concentric circles all the way up to the central medallion (fig. 55), the culmination of the iconographic program. The meaning of this imagery will be sought in a step-by-step analysis of its features, including the frame, portrait, attributes, and inscription. The place of the medallion within the three-dimensional space of the chapel will then be considered.

The position of Victor's image high in the centre of the dome echoes the position of the loculus where his bones once lay, more than fourteen metres below. His medallion portrait is framed by a large wreath or crown, tied at its narrowest point with a red ribbon which wraps around three times in each direction and then twists freely across the golden ground, before ending in two small ivy leaves, symbolic of death and also of immortality. Such heart-shaped leaves are common in the funerary context, for example, on the fifth-century sarcophagi of Ravenna.[20] The wreath is made up of plants: lilies and roses, ears of wheat, grapes on the vine, and branches of olives, which together symbolize the four seasons and hence the passage of time. Eternity is indicated by the circular shape of the crown, without end or beginning, where the seasons follow each other in an endless succession. Vegetal crowns, which in classical times were awarded as visible signs of personal victory, also have roots in Hebrew culture, where wreaths of plants were necessary components of the Feast of the Tabernacles.[21] Jean Daniélou noted the survival of this feast in the Christian rite of baptism, and showed that its decorations are as appropriate to a funerary structure as to a baptistery, since each is concerned with the passage into salvation.[22] In New Testament times crowns were awarded as victory prizes, and also had connotations of the afterlife.[23] The crown also embodied the 'four last things' – death and hell, judgment and resurrection – and symbolized eternal glory in both the Jewish and Christian traditions.[24] Outside the Judaeo-Christian tradition vegetal crowns were also considered to be both attributes of the Gods and constituents of the rites of death.[25] It seems appropriate that the crown and garland should play such a major role in the decoration of S Vittore in Ciel d'Oro, a role which underlines not only the idea of eternity, but the 'four last things' of eschatalogical thought.

Other details of the wreath at S Vittore in Ciel d'Oro are also significant. At the top a flame-like jewel is set in an oval frame right above the head of the saint.[26] The jewel, which seems to burn with a white heat at the centre, and is shaded to red, is clearly shown within an aureole of light, framed in gold. Jewels and flames shared a quality of light and radiance in the thought of Late Antiquity: this image may well allude to the Paschal candle, which is lit to symbolize that Christ is risen. By extension, the image refers to the martyr who imitates Christ in his sacrifice and his reward, and like him is represented by radiant light. In the context of S Vittore in Ciel d'Oro this martyr is Victor, shown in the midst of a 'golden sky,' visionary symbol of a state of glory. From earliest times, and through a variety of cultures, gold has represented celestial light.[27] In medieval art, gold mosaics in the vault capture and diffract the incident light and thus symbolically recreate the celestial light of heaven. All these levels of meaning of gold seem appropriate to the 'golden sky' of S Vittore in Ciel d'Oro: the vision of heaven, the victory of the spirit in martyrdom, the light this victory of the spirit brings to earth. And the location chosen for the bust of Victor, high in the apex of the vault of heaven, lit by burning radiance above the brow, and framed in a victory wreath, is not accidental. The intention is to stress the rewards that crown the martyr's sacrifice.

The saint's portrait is shown, not only within a crown of victory, but receiving another from the hand of God above. A jewelled crown, trailing a second set of ribbons, is held above Victor's head by a hand that emerges from the clouds of glory in the highest part of this high heaven, the home of God. This is an image of victory on several planes; victory earned in the struggle of martyrdom, victory bestowed by God and rewarded by him in a well-understood gesture, and, it seems likely, a play on words also, for on the open book held in the saint's left hand the word 'VICTOR' is written, both the given name of the saint himself, and the generic term for conqueror.[28]

Victor is shown as a fully frontal bust-length figure, with short hair and beard, tonsured and wearing a white tunic with dark blue *clavi*. He is not shown in the mosaic as either a soldier or an African: earthly realism was apparently not desired, especially when saints were shown victorious in heaven. We see this idealization quite frequently in the portraits above saints' tombs, a more usual location for such images, as funerary portraits were rarely placed in the centre of the vault, a space normally reserved for Christ or his symbol.[29] The placement of the dedicatory saint in the cupola at S Vittore in Ciel d'Oro is unique: perhaps other *cellae memoriae* followed the same formula, but their domes have not survived. Another puzzling feature of the composition is the unique form taken by the two crosses which flank the saint, and the inscriptions which these crosses bear. Victor holds a large, gold Latin cross in his right hand. Its upright shaft is split at either end: the top right half is elongated and bent over. The crossbar has extra vertical pieces on the ends, and bears the inscription 'PANECIRIAE.' The overall outline of the cross can be seen as a monogram, which reads 'IH,' the first two letters of Jesus, 'IHCOUC,' in Greek. Cryptic forms of Christ's name were among the very earliest symbols of the Christian faith to appear, and include the *sphragis*, a cryptic sign used to mark the Christian on the brow in the sacraments of baptism, confirmation, the Eucharist, and at the last anointing. This can be traced back to the time of the apostles, when it was used by individuals as protection against evil.[30] The earliest form of the *sphragis* was the letter *tau*, the last in the Hebrew alphabet. In the time of Christ, this letter could be written both as a T and as an upright or a diagonal cross. In Old Testament times, as well, the prophet Ezekiel records that God's messenger signed the foreheads of righteous men with the mark *tau*, which had already acquired the meaning Yahweh, God.[31] In New Testament times *tau* retained the same symbolic meaning, sometimes sharing it with the Greek letter *omega*, also the last letter of an alphabet. Aside from *tau*'s liturgical and personal use, by the early third century it had already appeared as a symbol in art,[32] and its meaning was discussed by the Church Fathers in terms of the prophecies of the Old Testament.[33] Study of *tau*'s development as a symbol reveals that it did not originally refer to the gallows cross or to crucifixion, but symbolized the word of God, which for Christians was embodied in Christ, the Logos, to whom they were dedicated in baptism.[34] Originally, then, the symbolism was attached to a Hebrew letter, and it was only later, and in the Greek world, that this letter lost its original meaning and acquired a pictographic sense from its likeness to the cross. It was in the Greek world, too, that the Hebrew *tau* came to be confused with the Greek letter which looked most like it, the letter *chi*, X, which also happened to be the first letter of the word *Christos*. From this point on, the process of attaching significance to letters was elaborated, and Daniélou finds the first reference to a primitive use of the symbol IH, standing for the first two letters of the name Jesus in Greek, as early as the late first century, in the *Epistle of Barnabas*, where the writer comments on the significance of the 'eighteen and three hundred' of Abraham's servants to be circumcised, as numerological equivalents to the letters of Jesus' name.[35] After this, the use of monograms proliferated, continuing through the fifth century, and then gradually disappeared.[36]

In view of this widespread interest in monograms in Early Christian times, it is almost certain that the cross in Victor's right hand is monogrammatic, the shaft representing *iota*, I, the crossbar with its terminations *eta*, H, the hooked character being a *rho*, R, and the cross itself, *chi*, X, giving IH and XR, Jesus Christ.[37] The exact form of this cross at S Vittore is unique among surviving monograms, but this does not pose a problem for an extraordinary number of variants are known from Early Christian funerary art and inscriptions, and many more must have been lost.

The cross on our right, which stands on the rim of the wreath, is slightly the larger of the two. Like its fellow it has split verticals and an inscription on the crosspiece. Here, though, the crossbar is framed by paired loops to give a unique configuration, which can be presumed to have a cryptic significance, as in the case of the left-hand cross. One possible clue to a hidden meaning lies in the fact that the name Jesus could also be symbolized by a monogram combining the cross with *waw*, the archaic sixth letter of the Greek alphabet. This obscure letter was considered to have a hidden significance: because it came sixth in the Greek alphabet, it represented the name of Jesus, *Ihcouc*, with its six letters.[38] A monogram combining the cross with *waw* was discussed by St Jerome (342–420), in his *De Monogramma XPI*,[39] a companion piece to his recension of the *Commentarius in Apocalypsim* of Victorinus (d. 304).[40] Jerome found the combination of the cross with the double curve of the letter *waw* to be reminiscent of the brazen serpent that Moses lifted up on a pole in the wilderness.[41] At S Vittore in Ciel d'Oro, the outer loop of the right-hand cross, which does not seem to have undergone restoration, terminates in a pointed 'tail' by the stem of the cross. This suggests that this double loop may also have represented Moses' serpent, to which Christ was likened in John 3.14, 'as Moses lifted up the serpent in the desert, so must the Son of Man be lifted up, so that whoever believes in him may have eternal life.' Daniélou stresses both the authority of this Gospel text and the interest of the Fathers in it and in the monogram with the cross and the serpent.[42] One must conclude that this second cross can also be read as a cryptogram of the name of Christ. This need not preclude a more mundane explanation, for on another level, the circles behind the cross may well represent *dona militaria*, given in the form of armbands, *armillae*, which were awarded in pairs for merit on the field of battle, and were often depicted on the funerary monuments of veterans.[43] After AD 212, when the *Constitutio Antoniniana* extended Roman citizenship to all free-born men, the eligibility for *dona* was also extended, and Victor, although he was only a low-ranked *miles* of African race, may actually have been the recipient of this award.[44] More likely, though, the armbands were included in the iconographic program as symbols of military merit, appropriate for a veteran victorious in martyrdom. Even the Church Fathers compared the cross to military trophies.[45] *Armillae* were, in fact, commonly fashioned in the form of snakes, which would also fit the context of the Gospel's comparison of Christ raised on the cross with Moses' raising of the brazen serpent. The cross could thus have embodied different levels of meaning: monogrammatic, military, and symbolic, which were not mutually exclusive, but separately and in sum represented Christ and his name, as well as the sacrifice in death of his martyr Victor.[46]

Daniélou has pointed out that the meaning of the cross as a symbol originates in an allusion to Christ's divinity and not as a reference to his passion.[47] This then is the overall meaning of these two crosses: they stress Christ's victory, having first named him by the cryptic language of the monogram. And by positioning Victor between these two symbols, it is made plain that the saint has joined Christ in his glory.

Another problem presented by the crosses at S Vittore in Ciel d'Oro is the meaning of the words which are inscribed upon them. The inscriptions, according to Reggiori, are original and unrestored.[48] They have never been satisfactorily explained. Wilpert, for example, suggested that 'PANECIRIAE' and 'FAUSTINI' are the names of donor families, who are thus recommended to God by Victor.[49] The genitive word forms would appear to support this interpretation, but who were these families? The name Panicyrius is known only from a single fourth-century funerary inscription in S Sebastiano, Rome.[50] Perhaps an alternative interpretation is possible, one which would give the word a meaning in the context of the overall composition. *Paneciriae* appears to be a composite word meaning 'Lord of All,' derived from *pan* and *kyrios*, the Greek words for 'all' and 'lord' written in Latin letters.[51] With regard to the inscription 'FAUSTINI,' previous attempts to identify it have also assumed that it is an individual or family name. The links to S Vittore in Ciel d'Oro of various individuals with this or similar names from fourth- and fifth-century Milan have been explored, but without much success. The similarity of Faustini to the name Faustus or Faustinus has suggested the chapel might be the 'Basilica Faustae' of Ambrose's letter to Marcellina.[52] According to one tradition, this Fausta was a child of Philippus, who, along with his children Portius and Faustus or Fausta, was an early Milanese convert of the apostle Barnabas.[53] He gave his garden, the Hortus Philippi, as the site of the Coemeterium ad Martyres, the Early Christian cemetery.[54] Alternatively, it has been suggested that the Basilica Faustae was named for Faustus, whose relative bishop Ennendius of Pavia wrote to him of his miraculous cure by the oil of the lamps which hung in the shrine of S Vittore in Ciel d'Oro.[55] However, the Basilica Faustae is now not usually identified as S Vittore in Ciel d'Oro, but as the ancient chapel of S Vitalis, where Mona, bishop between 306 and 314, was interred,[56] and neither of these solutions is very convincing. Perhaps here too an alternate explanation would allow the inscription 'FAUSTINI' to be understood literally, for *faustinus* means 'favourite,' 'of good omen,' 'attended by good fortune.' All these epithets could surely apply to St Victor. In summary, since neither of the names can be securely identified with a specific donor individual or family, I suggest the simpler solution, that of literal translation of the two mosaic inscriptions, one from Latin, the other from Greek.

The domes of Early Christian chapels typically were sustained at the base by the evangelist symbols, expressing the idea that the microcosmic vision of heaven was supported by the word of God as revealed in the Gospels. The cupola of S Vittore in Ciel d'Oro also adheres to this formula. The dome rests on horizontal granite beams, replacements for the wooden supports that until the mid-nineteenth century had bridged the corners of the trapezoid below. The original mosaics that covered the beams were lost at the same time. The restoration depends in part on their scanty remains, part of a single wing, and also on the drawings done by Giulio Ferrario in 1824, which were followed closely.[57] Ferrario depicted full-face evangelist symbols with outstretched wings, one pair to each, just as we see today (fig. 55). He showed the Beings without books or haloes, and with single pairs of wings. Unfortunately it is not possible to tell whether Ferrario's drawings copied the originals faithfully, as even in 1824 they were in the last stages of decay. All that is certain is that they occupied the triangular areas supporting the dome, and that if the copies are faithful, they were of an early type, similar to those at the Naples Baptistery and at the Mausoleum of Galla Placidia in Ravenna, both of which are usually dated to the first half of the fifth century. Another area of mosaic replaced at this time was the decoration of the triangular areas flanking the east and west arches below the dome. Here medallion portraits of the evangelists were appropriately positioned, each beneath his symbol. This type of replication, the portrait image and its symbol shown as a pair, though rare, is not unknown from the fifth century. For example, in the lunettes below the vault at the mid-fifth-century chapel of San Giovanni Battista at the Lateran Baptistery, Rome, the winged symbols were shown above the standing figures of the evangelists, who were named and carried open books (fig. 100).

One last major component of the mosaic program at S Vittore in Ciel d'Oro occupies the drum. It consists of the approximately life-sized, named figures of six standing saints, one in each interfenestration. Haloes and the title 'SCS' (Sanctus) are not used. On the right wall (when facing the present altar), Ambrose is flanked by Protase and Gervase, while on the left, Maternus stands between Felix and Nabor (fig. 55).

The meaning of these two matching compositions, each of three saints, is to be sought in the identity of the central figures, the Milanese bishops Ambrose (fig. 56) and Maternus.[58] Each of these men had searched for the remains of Early Christian saints for Milan, in each case with success. Ambrose had discovered the bodies of Gervase and Protase before the chancel screen of the chapel dedicated to Nabor and Felix, the Naboriana, and reinterred them in his own prepared tomb under the high altar of his church, later S Ambrogio. The Naboriana was the funeral chapel of the early-fourth-century bishop Maternus, who discovered the remains of Nabor, Felix, and Victor in Lodi. He brought their remains to Milan, burying Victor in S Vittore in Ciel d'Oro,[59] and the other two in the Naboriana, where he planned his own burial beside them.[60] Both Maternus and Ambrose therefore have links with Victor and with the chapel of S Vittore. Maternus was responsible for the original burial of St Victor, while Ambrose chose to bury his brother Satyrus beside him. Maternus appears between Nabor and Felix because he brought their bodies to Milan, honoured them with a memorial chapel, and chose it for his own burial. In the mosaics, each bishop is shown between his own patron saints, with whom he had arranged to await the Day of Judgment. In the real world, as in the space of this chapel, each of the four patron saints was also connected with Victor: Nabor and Felix directly, by being his companions in arms and in martyrdom, and Protase and Gervase indirectly, acquiring continuity with the earlier saints and hence with their companion in martyrdom, Victor, from their burial beside Felix and Nabor in the Naboriana.

To sum up, the iconographic program of S Vittore in Ciel d'Oro, a typical martyr shrine from around the turn of the fifth century, proclaims the reward of the martyr's sacrifice: his raising up to be with God in heaven. His status in heaven is marked by his wreath of victory and his crowning by God, by the radiance of light that proclaims his glory, and by his white robes that symbolize salvation. Victor's path to glory is expressed by the presence of Christ's monogram, as well as by the symbol of his death, the cross. The saint's image in the summit of the dome is positioned – surely not by chance – directly above his tomb many metres below in the crypt (fig. 53). Thus a powerful axis of sanctity is created between image and relics in the internal space of this little building: an invisible connection that explains the position of Victor in place of Christ in the vault. Relics and image constitute two different manifestations of the presence of the holy: the relics, once honourably wrapped and returned to the earth from which they came, the image a numinous symbol of the resurrection of that same body through faith and the power of the cross. Together they symbolize the martyr's victorious death and his reward: ascent to heaven by means of his imitation of Christ's death and passion.

It is clear that the space of the chapel from crypt to dome has been laid out specifically to symbolize the transition of Victor from the human condition, subject to death, to saint in glory. The stone-lined grave in the crypt where his bones lay represents his mortality. The marble revetments which once clad the chapel's walls came from the earth and mystically clothed its four corners. In the drum and vault overhead the double radiance of great arched windows and glowing blue mosaic represents the sky, inhabited by the transformed likenesses of the Milanese saints and bishops, who witness Victor's ascent to heaven. Beyond again, a glittering gold mosaic dome, representing the vault of heaven, captures and diffracts the incident light. It is pierced at the apex by a vision of the saint of the dedication, who is present by virtue of his image and his relics and who confers extraordinary spiritual power on the chapel's interior space. Earliest functions of this visionary space must have included both veneration of the saints' remains and their images, and supplication for their active help on behalf of the faithful. In addition, we learn from the example of Satyrus that such spiritually potent space was eagerly sought by those in positions of power who could invoke the protection of the saints for eternity. For although the chapel's program, as it survives today, confines itself to its primary role as a *cella memoriae*, S Vittore in Ciel d'Oro was not a martyr shrine pure and simple, but had a secondary role as the funerary chapel of Satyrus. This fact is recorded in the testimony of an Irish traveller, Dungalus (Dungall), who visited the chapel around the year 828, and wrote down the following epitaph, which has since disappeared.[61] It ran: 'URANIO SATYRO SUPREMUM FRATER HONOREM/ MARTYRIS AD LAEVAM DERULIT AMBROSIUS/ HAEC MERITI MERCES UT SACRI SANGUINIS HUMOR/ FINITIMAS PENETRANS ADBLUAT EXUVIAS.'[62]

The original decoration of the chapel may perhaps have included some reference to Satyrus which has not survived. Dungall, who stayed at Pavia around 820–30, wrote that Ambrose buried his brother beside Victor, but omitted to name the exact location: S Vittore in Ciel d'Oro, or S Vittore al Corpo, where Victor's body was apparently translated in the early Middle Ages. However, this question was dramatically decided by archaeology, when in 1922 a pair of stone-lined graves was discovered in the crypt of S Vittore in Ciel d'Oro. One, almost exactly below the centre of the dome, measured 1.15 by 1.08 metres and was a typical *loculus* for corporeal relics. The other was adjacent; a rectangular grave, measuring 0.84 by 1.36 metres, was separated from the central loculus only by a thin stone slab. Identification of these graves as those of Victor and Satyrus has been universally accepted.[63]

Ambrose's eulogy of his brother was spoken in S Ambrogio, and included an invitation to the mourners to accompany him to the nearby grave, presumably that in S Vittore in Ciel d'Oro. Satyrus's burial beside a martyr is an important example of a practice which must have been widespread.[64] Its documentation throws interesting light on fourth-century beliefs. Satyrus, to whom Ambrose was deeply devoted, as evidenced by his eulogy, *De Excessu*, had not adopted the religious life, and indeed had not yet received baptism. Nor did he die a martyr's death. As elder brother and head of the family, he took care of the family's far-flung estates, thus allowing his brother and sister freedom to follow the religious life. Yet Ambrose's action in arranging him burial *ad sanctos* was to have a profound effect on his future reputation in the Christian church and, presumably, on the outcome of his fate on Judgment Day. This efficacious burial, immediately in contact with the body of a martyr, whose blood would penetrate and redeem the body of any person interred beside it, was so full of spiritual power that within a few centuries Satyrus himself had acquired the status of a saint. He went on to become the patron of S Vittore in Ciel d'Oro itself, after the translation of the relics of Victor, and was honoured with other dedications, as well as with a cult of his own.

Ambrose's words, then, have been confirmed by the archaeologists who have shown that Satyrus's last resting place was indeed beside S Victor in S Vittore in Ciel d'Oro. There the iconographic program, when considered as a text, and subjected to interpretation, has revealed a wealth of information. The meaning of some parts of the decoration must have been immediately obvious to the Late Antique viewer. Other elements reveal an esoteric side to Christian thought, illustrated by its interest in the occult, as represented by numerology, as well as in cryptograms. These elements in the mosaics must have required a level of sophistication in the viewer, who could thus add depth to the surface level of meaning. Use of these cryptic modes of expression probably dates back to the times of persecution, when such signs proliferated, an era which matches the subject illustrated in the mosaics themselves, the resurrection in glory of a victim of those times.

It is these elements in the S Vittore in Ciel d'Oro mosaics which argue an early date for the decoration, since the content of the iconographic program, at both its obvious and cryptic levels of meaning, best relates to the troubled times which led Victor and his companions in arms to their heroic deaths. The period after Ambrose's death in 397 and before the court moved to Ravenna in 402 seems a possible moment for creation of these mosaics: as for the patron, in the absence of direct evidence, one may speculate that an early successor to Ambrose in the See of Milan, perhaps his successor, Simplicianus, a known patron of architecture, might have been responsible, even perhaps carrying out some unfulfilled plan of Ambrose himself. But whatever its exact date within the Early Christian period, its importance as a document of the period is incontestable: it is the sole intact survivor of a myriad of shrines built to commemorate the martyrs in the earliest years of organized Christianity. Decorated as a microcosm of earth and heaven, it is above all a celebration of Victor's glorious death and resurrection.

The S Matrona Chapel

We have found that the chapel of S Vittore in Ciel d'Oro at Milan shows all the hallmarks of a *memoria* in its decoration: the martyr Victor in glory in heaven, crowned and wreathed, holding Christ's cross, and supported by the symbols of the Christian faith, the four evangelists. These elements are set in a golden vault which re-creates a likeness of heaven in the chapel's internal space. The heavenly vault is integrated with earth and with the present day by the inclusion on the side walls of locally important saints and of the clerics who had cared for their remains and initiated their cults. However, S Vittore was not only a *memoria*; it evolved from memorial shrine to funerary chapel, and this phase of transition is documented in the writings of S Ambrose, who explains its secondary use for the burial of his brother. Thus the initial stage in the series *memoria*/funerary chapel/martyrium is clarified by reading the chapel's decoration as a document, and the second phase, that of burial chapel, is revealed in the writings of the patron himself.

The other early chapel that has survived to illustrate the martyr grave–funerary chapel sequence, the S Matrona chapel, differs in having virtually no documentation, except in the lives and legends of the saints. These sources are not securely dated and are not contemporary with the chapel. The chapel itself is not dated, and work is needed to determine whether it is contemporary with its mosaic decoration, or whether this was added to a preexistent structure. The patron, despite legendary tales of a saint and of her grateful community building this chapel as her tomb, cannot be said to have a firm, historical identity, and indeed the question of patronage remains wide open. Using the decorative program itself as a document, I shall suggest that the chapel, while it may originally have been constructed as a *cella memoriae*, was decorated as a burial chapel, whether of a local ecclesiastic or of the aristocratic leader of a local community of religious women. Whoever he or she may have been, there is no evidence in the decoration to support the conclusion that the occupant was either a saint or a martyr. Rather, the atmosphere generated by the decorative scheme may be compared to that of an aristocratic Christian grave in the catacombs. It is, however, entirely possible that, as at S Vittore in Ciel d'Oro, the chapel originally housed the remains of an early saint and was then chosen as a funerary chapel by a Christian desirous of *ad sanctos* burial, and that it was decorated to suit this purpose.

Actual evidence for this suggestion is scanty. The S Matrona chapel is attached to the parish church in the village of S Prisco near S Maria di Capua Vetere in Campania.[65] The village has grown up around this church, which occupies the site of an Early Christian funerary basilica in the cemetery of Capua. The building history of the church shows two early phases. A poorly documented seventeenth-century excavation found a building in the area in front of the present church, and identified it as the remains of the primitive basilica, which may perhaps have included the grave of St Priscus.[66] The present church is an eighteenth-century replacement for the second church, which was pulled down in 1759. According to legend this second church had been built at the request of Matrona herself. It, like the chapel, was once richly decorated with mosaics, which are known only from wood engravings published by Michael Monachus in his *Sanctuarium Capuanum* of 1630: he illustrates the apse and dome mosaics of the church (figs. 63, 64), and a view of a lost portion of the mosaics of the chapel (fig. 60).

There is no information about the physical relationship of the S Matrona chapel to the second church: this question must await a full archaeological survey. The caption to Monachus's one illustration of the chapel's mosaics implies that by the seventeenth century it was no longer free-standing, but was annexed to the church, as it is now.[67] Its physical relationship with the original basilica also remains a mystery.

In contrast to the situation at S Prisco itself, the S Matrona chapel retains a large part of its original mosaics. These cover, with some areas of loss, the entire vault and the four lunettes between its springings with a coherent series of images. Investigation of the decorative program reveals the chapel's purpose as a setting of great luxury, beauty, and spiritual power for Christian burial.

The chapel consists of a small, square room, crowned with a groin vault. The corners are provided with mismatched marble columns, evidently spoils. One is beige, two are of white marble veined with light grey, and a fourth is veined with dark grey. They bear a matched set of Corinthian capitals, which in turn sustain a plaster cornice, painted bright green in imitation of malachite. The bases of the columns are almost buried in a later pavement of marble intarsia squares in two shades of grey. There are two doors: the small, rectangular one opening into the nave of the church may be original; the other leads into the front of the right aisle, which is a later addition.

The groins of the vault frame four lunettes. Two, aligned with the main axis of the church, are framed in deep soffits. The others, being in shallower niches, are subtly deemphasized. The walls must once have been covered with marble revetment, which had disappeared by 1630.[68] No early inscriptions are recorded from the chapel itself or its church.[69] The chapel does, however, contain an antique *labrum* in beige marble, now used as the altar, and traditionally believed to be the sarcophagus of Matrona, the locally honoured saint who gives her name to the chapel.

Tradition tells that the chapel was built to house the grave of a Lusitanian princess, Matrona, who was cured at this place of a long-standing illness. Her flow of blood had lasted for twelve years when an angel led her to the bones of St Priscus, one of the seventy disciples of Christ who had come to Italy with the apostle Peter.[70] The angel told her to travel from her home to Campania, and to dig where she would find two untamed bullocks pawing the ground.[71] There Priscus's body was found, and it was there that the princess built a funerary basilica in his honour.[72] At the same site she also built a house, where she spent the rest of her life with her maidens, honouring the saint who had cured her, and following the example of the blessed Therasia, wife of St Paulinus of Nola.[73] When eventually she died there from natural causes, her community built the chapel onto the right nave of the basilica for her remains, which have lain there ever since.[74]

It is difficult to substantiate this legend. It seems that Rechiarius, king of the Suevi from 448 to 456, was the first barbarian king of the Lusitanian region to embrace orthodox Christianity. After 468, however, his successors fell under Visigothic, and hence Arian, control. Nothing at all is known of these rulers in the period between 470 and 550, though the royal house then again emerges as the local champion of orthodoxy.[75] Unfortunately, history does not record a daughter, Matrona, of this house. So the sole evidence for her existence comes from the chapel and its legends, and indeed the seventeenth-century chronicler, Michael Monachus, admits to having pieced together her story from the paintings of uncertain date which he saw in the basilica of S Prisco.[76] There seems to be no other inscription, nor any documentation for her life or even for her very existence, and the name Matrona itself is suspect, a generic term meaning 'matron,' 'wife,' 'widow,' or even 'young girl of superior rank.'[77] Even Priscus, although by tradition the first bishop of Capua, who lived and performed miracles at the place now called S Prisco, cannot be securely documented, while the sarcophagus within the chapel, when opened in the seventeenth century, proved to contain only a glass urn full of many small bones, rather than the entire body that was expected.[78] Nevertheless, the chapel's mosaic program tells, in general terms at least, of the purpose of its building and of the ideas and beliefs that are illustrated there. The evidence suggests that it was built and decorated as a funeral chapel, with this function taking precedence over its possible role as a *memoria*.

Émile Bertaux has suggested that the theme of the decoration is Christ, who appears in a medallion over the 'west' door, flanked by the apocalyptic alpha and omega (fig. 57).[79] This doorway into the aisle is a simple but imposing gothic arch, which must postdate the chapel. The original door was probably the one which opens into the nave of the basilica. The lunette above this door bears the throne and two apocalyptic creatures, Ox and Eagle (fig. 58): the remaining two, the Man and the Lion, the latter totally lost except for two fragments of its accompanying clouds of glory, flank the oval window in the opposite lunette (fig. 59). The altar occupies what is not only the most important position in the chapel today, the centre of the veneration of St Matrona, but the prime location, parallel to the east end of the basilica, where the high altar is situated.[80] The chapel's altar consists of the ancient *labrum*, a classical bathtub complete with nonfunctional, carved 'lifting rings' and a drain hole. The bath had been equipped for reuse as a sarcophagus by provision of a flat, recessed lid of matching beige marble, which now forms the altar top. Perhaps that was also its ancient use, since grave-tops were commonly used as altars for the sacraments in cemetery churches.[81] By the early fifth century, sanctification of altars by means of physical relics was beginning to take place. Paulinus of Nola (353–431), for example, wrote about his church at Fundi that 'the holy ashes of the blessed relics of apostles and martyrs will give their consecration in the name of Christ to this little church.'[82]

The lunette above the altar-sarcophagus of the S Matrona chapel, now empty of mosaic, contained the most significant part of the decoration, as we know from the wood engraving of Michael Monachus. It was the only part of the chapel which he illustrated in *Sanctuarium Capuanum* (fig. 60). The central subject was a cross, of flat, lobate form with five major jewels, standing upon a small hill. Four rivers flowed from its foot, and it was flanked by six doves on each side, arranged three and three. This composition may be a reference to Constantine's jewelled cross on Golgotha, which could also be the inspiration for Paulinus's lost apse designs at nearby Nola.[83] Paulinus explains these in his own writings,[84] and their layout has been reconstructed by Wickhoff, while Rizza has more recently proposed a rather different solution.[85]

Paulinus built the Basilica Apostolorum at Nola-Cimitile shortly before 403 over the grave of St Felix. The apse-mosaic included a large, central, jewelled cross. Below, the Lamb of God crowned the Hill of Zion, from which flowed the four rivers of Paradise. Paulinus, in his dedicatory poem upon the apse, explained the wreath-like circle of birds around the cross as 'the image of the apostles expressed in a chorus of doves,' a symbolic rendering of a motif that is well known from other fifth- and sixth-century chapels and churches.[86] Doves were also shown above the doorway of the church, and Paulinus equates these to the human soul, inscribing 'the doves perched above the heavenly sign [the cross] intimate that the Kingdom of God is open to the simple of heart,' and 'us too wilt thou make doves pleasing to Thee, Christ, if Thy followers have strength through purity of heart.'[87] The paired dove motif was common in Roman funerary art, the single dove a favourite element of Early Christian art in the catacombs. In funerary settings, these single doves often carry garlands or twigs in their beaks; at other times pairs of doves drink from vessels overflowing with water.[88] The role of the dove in both the Old and the New Testaments was to transfer the word of God from heaven to earth. Thus, the message of peace, the olive branch which Noah received heralding the retreat of the flood, was carried by a dove. In the New Testament, the Holy Spirit also appears as a hovering dove, and a gold or silver dove was suspended over the font to symbolize the descent of the Spirit at baptism. From the earliest period of Christian funerary art, doves also represented the soul that had attained celestial bliss.[89] All of these meanings are illustrated in the decorative program of the S Matrona chapel.

There, just as at Nola, the twelve doves must have represented the twelve apostles, and their position in the 'apse' indicates the influence of Paulinus's shrine of St Felix, which also portrayed the Cross, the Hill of Zion, and the four rivers. Another level of meaning of the doves, however, may also be suggested by Paulinus's writings, for the epigrams over the doors which he composed declare that the simplicity and purity of heart of the dove-like soul will lead to its ultimate reward: attainment of the kingdom of heaven. In short, for Paulinus a level of eschatological meaning existed within the symbolism of the dove. It is likely that this was also an important factor in the choice of doves for the St Matrona chapel, where the soul's fate was obviously of paramount interest.[90] Thus, behind an orthodox image of Christ's cross triumphant acclaimed by his apostles was hidden the message of hope for the fate of the individual soul in eternity, an appropriate concern in a burial place.

The rivers which flow from the foot of the cross also have several well-defined meanings in early Christian thought. First, they stand for the waters of baptism. As in the garden of Eden a single river gave rise to four, which watered all the earth,[91] so Christ is the River which is announced on earth by the four evangelists. The gospels are the rivers which flow from the foot of the cross, leading the faithful to baptism and through grace to salvation,[92] and these waters in art also represent the garden of Paradise, which the soul hopes to reach after death.[93] In addition, the rivers symbolize the blood of Christ, which gushes forth in the triumph of the cross,[94] for the redemptive cross, promising forgiveness of sins, is also the triumphant cross, victorious over death. The cross, the tree of Golgotha, has now become the new centre of the world at the hilltop site of the crucifixion, which is also the Hill of Zion. The cross is made of wood, as a tree,[95] yet is precious as gold and clothed with garnets as by a garment or by Christ's blood;[96] it grows from earth yet it is blazened with heavenly jewels: the dual symbolism is as profound and complex as the dual nature of Christ himself.

We have already compared the cross, as shown by Monachus, with the monumental crosses of the Holy Land, which are also reflected in the mosaics at S Pudenziana, Rome (ca. 390) and S Apollinare, Ravenna (ca. 550). These crosses are also embossed in miniature on the holy oil ampoules at Monza and Bobbio, souvenirs brought by pilgrims from the shrines of the Holy Land. But it is obvious that the huge, mosaic 'jewelled' crosses in the apses at Rome and Ravenna, as well as the cruder copies on the pilgrim flasks, are quite different in proportion and scale from the one in Monachus's drawing, with its flat, lobate shape. It seems that it was unimportant whether the cross was an exact copy of the Cross of Golgotha. This allowed it to take a variety of shapes, and follow a variety of models, which could include both liturgical crosses and jewellery. A cross similar to an early-sixth-century pendant now in Baltimore could well have been the inspiration at S Prisco.[97]

The medallion image of Christ, blessing and signed with the alpha and omega, which faces the altar (fig. 57), is of a type common to Early Christian decorative schemes in both Rome and Ravenna. It is an illustration of a specific text, one of Christ's metaphorical revelations of himself in the apocalyptic vision of St John. This text is identified by means of the alpha and omega as illustrating Christ's words 'I am the Alpha and the Omega, the beginning and the end,' words also given to God the Father in the same work, and so, perhaps, also illustrating that Christ is one with the Father.[98] The alpha and omega accompanying Christ's image or the chi-rho symbol also appear at the Naples Baptistery and on the Byzantine silver of the period. The use of this text fits the pattern of the earliest Christian art, which illustrates Christ's own words as recorded in the Gospels or the Apocalypse, rather than narrative scenes of his life.

In addition to this medallion, Christ's presence may have been symbolized in a second position in the vault, which is centred on a circular, though fragmentary, frame ornamented with the Greek key pattern (fig. 61). The contents of the frame have not survived. This frame takes the place of the vegetal wreath at S Vittore in Ciel d'Oro, but it is evident that it has a different iconographic content from that of a victory wreath in imperial imagery, and represents the bronze frame of an oculus in a domed building, which allows the sky to be seen through a central opening.[99] This sort of building was thought to represent a microcosm of the universe, with the vault as firmament, and the heavens as a higher region to be glimpsed beyond: this concept was also illustrated at S Vittore in Ciel d'Oro and the Archbishops' Chapel. At the S Matrona chapel, one would have looked through the illusory frame of the oculus in the vault into the limitless space beyond, the highest heaven where God resides.[100] Corrado Leonardi has suggested, on the precedent of S Vittore in Ciel d'Oro, that Priscus was depicted in glory in this space;[101] this would only have been possible if this chapel had been decorated as his *cella memoriae*, for which there is at present no evidence. By contrast, many precedents in chapel and catacomb decorations would suggest that the central frame in the S Matrona chapel contained the Lamb, the Cross, or the chi-rho symbol, all of which were seen as mystically equivalent to Christ,[102] or even the Good Shepherd, a popular composition in the vaults of catacomb *cubicula*.

Christ is not the only member of the Trinity to appear in the chapel, for in the left lunette the Dove of the Holy Ghost, wings outspread, occupies the throne's centre back (fig. 58). It is not clear whether God the Father was also present in the program to complete the Trinity, as André Grabar suggested.[103] Grabar interpreted this throne as a Trinitarian symbol, an attempt by Early Christian iconographers to portray the abstract idea of the Trinity in visual terms. According to Grabar's argument, the empty throne in the chapel symbolizes the presence there of God the Father,[104] just as the empty throne in the Roman law courts symbolized the earthly emperor. The scroll, Grabar suggested, stands for the Son and the Dove for the Holy Spirit, following the text in St John's Gospel: 'I saw the spirit descending from heaven like a dove.'[105] There are several problems with this theory. First, the Church Fathers had decided, after much debate, that the 'Nameless One' upon the throne was Christ the Logos, who would then be represented by his Word, the Gospels, and at the S Matrona chapel, this is confirmed by Christ's monogram, the *chrismon*, that appears on its armrests.[106] In addition, theologians had decided in the fifth century that the dove could represent both the Logos and the Spirit. Van der Meer suggested that at the S Matrona chapel the former is intended, making the throne there purely a Christological symbol. An extra layer of meaning could even hold that Christ and his spirit were visualized together with the Holy Spirit in the image of the dove.[107]

The Gospels, too, present problems since their usual iconography shows them as books or as evangelist symbols, rather than in the form of a *rotulus*. The scroll on the seat of the S Matrona throne, far from being a generic roll which could be interpreted in any way the observer chooses (perhaps even as the Gospels), is clearly distinguished by its markings, which are prominently legible as seven tapes with seals (fig. 58). This identifies it as the scroll of Revelation 5.1, which reads 'And I saw in the right hand of Him who was seated on the throne a scroll ... sealed with seven seals.' It is also the scroll of Ezekiel 2.9–10, 'containing the fixed purposes of God for the future,' both 'unalterable and unknown to others,' and prepared for the Messiah to open at the second coming.[108]

Therefore, the most logical interpretation of the triple image of throne, scroll, and dove is apocalyptic, with the scroll as the key to its meaning. The creatures that surround it confirm this interpretation, since they did originally represent the Creatures of the Apocalypse, and only later came to be thought of as symbols of the four evangelists.[109] The composition is an image of judgment, the earliest to survive on the inner surface of an entry wall. This meaning also ties in with the content of the rest of the program, which draws most of its elements from the Book of Revelation, appropriately enough for a funerary chapel.[110]

The side lunettes of the chapel are notable for their conspicuous renderings of the Four Creatures. Three of the four survive, with only the lion of St Mark missing. In the past, evangelist symbols have been employed in dating, using as criteria the presence or absence of nimbus and gospel book, and the form and number of the wings. These criteria remain valid in broad terms, since the early examples are closest to the apocalyptic texts which describe the Creatures, and include such details as their six wings, while later, perhaps under the influence of Jerome and his preface to the Vulgate, the Beasts acquired firm identities as symbols of the evangelists. The symbols at the St Matrona chapel, six-winged and without attributes, are shown in three-quarter view with their wings folded, fitting the constraints of space in the lunettes. An earlier example in the Naples Baptistery is dated to around 408:[111] a slightly later-dated mosaic funerary portrait in the catacomb of S Gennaro, Naples, portrays four six-winged, three-quarter-view symbols on the cover of a book held by a bishop, identified as Quodvultdeus, Bishop of Carthage, who died in Naples around the year 454. These symbols identify the book that they decorate as the gospels (fig. 62).[112] These Campanian examples suggest that the six-winged form without attributes was standard there in early-fifth-century decoration, and that the formula lingered on past mid-century. Therefore it cannot be used to prove a date earlier than the mid-fifth century for the mosaics at S Matrona. It seems that the plain, unadorned Creature could and did stand for the Evangelist and his Gospel in the South, perhaps with a second layer of meaning as Beast of the Apocalypse.

The lunettes in the chapel are related to each other in theme, particularly in pairs across the chapel. They are also tied together by the decorated vault above them, as well as by borders of abstract pattern, which contain their own symbolic meaning. The vault is covered with mosaic vine scrolls, bearing bunches of grapes. This vegetal schema is divided into four segments by palm trees, one following each of the four groins of the vault (fig. 61). The palm trees, fruiting date palms, symbolize paradise, and are rendered in the same way as those that arch above the lunettes at the Naples Baptistery. The scrolls in each quadrant of the vault arise from a large, centrally placed, golden *krater*, on either side of which a bird within the scroll pecks at the grapes. Above, the central oculus frames an empty space which must once have contained Christ's symbol.

This vault decoration descends directly from similar compositions found in the vaults of catacomb *cubicula* at Rome and Naples. Raffaella Farioli, for example, has drawn attention to the stucco vine which decorated the vault of a *cubiculum* in the cemetery of Apronianus, on the Via Latina in Rome.[113] There, cupids play among vines bearing grape clusters, which fill the quadrants of the vault. A similar decoration in mosaic at S Costanza, Rome, occupies sections of the ring vault of the ambulatory. Here, even more explicitly, *putti* gather the grapes and crush them: an allegory of harvest which can be endowed with Christian meaning in terms of Christ's words 'I am the True Vine, you are the branches.'[114] Thus the grapes which are to be pressed for the vintage are the newly baptized, the fruit of the gospels.[115] The vintage is obviously a metaphor for Christ's blood, shed for humanity.

These ideas are also illustrated at the S Matrona chapel. The deep blue of the vault tells of the sky-blue firmament; the oculus, of the realms beyond. Even the vase from which the grapevine springs may symbolize the Virgin's womb, which often appears in metaphor as a closed vessel, and in this vault by giving rise to the Vine suggests the idea of Christ's miraculous birth. The vine scroll with its leaves and fruit appears to be trained overhead as on a trellis, causing the physical confines of the billowing vault to seem dematerialized, and adding to the illusion of a heavenly vision. There are texts for this interpretation too: the words of St Zeno of Verona tell that the vine was planted by God to be 'conformable to his will, our mother the church.' 'He tended it ... and having suspended it on the blessed wood he trained it to bear an abundant harvest. And so today among your number, new shoots are trained along their trellises, bubbling like a sweet stream of fermenting must they have filled the Lord's wine-vault.'[116] And from the words of Asterius the Sophist, 'The divine and timeless vine has sprung from the grave, bearing as fruits the newly baptized, like bunches of grapes on the altar.'[117]

The metaphors embodied in these quotations and the many others to be found in the writings of the Church Fathers include Christ as the vine and as its support; Christians as shoots, bearing grapes, the product of the harvest. Christ's resurrection from the grave is visualized as a vine springing from a vase. The wide-mouthed *krater*, as well as symbolizing the Virgin's womb, is a form of vessel often shown in connection with water, even overflowing with it, making it a symbol of baptism, another form of rebirth, as well as a metaphor for the grave within the tomb.

On either side of the vessel in each quarter of the vault, the vine is also home to a pair of birds. They are well differentiated into separate species. In their naturalism, they remind us of the lifelike paired birds which flank fruit baskets in the vault of the Naples Baptistery. They also recall the pairs of doves which once flanked crosses above the doors at Nola, as well as the paired peacocks which, as sole surviving fragments of Paulinus's mosaic complex there, decorated the spandrels of a *fastigium* around the tomb of St Felix.[118] Lifelike birds seem to have been typical of Campanian mosaic work, and their abundance sets it apart from other regional schools of mosaic, including that of Rome. The origin of this naturalism is seen in Pompeian-style Roman painting, where numerous examples of birds set in their natural surroundings survive in secular and domestic settings.[119]

The S Matrona chapel contains another superb example of naturalism. In the intrados of each of the two deeper lunette niches, around the cross and around Christ, baskets give rise to leafy, fruit-bearing festoons or garlands on a cold yellow ground (fig. 57). The varied fruits and grains are easily recognized: they include citrus fruits, at this date probably citrons;[120] apples and pears; pomegranates; several sorts of figs; medlars; peaches; and apricots; as well as wheat and oats. Although garlands with fruits symbolizing the four seasons were commonly included in pre-Christian decorative schemes, it is not hard to see them reinterpreted in the Christian funerary setting as an illustration to Revelation 22.2, 'on either side of the river stood a tree of life which yields twelve crops of fruit, one for each month of the year.' Again the imagery is of paradise; the text is the Apocalypse.

The S Matrona chapel is also rich in ornament. Concentric border patterns frame the vault and the lunettes (figs. 57, 58). Between the fruit garlands and the east and west lunettes is a radial pattern of golden bowls or amphorae on a dark blue ground (now largely destroyed), while to the vault side of the garlands are three rich borders, one of a variant jewelled chain, jewels alternating with lilies; a second features large, S-shaped golden symbols back to back on dark blue; while the third, which outlines all the inner edges of the decoration, alternates paired *pelta* shields with golden circles containing each a leafy cross. These patterns are subtly different from those of Rome and Ravenna. They use much less gold, and there is a tendency even here to substitute plant forms for geometric details. The use of *pelta* and S-forms is also unique. Parallels must be sought among Campanian mosaics, of which so few survive. The closest parallels, again, are found in S Giovanni in Fonte, Naples. There, the whole dome is outlined with a band of back-to-back S-pattern, while the lower edge of the mosaic zone is demarcated by a pattern of bowl shapes. Further east, similar patterns occur at Salonica in the rotunda of St George, again suggesting a Greek influence on Campanian mosaic art, though this influence has not been precisely defined.

Further information can, however, be gained from both written accounts and drawings about other lost mosaics from Campania's Early Christian period. The most relevant, apart from Nola, are the lost decorations of the cathedral at S Maria di Capua Vetere, and the mosaics and paintings of the basilica of S Prisco itself.[121] The cathedral retained its apse mosaic into the eighteenth century. The whole apse was covered with vine scrolls, in the centre of which was seated a figure of the Virgin enthroned with her Child.[122] The inscription, 'SANCTAE MARIAE SYMMACUS EPISCOPUS,' which was written in large letters at the top of the mosaic,[123] dates it to the episcopate of Bishop Symmachus, of whom we know nothing except that he was present at the deathbed of St Paulinus at nearby Nola, on 22 June 431.[124] Evidently, he was also a patron of mosaic decoration. The date 431 is memorable as the year of the Council of Ephesus, in which Mary was declared to be the Mother of God. Symmachus's name in the mosaic, his active life as bishop around that date, and a composition centred on Mary and her Child in the centre of his apse, taken together confirm both his involvement as patron of the Capua Vetere apse mosaic, and a date soon after 431. If so, this composition would have been made about a quarter of a century after Paulinus's own apses at Nola and Fundi. Its use of vine scrolls to demarcate the heavenly zone in which the Virgin resides suggests a continuity of thought with the S Matrona chapel, and its subject matter with the original apse decoration at S Maria Maggiore, Rome.

I have already mentioned that the Early Christian church of S Prisco had mosaics in its apse and in the dome in front of its sanctuary, which were recorded by Michael Monachus in 1630,[125] and survived until the church was razed to the ground in 1759. The apse composition featured twelve men, two boys, and two women all named and all holding up objects in their outstretched hands (fig. 63).[126] Monachus's wood engraving fails to precisely identify these objects, which appear to be loaves of bread, rather than the traditional crowns of martyrdom. Perhaps they represent the loaves which Christians brought to the altar as their Eucharistic offerings. These were traditionally not only crown-shaped but known as *coronae*, allowing an elegant double layer of meaning in this composition.[127] Curiously there seems to have been a void at the centre of the composition, so that the saints appear to carry their enigmatic offerings towards each other. Perhaps they were thought of as bringing gifts to the altar which is shown below. Above the saints, a single dove, symbolizing the Holy Spirit, fluttered in the bowl of the apse. It was the central focus of the upper level of the mosaics, which consisted of a garland of olive branches and pomegranates, topped by eight tightly rolled scrolls, quite possibly the writings of the four evangelists and the four major prophets which the Holy Spirit had inspired.

The other mosaic composition at S Prisco decorated a dome immediately before the main altar of the church. The decorated dome is such an unusual feature for an Early Christian church in Italy that its presence alone may indicate that S Prisco was a martyrium where relics of the saints were venerated. Many saints were named and pictured in the dome mosaics, and most were local (fig. 64).[128] Above a wide girdling wreath with cupids, the whole ground was divided into zones like a checkerboard. Only alternate compartments were filled with mosaic, and the other areas originally bore paintings, though they were shown as empty by the engraver. A damask effect resulted, generically similar to the vault of the Naples Baptistery. At S Prisco, the mosaic panels of the two lower zones contained pairs of figures conversing. In the lowest zone eight pairs of saints sat upon rocks holding their crowns of martyrdom; above them, but alternating, pairs of standing prophets and apostles held books.[129] Above this again, the upper two zones alternated pairs of motifs, roses and the ubiquitous birds flanking vases. The whole scheme was crowned with a second garland framing an 'oculus,' through which an object on a starry background could be seen. Bertaux interpreted this as a throne, but Lehmann has more convincingly identified the object as a 'Sphere of Heaven' with a canopy, an astrological symbol taken straight from pagan iconography, where, for example, it occurred at Hadrian's villa at Tivoli.[130] The whole schema of this vault with its imitation coffering, has a strong classical component: roses, for example, were the standard sculptured infill of many a classical coffer vault, and roses of this elongated type are conspicuous elements in the painted stucco vault decoration of the second-century Tomb of the Pancratiae on the Via Latina, Rome. This relationship is not really surprising in an Early Christian composition. The choice of saints, too, is markedly Campanian, with six martyrs of Capua and four more from Campania, including Felix and Priscus, who occupy a single 'coffer.' In the absence of any other documentation, these images of local saints suggest that this funerary basilica in the graveyard of Capua was the *martyrium* of that city, built to shelter its graves and the collected relics of its saints. Probably the site was chosen specifically because it was the location of the grave or the first *memoria* of St Priscus.

It has been suggested by Giuseppe Bovini that S Prisco, far from being the work of an undocumented and legendary congregation of nuns, was part of the building program of a known patron, Symmachus, bishop of Capua, the donor of the apse mosaic of S Maria Suricorum, Capua, the cathedral of his diocese.[131] It is tempting to see that mosaic as but one of his gifts to his see, and to identify him as possible donor of the martyrium of S Prisco in the extramural cemetery on the Via Aquaria, and of its mosaic decoration. In this case, he may well have prepared its attached chapel as his own tomb. Although Michael Monachus records his tomb site in Capua's S Maria Maggiore in the seventeenth century,[132] burial within the walls of the city of Capua would not have been possible at the time of Symmachus's death sometime in the fifth century. His tomb may well have been moved into the city from the cemetery outside the walls at a later date.

To sum up, there is no physical evidence linking St Matrona with the chapel, though her relics may possibly have sanctified its altar, if indeed she existed at all. The most probable date for the chapel's mosaics, the mid-fifth century, certainly suggests a connection with Symma-chus, though that cannot be proved at the present time. The S Matrona mosaics would then fit into the series of surviving Campanian mosa-ics, all of which date between 403 and 431. Although scholars have put the S Matrona mosaics as early as the late fourth century, and as late as the first quarter of the sixth century,[133] Farioli, most recently, dates the chapel to the mid-fifth century, a date which seems well founded.[134] She sees the chapel as an integral part of the decor of the martyrium church: the basilica illustrating the glory of the martyrs in heaven and the chapel, the individual soul's salvation.

The chapel's decoration, then, re-creates the 'resurrection atmo-sphere' of a *cubiculum* in the catacombs,[135] and includes the same icon-ographic ingredients. The symbols of Christ, his Vine, the emblems of paradise, all are as old as the first Christian art. The texts, however, are precise and taken from the Apocalypse: texts about judgment and the hope of salvation, and about the mysteries of the vision revealed to St John. Thus the program derives from Western theology, since the Apocalypse did not enjoy early canonical status in the East. It seems that the S Matrona chapel is an aristocratic, above-ground survivor of the sort of Late Antique tomb which the catacombs copied in their carved-out tufa architecture and in their decorations. The S Matrona chapel, annex of a small and somewhat provincial cemeterial basilica, which nevertheless was probably an important regional martyrium, appears to reflect ordinary, upper-level patronage: the sort of setting which would be considered efficacious for the resurrection of an aris-tocratic Christian soul on Judgment Day.

CHAPTER SEVEN

Mausolea of the Rulers in the West

A survey of the *corpus* of funerary monuments built by the Christian emperors of the West in Late Antiquity has made it clear that the vast majority of them survive only in ruins and often in anonymity. Details of the decoration of the Mausoleum of Helena, for example, would hardly be known were it not for Bosio (fig. 42), while the enigmatic mausolea beside Old St Peter's present problems in their dating, patronage, and occupancy: not surprisingly, since both were destroyed during the rebuilding of St Peter's.

Nevertheless, several Late Antique mausolea of imperial or royal quality do survive in the suburbs of Rome, Milan, and Ravenna, and are joined by others in the hinterland of Tarragona (Tarraco) in Spain, and in the heart of Toulouse (Tolosia) in France, the latter known only from a very full seventeenth-century description of its mosaics, and some rather enigmatic plans. These are the mausolea of the daughters of Constantine (S Costanza in Rome); of the Theodosian dynasty in Milan (S Aquilino); the probable mausoleum of Constantine's youngest son Constans I near Tarragona; and of the Barbarian kings – the Visigothic rulers in Toulouse and Theoderic the Great in Ravenna – to which I propose to add the Mausoleum of Galla Placidia in Ravenna, a burial place which may well have been built for the interment of Placidia's eldest child, Theodosius, son of her marriage to the Visigothic king, Ataulf.

Each of these buildings will be discussed in depth in this chapter as examples of either the typical imperial mausoleum of Late Antiquity, of the structures built in imitation of the Roman imperial model by the Visigothic and Ostrogothic rulers, or, in the case of the Mausoleum of Galla Placidia, of an atypical funerary structure built by an imperial princess, perhaps with her own burial or that of her son in mind.

S Costanza

In contrast to the many losses at St Peter's and in Rome's suburban areas which were surveyed earlier in this book, a single Late Antique imperial mausoleum survives in Rome: S Costanza on the Via Nomentana (fig. 65). Not only does the building retain a substantial part of its original decoration, but much of what is lost can be reconstructed from drawings and descriptions made by Renaissance artists and antiquarians. S Costanza is the prime example of a decorated Late Antique imperial mausoleum. Its iconographic program is especially interesting because it was erected in the mid-fourth century, a pivotal time for the change from pagan to Christian iconography. In the interpretation of this decoration patronage must play an important part, as the ambiguous decor is best understood in terms of both the patron and those who would occupy the mausoleum in death.

Until recently, S Costanza, which was situated on imperial property outside the walls of Rome, was thought to have been built for Constantina, daughter of Constantine, as her mausoleum. This belief originated in a sixth-century text, the *Liber Pontificalis* biography of Pope Silvester, according to which Constantine constructed a basilica dedicated to St Agnes and an adjacent baptistery on the Via Nomentana site at his daughter's request.[1] Although the text specified a baptistery rather than a mausoleum, scholars proposed that a clerical error had substituted the word 'baptistery' for 'mausoleum' in the lost sources for the sixth-century text. This allowed S Costanza to be identified as Constantina's mausoleum, and to be dated to the period between 337 and 351, when she was a widow in Rome. She died in Bithynia in 354, at which time her body was returned to Rome for burial, a fact which is recorded by the contemporary historian Ammianus Marcellinus.[2]

Although Constantina was certainly buried somewhere on the Via Nomentana estate, it now transpires that her original burial place cannot have been in S Costanza, which was evidently not part of the original building campaign, since a structure has been discovered beneath it, and it is the brickwork of this lower building which is bonded to that of S Agnese, the Constantinian basilica. The lower building, a triconch,[3] was discovered during the 1992 excavations of David Stanley, and must be the building called a baptistery in the *Liber Pontificalis* text (plan, fig. 66).[4] Since burial within baptisteries did sometimes occur in Early Christian times, it may even have served both as a baptistery and as Constantina's original mausoleum.[5]

The discovery of the earlier building on this site raises a lot of questions. Foremost among them is the reason for replacing one plainly imperial building on imperial private property with another, within decades at most of its construction. Who could have done this, and why? Presumably only a leading member of the imperial family would have been empowered to pull down Constantina's baptistery, which occupied the best and most level site on the sloping terrain adjacent to the funerary basilica (fig. 67). As to the purpose of rebuilding on the site, Stanley has suggested that the 'second' building served as a *memoria* to St Agnes, whose tomb was in the catacomb nearby, though not directly below, and that it was sanctified, perhaps, by a contact relic.[6] Another possibility is that the second building, S Costanza, was a mausoleum built by the emperor Julian the Apostate (361–3) for his wife the empress Helena, the younger daughter of Constantine and sister to Constantina.[7] Helena's burial, as well as Constantina's, is documented to this location. She married Julian in 355, when he was Caesar, and died in Gaul in the winter of 360–1, shortly before her husband's unexpected assumption of sole power in November of 361. Her body was returned to the Via Nomentana villa, and interred beside that of her sister, according to Ammianus.[8] It is quite possible, and indeed likely, that Julian built her a new and grander mausoleum at the imperial villa. He may even have planned to be buried there beside his wife. The *Liber Pontificalis* text may indeed be accurate in stating that Constantine had built a baptistery at Constantina's request, and that this was the site where she and her aunt Constantia were baptized. If so, this baptistery was the building that the mausoleum replaced.

S Costanza owes its survival to its dedication as a church in or before the seventh century. It is the most important centrally planned imperial mausoleum to survive from the period of evolution of Christian imagery, when new beliefs were taking their place alongside the old in art. The result displayed in the decoration of S Costanza is an enigmatic mixture of two faiths and two traditions. This mixture not only confirms the extent of the two sisters' Christian belief, but sets it in a context of art forms taken over from pagan tradition. This subtle mixture, while it adheres to the tradition of the era when pagan imagery was being reinterpreted for Christian use, may also have a more specific meaning, if the patron were the emperor Julian. Julian was to announce his apostasy from the Christian faith shortly after his accession to sole power, but he had secretly been a pagan for many years.[9] If he were the patron of S Costanza, the ambiguity of its decoration would have suited both his own beliefs and those of his wife and sister-in-law, who were Christians. This pivotal monument, dating from the very earliest years of state Christianity, and quite possibly built at the command of a crypto-pagan emperor, will be compared with the other surviving imperial mausolea: Centcelles at Constanti near Tarragona, probably built for the burial of Constans I; S Aquilino in Milan, which is almost certainly dated to the late fourth century; and the Mausoleum of Galla Placidia at Ravenna, from the first half of the fifth century. These four monuments are the only funerary structures of the imperial family to survive intact from Late Antiquity. They display an evolution of imagery and symbolism in their architecture and decoration which reveals the growing certainty of the faith of the Christian emperors in the first hundred years after the death of Constantine. They also reveal that at the highest level of patronage, where expense was no object, salvation was the preferred subject of the funerary decorations, and in this there was no difference from the humbler decorations in the Roman catacombs. Comparison with the tombs of the barbarian kings will also prove to be illuminating.

S Costanza is a circular brick structure over 20 metres in diameter, which was entered from the funerary basilica of Sant'Agnese through a vestibule with lateral apses and a barrel vault, of which only traces remain (fig. 68). Its position beside a Christian church is analogous to that of the Mausoleum of St Helena on the Via Labicana and to S Aquilino in Milan. At S Costanza, the interior is dominated by the tall, windowed, central drum, supported on two dozen columns which are radially arranged in pairs (fig. 69). Outside the columns is a circular ambulatory, roofed with a ring-shaped tunnel vault. The ambulatory is articulated by sixteen niches and two small, lateral apses, and a turret rises on the main axis across from the entrance. It was there that until 1791 the imperial porphyry sarcophagus, now in the Vatican Museum, was situated. A rather subtle secondary symmetry is imposed on the primarily concentric ground plan, for the niches and the intercolumnations are only aligned on the cross axis, (see plan, fig. 66). This symmetry is that of the cross, which is thus inscribed in the circular plan. The sumptuous decorative scheme of the mausoleum included mosaics in the main dome, the tunnel vault of the ambulatory and its twin apses, and the turret over the sarcophagus. Between the windows and above the capitals the drum wall was revetted with marbles, the *opus sectile* designs carried out in purple and green porphyry and *giallo antico* (fig. 70). Decoration of the floor has not survived: a marble medallion which depicted Silenus upon a donkey in black and white intarsia was drawn and ascribed to S Costanza by P.S. Bartoli. Now lost, its provenance is not clear.[10]

Of all this splendour, only the ambulatory and lunette mosaics survive. The mosaics and marbles of the dome, drum, and turret were removed in 1620 and replaced by baroque paintings. These in their turn were removed in 1938–9, and the upper area was stripped down to bare brick.[11] Fortunately, the vanished dome mosaics had been recorded in watercolour by Francesco d'Ollanda in the years between 1538 and 1540 (fig. 71). Several other Renaissance artists, among them Antonio da San Gallo, also drew them, and they were described and roughly sketched in 1594 and again in 1608 by Pompeio Ugonio, who also recorded the turret mosaics.[12] The mosaic occupied all the space above the windows of the drum. In the lower zone, immediately above the windows, a river scene girdled the dome (fig. 71). The river contained marine life, octopus and squid, as well as fish: presumably the original inspiration was the Nile delta, and it sprang from the same tradition as the Nile mosaic at Palestrina. There was copious bird life, and the waters were populated by dozens of winged *putti*, who fished with nets or lines, rode in boats or on the backs of swans, tended fish weirs, or played with tridents.[13] The scene adheres to the pagan tradition in almost all respects. Although this tradition was to be taken over in Christian art, where such rivers would be reinterpreted as the River Jordan, here at S Costanza the version was still almost totally devoid of Christian meaning: its roots are fully visible as pagan and classical. This is underlined, also, by one almost discordant motif, observed by Ugonio, but unfortunately never illustrated. In a central location facing the entry, above the sarcophagus itself, a boat of a more serious sort set out on a journey across the water. It bore, not cupids, but a boatman in the stern and two figures 'dressed as the saints' sitting in its prow.[14] Here, surely, were the imperial dead, ferried by Charon across the Styx, frontier to the afterlife. And the 'silver waters' of the river just as surely separate the land of the living from the landscape of paradise, which was glimpsed along the far side of the water, by a trick of illusion stretching away into infinity.

As in the Palestrina mosaic, the far shoreline was the setting for a series of figural scenes. Here, these were framed and separated by a trellis formed of golden caryatids, raising candelabra above their heads and supported underfoot by paired panthers, animals dear to Bacchus. At the upper level, the golden network formed the architectural framework of a canopy of heaven, open in the centre to the real sky, as shown by the draughtsman known as the Anonymous Destailleur (fig. 70). The caryatid network, a twelve-part *pergula* of glittering splendour, once revealed on the lower level twelve groups of classically draped figures, some on the open shore, others set against backdrops of architecture. These precisely choreographed scenes have been identified as specific events from the Old Testament, rather surprisingly inserted into the framework of a pagan, overtly Bacchic, temple decoration. Above them in the lower part of the canopy area, twelve other scenes were shown: one only, the miracle of the centurion's servant, has been identified up to now.[15] This has been seen as the sole survivor of a New Testament cycle, which may perhaps have been paired with the Old Testament scenes below in a typological relationship. The portrayal of this Christian imagery within a pagan framework makes it clear that the transition from one life to the next was seen in similar terms in both old and new faiths as the crossing of a boundary, a boundary which was symbolized here by living waters. The *pergula* with its pagan overtones seems to have been a basic motif that represented luxury outdoor furnishings in both the real and the symbolic worlds.[16] The heaven glimpsed through the arches of the *pergula* at S Costanza, however, had been fully transformed into a Christian one, proving once and for all that at least one of the deceased was a devout believer in the Christian afterlife.

Some of the twenty-four biblical scenes had disappeared before they could be recorded, but the remaining scenes summarize Early Christian beliefs about the afterlife. Not all of the twelve Old Testament scenes, and the one scene from the New Testament, have been identified.[17] Henri Stern listed the securely identified scenes of Susannah and the Elders, and Tobias and the Fish, as paradigms of salvation; the sacrifice of Cain and Abel, and that of Elijah, as examples of God's answers to prayer; Moses striking water from a desert rock as God's intervention on behalf of his flock; and both Lot at the Gate of Sodom and Noah building the ark as symbols of deliverance. These last two were mentioned in the liturgical prayers for the dead, among them the *commendatio animae,* and thus were especially appropriate to a place of burial. Liturgical connections have also been identified for the sacrifice of Cain and Abel, cited at the Offertory in the Roman Canon of the

Mass.[18] But further research on the funerary liturgy has made it possible to identify the source of almost all the paradigms that were illustrated in the mosaics of S Costanza.

Although the earliest funeral mass has not survived intact, the compilation made by Damien Sicard from various early Roman and Gelasian liturgical manuscripts reveals some intriguing parallels between the salvation paradigms acclaimed in the funerary prayer *proficiscere anima*, the 'setting forth of the soul,' and the scenes illustrated at S Costanza.[19] '*Proficiscere anima de hoc mundo*' are the opening words of the prayers, which take the form of a litany for the salvation of the departing soul. These prayers are known from the Gellone Sacramentary of the Gelasian rite, sent to Charlemagne by Pope Hadrian I, and adhere to the Roman ritual used by the papacy between 784 and 791, as is clear from other Roman texts.[20] The *proficiscere anima* was a central part of the funeral liturgy in eighth- to tenth-century sources, including the earliest survivors.

All of the Old Testament scenes identified at S Costanza except Tobias and the Fish also occur in the eighth-century *proficiscere anima*.[21] Each intercession was introduced by the words 'O Lord, deliver the soul of your servant from many tribulations, as you have delivered.' The paradigms followed: 'Susannah – from false testimony; Elijah (and Enoch) – from the universal death of the world; Moses – from the hand of Pharaoh, king of the Egyptians; Lot – from Sodom and from the blazing fire; Noah – from the flood; Abel – through the pleasing sacrifice.'[22] The mosaics would then have represented visualizations of these prayers, ensuring their mystical repetition in the funerary space, to plead the cause of the deceased forever. They present independent evidence for the antiquity of the prayers of the *proficiscere anima*, which appear to have formed an integral part of the funerary liturgy as early as the mid-fourth century. The importance of these paradigms in the belief and ritual of the early church is underlined by their repetition in the exorcisms which catechumens underwent during the forty days of their initiation. This has led some scholars, notably Aimé Georges Martimort, to deny that the images of these scenes of deliverance, specifically those in the catacombs, illustrate the funerary rites. Martimort proposes instead that the series of deliverance images is general, not specific, and expresses the beliefs learned in Christian initiation.[23] Thus Martimort identifies the themes of vocation, faith, pardoning of sins, rebirth, salvation through water, and the Eucharistic meal in the art of the catacombs, the earliest Christian art, as illustrating the cate-

chism. Broadly speaking, though, exorcism is another form of deliverance from evil, and so one would expect this overlap in the
employment of deliverance imagery. However, in the narrower setting
of an imperial mausoleum built with one purpose in mind, the housing
of a deceased person in such a way as to invoke or even compel a
favourable life in the hereafter, the more specific meaning of intercession for the dead is paramount. This must be the primary meaning of
the images in a funerary setting, though these images may also fit the
broader context of catechismal belief in general.

Christian content has also been ascribed to the ambulatory mosaics,
although most of the panels could be interpreted in terms of either
faith. An obvious exception was the chi-rho symbol over the sarcophagus, in gold on a white background with stars, seen on the extreme
right in the Anonymous Destailleur drawing (fig. 70). Only fragments
survive of this panel, the only one to lack ambiguity of meaning. Next
to it, two panels bear scattered funerary imagery in gold and colours
on white: olive and myrtle branches and vessels for pouring libations
and perhaps also symbolizing purification, musical instruments for the
funerary rites, and all sorts of fruits and birds (fig. 74, L). The latter
included the standard peacocks and doves, partridges and pheasants,
whose meanings marked the paradise setting in much the same way in
pagan or Christian times. Fruits in a garden – here apples, pears, figs,
grapes and fir cones – also symbolized paradise.

The next pair of vaults, moving away from the sarcophagus, is decorated with a design of interlocking roundels containing busts, cupids
and psyches, and geometric motifs: elements typical of floor mosaics,
with many parallels in Roman art as far back as the first century and
floors at Pompeii (fig. 74, centre). Next come one of the most interesting panel pairs (fig. 73; 74, R). The vault is covered in each case with a
spreading vine which bears both grape and acanthus leaves, and
bunches of grapes which are being harvested by *putti*. In the centre
are two portrait busts, presumably representing the deceased. Since
one bust portrait appears to have been heavily restored using the other
one (a woman) as a model, we can only speculate about the identity of
the two figures: they could represent the daughters of Constantine or,
equally well, one of the two princesses and her husband. If the former,
they could date from the presumed reburial of Constantina beside her
sister at the time of Helena's death, and their sarcophagi could have
lain in the lateral apses of the mausoleum, in one of which a small porphyry sarcophagus (a classical bathtub) lay until the early seventeenth

century, when it was taken to St Peter's for use as an altar. The mosaics above these probable gravesites depict the vintage on either side of the vault: *putti* tread the grapes in a vat under a colonnade; oxen pull a cart heaped with grapes; a *putto* loads the fruit; another goads the oxen (fig. 73).

The grape harvest is part of the iconographic repertory of the Dionysiac mystery cult, and as such frequently occurs in Greco-Roman decorative schemes. It appears, for example, at Piazza Armerina (ca. 305), where a floor is adorned with a scene of *putti* harvesting grapes. It is, however, equally capable of Christian interpretation, as we have already seen at the S Matrona chapel. Christ as the True Vine, the grapes as the Christian souls, the vintage as the pouring out of the blood of the martyrs – all are concepts that were to be expounded by the Fathers, and this on a basis of Christ's own words in the gospels. The imagery, then, could not only express the hope of joyous immortality in Bacchic terms, but had a new significance in Christian terms, where the wine had a symbolic equivalence not only to the blood of the martyrs, but to Christ's blood as given in the Eucharist as the means of salvation: it meant the end of earthly life and rebirth into the next. Obviously this is a motif which would have fitted with Christian or pagan belief, according to interpretation. The Christian interpretation would have been the choice of the two princesses, who are known to have been devout Christians. Equally, had it been the emperor Julian's intention to be buried beside his wife in this mausoleum, as seems likely if it was built in the interval between Helena's death and his unexpected accession to power, this ambiguous imagery would have fit with his pagan beliefs, which he had previously kept secret. This would also explain his choice of seemingly Bacchic themes for the magnificent porphyry sarcophagus provided for the mausoleum's main burial site.

The next pair of vaults has an overall design of interlaced circles, enclosing octagons, similar to a standard floor design (fig. 75, above). The contents of the octagons are animals and birds; the circles frame *putti*, psyches, and figures bearing flowers and fruit. One panel is centred on a psyche, the other on a *putto*, which has been interpreted as a symbolic reference to the souls of the deceased and her husband.[24]

Beyond this, on either side of the entry, the vaults display geometric motifs and double pairs of dolphins attacking octopi in interlocking lozenges (fig. 75, main field). These dolphins are sometimes thought to embody Christian symbolism: the initials for the words Jesus Christ,

Son of God, Saviour standing for the Greek word ichthous, fish; the octopus representing evil, here overcome by Christ. Again this dolphin pattern is not unknown in the pagan world; here in the mausoleum, for example, paired dolphins are a part of the pagan framework in the dome through which the Christian heaven is glimpsed. So again an ambiguous imagery is presented, capable of being interpreted in terms of the old or the new faiths.

One last panel of the ambulatory vault remains: the entry area. A subtle geometric pattern, reminiscent of a floor pattern, and identical with a contemporary painted vault in the Catacomb of the Via Latina, it displays red, blue, and green octagons, stars and crosses on white (fig. 75 below). The cross was a motif frequently included in pagan floors: here, dominant in the design over the entryway, it may well have intentional Christian connotations and mark the entrance to what is, on analysis, a deeply Christian monument, however much veiled in the imperial paraphernalia of luxury and tradition.

The decoration of the mausoleum originally included other areas which were unambiguously Christian. Among these were the mosaics of the turret above the sarcophagus, which were described by Ugonio, and sketched by the Anonymous Destailleur (fig. 70, R). On the west wall, the haloed Lamb was represented, in front of a backdrop of buildings that may have represented Constantinian Jerusalem. The Lamb stood in the midst of six or seven wine jars, identifying the scene as the wedding at Cana. This, while often interpreted as a deliverance miracle, was also symbolic of the Eucharist.

Ugonio also mentioned the mosaics of the other walls of the turret: only one was identified, probably that of the south wall. This showed Christ among his disciples, a popular theme of the mid- to late fourth century, and one that would reappear at S Aquilino, Milan. The north wall had both seated figures and two standing, white-robed women, possibly representing the two princesses who were interred here.[25]

The ambulatory apses also retain their mosaics, heavily restored. Their grey-blue backgrounds and sparing use of gold have suggested dating them to the mid-fourth century, but technical studies have confirmed a much later date, probably the sixth century.[26] Since they do not form part of the original iconographic program, they will not be considered here, except to note that the overtly Christian subject matter, the Giving of the Keys and the Giving of the Law, departs from the ambiguity and pagan overtones of the earlier decoration and provides a Christian focus within the building that fits the later period.

Centcelles

Like S Costanza, the mausoleum at Centcelles, about five kilometres from Tarragona in Spain, can be dated to the mid-fourth century. It therefore belongs to the period when ancient forms of aristocratic and imperial burial were still in use, but were being readapted for Christian patrons.

The mausoleum is situated on the site of a Late Antique suburban villa, the usual location for an imperial mausoleum of the period (plan, fig. 76A). The villa lay close to the route of the Roman road that connected Tarragona (ancient Tarraco) with Saragossa. Apart from the mausoleum itself and an adjacent tetraconch, the villa has not been excavated. These two buildings may owe their survival to their consecration as a church, perhaps as early as the twelfth century.[27] The domed building is identified as a mausoleum by its mosaic and painted decoration, and by the presence of a tomb chamber (fig. 76B) under the floor.

Its identification as the tomb of the emperor Constans I, youngest son of Constantine the Great, cannot be proved, but is likely as its grandeur seems appropriate for the burial of an imperial personage, rather than a rural aristocrat. Reasons for attributing it to Constans are circumstantial. He was murdered in January 350 by order of the usurper Magnentius, at Helena (present day Elne), which lies at the southern end of the Pyrenees not far from Tarragona. Athanasius recorded that Constantius II was 'pretending to build' a mausoleum for his brother in the period 353–7, though its location was not recorded.[28] The fact that the village nearest to the villa site is called Constanti also suggests a connection to Constans, though another explanation cannot be ruled out. It may also be significant that the only porphyry sarcophagus in Spain, a *labrum*, is situated not far away from Centcelles at the Cistercian monastery of Santes Creus, where it had been reused for the burial of Pedro III of Aragon in 1285.[29]

The circular, domed chamber is set into a plain, square stone block (fig. 77), measuring 10.7 metres internally. The height of the chamber is 18 feet, and the interior is articulated by four niches which occupy the four corners of the outer block. Traces of the stucco setting bed suggest mosaics were once present in the four conches.

The lower wall of the main dome has painted decoration up to the level of the springing of the vault, which was marked by a cornice.

Only fragments of these paintings survive: the portrait of a woman (fig. 79), and fragmentary scenes with buildings and animals.

Above the cornice the mosaic decoration is in three registers with a central medallion (fig. 78). These mosaics are in fragmentary condition. Those of the central disc are almost completely lost and cannot be deciphered. Below, much damaged, is a register with four large and four small panels: the latter are devoted to the four seasons shown as young men with their seasonal attributes. Between them were four larger scenes depicting ceremonies, apparently imperial, but now damaged almost beyond recognition. One panel showed an enthroned figure, dressed in purple and gold, holding a diadem and flanked by other figures in court dress. Two other scenes appear to show similar groups of figures, which flank a prominent central personage who holds a *rotulus* or a *mappa*. Enough remains of these fragmetary scenes to make it probable that an important person, quite possibly a ruler, was depicted here.[30]

Below this level, and separated from it by a wide border of roundels containing crosses, is a wide register with biblical scenes illusionistically set into a mosaic framework of spiral columns crowned with ionic capitals, a framework which has already been discussed in the context of other mausolea in the second chapter (fig. 79). The spaces defined by these columns vary in size and it is unclear how many scenes were formerly depicted. Estimates vary from a low of twelve to a high of sixteen. The scenes depicted come from the Old Testament and represent the paradigms of salvation of the Early Christian church. In this, Centcelles parallels its contemporary, S Costanza, and the earlier mausoleum of Helena, in so far as its decorative scheme is known.

At Centcelles, the program of decoration includes Daniel in the Lions' Den (upper L., fig. 79) as well as two scenes from the narrative of the Three Hebrew Youths from the Book of Daniel: their refusal to worship the Golden Calf and their delivery from the Fiery Furnace, (centre, fig. 79) where they are accompanied by a succouring angel, as in the text.[31] Two of the three usual scenes of the deliverance of Jonah are included: Jonah thrown overboard and swallowed by the sea monster (far R, fig. 79) and Jonah at rest under the vine of gourds; Jonah thrown up alive from the creature's stomach was probably also depicted but has not survived.[32] Another panel illustrates Noah's Ark, while yet another is cautiously identified as Moses striking the Rock.[33] Adam and Eve and the Good Shepherd are also included, as well as, arguably, the Raising of Lazarus. Four of the panels are completely lost or so badly damaged as to be indecipherable. Judging by what survives, one may speculate that they also illustrated the paradigms of salvation.

Once again, as at S Costanza, the Christian elements appear in a pagan setting which displays strong imperial links with the past, the age-old idealized secular paradise which since Etruscan times had been the hope of the aristocrat facing death. This, to judge from the decorations of pagan tombs, was to be an existence in which the dead continued to enjoy their favourite activities. The Tomb of the Cacciatore, Tomb 3700 at Tarquinia, for example, which dates from around 500 BC, is painted with a hunter's paradise, both game roaming free and the trophies of the chase (fig. 105). Nearer the time of Centcelles, we find the magnificent inner doorway at S Aquilino, Milan, which is decorated with scenes of chariot races, while at S Costanza the dome was girdled with a river scene in which children fished and snared game. This was perhaps a gentler and more idealized version of hunting that was suited to the women who were entombed there.

At Centcelles, in the same tradition, a hunting scene takes pride of place in the dome. Right above the cornice a broad frieze of mosaic, almost a metre and a half high and over 33 metres in circumference, girdles the dome at its widest point. The subject is the hunt. Straight across from the entry, a group of five men is portrayed, grouped around a central figure who faces the viewer directly (fig. 80). This personage has been universally accepted as the owner-occupier of the tomb, though his identity has not been established, beyond the fact that his hair is cut in the style of the tetrarchs. On either side, scenes of the hunt follow on one another – deer are netted, snares are set, horses are led out, hunters gallop after prey, a rural villa is included. Surely the vision is still one of the hunter's afterlife, where he would continue to enjoy the aristocratic sports that had been his in life.

Imperial Mausolea at Milan: S Gregorio and S Aquilino

In Milan, two mausolea were raised outside the walls of the city by the imperial family during the years they held court there. One survives, S Aquilino at S Lorenzo; the other, nearby at S Vittore al Corpo, was surrounded by an octagonal walled precinct, and was later dedicated as a chapel to St Gregory. S Gregorio was demolished in 1576, when its church was rebuilt and reorientated: it is known from a drawing (fig. 16) and descriptions, as well as from recent archaeological studies, in which a segment of the foundations has been uncovered near the present entrance of the church of S Vittore (plan, fig. 81).[34] Parts of the precinct wall, which was towered but of light construction, have also been unearthed: these characteristics suggest that it was a *temenos* enclosure rather than a defensive fortification and suggest a pagan burial.[35] Silvia Lusuardi Siena has proposed that, with or without the mausoleum, this was a burial ground on imperial property, which was Christianized in the first half of the fourth century and provided with a basilica. The polygonal precinct was then built to protect the privileged burials.[36]

Curiously, the exact patron or occupant is not known in either case: it seems that the imperial family either presumed that their identity would never be lost, or used grave markers that were not permanent. S Gregorio has been proposed as the mausoleum of the emperor Valentinian II (375–92), who was murdered in Gaul but was returned to Milan for burial. It has also been attributed to his half-brother Gratian (367–83), in which case the brothers could have shared it in death, as Ambrose stated in his funerary oration for Valentinian, declaring that the brothers were inseparable in life and buried in adjacent tombs.[37] However, it is more likely that S Gregorio was the tomb of the tetrarch Maximian (286–305 and 307–8), who died in Gaul in 310. Its plan is similar to that of Maximian's colleague Diocletian in Split. Its construction methods are typical of Maximian's buildings, and although Maximian's place of burial is not known, he had lived in Milan for many years, and may well have prepared a mausoleum for himself there.[38]

The Stuttgart drawing of S Gregorio (fig. 16) shows that it resembled S Aquilino closely (fig. 17). Both mausolea were built in the form of tall brick octagons with corner buttresses. Each also had an external dwarf gallery on the upper wall below the roof.[39] S Gregorio was lit by at least one window below the blind arcade: at S Aquilino there is a window in each of the eight walls, giving light to an internal gallery. Inside, both mausolea were articulated with seven niches in the thickness of the walls, alternating rectangular and semicircular. Bonaventura Castiglioni, in 1553, described both S Gregorio's mosaics and the varicoloured cut marbles that formed friezes with birds and vases of flowers on its walls, while the notary Besta described the rotunda's eight altars and its connecting link with the main church.[40] S Aquilino, which still stands, has lost its revetments, which, as at San Gregorio, were of precious marbles and porphyry, as well as most of its mosaics, which covered the vaults and niches.[41]

S Aquilino also resembles S Gregorio in its total lack of information about function, patronage, and occupancy, due to the lack of early documentation of the mother church, S Lorenzo.[42] According to one theory S Lorenzo was the Arian cathedral, dating from the episcopate of Auxentius (355–72),[43] and S Aquilino was its baptistery, an idea supported by the presence of stone drains among the foundations. These, though, were probably installed to drain the marshy terrain.[44] So, despite its similarity to Ambrose's baptistery of S Giovanni at S Tecla, also a niched octagon with thick walls and a comparatively small inner space, more recent opinion is that S Aquilino never was a baptistery.[45] This is despite the iconography of its mosaics, which have sometimes been interpreted in baptismal terms. The decorations, though, are equally appropriate for a funerary chapel, and explained by the convergence of ideas between the passage from pagan to Christian life, and between life on earth and life after death, ideas which were often expressed in similar imagery, and were recurrent themes in early Christian art.

In fact, S Aquilino's mother church, S Lorenzo, perfectly fits the formula of a centrally planned palace church (plan, fig. 14). It was located close to the imperial palace, conveniently sited for court ceremonies and the imperial liturgy. The church's special status is marked by the unusually massive foundations of the church and its two early satellites, S Aquilino and S Ippolito. All three were set on huge granite blocks, which probably came from a great imperial building, perhaps the nearby amphitheatre of Mediolanum. These spoils contrast with the inexpensive foundation materials of Ambrose's churches, and suggest an imperial patron for S Lorenzo and its two early annexes.

S Aquilino was originally planned without a vestibule, but early in its construction the plan was altered, and a tall, square, twin-apsed atrium was inserted between the tetraconch and the octagon, which was moved back on its site. The dates of construction of the chapel and its vestibule remain as problematic as those of the church. Much of the dating argument centres on whether S Lorenzo was in fact the Basilica Portiana, which was disputed by the Arians and the orthodox Christians between 378 and 386. If it was, S Lorenzo must have been built before 378, probably in Gratian's reign sometime between 367 and 383. The mausoleum could have been built somewhat later, since the party wall is not bonded, unlike the junction wall of S Lorenzo with S Ippolito, the octagonal shrine behind the altar. Since the body of Valentinian I, who died in 375, was sent to Constantinople for burial, the mausoleum cannot have been finished by that date, and probably had not yet been started.[46] This would narrow the construction possibilities to the period between 375 and 392, the year of Valentinian II's death in Gaul, and of his burial beside his brother Gratian in Milan. The earlier part of that period, before Gratian's death in 383, is more likely, rather than the time of Valentinian, who died unexpectedly at the age of twenty-one, and was unlikely to have completed a mausoleum for himself or to have built one for Gratian before his early death. In fact, the patronage of Gratian seems the most plausible, making the mausoleum date to the years between 375 and 383. Gratian's body was held hostage by the usurper Maximus and was only returned to Milan sometime after 385–6, perhaps even as late as 387, after the death of Maximus himself. At that time, it would have needed an imperial burial place. It is also possible that the patron was the Arian empress Justina, the second wife of Valentinian I, and mother of Valentinian II.[47] She died in Milan in 388, and was probably buried in the mausoleum, where she was joined in death in 394 by her daughter Galla, the second wife of Theodosius I and mother of Galla Placidia.[48] It is likely that S Aquilino was the dynastic mausoleum for the entire imperial family of the West in the last quarter of the fourth century, before the court left Milan for Ravenna in 402.

Dating to the late fourth century is consistent with the decorative style of the mosaics in S Aquilino. The quality of the rich interior decoration is revealed both in the mosaics of the niches on either side of the altar bay, and in the fragmentary mosaics discovered in the atrium in the 1930s. Paintings also survive in the upper-level gallery, which is reached by a staircase from within the right bay of the chapel. The gallery has eight arches, which coincide with the eight openings below. They are decorated with small paintings of birds and animals (both sheep and goats) drawn on a white ground within red and yellow frames, as in the chapels of the Roman catacombs.[49] Drawings have also been found on the unplastered lower walls: interlocked circles, a horse and rider, and birds. The apparently neutral subject matter of these paintings is reminiscent of catacomb painting, and both can be read as having paradisical meaning.

The mosaics of the atrium consist of the remains of a double row of standing figures (fig. 82). High up on the entry wall and named in large gold letters above and to each side, apostles are arranged above, and so-called patriarchs, the representatives of the tribes of Israel, below. The composition continues onto the adjacent walls, where there are martyrs in place of the apostles. The figures stand in the natural poses of antiquity: their heads in three-quarter view, their faces individualized and well proportioned. A small genre scene of women and children enlivens a corner of one fragmentary panel. These figures are usually dated to the late fourth century, like the building they adorn.

The composition can be interpreted as an early iconographic variant of the scene of the twenty-four Elders of the Apocalypse, who, robed in white and bearing golden crowns, worship the One upon the throne, the Lamb.[50] As early as the fourth century, the Church Fathers taught that the twenty-four elders were made up of the twelve apostles and the twelve Sons of Judah, leaders of the tribes of Israel.[51] The fragmentary inscriptions name the apostles John and Philip, Matheus, Judas Zelotes and James Alpheus, and the tribes of Symeon and Zabulon were each represented by an individual standing in front of a continuous battlemented wall, the ramparts of the heavenly city. A remarkably similar wall appears as the backdrop of the Palace scene at S Apollinare Nuovo, Ravenna. The representative of the tribe of Symeon raises a golden crown on edge. On either side of each 'battlement' is an inscription: 'DE TRIBU SYMEON. DE TRIBU [ZABU]LON' and so on. Unlike the apostles and martyrs, these figures are not named as individuals and cannot be intended to portray the individual patriarchs, as is usually implied. Rather, the sense 'from the tribe of' implies that each young man shown is a representative of his people, and thus representative of a group chosen for salvation.[52] The Book of Revelation refers to a total of 144,000 saved, 12,000 from each of the twelve tribes of Israel.[53] These figures at S Aquilino, then, once twelve, represented the whole multitude of the saved, according to John's vision. Furthermore, the martyrs on the side walls must be those who cried out from their graves under the altar for vengeance, as the vision describes.[54] Of these, the only name to survive is Pelagia's. She was a young virgin and martyr of Antioch who died around 311, and was dear to both St John Chrysostom[55] and, even more relevantly, to Ambrose, who eulogized her, her mother, and her young sisters in his treatise 'About Virgins, to His Sister Marcellina.'[56] To Ambrose, Pelagia was the perfect example of a dedicated virgin, ready to die for her faith. The inclusion of this Eastern saint once again reveals Ambrose's influence on the formation of the faith of the imperial house, while he expounded the apocalyptic vision of the heavenly city in his De Virginitate ('On Virginity')[57] and In Psalmum CXVIII.[58] His text is illustrated by the S Aquilino mosaics, including as they do both the twelve patriarchs of the Old

Testament and the twelve apostles of the New, who together are the sources of the Church.[59]

The composition in the atrium of S Aquilino, then, illustrates the apocalyptic vision of St John. Its iconography does not adhere to the standard formula that would develop later in Rome, where the Elders of the Apocalypse are shown as a group of identical elderly men in white, raising their crowns on edge like quoits.[60] A different formula is not surprising at such an early period as the late fourth century, and the layout, with its clear inscriptions, relates more easily to the text than the Roman variant does. So clear an example of apocalyptic imagery leaves us in no doubt that S Aquilino and its atrium were prepared for Christian burial and illustrated with texts that described the second coming of Christ.

The atrium mosaics at S Aquilino form part of the same decorative program as those in the niches of the mausoleum itself. Two panels survive there of a program which formerly covered all the niches as well as the vault above.[61] The survivors are situated in the niches to either side of the sanctuary, which is a later addition. Like the paintings in the gallery, they illustrate subjects that were common in the funerary art of the catacombs. The subjects of the mosaics are as follows. On the left, the severely damaged scene portrays a group of shepherds and their flocks, resting on the grass among the rocks and flowers of a natural meadow, watered by streams and waterfalls, while above a chariot with snow-white horses ascends against a golden sky. Elijah, whose figure is almost totally lost, is carried up to heaven in a quadriga. The facing apse features a youthful Christ, nimbed in white with alpha and omega and a *scrinium* of scrolls. His arm is raised as in speech and he sits among the Twelve, who are set against the mystical gold of heaven (fig. 83). Both panels are edged by complex mosaic borders: the Christ panel by a twisted ribbon punctuated by slender arrows, above a strip of green bearing a repeated golden cross; the pastoral scene by interlocking circles, blue and green outlined with gold, on red.

Each of these compositions has an iconographic history that relates it not only to the earliest Christian art, but to the paintings of pagan antiquity. The group of Christ as teacher among the apostles is a direct descendant of the groups of sages, doctors, or philosophers that were popular in the apses of pagan monuments.[62] For example, there is a collective portrait of an anatomy lesson in one of the pagan *cubicula* of the Catacomb of the Via Latina, Rome, dating to the mid- to late fourth century. At S Aquilino the youthful Christ, nimbed with the alpha and omega that express his presence at the beginning and the end of time, holds a scroll partly unrolled, the subject of his discourse. This is the New Law, which is the way to salvation through Christ's own teachings and his words. Through these the Christian will rise to be with Christ.

The other panel is also concerned with resurrection. St Ambrose, in late-fourth-century Milan, expounded the meaning of Elijah, who 'went up by a whirlwind into heaven' by means of a fiery chariot and horses.[63] He saw this as foretelling Christ's own resurrection, with its promise of immortality for the Christian soul.[64] This is surely the meaning here, and the paradisical scene in which shepherds exclaim the vision while their flocks graze identifies the scene as a theophany vision with the witnesses who are needed to verify it. The choice of a quadriga, specifically, as the means of elevation of Elijah to the skies is also an allusion to the mausoleum's imperial patrons, and to their traditional apotheosis of the past, in which the divinized emperors rose in their chariots to dwell with the gods. This tradition was still alive as recently as the year 364, when the Christian emperor Jovian had been divinized on his death, in the last recorded ceremony of its kind. The pastoral setting of the S Aquilino mosaic is reminiscent of the scene above the entryway of Galla Placidia's mausoleum in Ravenna, but there are significant differences. In the Ravenna panel, Christ himself occupied the centre of the scene as shepherd, putting out his hand to one of the lambs in his care. In Joseph Wilpert's reconstruction of the S Aquilino mosaic, based on the *sinopia* visible where the mosaic has fallen, there would have been no room for Christ as shepherd, but his central place was taken by his typological equivalent, Elijah.[65] A further level of meaning may be inferred from the pagan context of an imperial apotheosis, which commemorated the deceased seated in a four-horse chariot, while a hand stretched down from above to receive him into heaven.[66]

The theme of Christ among his apostles, of which S Aquilino's is an early example, was popular in early Christian art.[67] Christ the Logos holds the scroll of resurrection partly opened, a symbol of his unique power to teach the new law. The apostles' scrolls are not yet unrolled – in this way their status as pupils is defined. This iconography seems to have been especially valued among the Arians: it appeared in the apse of the so-called chapel of the Monte della Giustizia, Rome, which was probably a small, fifth-century Arian church, as well as in two other

Roman churches built by the Arians, S Agata dei Goti[68] and S Andrea Catabarbara.[69] As far as I know, no explanation has been advanced for this Arian preference, and it may be purely coincidental that several Gothic examples of this iconography are known; however, since the Milan court had strong Arian connections during the minorities of Gratian and Valentinian II, it seems possible that Arian ideas were expressed at S Aquilino as well. This connection strengthens the case for the patronage of the Arian empress Justina, the second wife of Valentinian I and the mother of the young emperor Valentinian II.

The Mausolea of the Barbarian Kings: La Daurade at Toulouse and the Mausoleum of Theoderic at Ravenna

We have knowledge of two royal, but not imperial, mausolea built by the non-Roman successors of the emperors in the West: the rulers of the Visigothic and Ostrogothic kingdoms. One of these mausolea, long vanished but known from literary sources as well as enigmatic plans and drawings, stood beside the River Garonne within the walls of Toulouse (Tolosia), the capital of the Visigothic kings, who held court there from 418 to 507, the year of their defeat by the Franks under Clovis. Which of the Visigothic rulers was patron of this structure, known as La Daurade, is not known. The other mausoleum is still standing outside the walls of Ravenna. It is securely documented as the burial place of the Ostrogothic king Theoderic the Great, who reigned in Italy from 474 to 526. In both these buildings the kings copied the customary form of the Roman imperial mausoleum and adapted it for their own purposes. In both cases, the building continued the Roman tradition, where the mausoleum symbolized the grandeur of the ruler in death. Both patrons were interested in re-creating the tall, two-storeyed polygonal plan – the separate chamber for the sarcophagus, the temple-like interior for the rites – though both appear to have been willing to compromise in the details of the interior layout. In both cases, the rulers looked back at Roman custom, choosing to dedicate one storey of the structure as a 'temple,' in this case a Christian chapel, the other to the burial itself. Here they differed from the Christian rulers of Late Antiquity, who had built their burial places beside churches, which were used for the funerary rites. We shall see that the planners of La Daurade in Toulouse and the Mausoleum of Theoderic in Ravenna took rather different paths to achieve the same ends, almost certainly stacking the two chambers in opposite fashion from each other. The crypt at

La Daurade appears to have held the body, with the shrine above (as in Roman custom), while at Theoderic's mausoleum the shrine was probably at the lower level with the sarcophagus above in an inaccessible upper chamber, although arguments have also been advanced for the reverse orientation.

La Daurade

At La Daurade, the main chamber, which very likely also served as palace chapel, appears to have been built into a preexistent Roman temple, though there is controversy on this point. The presence of a crypt below the structure was recorded by Dom Chantelou in the mid-seventeenth century.[70] It was probably the site of the ruler's sarcophagus. A sarcophagus of the Visigothic period, which tradition says was the tomb of Ragnachilde, wife of Theoderic II (ca. 453–66), was present in the main chamber of the mausoleum until 1761, when the building was pulled down to make way for the present church of Notre Dame de la Daurade. The sarcophagus is now in the Musée des Augustins in Toulouse.

La Daurade maintains its extraordinary interest for us because it alone of all the vanished early medieval churches of France had a magnificent mosaic decoration which was recorded in scrupulous detail in the early seventeenth century.[71] The mosaics had originally covered the ten-sided interior from floor to ceiling, occupying shallow niches on three levels with compositions separated by small, antique colonnettes in a variety of styles (fig. 84). The number of sides of the building was reduced to seven when a Romanesque nave was added to the ancient decagon to form a basilica. This renovation probably took place around 1077, when the Cluniac monks of Moissac received La Daurade as a dependency. The remaining seven-tenths of the decagon were preserved as the choir of the new church.

By 1633, after more than a millennium of existence, the building itself had developed wide fissures in its walls and the mosaics were ob-scured by centuries of dirt. A member of the religious community, Dom Odon Lamotte, was put in charge of the repairs and also, with five of his fellow monks, took part in the campaign of restoration. Lamotte was keenly interested in the figures and inscriptions that were discovered during the cleaning and kept careful records of them. He identified each of the life-sized figures from the inscriptions, described their gestures and their interactions with each other, their clothing, each detail of the ornamental setting, and the exact positioning of each letter of each inscription.[72]

Each tier of mosaics at La Daurade expressed a different aspect of the faith of the Visigothic rulers, who were Arians. They had come into Roman territory as clients of the Romans, being allowed lands in south-western Gaul, where they set up their initial kingdom, centred on Toulouse. The top tier of mosaic decoration may well have commemorated their travels from eastern lands to Toulouse. This register of the decoration illustrated specific episodes from the infancy of Christ, and thus also of the life of the Virgin. In the central position, directly above the altar, the Nativity occupied four niches on either side of the east window. Lamotte notes that the Virgin, named as 'MARIA,' and her child were shown life-size, and were flanked on either side by a shepherd.

I have suggested elsewhere that all the other subjects depicted in this upper level of niches illustrated the biblical text of the Epiphany in St Matthew's gospel, a story with inherent interest to the Visigoths, who had also been rulers travelling from the east, as well as to the Arian theologians, who are epitomized by Maximinus, bishop and theologian, who wrote between 416 and 427.[73] Maximinus expounded the gospel in both sermons and commentary. His major work, the *Opus imperfectum in Matthaeum*, survived among the works of St John Chrysostom, to whom it was wrongly attributed, and was influential throughout the Middle Ages.[74] This work included a lengthy digression on the Magi in its Second Homily. The story of the Magi was not commonly illustrated in Early Christian art. The only other location where a similar, extended picture cycle survives is on the triumphal arch of S Maria Maggiore in Rome, built by Pope Sixtus III (432–40) immediately after the Council of Ephesus of 431. At La Daurade, the episodes seen by Lamotte were the Massacre of the Innocents (which is included in the gospel account), the Magi before Herod, and the Adoration of the Magi. The original cycle may well have included some of the following episodes: the Journey of the Magi, the Dream of Joseph, the Flight into Egypt, or even the apocryphal Christ adored in Egypt, as at S Maria Maggiore. Figure 85 shows the layout of the episodes in diagrammatic form.

The middle and lower registers of the decoration were also given over to Christian subjects at La Daurade, showing that the transformation of the traditional pagan structure to Christian use had now been completed (diagrams, figs. 86 and 87). The inclusion of pagan imagery and the reinterpretation of pagan iconography, which had been such an important part of the decorative formula of both S Costanza and Centcelles, had, in the intervening one hundred years, been relegated to history. Now the formula (perhaps modified to suit this preexistent building with its rigidly arranged tiers of shallow niches) only permitted the saints and holy figures a hierarchical placement in life-size iconic style, accompanied by naming inscriptions over and beside their heads. Any interactions of the figures were limited by the formal constraints of their arched compartments, though Lamotte is careful to note the occasional exceptions, when figures did appear to be communicating with each other.

The middle and lower tiers of mosaic should be read together. Above the altar in the east, Christ was named 'SALVATOR' in the mosaic and held an open book, on which Lamotte apparently saw the words 'PAX VOBISCUM.' Perhaps the inscription had already been damaged in Lamotte's day and had originally read 'PAX VOBIS,' Christ's words when he returned after his resurrection,[75] in keeping with the tendency in Early Christian art to attribute actual texts from the gospels or the apocalypse to Christ. An image of the Virgin on Christ's left, captioned 'SANCTA MARIA' rather than simply 'MARIA,' can perhaps be dated to the period after 507 and the rededication of the building to the Virgin under the Franks, explaining the use of 'SANCTA' just this once in the church, in contrast with the simple inscription 'MARIA,' which Lamotte records in all the other locations where she appeared.[76] A possible explanation is that Mary's image replaced a donor figure of the patron, an Arian heretic, whose portrait would have been unacceptable to the Franks, who were Catholics. Similar extirpations of the portrait of another Arian ruler, Theoderic the Great, in his palace church in Ravenna, now S Apollinare Nuovo, are recorded.[77]

The image of Christ Saviour was flanked by archangels and surrounded by all twelve of his apostles, named, and by two of the major prophets. How the decoration continued in the missing three sides of the decagon is not known.

The building's status as a funerary chapel is confirmed by the lowest register of images. Although Lamotte was unable to see what had been depicted in the east end of the church, since it was hidden behind the high altar, the imagery to either side of the altar illustrated the common funerary theme of salvation. On the left were Abraham and Isaac, while Noah, as well as the Hebrews in the Fiery Furnace, were depicted on the right. These salvation images commonly appeared in funerary settings and illustrated the prayers of the funerary liturgy, the *proficiscere anima*, following earlier models not only at S Costanza and at Centcelles, but at the burials of the more humble dead interred in the Roman catacombs.

One more element of the decoration is related directly to salvation: the portrayal in the embrasure of the south door of the Old Testament prophets Elijah and Enoch, who ascended directly into heaven without passing through death. Elijah was included in the decorative scheme at S Aquilino, Milan, at S Costanza, and in the Roman catacombs. Enoch appeared less often, but is mentioned in the same verse of the *proficiscere anima*: 'Hoenoch et Heliam – de communi mortem mundi'; the prayer asks that just as God had spared Enoch and Elijah from the ordinary death of the world, so he will spare the soul setting out on its journey beyond death from that same peril.

Finally, the iconographic program at La Daurade shared another rare feature with S Aquilino: a set of images of the twelve Sons of Jacob. Although only five survived at La Daurade, flanking the missing section at the west end, the other seven were undoubtedly also portrayed there. The similar set of Sons in Milan has already been discussed in terms of an apocryphal meaning, as illustrating the text of Revelation 7.4–8, where the chosen will consist of 12,000 members of each of the twelve tribes of Israel, descendants of Jacob's sons. These twelve individuals, then, epitomize these descendants. Furthermore, together with the twelve apostles, who were also shown in the upper register both here and at S Aquilino, they represented the twenty-four Elders of the Apocalypse.[78] This idea was expounded by the Fathers, among them Victorinus. Here at La Daurade, then, a rare descendant of this early iconographic variant of the Elders of the Apocalypse existed, a variant which was apparently peculiar to northern Italy and southern Gaul, and to Arian foundations. It would be superseded by the Roman iconography based on the facade of St Peter's, which spread through the early Roman basilicas such as S Maria Maggiore and the Lateran Basilica, and was subsequently copied by the Carolingian popes of the early ninth century.

In conclusion, the patron of La Daurade has not been precisely identified and its function as a mausoleum is known only from its mosaic decorations, which express the same prayers for salvation as the earlier mausolea of the Late Antique Christian emperors – the paradigms of salvation of the *proficiscere anima*. Its Early Christian date, its magnifi-

cent and royal materials, and its subtle references to Visigothic and
Arian concerns (such as the emphasis on the Magi in the upper register) combine to anchor it firmly in the period when the Visigoths held
court in Toulouse, between 418 and 507. The most likely patron from
the Visigothic years is Theoderic II (ca. 453–66), who received a Roman
education from Avitus, later the Western emperor (455–6), and is
known to have been interested in Roman forms and customs, a champion of both the Visigothic nobility and of Gallo-Roman interests.[79]

The Mausoleum of Theoderic the Great

The mausoleum of the Ostrogothic king Theoderic (ca. 455–526), which
still stands at Ravenna, bears witness to its undoubted imperial inspiration. It was built by a ruler who had carved out a kingdom in Italy
from the heartlands of the Roman empire. The desire for imperial
forms and symbols of power had probably been implanted in Theoderic during his childhood and adolescence as a hostage in Constantinople: formative years spent in the centre of the Christian and Roman
world. This desire for the Roman is the most evident feature of his
building program: Germanic influences appropriate to a Barbarian
chieftain, while sometimes sought by scholars, play a subsidiary role
in his patronage.[80]

The mausoleum, built outside the walls, and now located in the out-
skirts of Ravenna, is a two-storey building, made of huge, well-cut
ashlar blocks (fig. 88). It differs in material from most of the mausolea
of the emperors, who used stone only in exceptional circumstances
when it was freely available, either as the primary building material of
the region (Dalmatia: Diocletian's tomb) or as imperial spoils (Milan:
the remains of imperial structures, probably the Mediolanum amphitheatre, were used for the foundations of S Aquilino). Ravenna, a
region poor in quarries, customarily built in brick. Therefore, the
import of stone from the quarries of Pula, across the Adriatic, must
express Theoderic's desire to make a more noble architectural statement through the use of a more sumptuous building material. Already
only two or three decades after the Ostrogothic king's death, an anonymous writer who described the mausoleum remarked especially on
the use of stone. He wrote that Theoderic himself erected a monument
of marvellous size out of squared stone blocks as a funerary monument for himself, and had a monolithic vault stone of enormous size
made to cover it.[81]

The lower storey is a decagon, articulated on each of its ten sides with a Roman arch.[82] The remarkable roofing monolith of Istrian stone, which measures eleven metres in width and more than three metres in height, has twelve pierced spurs arranged radially around its perimeter. Each of these bears the name of an evangelist or an apostle, a possible reference to Constantine's mausoleum at the Holy Apostles in Constantinople, where he lay among the cenotaphs of Christ's twelve disciples. The spurs, though, must have had a practical use as well as a symbolic meaning, for they were surely used in the lifting of the huge monolith, and the names, if they were there from the beginning, may have been invoked in aid of the stupendous task of transport and elevation. Teutonic scholars see in this monolith a reference to the stone-covered mounds built by the king's Germanic ancestors as their tombs.[83]

The upper storey below the monolith is of smaller diameter than the lower storey. Like it, it is decagonal on the exterior, with a circular interior. It is decorated by a narrow, sculptured frieze of barbarian design, above a plain, shallow drum with tiny and infrequent windows; these include a remarkable cruciform window which throws a cross-shaped beam of light across the dark interior. The area below the drum bears the traces of an external construction which is now lost. It consisted of a loggia wrapped around the drum and occupying the edge of the flat top of the wider decagon below. Various reconstructions have been proposed: alternate round-headed and trapezoidal arches seem the most likely, each arch set upon paired colonnettes. At the front, a large door faces onto a void: if, as seems likely, this upper room was the actual tomb chamber, its inaccessibility may have been deliberate. At the back, the loggia must have been interrupted by the 'arcosolium' of the upper chamber. Examination of the upper storey shows that the construction of the loggia was not integrated with the walls of the drum: presumably it was added after the monolith had been safely installed above it.[84] This may explain why it has not survived. Figure 89 shows one proposed reconstruction, though it is also possible that the mausoleum was quite simply never finished.[85]

The mausoleum's lower storey consists of a cruciform chamber, heavily vaulted. Its function has been the subject of considerable discussion. Some scholars have seen it as the tomb chamber itself, while others have preferred to identify it as the chapel where the rites were performed, with the upper chamber as the funerary chapel. The cruciform chamber has been convincingly reconstructed by Guglielmo De

Angelis d'Ossat as a chapel.[86] Although the original floor had perished, he deduced the positions of the original furnishings from the insertion holes that had once taken the crossbeams of *pergula* and screening. Slots at the upper level suggested the presence of a simple *pergula* inside the entry arm, and of a jutting fastigium before the altar (fig. 90). The altar area was lit by two small windows, and the sole remaining sculptured decoration was situated on two pilasters high up in the rear corners of the room which had presumably held lamps, and consisted of two scallop shells, which have been interpreted as funerary motifs.

In addition, De Angelis d'Ossat argued that the tomb of the king was situated in the upper chamber of the mausoleum. Agnellus, in the ninth century, had seen a porphyry sarcophagus outside the building, and it is not clear whether this is the one which now lies broken in the upper *cella* and, if so, when it was replaced there.[87] A single niche in the east is adorned with a sculptured cross, but it is too small to have served as an arcosolium to house this sizeable sarcophagus. But rather than seeing the niche as an arcosolium, De Angelis d'Ossat suggested that the sarcophagus may have faced it at right angles, with the foot towards it. This arrangement would have ensured that Theoderic would rise on the day of judgment in a location where a carved cross – the sole enrichment of the stone – would meet his gaze, and where the cruciform window would beam a ray of light in the form of the cross before his eyes. The image of the cross was also placed where Theoderic could see it during his long wait for judgment day: the inside of the vault bears a huge *crux gemmata*, the largest such cross to survive from the Early Christian era, more than five metres across at the centre (fig. 91). De Angelis d'Ossat also suggested that twelve pilasters supporting a complex architrave of six radially arranged beams stood around the sarcophagus of the king: six cavities in the wall constitute the main evidence for this reconstruction (fig. 92). He has, moreover, found pilasters, plain at the foot, carved above, of the right height, though unmatched in size, reused as door jambs at the Arian cathedral, now S Salvatore, while a third of the set is in the collection of the Museo Nazionale di Ravenna. The pilasters are of two types: trapezoidal, which De Angelis d'Ossat suggests stood near the walls, and rectangular, which he believes supported the inner ends of the construction around the sarcophagus.

De Angelis d'Ossat's reconstruction of the two interior chambers of the mausoleum is convincing, being based on the physical evidence of original cavities in the stone walls, as well as on the existence of architectural elements (the pilasters) of exactly the right height, which have plainly been reused in their present locations.[88] The origin of these sculptures in the upper chamber is also supported by their peculiarities in size and decoration, with only the outer, trapezoidal ones bearing a monogrammed cross. The question then arises: what inherent reason is there for such a subdivision of internal space as De Angelis d'Ossat suggests, both the division into two chambers and the subdivision of the two chambers by *pergulae* and pilasters into carefully planned and furnished interiors?

The lower chamber, the more accessible, probably served as a chapel for the memorial rites, though even this is disputed. Its thick, cruciform walls, acting as supports for the actual tomb chamber above, speak of the support for the Christian soul offered by Christ's sacrifice upon the cross. The cross, which is embodied in the architecture of the lower floor and forms the foundations of the upper chamber where Theoderic lay, according to this interpretation also dominates the decorative scheme of the upper *cella*. It appears in both sculptured and painted forms and also in the dazzling light that entered the darkness of the tomb chamber through its cruciform window. The outer supports of the *pergula*, also, displayed the monogrammed cross on either side. De Angelis d'Ossat's reconstruction supposes a total of twelve pillars, matching the twelve spurs of the monolith above, and also, perhaps, corresponding to the 'twelve coffins' that Constantine caused to be set up in the Church of the Holy Apostles in Constantinople, 'like sacred pillars in honour and memory of the apostolic number, in the centre of which his own [Constantine's] was placed, having six of theirs on either side of it.'[89] Although Theoderic spent eight years of his youth in Constantinople, by this time the arrangement had long since given way to a separate burial place for Constantine in the annexed mausoleum.[90] Eusebius' description must, however, have been widely known, perhaps even to Theoderic's architect.

Many questions remain unanswered, among them the purpose of the monolithic roofstone, the arrangements of the external ambulatory and, perhaps, of the upper chamber with its somewhat hypothetical internal *pergula*. Barbarian influence seems limited to the shapes of the trapezoid arches and the details of the upper frieze, arches which may be compared to those on the diptych of the Vandal Stilicho in the treasury of Monza Cathedral. As for the monolith, it may have been the best way to achieve a very flat roof, with a rise of only 3.2 metres in eleven, on which to paint the giant jewelled cross. Flatness seems to have been desired as a quality for roofs, and the pursuit of it by conventional means sometimes led to disastrous results, as in the collapse of the original, shallow dome of Justinian's new H Sophia at Constantinople in 558. Of course, it is not entirely inconceivable that there is a barbarian element in this choice of a monolithic roofstone, but the idea seems unconvincing in light of Theoderic's professed enthusiasm for everything Roman, a taste which he probably acquired during his years as a hostage in Constantinople.

Rather, it seems that the mausoleum is a revival of the traditional two-storeyed imperial tomb. The inclusion of both tomb chamber and cult centre in the same tall cylindrical space is deeply traditional, and certainly refers back to pagan examples, such as the tombs of the tetrarchs Diocletian and Maxentius. Use of the space, however, if De Angelis d'Ossat's reconstruction is correct, is different, for tradition assumed the burial would be below, with the cult centre above. Whereas in the Christian period of Late Antiquity the tomb was invariably an annex to a church, where one may presume the funerary rites and remembrances would have taken place, Theoderic has returned to the solitary tomb, fortress-like in the cemetery.[91] He has provided it with its own cult centre, the chapel below, and with an innaccessible tomb chamber above, surrounded by an ambulatory as had been required by pagan ritual processions. He has prepared a sarcophagus of the symbolically powerful porphyry for himself, surrounded it with a *pergula* supported by the mystically appropriate twelve supports, and put himself literally and symbolically under the protection of the apostles and the cross to await eternity.

The Mausoleum of Galla Placidia at Ravenna

Finally we come to the last case study among the imperial and royal mausolea of Late Antiquity – the Mausoleum of Galla Placidia at Ravenna. Very different in form from the typical imperial mausoleum, with its emphasis on size, height, and grandeur, it nevertheless fulfills some of the criteria of a royal burial place. I will suggest that it was a funerary chapel built by a woman who was both an imperial princess and the bride of a barbarian king, for an occupant in whose veins the blood of both the Visigothic rulers and the Roman emperors was mingled: Theodosius, the infant son of Galla Placidia and her first husband, Ataulf. This child died in AD 415, in the first year of his life, and thus had no pretensions either to the Visigothic throne or to the imperial succession. I shall present evidence, nevertheless, that his mother, the only daughter of Theodosius the Great, mourned his death throughout her life, and ultimately chose to have his remains brought from Ravenna to be buried with her in the dynastic burial place beside St Peter's, though not before she had had this small but superb chapel built in Ravenna for his repose after death.

The chapel is situated inside the imperial quarter of Ravenna. It is built of brick, on a cruciform ground plan with a square tower over the crossing (fig. 93).[92] Its plain exterior, relieved only by blind arcading, gives no hint of the richness of the interior, which is ablaze with the colours of mosaic and of the precious marbles which panel the walls below (colour frontispiece).[93]

Obviously, its identification as an imperial mausoleum must depend on other evidence than its architecture. I will show from its iconographic program that it was designed as a funerary chapel. In addition, its privileged location within the imperial precinct at Ravenna is highly suggestive of imperial patronage. I shall also show that a precedent already existed in Constantinople for the mausoleum's new direction in size and architectural form. I will therefore discuss it in these terms, both as a mausoleum, and as an imperial one, a position which will be justified in the course of this chapter.[94]

The chapel differs from the imperial and royal mausolea discussed in the previous chapter in both its minuscule size and its cruciform shape, a choice which may be rooted in the growing piety of the imperial house, as well as their appropriation of the cross emblem as a symbol of victory.[95] There is no doubt that the mausoleum's presumed patron, the empress Galla Placidia (b. ca. 388–93, d. 450), was devoted to the cross, since she chose it for the dedication of her palace church in Ravenna and used it for its ground plan,[96] while she also enriched the Roman basilica of S Croce in Gerusalemme with mosaics.[97] She is also portrayed on her coinage and medallions with a monogrammatic cross upon her shoulder.[98]

In the early days of the church, major cruciform churches were built in Constantinople (the Holy Apostles) and Milan (the Basilica Apostolorum) as well as in Gaza, where Galla Placidia's sister-in-law Eudokia built a cruciform basilica in 401.[99] These churches were built as mausolea, or as *martyria* to shelter the relics of the martyrs. The cross was also the preferred architectural form for funerary chapels and for martyrs' *memoriae* in general in the early fifth century.[100] This is confirmed by archaeological studies, such as those at S Vitale, where the original *memoria* of Vitalis, an apsed rectangle, was converted into a cruciform building in the fifth century. More importantly in the context of the mausoleum of Galla Placidia, a precedent for a small cruciform mausoleum existed in the imperial burial precinct at Constantinople.[101] We learn that in addition to the well-known, centrally planned mausoleum that stood to the west of Constantine's cruciform church of the Holy Apostles, two other structures in the precinct also served for the burial of emperors and their consorts in Late Antiquity.[102] One of these chapels was the burial place of Galla Placidia's half-brother Arcadius, emperor of the East (395–408), his wife Eudokia, who died in 404, and their son Theodosius II (408–50). Downey suggests that this chapel was cruciform, with the burials in the ends of its three arms. In other words, it was very much like the mausoleum of Galla Placidia. Eudokia, who died first, lay in the east, with Arcadius in the south and Theodosius in the north. This mausoleum must have been known to Galla Placidia since it was the tomb of her brother and his family.

Unlike this possible prototype at the Holy Apostles, which is lost forever beneath the Mosque of the Conqueror at Istanbul, the chapel at Ravenna is one of the best-preserved Early Christian buildings to survive anywhere, and has been exhaustively studied.[103] Nevertheless, problems do remain, especially in the area of patronage. There is no contemporary evidence, for instance, that Galla Placidia, who died in Rome on 27 November 450, was actually buried in the chapel that bears her name in Ravenna, or even that she had it built. Since it almost certainly did not shelter her own tomb, were other members of the imperial family buried there, and if so, who? And how secure is the attribution of the structure to Galla Placidia? The first text to mention the empress in connection with the chapel is Agnellus's *Liber Pontificalis Ecclesiae Ravennatis*, which dates from almost 500 years after her death, and draws on verbal tradition only, as no inscription was then extant.[104] However, while there is no Late Antique documentation to suggest that Galla Placidia was the patron, some scholars have found the idea quite possible, as Friedrich Deichmann cautiously states,[105] or even 'universally accepted,' in the words of William Seston.[106]

A further mystery which may also have significance in terms of the chapel's patronage is iconographic. The decorative program is centred on an enigmatic mosaic panel which has until recently defied interpretation, though it is usually considered to represent the martyrdom of the Roman martyr Lawrence. However, this solution fails to explain the totality of images in the lunette, and has no special meaning in terms of Galla Placidia's life and interests.[107] By contrast, if the panel illustrates the martyrdom of the Spanish saint Vincent of Saragossa, as I have argued elsewhere, there are significant concordances with the empress' life, for she had both Spanish and Visigothic connections.[108] In addition, the images in the lunette are capable of a coherent interpretation.

The furnishings in the chapel might also include clues as to its occupancy. They consist of three magnificent antique sarcophagi which occupy the three short arms of the Latin cross. Their presence in the chapel has given rise to legends about the occupants that cannot be confirmed by documentation. One ancient tradition identified the tombs as those of Galla Placidia, in the centre, between her brother Honorius, who died in 423 in Rome, and is known to have been buried in the family mausoleum there, and her second husband Constantius III, who died in 421 in Ravenna.[109] On the other hand, a fourteenth-century commentator believed that she lay between her husband Constantius and her son Valentinian III, who was assassinated near Rome in 455 and presumably buried in the family mausoleum at St Peter's.[110] By the sixteenth century it was believed that she was interred with her two children by Constantius: Valentinian and Honoria.[111] Perhaps the best-known legend maintained that the central sarcophagus contained the mummified body of the empress, dressed in her imperial robes, and seated on a cedarwood throne. The body could be seen through a hole at the back of the sarcophagus,[112] this same hole being the port of entry of the taper of some curious children, who set the remains on fire in 1577.[113]

The legendary quality of all these theories is underlined by the fact that the sarcophagi do not form part of the chapel's original furnishings. They do not match in style, materials, or workmanship, as they should if they had been custom-made for the same location.[114] In fact, they differ from each other in style, degree of finish, and supposed dating. The central sarcophagus is rough-hewn and may once have been underground. The other two, though both of the figural type with symbolic lambs, do not match in decoration or design. Although both are only partly finished, even in this feature they are not a matched pair. The tomb on the left, of 'Constantius,' which has a design of lambs flanking the Agnus Dei on the front, has no decoration on its right end or back. The 'Honorius' tomb, on the other hand, is decorated with a design of three arches. A lamb in the centre stands in front of a cross flanked by doves, and the back bears an unfinished design. In addition, Marion Lawrence has dated the 'Honorius' sarcophagus to the sixth century on stylistic grounds, a century later than the chapel. The fact that there is a masonry foundation under each of the sarcophagi, between the two floor levels, also weighs against the theory that these sarcophagi were part of the original furnishings.[115] In fact, they were probably moved from the adjacent S Vitale site, when that church was built in the mid-sixth century. Since S Vitale rose on the site of several *memoriae*, one may even speculate that the sarcophagi came from these chapels,[116] though this cannot be proved any more than we can even confirm that the Mausoleum of Galla Placidia was originally furnished with sarcophagi.

Since the patronage of Galla Placidia is the reason for identifying this chapel as an imperial mausoleum, rather than as an ordinary funerary chapel, we must ask where she was buried, if not in her chapel. Again, there are numerous theories, none of which can be securely documented. There is no evidence that the empress' body was ever brought back to Ravenna from Rome, though the translation of the remains of emperors and bishops was quite common in the fifth century. It seems more likely that she was interred in the family mausoleum beside St Peter's, and archaeological evidence supporting, though not proving, this view, will be presented. In favour of Ravenna, Agnellus had written that she was buried before the altar in the '*monasterium*,' or chapel, of S Nazarius, which appears to have been the dedication of her mausoleum in the later Middle Ages.[117]

The first direct statement that claims Galla Placidia as the patron of the mausoleum named for her only dates to 1279, when Tommasso Tusco wrote that the empress had had 'this most beautiful chapel' built.[118] Soon after, in 1317, came another mention of Placidia having been buried in the chapel, now identified as being the one she had built at S Croce and dedicated to saints Nazarius and Celsus.[119]

As far as the chapel's date of construction is concerned, two periods have been favoured: the years of her marriage to Constantius III, between 417 and 421, when she travelled to Constantinople on his death; and the years after her return to Ravenna in 425, when she assumed the regency for her six-year-old son Valentinian III. The period after Constantius's death has been thought the most likely, precisely because there would have been a need for an imperial burial place at that time. This argument, though, could equally well favour

the earlier date when Placidia returned as a widow from Spain, need-
ing a burial place for the only child of her first marriage: Theodosius,
her infant son by the Visigothic king, Ataulf.[120]

The story of Galla Placidia's captivity among the Goths and her subsequent marriage to their king is relatively well known from the
account of their wedding in Narbonne in 414, celebrated in the Roman
style which the Visigoths admired.[121] The bare facts of their move to
Barcelona; of the birth of a son whom they named for Placidia's father,
the emperor Theodosius I; of the baby's death at a few months of age;
and of Ataulf's murder by a groom in his stable not long afterwards,
are also known. Both deaths occurred in 415, Ataulf's probably in September of that year. In addition, we learn that the baby was buried in a
silver coffin in a church outside the walls of Barcelona. After the death
of Ataulf, his successor Singeric forced Galla Placidia to walk on foot
out of Spain.[122] However, he died a mere seven days into his reign, and
his successor Wallia gave Galla Placidia sanctuary in Toulouse during
the negotiations for her release to Ravenna. Her stay in Toulouse lasted
well into 416, and she returned to Ravenna only in time to marry Constantius on 1 January 417, supposedly against her will.

There is evidence to suggest that Galla Placidia did not forget her
first child. In 424, she built a church dedicated to St John the Evangelist
at Ravenna, in honour of a vow she had made when she and her children were in danger from a storm at sea. Medallion portraits of her
family in mosaic were displayed upon the triumphal arch. Among
these portraits were those of three small boys. Two of them depicted
her brothers, Gratianus and Iohannes, who had died in infancy. The
third portrait, named as Theodosius Nepos ('THEODOSIUS NEP'),[123]
is presumed, in the absence of other candidates of that name, to have
been a representation of her infant son.[124] More tenuously, perhaps,
around the time of her death in Rome in November 450, a Theodosius
was interred in the family mausoleum there, with honours that
included the presence not only of a 'Placidia,' but of the pope and the
senate as well, marking it as the funeral of a member of the imperial
house.[125] It is to Stewart Oost that we owe the suggestion that the Theodosius mentioned here was Galla Placidia's baby son, on the grounds
that we know the burial places of the other imperial holders of the
name: Theodosius I, who died in Milan, but whose body was moved to
Constantinople in November 395, and Theodosius II, nephew of Galla
Placidia, who died at Constantinople 30 July 450 and was interred at
the Holy Apostles.[126] No other members of the imperial family with

that name are known. The presumption, if Galla Placidia transferred the body of her baby son to Rome, must be that she also planned her own burial in the family mausoleum there.[127] It was already late in the year of her own death, and she must have known that she was mortally ill.

If we accept that the baby's body was the one interred in Rome, we must make one further assumption, that Galla Placidia had the coffin with her in Ravenna. It is quite legitimate, therefore, to ask where it was kept during the years she resided there. I suggest that the tomb of an 'emperor' of that name recorded in the thirteenth century by Tomasso Tusco in Galla Placidia's 'capella pulcherrima'[128] may have been that of this child, despite the sword and standard and title 'imperator' which Tommaso says that he saw, for again the infant Theodosius seems to be the only one of that name who could have been buried here. A second record of a tomb of a Theodosius, inscribed 'TEODOSIUS IMPERATOR' in the pavement, was observed by Riccobaldo in a chapel at Honorius's palace church of S Lorenzo in Caesarea.[129] Speculatively, one may ask if the tombstone was engraved with 'INP,' 'IN PACE,' a common contraction in fifth-century epitaphs, rather than 'IMP,' short for 'IMPERATOR.' 'INP,' which had gone out of fashion as a contraction long before the thirteenth century, could then have been misread by these two early chroniclers. In this case, perhaps we have a reference to a temporary resting place of Galla Placidia's eldest child. This may have been at S Lorenzo or at her Mausoleum: we cannot exclude the possibility that the child's body rested at S Lorenzo while his mother had her 'most beautiful' chapel constructed for its final resting place.

A curious and late confirmation of the sequence of events outlined above is to be found in the diary of Nicolo della Tuccia, a native of Viterbo, who wrote a journal of happenings in Rome and its surroundings in the mid-fifteenth century.[130] Nicolo records a find made in the Honorian Mausoleum at St Peter's (S Petronilla) during excavations for the grave of a member of the clergy in the month of June 1458.[131] A marble sarcophagus of great beauty was found, enclosing two cypress-wood coffins, one large, the other small, and each sheathed in silver, with a combined weight of 832 pounds of the metal. The bodies in the coffins were covered with fine cloth of gold, weighing a total of sixteen pounds. Although it was immediately suspected that the bodies were those of Constantine and one of his infant children, this did not prevent the pope of the day from sending the precious materials – both gold and silver – to his mint.[132] Nicolo's brief notice is the sole record we have of this wonderful find.

We now know that there is no possibility that the burial was that of Constantine and his child. Constantine died in Constantinople and was buried at the Holy Apostles; no child of his is known to have died in infancy. Unfortunately, one can only speculate, on the basis of the evidence given above, on an alternative identity for these plainly imperial burials. To summarize the evidence in reverse order: the discovery of the silver coffins of an adult and a small child in the Honorian Mausoleum at St Peter's, Rome, in 1458; Galla Placidia's death in Rome in 450, and presumed burial there in the same year, which had also seen the interment of an imperial family member named Theodosius in the Honorian Mausoleum; Placidia's continued interest in her first-born son a decade after his death; inscriptions, now lost, attesting to the burial of a Theodosius in two separate imperial structures in Ravenna; and the baby Theodosius's original interment in Barcelona in a coffin made of silver, surely a most unusual material for the purpose. This chain of evidence, even though extremely tenuous, suggests that Galla Placidia took the coffin of her child from Barcelona to Toulouse and then to Ravenna, where it may have lain in a chapel at S Lorenzo or in the Mausoleum of Galla Placidia or in both in sequence; that she had it transported to Rome shortly before her death in 450; and that she was interred with the child in a marble sarcophagus, where they would rest together in the mausoleum, signed only with a simple cross,[133] until 27 June 1458, when the material evidence of their passing would be lost forever in the crucibles of the papal mint.[134]

Thus, while it is clearly not possible to establish the empress as patron, or to determine the intended occupant or occupants of the mausoleum in Ravenna with absolute certainty, it is very likely that Galla Placidia was the patron of this building. Analysis of the iconographic program will confirm that the chapel was designed for burial and that the intention was to build a funerary chapel with two burial places. The identities of the intended occupants will possibly never be known: however, it seems possible that one was the infant Theodosius, whose journey from Barcelona to Rome in his silver coffin must surely have been by way of Ravenna, where the Mausoleum of Galla Placidia may well have been built as a suitable setting for his coffin.

The Iconographic Program

It is now time to analyse the chapel's iconographic program, which, though seemingly mute as a document, reveals further important information about the chapel and the intentions of its patron.

The mosaic decoration of the chapel covers every surface of the vaults and shallow dome, as well as the walls above the marble revetment, which is a twentieth-century replacement (frontispiece). The complex cruciform shape with a vaulted drum above the crossing provides a number of areas for decoration.[135] The shallow dome rests on narrow pendentives, between which are four tall, arch-shaped sections of upper wall. Below these, four wide tunnel vaults open up, each roofing one arm of the cross. Each vault ends in a lunette. The marble sheathing reaches to the bottom of the springing of the tunnel vaults and the pendentives. Three of the lunettes and each of the upper wall sections contains a small rectangular window, fitted with a replacement pane in alabaster and set in a deep, decorated embrasure. The fourth lunette, windowless, is over the door. The artificially raised floor level, which alters the proportions of the building, also brings the mosaics closer to view than would otherwise be possible.

One of the most striking features is the decoration of the pendentive dome (fig. 94). Set with deep blue tesserae in imitation of the firmament, it is strewn with a multitude of golden stars, concentrically arranged to fill the space, and becoming larger as they near the bottom, creating an optical illusion of great height. In the centre is a plain Latin cross in gold, its long stem towards the arm on the left of the entry, the East.

The vault program is completed by half-length winged figures, one in each pendentive. These are also in plain gold, detailed in white. Each floats upon a bank of clouds. Eagle and Man flank the vault opposite the door, across from the Lion and Ox. They are the symbols of the evangelists, which have already been encountered in the Archbishops' Chapel in Ravenna and the S Matrona chapel at S Prisco, as well as in Milan and Vicenza, among many other examples.

We have already seen that these Beings, the winged beasts of the apocalypse, were thought also to symbolize the evangelists by St Irenaeus, writing in the late second century, and that his mystical ideas were further developed by St Jerome (d. 420).[136] The types of evangelist symbol found in the Mausoleum of Galla Placidia are typical of the early iconography, lacking the haloes and gospel books that were universally included by the mid-sixth century. However, they lack one important feature common to the very earliest evangelist symbols: the six wings that are described in the Book of Revelation. In the Ravenna chapel, each Being has only a single pair, in contrast to the situation in the Naples Baptistery (ca. 408) and the St Matrona chapel, which should probably be dated to the second quarter of the fifth century. It would seem that the loss of the extra pairs at the Ravenna mausoleum would fit well with a date within the span of Galla Placidia's patronage, say 416–50, especially considering Ravenna's position as capital, a likely point of origin for new imagery which would take time to reach the provinces.

The key to the meaning of the vault decoration is the cross which floats in the centre of the starry firmament. At a basic level it must symbolize the presence of Christ himself, the all-ruler, but a second and more specific meaning is suggested by the belief of fourth- and fifth-century theologians that a cross in the sky would be the first sign that Christ's second coming was imminent, and that the day of judgment was at hand.[137] The cross would go ahead of Christ in his triumph,[138] just as it was carried in front of the Byzantine emperor in procession, and when going to war.[139] It is significant that the cross at the mausoleum is shown to be on the same plane as the stars in the sky, and among them, a unique situation for an Early Christian vault symbol. It is not enclosed in a *clipeus* or wreath, as all the previous examples we have encountered are, which would reveal that the cross is located in a higher heaven where God resides in the celestial space beyond the stars.[140] This fine shade of difference suggests that the meaning of the cross within the program is eschatological: it is a sign of Christ's second coming.[141] This content is also confirmed by the orientation of the cross. Rather than following the north–south main axis of the chapel, it faces towards the East and Jerusalem, which in fourth- and fifth-century thought was the expected direction of Christ's return.[142]

The upper walls also have a deep blue background. Pairs of male figures, two flanking each window, making eight in all, gesture with their right hands towards the cross, which blazes among the stars in the height of the vault. They follow the standard iconography of the apostles, allowing recognition of Peter, Paul, and Andrew.[143] The four evangelists, present as their symbols, were probably seen as completing the mystical number twelve, as is also assumed at the Naples Baptistery.[144] The decorative formula of pairs of witnessing apostles was also known from the chapel of S Croce at the Lateran Baptistery, Rome, which was pulled down in 1588.[145] Information about the S Croce composition is limited, though it seems that there too the cross occupied the centre of the vault, and the two compositions appear to have illustrated the same concepts. At Ravenna the apostles are present as witnesses to the portent in the sky, the cross, to which they gesture, inviting the viewer, too, to follow their gaze.

Beneath the windows in each upper wall we see a pair of doves flanking an overflowing vase, or drinking from it. We have already seen that the dove may have represented the human soul in its struggle to attain the Kingdom of Heaven,[146] and that water overflowing from vessels was symbolic of baptism. This was a sacrament linked with death in the Early Christian mind, as both represented a farewell to an older, less perfect way of life, and rebirth into the Christian promise. The paired-bird motif, which derives ultimately from Roman painting, where it was extremely popular, is common to both funerary and baptismal settings, and also occurs at the S Matrona chapel.

The summit of each upper wall contains a shell-shaped motif. This is a device borrowed from sculpture to suggest the existence of a three-dimensional space below, emphasizing it like a niche. It also serves to set the scene within the heavenly realm above the sky.[147] Each 'shell' here is plainly an awning of gold cloth stretched between poles; at its summit is a looped rope of pearls, above which a dove's head, pointing down, emerges from the undulating border pattern. These doves must represent the Holy Spirit, the divine inspiration of the evangelists below. They illustrate the text from St John's Gospel: 'I saw the spirit descending from heaven like a dove.'[148]

The four arms of the cruciform building are roofed with tunnel vaults which are decorated as two pairs. Those of the lateral arms contain a sumptuous pattern of golden vegetal scrolls on a deep blue background, while the two on the main axis carry the symbolism of the sky further, and their deep blue background bears a profusion of complex stars like varied snowflakes.

The triple acanthus bases at either side of the vegetal side vaults give rise to grape branches with leaves and fruit. The acanthus represents the unbroken tie with classical tradition, while the grapevine, typical in pagan times of Dionysiac decorations, here has been imbued with the Christian symbolism that stems from Christ's words, 'I am the True Vine.'[149] Each volute base has a stiff central stem between its paired volutes; on this a golden prophet figure stands. The four together must represent the four major prophets. In the summit of each side vault is a chi-rho symbol, with alpha and omega, inside a laurel wreath, symbols of Christ's presence, his eternity and his victory. Each of these two vaults represents the arch of the firmament, where the vine has been stretched as on a trellis over the gravesite below, 'bearing as fruits the newly baptised,'[150] just as at the S Matrona chapel, and just as there the central and highest point is opened to allow a vision of the eternity of heaven to which the soul aspires. This symbolic setting for burial is completed by the decoration of the lunettes behind the sarcophagus sites (fig. 95). Each lunette is centred on a window with a deep embrasure decorated with double grape-bearing volutes. There is a pair of acanthus stems below each window, and, caught among the plants, like 'rams caught in a thicket,'[151] stags bend to drink from the stylized waters below, two horizontal streams on either side. The symbolism of these lunettes is clear. The reference is to baptism and to the words of Psalm 42.1: 'As a hart longs for flowing streams, so longs my soul for thee, O God,' a meaning that is confirmed by the mosaic panel from the baptistery at Salona in Dalmatia, where a pair of deer, drinking, are actually captioned with this verse. Use of this imagery in a funerary setting, together with doves and grapevines overhead, demonstrates the congruence in theologians' minds between death and the resurrection, which they hoped would follow, and the rebirth, which was already received at baptism, when the unregenerate soul dies and the Christian soul is born through 'water and the spirit.'[152] This congruence was also illustrated in the architectural forms, for some early baptisteries, among them the Early Christian Pula baptistery, were cruciform.[153] This was also the form chosen for some early immersion fonts, among them those at Salona, where the catechumens entered and were immersed in the water of the lateral arms of the font, while the priests stood at the head of the cross.[154] The submersion with water in the baptismal rite has even been equated with the throwing of earth on the coffin: 'submersion is a death, the waters close over the catechumen as the grave over the dead man; the catechumen dies away from the old Adam, buries himself in Christ in the closest intimacy with him, whose blood is symbolised by the baptismal water, and like Christ he is resurrected to a new life, reborn on stepping up from the piscina.'[155]

The program of the lateral arms of the chapel, identically decorated and complementing each other to make an iconographic whole, suggests that these areas were prepared as luxurious settings for burial. The mingling of baptismal imagery with the sepulchral confirms the thought behind the decoration, which stems from the words of Paul to the Romans: 'so many ... as were baptised into Jesus Christ were baptised into his death ... for if we have been planted together in the likeness of his death, we shall be also in the likeness of his resurrection,'[156] and the inclusion of the four rivers also gives a hint of paradise, for in the art of the fifth century these waters symbolized the paradise garden where the elect would join Christ.[157] At the Mausoleum of Galla Placidia the quality of the golden vegetation also suggests the realm of the blessed.

Each of the two lateral arms is approximately the size of a *cubiculum* in the catacombs, and excavation down to the original floor level should reveal, as there, the remains of a *trabeculum* before each sarcophagus site, marking it off as a burial chamber. In fact such a foundation was found in the left niche by Corrado Ricci in his excavations of 1898: he thought it the foundation of a *pergula*, but it could equally well be that of a *transenna*; in either case, it defines a *cubiculum*-like space, similar to those at the Catacomb on the Via Latina. The space is further defined and protected by the small Greek-key design which frames each side tunnel vault, and runs around the lateral arms just above the revetment: a maze or labyrinth in gold on blue. These, and the great multicoloured maze within the main arch, can be seen as defining those areas in which 'unwanted and possibly mischievous spirits' must be kept in their place.[158] This prompts the question, if the side arms of the chapel were burial sites, what was the function of the third, and most important, niche which faced the door of entry and was decorated with the panel which has been described as 'una delle più enigmatiche dell'arte cristiana'?[159]

Here, too, an approach which has borne fruit for the lateral arms of the chapel, which together form a whole, will be utilized, and the panel across from the door (fig. 96) will be considered together with its companion over the entryway (fig. 97). This latter shows a scene of paradise, set beyond a threshold of grassy, vertically cleft rocks which lend distance to the scene.[160] Christ, the Good Shepherd, dressed in gold and imperial purple, with a plain gold halo and holding a tall, golden cross, sits in an idealized landscape of grassy slopes and shrubs, tending six sheep, to one of which he extends his hand. The concept of Christ as Shepherd, an image of protection, was commonly illustrated in Early Christian times, and the iconography was taken over from classical painting.[161] Its inclusion is common to both funerary and baptismal programs, with the baptismal the earlier, and the funerary use following, perhaps under the influence of Psalm 23, which opens with the words 'The Lord is my shepherd.'[162] This congruence is summed up in Aimé Martimort's words 'the death of the Christian is a second baptism.'[163] In the Mausoleum of Galla Placidia, in addition to symbolizing the salvation of the individual Christian soul, to whom Christ puts out his hand, and the celestial bliss of those who are saved, the position of the image right over the entryway gives it a prophylactic function, guarding the doorway from any evil which might enter. Finally, and most importantly, in view of the image's place above the door, it illustrates Christ's words in John 10.7–9: 'I am the door ... through me whoever enters will be saved.'[164] Thus, there are many layers of meaning in this panel, which far from merely depicting a standard Early Christian paradise scene, the most typical of all funerary decorations, has an extra prophylactic meaning, as well as illustrating the personal hope of salvation. On this more personal level, it may be possible to identify another precise meaning hidden below the surface of this panel. If the chapel was built for Placidia's infant son Theodosius, the paradise imagery with Christ as Shepherd could well express a mother's hope for eternal life for her son. Since he was taken from her in infancy and before he had been capable of sin, in her eyes and those of the Church he would not await judgment, but would go directly to be with Christ, who had said 'Let the children come to me ... for to such belong the kingdom of heaven.' This panel may well symbolize these children, with Christ's hand reaching out to the infant Theodosius.

By contrast, the panel facing the door presents many problems which have been the subject of scholarly discussion. The three main subjects are presented in a unique juxtaposition of images which has no parallels in Early Christian art, so that a lack of comparative material compounds the difficulty of interpretation. In the centre, beneath the window, a wheeled grill sits in a vigorously burning bed of flames. On the right, a youngish man runs towards the fire. He carries an open codex on his left forearm, while his right hand supports a long-stemmed cross that rests on his shoulder. On the left, a cupboard is shown, its doors ajar. Within, labelled with their author's names (Marcus, Lucas, Matteus, Ioannes), the ribbon bedecked gospels lie, two to a shelf.

Attempts at identifying the running figure have fallen into two main groups. These either argue that the figure is Christ or identify him as a martyr who has met death upon the gridiron that is shown below the window. The most convincing of the 'Christ theories' is inspired by the idea that the panel should be seen in apocalyptic terms, as an image of Christ's second coming. This idea makes special sense in a funerary setting.

Among the apocalyptic theorists, the most recent, and the most credible, is William Seston, who saw the subject of the panel as Christ himself, hurrying to the second coming.[165] André Grabar was taken enough with his theory to call it 'très séduisante,'[166] and indeed, of all the suggestions, Seston's is the one which would best fit a funerary program. According to him, the panel is a Last Judgment composition. The gridiron, instead of being the symbol of martyrdom, is interpreted as the Jewish altar of holocausts, on which sinners will be immolated, in contrast to the altar of perfumes in the sky around which the blessed will cluster. This Old Testament imagery is seen as a prefiguration of the judgment that will follow Christ's second coming. The theory is based on the details of the holocaust altar as described in the Book of Exodus.[167] The account in the Vulgate version of St Jerome describes it as hollow, with horns and a grill on top; this description bears little resemblance to the flaming grill pictured in the chapel, which has wide-spaced bars and a leg at each corner, terminating in a wheel. By contrast, in the Syriac version of Exodus the altar differs in having its grill and lifting rings on the base.[168] Seston sees the wheels which terminate the legs of the chapel's grill as these rings, through which poles could be slid for lifting. One trouble with this theory is that it depends entirely on Eastern sources, the Syriac Bible and the commentaries of St Ephrem, a Syrian Father who has no known connection with Ravenna or with Galla Placidia.

Furthermore, and importantly, the figure is completely at variance with the Ravenna formula for Christ. All of the twenty-eight other images of him at Ravenna, including the Good Shepherd in the opposite lunette, are dressed in imperial purple and gold.[169] At the mausoleum, the figures in the opposing lunettes both carry processional crosses and have plain gold haloes, but these similarities could stress typological connections between Christ, the Good Shepherd, and the unknown 'saint' without implying that both are one and the same. The 'saint's' hairstyle and facial features are also quite inappropriate for Christ. As for the so-called altar, a better explanation for its wheels is that they are what they seem to be: wheels designed for moving the device around. They look more suitable for rolling than for lifting, especially since they are well below the centre of gravity. Pierre Courcelle has identified them as the wheels of a *craticula*, a kind of gridiron for roasting meats which the Fathers described as possessing wheels.[170] It seems clear that under Roman law a red-hot gridiron could be used for torture but was rarely used for an execution, as tradition describes in the martyrdom of St Lawrence.[171] But even for torture a grill large enough to lay a man on would be needed. Since a grill of this size would be unwieldy, it would need wheels for mobility. The identification of the grill as this sort of *craticula* has been confirmed by Jean Lassus, who has pointed out the similarity between the grill in the mosaic and a surviving Etruscan gridiron from Orvieto, dating from about 500 BC.[172] As in the mosaic, the short legs of this rectangular grill terminate in small wheels. Lassus describes the everyday use of such an object, for preparing meat away from the flames before wheeling it into position for cooking, and shows that such a structure reflects its function. For example, the Etruscan grill even has ornamental rings on top for securing the meat while moving the gridiron about. Lassus thinks there was an additional significance in the portrayal of this sort of grill. He suggests that, in the fifth century, memories of human sacrifice were not far distant, and that its use as a torture device would evoke memories of sacrifice to the pagan gods. Courcelle suggests one final level of meaning in the symbolism of the grill: the wheeled gridiron as the chariot on which the martyr's soul would rise to heaven at its resurrection. Thus it would be symbolically equivalent to the chariot of Elijah's ascension, or to that of Christ, when he is shown as Sun God.

But if the running figure is not Christ, he must presumably be both a saint, and a martyr, in view of the gridiron. An acceptable identification, though, must not ignore the other elements of the composition, and especially the presence of the gospel books. A specific reason is required for their presence. It is not enough to say that they are symbols of the Christian faith: a viable interpretation must provide adequate explanation of all the components of the composition, with nothing left over.

In actual fact, the books themselves have also given rise to a set of theories. According to the 'heresy theory,' the book-bearing figure, be he a saint or Christ himself, is running towards the grill to cast a heretical book into the flames.[173] The relevance of the suppression of heresy to a funerary program is not clear, nor can it be tied to any particular heresy, or to what is known of Galla Placidia.[174] Would a grill even be necessary for burning books? And even if it were, the book in this panel is being carefully held open as if it were displayed on the altar, and shows no sign of being consigned to the flames.[175] Moreover, the clearly written names on the books in the cupboard identify them as the gospels: they are not books of heresy. So it seems better to understand the books on literal terms, as four actual books, bound codices, rather than as divine revelations, the words of the evangelists. This distinguishes them from the 'Gospels as revelations,' which have their own iconography: they are always represented as the four Beings, the symbols of the evangelists.

This leaves us with the third group of theories about the running figure: those identifying him as a saint. The favourite choice, on account of the gridiron, is St Lawrence, a deacon like the mystery figure, with its attributes of processional cross and altar book. Above all, though, Lawrence was chosen because of the widespread conviction that he was the only one among the great Western saints who suffered on the gridiron.[176]

Nevertheless, this identification presents grave difficulties. Most importantly, scholars have totally failed to find a specific explanation for the presence of the gospel books. None of the texts that tell of Lawrence's martyrdom mention the gospels at all. Deichmann deals with this difficulty by interpreting not only the books, but the other images as well, in symbolic terms. The grill would then symbolize martyrdom; the running deacon, the faithful cleric and martyr; and the gospel books, the faith for which he died.[177]

At another, more literal, level of meaning, the books could represent the actual altar books, bound to the deacon's care. By a further allegory, they could also be symbols of the riches of the Church which, according to legend, Lawrence gave to the poor during the days before his death. But it is clear from early sources on the martyrdom of Lawrence, including Prudentius's poem in the *Peristephanon Liber*, that Lawrence identified the treasures of the Church for which he died as the Christian poor, whom he produced in place of the gold and silver that the judge demanded at his trial.[178]

The choice of Lawrence also poses an iconographic problem. Throughout the early Middle Ages he is portrayed on the gridiron, lying face down but rearing up on his elbows as he is held down by torturers. The famous moment when Lawrence challenges the torturers to turn him over and grill him on the other side is illustrated. Even the earliest surviving image of the martyrdom of Lawrence, on a fourth-century lead medallion from the catacombs at S Lorenzo *fuori le mura*, Rome,[179] employed this formula, and 500 years later the same iconography was still in use, virtually unchanged, in the crypt chapel at San Vincenzo al Volturno, Molise.[180] It is, in fact, the only early medieval iconographic formula known for this often-illustrated scene, if we exclude the composition at the Mausoleum of Galla Placidia. This, it seems, is so totally different, both from the known formula and from the details of literary accounts of Lawrence's martyrdom, that it must illustrate some other text altogether, perhaps even the sufferings of a different saint.

I have suggested elsewhere that there is another saint and another text that fit the mystery lunette perfectly in all its details.[181] This saint too is a deacon, tortured on a gridiron, and a martyr whose cult was popular throughout the Roman world in the early fifth century.[182] His also is a martyrdom sung by Prudentius in his *Peristephanon*, 'Crowns of Martyrdom.'[183] This individual is St Vincent of Saragossa, the premier martyr of Spain, who suffered death in the persecutions of Diocletian at the start of the fourth century. His passion is described in his *Vita*, as well as by Prudentius, and these two sources provide a remarkably accurate text for the mysterious images of the lunette.[184] It is clear that the lunette illustrates the story that Prudentius put into verse sometime around the year 400, dwelling on every grisly detail. The text explains all the constituents of the panel, making a coherent whole, and leaving nothing unexplained. There is no need to fall back on the symbolic content of the story, though that indeed could constitute a second level of meaning.

How likely is it that a saint from Spain, in the periphery of the Roman world, would be the main subject of an imperial decorative scheme in Italy? Prudentius's interest in Spanish martyrs in his *Peristephanon* has been explained by the fact that he himself was a Spaniard. It is less well known, perhaps, that Galla Placidia was also of Spanish descent, her father Theodosius I being from Spain. She also had the poignant connections with Spain that I have already described. But even in non-Spanish circles, the cult of Vincent was widespread by the fifth century. This is proved by the numerous sermons eulogizing the saint that survive among the works of both St Augustine and Pope Leo I.[185] On both these counts it seems natural that the cult should appeal to the empress and be included in the program of her mausoleum. She may well have acquired relics of St Vincent during her stay in Spain, and put them in the altar of her chapel, which presumably was beneath the lunette with the mysterious composition.

The lunette mosaic illustrates the main features of Vincent's martyrdom. He had defied the imperial order to sacrifice to the pagan gods, as promulgated by his judge Datianus, governor of Spain. His sentence was torture by hooks and rack. When he remained steadfast, he was ordered to disclose his 'secret writings' and 'hidden books,' that 'the teaching which sows the vicious seed may be burned with the fire it merits.'[186] Vincent replied that the destruction of the sacred books would be avenged by God, who would consign his judge to hell. Here surely is a precise text for the mosaic's gospel cupboard, a very satisfactory alternative to Deichmann's allegorical interpretation.

Next Prudentius tells of the judge's frenzied reaction to Vincent's counterattack. Datianus orders the last degree of torture 'with fire and bed and plates.'[187] The *grabato* or bed is the gridiron, sometimes described as with sharpened bars to cut the victim's flesh, and here as with spikes, 'its teeth wide spaced ... a cruel bed' where 'a great mass of coals exhales its burning breath.'[188] The text again applies to the mosaic scene: the flaming grill below the window fits the poem's words exactly. To this ultimate torture 'Vincent hurries with quick step. Joy gives him speed and he outstrips the very ministers of torture. Now they have reached the wrestling ground where the prize is glory.'[189] Here, too, the mosaic's hurrying figure illustrates the text, while the absence of torturers also fits the details of the poem.

Although Vincent does not die on the grill, he is released only as a prelude to fresh torture, which is precluded by his death: ultimately the result of his torture on the gridiron. Even then his ordeal was not ended, for the governor was determined that his body must not be allowed to find rest. First it was offered to the wild beasts, but to no avail, for God mercifully sent a raven to guard it from predation. At last it was sewn into a shroud and committed to the sea, a final attempt to deny Vincent's soul its resting place. And here another element of the story seems to have special significance for Placidia and her children, who had been saved from certain death at sea by divine intervention.[190] The body of Vincent, rather than being denied Christian burial, was borne by divine command towards the shore, flying through the water until it reached land at Valencia, where a sanctuary was built and the blessed bones were laid to rest.

Prudentius tells a story whose main events are perfectly illustrated by those mysterious images: the scriptures, the bed of coals, and the eagerly running saint. The images are explained separately, but, more importantly, their meaning is enhanced by their common relationship to the same text. The scriptures are not merely the gospels that symbolize the faith, but the secret books of Vincent's interrogation, the books he will willingly protect by undergoing further torture. The flaming grill is described by Prudentius down to the coals, crackling fire, and widespread teeth. The saint who runs so eagerly to martyrdom is so described in the poem, where Vincent is identified as a deacon, just as the mosaic portrays him, complete with altar book and processional cross. Finally, his deliverance even after death from the sea reflects what Placidia obviously regarded as a miracle in her own life. Her residence in Spain at a crucial period in her life provides a geographic context in which she could have acquired a devotion to Vincent, and even some relics of the saint. As we have seen, the cult of Vincent was well known in Italy during Placidia's lifetime. Relics of the saint were to be found in Ravenna a century after her death,[191] and by that time he had also attained inclusion in the Canons of both the Ambrosian and the Visigothic Mass, as well as in the Ravenna Litany. He had also been portrayed among the saints in procession on the nave wall at S Apollinare Nuovo.[192] This evidence makes it more than possible that Vincent was the subject of Placidia's devotion and her mosaic. Curiously, despite Vincent's popularity, no other images of him from this early period survive, except a gold glass *orant* figure inscribed with his name.[193] It was not until the later Middle Ages that his martyrdom became a popular subject for illustration.

One question remains: what exact purpose in the overall iconographic program of the chapel does this image fulfill? It seems obvious that the primary purpose of portraying a saint, the symbols of his passion, and a shortened narrative of his claim to glory must relate to the patron's need for his mystical presence in the chapel and for his help in fulfilling its purpose. This purpose was the facilitation of the occupants' passage to eternal life. We can only surmise what furnishings originally lay below this mosaic panel. Certainly, if the decoration betrays the function, as I believe, a third sarcophagus would not have been part of the original equipment. An altar for the funerary rites seems the most likely answer. The particular image chosen implies that this altar was sanctified with relics of an important saint: certainly the saint whose passion is so graphically illustrated above. If this saint is indeed Vincent of Saragossa, as seems likely, then his would be the relics enshrined below, brought here perhaps by Galla Placidia on her return from Spain in 416.

In view of its central position in the chapel, facing the entry door, the panel of Vincent, his gridiron, and the gospels should be the key to the chapel's decorative program. Its position, across from the Good Shepherd panel, links its meaning to that paradise scene and to the expected bliss of the hereafter.

The inclusion of Vincent must have had some special meaning in Placidia's life, and indeed several possible areas of significance for her in his story have been located, including his Spanish nationality and his delivery from the sea. In the realm of speculation, if this chapel were built not for the empress herself, but for her baby son, its Spanish connection would be well explained, as well as its position beside the palace church, where Placidia was wont to pray at night. Its difference in size, scale, and plan from other imperial mausolea in Italy would also be explained if it were built not for an emperor but for the child of a barbarian king. The changes could well be interpreted as personal choices made on behalf of an occupant who had no official status, and who therefore had no need of a mausoleum of vast dimensions, designed for the funerary and commemorative rites of an emperor. Galla Placidia's son could have been such an occupant, and would have had no need of such a setting. The change of chapel form from a polygonal to a cruciform shape was probably the personal choice of a pious Christian who, it has recently been suggested, sought to emulate in her devotion to the Cross the piety of Helena, the mother of Constantine.[194]

Thus the mausoleum of Galla Placidia can best be understood as a funerary chapel, decorated as a microcosm of heaven, and expressing in symbolic terms the Christian hope of life after death in the realms beyond the stars. In the chapel's assumption of the shape and symbolism of the cross, it states that the cross provides the way of salvation: in its devotion to St Vincent it shows the means whereby Christians by grace and sacrifice may tread the path to eternity. These must have been the aspirations of Galla Placidia as she commissioned this burial place, whether for herself or for her first-born son. There the deceased would have lain in their funerary chambers as in the chapels of the catacombs, surrounded by the imagery that would give Christian meaning and hope to their deaths. Galla Placidia died far away, and we shall probably never know for sure if any part of the planned use of the chapel was fulfilled, and whether any member of her family was buried there, though it seems likely that Placidia's first born lay there in his silver coffin for the remaining years of his mother's life, until he joined her on her death in a joint sarcophagus in the Honorian Mausoleum. At least it seems time to drop the 'so-called' from the chapel's usual name, and call this structure what it plainly is: the Mausoleum of Galla Placidia.

Study of the funerary structures that have survived with their decorations from Late Antiquity have revealed different aspects of the series *cella memoriae*, funerary chapel, martyr shrine, and it has been possible to explore the attitudes to death and burial current in the upper levels of Late Antique society through their decorative programs. The Mausoleum of Galla Placidia fits perfectly into this pattern, as a funerary chapel sanctified by the relics of a major saint, and decorated with imagery which would facilitate the occupant's passage to heaven. In this respect it shares many of the qualities of the funerary chapels discussed in the previous chapter, and adds to the understanding of these small burial places. In addition, it indirectly throws light on the chapels which were discussed much more briefly in the context chapters, on account of the incomplete data which restricted our knowledge of each building. All of the highlighted chapels, as well as the tombs of the Christian emperors and barbarian kings, reveal the aspirations of their creators both in their iconographic language, and, uniquely in the case of S Vittore, in the contemporary literary sources. But even where documentation has not survived, it has been possible to discover biblical, liturgical, and patristic texts related to the iconographic programs, texts which reveal the beliefs of the founders about death, burial, and the afterlife.

In addition, various conclusions may be drawn from this survey of the decoration of the imperial and royal mausolea of the Christian rulers of Late Antiquity. By chance the only ones to conserve their decorations all date from the fourth and early fifth centuries, and perhaps for this reason, the iconographic programs of the early examples in the West, of S Costanza, Centcelles, and S Aquilino, as well as of the fifth-century La Daurade, presumed mausoleum of the Visigothic rulers, are all similar in theme, concerned with salvation, the illustration of the funerary liturgy and Judgment Day. During this period, a new vision develops, where Christian examples take the place of pagan in the vistas of the life beyond death. But the formula is the same as has articulated such funerary interiors since Etruscan days, and we look through a veil, as if a curtain were drawn aside, to glimpse the hopes of the deceased for a blessed and immortal life after death. A little later, at the Mausoleum of Galla Placidia, a profoundly Christian program deals with judgment, paradise, the intercession of a sponsoring saint, and the mercy of Christ towards the deceased, who will wait here in the 'earthly paradise' for Judgment Day.

Where in this picture should we place the mausoleum of the Ostrogothic king, Theoderic the Great, the second example of a Romanophile barbarian ruler to base his funerary chapel upon the traditions of the Roman past? Whereas the decorative features of La Daurade as recorded in 1630 make it easy to fit it into the pattern of the mausolea of the Christian emperors of Late Antiquity, Theoderic's mausoleum shares only its most basic features with these buildings. Its superbly different interpretation of the Roman imperial burial tradition suggests a patron who, late in his life, was able to order a unique monument for himself that blended features from the Roman tradition with others from his own, non-Roman background, and produced a monument that is startling in its power and originality.

The next chapter will focus on chapels at the Lateran Baptistery, Rome, and their long-vanished counterparts at the Vatican Baptistery, using their decorative programs and surviving documentation to unravel the mystery of the purposes for which they were built.

CHAPTER EIGHT

Papal Chapels: The Chapels of Pope Hilarus at the Lateran Baptistery, Rome

Pope Hilarus I (461–8) built three chapels at the Lateran Baptistery, dedicating them to the two saints John and to the Holy Cross, and endowing them with exceptionally rich furnishings and adornments.[1] Two of the three chapels survive, with some modifications, and the Holy Cross chapel, which was pulled down in 1588, was recorded by numerous Renaissance architects and draughtsmen, and was also described by antiquarians.[2] The two surviving chapels of Hilarus, together with the seventh-century S Venanzio chapel of Pope John IV (640–2), which is the subject of the next chapter, constitute the most complete cluster of oratories grouped around a major ecclesiastical building to survive from among the many built in Early Christian times (fig. 98).

The accident of Pope Hilarus's chapels' survival, though, should not blind us to the priority assigned to them by their patron, which is underlined by their position in his biography in the *Liber Pontificalis*. There they head the record of his patronage. The complete set of chapels was also duplicated, at least in their dedications and furnishings, by Pope Symmachus (498–514) at the baptistery built at St Peter's by the mid-fourth-century pope, Damasus.[3] Some special significance of the trio of chapels in the context of papal politics must have been urgently clear to Symmachus, since he duplicated them at the Vatican, his seat of power, when he was excluded from the Lateran by a rival for the papacy.[4] Evidently, their possession in some sense conferred legitimacy upon a claimant to the throne of St Peter.[5] This question will be explored below, along with the other possible functions of the chapels, both spiritual and practical.

But even though the addition of matching sets of chapels to the papacy's most ancient and hallowed Roman baptisteries within a period of half a century is an obvious signal that they served an important purpose in the religious, practical, or political realm, or even in all of these simultaneously or sequentially, this purpose has not yet been determined. Indeed, the most recent author to mention the two smaller chapels at the Lateran (in 1995) remarks that there has been little evaluation of their function up to the present.[6] This chapter will explore the possible functions of Pope Hilarus's chapels using three main sources of information: the donation texts of the *Liber Pontificalis*, the chapels' decorative programs, and their inscriptions, both extant and recorded. Contemporary texts, more particularly the sermons of Hilarus's mentor Pope Leo the Great (440–61), who preceded him in the papacy, will also be considered.[7] Leo was the most influential theologian of the mid-fifth century in the West, and Hilarus both promoted his predecessor's statement of faith, the *Tomus*, and worked to confirm his vision of the preeminence of the See of Peter.[8] The sermon in which Pope Leo described the transformation of the Hebrew tabernacle into the central sanctuary of the Christian faith would be realized in brick and marble by Pope Hilarus, whose chapels beside the Lateran Baptistery perfectly illustrated Leo's words:

> Thou didst draw all things unto Thee, Lord, for the veil of the temple was rent, and the Holy of Holies existed no more for those unworthy high-priests [i.e., those who had condemned Christ]: so that type was turned into Truth, prophecy into Revelation, law into Gospel ... What before was done in the one temple of the Jews in dark signs was now to be celebrated everywhere by the piety of all the nations in full and open rite. For now there is a nobler rank of Levites, there are elders of greater dignity and priests of holier anointing: because Thy cross is the fount of all blessings, the source of all graces, and through it the believers receive strength for weakness, glory for shame, life for death. Now, too, the variety of fleshly sacrifices has ceased, and the one offering of Thy Body and Blood fulfils all those different victims: for Thou art the 'True Lamb of GOD, that takest away the sins of the world.'[9]

Early scholars, far from exploring the chapels' function in terms of these sources, attempted to assign them a function centred upon their possible role in the sacrament of baptism itself. This was not surprising, since the chapels were located at the baptistery. The suggestion of the late-seventeenth-century Maurist scholar Jean Mabillon that they were used as changing rooms for the candidates for baptism[10] was endorsed in the nineteenth century by Louis Duchesne, who repeated it in his *Origines du culte chrétien*.[11] Mabillon's theory was based on the ninth-century name of one of the chapels: San Giovanni 'ad Vestem,'[12] and Duchesne agreed that the name was suggestive, and proposed that since two comparable (though not identical) chapels, those of the two saints John, opened from the Baptistery itself, they could have been used as changing rooms for men and women respectively.[13]

There are problems with Mabillon's 'changing room' theory, since most Early Christian baptisteries were not equipped with annex chapels for disrobing.[14] The only known example is at the Dalmatian city of Salona, where Ejnar Dyggve found partitioned masonry benches like those which furnished bath buildings in a small annex of the baptistery, but even here the changing area does not appear to have been a consecrated chapel.[15] Extremely little is known about Early Christian baptismal practices, but it seems that men and women were baptized in separate or sequential ceremonies in the interests of modesty.[16] For the same reason, in Syria at least, female catechumens were anointed by deaconesses wherever possible, though evidence for this practice is missing for Rome.[17] It therefore seems unlikely that two changing rooms were needed. Need for even one may have been superfluous, as the catechumens' clothes could have been handled in some other way: for example, the clothing could have been slipped off at the font and handed to the godparents who accompanied the candidate there. Jean-Charles Picard, in his exhaustive study of the rites of baptism in the early Church, has failed to find any baptismal text which mentions changing rooms, and suggests that if the chapels were used for changing at all, it may have been the clergy who vested there in fulfillment of the requirements of the *Ordo* of Baptism XV.[18] Finally, the *vestis* of the medieval name of one chapel could even have referred to the garment of St John, a relic known to have been at the Lateran in the Middle Ages, which by the ninth century could well have been kept in the *confessio* of the chapel.

Although the comparative material for the Lateran Baptistery complex suggests that most Early Christian baptisteries did not have attached chapels, they were quite often surrounded by complexes of rooms. Again, the best-known complex of this type is at Salona, capital of Roman Dalmatia, a site that was abandoned in the seventh century. This has allowed excavation of the whole cathedral and baptistery complex and identification of its various rooms in terms of their function in the baptismal rite. In this, Ejnar Dyggve was helped by the built-in furnishings, such as clergy seating and mosaic floor inscriptions.[19] Salona remains the best guide to the layout of a complete baptismal complex in terms of the liturgy, although Annabel Wharton's study of the Neonian Baptistery in Ravenna is a comprehensive, recent study of a free-standing baptismal hall in similar terms.[20] Her findings, using the surviving catachetical literature, are that the basic elements of the baptismal rite were 'remarkably stable throughout the Early Christian world.'

What can we learn from the layout at Salona that might be relevant to the situation at Rome? At Salona, the essence of the ceremony consisted in assembly, disrobing, baptism, re-robing, confirmation, and communion, elements which must also have formed the central core of Christian initiation in Rome and elsewhere. I will attempt to assign specific roles to the various annexes and chapels at the Lateran Baptistery, to determine whether these buildings played an integral part in the baptismal ceremony, or whether they were self-contained entities, annexed to the baptistery for reasons other than liturgical necessity.

Assembly, one may suppose, took place in the monumental open portico which faced the basilica and formed the main entrance and antechamber to the baptistery (fig. 98). From there, the catechumens would have made their way to the font, pausing to disrobe, as the state of nakedness held a symbolic meaning: the candidate must put off the old garment that represented the sinful body, and stand as a child beside the font. Equally, he or she by undressing eliminated the 'badges of social difference.'[21] The candidates next stepped down into the font, for baptism was by total immersion in one of the streams of living water which gushed from the mouths of silver stags around the font.[22] Deacons, or possibly deaconesses if the candidates were female, carried out the ritual.[23] Leaving the font by the other side, a typological reference to the Crossing of the Red Sea as described in the Book of Exodus, the newly baptized were robed in white, symbolizing their new-found purity, and then proceeded to the *consignatorium* for their confirmation by the bishop, who laid his hands on them to transfer spiritual power and signed them on the brow with chrism. The newly initiated Christians then left the baptistery complex and made their way across the square to the cathedral for the ultimate Christian mystery, the Eucharist, which had previously been barred to them.

Any function that the two smaller chapels might have had in the baptismal rite must be seen in the context of the Easter baptism, the most important initiation ceremony of the Roman Church, which still attracted large numbers of candidates every year, although by the mid-fourth century several other baptisteries in and around the city had been built to share the load.[24] At the Lateran, it is clear that spacious rooms would have been needed at every stage of the ritual if the catechumens were to pass freely. One must conclude that the small size of the chapels and their restricted entries would have dangerously impeded circulation if their primary function was to serve the candidates for baptism at any stage of the ritual itself.

It seems that the function of the chapels must have lain outside the baptismal rite itself, despite their location at the baptistery. Early on, a non-baptismal function was suggested to several sixteenth-century antiquarians by a text of Pope Hilarus's entry in the *Liber Pontificalis* which stated that he founded two libraries *'in eodem loco.'*[25] Could 'that place' have been the Lateran Baptistery, and if so, could the St John chapels have been these libraries? Two versions of the text confused the issue. That preferred by Duchesne stated that the libraries were built at 'St Lawrence's,' where Hilarus also built a *praetorium*, or country retreat, a natural location for the traditional paired libraries. Duchesne located the *praetorium* close to the south-east corner of S Lorenzo *fuori le Mura*,[26] a reading endorsed by Guy Ferrari.[27] However, a second group of *Liber Pontificalis* manuscripts which implied that the libraries were actually at the Lateran was favoured by the antiquarians,[28] among them Ugonio, who decided on that basis that the St John chapels at the Lateran Baptistery must have housed the libraries.[29] Since Duchesne's text 'A' is now considered to be closest to the original, the 'library theory' has been discarded. There is also no evidence that special provisions for books existed at the Baptistery chapels. We have already seen that diagnosis of a space as a book storage area requires that it be elevated, dry and airy, or have a heating system. It should also have evidence of slots for shelving.[30] None of these conditions appears to have been met at the Lateran chapels,[31] though it is possible that books were stored in Hilarus's chapels in free-standing cupboards such as the one depicted in mosaic in the Mausoleum of Galla Placidia in Ravenna (fig. 96).

It therefore seems that neither of the service functions proposed for the chapels, whether as libraries or changing rooms, can be confirmed as the primary reason for their existence, and I will now argue that one real purpose of these chapels is to be found in the donation text of the

Liber Pontificalis, which lists the gifts with which the chapels were endowed. Each of them received a golden cross and a *confessio*, a place for the storage of relics beneath the altar, as well as lamps and other furnishings. With regard to relics, they were not yet in Hilarus's time required for the consecration of altars: this regulation was adopted more than a century later, in the time of Gregory the Great (590–604).[32] Yet relics were undoubtedly stored in the *confessiones* of Hilarus' altars in surroundings of considerable luxury, as they were also in Pope Symmachus's chapels at the Vatican, underlining their status as treasures in their own right. To house these treasures, each of Hilarus's St John chapels possessed a *confessio* weighing 100 pounds of silver, while each chapel's portal was closed by bronze doors chased with silver.[33] S Croce, which housed a fragment of the Cross of Christ, was also endowed with a silver-doored *confessio*, as was the Vatican Holy Cross chapel. In addition, all three of the Lateran oratories received golden crosses; that of S Croce was jewelled and weighed twenty pounds: the Symmachan Holy Cross oratory also held a jewelled cross weighing ten pounds of gold and containing a fragment of the cross.[34] Hilarus's Holy Cross chapel was the largest and most important of the three oratories at the Lateran, and received the greatest number of precious gifts.[35] Among these was a Lamb of two pounds' weight of solid gold, standing on a four-pound golden arch which itself was supported above the *confessio* on onyx columns. A golden crown weighing five pounds, in the form of a lamp with dolphins, hung in front of the *confessio*. Although it is clear that Hilarus's S Croce chapel housed a relic of the cross, there is no information in his biography on what his other two chapels contained in addition to the cross itself. However, it is reasonable to assume that since the chapels were provided with *confessiones*, they contained relics of the titular saints, although in the absence of precise contemporary documentation we can only speculate as to what precise form these may have taken.[36] By the turn of the seventh century, though, contemporary sources do confirm that the papacy owned such an abundance of relics of the Baptist that some could be spared for gifts: Gregory the Great gave hairs from the beard of St John the Baptist to the Visigothic king, Rechared,[37] and sent Theodelinda, the Lombard queen, a phial of blood, ashes, hair, and a tooth of the Baptist.[38] Presumably these were the relics for which the sumptuous, jewelled reliquary in the treasury of Monza cathedral was made.[39] By the twelfth century, the Baptist's camel-hair garment was also among the Lateran's possessions.[40]

Twelfth-century documentation records the presence of two major relics of St John the Evangelist at the Lateran: the saint's tunic and a vessel full of the manna that issued from his body in the grave.[41] Hilarus himself probably visited John's gravesite in Ephesus, when he served as papal legate to the Second Council of Ephesus in 449. Indeed, the dedicatory inscription of his chapel of the Evangelist credits St John with saving him from a menacing crowd there.[42] Hilarus might possibly have obtained the manna himself, since the flow started immediately after John's death, and continued unabated into the second century and perhaps beyond: obviously the total quantity was considerable.[43] John's tunic was discovered during the reign of Hadrian I (772–95) in an ancient altar of the Virgin which was moved from the atrium into the chapel of S Giovanni Evangelista at the Lateran.[44] John the Deacon recounts that the altar contained two small, sealed boxes, one of which housed two garments, a dalmatic and a tunic. Of these, he attributed the tunic to the Evangelist. However, its earlier history is complicated by Gregory I's letter asking John, abbot of S Lucia in Sicily, to send him a garment of St John which was in his possession.[45] Unfortunately, we do not know if the abbot complied; if he did, obviously this garment could have been the one that was at the Lateran in the eighth century. All we can say for sure is that on the evidence of the *confessiones* alone the papacy must have owned relics of both the saints John in the mid-fifth century, and housed them in the altars of the St John chapels, which by this means took on the character of reliquary-shrines.

This assumption is also supported by the architectural form of the chapels and by the iconographic content of their vault mosaics. The mosaics are still extant in the Evangelist's chapel (fig. 99), and an engraving by Giovanni Ciampini illustrates the related vault of the Baptist's chapel, which is lost (fig. 100). The vault mosaic of S Croce is known only from Renaissance drawings and antiquarian descriptions.

While all three of Hilarus's chapels were cruciform, S Croce differed from the St John chapels in apparently having been inserted into a pre-existent building. Although Richard Krautheimer has suggested that it originated as a second- or third-century garden pavilion,[46] it could equally have been an ancillary building of the nearby private baths, part of which lie under the Lateran Baptistery itself.[47] Building by the imperial family continued at the Lateran Palace, which remained their residence well into the mid-fourth century, and recent excavations have discovered buildings dated to their occupancy. Among them are remains of a fourth-century chapel with Christian paintings as well as statue bases of imperial family members.[48] Mark Johnson has recently argued that S Croce was indeed a fifth-century structure and built by Pope Hilarus. This point of view is supported by evidence that *tubi fitilli* were used in its vault, as was typical of the construction methods of the late fourth to late fifth centuries.[49] Presence of this vault technology, though, could be equally well explained as the result of fifth-century re-vaulting of an earlier building. Unfortunately, the extensive excavations of the Campus Lateranus undertaken in recent years by Valnea Santa Maria Scrinari have failed to reach the site of S Croce, which therefore remains problematic.[50]

The plan of S Croce was distinctive: it had a cruciform core with equal arms, between which four small polygonal chapels were inserted, giving seven chapels and an entryway (fig. 101). The two St John chapels open off the baptistery by their original portals, which are formed of precious *spolia*.[51] That of the Baptist was entirely remade in 1780 by Francesco Matteo di Giove. In its present form it is rectangular on the outside and has a small, oval, vaulted interior with two apses. In Panvinio's time its vault was supported by reused columns of alabaster and marble in the four corners, giving it a cruciform interior.[52] Its mosaic vault had 'an elegantly stuccoed little apse' beneath it, and two other apses at the sides with later paintings.[53] Ciampini's engraving (fig. 100) gives a good idea of the design of the vault mosaics, which in many ways were comparable to those of S Giovanni Evangelista. By contrast with the Baptist's chapel, that of the Evangelist takes the form of an equal-armed Greek cross with a full-width atrium before the main door. The cruciform plan was preferred in the fifth and sixth centuries for both funerary chapels and martyrs' *memoriae* on account of its symbolism: relic shrines also frequently followed this ground plan.

Although it is unlikely that the St John chapels at the Lateran were funerary chapels, since burial within the city was still forbidden by law in the fifth century,[54] we have seen that they probably housed contact or associative relics, and on one level should be seen as *memoriae*: shrines dedicated in honour of these relics. But the conventions of the mid-fifth century which ruled the decoration of sacred spaces included the idea that multiple layers of meaning could coexist, and that literal and obvious interpretations could hide deeper, allegorical meanings from sight.[55] Thus analysis of the vault designs will be found to reveal layers of meaning which will not only throw light on the chapels' functions, but will also help to explain their importance to the fifth-century papacy: the analysis will also be supported by the papal donation lists.

First of the decorative programs to be considered will be that of S Croce. Study of it is hampered by the lack of any complete, detailed drawing of its vault. The chapel is recorded only in the brief descriptions and sketches of antiquarians and architects who saw it before it was destroyed in 1588. Unfortunately, these records are limited in detail, and often conflict with one another.[56] Many of the most reliable draughtsmen omit the vault entirely. Onophrio Panvinio, writing before 1562, describes it as featuring an image of the cross held up by four angels on a golden ground.[57] Pompeio Ugonio, whose account is based largely on Panvinio's, also described these four angels, and noted that varicoloured birds and foliage were included in the design.[58] He is the only writer to mention them. Birds do appear in Antonio Lafréri's engraving of 1568, though the angels do not (fig. 102). By contrast, the angels holding up the cross appear in the drawing of Giuliano da Sangallo (fig. 103), but without the birds and foliage. Giuliano does not show the cross itself: the angels support an apparently empty oculus. Baldassare Peruzzi's drawing of a corner chapel interior also depicts an empty oculus, suggesting that the original building was equipped with an oculus in each of its five rooms (fig. 101, A). Giuliano shows the 'angels' as semi-naked *putti* in the classical tradition, set among curlicues: this may indicate that the decoration antedated the Christian phase of the chapel, although it is also possible that he saw an Early Christian scheme through the classicizing eyes of the Renaissance. The curlicues are a common feature of Late Antique decorative schemes, such as those in the vaults of Hilarus's other two chapels, and the iconographic formula in which diagonal figures hold up a symbol in the centre of a vault had a long history in the ancient world, being employed in the tombs of the Etruscans.[59] If the design dates from the time of Hilarus, S Croce is the first-known site where this iconography was used in a Christian setting, with the symbol being that of Christ. Its descendants were to be numerous.

The drum decoration of S Croce is known from a single written source, Panvinio's description. The drum was the site of four broad windows, between which, according to Panvinio, four pairs of apostles and saints were depicted in mosaic.[60] These were Peter and Paul, the two Saints John, Lawrence and Stephen, and James and Philip. None of the artists who drew the interior of S Croce showed the saints, though Lafréri's engraving shows some shadowy figures above the windows on the vault (fig. 102). The figures aside, Lafréri's version of the vault closely resembles those of the St John chapels in layout, with candelabra in the groins of the vault, and with curlicues and birds between. The similarity of Lafréri's design to the St Johns' vaults, rather than to either Panvinio's or Ugonio's descriptions, or to the Sangallo drawing, suggests that it may have been based on the decorations of the other chapels, rather than on S Croce itself.

On the upper walls of the S Croce crossing, Giuliano da Sangallo shows tall, Latin crosses in intarsia over the corner doors (fig. 103), and these, as well as the symbolism of the architectural form, led some scholars to believe that from the beginning Hilarus's Holy Cross Oratory functioned as the *consignatorium*, where the sacrament of confirmation took place.[61] Picard, though, has recently pointed out that there is no mention in the baptismal texts of a dedicated room for confirmation before the ninth century. He suggests that confirmation probably took place in the Lateran basilica itself, perhaps where the pope had his *cathedra*.[62] Ugonio informs us that an ancient custom was revived in his day, that of confirmation in the S Venanzio chapel, an open portico in the time of Hilarus.[63] A third location has also been suggested for the laying on of hands: the right apse of the baptistery portico, now known as the chapel of saints Ruffina and Secunda. In this apse, the mosaic has a design of acanthus scrolls, enriched with numerous small crosses, and mosaic crosses are also shown hanging in a row from the pleated 'canopy of heaven' above (fig. 104).[64] There are precedents at other Early Christian baptisteries for placing the *consignatorium* in a niche close to the font itself: S Gennaro, Naples, and Salona are two important examples. In favour of the latter two locations for the Lateran *consignatorium* is their position on the direct route between the font and the basilica, where the neophytes would partake of the Eucharist immediately after their confirmation. By contrast, S Croce was behind the baptistery and thus away from the probable circulation.[65]

The St John chapels' vault mosaics are variations on a common theme, each adapted to the contours of its vault (figs. 99 and 100). Both decorations are centred on the Lamb, which occupies the highest point of the vault and is haloed and enclosed in a wreath of seasonal fruits and flowers. In the Baptist's chapel, the vault was subdivided into fields by intersecting bands of decorative mosaic. The axes of a central square around the Lamb and its wreath were prolonged until they intersected with the frames of the two lunettes, and this rectangular network interlocked with a wide, diamond-shaped frame whose points touched the upper extremities of the same lunettes (fig. 100). A candelabrum motif bearing peacocks occupied each of the responds of the vault: birds and flowers inhabited the triangular spaces created by the vaults' mosaic framework. Doves and peacocks, partridges and parrots, lilies and acanthus filled these spaces. In each end lunette a window was flanked by standing evangelists with haloes and open books: Matthew and Luke facing Mark and John, named by inscription and further identified by their symbols, which reared up from the clouds above their heads.

The Evangelist's chapel possesses the only surviving vault mosaic of the three (fig. 99): it reveals a wealth of detail and colour, details which almost certainly applied to the Baptist's chapel vault as well. The mosaic details vividly confirm that the chapels illustrated contemporary ideas, such as those of Leo the Great, on the transformation of the Hebrew tabernacle into the sanctuary of the Christian faith through substitution of the holiest symbols of the Christian faith for those of the Hebrews.

In the Evangelist's chapel, the Lamb in the golden vault, symbolizing the One Sacrifice offered on the Christian altar, is framed by a leafy wreath which contains seasonal flowers and fruits, olives, wheat and grapes, a timeless composition popular in other media in the fifth century.[66] The Lamb, though, is the central feature of a composition which represents the wooden framework of a tent, the structure which, draped in cloth, would support a temporary dwelling. Such were the tents which the Jews built in the wilderness for the feast of Tabernacles. To convey this impression, the Lamb is surrounded by a square, brown framework. A similar border frames each of the four lunettes, and is joined by a vertical to the square above. In the groins of the vault, further brown uprights bear ornamental candelabra, springing from shieldlike motifs and topped by finials.

It is this framework of eight supports raising a central framework and holding rich garlands that represents the tent frame. Tents had deep symbolic significance in both Hebrew and Early Christian thought.[67] In the Psalms we find 'tent' used as a poetic synonym for the Temple in Jerusalem, and more particularly for the Tabernacle or Holy of Holies.[68] It is no coincidence that Hilarus chose this text from the Book of Psalms to inscribe over the doorway of S Croce: 'I will come into Thy house, I will worship towards thy holy temple in thy fear,' a choice which unequivocally confirms the connection between these chapels and the temple in Jerusalem.[69] Christians also saw the tent and the temple as prefigurations of the vision of the New Jerusalem that was a key topic of the Book of Revelation,[70] and they borrowed images of the desert tents of the Feast of Tabernacles from Jewish art.[71] They saw the tabernacle as a prefiguration of the new covenant of Christ, the Church which they entered into through baptism: 'their guilty hearts sprinkled clean, (their) bodies washed with pure water,' a concept which may help to explain the location Pope Hilarus chose for his chapels, beside the Lateran Baptistery.[72] The garlands hanging from the tent frame above also contain an allusion to baptism, for in the baptismal hymns of the *Odes of Solomon*, the neophyte is urged to 'come into his Paradise and make a garland from its tree and put it upon (his) head,' a reference to the crowning of the catechumens with wreaths of flowers in the baptismal rite. These *Odes*, a series designed to be sung on the forty days of Lent,[73] are replete with references to garlands and were known in a Latin version by the year 310.[74] Evidently, the vault mosaics at the St John chapels contained allusions to Christian initiation as well as to the sacred mysteries which were celebrated beneath them on altars which were typologically equivalent to the ark of the covenant, the 'arks of the Christian church.'[75] Furthermore, centrally placed within each chapel was the papal gift: a cross of pure gold which symbolized the presence of Christ himself within each sacred space.[76]

While the tent structures themselves express the ideas of the continuity and reinterpretation of the Hebrew scriptures in the Early Christian period, the space around them resonates with meanings drawn from the pagan past, from Roman and Etruscan ideas of the hereafter. The eight uprights of the tent frame define eight golden areas, as if one looked out from inside the tent through a transparent veil into an infinity beyond, the infinity of heaven symbolized by the mystic gold chosen to represent it, and the veil defined by the blue cusped band of its hem or border. In each segment of the vision of infinite space a green platform floats, perhaps representing the green fields of paradise. On each platform two pairs of birds peck at fruits piled in a high-footed vase. The choice of birds – partridges, doves, parrots, and ducks – symbolizes the ancient idea of the four elements: earth, air, fire, and water,[77] made up of the three states of matter, and the agent – fire – that transforms them. These are the constituent elements of the universe, which represent the infinity of God's creation.

We have seen that the tent frame depicted on the vault of the Evangelist's chapel represents, on one level, the Hebrew tabernacle, as it was redefined in Christian thought. It arches over the sacred contents of the chapel's interior space just as it had over the Holy of Holies with its symbolic contents. But the design also expresses continuity with the pagan past, an interpretation suggested by its colour, the natural brown of wood, by the trophies displayed upon its corner posts, and by the garlands suspended from its roof frame, all of which further define it as the framework of a pavilion. But far from being an ordinary hunting pavilion, this is a visionary dwelling from which one looks out at the infinity of heaven, symbolized by the golden dome of the vault. This idea of a vision of paradise glimpsed from within a defined space that represents the world of the present is not an invention of Christian or even of Roman art, and the only thing in the mosaics which distinguishes the Christian version from its pagan antecedents is the central vision of the Lamb: the one sacrifice which replaces the blood sacrifices of the past. However, the mechanism for defining this sort of revelation remains constant and can be traced back, ultimately, into the funerary art of the Etruscans. Many Etruscan tombs feature painted tentpoles and ridgepoles, which define the interior space and delimit it from the beyond, which although different in meaning and content from the Christian heaven, yet shares with it an iconographic language which is expressive of the soul's journey after death and of human hope of happiness in that realm. The Tomba del Cacciatore at Tarquinia (fig. 105), for example, takes the form of a room with an inner ceiling and upper wall frieze.[78] The ceiling is decorated with squares of red, blue, and white, reminiscent of fabric, finished at the lower edges by a frieze of animals in the same colours. The tent's support structure is clearly indicated in red-brown: a tentpole in the centre of the end wall articulates with a ridgepole; beams or trusses hold the squared 'fabric' taut; and the gable end is further supported by a pair of horizontal struts. From the lower edge of the roof awning hangs the transparent curtain through which the paradise of the hunter is glimpsed: undulating hills, with trees and game animals, while from the curtain rail dead ducks hang by their beaks as trophies. The curtain's transparency is indicated by repeated motifs, a small red square circumscribing a cross, imitating the medallions that were sometimes woven into plain gauzes.[79] The transparent curtain defines the invisible boundary between the Here and the Other, a concept which the Romans inherited and which was still expressed in the same visual formula almost a millennium later in the time of Pope Hilarus.

In the choice of such an ancient model for the re-creation of heaven within the interior of these chapels, Hilarus and his advisers were following what appears to have been the natural route of the times: the borrowing of well-known formulas, which were then reinterpreted in Christian terms, and the addition of key symbols as cryptic messages to the viewer that although the iconography may have been ancient, familiar and easy to read, the new context is Christian, and the meaning is to be understood on those terms. The key symbols in Hilarus's chapels are those which are allegories for Christ. Each is framed in the centre of its vault, and each, whether cross or Lamb, symbolizes his sacrifice for humanity. Presence of the paired evangelists in the zone below at S Giovanni Battista, and of the four pairs of saints below the vault at S Croce, again call to mind the dome mosaic of the Early Christian basilica at S Prisco in the Capua cemetery (fig. 64), with its pairs of martyrs, saints, and prophets. An early-fifth-century example of the Christian formula, also from Campania, is found at S Giovanni in Fonte, the Naples baptistery. Here the central chrismon which represents Christ is set on a starry ground and enclosed in a broad vegetal wreath with birds, and here, too, paired saints are shown below.[80] These examples, as well as the Lateran chapels themselves, reveal that the development of specifically Christian imagery was extremely gradual. Christian concepts were at first expressed in the traditional imagery of pagan times, as was demonstrated in S Costanza, Rome. The fifth-century chapels of Pope Hilarus give us reason to extend this period of transition for a further century.

How widespread was the depiction of the vault of paradise in Early Christian art? Was it restricted to particular groups of buildings or did its use depend on the architectural form, the creation of the illusion of the vault of heaven being fully possible only on masonry vaults and domes? The evidence relies on a small group of centrally planned buildings of the Early Christian period, those which not only have vaults suitable for mosaic decoration, but have retained enough of their decorative schemes to be capable of analysis. Three baptisteries, including the Naples baptistery and those of Ravenna, meet these criteria. Chapels with the same sort of vault decorations include one palace chapel, and several others used in various ways in the funerary and martyr cult, ways which often overlap. Regardless of their individual functions, the basic vocabulary of the vaults' decoration is the same, and expresses the vision of heaven, peopled by holy beings, set against the transcendental gold of the sky. The purpose is the creation of a sacred space which symbolizes within its own walls and under its own arched vault, so reminiscent of the dome of heaven, a microcosm of the whole universe. This decoration sanctifies the inner space of the building, creating an appropriate setting for the sacred activities which take place beneath, the celebration of the sacraments and the housing of the relics of the saints and of the symbols of the faith. I would suggest that in these small vaulted structures, the early stages in evolution of the system of decoration of the vaulted Middle Byzantine church are preserved.[81]

This, then, is another layer of meaning expressed by the mosaics of the vaults and upper walls of Hilarus's chapels, where symbols such as the 'sphere of heaven' have given way to another vision, another universal symbol: that of Christ in the heavens,[82] while in other respects, the Late Antique paradise is depicted much as before: peopled with birds, flowers, and fruit, with concepts such as time and eternity expressed by the depiction of the passing seasons as symbolized by their typical flowers and fruits.

In addition to the traditional re-creation of the microcosm of heaven, though, Hilarus's St John chapels reveal a more subtle interaction of the ideas of the Jewish and of the traditional Roman past. In these two chapels interpenetrating layers of meaning are visualized in the decoration of the chapels' vaults, where the illusionary golden vista of heaven is glimpsed through a transparent veil hanging over the tent-like structure which signifies the tabernacle. This is the sign that what lay below – altar, relics, the cross of Christ, the sacraments – surpassed the Old Covenant of the Hebrews, which in Christ's incarnation had been fulfilled. Moreover, these conclusions are strengthened by examination of the inscriptions which Hilarus placed in his chapels and the dedications which he chose for them.

First, the three dedications. John the Baptist was the traditional patron of an Early Christian baptistery.[83] Relics of St John could best have been revered in a special shrine beside the baptistery. The choice of St John the Evangelist was more personal: Hilarus's devotion to St John is recorded in the inscription on the lintel to this day. In the case of the Holy Cross chapel, the preexisting architectural form of the building may have suggested both the choice of relic, a major fragment of the True Cross, and the building's function as its shrine.[84]

The evidence of the contemporary written word holds a special place in the history and interpretation of any building, and this is true above all for inscriptions which form part of its original furnishings. All three of Hilarus's chapels were originally richly endowed with inscriptions; some survive, others are documented. The Baptist's chapel once had two dedicatory statements in addition to that on its surviving fifth-century bronze doors: 'Bishop Hilarus, servant of God, makes this offering in honour of Saint John the Baptist.'[85] An almost identical dedication is recorded from the apse mosaic, which had already been lost by the sixteenth century.[86] In addition, an extant inscription on the stone lintel over the door reads 'Bishop Hilarus to the Holy People of God.'[87] More revealing, perhaps, than these self-explanatory dedicatory messages, are the verses from the Book of Psalms which Pope Hilarus chose to place over the doorways of the chapels of the Baptist and S Croce, respectively. These read 'Lord, I have loved the beauty of thy house' at S Giovanni Battista (Psalm 26.8),[88] and 'I will come into thy house, I will worship towards thy holy temple in thy fear' at S Croce (Psalm 5.7).[89] On the surface these inscriptions refer to the chapels themselves as places of worship and beauty. They also record Hilarus's belief that each chapel was the dwelling place of God, just as he dwelt in the Holy of Holies in Jerusalem. Thus, the texts confirm the interpretation of the interior space of the chapels as re-creations of the tabernacle sacred to the Hebrews, perhaps the most significant of the vaults' many-layered meanings. But it cannot be a coincidence that both these verses are also quotations from psalms that are 'prayers for deliverance from personal enemies.'[90] I suggest that their veiled message is related to Hilarus's inscription at the Evangelist's chapel, in which he thanks St John for liberating him from danger, and that here in his other two chapels Hilarus, remembering his narrow escape in Ephesus, records his prayer that God will continue to protect him in a dangerous world. The inscriptions may also be read as apotropaic messages for the chapels themselves, forbidding evil to find entry, in view of their placement over the main doorways.

In summing up the evidence of the donation texts, the mosaic decoration of the vaults, and the inscriptions of the donor pope, the main themes that emerge are spiritual. The donor's gifts of Christ's symbols, the cross and the Lamb, fashioned in pure gold and in golden mosaic, are Christian equivalents of the sacred symbols of the Jewish faith which were hidden from view in the Holy of Holies of the temple: the ark of the covenant and the menorah. The vaults re-create in a new setting the desert tabernacles of the Jews, but now shelter the symbols of the new covenant: the cross, the Lamb and the Christian altar, lit by splendid lamps whose light sparkled from the thousand golden facets of the mosaics overhead. Further treasures which added their lustre to the sacred space were the relics of the saints enshrined in the chapels' *confessiones*. The details of the heavenly space were expressed in the traditional vocabulary of Roman tradition and of the Etruscans before them; the meaning though was taken from Judaeo-Christian tradition, and expressed the belief of the Early Church that Old Testament prophecies of the Messiah were now fulfilled in Christ.

As for the placement of the chapels at the residence of Pope Hilarus, Bishop of Rome, I suggest that these sanctuaries were built beside his cathedral and baptistery not only as re-creations of the Hebrew tabernacle, where only the high priest entered on one single annual occasion, but as the signifiers of the new, Christian 'high priest,' the descendant of St Peter, on whom the Christian church was founded. Here we must return to the writings of Pope Hilarus's mentor and predecessor in the papacy, Pope Leo I. In a sermon which he delivered on the anniversary of his election to the pontificate, Leo returned to a theme which was close to his heart.[91] This was the position of the successors of St Peter as the heirs of the high priest Melchizedeck. Leo declares that although Melchizedeck prefigured Christ as the eternal high priest, the mystery of the divine priesthood was now delegated to the human race, through the agency of the Holy Ghost. The divine nature of this choice precluded any chance that there would be succession to the See of Peter through inheritance, Leo argued. Rather, the candidates would be prepared for their task through divine grace.[92] The existence of chapels at the Lateran, which on both theological and political grounds symbolized the primacy of the pope as high priest of the Christian church, would surely explain the desire of Pope Symmachus to create his own set of identical symbols, the Damasus Baptistery chapels, beside his residence at the Vatican. The intention was to support his claim to the papal throne. To these ends he endowed the chapels with the gifts of crosses, altars, relic shrines, and lights, which, besides being identical to those of the Lateran chapels, were appropriate for the re-created Holy of Holies of the Christian church, with himself its would-be high priest.[93] The choice of the Vatican as their location fortuitously marks not only the location of Symmachus's residence and papal administration, but the shrine of St Peter itself, which would come to surpass the St John's Lateran as the holiest site in Western Christendom.

CHAPTER NINE

A Collective Funerary *Martyrium*: The S Venanzio Chapel, Rome

The desire for burial inside the structures that were raised to commemorate the martyrs was a natural consequence of the rise of the martyr cult itself, and of widespread belief in the power of the saints to help the individual in his lifetime and more particularly after his death, when burial beside a saint could be counted upon to ensure salvation. In addition, both cities and the Church believed that the martyrs could help them on a communal scale. Christians felt that the martyrs were the only power for good in a world that had become increasingly full of danger. This need for a system that would protect the community as well as the individual led to a further development of the martyr cult: the erection of buildings in which the martyr relics were centrally collected so that their power would be concentrated and enhanced for the common good. The earliest surviving example of a building founded to house the remains of saints who had been gathered together far from their homes and their places of martyrdom is the S Venanzio chapel, founded at the Lateran Baptistery in Rome by the mid-seventh-century Pope John IV (640–2). John, himself a Dalmatian, came to the papal throne in a time of great unrest in his homeland, which was overrun by the Avars and the Slavs, causing fears in Rome both for the safety of Dalmatia's Christians and for the safety of the relics of the saints and martyrs, the protectors of Dalmatia itself. Pope John's chapel epitomizes the final stage of development of the architecture of the martyr cult at the beginning of the Middle Ages.

The twin cults of the martyrs and of their relics were marked from their beginning by distinctive architecture, which, like the concept of venerating heroes by building shrines in their memory, was taken over from pagan tradition. These Christian shrines are known as *mar-*

tyria. André Grabar, in his magisterial work, *Martyrium*, defined the earliest *martyria* as monuments built with two purposes: the marking of the location of the martyrs' tombs and the organization of space around their graves for the use of the cult and for sheltering the faithful.[1] The broadness of this definition, though, can be confusing. For example, the word *martyrium* may describe both the earliest monument erected over a martyr's grave in connection with his or her cult and any shrine where the martyr's relics are venerated, even if the only connection between the location and the saint is that the relics have been moved there for veneration. It is obviously necessary to clarify the relationships of the various buildings raised in connection with the martyr cult in the earliest days of Christianity. Richard Krautheimer has drawn attention to the need for establishing some 'family trees' within the broad framework outlined by Grabar.[2] The case of the S Venanzio chapel and its antecedents in Dalmatia traces one such tree, a branching structure which leads from the earliest commemorative graves through *cellae memoriae* and funerary chapels to the collective shrines. The connecting links consist of the cults of a specific group of martyrs, each expressed in the architectural forms which best suited its needs.

The word *martyrium* will not be used for the early shrines. These will be referred to as 'martyr shrines' or *memoriae, cellae memoriae*, words which will be reserved for the primary buildings erected over sites specifically connected to the martyr's life or death, or over his or her grave. In the course of evolution, the primary sites acquired secondary uses: we have seen that it was common for important Christians to be buried beside a saint so that on Judgment Day that saint would help them reach paradise. Since the Western tradition forbade relocation of the bones of the martyrs except in very special circumstances, martyr shrines and burials *ad sanctos* were typically to be found in the suburban graveyards rather than elsewhere. It was not until the laws about burial within the city were relaxed in the late sixth century, and translations of relics from their original places of burial became possible, that a further step in the evolution of the martyr shrine became possible: the creation of buildings specifically for the veneration of relics, at locations other than the primary sites of the martyrs' lives and deaths. I suggest that the word *martyrium* should be reserved for these secondary shrines, built specifically for the veneration of relics of one or many saints in a place that was previously unconnected to the cult.[3] These buildings represented the culmination of the sequence of devotional building in connection with the martyr cult and commonly became sites of pilgrimage.

An important early example of a *martyrium* in the sense just defined is the S Venanzio chapel at the Lateran Baptistery, Rome, which was built by the Dalmatian Pope John IV. The circumstances of its building are recorded in the *Liber Pontificalis*, where we read that John feared for the fate of his countrymen, whose land had been overrun by the Avars, and for the remains of the saints who lay in its cemeteries. He therefore sent an envoy, Abbot Martinus, to Dalmatia and Istria, giving him money to ransom the captives taken by the invaders. Martinus was also charged with bringing the relics of the region's numerous saints back to Rome.[4]

The first part of the mission has left no records, and we do not know whether any captives were liberated, and if so, how many. Martinus's second charge resulted in the creation of a *martyrium* in the heart of the pope's domain in Rome. Its altar became the resting place of the relics of the Dalmatian saints, and its apse wall and apse were decorated with mosaics, which included a papal inscription commemorating the event.[5] These decorations reveal a great deal about the saints who are commemorated in the S Venanzio chapel, adding a further dimension to the building's considerable interest as one of the earliest surviving, decorated *martyria*, one, moreover, which has been in continuous use since its founding. The survival of the mosaics and the documentation also provides us with a unique opportunity to trace the connections between the seventh-century Roman *martyrium* and the martyrs' death sites, graves, and *cellae memoriae* in Early Christian Dalmatia. It is fortunate for our study that the site of Salona, capital city of Roman Dalmatia, was never again built on after the Avar conquest. At that time the population fled and took refuge in the strongly fortified palace of Diocletian four miles away at Aspalathos (Spalato, Split) or in the coastal islands. The abandonment of Salona, where all but one of the Dalmatian saints met death, has allowed unparalleled opportunities for confirming their existence. They are recorded in a variety of contexts. We know their places of martyrdom (in most cases the Salona amphitheatre), their gravesites in the cemeteries outside the walls of the city, and their original *memoriae* (plan, fig. 106), which have all been revealed by archaeological studies.[6] In addition, the images of some of the saints, named by inscription and painted not long after their deaths, were found on the walls of the east gladiator chapel at the Salona amphitheatre, and can be compared with their mosaic likenesses in Rome. Tradition has also preserved some of the details of their martyrdoms, as well as of their role as protectors and patrons of the communities along the eastern shore of the Adriatic. We also know the identity of some of those who chose to be buried beside them. We can, in fact, trace the evolution and elaboration of these saints' cults from their beginnings in Salona to their culmination across the sea in Rome, as a result of a unique combination of circumstances: Salona's abandonment and the survival of the S Venanzio chapel as part of the Lateran Baptistery complex at Rome.

The S Venanzio chapel has existed in its present form since the mid-seventh century (plan, fig. 98A) and still contains the relics and displays the mosaic decorations that were given to it by the founder. The mosaics show the donor pope and his successor as well as the named images of ten saints from the Adriatic's farther shore whose relics are venerated in the chapel (fig. 107). The Dalmatian saints are included in the composition as witnesses to the central event, portrayed in the bowl of the apse: a theophany vision which may well be modelled on the original design of the apse at St John's Lateran.[7] The *martyrium* also reveals the attitudes of two seventh-century popes to the martyr cult and the relics of the saints.

This chapter will explore the history of the S Venanzio chapel in the light of its antecedents in Dalmatia. The iconographic program of its mosaics will be analysed, and their meaning elucidated. The identity of the Dalmatian and Istrian martyrs will be established, as well as their place in the history of their homelands.

Papal attitudes to the translation of relics will also be discussed. The ideas of Pope Gregory I, revealed in his correspondence at the turn of the seventh century, will be compared with those current at the Lateran when the Dalmatian relics were moved there a scant forty years later. The physical nature of the relics acquired by Pope John's envoy will also be considered; this is possible since a recognition of the relics was carried out in 1962. It will become clear that, far from being a *martyrium* created *de novo* as the *Liber Pontificalis* text suggests, Pope John's foundation in Rome was the culmination of a sequence of shrines dedicated to the martyrs across the Adriatic in Salona and Poreč. The archaeological finds in Salona have revealed, for one or another of the martyrs, all the stages in the typical evolution of the martyr shrine. The simple martyr grave, perhaps marked by an inscription, came to be isolated in an apse or enclosure, and honoured with a *mensa* or altar.[8] The next stage of veneration of the grave came when a simple memorial chapel or *cella memoriae* was erected over it, and this was quickly followed by adoption of the *memoria* as a funerary chapel for burial of rich or powerful patrons beside the saint. As the cult grew, it was necessary to provide more space for pilgrims, and this development also occurred in Salona. The establishment of the martyrs' cults increased the need for physical manifestations of the holy in the form of relics. These could consist not only of the martyrs' physical remains, but of substances or objects which had been in contact with the remains such as *brandea*. Such contact relics were not subject to the rules which limited the transfer of human remains and could be dispersed to sanctify other burial places. The final stage of the process occurred when the relics, whether corporeal or contact, were brought together and placed in a building designed with a single aim: the veneration of the remains of the martyrs. This final building is the *martyrium*, defined as a central shrine holding the relics of a whole city or region, what Grabar, in a somewhat different context, called a 'collective *martyrium*.'[9] The veneration paid to the Dalmatian and Istrian martyrs was expressed sequentially in all these types of buildings and is atypical only in having taken place in two geographically separate locations: the earlier part of its history took place in the eastern homelands, while the climax of devotional building happened in Rome, thanks to the intervention of John IV. The early buildings have perished, but the series can be reconstructed from Salona's archaeological records, while the culmination of the series, the *martyrium*, rises far from its roots in foreign soil beyond the Adriatic Sea. This is the S Venanzio chapel: almost miraculously preserved, it can be studied in its original form, complete with documentation and a major part of its decorative program.

The building history of the S Venanzio chapel will be briefly summarized. The brickwork reveals two campaigns of building prior to that of John IV. The lower half of the apse wall can be dated to the third century, while the upper levels of the wall and its three windows are of fifth-century brick and tufa construction.[10] Brickwork studies also reveal that the apse itself was a seventh-century insertion and therefore probably dates from the time of John IV.

The fifth-century phase must be that of Hilarus I (461–8), whose St Stephen chapel appears to have been situated in a small room between the chapel of S Giovanni Evangelista and an open colonnade (fig. 98, B).[11] The latter was a continuation of the main portico of the Lateran Baptistery, and it was this extension which was walled off as the site of the S Venanzio chapel. Elements of the earlier building can still be traced not only in the apse wall but on the side walls of the chapel, where remnants of the columned portico are embedded in the walls of John IV's chapel. These walls were made by blocking up an arcade of five openings on the Lateran side and a pair of arches near the altar on the other side, towards S Giovanni Evangelista. Presumably the paired opening was the entrance to the inner sanctum of Hilarus's chapel. The central column of this opening survives, rising from a base at the lower floor level, and with its full height embedded in the wall. Panvinio, writing in the late sixteenth century, mentioned the 'ancient and not inelegant' pictures that clothed all walls apart from the apse, and especially that on the left.[12] Some unreadable traces of paint and plaster are all that survive of these. However, at a depth of about five feet below the present floor level, a black and white mosaic floor has been found, together with the lowest register of the early painted decoration of the chapel. This consists of an imitation in paint of red and green marble panels, a well-known decorative scheme for the dado in the early Middle Ages. For example, the Roman church of Santa Maria Antiqua has a comparable dado in the sanctuary which dates to the papacy of John VII (705–7).

The character of the S Venanzio chapel as a *martyrium* is made clear not only by the inscription and the *Liber Pontificalis* text, but by the mosaic decoration itself. Both the apse and its surrounding wall are covered with mosaics (fig. 107). The decoration of the apse is in three registers: Christ between angels in the clouds above; standing saints and donor popes on either side of an orant Virgin, a total of seventeen figures in the middle band; and the donor inscription below. The row of standing saints extends onto the arch wall on either side. The decoration is completed by two compositions on the upper part of the east wall: the cities of Bethlehem and Jerusalem in the outer corners and, framing the window above the apse, the single-winged symbols of the evangelists, complete with books and haloes. Spaces around the figural mosaics are filled with acanthus scrolls, and there is a wide band of formalized ornament containing crosses and lilies around the opening of the arch.

The bowl of the apse is the site of the most important and therefore largest figures, those of Christ and his archangels, which float imposingly above the heads of the smaller figures below. Backed by visionary gold, and supported by the red, blue, and white clouds from which they emerge, they provide the key to the whole iconographic program:

all the other figures on the lower apse are there to acclaim and bear witness to the vision above.[13]

The saints and martyrs who were transferred to the chapel by Pope John take their places below the visionary zone. Their images are accompanied by two unnamed popes, presumably the donor, John IV, and his successor Theodore (642–9), who finished the work. Only two of the ten saints are shown within the curved, central area of the apse: Domnius and Venantius, who stand beside the popes. Closer again to the centre stand the two saints John, honoured at the nearby baptistery, basilica, and chapels, and Peter and Paul, patrons of Rome. In the centre stands the Virgin, her hands raised in a gesture of prayer.

Who were these martyrs, lined up here like a guard of honour for our inspection, their forms and features brought along with their relics from their homeland across the Adriatic? Within the apse, Salonitan bishops Venantius and Domnius both carry books, and each stands beside a pope, probably John IV on the left holding a model of the church, and Theodore on the right holding a book. John reigned for less than two years; obviously the work on the S Venanzio chapel was carried to fruition by his successor, Theodore. Venantius, whom Frane Bulić presumed to have been the first bishop of Salona, a somewhat shadowy figure, may have been a missionary to the Dalmatians, who died among them in the time of the emperors Valerian (253–60) or Aurelian (270–8). Bulić believed Venantius met his death at Delminium, in present-day Herzogovina, in the spring of AD 270. More recent opinion is that Venantius was a bishop, but not necessarily bishop of Salona.[14] His position as patron of the chapel probably honours Pope John's father, another Venantius.[15] St Venantius's grave was formerly identified at Salona's Manastirine cemetery (plan, fig. 106) from an incomplete inscription, but this identification is now rejected.[16] His successor in the bishopric, Domnus or Domnius (Domnio), came from Nisibis in Mesopotamia and died in the Salona amphitheatre on 10 April 304, in the persecutions of Diocletian.[17] An inscription suggests that he also was originally interred at Manastirine, among the graves of other early bishops of Salona, where Bishop Primus (ca. 325) chose ad sanctos burial beside him.[18] Domnius was to become the patron saint of Aspalathos (Split), with his tomb in the cathedral. This church, by an ironic twist of fate, was the former Mausoleum of Diocletian, which was dedicated to St Domnius before the year 950, according to Constantine Porphyrogenitos.[19] The apparent duplication of Domnius's remains in Split and Rome has been explained since the early Middle

Ages by the existence of a second – and earlier – Bishop Domnius in Salona, a disciple of St Peter who suffered martyrdom under the emperor Trajan. This legend of an apostolic origin for St Domnius seems to have developed during the struggle for ecclesiastical primacy in Dalmatia in the seventh to tenth centuries, with Split basing its claim on the supposed apostolic foundation of Salona, to which it fell heir.[20]

The other five martyrs of the Salona amphitheatre – the priest Asterius and four soldiers of Diocletian's personal bodyguard, Antiochianus, Gaianus, Paulinianus, and Telius – are also pictured in the S Venanzio chapel. They too died in the persecutions of April 304. Diocletian was probably in residence at that time, since his bodyguards were there and their duty was to accompany his person. His known itineraries in the last two years of his reign confirm this possibility. He celebrated his *vicennalia* in Rome in late November 303, left Ravenna on 1 January 304, and arrived back in Nicomedia, his capital, on 28 August of the same year.[21] It is likely that he stopped at Salona on his way east, to visit the palace at nearby Aspalathos, which was being built for his retirement in 305.[22] Tradition recounts that the four palace guards were sent to arrest Bishop Domnius; refusing, they suffered martyrdom with him on 10 April 304.[23] In the mosaic the four saints are shown in the court dress of the emperor's personal bodyguard, white with distinctive black tablions, and are also distinguished by their identical and unusual haircuts, bushy at the sides and flat on top. Each holds his crown of martyrdom. Their sarcophagi were at first placed in the middle of the sanctuary at Kapljuć (plan, fig. 106) surrounded by benches for the funerary meal. The floor was raised fifty years later when the funerary basilica of Kapljuć in the Coemeterium Quinque Martyrum near the Salona amphitheatre was built around the martyr graves: these remained intact, their tops level with the new floor.

The fifth martyr of the Kapljuć cemetery was the priest Asterius, whose date of martyrdom is not known: Bulić has suggested 304 for him also, since it was a year in which many priests died in Salona.[24] Asterius was buried in the apse of the Kapljuć basilica, which became his *cella memoriae*, complete with the *mensa* for his funerary meal, which had plates carved into its surface and perforations for the pouring of libations of wine and oil, as well as for insertion of strips of cloth into the tomb for use as contact relics.[25]

Another clerical martyr shown in the mosaic is Septimius, a deacon, clad in a dalmatic and holding a book, who died in Salona on 18 April

304. His remains were installed under the main altar at Manastirine, where archaeology has revealed his *confessio*: Bishop Gaianus (d. ca. 391) was buried *ad sanctos* beside him.[26]

Flanking the curved apse wall on either side are two last saints: the Istrian bishop Maurus on the right, St Anastasius on the left.

According to tradition, Anastasius was a wealthy fuller, a native of Aquileia, who heard that persecutions were under way at Salona, and hurried there to give himself to martyrdom.[27] When he arrived, he deliberately advertised his Christian belief by signing his door with a cross. As he wished, he was condemned to death, tied to a millstone, and drowned in Salona bay on 26 March 304.[28] The earliest sources for both his trade and his nationality date from more than 700 years after his death: the evidence of the mosaics and of his burial suggest he was an aristocrat, for Anastasius appears in golden garments, unlike the other saints, who are dressed in white.[29] His burial also points to his aristocratic origins: his remains were at first hidden on the island of Pharia (Lesina, Hvar) off Split; a noble lady, Asclepia, and her husband then transferred his remains to their private mausoleum at Marusinac, a short way from Salona's northern boundary. In the fifth century a cemetery church was dedicated to him at Marusinac, and he was reinterred there beneath the main altar. Soon after 400 the attacks of the Goths and Huns became more frequent, and both Manastirine and Kapljuć were destroyed, their graveyards despoiled, and their sarcophagi broken open. In each case the martyrs' graves were consolidated into a smaller sacred area, an 'emergency church' within the great basilica, and the saints were moved to safety.[30] The emergency church at Manastirine consisted of the transept of the great basilica, walled off and buttressed: the nave at Kapljuć received the same treatment.

One more saint, Maurus of Parentium (Parenzo, Poreč), represents Istria in the S Venanzio chapel, fitting the text of the *Liber Pontificalis*, which specifically mentions relics of Istrian saints. Patron of his city, Maurus by long tradition had a corporeal presence there in the Basilica Euphrasiana, where a fourth- to fifth-century inscription connects him to the site.[31] His remains were stolen from Poreč by the Genoese in 1354 and reinterred in S Matteo, Genoa, in 1356, whence they were returned to Poreč in 1934.[32] For this reason, as well as his status as patron saint of his city and diocese, it seems unlikely that Pope John's emissary managed to take the saint's body to Rome, just as historical evidence makes it seem unlikely that the people of Aspalathos parted with the body of St Domnius.

Thus, Salona has offered unique opportunities to archaeologists to confirm the existence of the martyrs who are portrayed in the S Venanzio apse mosaic, and the events recorded in their legendary *Lives* have in many cases been corroborated by archaeological findings. This confirms that the Salona martyrs were interred, according to Roman law, in various of the graveyards that surrounded their city, and that *memoriae* were raised over their actual gravesites. The simple chapels became the centre of their cults, and larger buildings were added to provide accommodation for devotees and pilgrims. The martyrs' remains could be moved, either to larger quarters to accommodate their growing cults, as in the case of Anastasius, or to smaller, more defensible buildings to protect the remains in times of danger, as with the Manastirine and Kapljuć 'emergency churches.' However, archaeology has revealed a further type of veneration at Salona: the commemoration of the martyrs at the actual place of their deaths, the amphitheatre. There, a chapel dedicated to them came to light in 1911: the south-east chapel of the Salona amphitheatre.[33] Its position was analogous to that of the gladiator shrines common to amphitheatres, which in the pre-Christian era would typically have been dedicated to the goddess Nemesis.[34] Other nearby sites in Dalmatia and Pannonia retain traces of this cult, among them Pula (Pola), Carnuntum (Bratislava), and Aquincum (Budapest), and at Salona, too, an altar inscribed to Nemesis was discovered in the amphitheatre itself.[35] In the 1940s, the chapel still had barely legible, early medieval frescoes of saints on its walls, overwhelming evidence that it had been put to Christian use, although its precise purpose could not be determined owing to its poor condition. The decoration of the west wall, the best preserved, consisted of a row of standing saints, three-quarters life-sized, on a layer of pink-painted plaster that was itself superimposed on an earlier layer painted in imitation of marble (fig. 108). Best preserved was the image of Asterius; less distinct were the images of two more saints, one a palace guard, named by inscription Telius.[36] When the amphitheatre chapel was first excavated, Bulić recorded traces of a smaller figure, perhaps a boy, beside the saints.[37] Ivanka Nikolajević has suggested that this may have been a donor figure on a smaller scale, comparable to those at Dürres, where the amphitheatre chapel also contained votive images, in mosaic, complete with donors.[38] Since the Salona saints bore a remarkable likeness to those on the apse wall in the S Venanzio chapel, Ejnar Dyggve proposed that the emissary of John IV brought back not only the relics from Dalmatia, but the likenesses of the martyrs as well. By 1987 these paintings, which were in an unroofed location, had entirely disappeared, leaving only a few painted plaster fragments to mark their former location.

Detailed iconographic resemblances between these gravely damaged figures and the S Venanzio saints convinced all the scholars who saw the paintings that they were indeed the source for the Lateran 'portraits.' Among these scholars were Bulić, Bröndsted, and Dyggve.[39] However, they did not agree on the date to be given to the paintings, on the evidence of the plaster layers. Estimates spanned two centuries, from Bröndsted's choice of the first half of the fourth century to Dyggve's estimate of the early sixth century, a date supported by the style of the clothing. The conversion to Christian use of the gladiator chapel at the Dyrrachium (Dürres) amphitheatre has been dated to the same period by Nikolajević.[40] For Salona, Dyggve suggested a specific occasion, the visit of Justinian's general Constantianus in 536 in connection with improvements to the city's defences, which have plasterwork comparable to that of the amphitheatre chapel. If we accept the sixth-century date, the saints' likenesses cannot have been taken from life; nevertheless, their quality of ancient authority may have suggested their use as models by the emissaries of John IV a century later, and the many stylistic details shared with the S Venanzio chapel mosaics support this idea. These include the size of the haloes in proportion to the faces, the gold or yellow martyr crowns, the distinctive styles of hair and beard, and, most important, the clothing. For example, in both Rome and Salona Asterius appears as an older man with a pointed beard and a tonsure, while Telius has thick, dark hair and a white garment with a shoulder patch. Little remained of the third saint but tiny fragments of halo and of a light yellow garment. Indistinct painted remnants on the facing wall including a terracotta-coloured garment and a cruciform ornament, suggested a further set of three saints there: the slope of the roof would have limited the composition to three saints on each side. The matching south-west chapel may have had a similar decoration, bringing to twelve the number of saints portrayed. The facial features show no stylistic differences between the representation of a living pope and that of a canonized and martyred bishop.[41] Each individual appears to gaze out at the viewer; each is dematerialized in the manner of the S Venanzio mosaics, as well as of others from the same period at S Agnese *fuori le Mura*, Rome (ca. 625) and at St Demetrius, Thessaloniki, likewise from the early seventh century.

It seems very likely on the basis of these findings that John IV

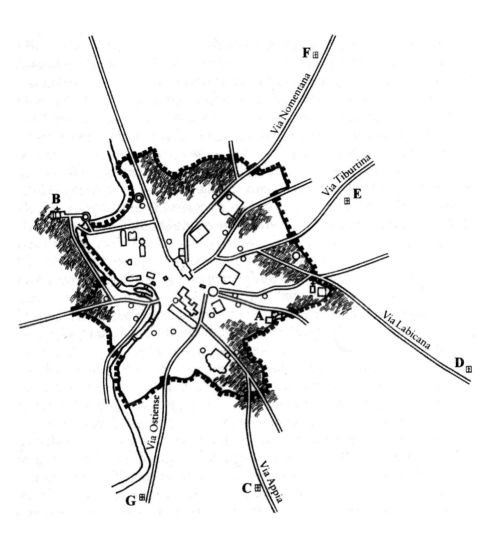

Fig. 1 Rome, Constantinian martyr churches and cemetery basilicas (after Krautheimer, *Three Christian Capitals* © The University of California Press). A – Lateran Basilica; B – St Peter's; C – S Sebastiano; D – SS Marcellino e Pietro; E – S Lorenzo; F – S Agnese; G – St Paul's.

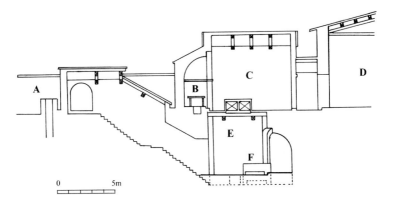

Fig. 2   The Shrines of Sts Peter and Marcellinus and of St Tiburtius at the Catacomb of SS Marcellino e Pietro, Rome. (Longitudinal section, courtesy of Guyon.) A – portico; B – altar-tomb of St Tiburtius; C – upper mausoleum; D – Constantinian basilica; E – underground room containing F – altar-tomb of Sts Peter and Marcellinus.

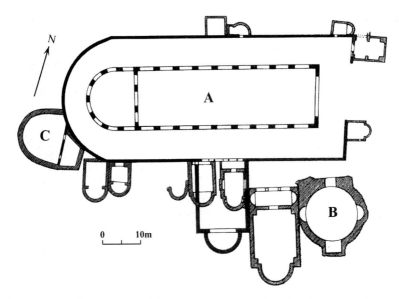

Fig. 3   Rome, Basilica Apostolorum (now S Sebastiano) and its chapels, plan (after Deichmann and Tschira, 1957). A – apse of basilica; B – mausoleum of the Uranii; C – 'Platonia.'

Fig. 4   Rome, S Sotere in the nineteenth century (after Grabar, following De Rossi 1854).

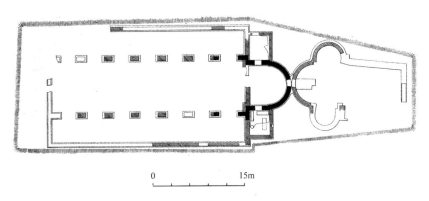

0   15m

Fig. 5   S Sinferosa, plan (after Stevenson, 1878).

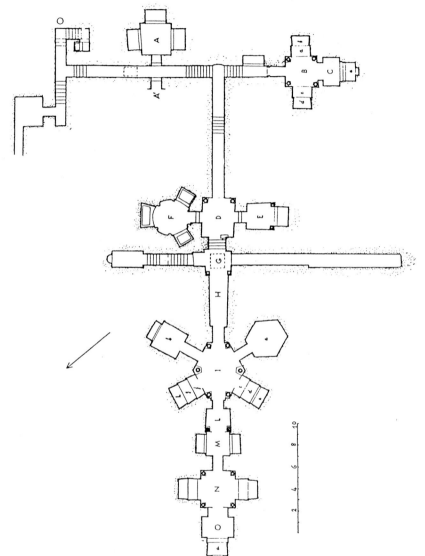

Fig. 6   The Via Latina Catacomb, plan (courtesy of Tronzo and of Ferrua).

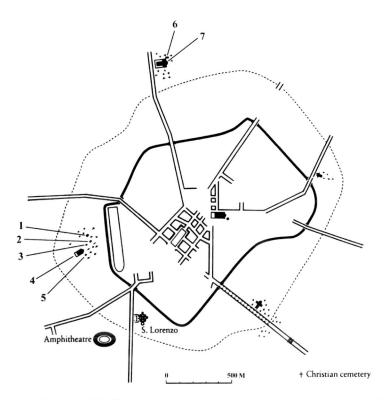

Fig. 7   Milan ca. 400. Plan showing locations of churches and chapels (after Krautheimer, *Three Christian Capitals* © The University of California Press). 1 – SS Nabore e Felice; 2 – S Valeria; 3 – S Vitale; 4 – Basilica Ambrosiana; 5 – S Vittore in Ciel d'Oro; 6 and 7 – S Simpliciano and its chapel.

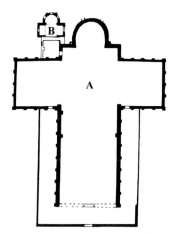

Fig. 8   S Simpliciano, Milan, and its chapel. Plan (after Krautheimer, *Three Christian Capitals* [© The University of California Press]). A – chapel; B – basilica.

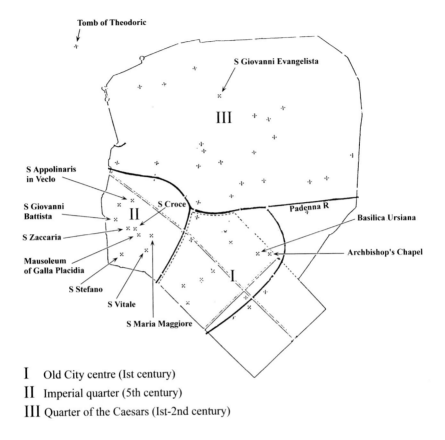

Tomb of Theodoric

S Giovanni Evangelista

III

S Appolinaris
in Veclo

S Giovanni
Battista

S Croce

II

Padenna R

Basilica Ursiana

S Zaccaria

Archbishop's Chapel

Mausoleum
of Galla Placidia

I

S Stefano

S Vitale

S Maria Maggiore

I   Old City centre (Ist century)

II   Imperial quarter (5th century)

III Quarter of the Caesars (Ist-2nd century)

Fig. 9   Ravenna, plan of city, ca. AD 500 (after Testi-Rasponi).

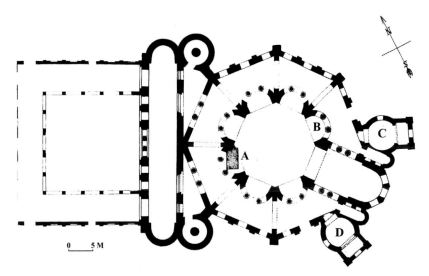

Fig. 10 S Vitale, Ravenna, plan (after Gerola), showing location of earlier chapels. A – site of S Vitale *memoria*; B – site of St Ursicinus *memoria*; C – Sts Gervasius and Protasius; D – Sts Nazarius and Celsus.

Fig. 11 Mosaic floor of *memoria* of St Vitalis below the pavement of S Vitale, Ravenna, showing relic container beneath the altar, and the position of its four supports (after Farioli, courtesy of Longo Editore).

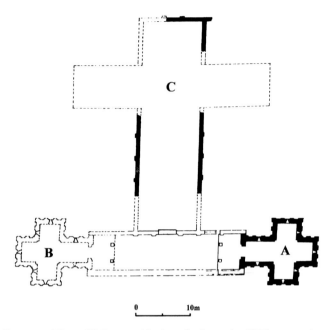

Fig. 12   Ravenna, Plan of S Croce with chapels, from the 1926 excavations (after Di Pietro). A – Mausoleum of Galla Placidia; B – Chapel, probably S Zaccaria; C – S Croce.

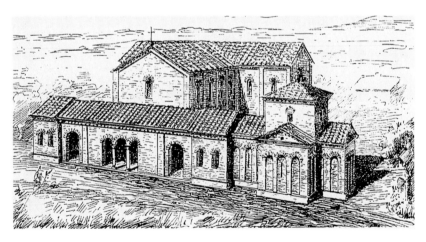

Fig 13   S Croce and the Mausoleum of Galla Placidia, before 1602, as reconstructed by Ricci. Courtesy of the Soprintendenza ai Beni Architettonici e Culturali di Ravenna.

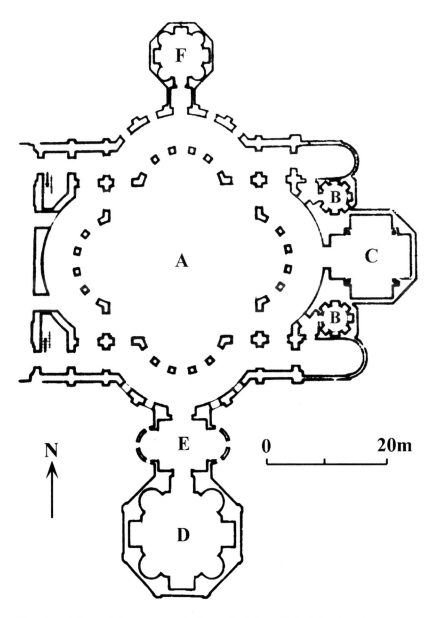

Fig. 14   Milan, S Lorenzo and Chapels (after Chierici). A – S Lorenzo;
B – 'Sacristy chapels'; C – S Ippolito; D – S Aquilino with E – atrium; F – S Sisto.

Fig. 15   S Lorenzo from the SE. Foreground, L, S Aquilino. Distance, R, S Ippolito.

Fig. 16 S Vittore al Corpo, Romanesque basilica: drawing by an anonymous Dutch artist (ca. 1570), Stuttgart, Staatsgalerie, Graphische Sammlung, Inv. 5781r. L to R in middle distance: Campanile and apse of S Vittore; imperial mausoleum, possibly that of Maximian, subsequently a chapel dedicated to S Gregorio. Courtesy of Staatsgalerie, Stuttgart.

Fig. 17   Milan, S Aquilino at S Lorenzo.

Fig. 18   Milan, S Ippolito at S Lorenzo.

Fig. 19   Milan, S Sisto at S Lorenzo.

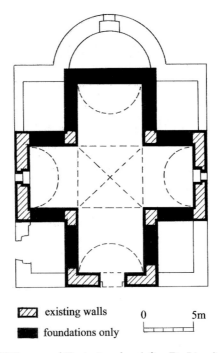

██ existing walls   0   5m

██ foundations only

Fig. 20   Verona, SS Tosca and Teuteria, plan (after Da Lisca).

Fig. 21   Verona, SS Tosca e Teuteria, exterior from south.

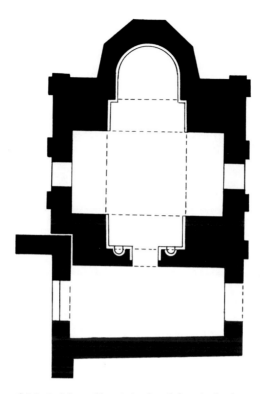

Fig. 22   Vicenza, S Maria Mater Domini, plan (after Arslan).

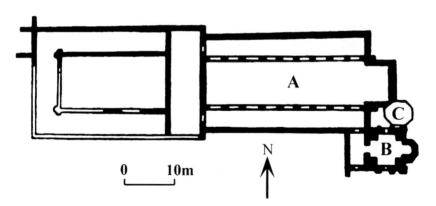

Fig. 23   Vicenza, SS Felice e Fortunato complex, plan (after Krautheimer).
A – SS Felice e Fortunato; B – S Maria Mater Domini; C – possible site of funerary chapel.

Fig. 24   Vicenza, S Maria Mater Domini, Mosaic, Lion of St Mark.

Fig. 25   Vicenza, S Maria Mater Domini, mosaic, saint.

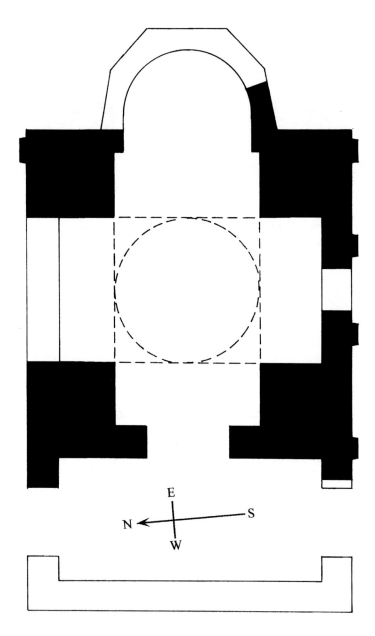

Fig. 26   Padua, S Prosdocimo, plan (after Arslan).

Fig. 27   Padua, S Prosdocimo, interior.

Fig. 28   Padua, S Prosdocimo. Tympanum with Opilio inscription.

Fig. 29   Padua, S Prosdocimo. Plaque: Bishop Prosdocimus.

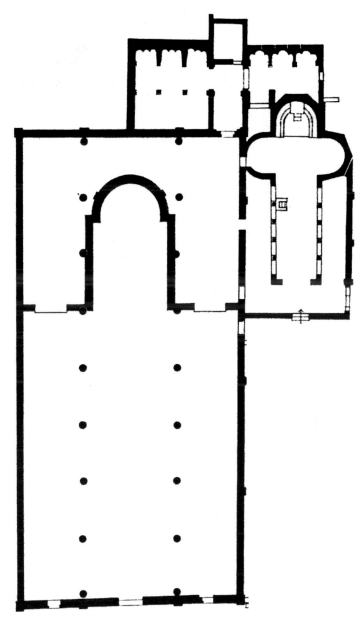

Fig. 30   Concordia, plan of the Early Christian Complex (after Furlan).

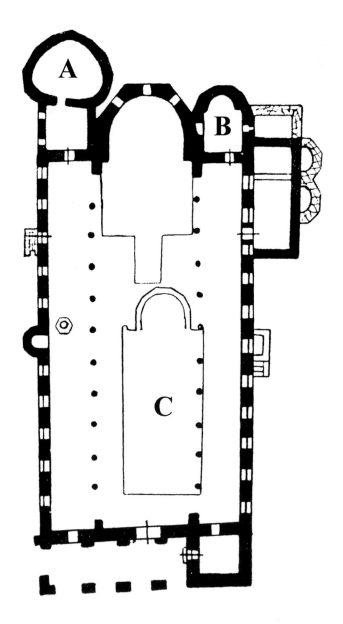

Fig. 31   Grado, S Eufemia, plan (after Zovatto). A – Trichora; B – 'Sacristy Chapel'; C – original church on site.

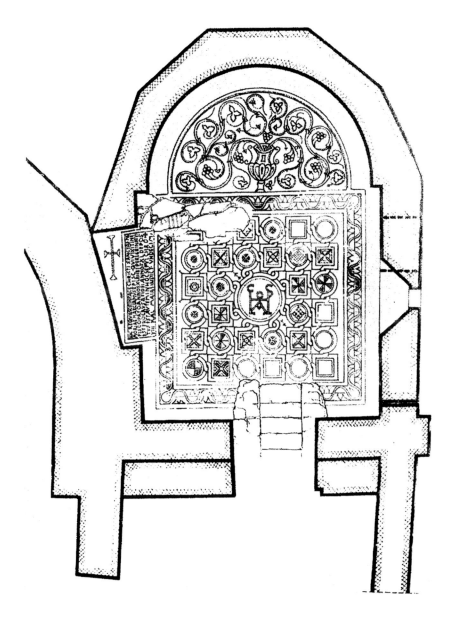

Fig. 32   S Eufemia, 'Sacristy Chapel,' floor mosaics. Grave of Bishop Marcianus
on L, monogram of Elia in centre (after Zovatto).

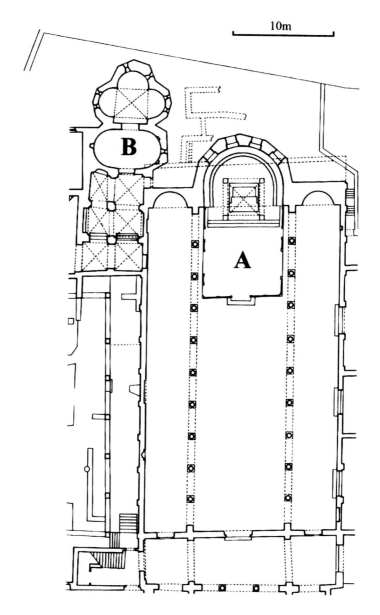

Fig. 33   Poreč, Basilica Eufrasiana, plan (after Prelog). A – basilica; B – Chapel
of S Andrea.

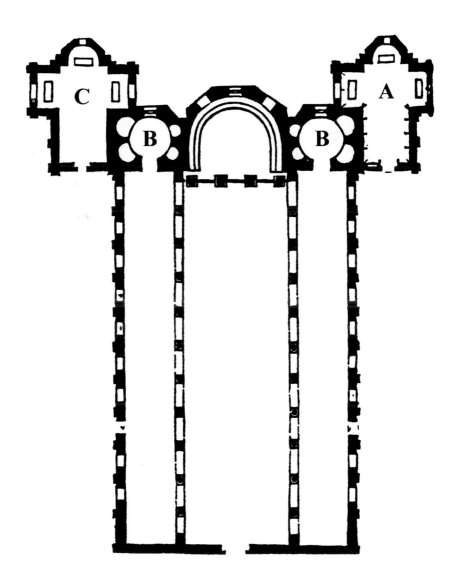

Fig. 34   Pula, S Maria Formosa, plan (after Kandler). A – Chapel of S Maria del
Canneto (or Formosa); B – sacristy chapels; C – Chapel of St Andrew.

Fig. 35   S Maria del Canneto, from south.

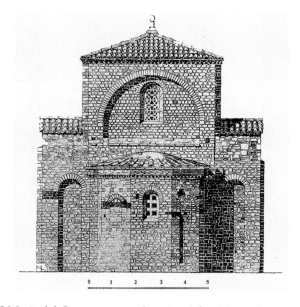

Fig. 36   S Maria del Canneto, apse elevation (after Morassi).

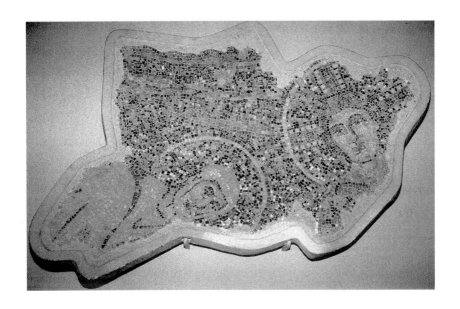

Fig. 37 Apse mosaic, fragment, Christ and Peter, from S Maria del Canneto, Pula.

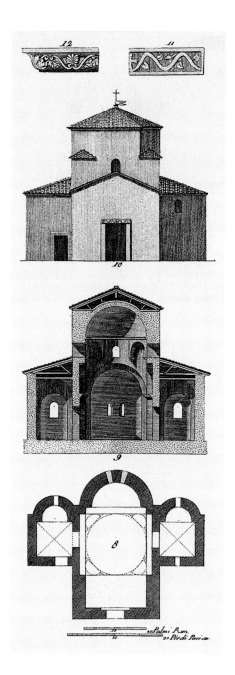

Fig. 38 Pula, S Caterina, exterior; section; plan; architectural details (after Seroux d'Agincourt, 1825).

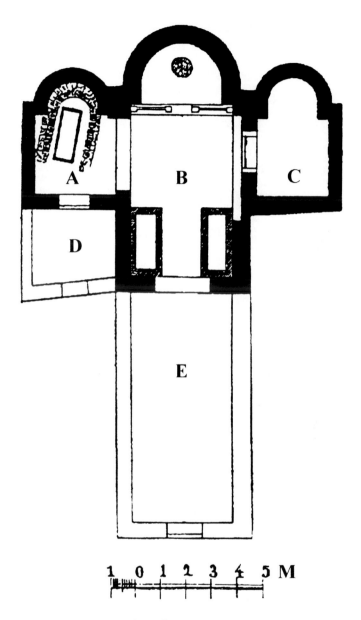

Fig. 39   Pula, S Caterina, plan of 1910 excavations. A, C, – side chapels;
B – nave; D and E – later additions (after Gnirs, 1911).

Fig. 40   Split, Diocletian's Mausoleum.

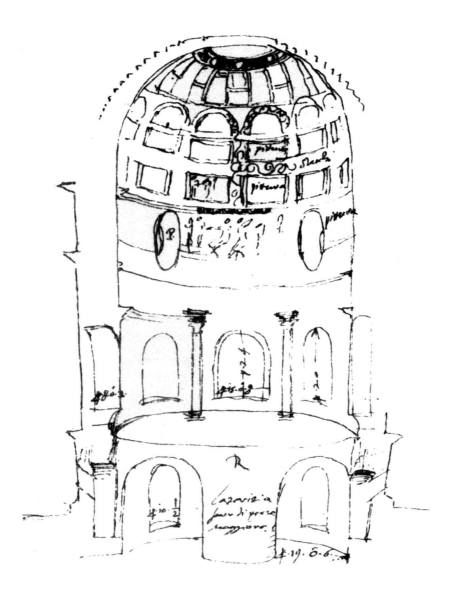

Fig. 41   Rome, Baldasarre Peruzzi, Tor de Schiavi, Gabinetto disegni e stampe degli Uffizi, A 668 (detail). Photo courtesy of the Uffizi Gallery, Florence.

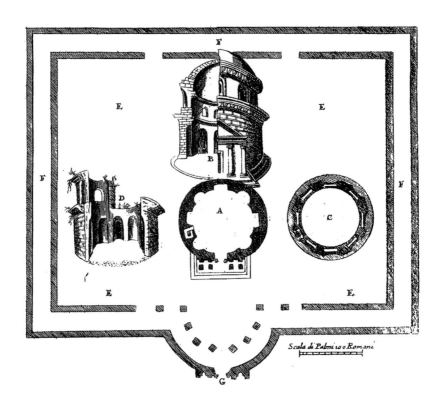

Fig. 42   Mausoleum of Helena (after Bosio, 1632).

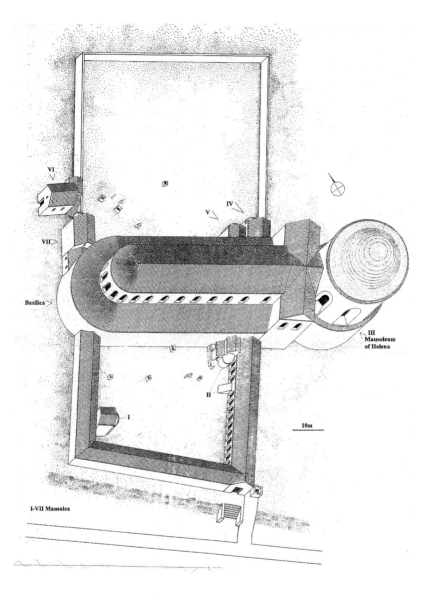

Fig. 43   Mausoleum of Helena at the Basilica of Sts Peter and Marcellinus on the Via Labicana, Rome, plan (courtesy of Guyon). III – Helena's mausoleum; VII – Chapel of St Tiburtius.

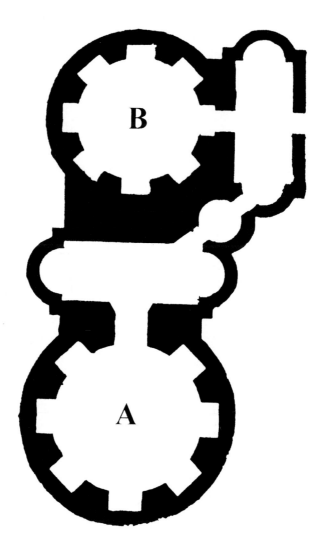

Fig. 44 Plan of imperial mausolea at St Peter's, ca. 1514, by an anonymous
Italian artist. A – Vatican Rotunda, later S Andrea; B – Mausoleum of Honorius,
later S Petronilla. Redrawn after UA 4336, courtesy of the Uffizi Gallery,
Florence.

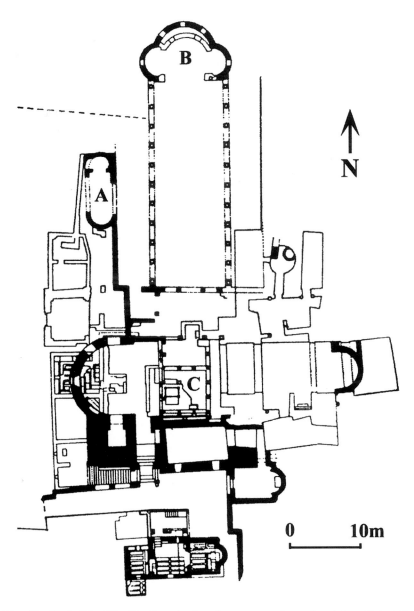

Fig. 45 Nola-Cimitile, Paulinus's churches, excavation plan (after Chierici).
A – chapel; B – apse of Basilica Apostolorum C – Shrine of St Felix.

Fig. 46   Rome, S Stefano Rotondo, Chapel of Sts Primus and Felicianus, apse mosaic.

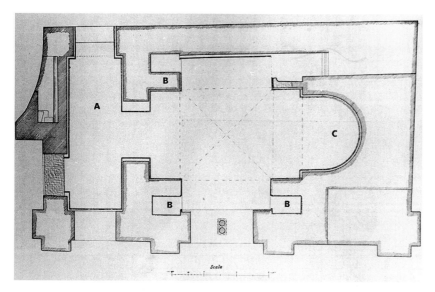

Fig. 47   Ravenna, Archbishops' Chapel, plan (after Gerola). A – narthex;
B – cupboards; C – apse.

Fig. 48   Ravenna, Archbishops' Chapel, narthex with mosaics and dedicatory
inscription.

Fig. 49   Ravenna, Archbishops' Chapel, main vault.

Fig. 50   Ravenna, Archbishops' Chapel, interior, view towards apse.

Fig. 51   Milan, S Vittore in Ciel d'Oro, dome: St Victor (after Wilpert). Courtesy
of the Pontificio Istituto di Archeologia Cristiana, Rome.

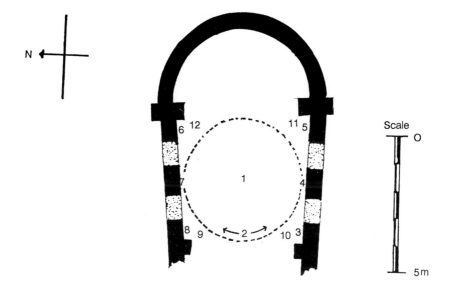

N ←

Scale

0

5 m

Location of the Mosaics

1. Victor
2. frieze
3. Protase
4. Ambrose
5. Gervase
6. Nabor
7. Maternus
8. Fellx
9-12. Evangelist symbols and portraits.

Fig. 52 Milan, S Vittore in Ciel d'Oro, plan (redrawn after Reggiori).

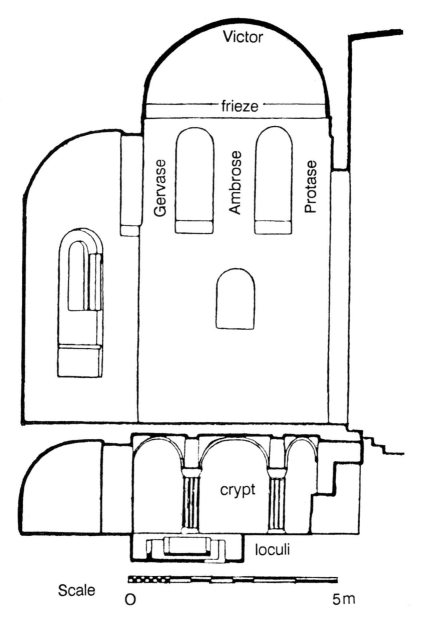

Fig. 53   Milan, S Vittore in Ciel d'Oro, section (redrawn after Landriani).

Fig. 54   Milan, S Vittore in Ciel d'Oro, mosaic frieze of dome (after Wilpert).

Fig. 55   Milan, S Vittore in Ciel d'Oro, view of dome and upper walls with saints.

Fig. 56   Milan, S Vittore in Ciel d'Oro, St Ambrose (after Wilpert).

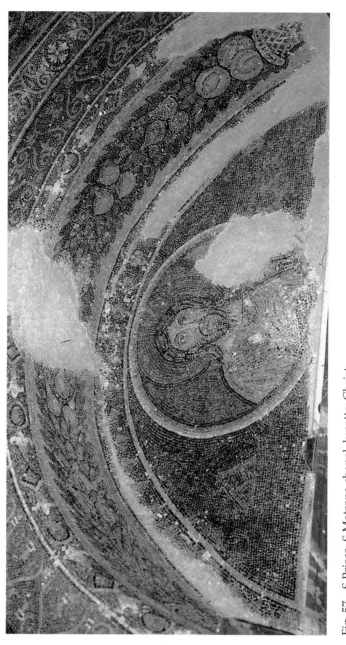

Fig. 57 S Prisco, S Matrona chapel, lunette: Christ.

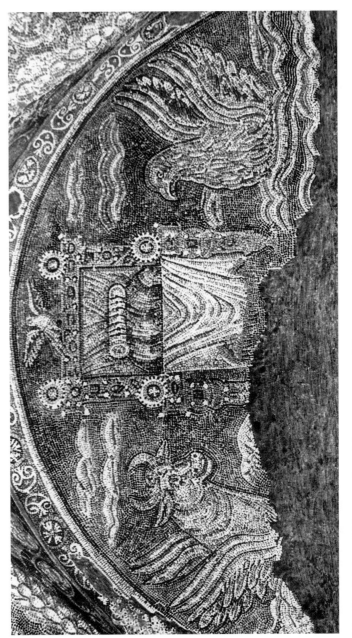

Fig. 58   S Prisco, S Matrona chapel, lunette: prepared throne, ox and eagle.

Fig. 59   S Prisco, S Matrona chapel, symbol of St Matthew.

Fig. 60   S Prisco, S Matrona chapel, M. Monachus engraving. Photo courtesy
Biblioteca Apostolica Vaticana.

Fig. 61   S Prisco, S Matrona chapel, groin of vault with palm tree and partial oculus.

Fig. 62 Naples, Catacomb of S Gennaro, funerary portrait of Quodvultdeus, Bishop of Carthage.

Fig. 63   S Prisco, apse mosaic of the basilica, M. Monachus engraving. Photo courtesy Biblioteca Apostolica Vaticana.

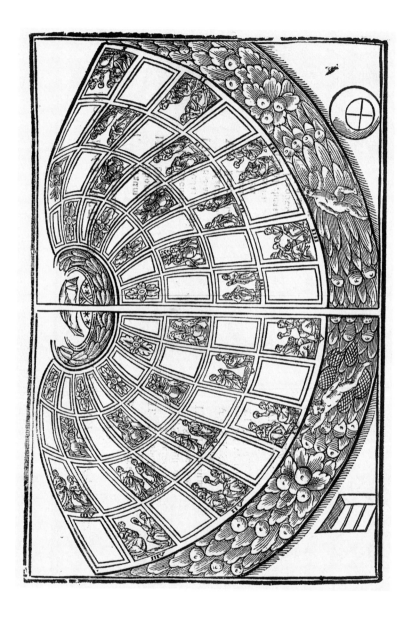

Fig. 64   S Prisco, dome mosaic of the basilica, M. Monachus engraving. Photo courtesy Biblioteca Apostolica Vaticana.

Fig. 65   Rome, S Costanza. Exterior.

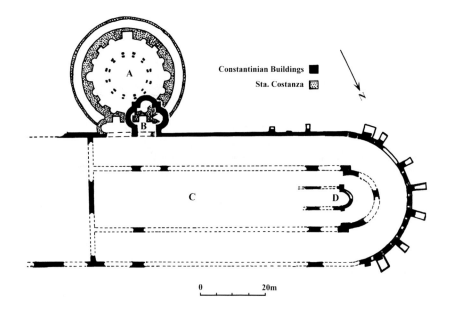

Constantinian Buildings ■
Sta. Costanza ▨

A

B

C

D

N

0   20m

Fig. 66   Rome, plan of Cemetery Basilica of Sant'Agnese with 'trichora' and
S Costanza.

Fig. 67   Rome, view of S Agnese and S Costanza in 1910. Photo courtesy of the
Archivio fotografico dei Musei Vaticani.

Fig. 68   S Costanza, atrium area to R of main entry: site of excavations.

Fig. 69   S Costanza, interior. Photo Sansaini, neg. 54.52, courtesy of the Deutsches
Archaeologisches Institut, Rome.

Fig. 70   S Costanza, section, Anonymous Destailleur, ca. 1500. Photo courtesy of Staatliche Museen zu Berlin-Preussischer Kulturbesitz Kunstbibliothek.

Fig. 71 S Costanza, part of decoration of dome, watercolour of Francesco d'Ollanda (after Wilpert). L to R: Tobias and the Fish; Lot and the Angels at the Gates of Sodom; Susanna and the Angels; The Offerings of Cain and Abel.

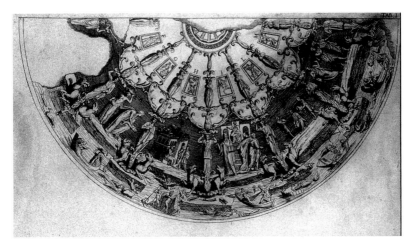

Fig. 72 S Costanza, Dome Mosaics (after Ciampini).

Fig. 73   S Costanza, ambulatory mosaics: vintaging.

Fig. 74   S Costanza, ambulatory mosaics. L to R: paradise imagery; cupids and psyches; vintaging.

Fig. 75   S Costanza, ambulatory mosaics: towards entryway.

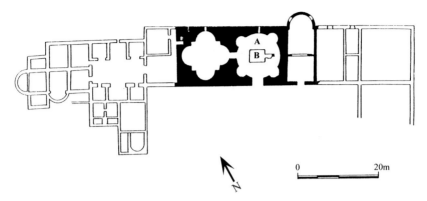

Fig. 76 Centcelles, plan of mausoleum and adjacent villa (after Schlunk and Hauschild, as redrawn by Johnson). A – funerary chamber; B – crypt.

Fig. 77 Centcelles, exterior from north.

Fig. 78   Centcelles, mosaics of the vault.

Fig. 79 Centcelles, mosaics and paintings: hunting scenes below, Christian scenes above. Lower centre: wall painting of female figure.

Fig. 80 Centcelles, mosaic detail: the patron and his companions.

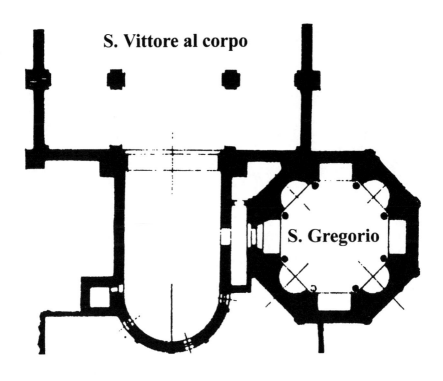

Fig. 81 Milan, S Gregorio at S Vittore al Corpo, plan (after Mirabella Roberti).

Fig. 82   Milan, S Aquilino, atrium. Mosaic patriarchs (after Chierici).

Fig. 83   Milan, S Aquilino, Mosaic: Christ and his apostles.

Fig. 84   Toulouse, La Daurade, section and plan, Jacques Martin, *La religion des Gaulois* (Paris, 1727) (after Jules de Lahondès, *Les monuments de Toulouse*, 1920, courtesy Éditions Privat, Toulouse).

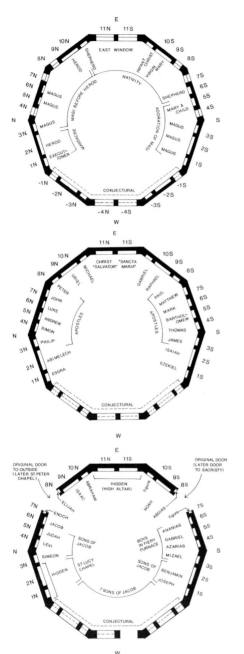

Fig. 85　La Daurade, upper tier of mosaics, layout (A. Murphy).

Fig. 86　La Daurade, middle tier of mosaics, layout (A. Murphy).

Fig. 87　La Daurade, lower tier of mosaics, layout (A. Murphy).

Fig. 88   Ravenna, Mausoleum of Theoderic, aerial view.

Fig. 89   Ravenna, Mausoleum of Theoderic, reconstruction of exterior (after Buchkremer).

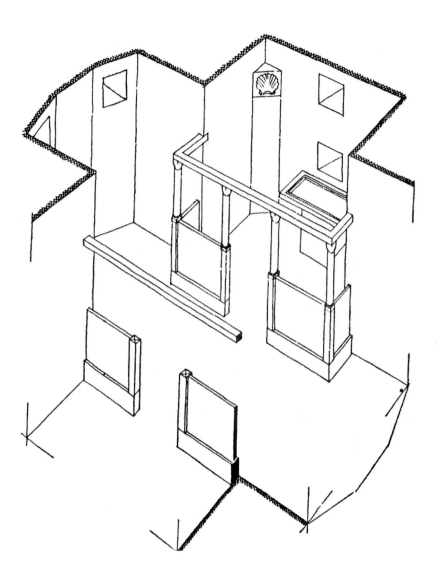

Fig. 90   Ravenna, Mausoleum of Theoderic, lower chamber with furnishings
proposed by De Angelis d'Ossat.

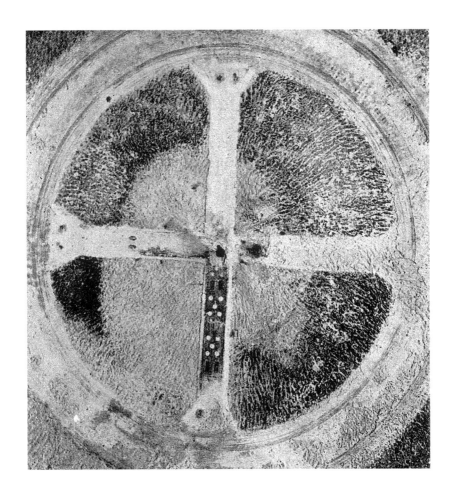

Fig. 91   Ravenna, Mausoleum of Theoderic: upper chamber, *Crux gemmata* on vault.

Fig. 92   Ravenna, Mausoleum of Theoderic, upper chamber with furnishings proposed by De Angelis d'Ossat.

Fig. 93 Ravenna, Mausoleum of Galla Placidia, exterior.

Fig. 94   Ravenna, Mausoleum of Galla Placidia, mosaics of the vault.

Fig. 95   Ravenna, Mausoleum of Galla Placidia, east arm lunette, deer drinking
from Rivers of Paradise.

Fig. 96 Ravenna, Mausoleum of Galla Placidia, south lunette, saint running to martyrdom.

Fig. 97   Ravenna, Mausoleum of Galla Placidia, north lunette, Christ as Good
Shepherd.

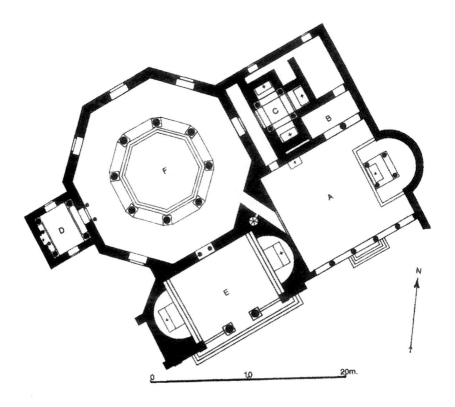

Fig. 98 Rome, Lateran Baptistery Complex, plan (after De Rossi, following Rohault de Fleury). A – S Venanzio Chapel; B – site of St Stephen's Chapel; C – S Giovanni Evangelista; D – S Giovanni Battista; E – portico, with SS Ruffina e Secunda in right apse; F – baptistery.

Fig. 99   Vault mosaic, S Giovanni Evangelista *in Laterano*.

Fig. 100   Vault and lunette design of S Giovanni Battista (after Ciampini).

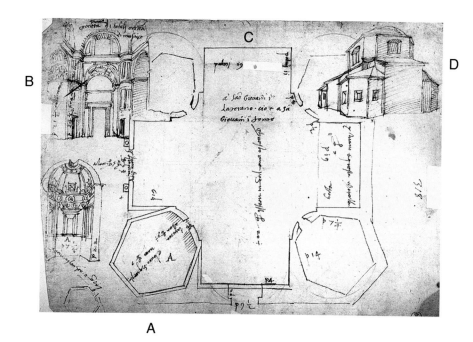

B

C

D

A

Fig. 101   S Croce, ground plan and 3 views, Baldasarre Peruzzi, S Croce *in Laterano*, Galleria degli Uffizi, Florence, U438A. Photo courtesy of the Uffizi Gallery. A – interior, corner chapel, also marked 'A' on the plan; B – interior of main room, facing entry; C – plan; D – exterior.

Cana

Fig. 102   S Croce, interior, from Antonio Lafréri, *Speculum Romanae magnificentiae*, Rome, 1568. Photo courtesy of the Pontificia Commissione di Archaeologia Sacra, Rome.

Fig. 103   Santa Croce, interior, entry wall and vault, Giuliano da Sangallo.
Photo courtesy of Biblioteca Apostolica Vaticana.

Fig. 104 Chapel of SS Ruffina e Secunda at the Lateran Baptistery, apse mosaic.

Fig. 105   Tarquinia, Tomba del Cacciatore, interior. Courtesy of the soprintendenza archeologica per l'Etruria meridionale.

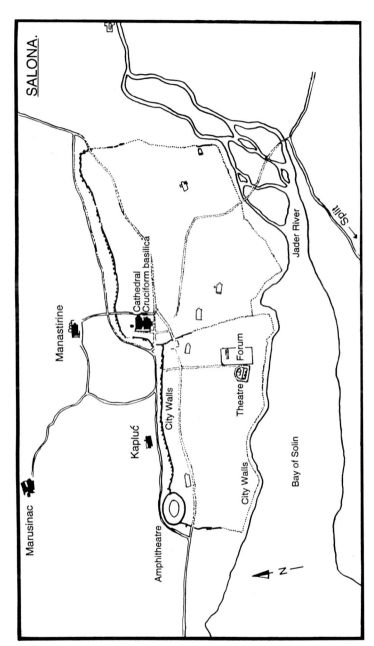

SALONA.

Marusinac

Manastirine

Kapluć

Cathedral
Cruciform basilica

City Walls

Amphitheatre

Theatre

Forum

City Walls

Bay of Solin

Jader River

Split →

N

Fig. 106   Plan of Salona (after Bulić and Dyggve, as edited by Marin).

Fig. 107　S Venanzio Chapel, altar wall, during renovations. Photo courtesy of the Archivio fotografico dei Musei Vaticani.

Fig. 108 Salona, east gladiator chapel in amphitheatre: saints (after Nikolajević, following Dyggve).

Fig. 109   Portal of S Giovanni Battista at the Lateran Baptistery, Rome.

Fig. 110   Mosaic floor of St Stephen's, the Chapel on the Corso Garibaldi in Ancona (after De Rossi).

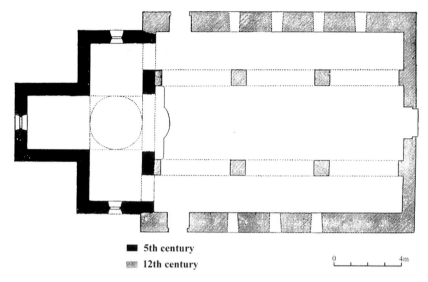

0   4m

Fig. 111   Plan of S Maria della Croce at Casaranello, Puglia. Original 5th-century chapel, truncated, with 13th- and 14th-century nave and aisles (after Bartoccini).

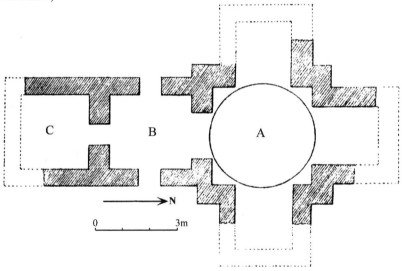

Fig. 112   Camerana, near Siracusa, Sicily, chapel known locally as Bagno de Mare (after Orsi). A – domed central chamber; B and C – vaulted rooms.

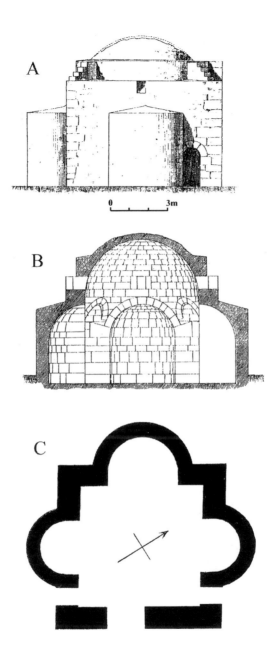

Fig. 113 Trigona di Maccari, near Siracusa. Plan, elevation, and interior (after Orsi).

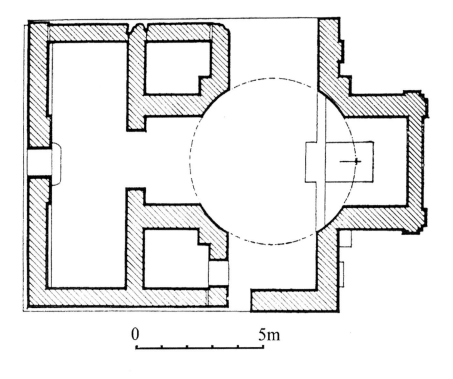

0   5m

Fig. 114   Rimini, S Andrea, plan (after Tonini).

received information, probably in the form of sketches, about the physical appearance of the saints, based on their pictures in the shrines at their place of martyrdom. Despite their dematerialized style, in Rome each saint is individualized through close attention to rank, colour, and ornament, and these images have come to be used as paradigms of seventh-century costume. For example, although the four palace guards are of necessity identically clothed in sumptuous uniforms, they are sharply individual in face, hair colour, and complexion.[42] The S Venanzio mosaics suggest that the models in Salona had already developed a separate iconography for each saint.

The S Venanzio chapel is the most fully dated and documented martyr chapel to survive complete with relics and a major part of its decoration. It is therefore one of the best sites at which to explore the attitude of the papacy and the church to relics in the mid-seventh century, a time of change and uncertainty. Obviously, in the particular circumstances of danger that surrounded the translation of the Dalmatian saints, it was acceptable to move the relics and to honour them with a magnificent new chapel in the pope's own establishment at the Lateran. However, very soon afterwards a translation occurred within the peaceful milieu of Rome itself. We have already seen that John IV's successor, Theodore I (642–9), who had shared the patronage of the S Venanzio chapel and like John was of Eastern origin, built a funerary chapel for his father, Bishop Theodore of Jerusalem, which was inside the Roman church of S Stefano Rotondo. The chapel was sanctified with the remains of two saints translated from the Roman catacombs, Primus and Felicianus, thus providing an *ad sanctos* burial for the bishop.[43] This is the first time that such a translation is recorded in Rome, and the circumstances have important elements in common with the S Venanzio chapel: most important, perhaps, the participation of Pope Theodore I; the translation itself (here from mile 14 of the Via Nomentana); and the honouring of a pope's father. Evidently, the crucial break with tradition took place at the S Venanzio chapel, rather than the chapel of Saints Primus and Felicianus at S Stefano Rotondo. However, the translations of saints' relics at these two chapels set a pattern which would be followed by many more and, indeed, was to become standard practice.

The circumstances of the pagan conquest of Dalmatia have been shrouded in mystery, as has the actual nature of the relics in the S Venanzio chapel. These are called *reliquias* in the early sources. When they were rehoused in 1698, however, they were described as *corpora*

on the lead cover of their casket. The casket occupies a small sarcophagus inside the altar of the S Venanzio chapel. What exactly was meant
by *reliquias* and *corpora* as applied to these martyrs, and what form did
the relics that John IV honoured in his chapel take? How available to
relic hunters were the bones of the saints in Dalmatia, and how acceptable was it at that time to move them from one place to another? Were
there guidelines governed by the needs of the saint, of the congregation, or of the church hierarchy that determined what might be done in
the way of translations? Did the acceptability of translation depend on
the motivation of the mover, with service to one's own purposes in
building a place of prayer or burial for oneself perhaps contrasting
with service to the martyr, the protection of his or her remains from
danger? Was the moving of remains complicated by the desire of those
who owned them not to lose their powerful *praesentia* and power for
good,[44] a question particularly apposite in the case of the patrons of
important cities such as Domnius and Maurus?

Much confusion has been generated by the belief that the word *reliquias* of the *Liber Pontificalis* statement must refer to *reliquias ad corpora*
or corporeal relics, bodies or bones of saints, for if Abbot Martinus took
the actual bodies of the saints to Rome around 641, then obviously
their homelands were deprived of them, providing, that is, that at least
in the West saints' bodies were not being dismembered and distrib-
uted in pieces as relics.[45] Our authority for this supposition is the papal
correspondence of a half-century earlier, which reacted to requests
from the rulers in Byzantium for corporeal relics of the apostles Peter
and Paul. As early as 519, the papal legate in Constantinople had
responded to a request by Justinian for relics of the apostles and St
Lawrence by asking Pope Hormisdas to send contact relics, objects that
had been in contact with the tombs of the saints, rather than corporeal
relics, and Justinian was told that it was contrary to Roman custom to
provide bodily relics of the saints.[46] A second instance, much closer to
the date of the S Venanzio chapel, is Gregory the Great's reply to the
request of Constantina, wife of the Byzantine emperor, for the head of
St Paul to sanctify a chapel she had built.[47] He told her that it was
totally contrary to Roman custom to disturb the bones of the saints,
and that he neither could, nor did he dare to do so, because of the danger of such intervention, which he illustrated graphically with examples. Indeed, he continued, one ought not to dare even to look at the
bodies of the saints. Instead, new relics could be created by placing
cloths by the body in the tomb. Relics so created were as powerful as

the saints' bodies themselves and were used for the same purpose, for the sanctification of altars.[48]

There has always been some doubt about whether this letter should be taken at face value, or whether Gregory was exaggerating the position of Rome so as to justify refusing an imperial request that the papacy relinquish the major relics that were central to its power. Does this letter, then, reflect actual practice in the West, as Gregory seems to claim? McCulloh has examined Gregory's correspondence and his *Dialogues*, to discover his attitudes to translations or dismemberments of saints' bodies, attitudes which might contradict the position he takes in his letter to Constantina.[49] He found many references to tombs and burials, but only a single reference to a translation, that of St Donatus, whose remains were carried away by the bishop and congregation of Euria in 603–4, when invaders forced them to flee their homes.[50] Gregory granted them permission to bury the saint's body in their camp and return for it when things returned to normal. This, the only place where Gregory mentions a translation, is comparable to the situation in Salona in the early seventh century, where saints were exhumed and reburied in safer places in times of emergency by their own congregations. The action was at least partly altruistic, the aim being to save the remains from loss or desecration during times of exceptional danger. On the other hand, earlier Salona practice suggests that the saints' remains could be disturbed for no better reason than to provide new and grander settings for them, perhaps in association with a bishop's burial *ad sanctos*. The bodies were also disturbed when their shrines were consolidated and made more secure. However, the primary service was to the saint in all these cases, and there is no record of the evil consequences that Gregory reports from Rome as sequels to the disturbance of the bodies of the saints. We know that practice differed from one place to another even in the West: for example, St Ambrose moved saints' bodies into Milan from Lodi, as well as disinterring the bodies of saints Gervasius and Protasius, which he discovered in the chapel of Nabor and Felix in the Coemeterium ad Martyres in Milan. He intended to use the relics to sanctify the altar of the church he was building, which would later become S Ambrogio. Ambrose tells of his apprehension at doing so, though, in a letter to his sister Marcellina.[51] On the question of 'relics' (such as those of the Salona martyrs whose *reliquias*, we are told, were put in the S Venanzio chapel), the texts of Gregory confirm that *reliquias* had two distinct meanings: parts of a saint's body, corporeal relics, and contact relics such as *brandea*, cloths which had been saturated with the holiness of proximity to a saint's remains. Since Gregory deplored the dangerous practice of touching a saint's body, while admitting that the Greeks allowed it, he was left with contact relics, which could be created and were as holy and powerful as the bodies themselves, to use on all occasions that required sanctification or the special protection and blessing of the saints. This then was the position around the turn of the seventh century: translations were rare and undertaken only in unusual circumstances; *reliquias* meant contact relics much more often than corporeal fragments.

The question of what exact form the relics of the Dalmatian saints took acquires new importance in this context, as evidence of papal attitudes that would either agree with Gregory's official position or disprove it. The interval of just under forty years is not long, and it would seem unlikely that papal policy would have changed in the interval. The ingredients for a physical transfer of bodies were there: a time of great danger when the saints' remains might have been lost or desecrated. Discussion of the contents of the relic container in the S Venanzio chapel has until recently been hampered by lack of tangible evidence. Consensus of opinion from the late Middle Ages through the Renaissance was that the actual bodies – *corpora* – were present in the chapel. According to the inscription on the lead cover of the casket[52] to which the remains, in their cherrywood box, were transferred in 1698, as well as to the words of Panvinio (1570), the ten bodies were physically present.[53] There was a recognition ceremony in 1713, but apparently no records were kept. Bulić, despite repeated efforts through his long life, was denied permission to investigate the contents of the casket. It was not until 1962 that the ecclesiastical authorities agreed to another recognition of the relics. The sealed reliquary was opened and the contents examined at the request of the bishops of Split and Poreč.[54] Surprisingly, the box contained less than a half-kilogram of small bones, both human and animal, plus dust and two small, illegible Byzantine coins. There were no documents. The relics included neither skulls nor long bones. It seems very unlikely that all the major bones were formerly there and then given away as relics. We are forced to the conclusion that Abbot Martinus brought back either tiny corporeal relics, contact relics such as *brandea*, soil or dust from the tombs, or even animal bones gathered up in ignorance from the ruined shrines, which were pillaged during the barbarian invasions, probably after being emptied of relics by the fleeing Christians. In such unsettled conditions, nothing outside the walls was safe, and archaeologists found very few of the numerous large stone sarcophagi in the Salona cemeteries to be intact.[55] In these circumstances, it is obvious that the martyrs' remains were taken to safety by the retreating population, either to Aspalathos (Split), to Iader (Zadar), or to the islands off the Dalmatian coast, which remained under Roman control and were administered from Iader for Ravenna as the Theme of Dalmatia.[56]

It has recently been proposed that the fall of Salona, far from happening soon after the last recorded burial at Salona in 612, took place only a year or two before the accession of John IV. John's delegation, it will be remembered, was charged with a double mission. It was not only to rescue the relics of the saints but to ransom Christian prisoners from the invaders. Ivan Marović has pointed out that prisoners taken soon after 612 are unlikely to have survived almost three decades until 640, so as to have needed ransom then.[57] The existence of the prisoners in 640 in fact implies that they were captured not long before this date, that is, not much earlier than 630. The entire period during which Salona could have fallen to the Avars was covered by the reign of Heraclius (610–41). For this reason Marović has analysed the distribution of coins of Heraclius found in Salona. He concluded that commerce continued to take place at Salona long after 614, the date previously suggested for its destruction, and that the city was therefore still inhabited after that date. The latest coin in a hoard found in a water drain of a Late Antique complex of buildings at Solin (Salona) in 1979 is dated to 630–1.[58] Although this evidence cannot be used to give a *terminus post quem* for the fall of Salona, as Marović suggests, the presence of this scatter of Heraclian coins, some from late in the reign, does imply that there was occupation of the site at least until well into the 620s. In support of this, a recent topographical analysis of the account of the fall of Salona in Constantine Porphyrogenitos's *De Administrando Imperio* has suggested a date of 626 for the fall of the city.[59] Its end may have come even later than this, if prisoners were still awaiting ransom in 642.

Abbot Martinus then would have found a dispersed Christian community on the islands and in Aspalathos, and the martyrs reinterred in new and safer surroundings. This would explain the enduring belief of the Croatians that they have, and have always had, the bones of their martyrs in the cathedral at Split. The Parentines' beliefs about Maurus's relics would likewise be vindicated.

So the S Venanzio chapel was probably sanctified with contact relics. These were tokens of the saints whose spiritual power they represented and symbols of the beleaguered churches across the Adriatic which, till then, had always been within the sphere of influence of Rome. The presence of these relics of the Istrian and Dalmatian martyrs and of their 'authentic' portraits in Rome guaranteed they would protect, assist, and intercede for the pious souls who had installed them there. Moreover, invisible threads of contact across the Adriatic were forged, which bound Istria and Dalmatia mystically to Rome, just as the images themselves looked West into the heart of the city, where all roads led, and where the pope was the vicar of Christ on earth. The political implications of this are clear: the mosaic is a statement that as the Illyrian saints looked to and protected Rome, so would the papacy care for Christians in the beleaguered homelands across the sea, which indeed have remained within the orbit of Rome until the present day.

The S Venanzio chapel owes its clarity of purpose to the fact that it was founded as a *martyrium* in the sense of a chapel built for the housing of relics of the martyrs which have been gathered into a central shrine for veneration. Because it fulfilled this purpose from the beginning, its original documentation remains fully relevant. This type of *martyrium*, though, seems to have been a late development in the evolution of the martyr shrine or *cella memoriae*. To sum up, the earliest of all these shrines were built over the actual gravesites of the saints or, less commonly, at the places of their martyrdoms or of episodes in their passions or at other sites which are closely connected with their life histories. Salona is rich in examples of all these types of shrines. The earliest were clearly *cellae memoriae*, comparable to the surviving early-fifth-century S Vittore in Ciel d'Oro in Milan, the most complete and well-documented surviving example of a shrine raised over a martyr's grave. Such chapels did not go unnoticed by those who sought a holy and powerful burial place for their own use, and the Early Christian shrines were favourite sites for the graves of pious Christians, who clustered around the saints in death as they had in life. The grave of St Peter on the Vatican Hill is a famous early example of this development, while the burial of Satyrus, brother of St Ambrose beside St Victor in S Vittore in Ciel d'Oro is a well-documented example of burial *ad sanctos*, burial beside the saints. Such burials are also known from Salona, where we find St Anastasius buried in the private funerary chapel of the noble lady Asclepia and her husband, who by this action not only honoured and benefited the saint, but also reserved his spiritual power and presence for themselves, to help them at the threshold of heaven. Clerics also chose this option, and we know that the sarcophagi of at least four early Salonitan bishops were placed beside the graves of martyrs.[60] The building of a basilica at Kapljuć illustrates another stage in the evolution of the martyr shrine: recognition that the cult has so grown that provision must be made at the graveside for the crowds of devotees. There is, however, a third stage illustrated in Salona in the journey towards the type of *martyrium* represented by the S Venanzio chapel. This is the choice of a martyr's *memoria*, which may or may not also be the funerary chapel of one or more important lay-people or clerics, as the central location to which other holy relics are brought, perhaps from the whole region surrounding the shrine. This consolidation also occurred at Salona, where the martyrs' bodies were gathered together in small, secure shrines at the suburban cemeteries. This has been interpreted until now as an early-fifth-century response to insecure times, when the great cemetery churches were destroyed by the Goths and the Huns. However, it also fits in with developments elsewhere in the sixth century, when regulations concerning the moving of the saints' bodies seem to have been altered in connection with the need for relics to use in the consecration of altars. The insecurity of the graveyards must have gone along with the changing image of the relic, which, as it lost its dread reputation as a dangerous and untouchable talisman, became an object of enormous commercial value. An almost limitless market developed as more and more churches were built, especially in the newly Christian lands north of the Alps, and as altars also proliferated, each one in need of a fragment of a saint for consecration. The way was open for development of trade in relics, fed from both legal and illegal sources, among the latter theft from the suburban cemeteries.[61]

So we see that the S Venanzio chapel, far from being a simple shrine built to house and revere the relics of the Dalmatian and Istrian saints which had been brought from afar, was in fact the last in an orderly and logical series of shrines commemorating this group of saints. Starting with local, small-scale veneration in their homelands, their cults grew and prospered and evolved through all the stages of such shrines: the *cella memoriae*, the funerary chapel with burial beside the saints, the shrine with added accommodation for pilgrims and devotees, the memorial chapel at the scene of martyrdom, and the full-blown regional *martyrium*. This last probably rose at Salona, not long before the final destruction of the city in the early seventh century. It may be identified as the cruciform basilica, which was raised beside the cathedral in the mid-sixth century (fig. 106) and which was probably dedicated to the cult of relics. It was at this point that chance provided both an expatriate pope, John IV, with the means and the will to save and commemorate these martyrs, and a homeland so changed forever by the invasions that its capital city would never rise again from its ruins. This has allowed the rediscovery of tangible memorials of its saints, which link their deaths, graves, and memorials to the S Venanzio chapel in Rome forever.

CHAPTER TEN

The Chapel Revisited: A Synthesis

The information that has been gathered here, fragmentary though much of it is, has the potential to give a picture of the furnished chapel as it must have looked and functioned in its own time. The case studies of individual chapels which have survived in a more or less complete form have been set into a context of information about the distribution of chapels in the capital cities of the empire as well as the smaller centres; of chapels that are still extant and those that are lost. Chapels that survive below ground in the Roman catacombs or in archaeological sites elsewhere exemplify those that have failed to survive in the cemeteries above ground. The exteriors of chapel buildings, the walls and roofs, the doors and portals, the windows with their traceries, have all been discussed, together with the interiors, with their brightly polished marble revetments, their pavements of mosaic in durable stone, and their upper walls and domes clad in the brilliance of glass mosaics. It remains to explore the built-in furnishings, which have almost always been lost in campaigns of refurbishment, but can be visualized from the few that do survive, and the portable treasures, recorded in the gift lists of many of the early medieval popes, as well as in early texts and chronicles, such as the ninth-century Ravenna *Liber Pontificalis* of Andrea Agnellus. Finally, we will consider here the interface between chapels and the outside world as expressed in doors and windows and their surrounds.

The almost total lack of contemporary written documentation for the chapels considered here has obliged us to analyse all the other sources of information that might throw light on the function and meaning of each building. Among these are the lists of gifts given to Roman churches and chapels by individual popes, as recorded in their biographies, which, while not contemporary with the earliest of the popes, are based on the original documents which once recorded their expenditures but are now lost.[1] The architecture itself is equally informative, as are surviving inscriptions, as well as others which are known from the records of antiquarians and travellers. But above all, each chapel's decorative program is a rich source of information. Architectural sculptures have been considered along with both paintings and mosaics. The superior durability of mosaic over wall painting has given it a better chance of survival, though early restorations may be hard to distinguish from the original. The presence of mosaic, the most expensive of artistic media, in itself suggests the highest level of artistic patronage, and slants the resulting survey towards a group of chapels which includes some of the most luxurious and venerated Early Christian shrines ever to be built. These superb examples are the source of a disproportionate amount of our information. The mausolea of the Christian emperors, here considered as funerary chapels at the top level of patronage, also express the almost unlimited resources of the rulers and their families. These mausolea have a different focus from the ordinary chapel: rather than being concerned primarily with the cult of the saints, they express the private aspirations of the ruler himself, the patron. Thus, from their earliest days in the fourth century, they concentrate on the Christian afterlife and salvation, themes which they share with almost all other early Christian burials. In this, they forsake the long tradition whereby the emperor would himself be deified and join the gods in death.

Early Christian chapels have endured the perils of around a millennium-and-a-half of existence, among them war, fire, and earthquake. They have also frequently been subject to rebuilding and renovation, which may have disguised or even destroyed their early medieval characteristics. The hazards of existence in an earthquake zone have favoured the survival of small and stable, vaulted structures built of stone or of brick-faced concrete, while structures built of less durable or more flammable materials have perished, as have many larger structures, such as the basilicas to which the chapels were originally annexed. The surviving chapels were built of expensive materials, and with reason, since almost all of them were associated with the cult of the martyrs and with the funerary cult which sprang up in association with it. No expense was thought to be too great to honour the saints, who could be called upon to protect the individual or the whole community. The wish to honour the saints is also the reason why the surviving chapels were maintained and repaired through the centuries, since enthusiasm for the saints and their cults continued unabated. These chapels, which illustrated the presence of the martyrs in their decorations, as well as by the powerful presence of their relics, continued to provide a focus for the devotion of Christians to their protectors in a dangerous and unstable world. In this devotion it is surely possible to see the beginnings of the custom of pilgrimage, which was to assume such importance in the later Middle Ages.

The random nature of the survival of early chapels, and the special nature of their veneration, have caused there to be a preponderance of examples connected with the cult of the dead: martyr shrines, funerary chapels, and collective martyria, and indeed even among the lost examples which are known to us from archaeology or literary sources, these are in the majority. Private chapels, which are mentioned in passing in the literature, have totally disappeared. Nevertheless, one splendid example of an oratory from a bishops' palace, the Archbishops' Chapel at Ravenna, is still extant, and papal chapels built at the Lateran and the Vatican by various early medieval popes in their role as bishops of Rome, and with no funerary purpose in mind, have been considered here as oratories for the private prayer of clerics and as shrines for relics; other papal foundations at Old St Peter's come into the category of funerary chapels and have been discussed in that context.

The archaeological record is a valuable source of information about the layout of chapel furnishings made of stone. For example, put-holes in the walls of Theoderic's Mausoleum at Ravenna suggested a new and credible interpretation of the interior space to Giuglielmo de Angelis d'Ossat (figs. 90, 92). Evidence for existence of such features as a *pergula* in front of the altar, which would have supported both the hanging lamps and the carved *plutei* which delineated the sacred space around the altar, can be tied in with architectural fragments which may survive in the area surrounding the chapel, or even under its pavement, but detached from their original contexts. An immured *pergula*, for example, was still present in the chapel of S Prosdocimo in Padua and has been restored to its original position (fig. 27); foundations of another were found by archaeologists in the sixth-century remains of S Caterina in the bay at Pula (fig. 39). At the chapel of S Maria Mater Domini in Vicenza a seventeenth-century record preserves the sixth-century donor inscription from a similar *pergula*, and, together with fragments of a *pluteus* slab found beneath the floor, has allowed a convincing reconstruction of the altar enclosure that was destroyed in a Baroque rebuilding. The biography of Pope Gregory III discusses the *pergula* he supplied for his chapel in St Peter's in terms of the lamps and other gifts in gold and silver which it would support. The sarcophagi, ultimate furniture of the deceased, have frequently been the targets of reuse: their provenance, especially in the case of those from the tombs of the emperors, can sometimes be traced, as in the case of the two porphyry sarcophagi from Helena's mausoleum and S Costanza in Rome respectively, which are now in the Vatican Museum. Excavations at other more modestly sized chapels have also given evidence of the sarcophagi with which they were once furnished. The chapel of S Prosdocimo in Padua, for example, contains an Early Christian sarcophagus, reworked in 1564 in Renaissance style, while the catacomb on the Via Latina shows in some of its *cubicula* the way the arcosolia were furnished with the carved front panels of strigillated sarcophagi, which were sometimes isolated from neighbouring burial chambers by low barriers constructed of paired stone lattices, *trabeculae*, framing a central entryway.[2]

Although the written records of papal gifts to the chapels they built are a rich source of evidence about the furnishings of an Early Christian chapel, the portable furnishings that are recorded have almost never survived. For this reason the records in the *Liber Pontificalis* are especially valuable since they provide almost the only evidence that chapels were the recipients of spectacular portable gifts from their patrons. These gifts of furnishings, so proudly listed in detail in the papal biographies, complete with their weight in precious metals, both gold and silver, have not survived the centuries, since their intrinsic value in precious metal and their portability have lured robbers, among them the successive waves of barbarian invaders from the East.[3] The sack of Rome in 455 by the Vandals under Gaiseric, for example, resulted in the loss of all the silver altar vessels from the twenty-five *tituli* or parish churches of Rome. These were replaced by Pope Leo I (440–61), who melted down the weighty silver water jars that Constantine had given to the great Roman basilicas he had founded so as to reuse the metal.[4] Leo's successor, Pope Hilarus (461–8), gave yet more relacements of plate to the churches, but prudently decreed that the silverware should be kept safely at the Lateran or at S Maria Maggiore except when actually in use. But even when these church and chapel furnishings escaped robbery, they sometimes did not survive their fate as a source of wealth to be melted down for coinage in papal emergencies. None of the vessels and ornaments listed in the *Liber Pontificalis* survives today.

The scale of papal munificence, though obvious from the recorded weights, is underlined still further by the listing of the popes' gifts as among their most important achievements. We have already seen that the biography of Pope Hilarus, as one example, recorded the gifts he had given to the three chapels he built at the Lateran Baptistery.[5] To recapitulate, these included *confessiones* weighing 100 pounds of silver each for the two chapels of the saints John, and a third for S Croce of unspecified weight, but having silver doors weighing 50 pounds; from these gifts we can surmise that the display and protection of relics of the saints were one of the primary functions of chapels and that their furnishings reflected this. Each of the two smaller chapels at the Lateran received a golden cross; a third for S Croce, which contained as relic a piece of the wood of the True Cross, was jewelled and weighed 20 pounds. A golden arch above the *confessio* in S Croce weighed four pounds of gold and supported a two-pound golden lamb on onyx columns. It is clear from these records that since the Cross and the Lamb were among the most sacred symbols of Christ's presence within the chapel's interior space, they deserved to be formed of the most precious materials. The S Croce *confessio* was lit by a lamp weighing five pounds of gold, flanked by golden lamps on either side which each weighed two pounds. For the three chapels these gifts totalled in excess of 39 pounds of gold and 250 pounds of silver. Again, the symbolic importance of light as well as the practical needs of illumination of these interiors are inferred. The artificial light provided by lamps and candles not only lit the sacred spaces of the chapel interiors, but streamed out from the traceried windows into the dark surrounding world, providing a beacon and focus of heavenly light for those who were excluded from sharing the microcosm of heaven inside the chapel walls.

The gifts provided by Pope Symmachus at the Vatican for the three chapels he built there, which, like those at the Lateran, were dedicated to the two saints John and to the Cross, also focused on precious relics, and consisted of *confessiones* surmounted by arches: the three chapels received gifts totalling 60 pounds in silver plus a ten-pound golden cross for S Croce.[6] Symmachus also inserted seven chapels into the niches of the imperial mausoleum nearby, expending 599 pounds of silver all told for *confessiones* and arches: there is no mention of lamps or crosses here, but perhaps they were made of cheaper materials such as bronze, since Symmachus had been denied access to the Lateran and may well have been relatively short of money.

Like the presence of a *confessio*, the gifts of communion plate to a chapel signify that an altar was present there. Such an altar may have left no mark because it was portable; on the other hand, the supports for an altar are among the most frequent traces of liturgical use to be detected in the archaeological remains of former chapels: we may cite here the indications of altar posts in the *memoria* of S Vitalis that lies beneath S Vitale in Ravenna. Even the small chapel in the Roman catacombs commemorating the martyr Felicity and her sons, the site where Pope Boniface (418–22) had stayed during his rivalry for the papacy, received gifts of silver communion plate from him: a paten of 20 pounds weight; *scyphae* or wine containers, and chalices, totalling 31 pounds as well as three hanging crown lamps, totalling 45 pounds: 95 pounds of silver in all.[7]

Nor was the papacy the only source of endowment for liturgical plate: Agnellus recorded the gift of a chalice to the chapel of S Zaccaria in Ravenna, which was engraved with the name of the empress Galla Placidia, and in Agnellus's time had already survived 400 years and been moved to Ravenna's cathedral. Its present whereabouts are unknown, if indeed it has survived.[8] Agnellus also informs us that Galla Placidia gave many other gifts to Ravenna's churches, including golden candelabra.[9] It is not surprising that chapels and churches were built with hidden spaces for the concealment of their treasures, spaces which have been discovered empty in recent times in the early churches and chapels of Ravenna, most notably in the Archbishops' Chapel and at S Vitale and S Apollinare in Classe.[10] Other churches were built with strongly fortified sacristies, such as those beside the altar at S Maria Formosa in Pula.

The amounts disbursed by patrons for the furnishing and lighting of chapels pale into insignificance in comparison with the endowments given by the emperors to their family mausolea. We are particularly well informed about Constantine's gifts to the mausoleum of his mother Helena in Rome, which are listed in the biography of Pope Silvester (314–35).[11] The mausoleum, a substantial building with an internal diameter of about twenty metres, obviously needed imposing fittings and generous lighting. Constantine's endowment included silver furnishings totalling 600 pounds, among them an altar weighing 200 pounds to place in front of Helena's porphyry tomb, and twenty chandeliers, each of 20 pounds' weight of silver. The liturgical plate was of solid gold and included a 35-pound paten, three 10-pound golden chalices with jewels, and two golden *scyphae* weighing 40 pounds each. There was also a huge gold crown chandelier, fitted with 120 lights and weighing 30 pounds of gold, and four 12-foot candelabra, in silver chased with gold, which weighed 200 pounds each.

S Costanza also, tomb of Constantine's daughters Constantina and Helena, gives some indication of the scale of its furnishings. In addition to its porphyry sarcophagus and the huge oval slab of pink granite on which it must once have stood, the furnishings included a second, plainer, and much smaller porphyry sarcophagus, once a tub or *labrum*, which now serves as an altar in St Peter's. Several huge, sculptured marble candlesticks also survive: one serves for the paschal candle in nearby S Agnese *fuori le mura*, while the others are in the Vatican Museum. No record survives of the furnishings in gold and silver which must once have been present.

The early chapel was a free-standing structure, often situated in the Christian cemetery outside the walls of the city, as required by Roman law if it contained a dead body or corporeal relics. Although it must have been to some extent protected by its sacred character from the activities of robbers, its position outside the city walls made it vulnerable to attack, and the rewards were great, since it housed not only valuable relics of the saints but furnishings made of precious materials, including gold and silver. All chapels must have had heavy doors for security. A few early chapels retain their original doorways, as at Poreč in Istria, where the door frame of the martyr chapel at the Basilica Euphrasiana consists of lintel and matching door jambs of marble, all deeply incised with profiling grooves, topped with a projecting cornice.[12] Others are known from drawings: the chapel of S Caterina in the bay at Pula had a lintel carved with a meander supported on plain doorjambs (fig. 38). While some chapels, such as S Caterina, which was an aristocratic funerary chapel, maintained their integrity as separate buildings, others in course of time became too small to serve the needs of devotees and pilgrims. Then a church was often built alongside, with the original chapel attached to it as a shrine. The shrine still required a door and perhaps a vestibule as well, to comply with Canon law that forbade more than one altar to a church. The door defined the chapel as a separate building and allowed it its own altar. Obviously, substantial doors were part of the furnishings of every chapel, whether an annex or a free-standing entity, and were often provided with monumental portals which foretold the grandeur of the sacred space within. Portals provided room for inscriptions, for messages carved into the stone, which acted as a sacred billboard displaying texts from the scriptures or recording the patron's motivation. Such doorways have occasionally survived. The most complete examples are at the chapels which Pope Hilarus built at the Lateran Baptistery: these will give some idea of other doors and portals which are now lost.

Both of the surviving chapels at the Lateran were provided with elaborate entrances from the baptistery itself. Marble door surrounds with elaborate profiles were framed in portals composed of spoils from classical buildings. These included imposing sculpted architraves supported both inside and out by columns of *verde antico* and reused Corinthian capitals. The lintels were inscribed with appropriate texts from scripture and personal dedicatory inscriptions. The importance of Pope Hilarus's doorways is emphasized by texts on the inner and outer faces of the lintels and on the doors themselves, which provide clues as to the meaning of the interior: at the chapel of the Baptist an inscription dedicates the chapel to the 'people of God,' while a second proclaims 'Lord, I have loved the beauty of your house' (fig. 109).[13] The same theme was taken up at Pope Hilarus's third chapel, S Croce, which has not survived, where the portal was inscribed with a text from Psalm 5, which described the chapel as the temple and dwelling place of God. The psalms from which these texts are taken have both been identified as prayers for deliverance from enemies, linking the messages on these two doorways with the votive inscription on the lintel at the Evangelist's chapel in which Hilarus describes the Evangelist as his 'liberator'; we have already seen that Hilarus had been saved from a mob in Ephesus by the intervention of the saint, and had vowed him a chapel as a thank-offering.

The portals were enhanced by magnificent doors which were probably also classical spoils: Hilarus's biography tells us that both of the St John chapels originally possessed 'bronze doors, chased with silver.' One pair survives, those of the Baptist's chapel, and these too bear Hilarus's dedication (fig. 109).

But doors and portals were also seen to have wider symbolic functions as guardians of the doorway. While the closed doors quite literally barred the entry of evil people, symbolic protection was also embodied in their texts and decoration: the mosaic mazes in the Mausoleum of Galla Placidia function in just this way, blocking the entry of spirits which may be mischievous or even evil. But above all, Christ himself declared that he was 'the door ... if anyone enters by [him], he will be saved.'[14] Christ's declaration stresses a mystical level of meaning to the door, which symbolizes the way into the sacred space of the chapel, marking it as a re-creation in this world of the Holy of Holies and the dwelling place of God and, in general and universal terms, as the entry into Christian life and salvation.

The decoration which surrounded the doors on the inside was also full of symbolic meaning. Often, there was room for a lunette above the lintel. In the three examples that I have considered, the lunette was decorated in mosaic, placing important messages right on the interface between the sacred interior and the world outside. These messages were designed for those who passed beneath them. For example, the joys of paradise are represented by the composition of the Good Shepherd, who tenderly cares for his flock,[15] as in the Mausoleum of Galla Placidia at Ravenna (fig. 97), where the subject constitutes a message of hope of paradise for those who were to be interred there, in this case perhaps Galla Placidia's little son, who had died in infancy. The empress, as she left the chapel, would then have been reassured by Christ's promise 'Let the children come to me, do not hinder them; for to such belongs the kingdom of God.'[16]

On the other hand, the stark image of an empty throne, marked as Christ's by his monograms on its armrests, and as a judgment image by the scroll of the seven seals that lay upon its seat, gives out a message of warning about Christ's return in judgment.[17] This is a warning that must have reflected the concerns of the patron who ordered it placed there, often in the burial place he had planned for himself. The empty throne must also have reminded the living to ask God's mercy on the departed soul. Among early chapels, this iconography is represented by the mosaic image on the inner entry wall at the fifth-century S Matrona chapel at S Prisco: the earliest surviving example of judgment imagery above the inner lintel (fig. 58). The iconography was still in use in the ninth century, when it was placed in the same position, on the inner side of the entry door, at the funerary chapel which Pope Paschal I built for his mother in Rome. This position would continue to be a prime location for this iconography throughout the Middle Ages.

A third subject, this time in a nonfunerary structure, occupies the same location in the palace-chapel built by the archbishops of Ravenna around the turn of the sixth century. Above the exit door of the chapel, where the archbishops would have seen it every time they went out, is a representation of Christ's victory over evil, which is symbolized by his trampling of the lion and the adder, as foretold in Psalm 91: 'You will tread on the lion and the adder, the young lion and the serpent you will trample under foot' (fig. 48). How was this relevant to the Ravenna archbishops? I have already suggested that Christ's trampling of the beasts is depicted in the Ravenna Chapel as a model to be imitated by the church militant in its earthly struggle. It therefore reminds each archbishop, every time he leaves the sacred space of his private oratory, of his responsibilities and battles as a leader of the church in this world, rather than reminding him of personal hopes and fears for the life to come, as in the other two examples we have considered

Chapels were also provided with windows. Just as doors fulfilled a practical and symbolic role in conducting Christians, both the living and the deceased, through the chapel's walls, windows were also specialized for the entry and exit of an entity, but this time, a nonliving, noncorporeal entity: light. They were concerned with the transmission, channelling or blocking, of light into the chapel's interior. This light was the direct or diffused light of the sun. Light might be blocked from some part of the interior for security reasons: windows might be situated only in the upper storey, far above the ground, as is well shown in the imperial mausolea, with their rich furnishings Other chapels are known to have been provided with only minimal light, perhaps marking their function as strong rooms or treasuries. For example, according to an anonymous visitor who saw them in the late sixteenth century, the paired circular chambers beside the altar at the lost basilica of S Maria Formosa, Pula, are reported to have had 'windows that gave very little light,' as well as most beautiful doors.[18] The majority of windows were covered with stone traceries which served also to diffuse the light. Three of the original *transennae* can still be seen at the sixth-century funerary chapel of S Maria del Canneto, which is the only part of S Maria Formosa to survive. Two have a simple rectangular design, while above, in the east wall of the central tower, is a large window with a tracery based on interlocking circles (fig. 36). These *transennae* must have fulfilled several functions: not only did they discourage thieves, but they allowed the use of the relatively small pieces of window glass which were available to light the interior and exclude the elements.[19] Thin sheets of alabaster could also be used as windowpanes, as at the Mausoleum of Galla Placidia in Ravenna. The designs of the stone traceries and the lacy patterns in the alabaster added an aesthetic quality to the incident light by interrupting and diffracting its rays.

Lighting is an important aspect of the interior of any chapel. Two different modes of illumination are possible: natural light, which enters through a transparent medium during daylight hours, and may highlight some area of the decoration, depending on the orientation of the chapel to the sun; and artificial light, the light of lamps and candles, which overrides the orientation and provides its own internal focus. When the interior of the chapel is decorated with mosaics, the aesthetic of the golden vault in which each tessera is set to reflect light in a slightly different direction comes into play. The lamp-lit effect recreates the shimmering light of the vault of heaven and becomes an important symbolic element of the decoration. This effect was plainly intentional, and helped create the illusion that a microcosm of heaven and earth existed inside the chapel's sacred space.

The furnishings of precious metals, which in the long run proved to be ephemeral, were matched by the transitory gifts of luxurious and costly fabrics with which the chapels and mausolea must have been adorned, and which were subject to the ravages of time as well as to the activities of robbers. The sarcophagus of Diocletian at his mausoleum in Split was covered with a purple drapery, which is only recorded because thieves made away with it, according to Ammianus.[20] We can presume that similar palls will have covered other imperial burials, but none has survived. Their portability will have made them especially vulnerable, and in a location such as the crypt of Diocletian's mausoleum, where the porphyry sarcophagus seems to have been immured during the construction of the building, making it impossible to remove it intact, the pall may well have been the only portable loot. This sort of purple pall was also given to the most important Christian heroes: for example, Gregory I (590–604) provided one to cover the body of St Peter, and covered it with 100 pounds of the finest gold.[21] We know that by the late eighth century draperies had become part of the furnishings of both churches and chapels, as they were given in great abundance by Leo III (795–816) and are listed in the records of his donations.[22] In his era, sets were given to veil the altar, to hang between the columns of the sanctuary, and to enrich the main arcade and the entrance itself. Although the donation lists of the earlier popes do not record gifts of hangings in this detail or on this scale, draperies were almost certainly in use, and formed part of the expensive furnishings of chapels and churches. For example, although gifts of curtains to chapels are not specifically mentioned, Benedict II (684–5), a Roman by birth, gave precious silk altarcloths to various churches, including S Maria *ad martyres*, the Pantheon. The Syrian pope, Sergius I (687–701), gave eight veils to hang around the altar of St Peter's, and altar cloths 'for various churches'; these gifts may have reflected Syrian custom. His Greek successor John VI (701–5) gave a similar gift to St Paul's. We can presume that by the turn of the eighth century the well-furnished chapel will have owned at a minimum an altar cloth of rich fabric, and possibly special hangings to adorn the sanctuary as well. This supposition is hinted at by the gifts of Gregory III to his funerary chapel inside St Peter's, which included items 'assigned for the adornment of the *pergula* and as altarcloths'; most likely all of these were made of luxurious fabrics.[23]

The picture of a chapel in use in Early Christian times is completed by a pavement made of durable materials, stone mosaic or *opus sectile*. These materials, and all the other furnishings and embellishments, contrast marvellously with the exteriors of these buildings, which adhere to the Early Christian aesthetic of the plain exterior and the richly decorated interior. The exterior wall surface was austere, usually in brick, sometimes in stone, with a roof covered with Roman rooftiles and topped with a funerary finial. Decoration was usually limited to blind arcading, elaborate portals, and window traceries carved from stone and glazed with small panes of transparent glass or mica. These will have protected the inner space from the weather, while allowing the transmission of light into the interior. This light streaming into the dark interior symbolized the presence of Christ, who had called himself the Light of the World.[24] Light was necessary for practical as well as symbolic reasons, though, as it played over the surface of the mosaics inside, imparting brilliance and bringing them to life. We have seen that one of its special qualities was to linger on the many tesserae which had been set at varying angles so as to catch the incident rays and diffract them. Each interior will have been rich with rare materials: marble, mosaic, and precious metal, fitted with carved marble furnishings and hung with golden lamps and rare fabrics. In their present condition no single chapel can give an idea of all this splendour, and it is only when the fragments of information about the many chapels that we know of are put together that we can obtain some idea of the aims of the founders and the way in which they expressed their faith and their hopes for a blessed outcome on Judgment Day.

Appendix

A Short Catalogue of Chapels Mentioned in This Book

(This catalogue does not claim to be exhaustive.)

ANCONA

ST STEPHEN: THE 'ORATORY on the CORSO GARIBALDI'

Bibliography

G. Bovini, 'La "memoria antiqua S Stephani," e l'oratorio paleocristiano di Corso Garibaldi di Ancona,' *CorsiCRB* 13 (1966), 12–13 and fig. 1. Older bibliography listed in 12, note 21.

G.B. De Rossi, 'Ancona – Cubicolo sepolcrale cristiano di diritto privato e musaico del suo pavimento,' *BAC* (1879), 128–32, and pl. IX–X.

Location 3.5 m below street level on Corso Garibaldi.

Plan A rectangular room 11 × 8 m, with apse. Apse mosaic, fig. 110 (after De Rossi).

A mosaic vine scroll and inscription in the apse were intact. Inscription reads 'VINEA FACTA EST DILECTA IN CORNUM IN LOCO VBERI' (Isaiah 5.1). Dated to the late fourth century by Bovini, who suggested it may have been a small church rather than a chapel.

BOLOGNA

S CROCE AT S STEFANO

Bibliography

L. Donini and G. Belvederi, *Gli scavi nella chiesa di S Stephano, Bologna* (Bologna, 1914).

Robert G. Ousterhout, *The Church of S Stefano: A 'Jerusalem' in Bologna*, unpublished Master's thesis (University of Cincinnati, 1977).

Luciano Serchia, ed., *S Stephano di Bologna. Restauri, ripristini, manutenzioni* (Vigevano, 1987), 255, and plan p. 261.

Location Outside the city walls of Bologna on the Via Emilia.

Plan See Ousterhout, fig. 2; Serchia, 261.

Built ca. 432–50. Restored to original condition in 1930, on the ancient foundations. May have been a copy of Calvary, complete with a copy of the True Cross and a nail from the Crucifixion housed in a temple-like shrine to simulate the New Jerusalem. Also housed the tomb of an aristocratic lady of the fifth century, Giuliana Afrodite

BRESCIA

ST FILASTRIUS

Bibliography
A. Grabar, *Martyrium*, I, 406, and note 4, referring to:
Mottes, *Die Baukunst d. Mittelalters in Italien*, I, 243, fig. 76.

A cruciform martyr chapel found in excavations below St Filastrius, Brescia, and dated to the fifth century.

S STEFANO IN ARCE

Bibliography Adriano Bausola ('A. B'), in *Milano, Capitale*, 2. b. 4, p. 155.

A late-sixth-century martyrium, dedicated to S Stefano, was an apsed square with a relic chamber, and became the crypt of a later church on the site.

BRINDISI

SAN LEUCIO (no longer extant)

Bibliography R. Jularlo, 'Un Martyrium a Brindisi,' *RAC* 45 (1969), 89–95.

CAESAREA (See also Classe and Ravenna)

S PETRONILLA (no longer extant)

Bibliography Agnellus, *CPER*, XV, Florentius, 61.

Location On Via Caesarea, outside walls, and later annexed to the Basilica Apostolorum (S Francesco).

Burial chapel of Bishop Florentius. Possibly on his private estate (patrimony) rather than in a public cemetery.

SAINTS STEPHEN, PROTASE, AND GERVASE (no longer extant)

Bibliography Agnellus, *CPER*, XXI, Iohannes I, 94–7.

Location One of many funerary chapels at the basilica of S Lorenzo, built by an imperial official, Lauricius, in the cemetery outside the walls of Ravenna.

Dedicated 29 September 435. Funerary chapel of Lauricius.

Decoration in mosaic, marble, and stucco was recorded by Agnellus. Pulled down in 1553.

S PULLIONE (no longer extant)

Bibliography Agnellus, *CPER*, XV, Florentius, 61.

Location Outside the walls of Ravenna, not far from Porta Nova.

Funerary chapel of Liberius II, late-fourth-century bishop of Ravenna.

CASARANELLO (Puglia)

S MARIA DELLA CROCE

Bibliography

Renato Bartoccini, 'Casaranello e i suoi mosaici,' *FR*, n.s., IV, 45 (1934), 157–85.

M.M. Trinci Cecchelli, 'I mosaici di S Maria della Croce a Casaranello,' *Puglia paleocristiana*, 3 (Bari, 1979), 414–48.

Plan Fig. 111 (after Bartoccini).

A chapel with Early Christian mosaics on its vault is incorporated as the sanctuary and crossing of the parish church.

CLASSE

S RUPHILUS (no longer extant)

Bibliography

Agnellus, *LPER*, 288.

J.-C. Picard, *Souvenir des évêques*,132–43.

Plan M. Mazzotti, 'Chiese ravennati scomparse,' *Almanacco Ravennate* (1958), 368; reprinted in G. Cortesi, 'La chiesa di Santa Croce di Ravenna alla luce degli ultimi scavi e ricerche,' *CorsiCRB* 25 (1978), 47–76, esp. 67, fig. 1.

The chapel dedicated to St Ruphilus was built in an adjacent room to the original burial place of St Severus, first bishop of Ravenna (mid-fourth century), in a room of his family villa. The funerary basilica of St Severus was built beside the two chapels in the late sixth century by Bishop Giovanni II Romanus.

Site found in 1963 and excavated in 1967 by G. Cortesi, as above.

CHAPELS OF ST JAMES, ST MATTHEW (no longer extant)

Bibliography Agnellus, *CPER*, XVIII, Petrus I, 223–4.

Location: Both beside the baptistery of the Basilica Petriana. Neither church, baptistery, nor chapels survive.

The chapel of St James later became the burial chapel of Bishop Petrus II (494–518/19), seen lying in his tomb by Agnellus, and identified by portrait and inscription. Both chapels had apse mosaics given by Archbishop Agnellus (556–569)

SS MARCUS, MARCELLUS E FELICULA (No longer extant)

Bibliography
Agnellus, *CPER*, XXX, Iohannes II, 245.
Picard, *Souvenir*, 180–4.

Location beside S Apollinare in Classe, probably either at the south end of the narthex, where a ruined structure is recorded from the sixteenth century, or beside the north flank of the church.

Built by John II Romanus (578–595), who was buried there, the chapel subsequently became the communal burial place of the archbishops of Ravenna. Last seen in the early sixteenth century, it had vanished by 1589.

CONCORDIA

Bibliography P.L. Zovatto, 'La trichora paleocristiana nel nuovo complesso monumentale di Concordia,' *FR* 86 (1962), 74–95
Italo Furlan, 'Architettura del complesso paleocristiano di Iulia Concordia: Revisione e proposte,' *Scritti storici in memoria di Paolo Lino Zovatto* (Milan, 1972), 79–95, esp. 88, fig. 5.
R. Canova dal Zio, *Chiese*, 46–7, with bibliography to 1986.

Plan Dal Zio, *Chiese*, 42; Furlan, 'Architettura,' 88, fig. 5, and see fig. 30, above.

Location Outside the Roman city of Iulia Concordia Sagittaria, near Portogruaro, which was devastated by the Huns in 452, and finally destroyed in the floods of 586.

The triconch chapel was probably a *memoria* to an unknown saint. Later it was annexed to the sanctuary of the Basilica Apostolorum, and later still, perhaps soon after 452, it was enlarged by the addition of a nave.

GRADO

TRICHORA AT S EUFEMIA

Bibliography
G. Cuscito, *Grado e le sue basiliche paleocristiane* (Bologna, 1979).
T.G. Jackson, *Dalmatia, the Quarnero and Istria*, III (Oxford, 1887), 431.
P.L. Zovatto, *Grado, antichi monumenti* (Bologna, 1971).

Plan Jackson, *Dalmatia*, fig. 125. See also fig. 31, above.

Possibly originally dedicated as a *memoria* to saints Ermacora and Fortunatus, the evangelists of the Veneto, from ca. 630, the trichora was dedicated to St Mark. By the late nineteenth century, all that remained was the original mosaic floors. A chapel in Early Christian style was built over them in the twentieth century.

'SACRISTY CHAPEL' AT S EUFEMIA

Bibliography As for trichora, above.

Plan Figs. 31 and 32, above.

Location At apse end of south aisle at S Eufemia

Possibly the original sacristy. The mosaic pavement was given by Bishop Elia (571–586). The tomb of a bishop Marcianus (possibly bishop of Augusta), who spent forty years in exile here, and died in 578, was discovered intact there in 1966.

CHAPEL at the 'BASILICA OF PIAZZA VITTORIA'

Bibliography
G. Brusin and P.L. Zovatto, *Monumenti paleocristiani di Aquileia e di Grado*, Udine, 1957, figs. 57–8; 487–9.
G. Cuscito, *Grado e le sue basiliche paleocristiane* (Bologna, 1979).
P.L. Zovatto, *Grado, antichi monumenti* (Bologna, 1971).

Plan Zovatto, 74, fig. 107; Brusin and Zovatto, 487–9, figs. 57–8.

This chapel, possibly the church's sacristy, appears to have been renovated by Bishop Elia, perhaps for the veneration of the relics which he gave to Grado's churches. There is no proof that it was Elia's funerary chapel, and his grave has not been found there.

MILAN (Mediolanum)

S GREGORIO (no longer extant)

Case study, discussed in Chapter 7.

Bibliography
M.J. Johnson, *Imperial Mausolea*, 55–9.
S. Lewis, 'San Lorenzo Revisited: A Theodosian Palace Church at Milan,' *JSAH*, 32 (1975), 197–222.
M. Mirabella Roberti, 'Il mausoleo romano di S Vittore a Milano,' *Atti del VI*

Congresso nazionale di archeologia cristiana, Pesaro/Ancona, 1983 (Ancona, 1985), 777–83.

Plan See fig. 81, above.

Location In the cemetery outside the walls of Mediolanum, inside a fortified precinct.

Built for an emperor, possibly the tetrarch Maximian, who died in AD 310, the mausoleum was later incorporated as a chapel beside the apse at the Romanesque basilica of S Vittore al Corpo. It was destroyed when this church was replaced in 1512. Known from partial archaeological remains and from the Stuttgart drawing by an anonymous Dutch artist, fig. 16, above.

S AQUILINO at S Lorenzo

Discussed in chapter 7, as an imperial mausoleum, probably that of the Theodosian dynasty; see figs. 14, 15, 17, and 82–3, above.

Bibliography

Dale Kinney, 'Le chiese paleocristiane di Mediolanum,' in *Milano, una capitale da Ambrogio ai Carolingi*, ed. C. Bertelli (Milan, 1987).
– 'The Evidence for the Dating of S Lorenzo in Milan,' *JSAH* 34 (1972), 92–107.
Suzanne Lewis, 'San Lorenzo Revisited: A Theodosian Palace Church at Milan,' *JSAH* 32 (1973), 197–222, esp. 218–22.

S IPPOLITO at S Lorenzo

Bibliography Dale Kinney, 'Le chiese paleocristiane di Mediolanum,' in *Milano, una capitale da Ambrogio ai Carolingi*, ed. C. Bertelli (Milan, 1987).
– 'The Evidence for the Dating of S Lorenzo in Milan,' *JSAH* 34 (1972), 92–107.
Suzanne Lewis, 'San Lorenzo Revisited: A Theodosian Palace Church at Milan,' *JSAH* 32 (1973), 197–222, esp. 211–18.
Picard, *Souvenir*, 62–5.
Ann Terry, *Early Christian Cruciform Annex Chapels*, MA thesis (University of Illinois, 1979), 102–6.

Plan See plan of S Lorenzo complex, fig. 14. The hexagonal exterior (fig. 18) enclosed a groin-vaulted Greek cross which was originally covered by a pendentive dome.

The date of the chapel must depend on the contentious dating of S Lorenzo, to which its stonework is bonded, and is usually placed in the period 355–74. Situated directly behind the high altar of the church, it was flanked by a pair of circular structures that have not survived. It probably functioned as a martyrium, possibly honouring St Lawrence. Subsequently served as the funerary chapel of two bishops: Theodore, who died in 489, and his successor, Lawrence I.

S SISTO at S Lorenzo

Bibliography
S Lewis, 'San Lorenzo Revisited,' 211–15.
Picard, *Souvenir*, 62–4.

Plan An octagon containing an inscribed cross. See fig. 14, for plan of S Lorenzo complex, and fig. 19, exterior.

Built in the early sixth century, S Sisto functioned as the communal burial chapel of Milan's bishops.

S VITTORE IN CIEL D'ORO

The chapel is introduced in chapter 1 and fully treated in chapter 6. See also figs. 51–6, above.

Bibliography
Picard, *Souvenir*, 36–41, with full bibliography on 36, note 61.
F. Reggiori, *La Basilica Ambrosiana. Ricerche e restauri, 1929–1940* (Milan, 1941).

Location Incorporated into the Basilica Ambrosiana, beside the apse on the south side.

Plan Fig. 52.

S VALERIA (no longer extant)

Bibliography
M. Mirabella Roberti, *Milano Capitale*, 433.
Caterina Occhetti Viola ('C. O. V.') *Milano Capitale*, 124

Location Site discovered in 1969 on Via Valeria, identified by fragment with letters VAL. See *Milano Capitale*, 474, plan 2a. 25. The remains of this chapel have been found under S Francesco Grande at the Catholic University.

SS NABOR e FELIX, the Naboriana (no longer extant)

Bibliography
Ambrose, Epistola XXII, Letter to Marcellina, *PL* 16, col. 106.
A. Calderini and F. Reggiori, 'Scavi alla ricerca dei SS Nabor e Felice,' *Ritrovamenti e scavi per la Forma Urbis Mediolani*, 2, *Quaderni di Studi Romani*, 3 (Rome, 1951) 3–5.

Location South of Via Vercellina, under S Francesco Grande at the Catholic University

Built by Bishop Maternus in the early fourth century to shelter the remains of

Sts Nabor and Felix, which he had brought to Milan from Lodi, and eventually chosen for his own burial.

S VITALIS
Bibliography
Picard, *Souvenir*, 28–9.
Location: in Coemeterium ad Martyres, outside the walls of Milan (see plan, fig. 7). Funerary chapel of Bishop Monas. Pulled down in 1577.

CHAPEL at S SIMPLICIANO (perhaps originally dedicated to the Trentine martyrs Sisinnius, Martirius, and Alexandrus)
Bibliography
G. Traversi, *Architettura paleocristiana milanese* (Milan, 1964), 38–40.
P. Verzone, *Architettura religiosa dell'alto medioevo nell'Italia settentrionale* (Milan, 1942), 65.

Location At S Simpliciano (formerly the Basilica Vergine) outside the walls of Milan on the Via Comasina.

Plan See fig. 8, above.

A cruciform structure, without atrium, attached to the east side of the left transept, but formerly free-standing, and probably pre-Ambrosian, since it incorporates much reused material. Appears to have been rebuilt by Bishop Simplicianus (397–400) as a *memoria* for the Trentine martyrs Sisinnius, Martirius, and Alexandrus, whose bodies were sent here at the end of the fourth century from Trento.

SS NAZARIUS and CELSUS
Bibliography
Paulinus Diaconus, *Vita Ambrosii*, tr. Lacey, 33–66, esp. 32–3.
Picard, *Souvenir*, 52–3.

Location Outside the Porta Romana of Milan at a place called 'tres moros.'

The first *memoria* over the graves of the two saints was dated to AD 57 and the persecutions of Nero. Celsus's relics remained there in the chapel; those of Nazarius were moved by Ambrose to the Basilica Apostolorum.

Memoriae below S CALIMERO and S EUSTORGIO

Bibliography Picard, *Souvenir*, 25–6 (S Calimero) and 41–4 (S Eustorgio).

NARNI

EPISCOPAL CHAPEL (no longer extant)
Bibliography
Gregory I, *PL* 76, *Homil. in Evang.* II, Homily 37, 9, col. 1281.

SAN GIOVENALE

Bibliography
Adriano Prandi, 'Il volto di Narni' in *Narni* (Rome, 1993).
M. Bigotti, G.A. Mensuelli, A. Prandi, 'Narni nel medioevo,' in Prandi, *Narni*, 198–206.
M. Salmi, 'Un problema storico-artistico medievale,' *Bolletino d'arte*, n.s., 3 (1958), 213–31.

Plan Salmi, 'Problema,' fig. 11.

Location Built in the cemetery outside the walls of Narni as the *cella memoriae* of the early bishop, Giovenale.

Chosen for burial by Giovenale's successors in the bishopric in the late fourth and fifth centuries. Later dedicated to the sixth-century Bishop Cassius. Giovenale's remains were stolen in 878 and taken to Lucca by Adalbert Margrave of Tuscany, but later returned and reinterred in the chapel.

PADUA

S PROSDOCIMO (see chapter 1, p. 40, and figs. 26–9, above).

Bibliography
R. Canova dal Zio, *Chiese* (1986), 91–4.
Maria Tonzig, *La basilica romanico-gotica di Santa Giustina in Padova* (Padua, 1932).

Plan See fig. 26. For original layout, see Tonzig, 30, fig. 6.

Location Originally a free-standing chapel in the cemetery outside the walls of Padua, now attached by a complex of buildings to the much later basilica of S Giustina.

Probably a *memoria* built in honour of the local martyr Justina, and chosen for the burial of the early bishop, Prosdocimus, it was rebuilt by the patrician Opilio in the early sixth century.

POREČ (Parenzo)

S ANDREA (see fig. 33)

Bibliography
Verzone, *Architettura*, 50–3.
M. Prelog, *The Basilica of Euphrasius in Poreč* (Zagreb, 1963).

Location Annexed to the left (north) of the apse of the Basilica Eufrasiana (539–50).

Plan Verzone, *Architettura*, 51, fig. 21.

A triconch, with oval atrium and tower, and polygonal apses, round on the interior. Probably the *memoria* of Maurus and Eleutherius, the patron saints of Poreč, and originally dedicated to them. May also have been the funerary chapel of Euphrasius, the patron.

PULA (Pola, Parenzo)

BETIKA (near Poreč and Pula)

Bibliography

Rajko Bratož, 'The Development of the Early Christian Research in Slovenia and Istria between 1976 and 1986,' *Actes du XI Congrès international d'archéologie chrétienne*, 2345–88, esp. 2379–82.

Plan Bratož, 2380, fig. 7.

A triconch chapel, dating to early fifth century. The dedicatory inscription in the south apse *in honore beatorum sanctorum* identifies it as a martyrium. Pavement with black and white mosaics.

CHAPELS AT THE CIMARE CEMETERY, PULA

Bibliography Rajko Bratož, 'The Development of the Early Christian Research in Slovenia and Istria between 1976 and 1986,' *Actes du XI Congrès international d'archéologie chrétienne*, 2369f.

Five *memoriae* with semicircular apses and floor mosaics, discovered in the late nineteenth century.

S CATERINA (no longer extant)

See figs. 38 and 39, above.

Bibliography

A. Gnirs, 'Forschungen in Istrien,' *Jahreshefte des Osterreichischen Archäologischen Institutes in Wien* 14 (1911), 188–96.

P. Kandler, *Osservatore Triestino* (n.d.); repr. *Notizie Storiche di Pola* (Poreč, 1876), 230–2.

Ibid., 187, letter to Dom Domenico Bronzin at Parenzo: 'S Andrea o scoglio grande di Pola. '

Location On islet of the same name in Pula harbour, adjacent to island monastery of S Andrea, and attached to it by a bridge over the canal between the two islands. The monastery was destroyed in 1805 and replaced by a Venetian fortification; at that time S Caterina was deserted but still intact.

Plans Fig. 38, after Seroux d'Agincourt, *Storia dell'Arte* (Milan, 1825), II, pl.

XXVI (drawn by S. Dufourney), 8, ground plan; 9, transverse section; 10 exterior. Fig. 39, after A. Gnirs, 1911, shows plan of excavation, including sarcophagi.

Probably built in the sixth century, the chapel was seen by Kandler in the mid-nineteenth century when already in ruins. He noted the presence of fallen mosaic tesserae both inside and around the perimeter. The site was excavated by Gnirs in 1910, and identified as a funerary chapel by the presence of three sarcophagi.

S MARIA FORMOSA (or del Canneto)

See the section entitled 'Chapels in the North-East' in chapter 1, and figs. 34–7.

Bibliography
Pietro Kandler, 'Della basilica di S Maria Formosa in Pola,' *L'Istra* (1847); reprinted in *Notizie storiche di Pola* (Poreč, 1976), 171–6.
Antonio Morassi, 'La Chiesa di Santa Maria Formosa o del Canneto in Pola,' *Bolletino d'Arte del Ministero della pubblica istruzione*, 1 (1924–5), 11–25.

Location Inside the walls of Pula, last remnant of the destroyed sixth-century church of S Maria Formosa.

Plan Fig. 34, after Kandler.

S FIORANO and S SABBA (on island of S Fiorano in Pula bay)

Bibliography These chapels are known only from Pola Anonymous (Pietro Dragano), *Dialoghi due sulle antichità di Pola del 1600*, ed. Pietro Kandler as *Cenni del forestiero che visita Pola* (Trieste, 1845), 125–6.

Location S Fiorano on the high point of the island, S Sabbas below.

Plan No information survives.

CHAPELS IN PULA REGION:
at Fažana, Chapel of Sv. Elizej (plan, Marušić, 25–6)
at Vrh, near Pula: Sv. Kliment
on Brioni I: St Peter
in Pula: Sv. Nikola
in Rovinj: Sv. Toma
in Galižana, Sv. Lucija ; Sv. Maver (Mauro).

Bibliography
R. Bratož, 'Early Christian Research,' 2377–8.
B. Maružić, *Kasnoantička i bizantinska Pula* (Pula, 1967) (German edition: Spätantike und bysantinische [sic] Pula [Pula, 1967]).

RAVENNA (see also Caesarea and Classe)

S APOLLINARIS *IN VECLO* (no longer extant)

Bibliography
Agnellus, *LPER*, 353.
G. Cortesi, 'I principali edifici sacri ravennati nei secc. V e VI,' *CorsiCRB*
   29 (1982), 63–107.

Location Near the west gate of Ravenna and the public mint.

Built in the time of bishop Reparatus (671–7). Cruciform, therefore probably a funerary chapel. Part of a monastery by the late 8th century.

ARCHBISHOPS' CHAPEL: S ANDREA
 Introduced in chapter 3 and fully discussed in chapter 5. See also figs. 47 (plan) and 48–50.

ARIAN ARCHBISHOPS' CHAPEL (S APOLLINARIS) No longer extant.

Bibliography
Agnellus, *LPER*, 334. Also, *CPER*, 217: '... et sancti Apolenaris monasterio, quod in superiora domus structum, episcopium ipsius ecclesie fuit. '

MAUSOLEUM OF GALLA PLACIDIA

See chapter 7, 'Mausolea of the Rulers in the West'; frontispiece; and figs. 12, 13, and 93–7)

Plan For S Croce complex, see S Zaccaria, below; and also C. Ricci, *Mausoleo di Galla Placidia*, fig 23. For reconstruction drawing of S Croce complex: Ricci, fig. 21, and for section, Ricci, *Mausoleo*, fig. 35.

S GIOVANNI BATTISTA (no longer extant)

Bibliography Agnellus, *CPER*, XXII, Petrus II, 151 and notes 9–10, and ibid., 121

Plan No information.

Galla Placidia chose this as the funerary chapel of her confessor, Barbatianus, who later achieved sainthood and the dedication of the chapel. It was demolished in the early sixteenth century.

S ZACCARIA

Bibliography
Agnellus, *CPER*, XXI, Iohannes I, 119.
G. Cortesi, 'I principali edifici sacri ravennati in funzione sepolcrale nei secc.
   V e VI,' *CorsiCRB* 29 (1982), 63–107, esp. 103–4, and 94, fig. 9.

Location: Built soon after AD 415, close to Galla Placidia's palace church, S

Croce. Identified by Cortesi as the cruciform chapel discovered by archaeologists in 1926, at the north end of the S Croce narthex.

Plan Reconstruction by F. Di Pietro reproduced by Cortesi, 55, fig. 3. See also fig. 12B, above.

Functioned as a funerary chapel, possibly for Sounigilda the wife of Odovacar. Received a set of inscribed liturgical plate from the empress, which was moved to Ravenna's cathedral, the Basilica Ursiana, by the ninth century at latest.

CHAPELS (*memoriae*) BENEATH S VITALE

See fig. 11 for mosaic floor and foundations of the *memoria* of S Vitalis.

Bibliography
G. Gerola, 'Il sacello primitivo in San Vitale,' *FR* 2 (1913), 427–34 and 459–71, esp. 461–3.
F. di Pietro, 'Il prisco sacello di S Vitale,' *Bolletino d'Arte*, ser. 2, 5 (1926), 241–51.

Plan Fig. 10 (after Gerola), and F. di Pietro, 243, fig. 1, for plan of excavations.

S VITALE: DOMED SIDE CHAPELS

Bibliography
C. Ricci, 'La cappella detta Sancta Sanctorum nella chiesa di S Vitale in Ravenna,' *Rassegna d'Arte* 4 (1904), 104–8.

Plan Fig. 10, after Gerola.

Remains of the original memorial chapels may lie beneath the domed side chapels of the mid-sixth-century church of S Vitale, together with those dedicated to S Ursicinus and to S Vitale (see above); the new church would then have been planned to cover all four of these *memoriae*.

Chapel of S STEFANO

Bibliography Mentioned in Agnellus, *CPER*, ed. Testi-Rasponi, XXI, Iohannes I, 119–21, note 9.

Location Probably on the site of Maximinian's lost church of S Stefano in the imperial quarter.

S MARIA MAGGIORE

Bibliography Agnellus, *CPER*, ed. Testi-Rasponi, 165, note 2.

Location In imperial quarter, close to S Vitale.

Ground plan Verzone, *L'architettura religiosa*, 66, fig. 31.

Built soon after 431 as a dodecahedron, and transformed into a church by addition of a nave and provision of mosaic decoration in apse by Bishop Ecclesius around 534. This involved loss of three sides of the chapel. Apse mosaics lost in sixteenth century.

RIMINI

S ANDREA

Bibliography
Luigi Tonini, 'La chiesa di S Andrea presso Rimini,' *Atti e memorie della R. Dep. Di Storia Patria per le provincie di Romagna* (1863), 76f. and 1865, 108f.
P. Verzone, *L'architettura religiosa*, 28–30.

Location In the Christian cemetery outside the walls of Rimini.

Plan A Greek cross: fig. 114, above (after Tonini).

S GREGORIO

Bibliography Carlo Cecchelli, 'Un ignorato monumento riminese,' *Festschrift Friedrich Gerke* (Baden-Baden, 1962), 73–5.

Location Outside the walls of Rimini.

Plan Cecchelli's fig. 1 shows plan, section, exterior and mosaic decorations of this chapel, after an unidentified nineteenth-century manuscript in the Biblioteca Civica of Rimini.

S Gregorio was constructed around 523 (as dated by the tomb of a certain Leo) and completely destroyed, including the foundations, in 1834.

ROME

For the chapels at the Constantinian cemetery basilicas, see the entries under the various basilicas in R. Krautheimer et al., *Corpus Basilicarum Christianarum Romae*, 5 vols. (Vatican City, 1937–77). A representative selection only will be entered here.

CHAPEL OF S LEO AT S LORENZO f. l. m. (no longer extant)

Bibliography
Krautheimer et al., *CBCR*, II, 120–1, also pl. 2 and fig. 90.
G. De Rossi, 'Il monumento d'un ignoto S Leone, Vescovo e martire, nell'agro verano,' *BAC* 2 (1864), 54–6, and text illustration, 55.

Plan A trichora: see references above.

Location Near north corner of quadriporticus of S Lorenzo *fuori le mura*.

Built around 384 as *memoria* of a Bishop Leo, whose epigraph was discovered and recorded by De Rossi. In use until the late eighth century, when it was repaired by Hadrian I (772–95). Discovered in 1857 and now again lost.

The Roman Catacombs:

ORATORY OF S FELICITAS and her son SILVANUS

Bibliography

G. B. De Rossi, 'Scoperta d'una cripta storica nel cimitero di Massimo *ad sanctam Felicitatem* sulla via Salaria Nuova,' *BAC* 3–4 (1884–5), 149–84.

LP, I, 227, Boniface I (418–422): 'Hic fecit oratorium in cymiterio sanctae Felicitatis, iuxta corpus eius, et ornavit sepulchrum sanctae martyris Felicitatis.'

J. Osborne, 'The Roman Catacombs in the Middle Ages,' *PBSR* 53 (1985), 278–328, and plates XVI–XXII, esp. 316–17.

Location In the Catacomb of St Felicitas, on the Via Salaria Nuova.

The burial place of Felicitas was chosen by Pope Boniface I (418–22) as his place of refuge during his dispute over the papacy, and he had the chapel built, endowed it with gifts, and was buried nearby. It became a place of pilgrimage around the sixth century. For Pope Boniface's gifts of liturgical plate to this oratory, see chapter 10. For the chapel's early medieval paintings, see De Rossi, plates IX–X, and Osborne, plate XXa, who date them to the eighth century. They cover earlier mural paintings, which may date to the first campaign of decoration under Boniface.

Oratories outside the city walls:

ORATORY OF ST EUPLUS (no longer extant)

Bibliography

LP, I, Theodore (642–49): 'Fecit et oratorium beato Euplo martyris, foris porta beati Pauli apostoli, quam etiam ornavit.'

Location Near the Pyramid of Cestius, in the portico leading from the Porta Ostiense to S Paolo f. l. m. *LP*, I, 334, note 12.

Built by Theodore (642–49), it was repaired by Hadrian I (772–95), and survived until 1849 with a new dedication to S Salvatore.

Oratories at Old St Peter's:

S ANDREA

Bibliography

Joseph Alchermes, 'Petrine Politics: Pope Symmachus and the Rotunda of St Andrew at Old St Peter's,' *Catholic Historical Review* 81 (1995), 1–40.

LP, I, 261: 'Hic fecit [Symmachus] sancti Andreae apostoli apud beatum Petrum, ubi fecit tiburium ex argento purissimo et confessionem, pens. Lib. CXX; arcos argenteos III, pens. lib. LX; [the other donations follow].'

Plan Fig. 44.

The Vatican Rotunda was built as a mausoleum for an unknown imperial personage in the third century. Its site lay on the *spina* of the Circus of Nero, and was adjacent to the future location of St Peter's basilica. Pope Symmachus (498–514) converted it into a chapel complex, dedicating each of the seven niches to a different saint, among them Thomas, Protus and Hyacinthus, Apollinaris, Cassianus, Sossius, and possibly Lawrence and Vitus. The dedicatory inscriptions of several of these chapels have been recorded: *LP*, I, 265–6, notes 17–19. S Andrea was later rededicated as S Maria delle Febbre in honour of its miracle-working icon.

CHAPEL OF JOHN VII in St Peter's

Bibliography

LP, I, 385, Iohannes VII: 'Hic fecit oratorium sanctae Dei genetricis intro ecclesiam beati Petri apostoli, cuius parietes musibo depinxit, illicque auri et argenti quantitatem multam expendit et venerabilium Patrum dextra levaque vultus erexit.'

Giacomo Grimaldi, *Descrizione della basilica antica di S Pietro in Vaticano*, Cod. Vat. Barb. Lat. 2733; facsimile, ed. Reto Niggl (Vatican City, 1972).

William Tronzo, 'Setting and Structure in Two Roman Wall Decorations of the Early Middle Ages,' *DOP*, 41 (1987) 477–92.

Location Inside east (entry) wall of Old St Peter's.

Built by John VII (705–707), and demolished to make way for the new basilica on the site. The chapel is discussed in chapter 4, 'Chapels within the Confines of Churches.'

Memoriae in cemeteries:

SS SISTO e CECILIA, and S SOTERE

Bibliography

Antonio Baruffa, *Le Catacombe di San Callisto* (Turin, 1988), 34–6, for S Sotere, and colour plate 2, for its restored condition.

U.M. Fasola, 'Le ricerche di archeologia cristiana a Roma fuori le mura,' *Actes du XI congrès international d'archéologie chrétienne, 1986*, III (1989), 2149–76, esp. 2153 on the western triconch, excavated in 1908 and again in 1979–80.

O. Marucchi, 'La cella trichora detta di santa Sotere,' *NBAC*, XIV (1908), 157–95.

Plan and topography of site in Marruchi's paper.

Lateran Palace Chapels:

ST SEBASTIAN
Built by Pope Theodore (642–649).

Bibliography *LP*, Davis tr. 68.

ST SYLVESTER

Location In portico to right of the great entrance. In existence by 687.

Bibliography *LP* I, 371 and 377.

ST PETER

Bibliography

LP I, 402.

O. Panvinio, in *Le Palais du Latran*, ed. P. Lauer (Paris, 1911), 486.

The chapel dated from before the time of Pope Gregory II (715–31), who redecorated it. It survived into sixteenth century and was described by Panvinio.

Chapels inside other Roman churches:

SS PRIMUS AND FELICIANUS in S Stefano Rotondo

Bibliography

Carlo Ceschi, 'S Stefano Rotondo,' *Atti della pont. acc. rom. di arch.*, ser. II, *Memorie*, 15 (1982) entire volume, especially 94–5.

Caecilia Davis-Weyer, 'S Stefano Rotondo in Rome and the Oratory of Theodore I,' in *Italian Church Decoration of the Middle Ages and Early Renaissance. Functions, Forms and Regional Traditions*, ed. W. Tronzo (Bologna, 1989), 61–80.

R. Krautheimer et al., *CBCR*, IV, 223–6 and 237.

LP, I, 332.

Location In north-east arm of S Stefano Rotondo.

Plan See Davis-Weyer, fig. 3 (after C. Ceschi).

Dates to the reign of Theodore I (642–9). For details see chapter 4, 'Chapels within the Confines of Churches.'

SAN PRISCO, near S MARIA DI CAPUA VETERE

S MATRONA CHAPEL
Fully discussed in chapter 6; see also figs. 57–61

Location Annexed to the Parish Church, S Prisco, in the centre of the village.

Plan Not available.

SICILY

Near SIRACUSA. Two chapels near S CROCE IN CAMERINA, known locally as 'Vigna de Mare' and 'Bagno de Mare.'

Bibliography Paolo Orsi, 'Chiese bizantine del territorio di Siracusa,' *BZ*, 7 (1898), 1–28.

Plans The buildings are very similar. Both are cruciform with a central dome formed of *tubi fitilli*, which get smaller at the summit. In each, the entry arm is prolonged to form a Latin cross. For plan of Bagno de Mare, see fig. 112, above (after Orsi).

Location Vigna de Mare is located in the Caucana quarter on the banks of the Pantano, and Bagno de Mare, in a marshy area called Mezzagnone below S Croce in Camerina.

Probably dated to the sixth century. No traces of dedication or decorations survive, and the present condition is not known.

TRIGONA DI MACCARI, near NOTO

Bibliography See Orsi, above.

Plan A three-apsed structure with thick walls and small rectangular windows over the springing of the apses. See fig. 113, A–C (after Orsi), for its condition in 1898.

Location. The trichora is situated at the north end of the ruined Early Christian/early Byzantine city of Maccari, near Noto.

Probably of sixth century date. Present condition unknown.

TRIESTE REGION: San Canzian d'Isonzo; S Giovanni al Timavo; S Proto

Bibliography

G. Bovini, *Antichità cristiane di S Canzian d'Isonzo, S Giovanni al Timavo, e Trieste* (Bologna, 1973).
M. Mirabella Roberti, 'I mosaici di San Canzian d'Isonzo,' *Antichità altoadriatiche* 8 (1975), 235–44, fig. 1.

Plan Mirabella Roberti, fig. 1, shows 1959–60 excavations at S Proto, with the *memoria* underlying the SW corner: a rectangle with geometric mosaics framing crosses and a fish, probably marking the altar site.

TRIESTE

S MARIA DEL MARE

Bibliography Gabriella Pross Gabrielli, *L'oratorio e la basilica paleocristiana di Trieste (Via Madonna del Mare)* (Bologna, 1969).

Plan Gabrielli, pl. II, shows all three phases of its existence.

Location Outside the walls of Trieste in the suburban cemetery.

Orientated to the east, and rectangular, it was destroyed by fire in the mid-fifth century, and replaced by a second rectangular structure (6 by 7.5 m). It was later enlarged by the addition of an apse and side-arms to form a Latin cross.

VERONA

SS TOSCA E TEUTERIA
See chapter 1 and figs. 20 and 21.

Bibliography

P. Verzone, *L'Architettura religiosa*, 14–15.

P.L. Zovatto, 'Il sacello paleocristiano delle SS Tosca e Teuteria a Verona,' *FR* 33 (1961), 133–42.

Location On the site of an Early Christian cemetery on the Roman decumanus of Verona, outside the Porta dei Borsari of the city, beside the apse of the church of SS Apostoli.

Plan Verzone, 13, figs. 3 and 4, representing the Da Lisca excavations of 1912, and the present structure respectively.

Probably built around the turn of the sixth century, with an early dedication to St Apollinaris. Rededicated to the Early Christian saints Tosca and Teuteria (martyred in 263) when their remains were discovered in 1162. Original form a domed Greek cross, later converted to an apsed three-aisled basilica, perhaps in the extensive renovations of 1160, when it was enlarged for use as a family mausoleum.

SS NAZARO E CELSO

Bibliography

F. Dal Forno, *La chiesa dei santi Nazaro e Celso in Verona* (Verona, 1982), 19–37. See also R. Dal Zio, *Chiese*, 173–5.

Location Adjacent to the fifteenth-century basilica of the same name.

Plan dal Zio, 173. Cruciform with a vestibule and side arms.

Probably built in the sixth or seventh century. Partly cut into the tufa of Monte Costiglione, and only this part survives. A mosaic pavement survives in the central area.

VICENZA

S MARIA MATER DOMINI
See chapter 1 and figs. 22–5.

Bibliography

AAVV, *La basilica dei santi Felice e Fortunato in Vicenza*, 2 vols. (Vicenza, 1979–80).

Edoardo Arslan, *Catalogo delle cose d'arte e di antichità d'Italia, Vicenza*, I: *Le Chiese* (Rome, 1956), 88–9. Bibliography on chapel, 72.

Giovanni Lorenzon, 'Il gruppo monumentale dei martiri Felice e Fortunato di Vicenza,' in G.P. Bognetti, B. Forlati Tamaro, and G. Lorenzon, *Vicenza nell'alto Medio Evo* (Venice, 1959).

Location At SS Felice e Fortunato on the Via Postumia outside the walls of Vicenza.

Plan Figs. 22 and 23, above, for plan of chapel and basilica.

Probably built as a martyrium beside the earlier basilica of SS Felice e Fortunato in the mid-sixth century.

Notes

Introduction

1 For discussion of this change from pagan to Christian patronage, see Bryan Ward-Perkins, *From Classical Antiquity to the Middle Ages: Urban Public Building in Northern and Central Italy, AD 300–850* (Oxford, 1984), esp. chapters 3 and 4.

2 See Johannes Baptista Gattico, *De Oratoriis Domesticis et de usu altario portatalis* (Rome, 1746, 2nd ed. 1770), chapter 2, 'De Nomine Capellae,' p. 8. See also F. Cabrol and H. Leclercq, *Dictionnaire d'Archéologie chrétienne et de Liturgie (DACL)* (Paris, 1914), 3/1, cols. 407–10, and, for the cloak itself, cols. 381–90.

3 J.F. Niermeyer, *Mediae Latinitatis Lexicon Minus* (Leiden, 1976), 130.

4 In addition to Niermeyer, *Lexicon*, see R.E. Latham, *Revised Medieval Latin Word-List* (Oxford, 1965); A. Souter, *Glossary of Later Latin to 600 AD* (Oxford, 1949), and the *Oxford Latin Dictionary*, 2 vols. (Oxford, 1968–76).

5 See Niermeyer, *Lexicon*, 702–3, for a total of nine meanings for the word *monasterium* in the ninth to eleventh centuries, including 'chapel adjacent to a church.' Two editions exist of Agnellus's chronicle: *Liber Pontificalis Ecclesiae Ravennatis*, ed. O. Holder-Egger, *MGH, ScriptRerLangobard* (Hanover, 1878); and *Codex Pontificalis Ecclesiae Ravennatis*, ed. Alessandro Testi-Rasponi (Bologna, 1924), unfinished, but the preferred edition.

6 See Joseph Braun, *Der christliche Altar in seiner historischen Entwicklung* (Munich, 1924), 369.

7 Cabrol and Leclercq, *DACL*, 1/2, 'Autel,' cols. 3185–7, esp. 3185.

8 See Raymond Davis, tr. and ed., *The Book of Pontiffs (Liber Pontificalis)* (Liverpool, 1989), 107, 'altar.'

9 Niermeyer, *Lexicon, altare*, 38, 1: 'Christian altar'; 3: 'lateral chapel of a

church,' with Niermeyer's example dating from 844; the beginnings of this usage will be discussed in chapter 4.

1 Martyr Shrine to Funerary Chapel

1 For general information, see J.M.C. Toynbee, *Death and Burial in the Roman World* (London, 1971). For specific laws, see *The Theodosian Code*, tr. Clyde Pharr (Princeton, 1952), esp. 240, 9.17.6, of emperors Gratian, Valentinian, and Theodosius, 30 July 381, banning the bodies of apostles and martyrs from the city, on pain of penalties that included heavy fines and the removal of the remains.

2 Ibid., 240, 9.17. 7, same emperors, 26 February 386, 'No person shall transfer a buried body to another place. No person shall sell the relics of a martyr; no person shall traffic in them.'

3 See chapters 2 and 7.

4 R. Krautheimer, S. Corbett, and W. Frankl, *Corpus Basilicarum Christianarum Romae, The Early Christian Basilicas of Rome IV–IX Centuries*, 5 vols. (Vatican City, 1937–77), II, 196–8. St Tiburtius is first recorded from this catacomb in an epigram of Pope Damasus (366–84). See *ActaSS*, 2 June, 173f., and also Jean Guyon, *Le Cimetière aux Deux Lauriers* (Rome, 1987), 208, fig. 115, which shows the overall plan of the excavations between 1896 and 1984. His 'VII' is the chapel of St Tiburtius.

5 Guyon, ibid., 440–5, esp. 449, and fig. 244, 'La basilique inférieure,' the *basilica ad corpus* of Peter and Marcellinus.

6 P. Crostarosa, 'Le Catacombe Romane,' *NBAC* 3 (1897), 113–30, esp. 122–5.

7 Krautheimer, Corbett, and Frankl, *CBCR*, II, 196. A. Bosio, *Roma sotteranea* (Rome, 1632), 322f. Also see Guyon, *Cimetière*, 21–9, for an account of the excavation of 'mausoleum XII,' which, on the evidence of its floor mosaics, probably dated from the second century.

8 For P. Ligorio, Bibl. Naz. Napoli, Cod. XIIIB 10, Libro 49, see Guyon, *Cimetière*, 28, fig. 25, and 29, fig. 26.

9 G.B. De Rossi, 'Sepolcri antichi nell'agro Verano,' *BAC* 1 (1863), 16.

10 G.B. De Rossi, 'Il monumento d'un ignoto S Leone, vescovo e martire, nell'agro Verano,' *BAC* II (1864), 54–6, and text illustration, p. 55; Also Krautheimer, Corbett, and Frankl, *CBCR*, II, 120–1, and pl. 2, and fig. 90.

11 *LP*, I, 508, 'Immo et aecclesiam sancti Stephani iuxta eas sita, ubi corpus sancti Leonis episcopus et martyris quiescit, similiter undique renovavit una cum cymiterio beatae Cyriacae seu ascensum eius.'

12 Krautheimer, Corbett, and Frankl, *CBCR*, II, 107–8.

13 For the annexed chapels discussed in this paragraph, see Krautheimer, Corbett, and Frankl, *CBCR*, IV, 136–9 and pl. VII.

14 See Antonio Baruffa, *Le Catacombe di San Callisto* (Turin, 1988), 34–6, for the 'western trichora' (S Sotere), and colour plate 2, for its restored condition. This is probably one of the structures drawn by G.-B. Montano, *Scielta de varii Tempietti antichi* (Rome, 1624), no. 10, 'Tempio antico nella Via Appia, poco lontano da capo di Boue,' or 20, 'Tempio antico fuori di Roma nella Via Appia, a mano manca passato Capo di Boue.'

15 U. Fasola, 'Le ricerche di archeologia cristiana a Roma fuori le mura,' *Actes du XI congrès international d'archéologie chrétienne, 1986*, III (1989), 2149–76, esp. 2153 on the western triconch, excavated in 1908 and again in 1979–80. See also A. Grabar, *Martyrium, recherches sur le culte des reliques et l'art chrétien antique*, 3 vols. (Paris, 1946), III, pl. 1:1 (St Sixtus) and 1:2 (St Soter).

16 E. (Henri) Stevenson, 'Découverte de la basilique double de Ste Symphorose et de ses sept fils au neuvième mille de la voie tiburtine,' *BAC*, ser. III (1878), 80–7 and pl. IV.

17 Grabar, *Martyrium*, I, 103–4.

18 D. Thierri Ruinart, *Acta Sincera* (1711), 23, places the cult of Sinferosa and her sons at the ninth mile of the Via Tiburtina, which was still popularly known as 'a sette fratte' in the seventeenth century. A. Bosio, *Roma sotteranea* (Rome, 1632), 401.

19 I. Lavin, 'The House of the Lord. Aspects of the Role of Palace Triclinia in the Architecture of Late Antiquity and the Early Middle Ages,' *ArtBull.* 44 (1962), 1–27, esp. 21, note 170.

20 Rediscovered by G.B. De Rossi in 1856, 'Scoperta d'una cripta storica nel cimitero di Massimo *ad sanctam Felicitatem* sulla via Salaria Nuova,' *BAC* 3–4 (1884–5), 149–84, and pl. IX–X (drawn by Mariani). *LP*, I, 227: 'Hic fecit oratorium in cymiterio sanctae Felicitatis, iuxta corpus eius, et ornavit sepulchrum sanctae martyris Felicitatis et sancti Silvani.' See also J. Osborne, 'The Roman Catacombs in the Middle Ages,' *PBSR* 53 (1985), 278–328, esp. 316–17.

21 See De Rossi, 'Scoperta,' pl. XI, XII, and Cabrol and Leclercq, *DACL*, 5/1, fig. 4327, cols. 1283–4. Grabar, *Martyrium*, III, pl. XIX, mistakenly attributes this drawing to Ruspi and places it in the catacomb chapel. Its actual site was in the chapel on the Oppian Hill.

22 Grabar, *Martyrium*, II, 17, note 2, 'cette fresque du VIIe siècle décore la niche absidiale de l'oratoire-martyrium de Sainte-Félicité.' Also, Krautheimer, Corbett, and Frankl, *CBCR*, I, 219. See also Christa Ihm, *Die Programme der christlicher Apsismalerei vom vierten Jahrhundert bis zur mitte des achten Jahrhunderts* (Wiesbaden, 1960), pl. XXVI/3.

23 See W. Tronzo, *The Via Latina Catacomb* (University Park, PA, 1986), esp. chapter 2, 'The Building of the Catacomb,' and A. Ferrua, *Le pitture della nuova catacomba di Via Latina'* (Vatican City, 1960).

24 Tronzo, *Catacomb*, 10.

25 Ferrua, *Le pitture della nuova catacomba*, pl. LIV, for tunnel vault of corridor H; Tronzo, *Catacomb*, fig. 26, for cubiculum I, and figs. 27, 28 for cubiculum N and the S Costanza vault.

26 For the chapels of north-east Italy and Istria, see the section 'Chapels in the North-East,' in this chapter. For the north-west, see Ward-Perkins, *From Classical Antiquity to the Middle Ages*, 79–80.

27 For these chapels see the Appendix.

28 Ambrose, *Exhortatio Virginitatis*, I, *PL*, 16, cols. 351–2.

29 Ambrose, *Epistola XXII*, 'To His Sister Marcellina,' *PL*, 16, cols. 1062–9, esp. 1063, 'transtulimus vespere jam incumbente ad basilicam Faustae: ibi vigiliae tota nocte manus impositio.' See also M. Mirabella Roberti, ed., 'Architettura paleocristiane a Milano,' *Milano, Capitale dell'impero romano, 286–402 d.c.* (Milan, 1990), 433–9, esp. 436.

30 Galvano Flamma (Galvanei Flammae), *Chronicon Maius*, in *Miscellanea di storia italiana*, 7 (Turin, 1869), 506f.

31 The *Acts* of Vitalis are based on the fifth-century *Letter of Pseudo-Ambrose*, *PL*, 17, *Epistola* II (alias LIII), cols. 821–5, which creates a dynasty of saints for Ravenna, borrowing the patrons of Milan and other places and setting up a place of martyrdom for them to rival the Colosseum, at a site which supposedly now lies under the church of S Vitale.

32 V. Forcella, *Seletti iscrizioni cristiane in Milano anteriori al IX secolo* (Cologne, 1897), 34, inscription 37.

33 For S Valeria chapel, see Appendix.

34 Ambrose, 'To his sister Marcellina,' col. 1063: 'eo loci, qui est ante cancellos sanctorum Felicis atque Naboris,' tr. H. de Romestin, *N&PNF*, 10, 436. The recognition of the saints by their larger-than-life-size bones, as Ambrose recounts, is reminiscent of the return to Sparta of the bones of Orestes, son of Agamemnon, which were also recognized by their heroic size. Herodotus, *History*, I, 67–8 (Loeb ed.,1926), 79–83.

35 F. Savio, *Gli antichi vescovi d'Italia: Milano* (Florence, 1913), 147–8. For Vigilius' letter describing the martyrdoms, see *Bibliotheca Hagiographica Latina Antiquae et Mediae Aetatis* (Brussels, 1898–1901), 7994–6.

36 See G. Traversi, *Architettura paleocristiana milanese* (Milan, 1964), 38–40.

37 P. Verzone, *L'architettura religiosa dell'alto medioevo nell'Italia settentrionale* (Milan, 1942), 65. Also A. de'Capitani d'Arzago, 'L'architettura cristiana in

Milano,' *Actes du VIIe congrés d'études Byzantines* (Paris, 1948), II, 1951, 67ff., esp. 75.

38 Ann Terry, 'Early Christian Cruciform Annex Chapels in Northern Italy: A Family of Martyria-Mausolea,' master's thesis (University of Illinois, 1979), 111, points out the presence of three recesses, 1.8 metres in length by 3 metres deep, cut into the north and south arms and filled with later masonry, as possible sites for the relics of the three saints.

39 *ActaSS*, July, VI, 508; also M. Caffi, *Storia di Milano* (Milan, 1953–4), 623.

40 Paulinus Diaconus, *Vita Ambrosii*, PL, 14, 10, col. 32, 1432–3. Jean-Charles Picard, *Le souvenir des évêques: Sépultures, listes épiscopales et culte des évêques en Italie du Nord des origines au Xe siècle* (Rome, 1988), 52–3, gives the probable date of Ambrose's discovery of Nazarius as 28 July 395.

41 See Picard, *Souvenir*, 41–4, for the excavations at S Eustorgio. A *memoria* was found, but without any indication that it was that of the saint.

42 F. Reggiori, *La Basilica Ambrosiana. Ricerche e restauri, 1929–1940* (Milan, 1941), 244, 248.

43 Reggiori dates the change to the late fifth or early sixth centuries. Ibid., 181f. and fig., p. 83; also Verzone, *Architettura religiosa*, 64.

44 Reggiori, *Basilica Ambrosiana*, 177; also G. Bovini, 'Gli edifici di culto milanesi d'età pre-ambrosiana,' *CorsiCRB* 8 (1961), 47–72, esp. 69.

45 See Picard, *Souvenir*, 36–41, for burial of Victor and Satyrus at San Vittore and 36, notes 61–2, for bibliography of chapel.

46 See also my 'Symbolism and Purpose in an Early Christian Martyr Chapel: The Case of San Vittore in Ciel d'Oro,' *Gesta* 34 (1995), 91–101.

47 F. Savio, *Vescovi*, 10, places his twelve-year bishopric within the period 314 to 343.

48 Ibid., 94.

49 Codex Vindobonensis, folios 184–91, esp. 186, cited by Picard, *Souvenir*, 19.

50 Picard, *Souvenir*, 46; also 22–4 on the itinerary and the seventh-century translation of Simplicianus's remains, which were discovered in the tenth century in S Simpliciano.

51 Apparently Calimerus lay in a *memoria* near the Porta Romana which was subsequently replaced by a church in his name. For both Calimerus and Eustorgius see Picard, *Souvenir*, 25–6.

52 For the Trentine martyrs see Picard, *Souvenir*, 68, and for Maternus, 39–41.

53 S Maria Maggiore appears to have been founded on land given to the bishop by Honorius. Agnellus, *LPER*, 318: 'in sua proprietatis iura haedificavit ecclesia.' See also *CPER*, 163–5, note 2.

54 P. Verzone, 'Ipotesi di topografia ravennate,' *CorsiCRB* 13 (1966), 433–44,

esp. 441, and Neil Christie, 'The City Walls of Ravenna: The Defence of a Capital, AD 402–750,' *CorsiCRB* 36 (1989), 113–38, esp. 136–7.

55 Peter Brown, *The Cult of the Saints* (Chicago, 1981), 86.

56 Ambrose did receive a sign, a vision or dream, that his action was pleasing to God, as Augustine recounts in his *Confessions*, Lib. IX, cap. 7, and *De Civitate Dei*, Lib. XXII, cap. 8, and was further reassured by miracles at each resting place of the remains. Ambrose, *Epistola* XXII, *PL*, 16, col. 1063.

57 Ibid., col. 1063, 'formidantibus etiam clericis jussi eruderari terram eo loci, qui est ante cancellos sanctorum Felicis atque Naboris.'

58 Ibid., col. 1062. The congregation was asking him to consecrate the church in the same way as he had consecrated the Basilica Apostolarum.

59 Ibid., col. 1066. 'Hunc ego locum praedestinaveram mihi; dignum est enim ut ibi requiescat sacerdos, ubi offerre consuevit: sed cedo sacris victimis dexteram portionem, locus iste martyribus debebatur.'

60 Gregory I, *Epistola* XXX, 'Ad Constantinam Augustam,' *PL*, 77, Lib. IV, cols. 700–5.

61 J.M.M. McCulloh, 'The Cult of Relics in the Letters and Dialogues of Pope Gregory the Great: A Lexicographical Study,' *Traditio* 32 (1975), 158–84.

62 Ambrose, *Epistola* XXII, cols. 1064–5: 'Cognovistis, imo vidistis ipsi multos a daemoniis purgatos: plurimos etiam, ubi vestem sanctorum manibus contiguerunt, iis quibus laborabant, debilitatibus absolutos: reparata vetusti temporis miracula ... umbra quadam sanctorum corporum plerosque sanatos cernitis. Quanta oraria jaclitantur! quanta indumenta super reliquias sacratissimas et tactu ipso medicabilia reposcuntur! Gaudent omnes extrema linea contingere; et qui contigerit, salvus erit.'

63 Gregory I, *Epistola* XXX, cols. 700–5.

64 G. Gerola, 'Il sacello primitivo in San Vitale,' *FR* 2 (1913), 427–34 and 459–71, esp. 461–3.

65 Ibid., esp. 430. See also R. Farioli, *Pavimenti musivi di Ravenna paleocristiana* (Ravenna, 1975), 73, fig. 26.

66 For the 1911 excavations, see Gerola, 'Sacello,' 459–63. For subsequent work, see F. Di Pietro, 'Il prisco sacello di S. Vitale,' *Bolletino d'Arte*, ser. II, 5 (1926), 241–51, and 243, fig. 1, for a plan of the excavations.

67 Gerola, 'Sacello,' 427. The date 393 constitutes a *terminus post quem* for the 'Letter of Pseudo-Ambrose': see note 68, below. See also Paola Porta, 'Due sarcophagi nel tempo' in *7 colonne e 7 chiese. La vicenda ultramillenaria del complesso di santo Stefano* (Bologna, 1986), 88–99, esp. 89.

68 Pseudo-Ambrose, *Epistola* II, alias LIII, *PL*, 17, cols. 821–5. See also *Passio sanctorum Vitalis, Valeriae, Gervasi, Protasi et Ursicini*, in *Bibliotheca Hagiographica Latina* (Brussels, 1901), 524, 1216, and 1255f; and also *ActaSS*

(April), III, 562–5. The letter has been variously dated: after the arrival of
the Augusti in Ravenna in 402; after 425 (Savio); 'much later' than 393
(Gerola); after 526 (Testi-Rasponi); but anyway before 548 (the verses of
Venantius Fortunatus forming a *terminus ante quem*).

69 F. Savio, 'Due lettere falsamente attribuite a S Ambrogio,' *NBAC* 3 (1897),
153–78, esp. 166.

70 A theme developed by Brown in *Cult of the Saints.*

71 Agnellus, *CPER,* XXIV Eclesius, 163–5. Testi-Rasponi's 163, note 6, gives the
date of construction of S Vitale as soon after 526.

72 Di Pietro, 'Sacello di S. Vitale,' 245, and Gerola, 'Sacello,' 465.

73 Agnellus, *CPER,* XXI Iohannes I, note, 120–1.

74 Gerola, 'Sacello,' 464. See also C. Ricci, 'La cappella detta Sancta Sanctorum nella chiesa di S. Vitale in Ravenna,' *Rassegna d'Arte* 4 (1904),
104–8.

75 'A crown of chapels, which recall the sanctuaries that were not far from the
imperial palace in Milan.' See Agnellus, *CPER,* XXI Iohannes I, 120, and
Testi-Rasponi's note 9, 119–21, which covers the whole group of chapels
in detail, and discusses their probable dates. See also his note 6, p. 163,
'Questa parte della città (il quartiere della domus Augustae), che la pietà
del principi aveva disseminato di modesti sacelli, noi ne contiamo sette, nel
V secolo apparteneva al fisco imperiale, forse piutosto al patrimonio privato del sovrano, sotto la giurisdizione del comes privatorum.'

76 Agnellus, *CPER,* XXVII Maximian, 190.

77 See Mackie, 'New Light on the So-Called St Lawrence Panel at the Mausoleum of Galla Placidia in Ravenna,' *Gesta* 29 (1990), 54–60.

78 Testi-Rasponi in Agnellus, *CPER,* 165, note 2, suggests that Ecclesius's
alterations date to the period soon after 526. The mosaics are known from
the description of Girolamo Rossi (= Hieronymus Rubeus), *Historia Ravennatis libri decem* (Venice, 1689), 153–4; they were already ruined in 1550.
Rossi wrote 'Eiusdem (Ecclesii) imago, templum d. Mariae Virgini ac
infanti Christo Deo offerentis, in d. Mariae Maioris cernitur, opere picta
vermiculato, annos referens circiter quadraginta, sed ita corrupta, ut nisi
eorum, qui praesunt, liberalitas latus pateat, paucio abhinc annis penitus
collapsura sit.'

79 R. Krautheimer, 'Sancta Maria Rotunda,' in *Arte del primo millenio* (Turin,
1950), reprinted in idem., *Studies in Early Christian, Medieval and Renaissance
Art* (New York, 1969), 107–14, esp. postscript, 113–14.

80 Bernardus Monachus Francus, *Itinerarium in Loca Sancta, PL,* 121, cols.
569–74, esp. 572–3: 'De Hierusalem in Valle Josaphat milliari, et habet vil-
lam Gethsemani cum loco nativitatis sanctae Mariae, in quo est in honore

ipsius ecclesia permaxima. In ipsa quoque villa est ecclesia sanctae Mariae rotunda ubi est sepulchrum illius, quod supra se tectum non habet, pluviam minime patitur.'

81 *Breviarius Hierosolyma* (*Itinera Hierosolymitana*), ed. P. Geyer, *CSEL* 39 (Vienna, 1898), 155, 'refers to two distinct structures, the "Basilica sanctae Mariae" and, introduced by a new "ibi," her tomb, "sepulchrum eius."' See Krautheimer, 'Sancta Maria Rotunda.'

82 Staale Sunding Larson, 'Some Functional and Iconographical Aspects of the Centralised Church in the Italian Renaissance,' *Acta R.Norv.* 2 (1965), 203–53, esp 220, 'Iconographical aspects in centralised buildings.'

83 See *The Book of James*, a mid-second-century infancy gospel of Mary, in M.R. James, *The Apocryphal New Testament*, 2nd ed. (Oxford, 1953), 38–49. Also, *ODCC*, 723.

84 Agnellus, *CPER*, 119, the words imputed to Singledia: 'in illo loco non longe ab ... Sancta Crucis ecclesia ... quantum iactum sagita est, construe michi monasterium.'

85 Galla Placidia had two brothers: Honorius was childless, Arcadius's children did not include a Singledia.

86 A. Testi-Rasponi, 'Note Agnelliane,' *FR* 18 (1915), 773–89, esp. 782.

87 G. Cortesi, 'I principali edifici sacri ravennati in funzione sepolcrale nei secc. V e VI,' *CorsiCRB* 29 (1982), 63–107, esp. 103–4, and 94, fig. 9.

88 Agnellus, *CPER*, XXI, Iohannes I, 123; text in chapter 3, note 5.

89 Ibid., 121, note 9.

90 Agnellus, *CPER*, XXII, Petrus II, 151: 'Temporibus Galle Placidie auguste, sicut scriptum reperimus, corpus beati Barbatiani, idem Petrus Crisologus cum predicta augusta aromatibus condiderunt et cum magno honore sepelierunt, non longe ad posterulam Ovilionis; consecravitque ecclesiam sancti Iohannis Barbatiani quam Baduarius hedificavit.' According to Testi-Rasponi, 'Note Agnelliane,' note 10, S Giovanni Battista was certainly one of the many founded around the palace by the Augusti: the attribution to Baduarius he explains as perhaps recording an epigraph from the place where Barbatianus's body was later kept.

91 Ibid., 151.

92 Agnellus, *LPER*, 353: 'De monasterio sancti Apolenaris quae situs est, hic Ravenna non longe a posterula Ovilionis in loco qui vocatur Moneta publica, exinde abba fuit. Et istius ecclesiae vicedominus fuit, post pontificem similiter tenuit principatum.'

93 Cortesi, 'Principali edifici,' 106.

94 Agnellus, *LPER*, 383: 'Ex monasterio beati Apolenaris (Gratiosus) abba fuit, quod est fundatum non longe ab ecclesia sanctae redemptricis Crucis ad Monetam veteram, unde sanctissimus Reperatus fuit.'

95 Ibid., 94–6, esp. 96: 'Sepultus est in monasterio sancti Gervasi et Protasi, iuxta predictam eclesiam, mirabiliter decoratam musiva auream et diversarum lapidum genera singullaque metalla, parietibus iuncta.'

96 Agnellus, *CPER*, XXI Iohannes I, 97. The inscription read: 'STEPHANO PROTASIO GERVASIO BTO MARTIRIO ET SIBI MEMORIA ETERNA LAURICIUS HUIUS DEDICAVIT SUB DIE TERCIO KAL. OCTUBRIS THEODOXIO QUINTO DECIMO ET PLACIDO VALENTINIANO.' The date reads 29 September 435.

97 H.L. Gonin, *Excerpta Agnelliana. The Ravennate Liber Pontificalis as a Source for the History of Art* (Utrecht, 1933), 73.

98 Pseudo-Ambrose, *Epistola* II, cols. 747–9.

99 The scene occurs in the Catacomb of Priscilla, for example. J. Wilpert, *Die römischen Mosaiken und Malereien der kirchlichen Bauten vom IX–XIII Jahrhundert* (Freiburg, 1917), pl. 78:1. The scene probably also occurred at the Mausoleum of Helena, Rome, as well as at Centcelles, Spain.

100 Agnellus, *CPER*, XXI Iohannes I, 94–7, esp. 95.

101 Picard, *Souvenir*, 132–43.

102 Agnellus, *CPER*, XV Florentius, 61, notes 4–7: 'Sepultusque est in monasterio Sancti Pulionis quem suis temporibus edificatum est, non longe a porta que vocatur Nova, cuius sepulchrum nobis cognitum est.' See also *LPER*, 288, note 4: 'in regione S. Salvatore prope murum civitatis sito.' Also M. Fantuzzi, *Monumenti Ravennati*, 6 vols. (Venice, 1801), I, 336; VI, 248.

103 Agnellus, *LPER*, 288: 'Pulcher fuit in forma, clarior in sensu.' See also G. Bovini, 'Le "imagines episcoporum Ravennae" ricordate nel *Liber Pontificalis* di Andrea Agnello,' *CorsiCRB* 21 (1974), 53–63, which analyses the physical descriptions of the bishops of Ravenna given by Agnellus, and finds that monumental sources are recorded for the physiognomy of fourteen bishops among the total of forty-six listed (ending with Archbishop George, d. 846). Of the remaining thirty-two, sixteen were not described, and possibly Agnellus had no pictorial source for them. The other sixteen descriptions may have been based on minor arts, including a portrait on a processional cross, and the embroidered *endothis* or altar cloth commissioned by Maximinian that showed his predecessors in the see. It has not survived, though the so-called Velum of Classis in the National Museum, Ravenna, is a similar cloth with portraits of the bishops of Verona. See G. Bovini, 'Le "tovaglie d'altare" ricamate ricordate da Andrea Agnello nel *Liber Pontificalis Ecclesiae Ravennatis*,' *CorsiCRB* 21 (1974), 77–90.

104 U.M. Fasola, *Le Catacombe di S. Gennaro a Capodimonte* (Rome, 1975), 131–60, and colour plates XI, a and b, XII and XIII.

105 Agnellus, *CPER*, XV Florentius, 61: 'Sepultus est hic sanctus vir in monasterio sanctae Petronillae, haerens muris ecclesiae Apostolorum.'

106 Agnellus, *CPER*, III Eleuchadius, 32: 'Sepultus est extra muros Classis, ubi usque hodie laudem et nominis eius ecclesia hedificata et Deo consecrata.'

107 M. Mazzotti, 'Chiese ravennati scomparse,' *Almanacco Ravennate* (1958), 365.

108 Agnellus, *LPER*, 366; Also R. Farioli, 'Ravenna paleocristiana scomparsa,' *FR*, 31 (1960); 32 (1961), 5–88.

109 Picard, *Souvenir*, 179–84, quoting Vitale Aequedotti, an early-sixteenth-century source.

110 The Arian Cathedral of the Anastasis, now S Salvatore, and its baptistery, are obvious exceptions. So are the Mausoleum of Theodoric, and the lost S Andrea Gothorum.

111 M.J. Johnson, 'Toward a History of Theoderic's Building Programme,' *DOP* 42 (1988), 73–96.

112 For instance, S Vittore in Ciel d'Oro was rebuilt, and the chapel of S Sisto, burial place of Milan's bishops, was added at S Lorenzo.

113 See J.C. Smith, 'Side Chambers,' and 'Church Libraries.'

114 Agnellus, *CPER*, 173, note 4.

115 Cortesi, *Principali edifici*, 65.

116 Gerolamo Fabri, *Le sagre memorie di Ravenna antica* (Venice, 1664), 98–9: 'Le reliquie dei santi ... sotto un altare a loro nome ... sotto il portico ... a mano destra entrando.'

117 Agnellus, *CPER*, XXX Iohannes II, 245.

118 This was not the first joint burial place of the bishops. Maximinian had buried some of his predecessors beside the body of St Probus in the cemetery church of S Probo in Classe, Agnellus, *LPER*, 330. When Classis declined as a port, these burials were moved by way of S Apollinare in Classe and S Severo in Caesarea to the Ravenna cathedral, the Ursiana, *CPER*, 200, note 2. This transfer had occurred between the seventh century, when burial became acceptable inside the city, and Agnellus's time, the mid-ninth century.

119 Agnellus, *CPER*, XXX Iohannes II, 247.

120 Gregory I, to Castorius, his notary, *Registrum Epistolorum*, IX, 169.

121 Farioli, *Ravenna scomparsa*, 31–2.

122 Agnellus thought it was a portrait of Petrus I, but this is improbable since the title Archiepiscopus was not used in the first half of the fifth century. Agnellus, *CPER*, 74; also 103–8. Petrus III was buried in the narthex at S Probo (*CPER*, 241).

123 Agnellus, *CPER*, XXVIII, 223–4: 'Monasterio vero in civitate Classis, que

lateribus fontique eclesia Petriana iuncta sunt, sancti Mathei et Jacobi, ipse tessellis ornare iussit.' According to Testi-Rasponi, Agnellus was responsible for the decoration of both chapels. The inscription in S Matteo ran: 'SALVO DOMNO PAPA AGNELO DE DONIS DEI ET SERVORUM EIUS QUI OPTULERUNT AD HONOREM ET HORNATUS QUORUM APOSTOLORUM ET RELIQUA PARS DE SUMMA CERVORUM QUI PERIERANT ET DEO AUTORE INVENTU SUNT HEC ABSIDA MOSIVO EXORNATA EST.'

124 S. Lewis, 'San Lorenzo Revisited: A Theodosian Palace Church at Milan,' *JSAH* 32 (1973), 204–5.

125 The resemblance has been made clear both by excavation and by identification of a drawing by an anonymous Dutch artist (ca. 1570), Stuttgart, Staatsgalerie, Graphische Sammlung, Inv. 5781r, and shown in my fig. 16. See C. de Fabriczy, 'Vedute cinquecentistiche di alcuni monumenti milanesi,' *Rassegna d'Arte* 6 (1906), 87–90.

126 See M.J. Johnson, *Late Antique Imperial Mausolea*, PhD dissertation (Princeton University, 1986), 55–9, and, for Maximian, 261–3.

127 Ambrose, Hymns: LXXII, 'De S. Sixto,' and LXXIII, 'De S. Laurentio,' *PL*, 17, cols. 1253–4. Also, *De Officiis, PL*, 16, cols. 90–2, and *Epistola* 37, to Simplicianus, cols. 1129–42, esp. 1139.

128 Picard, *Souvenir*, 62–4.

129 Lewis, 'San Lorenzo Revisited,' 211–15.

130 Grabar, *Martyrium*, I, 347.

131 Lewis, 'San Lorenzo Revisited,' 214: 'From the eighth century *Laudes Mediolensis Civitatis* through the eleventh century chronicles of Benzonis Albensis and Arnulphus, the martyrium of S. Lawrence is described as being covered with gold mosaics.'

132 Ibid., 213; see also *Catalogus Archiepiscoporum Mediolanensium*, ed. W. Wattenbach, *MGH, Scriptores* (Hanover, 1848), VIII, 102f.

133 Magnus Felix Ennodius, *Opera Omnia*, ed. F. Vogel, *MGH, AA*, VII (Berlin, 1885), 120, XCVI, Carmen 2, 8: 'Versus in basilica sancti Syxti, facti et scripti, quam Laurentius episcopus fecit.'

134 Verzone, *Architettura religiosa*, 14–15.

135 The translation is recorded on two lead sheets in the urn, giving the date and recording the inscriptions on the burials: TUSCA INNOCENS and THEUTERIA VIRGO.

136 These documents, from the *Psalter* of the SS Apostoli, are discussed by Verzone, *Architettura religiosa*, 15.

137 See AAVV, *La Basilica dei Santi Felice e Fortunato in Vicenza*, 2 vols. (Vicenza, 1979–80), I, 76–7, for section and plan.

138 For dating, see E. Arslan, *Catalogo delle cose d'arte e di antichità d'Italia, Vicenza.* I: *Le Chiese* (Rome, 1956).

139 Giovanni Lorenzon, 'Il gruppo monumentale dei martiri Felice e Fortunato di Vicenza,' in G.P. Bognetti, B. Forlati Tamaro, and G. Lorenzon, *Vicenza nell'alto Medio Evo* (Venice, 1959), 15ff., esp. 28: 'il sacello ... raccoglieva le reliquie dei Martiri di tutto il territorio.' Also see Grabar, *Martyrium*, I, 406, 423; and Arslan, *Catalogo*, 88–9.

140 'The blessed martyrs Felix and Fortunatus,' G.B. De Rossi, *Roma sotteranea cristiana descritta ed illustrata* (Rome, 1854), III, 436. Lorenzon, 'Gruppo monumentale,' 23, dates the sarcophagus to 310–20, though others, such as B. Tamaro Forlati, prefer the sixth century. The sarcophagus, now in the crypt of SS Felice e Fortunatus, is illustrated in R. Canova Dal Zio, *Le Chiese delle tre Venezie anteriori al mille* (Padua, 1986), 129.

141 Lorenzon, ibid., 23.

142 A formal 'recognition' in 1979 confirmed the contents of the casket. Lellia Cracco Ruggieri, in A. Broglio and L. Cracco Ruggieri, *Storia di Vicenza*, I (Vicenza, 1987), 299f.; and AAVV, *Basilica* (Vicenza, 1979), 121 and pl. 80, p. 120.

143 Venantius Fortunatus (b. ca. 530), *Vita S. Martini*, II, vv. 658–60, *MGH, AA*, IV, I. Also, *Carmina*, 8/3, *PL*, 88, vv. 165–6.

144 Francesco Barbarano de Mironi, *Historia ecclesiastica della città, territorio, e diocesi di Vicenza* (Vicenza, 1649), I, 13, and 28–9, not available to me; cited by Arslan, *Catalogo*, 88. See also F.W. Deichmann, 'Per la datazione dell'epigrafe dedicatoria di S. Maria Mater Domini a Vicenza,' *FR*, 3 ser., 62 (1953), 48–50, esp. 48.

145 'Gregorius, *Sublimis Vir* [and] *Referendarius*, built this chapel of the Blessed Mary, Mother of the Lord, from the foundations [and] dedicated [it] in the name of Christ.'

146 Barbarano, ibid. Niermeyer, *Lexicon*, 898, *referendarius*: 'a court dignitary who receives petitions.' See also *ODB*, ed. Alexander P. Kazhdan, vol. III (New York and Oxford, 1991), 1778.

147 G. Frasson, 'Di un importantissimo monumento paleocristiano a Vicenza,' *Atti del R. Istituto Veneto di S.L.A.* 96, 2 (1936–7), 459–62. See also Arslan, *Catalogo*, 88–9.

148 This Gregorius does not occur in J.R. Martindale, ed., *The Prosopography of the Later Roman Empire*, vol. II: AD 395–527 (Cambridge, 1980), and vol. III: AD 527–641 (Cambridge, 1992).

149 Attilio Previtali, *San Felice: Una dimora dello spirito*, II: *Martyrion* (Vicenza, 1988), and idem, in AAVV, *Basilica*, I, 69–116 and pl. IX, X, and XI; bibliography in *Basilica*, vol. I, note 1, p. 72 (on chapel), and vol. II, 432–3 (gen-

eral). See also M. Mirabella Roberti, 'La basilica dei SS Felice e Fortunato in Vicenza,' 89–92, in the same volume.

150 Paolo Lino Zovatto, 'L'oratorio paleocristiano di S Giustina a Padova,' in *La Basilica di Santa Giustina Arte e storia* (Castelfranco Veneto, 1970), 18–63.

151 As seen by Guglielmo Ongarello, *Chronica di Padova*, 1441, Bibl.civ.Padova, segnato BP, 396, 33v.: 'la quale è su do collone sopra la porta la quale va la cappella de S.Prosdocimo.' Text in Maria Tonzig, *La basilica romanico-gotica di Santa Giustina in Padova* (Padua, 1932), 5.

152 For example, the border on the 'Lamb' sarcophagus in S Apollinare in Classe. M. Lawrence, *The Sarcophagi of Ravenna* (New York, 1945), 33, and pl. 54–6.

153 A. Simioni, *Storia di Padova* (Padua, 1968), 138. Actual text: '+ OPILIO VC/ET IN L.PP ADQ/PATRICIUS HANC.BASILICAMVEL ORA/TOR-IUM IN HONORE SCAEIUSTINAE MARTYRIS A FUNDAMENTIS/ COEPTAM.DED. IU/VANTE PERFE/+CIT+.' 'Opilio, *Vir Clarissimus* and Prefect *inluster* and *Praetor* [or *Patricius*], undertook eagerly [to build] this basilica and also [this] chapel from the foundations in honour of S. Justina the Martyr [and] accomplished [it] in the time of youth.'

154 The title *inluster*, originally reserved for consuls, in the Christian period could be given to other exalted personages. Andrea Gloria, 'Nuove esame della donazione di Opilione alla chiesa di S. Giustina in Padova,' *Rassegna Padovana di Storia, Lettere ed Arti*, 1 (1891), 101.

155 These inscriptions, found at Gemona and Milan, match the epigraphy of the S Prosdocimo lintel. Simioni, *Storia di Padova*, 38.

156 Opilio is cited as Venantius Opilio 5 in *LPRE*, 808–9. The S Prosdocimo inscription does not mention that Opilio was consul in 524. It must ante-date the honour.

157 Three eleventh-century documents in the Archives of the Padua Museo Civico record this gift. They consist of two copies of the donation, and a request that Opilio be permitted to rent back the lands of his gift. Despite the late date, and eleventh-century phrasing, Gloria argues for an authen-tic original, destroyed perhaps in the sack of 899, and rewritten from memory. Gloria, 'Opilione,' 97 and 102–3.

158 Simioni lists its destruction in 452 by the Goths, in 601 by the Lombards, and in 899 by the Huns. *Storia di Padova*, 116.

159 G. Ongarello, *Chronica di Padova*, 33: 'Edificò ancora S. Prosdocimo uno Oratorio Grande in lo quale repuose el corpo di S Justina Verzene et mar-tire Rezina di Padova.' See Alessandro Scrinzi, 'Di un tempietto bizantino del VI secolo a Padova,' *L'Arte* 29 (1926), 75–84, esp. 78.

160 See *ActaSS*, Justina, October, III, 790–826; Prosdocimus, *ActaSS*, November, III, 350ff.

161 Venantius Fortunatus, *Carmina*, VIII, 3, 169.

162 According to the earliest list of Paduan bishops, in the *Cronica di Rolandino Patavini*, *RIS*-n.s., VIII, appendix 4, 'La serie dei vescovi di Padova edita dal Muratori.' This dates from 1267 or 1268, cited by Simioni, *Storia di Padova*, 116. He believes the list, while full of inaccuracies, kept the tradition of Prosdoscimus's apostolic connection alive. Picard, *Souvenir*, 643, points out that it is not even clear whether Prosdocimus was first bishop. At any rate, he was not contemporary with Opilio, for his inscription has more of the character of an epigraph than a funerary inscription. Picard suggests that Prosdocimus was buried in the nearby cemetery and given a new sarcophagus and burial beside S Giustina when Opilio's basilica was built.

163 'Saint Prosdocimus/Bishop and Confessor.' The title 'confessor' was sometimes given to a martyr in the Upper Adriatic area. P.L. Zovatto, 'La pergula paleocristiana del sacello di S. Prosdocimo di Padova e il ritratto del santo titolare,' *RAC* 34 (1958), 165, note 37: 'in epigrafe paleocristiane il termine *confessor* talvolta é sinonimo di *martyr*.' He gives other examples of episcopus and confessor or martyr used together, including an inscription under the high altar at Poreč, stating that Maurus 'episcopus et martyr est factus.'

164 Picard, *Souvenir*, 643. See also G. Cuscito, 'Opilione e le origine del culto martiriale a Padova,' *Memoriam sanctorum venerantes, Miscellanea in onore di monsignor Victor Saxer*, in *Studi di Antichita cristiana*, 48 (Vatican City, 1992), 163–81, esp. 180–1, with bibliography in note 76.

165 Zovatto, 'Pergula,' 158, calls this the oldest and best preserved of the pergula type where the straight architrave is interrupted by a central arch in direct reflection of the palace peristyle, the setting for imperial ceremonials. He describes this as the pre-Byzantine ancestor of the Byzantine iconostasis.

166 'IN HOC LOCO CONLOCATAE SUNT RELIQUIAE SANCTORUM APOSTOLORUM ET PLURIMUM MARTYRUM QUI PRO CONDITORE OMNIQUE FIDELIUM PLEBE ORARE DIGNENTUR.' 'In this place are gathered together relics of saints, apostles, and many martyrs who deign to pray for the founder and all faithful people.'

167 For Urius, who was himself formerly buried in the chapel, see *ActaSS*, Justina, October, III, 816.

168 See also Simioni, *Storia di Padova*, 142–3.

169 'Oratorium sive templum mire pulchritudinis constructum in honore Dei

et beatae Mariae semper Virginis et plurimorum Apostolorum, in quo S. Prosdocimi corpus tumulatum jacet cuius parietes humo tenus in circuito vario suis marmoree crustati, pars vero superior que testudineo clauditur arcu longe lateque deaurata relucet, et opere Musoleo depicta quasi celeste Palatium ac viridantia Paradisi prata demonstrat.' F.S. Dondi Dall'Orologio, *Dissertazione sopra i riti, discipline, costumanze della chiesa di Padova sino al sec. XVI* (Padua, 1816).

170 Girolamo Da Potenza, *Cronica Iustiniana* (1598), Padova, Museo Civico, BP 829c13, p. 13f.: 'era tutta crustata di marmi da capo a basso di bellissimi lastroni: il cielo o testudine di sopra tutto mosiato, isculti li dodici apostoli.' Cited in S. Bettini, *Monumenti paleocristiani delle Venezie e della Dalmazia* (Padua, 1942), 231. See also Verzone, *Architettura religiosa*, 25–6, 'Padova, la cappella di S. Prosdocimo.'

171 Tonzig, *Basilica*, 100, states that since very few figural fragments were among the great quantities of mosaic fragments found in the excavations of 1928, the apostle mosaic could be immured under the painted replica of 1565.

172 The present revetment is a replacement following the traces of the original of Opilio's day. L. Michelotto, 'L'oratorio paleocristiano di Opilione,' *Palladio*, n.s., 4 (1954), 179–84, esp. 182.

173 For Concordia, see Regina Canova Dal Zio, *Le chiese delle tre Venezie anteriori al mille* (Padua, 1986), 42–7; bibliography, 46–7.

174 T.G. Jackson, *Dalmatia, the Quarnero and Istria*, 3 vols. (Oxford, 1887), III, 431, and plan, 413, fig. 125.

175 G. Cuscito, *Grado e le sue basiliche paleocristiane* (Bologna, 1979), n.p.

176 P.L. Zovatto, *Grado, antichi monumenti* (Bologna, 1971), 21, figs. 69, a, b.

177 Grado had two thrones: one, 'of St Mark,' had been 'taken from Alexandria to Constantinople and offered to the Patriarch of Grado by the emperor Heraclius in 630.' D. Gaborit-Chopin, 'Sedia di San Marco,' *The Treasury of San Marco, Venice* (Milan 1984), 98–105, esp.105. Bibliography of Heraclius's gift in S. Tavano, 'Le cattedre di Grado e le culture artistiche del Mediterraneo orientale,' *Antichità Altoadriatiche* 12 (1977), 445–89.

178 '+AD HONORE BEATI MARCI E(VANGELIS)TE IOHANNIS IUNIOR SOLA DE(I) SUFFRAGENTE GRATIA D(...X)V IN D(ICTIONE).' Cuscito, *Grado*, fig. 42 and text beside fig. 43.

179 The so-called Throne of St Mark, once in Grado (see Cuscito, *Grado*, figs. 44–5), takes its name from its present location, S Marco, Venice, where it was placed after the dissolution of the Grado patriarchate in 1451, and is not believed to be the reliquary chair of St Mark which Heraclius gave to the Patriarch of Grado in 630, for that one was covered with ivory plaques.

For relics of other saints, some contained in fifth- and sixth-century reliquaries, see Cuscito, *Grado*, figs. 31–9.

180 See ibid., n.p.: 'HIC REQUIESCIT IN PACE CHRISTI SANCTAE ME/
MORIAE MARCIANUS EPISC(OPUS) QUI VIXIT IN E/PISCOPATO
ANNOS XLIIII ET PEREGRINATUS/EST PRO CAUSA FIDEI ANNOS
XL. DEPOSITUS AUTEM IN HOC SEPULCHRO +/VIII KAL(ENDAS)
MAIAS INDICT(IONE) UNDECIMA.' Marcianus may have been the
bishop of that name consecrated in 534 to the see of Augusta (Augsburg),
capital of Rezia Secunda, then under Vandal rule, by Macedonius, bishop
of Aquileia.

181 See Zovatto, *Grado*, 21; G. Brusin and P.L. Zovatto, *Monumenti paleocristiani di Aquileia e di Grado* (Udine, 1957), figs. 57–8; 487–9.

182 J.E. Cirlot, *A Dictionary of Symbols*, trans. J. Sage (New York, 1962), 164: 'the
sign for infinity [is] at once interlaced and also knotted'; and Ferguson,
Signs and Symbols, 153, who states that the circle or ring is 'universally
accepted as the symbol of eternity and never-ending existence.'

183 John 15.1: 'I am the true vine, and my Father is the husbandman.'

184 Hippolytus, *On the Benedictions of Isaac, Jacob and Moses*, ed. R. Graffin,
trans. M. Brière, L. Mariès and B. Ch. Mercier, *Patrologia Orientalis*, 27
(1954), 99: 'La vigne spirituelle, c'était le Sauveur, les sarments et les pam-
pres ... sont les saints, ceux qui croient en Lui; et les grappes, ses martyrs.'

185 See Zovatto, *Grado*, 98.

186 Brusin and Zovatto, *Monumenti*, 503–10. For Elia's gifts of relics to Grado's
churches, see Andrea Dandalus, *Chronicon Venetum*, in *RIS*, 12 (1728), col.
102.

187 Zovatto, *Grado*, 70–1; 77, fig. 119, and 74, fig. 107 (plan). See also P.L.
Zovatto, 'La prothesis ed il diaconicon della basilica di Santa Maria di
Grado,' *Aquileia Nostra* 22 (1951), 74–95, and Canova dal Zio, *Chiese delle tre
Venezie*, 280 f.

188 Gabriella Pross Gabrielli, *L'oratorio e la basilica paleocristiana di Trieste (Via
Madonna del Mare)* (Bologna, 1969). M. Mirabella Roberti, 'I musaici di
san Canzian d'Isonzo,' *Antichità altoadriatiche* 8 (1975), 235–44, and fig. 1.
G. Bovini, *Antichità cristiane di S. Canzian d'Isonzo, S. Giovanni al Timavo e
Trieste* (Bologna 1973), 2, for *memoria* of St Proto; 22–3 for San Canzian;
and 29 for S Giovanni al Timavo.

189 Illustrated in M. Prelog, *The Basilica of Euphrasius in Poreč* (Zagreb, 1986),
pl. 63, 64.

190 The status of Maurus's remains is unclear. They were stolen by the
Genoese in 1354, and supposedly remain in S Matteo, Genoa. They are
also claimed by the Lateran Baptistery chapel of S Venanzio, Rome.

191 Verzone, *Architettura religiosa*, 53.
192 Ann Terry, 'The Sculpture at the Cathedral of Eufrasius in Poreč,' *DOP* 42 (1988), 13–64, esp. 30–1 and fig. 56.
193 Cabrol and Leclercq, *DACL*, 12/2, cols. 2346–72, 'Oratoire,' esp. 2363 f., fig. 9120. Also O. Marucchi, 'Le recenti scoperte nel duomo di Parenzo,' *NBAC*, 2 (1896), 19. A fish illustrated in colour in Prelog, *The Basilica of Euphrasius*, pl. 58, captioned 'Fourth century mosaic with a symbolical fish,' appears to be a detail from this pavement; however, the date is disputed.
194 Rajko Bratož, 'The Development of the Early Christian Research in Slovenia and Istria between 1976 and 1986,' *Actes du XIe Congrès international d'archéologie chrétienne*, III (Rome, 1989), 2369–88 for Poreč chapels; for Betika, see 2379–82, and plan, 2380, fig. 7.
195 Agnellus, *CPER*, XXVII Maximian, 193–4; also *LPER*, 329: 'Aedificavitque ecclesiam beatae Mariae in Pola quae vocatur Formosa, unde diaconus fuit, mira pulcritudine et diversis ornavit lapidis.
196 The alabaster columns of its ciborium are now in the Holy Sacrament chapel in San Marco in Venice. See Marzia Vidulli Torlo, 'Analisi spaziale della basilica di Santa Maria Formosa in Pola,' *Atti e memorie della società istriana di archeologia e storia patria (AMSI)*, n.s. 36 (1988), 4–21, esp. 7–10, citing R. Gallo, 'Iacopo Sansovino a Pola,' *AMSI* 38 (1926), 62–4.
197 Pietro Kandler, 'Della basilica di S. Maria Formosa in Pola,' *L'Istra* 32 (1847), reprinted in *Notizie storiche di Pola* (Poreč, 1876), 171–7, esp. 176.
198 Kandler, ibid., 130, notes the presence of a bishop's sarcophagus in the chapel in the sixteenth century. This had been recorded by the Anonymous of Pola (now identified as Pietro Degani), in his *Dialoghi due sulle antichità di Pola del 1600*, ed. P. Kandler, as *Cenni al forestiero che visita Pola* (Trieste, 1845), 76.
199 Antonio Morassi, 'La chiesa di S. Maria Formosa o del canneto in Pola,' *Bolletino d'Arte*, ser. II, 4 (1924), 11–25, esp. 16, and plate p. 23, for the mosaic. See also S. Tavano, 'Mosaici parietali in Istria,' *Antichità adriatiche*, 8 (1975), 245–52, and figs. 1, 2.
200 Agnellus, *CPER*, 194, note 17, lines 18–23: 'È rimasto anche il rudere di uno di due *monasteria*, portante un frammento, a composizione musiva, colla testa del Redentore imberbe cinto dal nimbo crociato, e avente ai fianchi due figure che sembrano essere gli apostoli Pietro e Paolo, forse la scena della *traditio legis* così frequente sui nostri sarcofagi.'
201 Morassi, 'La chiesa di S. Maria Formosa,' 17–20. Morassi, who saw them in a ruined condition, thought the paintings could have been part of the original decor.

202 Though the sculptures on Ravenna sarcophagi of the fifth century, such as the two in S Francesco, Ravenna, the former *Basilica Apostolorum*, frequently portrayed this theme, showing the apostles standing in arcades of the type Morassi describes, the arches are always semicircular.

203 Morassi, 'La chiesa di S. Maria Formosa,' note 5; Kandler, 'S. Maria Formosa in Pola,' 32, repr. *Notizie*, 172.

204 *ODB*, II, 1321.

205 Agnellus, *LPER*, 332: 'sepultusque est in basilicae sancti Andreae apostoli iuxta altarium, ubi barbas praedicti apostoli condidit.'

206 Agnellus, *LPER*, 325; *CPER*, 193–4. Kandler, 'S. Maria Formosa,' 32, repr. *Notizie*, 172: the 'Pola Anonymous' saw this document in Pula in 1657.

207 Agnellus, *LPER*, 326. Agnellus believed that the whole treasure was sent to Justinian, who rewarded the deacon's honesty with the appointment to the Ravenna See.

208 According to the 'Pola Anonymous,' writing in the late sixteenth century, paraphrased by Kandler, 'S. Maria Formosa,' 32, repr. *Notizie*, 174, 'sono queste due celle perfettamente rotonde, a volta, con finestra che dà scarsa luce, con quattro nicchie che s'aprono nel grosso del muro di dimensioni differenti. Erano queste celle rivestite nel pavimento e nelle muraglie di mosaici a belle figure e scompartimenti, dei quali siamo giunti in tempo di vedere frammenti. Avrebbero dovuto sevire per deposito di sacri arredi e di sacri libri ... l'Anonimo ... assicura che in quelle nicchie vi fossero collocati statue, e che le porte in queste celle fossero bellissime.'

209 Kandler, *L'Istra*, 16, 1852, repr. *Notizie*, 179.

210 All discussed by B. Marušić, *Kasnoantička i bizantinska Pula* (Pula, 1967), 26–35.

211 Ante Šonje, 'La chiesa paleocristiana nella insenatura marina di Šepen presso Castelmuchio (Omišalj) sull'isola di Veglia (Krk),' 1, *FR* 111 (1976), 137f., esp 152f. Apparently these chapels have lost their decorations.

212 G.B.L.G. Seroux d'Agincourt, *Storia dell'Arte*, II, (Milan, 1825), pl. XXVI, figs. 8–12.

213 P. Kandler, *Osservatore Triestino*, n.d., repr. *Notizie Storiche di Pola* (Poreč, 1876), 232: 'Era questo tempietto cosi nell'interno come nell'esterno coperto da mosaici a tesselli vitrei colorati, come la facciata della basilica Eufrasiana di Parenzo, e come la Marciana di Venezia, quanto alla materia di rivestitura delle pareti; quanto alli disegni eseguiti col mosaico, nessuno traccia, dacchè i tesselli erano tutti staccati ed ingombravano il terreno interno e circostante. A sole lucente l'aspetto deve essere stato maravglioso.' See also *Notizie*, 187, reprinted from *Conservatore*, N. 517A (1871), 'S. Andrea o scolgio grande di Pola,' with details of chapel.

214 Anton Gnirs, 'Forschungen in Istrien, III, Grabungen auf dem Scoglio S Caterina bei Pola,' *Jahreshefte des Osterreichischen Archäologischen Institutes in Wien* 14 (1911), 188–96, and fig. 114.

215 The flowering of these architectural forms on the eastern Adriatic coast is thought to have led to the development of the typical centrally planned early Croatian churches, such as Sv.Krz at Nin (Anaunia) and Sv.Donat, Zadar (Jader). See Šonje, 'La chiesa paleocristiana,' 153.

216 Ward-Perkins, *From Classical Antiquity*, 79f., discusses a cluster of annexed mausoleum chapels built by the Lombard rulers in Pavia: among others, the son (d. 688), grandson (d. 700), and great-grandson (d. 712) of Aripert I (653–61) were buried in a mausoleum beside S Salvatore; Ansprand (d. 712) and Liutprand (712–44) were buried in S Adriano beside S Maria in Pertica.

2 The Mausolea of the Imperial Family in the West

1 See M.J. Johnson, *Mausolea*, for details of each mausoleum and of the circumstances of the deaths and burials of the emperors and their consorts who were buried in them.

2 R. Krautheimer, *Early Christian and Byzantine Architecture* (Harmondsworth, 1965, rev. paperback ed., 1975), 66.

3 See J. and T. Marasović, *Diocletian Palace* (Zagreb, 1970), 17–18, and plates 50–90, and J.J. Wilkes, *Diocletian's Palace, Split: Residence of a Retired Roman Emperor* (Sheffield, 1986, reprinted with corrections 1993), 46–52.

4 P.S. Bartoli, *Gli antichi sepolcri* (Rome, 1699). See Harold Mielsch, 'Zur stadtrömischen Malerei des 4. Jahrhunderts ...,' *Römische Mitteilungen* 85 (1978), 151–207, esp. 154–6 and pl. 8,1, for his argument that the Bartoli drawing was of the Tor de' Schiavi vault, rather than a vault of Nero's Domus Aurea.

5 See Francesco Tolotti, 'Le basiliche cimiteriali con deambulatorio del suburbio romano: Questione ancora aperta,' *Römische Mitteilungen* 89 (1982), 153–211, esp. fig. 9, p. 179, plan of Tor de' Schiavi (= 'Basilica anonima sulla via Prenestina') and fig. 1, p. 157, on the Tor de' Schiavi's place among these funerary complexes.

6 A. Bosio, *Roma sotteranea* (Rome, 1632), 323.

7 This mausoleum survives in ruins as a two-storey circular structure within a walled precinct. Maxentius buried his son Valerius Romulus there in 309. This provenance of the sarcophagus was suggested by Johnson, *Mausolea*, 73.

8 Johnson, *Mausolea*, 79–80.

9 A possible intermediary stage exists at the Tor de Schiavi, where the mausoleum lay beside a basilica, but not attached to it. See note 5.

10 Tolotti, 'Basiliche cimiteriali,' 154.

11 Bosio, *Roma sotteranea*, 321.

12 F.W. Deichmann and A. Tschira, 'Das Mausoleum der Kaiserin Helena und die Basilika der heiligen Marcellinus und Petrus an der via Labicana von Rom,' *Jahrbuch der deutschen archäologischen Instituts* 72 (1957), fig. 20.

13 A. Recio-Vegazones, 'Una posibile escena musiva paleocristiana vista por Bosio en el mausoleo de Sta. Helena,' *RAC* 53 (1977), 137–53, esp. 146–53.

14 See Recio-Vegazones, ibid., and F. Camprubi, 'I mosaici della cupola di Centcelles nella Spagna,' *RAC* 19 (1942), 87–110, esp. 95, fig 8. Also, Johnson, *Mausolea*, 101–8, on the mausoleum, and 279–80, on Constans, with bibliography.

15 Camprubi, ibid., 89–90, figs. 3–4, for the layout of the fragmentary scenes.

16 The classical account of La Daurade is that of Helen Woodruff, 'The Iconography and Date of the Mosaics of La Daurade,' *ArtBull.* 13 (1931), 80–107. The building, which had a five-foot oculus, was almost certainly Roman, and was converted subsequently into a church or mausoleum. The decoration is primarily known from the seventeenth-century description of Dom Odon Lamotte, which Woodruff transcribes almost in entirety. The colonnettes are divided between the Toulouse Museum and the Metropolitan Museum, New York.

17 G. Mackie, 'La Daurade: A Royal Mausoleum,' *CahArch* 42 (1994), 17–34.

18 The crypt was recorded by Dom Chantelou, *Mémoire de l'église Notre Dame de La Daurade à Toulouse* (Toulouse, 1621), Paris, Bibl. Nat. Lat. 13845, f. 47–99, esp. 48–9.

19 F. Tolotti, 'I due mausolei rotondi del vecchio S. Pietro,' *RAC* 64 (1988), 287–315.

20 Ferdinando Castagnoli, 'Il circo di Nerone in Vaticano,' *RendPontAcc* 32 (1959–1960), 97–121, esp. 104. Masonry techniques support a third-century date.

21 Krautheimer, *ECBA*, 56, figs. 21 and 22, isometric reconstruction and plan of the mausolea and basilica, and Johnson, *Mausolea*, 38–43, 'Vatican Rotunda,' and 118–22 on Mausoleum of Honorius.

22 This rubble was found *in situ* by Castagnoli at the Vatican Rotunda.

23 Most notably those of G.A. Dosio, whose drawings in the Uffizi Gallery, Florence, 2535, 2536, and 4345, are reproduced in A. Bartoli, *I monumenti antichi di Roma nei disegni degli Uffizi di Firenze*, 6 vols. (Rome, 1914–22), V, plates 817, 816, and 818.

24 Cesare D'Onofrio, *Gli obelischi di Roma*, 2nd ed. (Rome, 1967), 30; also see Johnson, *Mausolea*, 38.

25 Symmachus, *LP*, I, 260–1. See also Joseph D. Alchermes, 'Petrine Politics: Pope Symmachus and the Rotunda of St Andrew at Old St Peter's,' *The Catholic Historical Review* 81 (1995), 1–40.

26 Castagnoli, 'Circo di Nerone.'

27 T. Alpharanus, *De Basilicae Vaticanae antiquissima et nova structura*, ed. D.M. Cerrati, Studi e Testi, 26 (Rome, 1914). 'De Templo B. Petronillae, 133–9, describes S Petronilla just before the demolition of the building in 1514, while 139–45 describes Sant'Andrea, which he calls S.M. de Febribus.

28 Walter N. Schumacher 'Das Baptisterium von Alt-St Peter und seine Probleme,' in *Studien zur spätantiken und byzantinischen Kunst Friedrich Wilhelm Deichmann gewidmet*, ed. Otto Feld and Urs Peschlow, 3 vols. (Bonn, 1986), I, 215–33.

29 Prudentius, *Opera*, II, *Peristephanon Liber*, XII: 'Passio apostolorum Petri et Pauli,' tr. H.J. Thomson (Loeb edition, London and Cambridge, MA, 1953, repr. 1961), 322–7, esp. 324–7.

30 The empress Maria's burial was discovered intact on 3 February 1544.

31 See M.J. Johnson, 'On the Burial Places of the Theodosian Dynasty,' *Byzantion* 61 (1991), 330–9.

32 Hartmann Schedel, *Das Buch der Chroniken* (*Nuremberg Chronicle*) (Nuremberg, 1493).

3 The Domestic Oratory

1 For floors in Rome, see Cabrol and Leclercq, *DACL*, 12/2, cols. 2346–72, esp. col. 2357f., 'Oratoires privés.' For those in Aquileia, see Canova del Zio, *Le chiese delle tre Venezie*, 248, 'Gli oratori privati.' She draws attention to ten rectangular floors, all about 10 by 6 metres, which date from the first half of the fourth century or before. Apses, where present, are later additions, and she suggests the use of portable, wooden altars. These buildings appear to have functioned as places of worship but not necessarily as private chapels.

2 G.B. De Rossi, 'D'un oratoire privé du quatrième siècle découvert sur le mont dit della Giustizia, près les Thermes de Diocletien,' *BAC*, ser. III, 1 (1876), 45–63, esp. 45–6, and plate VI, facing p. 88.

3 P. Testini, 'L'oratorio scoperto al "monte della giustizia" presso la Porta Viminale a Roma,' *RAC* 44 (1968), 219–60, esp. 250–1.

4 M. Rampolla del Tindaro, ed., with commentary, *S. Melania giuniore, senatrice romana* (Rome, 1905), 5–6: 'Occasio evenit ut dies solemnis et commemoratio S. Laurentii martyris ageretur. Beatissima vero fervens spiritu

desiderabat ire et in sancti martyris basilica per vigilem celebrare noctem; sed non permittitur a parentibus, eo quod nimis tenera et delicati corporis hunc laborem vigiliarum ferre non posset. At illa timens parentes et desiderans placere Deo, permansit tota nocte vigilans in oratorio domus suae, curvans genua usque in mane ac deprecans Dominum cum multis lacrimis ut cordis sui desiderium adimpleret Dominus.'

The occasion was the vigil of St Lawrence at S Lorenzo fuori le mura, Rome, which the young Melania's parents had not allowed her to attend: she must have been less than fourteen years old, since she was married in 397 at the age of thirteen to Valerius Pinianus.

5 Agnellus, *LPER*, 306; *CPER*, 123: 'Et dicunt quidam, quod ipsa Galla Placidia augusta super quatuor rotas rubeas marmoreas, quae sunt ante nominatas regias, iubebat ponere cereostatos cum manualia ad mensuram, et iactabat se noctu in medio pavimento, Deo fundere preces, et tamdiu pernoctebat in lacrimis orans, quamdiu ipsa lumina perdurabant.'

6 Paulinus Diaconus, *Vita Ambrosii*, 10, *PL* 14, col. 32: 'per idem tempus cum trans Tiberim apud quamdam clarissimam invitatus, sacrificium in domo offeret, quaedam balneatrix quae paralytica jacebat, cum cognovisset Ibid.em esse Domini sacerdotem, in sellula se ad eamdem domum, ad quam ille invitatus venerat, portari fecit, atque orantis et imponentis manus vestimenta attigit.'

7 Gregory of Nazianzus, *Oratio VII*, 'In Laudem Sororis suae Gorgoniae,' 8 (al. 11), 18; *PG*, 35, cols. 810–11, tr. C.G. Browne and J.E. Swallow, *N&PNF* 7 (1894), 243, 'On His Sister Gorgonia': 'Resting her head ... upon the altar ... she then applied her medicine to her whole body, viz. such a portion of the antitypes of the Precious Body and Blood as she treasured in her hand.' The translators date this between 369 and 374 (p. 238). It appears to be an allusion to the rite of baptism as practised in Antioch, where the priest anointed the entire body of each catechumen before baptism. See St Cyril of Jerusalem, *Catechetical Lectures*, XX, *On the Mysteries*, II: 'Of Baptism,' tr. E. Gifford (Oxford 1893, repr. 1996), 147: 'Then, when ye were stripped, ye were anointed with exorcised oil, from the very hairs of your head to your feet.'

8 Eusebius, *De Vita Constantini*, *PG*, 20, cap. XIV, cols. 910–1234, esp. 992; tr. *N&PNF* (2nd series) 1 (New York, 1890, repr. 1997), 405–580, esp. 503–4; Socrates Scholasticus, *Historia ecclesiastica*, *PG*, 67, col. 124, trans. A.C. Zenos, *N&PNF* (2nd series) 2 (Oxford, 1891, repr. 1997), 1, XVIII, 22.

9 Sozomen, *Historia ecclesiastica*, *PG*, 67, col. 80, trans. C.D. Hartranft, *N&PNF* (2nd series), 2 (Oxford, 1891, repr. 1997), 245: 'He erected a house of prayer in the palace.'

10 Cabrol and Leclercq, 'Oratoire,' *DACL*, 12/2, cols. 2346–72, esp. 2355–7.

11 G.P. Kirsch, 'I santuari domestici di martiri nei titoli romani ed altri simili santuari nelle chiese cristiane e nelle case private di fedeli,' *RendPontAcc* 2, (1924), 27–43, esp. 28–9 and 36.

12 Ibid., 28–9.

13 Ibid., 34.

14 Tertullian, *De Fuga*, *PL*, 2, ch. 14. In this passage Tertullian answers the objection that those who fled persecution would miss the sacraments by suggesting that they rely on faith or, as a last resort, that they assemble at night.

15 Eusebius, *De Vita Constantini*: 'He [Constantine] pitched the tabernacle of the Cross outside and at a distance from his camp, and there passed his time in a pure and holy manner, offering up prayers to God.'

16 Exact date unknown, but not earlier than 345, and probably at least twenty years later. See F.L. Cross and E.A. Livingstone, *ODCC*, 2nd ed. (Oxford, 1983), 799, 'Laodicea.'

17 H.R. Percival, tr., *The Seven Ecumenical Councils of the Undivided Church*, *N&PNF* 14 (Oxford, 1900), 158. The twelfth-century Byzantine canonist and historian Zonaras, commenting on this Canon, says 'The faithful can pray to God and be intent upon their prayers everywhere, whether in the house, in the field, or in any place they possess: but to offer or perform the oblation must by no means be done except in a church or at an altar.' Ibid., xxi, citing Z.B. Van Espen, *Tractatus de Promulgatione legum ecclesiasicarum, etc* (Brussels, 1712).

18 Ibid., 94.

19 *ODCC*, 549, 'Gangra.' Also, *N&PNF*, 14, 94.

20 This was repeated in the African Code, *Codex Canonum Ecclesiae Africanae*, of AD 419: *N&PNF*, 14, 447, Canon X.

21 *N&PNF*, 14, 270–1.

22 Council of Chalcedon, 451, Canon V declares that the Canons also apply to bishops and priests who travel from city to city; Canon VI (ibid., 270–1) states: 'Neither presbyter, deacon, nor any of the ecclesiastical order shall be ordained at large, nor unless the person ordained is particularly appointed to a church in a city or village, or to a martyry, or to a monastery. And if any have been ordained without a charge, the Holy Synod decrees, to the reproach of the ordainer, that such an ordination shall be inoperative, and that such shall nowhere be suffered to officiate.'

23 J. Hefele, *Histoire des Conciles*, 2/1, tr. H. Leclercq (Paris, 1908), 260–4.

24 Cabrol and Leclercq, *DACL*, 12/2, cols. 2359–60; P. Coustant, *Epistolae Romanorum Pontificum* (Paris, 1721), *Epistola* IX, dated 430, col. 1094–9, esp. 1098–9.

25 *N&PNF*, 14, 379.

26 The primary source for Ravenna is Agnellus, as in Introduction, note 5. Secondary literature on the Archbishops' Chapel includes Giuseppe Gerola, 'Il ripristino della cappella di S. Andrea nel palazzo vescovile di Ravenna,' *FR*, n.s., 3 (1932), 71–132, esp. 86. See also Anna Maria Iannucci, 'Restauri ravennati: L'oratorio di S. Andrea nell'episcopio,' *CorsiCRB* 38 (1991), 229–33, for a commentary on the restorations. See also F.W. Deichmann, *Ravenna. Haupstadt des spätantiken Abendlandes*, vol. II/1 (Weisbaden, 1969–89), 201–7; Clementina Rizzardi, 'Note sull'antico episcopio di Ravenna: Formazione e sviluppo,' *Actes du XIe congrès international d'archéologie chrétienne*, I (Rome, 1989), 711–32; Maureen C. Miller, 'The Development of the Archiepiscopal Residence in Ravenna, 300–1300,' *FR* 141 (1991; appeared 1997), 145–73.

27 For the Arian episcopal chapel (St Apollinaris) see Agnellus, *LPER*, 334; *CPER*, 217: 'Infra urbem vero Ravenam, eclesiam sancti Theodori non longe a domo Drocdonis, qua domus una cum balneo et sancti Apolenaris monasterio, quod in superiora domus structum, episcopium ipsius ecclesie fuit.'

28 Miller, 'Archiepiscopal Residence,' believes the position of the Archbishops' Chapel inside the Episcopium is very unusual, and that chapels 'did not become common features of medieval episcopal residences in Northern Italy until the eleventh or twelfth centuries' (157–8). Quoting archaeological evidence from Asia Minor, from the survey of Wolfgang Müller-Wiener, 'Riflessioni sulle charatteristiche dei palazzi episcopali,' *CorsiCRB* 17 (1970), 103–45, Miller found that only one bishops' palace of the period, that of Side, had a chapel. However, in view of the situation at Ravenna, where the chapel was upstairs and would not have left traces in the building's ground plan, her conclusions seem unjustified.

29 Gregory of Tours, *History of the Franks*, vol. I, tr. O.M. Doulton (Oxford, 1927), 255; also Gregory of Tours, *Liber Vitae Patrem*, *PL* 71, cap. II/3, col. 1019: 'Dedicaverat igitur oratorium infra domum ecclestiaticam urbis Turonicae in primo sacerdotii suo anno, in quo cum reliquorum sanctorum pignoribus hujus antistitis reliquias collocavit.'

30 Gregory I, *Homiliae in Evangelia*, II, *Homilia* XXXVII/9, cols. 1279–81, esp. 1281.

31 *LP*, I, 371, The election of Sergius (687–701) took place 'in oraculum beati Caesarii Christi martyris, quod est intro suprascriptum palatium,' R. Davis, tr., *Book of Pontiffs*, 83. See also *LP*, I, 386, note 1.

32 Davis, ibid., 68: 'He also built an oratory to St Sebastian inside the Lateran Episcopium, and there too he bestowed gifts.'

33 *LP*, I, 371, and 377, note 8; Davis, *Book of Pontiffs*, 83: 'Paschal held the outer parts (of the patriarchate) from the oratory of St Silvester.'

34 *LP*, I, 402. This chapel survived until the destruction of the Lateran Palace, and was described by Panvinio. See P. Lauer, *Le Palais du Latran* (Paris, 1911), 486.

35 Gerola, 'Ripristino,' 86.

36 J.C. Smith, 'Form and Function of the Side Chambers of Fifth-and Sixth-Century Churches in Ravenna,' *JSAH* 49 (1990), 181–204, sets out the conditions needed for book storage at this period: the space should be dry, ventilated, and for preference upstairs. She cites the upper chapels at the altar end of S Vitale.

37 See the *LP* entries for Pope Hilarus I (461–8) and Pope Symmachus (498–514) for lists of their donations to their chapels at the Lateran Baptistery and the Baptistery of Damasus, respectively.

4 Chapels within the Confines of Churches

1 Paulinus, *Epistola* 32, text and translation from R.C. Goldschmidt, *Paulinus' Churches at Nola* (Amsterdam, 1940), 40–1.

2 Ibid.: 'Cubicula intra porticus quaterna longis basilicae lateribus inserta secretis orantium vel in lege domini meditantium, praeterea memoriis religiosorum ac familiarium accommodatos ad pacis aeternae requiem locos praebent.'

3 Ibid.: 'Omne cubiculum binis per liminum frontes uersibus praenotatur, quos inserere his litteris nolui.'

4 G. Chierici, 'Recenti lavori ... alle basiliche paoliniane di Cimitile,' *RAC* 16 (1939), 51–73, esp. 60, fig 5.

5 Paulinus, *Carmen* 27, in Goldschmidt, *Churches*, 52–69, esp. 63–5.

6 Prudentius, *Peristephanon Liber*, XI: *Ad Valeriam Episcopum de Passione Hippolyti Beatissimae Martyris*, tr. H.J. Thomson (Loeb ed., London and Cambridge, MA, 1953, repr. 1961), v. 171f., esp. 227f.: 'plena laborantes aegre domus accipit undas,/artaque confertis aestuat in foribus,/maternum pandens gremium, quo condat alumnos/ac foveat felos adcumulata sinus.'

7 Jerome, *Epistola* 108, 'Ad Eustochium Virginem,' *PL* 22, cols. 878–906, esp. 889; see also Peter Brown, *The Cult of the Saints* (Chicago, 1981), chapter 6, 'Potentia,' esp. 106f.

8 *LP*, I, 375, and note 33: 'Hic tegnum et cubicula quae circumquaque eiusdem basilicae sunt, quae per longa tempora stillicidiis et ruderibus fuerant disrupta, studiosus innovavit ac reparavit.'

9 Ibid., 375: 'Hic tegnum et cubicula universa in circuitu basilicae beati Pauli

apostoli quae longa per tempora vetustate confecta fuerant, studiosus innovavit ac reparavit.'

10 Paulinus, *Carmen* 27, 395–406, in Goldschmidt, *Churches*, 54–5.

11 See Appendix: Rome, for *memoria* of S Felicitas.

12 *LP*, I, 262, Symmachus (498–514): 'Item ad sanctam Mariam oratorium sanctorum Cosmae et Damiani a fundamento construxit.'

13 The Oratory of St Euplus; see Appendix: Rome.

14 The two chapels of St John, and the S Croce chapel, all of Hilarus (461–8), as well as the S Venanzio chapel of Pope John IV (640–2), finished by Pope Theodore (642–9), are discussed in chapters 8 and 9.

15 See Appendix: Rome.

16 *LP*, I, 261–2, Symmachus (498–514): 'Item ad fontem in basilica beati Petri apostoli ... oratorium sanctae Crucis ... fecit autem oratoria II, sancti Iohannis Evangelistae et sancti I. Baptistae ... quas cubicula omnes a fundamento perfecta construxit.'

17 For early baptisteries in Rome, and baptism at locations other than the Lateran, see M. Andrieu, *Les Ordines Romani du Haut Moyen Age*, II (Louvain, 1965–74), 408–13. For the Alfarano plan, see Tiberius Alpharanus, *De Basilicae Vaticanae*, ed. D. Michele Cerrati, Studi e testi, 26 (Rome, 1914), pl. II, and xxvii, f. The chapels are numbered 35, 32, and 30 respectively on Alfarano's plan, showing as altars attached to the west and north walls of the north transept.

18 The liturgist M. Andrieu accepts the Alfarano plan, postulating that the chapels were at first temporary structures, thrown up hastily in response to a sudden need, and only later acquiring permanent status. Andrieu, *Ordines Romani*, III: *Les textes, Ordines XIV–XXXIV*, esp. Ordo XIV (Baptism). The arrangement probably dates from shortly before the mid-fifteenth century, when the building of the new choir at St Peter's necessitated the destruction of the old baptistery complex.

19 P. Albert Février, 'Baptistères, martyrs et reliques,' *RAC* 62 (1986), 109–38, esp. 131f.

20 P. Mallius (writing 1159–1181), *Descriptio Basilicae Vaticanae*, in *Codice topografico*, ed. R. Valentini and G. Zucchetti, III, FSI, 90 (Rome, 1946), 382, 'De oratorio sanctae crucis,' and 'De ecclesia sancti Iohannis ad fontes.'

21 Prudentius, *Peristephanon Liber*, XII: '... de passione Hippolyti ...,' v. 171f.

22 Février, *Baptistères*, 133.

23 Mallius, *Descriptio*, 35, 'De Oratorio sanctae Crucis,' 422: 'Ab alia parte est ecclesia sanctae Crucis, quam construi fecit beatae recordationis Symachus papa, cuius absidam columnas porfireticus et optimo mosibo decoravit, et X libras ligni sanctae Crucis in ea recondidit.' See also chapter 8.

24 See also my 'The Santa Croce Drawings: A Re-Examination,' *RACAR* 24 (1997), 1–14.
25 Ignatius of Antioch (ca. 35–ca. 107), *Ad Philadelphenses*, IV, I, ed. Funk, I, 226. tr. Quasten, *Patrology*, I (Utrecht, 1950), 66: 'Take care, then, to partake of one Eucharist; for one is the Flesh of our Lord Jesus Christ, and one the cup to unite us with His Blood, and one altar, just as there is one bishop assisted by the presbytery and the deacons, my fellow servants.'
26 Eusebius, *The Ecclesiastical History*, 10, 37–45, tr. J.E.L. Oulton (Loeb ed., London and Cambridge, MA, 1926, repr. 1953–7). The tenth book of Eusebius's *History* was probably written in 323: *ODCC*, 481.
27 J. Braun, *Der christliche Altar in seiner historischen Entwicklung* (Munich, 1924), 368.
28 Some earlier references are ambiguous, as the plural form *altaria* of *altare* could also have a singular meaning. For example, Paulinus of Nola, *PL*, 61, *Epistola* XXXI, col. 329: 'et aureis dives altaribus.'
29 Gregory I, *Epistola* XLIX, 'Ad Palladium Episcopum,' *PL*, 77, lib. I, VI, col. 834: 'atque illic tredecim altaria collocasse.' Date of letter taken from Thomas Hodgkin's autograph copy of *PL* 77 in the library of the British School at Rome.
30 Cabrol and Leclercq, *DACL*, 1/2, col. 3186, 'Autel.' Texts which might be read to refer to multiple altars can all be explained by the possible use of *altaria* to mean altar in the singular.
31 See Eugenia Chalkia, *Le mense paleocristiane. Tipologia e funzioni delle mense secondarie nel culto paleocristiano*. Studi di antichità cristiana, XLVI (Vatican City, 1991), esp. chapter 4, 111–28, on the use and function of the mensa and altar.
32 Ejnar Dyggve, 'L'origine del cimitero entro la cinta della città,' *Atti dello VIII Congresso di studi bizantini* (Palermo, 1951), repr. *Studi bizantani e neoellenici*, 8 (Rome, 1953), 137–41. See also E. Dyggve, 'The Origin of the Urban Churchyard,' *Classica et Mediaevalia* 13 (1952), 147–58, esp. 152.
33 Athanasius, *Apologia ad Constantium*, 14, *PG*, 25, col. 412; A. Robertson, tr., *N&PNF*, 4, 243–5.
34 J.D. Mansi, *Concilium omnium amplissima collectio*, IX (Graz, 1960), col. 913, *Concilium Autisiodorense*, Canon X: 'Non licet super uno altario in una die duas missas dicere: nec altario ubi episcopus missas dixerit, ut presbyter in una die missas dicat.'
35 See Jean Croquison, 'L'iconographie chrétienne à Rome d'après le *Liber Pontificalis*,' *Byzantion* 34 (1964), 535–606, for an analysis of the iconography of papal gifts to churches and chapels in the Early Middle Ages.
36 Krautheimer, Corbett, and Frankl, *CBCR*, IV, 237.

37 Cecilia Davis-Weyer, 'S Stefano Rotondo in Rome and the Oratory of The-
    odore I,' in *Italian Church Decoration of the Middle Ages and Early Renaissance.
    Functions, Forms and Regional Traditions*, ed. W. Tronzo (Bologna, 1989),
    61–80.
38 Two inscriptions, now lost, were recorded by G.B. De Rossi, *Inscriptiones
    Christianae Urbis Romae*, II (Rome, 1888), 152, no. 30: 'EXQUIRENS PIETAS
    TECTUM DECORARE SACRATUM/ PASTORIS SUMMI THEODORI
    CORDEM EREXIT/ QUI STUDIO MAGNO SANCTORUM CORPORA
    CULTU HOC DEDICAVIT NON PATRIS NEGLECTA RELIQUIT.' 'Piety
    inspired the heart of pope Theodore, who wished to decorate this sanctu-
    ary. He applied all his zeal to honouring the bodies of the saints by this fine
    decoration, nor did he forget the remains of his father,' tr. W. Oakeshott,
    The Mosaics of Rome (Greenwich, CT, 1967), 153.
39 See A. Grabar, *Les Ampoules de Terre Sainte (Monza-Bobbio)* (Paris, 1958).
40 Tr. Oakeshott, *Mosaics*, 153.
41 Archaeological data from Carlo Ceschi, 'Santo Stefano Rotondo,' *Atti della
    pont.acc.rom.di arch.*, ser. III, *Memoriae* 15 (1982), 7 to end of volume.
42 Davis-Weyer, *S Stefano Rotondo*, 79.
43 R. Davis, ed. and tr., 'Lives,' 9.
44 *LP*, I, 465: 'et infra ecclesiam beati Petri apostoli foris muros civitatis Roma-
    nae, noviter oraculum ... construxit, iuxta oratorium beati Leonis papae.'
    Duchesne, *LP*, I, 379, note 35, establishes this connection.
45 De Rossi, *Inscr.christ.* II, 201–2.
46 *LP*, II, 379, note 35: 'HINC VATUM PROCERUMQUE COHORS QUOS
    CERNIS ADESSE/MEMBRA SUB EGREGIA SUNT ADOPERTA DOMO.'
47 *LP*, I, 417; see also R. Davis, ed. and tr., *The Lives of the Eighth-Century Popes*
    (Liverpool, 1992), 22–3.
48 These crowns, including that of Receswinth, are illustrated in *The Art of
    Medieval Spain AD 500–1200*, Metropolitan Museum of Art (New York,
    1993), 53–9.
49 Petrus Mallius, Vat.Lat. 3627, *Descriptio Basilicae Vaticanae*, in R. Valentini
    and G. Zucchetti, eds., *Codice topografico della città di Roma*, III, FSI, 90
    (Rome, 1946), 375–442, esp. 388.
50 P.J. Nordhagen, 'Icons Designed for the Display of Sumptuous Votive
    Gifts,' *DOP* 41 (1987), 453–60.
51 P.J. Nordhagen, 'The Mosaics of John VII, 705–707,' *Acta R. Norv.* 2 (1965),
    143–65
52 William Tronzo, 'Setting and Structure in Two Roman Wall Decorations of
    the Early Middle Ages,' *DOP* 41 (1987), 477–92.
53 A. van Dijk, 'The Oratory of Pope John VII (705–707) in Old St Peter's,' PhD

dissertation (Johns Hopkins University, 1997), and 'Domus Sanctae Dei Genetricis: Art and Liturgy in the Oratory of Pope John VII, 705–707,' *Byzantine Studies Conference Abstracts* 21 (1995), 76.

54 A further fragment, Joseph from the Nativity, has recently been identified in Moscow. Illustrated in G. Matthiae, *Pittura Romana del Medioevo, Secoli IV–X* (Rome, 1987), part 2, 'Aggiornamento scientifico e bibliografia di Maria Andaloro,' colour plate 2.

55 Giacomo Grimaldi, *Descrizione della basilica antica di S Pietro in Vaticano*, Cod. Vat. Barb. Lat. 2733; facsimile, ed. Reto Niggl (Vatican City, 1972).

56 Tronzo, 'Roman Wall Decorations,' 491–2.

57 This latter use was not usually possible in city churches while the Roman laws forbidding burial within the city were in force, that is, before about the seventh century. An early example is the late-sixth-century burial of Bishop Marcianus in S Euphemia, Grado, discussed in chapter 1, and in the Appendix, under Grado: 'sacristy chapel.'

58 *LP*, II, Paschal I; 53 and 58.

59 See J.C. Smith, 'Side Chambers,' 181–2, with bibliography.

60 Krautheimer, *ECBA*, 69, 361–2.

61 Djordje Stričević, 'The Diakonikon and the Prothesis in Early Christian Churches,' *Starinar*, ser. 4, 9 (1959), 59–66, in Serbian with a summary in English, p. 66.

62 Smith, 'Side Chambers,' 181.

63 Paulinus, *Letter* 32 to Sulpicius Severus, in Goldschmidt, *Churches*, 41.

64 Paulinus, in Goldschmidt, *Churches*, 38: 'reliquiis apostolorum et martyrum intra absidem trichoram sub altaria sacratis.' Goldschmidt (ibid., 125–8) discusses the meaning of the phrase *absis trichora*, which is also discussed by F.W. Deichmann, 'Cella trichora,' *Reallexicon für Antike und Christentum*, II (1954), cols. 944–54.

65 Paulinus, *Epistola* 32, *PL* 61, col. 338.

66 Chierici, 'Recenti lavori,' 51–73, esp. 60, fig.5.

67 Paulinus, in Goldschmidt, *Churches*, 40: 'Una earum (conchula) immolanti hostias iubilationis antistiti patet, alia post sacerdotem capaci sinu receptat orentes.'

68 Ibid., 44: 'Si quem sancta tenet meditandi in lege voluntas,/hic poterit residens sacris intendere libris.'

69 Much evidence for the large collections of silver vessels of even quite modestly sized churches has come to light in the numerous hoards found in Syria and Turkey, and inscribed with the names of particular churches.

70 J. Lassus, *Sanctuaires chrétiens de Syrie* (Paris, 1947), 162f.

71 See G. Descoeudres, *Die Pastophorien in syro-byzantinischen Osten*, PhD thesis (Wiesbaden, 1983), 13–25, for a discussion of other functions which were sometimes carried out in pastophories in the East, such as baptism, burial, and housing of martyr relics.

72 Thomas F. Mathews, *The Early Churches of Constantinople. Architecture and Liturgy* (University Park, PA, 1971).

73 Robert F. Taft, 'The Great Entrance,' *Orientalia Christiana Analecta*, 200 (Rome, 1975). N.K. Moran questioned Taft's conclusions, on the basis that the longer Mass of St Basil was in more widespread use than that of St John Chrysostom, and hence would have formed a more valid basis for analysis. Neil K. Moran, 'The Skeuophylakion of the Hagia Sophia,' *CahArch* 34 (1987), 29–32, esp. 29.

74 Taft, ibid., 181.

75 Palladius, *Dialogus de Vita S Ioannis Chrysostomi*, PG, 47, 5–82, esp. 36. This was written ca. 408. See Quasten, *Patrology*, III, 179; also Taft, *Great Entrance*, 185.

76 Mathews, *Churches*, 161. For the skeuophylakion at H Sophia, 16–17, figs. 2 and 3, and pl. 16.

77 This idea, however, has been challenged by Moran, 'Skeuophylakion,' who proposes that a curtained-off corner of the north-east conch of the church would have been a more convenient gathering place for the procession. In either case, the skeuophylakion would have functioned as a secure accessory building for storage of the treasures of the church, and would have served its liturgical needs.

78 Taft, *Great Entrance*, 181; Mathews, *Churches*, 109.

79 A. Calderini, G. Chierici, and C. Cecchelli, *La Basilica di San Lorenzo Maggiore* (Milan, 1952), pl. XXXIII. Also, Traversi, *Architettura paleocristiana milanese*, 70

80 M. Mirabella Roberti, *Milano romana* (Milan, 1984), 137, 138, and plan: fig. 138.

81 See Picard, *Souvenir*, 166–73.

82 Tomasso Tomai, *Historia di Ravenna* (Ravenna, 1580), 23–6.

83 Some were sent to Venice, where they were used to repair and augment the Pala d'Oro. This dates the find to the period 1527–30, when Ravenna was under the rule of Venice. Other jewels were used to ornament three mitres, which were lost in the early nineteenth century.

84 For the dimensions of the niches in the domed chambers of S Vitale in terms of sarcophagus size, see Smith, 'Side Chambers,' 186–7.

85 C. Ricci, *Il mausoleo di Galla Placidia in Ravenna* (Rome, 1914), 30: 'il ricordo del tesoro rinvenuto richiama la nostra mente all'uso antico di seppellire le persone cospicue con le loro cose più preziose e rafforza la

tradizione, per non dire il fatto, esser quel monumento un sepolcro imperiale.'

86 The reports of the discovery of Maria's tomb and its contents in the Honorian Mausoleum, Rome, in 1544 have been collected by Johnson, *Mausolea*, 322–34, Appendix C, 3–12.

87 I have not found any reference to mosaic fragments being found in restorations of this chapel.

88 Smith, 'Side Chambers,' 189–90.

89 These funerary chapels (originally two) opened only to the exterior and are unlikely to have served the functions of sacristies.

90 Anonimo di Pola, *Dialoghi sulle antichità di Pola del 1600*, ms. in Bibl. Marciana, Venice, repr. in P. Kandler, ed., *Cenni al forestiero che visita Pola* (Trieste, 1845), 59–158, esp. 78: 'l'entrate delle quali hanno dei bellissimi portoni,' and 'finestra che dà scarsa luce.'

91 Kandler, 'Della basilica di S. Maria Formosa in Pola,' repr. in *Notizie Storiche di Pola*, IX Congresso Generale, Città di Pola (Parenzo, 1876), 171–7, esp. 174.

92 Anonimo di Pola, *Dialoghi*, in Kandler, ed., *Cenni*, 78: 'lavorate et sotto nel pavimento et sopra nella concavità di volti a mosaico, di opera segnalatamente ricca e vistosa ... dimostrano a'concavi ovati che in finissimo marmo vi si veggono, essere già state ornate di belissime statue.'

93 Marzia Vidulli Torlo, 'Analisi spaziale della basilica di Santa Maria Formosa in Pola,' *Atti e memorie della società istriana di archaeologia e storia patria*, n.s., 36 (Trieste, 1998), 4–21, esp. 13.

94 Krautheimer, 'Introduction to an "Iconography of Medieval Architecture,"' repr. in Krautheimer, *Studies in Early Christian, Medieval and Renaissance Art* (New York, 1969), 115–50, esp. 125–6.

95 Smith, 'Side Chambers,' esp. 193–200; idem,'The Side-Chambers of San Giovanni Evangelista in Ravenna: Church Libraries of the Fifth Century,' *Gesta* 29 (1990), 86–97.

96 Krautheimer, Corbett, and Frankl, *CBCR*, IV, 49, 538–45.

97 Ibid., I, 78–81. The fresco is reproduced there as fig. 56; these sacristies apparently remained in use until 1702.

98 Ibid., I, 315, and 313, fig. 165.

99 Ibid., 318. Marzia Vidulli Torlo has established that the Byzantine foot was used as the unit of measurement at both S Maria Formosa in Pula (see note 90) and at the Basilica Euphrasiana in Poreč. See Vidulli Torlo, 'Valori spaziali proporzionali della Basilica Eufrasiana di Parenzo,' in *Quaderno Giuliani di Storia*, 1 (1985), 56.

100 Mosaic floors on the site at a lower level reveal the presence of fourth- and fifth-century churches on this site.

101 Verzone, *Architettura religiosa*, 45, fig. 18. A different layout for the space is given in Brusin and Zovatto, *Monumenti*, 435, fig. 22, and plan fig. 15. For relics given by bishop Elia, see note 101, below.

102 Andrea Dandalus, *Chronicon Venetum*, col. 102, XIV–XVI. Relics went to Elia's S Eufemia, S Maria, S Giovanni Evangelista, and S Vitalis. Perhaps the Piazza Vittoria church was one of the latter two.

103 G. Bovini, *Memorie cristiane scomparse dell'antica città di Classe* (Ravenna, 1965), 69.

104 Ibid., 92.

105 Ibid., 35. Bovini thinks the trichoran apse may date from the mid-sixth century.

Part Two The Survivors

1 Many of these will be found in the Appendix.

2 See chapter 7 for the imperial mausolea, and also my 'The Zeno Chapel: A Prayer for Salvation,' *PBSR* (1989). See also Sicard, *Liturgie de la Mort*, 361ff.

3 John 1.18: 'No one has ever seen God; the only Son, who is in the bosom of the Father, he has made him known'; and 6.46, in Christ's own words: 'Not that any one has seen the Father except him who is from the Father.'

4 Ernst Kitzinger, 'The Cult of Images in the Age before Iconoclasm,' *DOP* 8 (1954), 83–150, esp. 90f. For an opposing view, see T. Mathews, *The Clash of the Gods* (Princeton, 1993).

5 Kitzinger, ibid., 89.

6 Perhaps significantly, the *Liber Pontificalis* text refers to it as an *ecclesia*: 'eodem tempore fecit ecclesiam beatis martyribus.' See chapter 9, note 4, for complete text.

7 See E. Kitzinger, *Byzantine Art in the Making* (London, 1977), esp. 62.

8 Kitzinger, 'Cult of Images,' 117–20.

9 Otto Demus, *Byzantine Mosaic Decoration* (London, 1948), 5f.

10 The history of the Middle Byzantine decorative system is discussed by Demus, ibid., chapter II.

11 A mid-sixth-century text, a hymn probably written for the reconsecration of H Sofia, Edessa (Urfa), is the earliest source in writing which describes the church building as a microcosm of the universe. See Kathleen E. McVey, 'The Domed Church as Microcosm: Literary Roots of an Architectural Symbol,' *DOP* 37 (1983), 91–123, esp. translation of hymn, 95, and commentary, 96–106. See also Krautheimer, *ECBA*, 230.

12 See Brown, *Cult of Saints*, chapter 3, 'The Invisible Companion.'

5 A Sole Survivor

1 See chapter 3, 'The Domestic Oratory,' note 26, for bibliography.

2 G. Gerola, 'Il ripristino della cappella di S Andrea nel palazzo vesco-vile di Ravenna,' *FR*, n.s., 3 (1932), 71–132, esp. 122, with plan of 'intermediate floor.' This shows three rooms, one a closed space under the narthex.

3 J.C. Smith, 'Side Chambers of ... Churches in Ravenna,' 199–200.

4 Gerola, 'Ripristino,' 76.

5 'Dum sederet ad mensam post tribunal ecclesiae super vivarium,' Agnellus writes of Johannes VIII, *LPER*, 382. See also C. Ricci, 'Il vivaio dell'arcivescovado di Ravenna,' *Bolletino d'Arte* 13 (1919), 33–6; Deichmann, *Ravenna*, II/1, 196; and Miller, 'Archiepiscopal Residence,'150–1.

6 Gerola, 'Ripristino,' 76–8.

7 Agnellus, *CPER*, XXII Petrus II, 149, note 1: 'Fecitque non longe ab eadem domo monasterium sancti Andree apostoli; suaque effigies super valvas eiusdem monasteri est inferius teselis depicta.'

8 Ibid., 148–9: 'Iterumque fundavit domum infra episcopium Ravennae sedis, que dicitur Tricoli, eo quod tria colla contineat; que hedificia nimis ingeniossa inferius structa est. Fecitque non longe ab eadem domo monasterium sancti Andree apostoli; suaque effigies super valvas eiusdem monasteri est inferius teselis depicta.'

9 Ibid., 149: 'Totis vero parietibus proconissis marmoribus decoravit, et in ingressu ianue extrinsecus super liminare versus metricos continentes ita, videlicet.' The verses read:

> Aut lux hic nata est, aut capta hic libera regnat.
> Lux est ante, venit caeli decus unde modernum,
> Aut privata diem pepererunt tecta nitentem,
> Inclusumque iubar secluso fulget Olimpo.
> Marmora cum radiis vernantur, cerne, serenis
> Cunctaque sidereo percussa in murice saxa.
> Auctoris pretio splendescunt munera Petri.
> Huic honor, huic meritum tribuit, sic comere parva,
> Ut valeant spatiis anplum superare coactis.
> Nil modicum Christo est. Artas bene possidet aedes,
> Cuius in humano consistunt pectore tenpla.
> Fundamen Petrus, Petrus fundator et aula.
> Quod domus, hoc dominus, quod factum, factor et idem,

Moribus atque opere. Christus possessor habetur,
Qui duo consocians mediator reddit et unum.
Huc veniens fundat parituros gaudia fletus,
Contritam solidans percusso in pectore mentem.
Ne iaceat, se sternat humo morbosque latentes
Ante pedes medici, cura properante, recludat.
Saepe metus mortis vitae fit causa beatae. (*LPER*, 313)

10 Gerola, 'Ripristino,' 107.
11 Agnellus, *CPER*, 149–50: 'AUCTORIS PRECIO SPLENDESCUNT
MUNERA PETRI ... FUNDAMEN PETRUS, PETRUS FUNDATOR ET
AULA.'
12 The following is a chronology of Ravenna archbishops named Peter. The
dates are taken from A. Carile, ed., *Storia di Ravenna*, II, 2 (Ravenna, 1992).
Petrus I (Petrus Chrysologus): ca. 426 to 432–ca. 450 to 452
Petrus II: 494–518 or 519.
Petrus III: 570–578
13 Agnellus, *CPER*, XVIII Petrus I, 70, note 2, and XXII Petrus II, 138, note 3.
14 Gerola, 'Ripristino,' 72.
15 F.W. Deichmann, 'Studi sulla Ravenna scomparsa,' *FR* 103 (1972), 61–112,
esp. 66, note 25, strongly supports this idea. Raffaella Farioli, 'Ravenna
paleocristiana scomparsa,' *FR*, ser. 3, 31 (1960), and 32 (1961), 5–88, suggests a dedication to All Saints, on the basis of the medallion saints in the
soffits and of the inscription on the two capitals in the chapel – 'PETRUS
EPISC. SCE. RAVENT COEPTUM OPUS A FUNDAMENTIS IN HONORE
SCORUM PERFECIT' – though she herself admits the provenance of the
capitals is dubious.
16 See Agnellus, *CPER*, XXVII Maximian, 195, for relic of Andrew's beard.
Testi-Rasponi's note 2, p. 189, describes Maximian's frequent visits to Constantinople. The remains of Andrew, along with those of Timothy and
Luke, had been found at the Church of the Holy Apostles, Constantinople,
on 28 July 548, as recorded by Procopius, *Buildings*, I/4, 18, and Maximian
must have obtained his relics after this date. See also *CPER*, 192, note 17.
17 The date of Maximinian's S Andrea Maggiore was 557. This appears to be
the first authenticated case of a bishop being buried inside the city of
Ravenna. See Picard, *Souvenir*, 347 and 355, for a general discussion of
bishop burials inside the city.
18 Agnellus, *CPER*, XXVII Maximian, 191.
19 Details of building history in Gerola, 'Ripristino.'

20 These fragments are displayed in the Archiepiscopal Museum in Ravenna. See G. Gerola, 'Il mosaico absidiale della Ursiana,' *FR* 1, 5 (1912), 177–90, for the history of the mosaic, which was dated to 1112, and 180, pl. 13, for a copy of a drawing (now lost) by Gianfrancesco Buonamici of the apse and tribune mosaics *in situ*. This identifies the portions saved in the Archbishops' Chapel.

21 Gerola, 'Ripristino,' 104–5.

22 Illustrated in Deichmann, *Ravenna*, III, plates 219–43.

23 The mosaics of the north and south lunettes were replaced by Luca Longhi's paintings in the mid-sixteenth-century renovations of Archbishop Cardinal Giulio della Rovere. Gerolamo Fabri, *Le sagre memorie di Ravenna antica* (Venice, 1664), 59, and 383.

24 Gerola, 'Ripristino,' 111.

25 A. Grabar, 'L'iconographie du ciel dans l'art chrétien de l'Antiquité et du Haut Moyen Age,' *CahArch* 30 (1982), 5–25; and K. Lehmann, 'The Dome of Heaven,' *ArtBull.* 27 (1945), 19.

26 Gerola, 'Ripristino,' 107–8. The extent of the original is shown in Corrado Ricci, *Monumenti. Tavole storiche dei mosaici di Ravenna*, V: *Cappella Arcivescovile* (Rome, 1934), pl. XXXVII, XXXVIII, XXXIX, and, esp., XL.

27 A. Gonosovà, 'The Formation and Sources of Early Byzantine Floral Semis and Floral Diaper Patterns Reexamined,' *DOP* 39 (1988), 227–37, esp. 230. See also the mosaic of Theodora's court in San Vitale, Ravenna, mid-sixth century: the court lady second from Theodora wears a dress of fabric patterned with birds facing alternate ways and alternating with crosses. For illustrations, see G. Bovini, *I mosaici di Ravenna* (Milan, 1956), pl. 36, and Deichmann, *Ravenna*, III, 216–18. E. Kitzinger, *Byzantine Art in the Making*, 54, and 138, note 24, has also proposed a textile model for the starry vaults at the Mausoleum of Galla Placidia, though no precisely similar textiles have survived. See also Deichmann, *Ravenna*, II, 1, 88.

28 The Lateran Baptistery chapels of Pope Hilarus are discussed in chapter 8.

29 See H. Maguire, *Earth and Ocean, The Terrestrial World in Early Byzantine Art* (University Park, PA, and London, 1987), 30–1.

30 John 14.6: 'Jesus said to him "I am the way, the truth and the life; no one comes to the Father, but by me."'

31 As shown in J. Wilpert, *Die römischen Mosaiken*, vol. 3, fig. 89, where, however, Wilpert envisaged the lion on the right, the serpent on the left, rather than the reverse, as actually reconstructed.

32 See Spiro K. Kostof, *The Orthodox Baptistery of Ravenna* (New Haven and London, 1965), figs. 76 and 80.

33 Gerola, 'Ripristino,' 108. Ricci, *Tavole*, V, pl. XXXV.
34 As suggested by S.J.B. Barnish in his review of M. McCormick, *Triumphal Rulership in Late Antiquity, Byzantium and the Early Medieval West* (Cambridge, 1986), in *J.Eccl. Hist.* 41 (1990), 79–81.
35 McCormick, *Triumphal Rulership*, 57–8.
36 See ibid., 70–3, for discussion of these examples of ritual trampling.
37 G. Ferguson, *Signs and Symbols in Christian Art* (Oxford, 1954): 15, 23, 28, 37.
38 The status of Paul at Ravenna is discussed by J.M. Huskisson, *Concordia Apostolorum. Christian Propaganda at Rome in the Fourth and Fifth Centuries. A Study in Early Christian Iconography and Iconology*. BAR, 148 (Oxford, 1982), 29. He attributes Paul's status in Ravenna to a special devotion of the Theodosian house, previously manifested in their building of S Paolo *fuori le Mura*, Rome, and shown in Ravenna in Paul's position on such sarcophagi as the Liberius sarcophagus used as a high altar in S Francesco, Ravenna, where he receives the Law from Christ in place of Peter, and the early-fifth-century example in S Maria in Porto Fuori, where Paul alone is shown receiving the Law.
39 J.E. Cirlot, *A Dictionary of Symbols*, tr. J. Sage (New York, 1962), 130, on haloes, and 50–7 on the mystical significance of colours, esp. 55–6, on white: 'The function of white is derived from that of the sun ... it comes to signify intuition in general, and, in its affirmative and spiritual aspect, intuition of the Beyond.' Cirlot's work draws upon wide and varied sources to unravel the ancient beliefs of many cultures, some of which were influential upon the thought of the early church. See introduction, and esp. xix–xxii, 'Symbolism in the West.'
40 Illustrated in Michael Gough, *The Origins of Christian Art* (London, 1973), 19, pl. 10.
41 Agnellus, *LPER*, 327–8: 'Collocavit autem hic merita apostolorum et martirum, id est ... sanctae Eufimiae ... sanctae Eugeniae, qui orent pro nobis.'
42 Alchemy, perhaps coincidentally, found the series black–white–red–gold to denote the path of spiritual ascension. Cirlot, *Symbols*, 53.
43 E. Arslan, *Catalogo delle cose d'arte e di antichità d'Italia – Vicenza*, I: *Le chiese* (Rome, 1956), 88–9.
44 Attilio Previtali, *San Felice: Una dimora dello spirito* (Vicenza, 1988), n.p.
45 Referring to Revelation 1.8: '"I am Alpha and the Omega," says the Lord God.'
46 John 1.21.
47 See Elizabeth Lipsmeyer, *The Donor and His Church Model in Medieval Art from Early Christian Times to the Late Romanesque period*, PhD dissertation (Rutgers University, 1981).

6 Commemoration of the Dead

1 Ambrose, *Victor, Nabor, Felix pii*, Ambrose, in *Ambroise de Milan: Hymnes*, ed. Jacques Fontaine (Paris, 1992), 445–83, esp. 454–7, for text and French translation of this hymn (no. 10). English translation in F. Van der Meer and C. Mohrmann, *Atlas of the Early Christian World* (London, 1959), 151. See also F.J.E. Raby, *A History of Christian Latin Poetry from the Beginnings to the Close of the Middle Ages*, 2nd ed. (Oxford, 1953), 34, note 1, where Raby includes it among the eighteen genuine hymns of Ambrose.

2 Ambrose, *De Excessu Fratris sui Satyri*, PL 16, cols. 1345–1414, tr. H.de Romestin, *N&PNF*, 10 (Oxford and New York, 1896).

3 Although Ernst Dassmann, 'Ambrosius und die Märtyrer,' *Jahrbuch für Antike und Cristentum* 18 (1975), 49–68, summarizes Ambrose's writings on the martyr cult, he does so without reference to the associated buildings. The classic work on the chapel is F. Reggiori, *La Basilica Ambrosiana. Ricerche e restauri, 1929–1940* (Milan, 1941). Recent sources include: Carlo Bertelli, 'Mosaici a Milano,' *Atti del 10° congresso internazionale di studi sull'alto medio evo* (Spoleto, 1986), 333–51; Angela Surace, 'Milano, Basilica di S Ambrogio, Cappella di San Vittore in Ciel d'Oro. Restauro dei mosaici.' In *Notiziario*, Soprintendenza Archeologica della Lombardia (1988–9), 322–3, with recent restoration bibliography; C. Ferrari da Passano, 'Il restauro statico e conservativo della cappella di San Vittore in Ciel d'Oro, Basilica di Sant'Ambrogio (1989), 6–11. The material in this chapter first appeared in the author's paper 'Symbolism and Purpose in an Early Christian Martyr Chapel: The Case of San Vittore in Ciel d'Oro, Milan,' *Gesta* 34 (1995), 91–101. It owes a great deal to the helpful comments of Anne Marie Weyl Carr, the former editor of *Gesta*.

4 Reggiori, *Basilica Ambrosiana*, 254, found this inscription was original and unrestored.

5 Ambrose, Hymn, 'Victor, Nabor, Felix,' and *ActaSS*, Victor, May, II, 285, states: 'Erat autem ibi quidam miles, Maurus genere, nomine Victor.' See also V. Saxer, 'Victor, Titre d'honneur ou nom propre?' *RAC* 44 (1968), 209–18.

6 Ambrose, *Victor, Nabor, Felix pii*.

7 Matthew 13.31. Ambrose, *Expositio evangelii secundum Lucam*, PL, 15, col. 1746: 'Granum sinapis martyres nostri sunt Felix, Nabor et Victor ... Venit persecutio, arma posuerunt, colla flexerunt, contriti gladio per totius terminos mundi gratiam sui sparsere martyrii, eit jure dicatur "in omnem terram exivit sonus eorum"' (Psalm 18.5).

8 *ActaSS*, Victor, May, II, 286–90, esp. 288, legend of St Victor, and 290, for statement that Maternus was builder of the chapel: 'Postquam vero permissum est, ut sepeliretur corpus Martyris, abiit sanctus et beatissimus vir Maternus et invenit ... ipsum, quasi eadem hora fuisset decollatus ... et sepelierunt in pace.' The author makes Victor contemporary with Maternus, though this would have made him die after the Peace of the Church, for Maternus held office sometime between Mirocles (313–14) and Protase (342–4). See also Savio, *Vescovi: Milano*, 101.

9 *Passio* of St Victor, *AASS*, II (May), 290. See also F. Savio, 'De alcune chiese di Milano anteriori a S Ambrogio,' *NBAC* 2 (1896), 166, note 2. Savio believes Maternus buried the saint and built the first chapel over his grave, even if Victor's death had occurred at an earlier period.

10 Details from Reggiori, *Basilica Ambrosiana*, 177, and 244–8.

11 For a summary of early opinion on the dating of the mosaics at S Vittore in Ciel d'Oro, see Reggiori, ibid., 228, 234, and 236–8. See also Bertelli, 'Mosaici a Milano,' and E. Kitzinger, *Byzantine Art in the Making*, 61–2.

12 These letter forms point to the fourth or early fifth centuries. See A. Ratti, 'Il più antico ritratto di S Ambrogio,' *Ambrosiana; scritti varii pubblicati nel XV centenario dalla morte di S Ambrogio* (Milan, 1897), 1–74, esp. 26–32.

13 E. Battisti, 'Per la datazione di alcuni mosaici di Ravenna e di Milano,' *Scritti di storia dell'arte in onore di M. Salmi*, 3 vols. (Rome, 1961), I: 101–23, esp.119–23.

14 Reggiori, *Basilica Ambrosiana*, 225

15 Ratti, 'Ritratto,' 22.

16 See Reggiori, *Basilica Ambrosiana*, 220 f., for state of mosaics. Restorations include, in the central medallion, two areas of Victor's clothing and one of his cheek, and in the side walls, the hand of St Nabor, while the frieze at the base of the dome has suffered serious cracking.

17 O. von Simson, *Sacred Fortress* (Chicago, 1948), 81.

18 For the symbolic meaning of the dove, see Paulinus's inscriptions beside the door of his church of St Felix at Nola, which twice referred to Christian souls as doves. R.C. Goldschmidt, *Paulinus' Churches at Nola* (Amsterdam, 1940), 42–3, for text and translation: 'QUAEQUE SIGNUM RESIDENT CAELESTE COLUMBAE/ SIMPLICIBUS PRODUNT REGNA PATERE DEI' ('The doves perched above the heavenly sign/intimate that the kingdom of God is open to the simple of heart') and 'NOS QUOQUE PERFICIES PLACITAS TIBI, CHRISTE, COLUMBAS SI VIGEAT PURIS PARS TUA PECTORIBUS' ('Us too wilt Thou make doves pleasing to Thee, Christ, if thy followers have strength through purity of heart').

19 See Rev. 3.5, *NOAB*, 1496, also Rev. 21.12; a similar thought inspires the

marble inscription at Santa Prassede, Rome, which records the unnamed
martyrs transferred to the church by Paschal I on 20 June 817. *LP*, II, 64,
'Quorum nomina sunt in libro vitae.'

20 See Jean-Louis Maier, *Le baptistère de Naples et ses mosaïques* (Fribourg, 1969),
fig. 3, and M. Lawrence, *The Sarcophagi of Ravenna* (New York, 1945), 23 and
30.

21 See Jean Daniélou, *Primitive Christian Symbols*, tr. D. Attwater (Baltimore,
1964), 1–25, 'The Palm and the Crown,' esp. 4–9. This feast took place at the
vintage, and had an extended meaning which was rooted in the Book of
Exodus. The celebration referred both to the Jews' deliverance from Egypt
and to the coming of the Messiah and the joys that were expected thereaf-
ter. The special celebrations included the building and the garlanding of
tabernacles, which were symbols of the life to come.

22 Ibid., 17–18.

23 Contrast 1 Cor. 9.24–5, 'in a race all the runners compete, but only one
receives the prize ... they do it to receive a perishable wreath, but we an
imperishable ...' and Revelation, 2.10, 'Be faithful unto death, and I will
give you the crown of life,' where the crown clearly has eschatalogical significance.

24 Daniélou, *Symbols*, 18–23.

25 See, for example, the gold wreath with oak leaves and acorns from the
burial of Philip II of Macedon. See *The Search for Alexander, an Exhibition*, ed.
K. Rhomiopoulou, A. Herrmann, and C. Vermeule (New York, 1980),
colour plate 36.

26 M. van Berchem and E. Clouzot, *Mosaïques Chrétiennes* (Geneva, 1924), 111:
'une pierre précieuse ovale'; Reggiori, *Basilica Ambrosiana*, 220: 'una grossa
gemma variopinta.'

27 René Guénon, *Man and His Becoming According to the Vedanta*, tr. R.C.
Nicholson (London, 1945), 101, note 1. Guénon describes the origin of the
cosmic light from the *hianyagarbha*, literally the 'golden embryo,' Brahma.
Guenon also points out the remarkable, presumably coincidental, similarity
of the Latin word *aurum*, gold, to the Hebrew *aor*, light. In alchemy, too, the
metal gold corresponded to the light of the sun: see C.G. Jung, *Collected
Works*, vol. 12: *Psychology and Alchemy* (London, 1932).

28 During the controversy in the early years of the twentieth century between
the Ambrosiana and S Vittore al Corpo over the possession of the relics of
Victor, the image was interpreted as representing Christ Victorious. See
Reggiori, *Basilica Ambrosiana*, 237–8, for discussion and total rejection of this
idea. Achille Ratti's arguments for the interpretation as Christ are summarized by F. Savio, *Vescovi: Milano*, 765, note 1.

29 A dark complexion was certainly possible in another context. See the mosaic funerary portrait of Quodvultdeus, mid-fourth-century bishop of Carthage, in the catacomb of S Gennaro, Naples, which shows him as an African (fig. 62). U.M. Fasola, *Le Catacombe di S Gennaro a Capodimonte* (Rome, 1975), 155–60, and colour plate XIII.

30 Daniélou, *Symbols*, 136.

31 Ezekiel 9.3–4, *NOAB*, 1008, note v. 4. See also Daniélou, *Symbols*, 136–45, for the meaning of *tau*.

32 See examples in Cabrol and Leclercq, *DACL*, 3/2, cols. 3056–60, 'Croix et crucifix.' Leclercq found about twenty representations of the cross which dated from before the start of the fourth century, suggesting that the earliest was in the Hypogeum of Lucina, Rome (fig. 3360). This example is of a Greek cross and, despite Leclercq's placing it in the second century, cannot be dated before the early-third-century date of the earliest catacombs. The *tau* cross occurs on two marbles in the Cemetery of Callixtus: De Rossi, *Roma sotteranea*, II, pl. 39, and pl. 43:14.

33 Among them Tertullian (c. 160–c. 225), *Adversus Marcionem*, ed. and tr. Ernest Evans, III, 22, 240–1 (Oxford, 1972): 'and afterwards all the faithful, sealed with that mark of which Ezekiel speaks ... for this same letter *tau* of the Greeks which is our T, has the appearance of the Cross, which he (Ezekiel) foresaw we should have on our foreheads in ... Jerusalem ... all these are found in use with you also, the sign on the foreheads and the sacraments of the churches.'

34 Daniélou, *Symbols*, 141–2.

35 *Epistle of Barnabas*, 9, 'Of Circumcision,' in *Early Christian Writings, the Apostolic Fathers*, tr. Maxwell Stamforth (Harmondsworth, 1968), 205–6. Also see Daniélou, *Symbols*, 143. The *Epistle* dates from 70 to 100 AD. *ODCC*, 134.

36 Max Sulzberger, 'Le symbole de la croix et les monogrammes de Jésus chez les premiers chrétiens,' *Byzantion* 2 (1925), 337–448, esp. 448.

37 Van Berchem and Clouzot, *Mosaïques*, 112, also suggested, without further explanation, that this cross was monogrammatic, and contained the first two letters of the names of Jesus and of Christ. I have looked for parallels to this particular cross without success. The monogram cross with an open *rho* occurs on numerous Ravenna sarcophagi: see Lawrence, *Sarcophagi of Ravenna*, figs. 54–6 and 58.

38 Daniélou, *Symbols*, 143.

39 This text, on the monogram of Christ, is known from both British Museum, cod. Harl. 3049, and Oxford, Merton College cod. 26. It was first attributed to Jerome by D. Germain Morin, 'Hieronymus de Monogrammate,' *Revue Bénédictine* 2 (1903), 225–36, an attribution accepted by later scholars such

as Daniélou. See Morin, ibid., 231, for Jerome's additions to Victorinus's text 'Sign of the Cross,' and 232, where he discusses the text of Cod. Harl. Mus. Brit 3049, in which there is a marginal monogram of combined cross and *waw* added by Jerome.

40 Victorinus, *Commentarius in Apocalypsim, Victorini Episcopi Petavionensis Opera*, ed. J. Haussleiter, CSEL 49 (Vienna, 1926).

41 A. Dupont-Sommer, *La doctrine gnostique du 'waw'* (Paris, 1946), ch. 3, 'De la mystique des lettres,' 72. Dupont-Sommer discusses the variants of the letter *waw*, among which are forms where the letter was formed like a serpent 'dressé sur sa queue,' and others where the ends of the 'serpent' were joined to form a circle.

42 Daniélou, *Symbols*, 144.

43 Valerie A. Maxfield, *The Military Decorations of the Roman Army* (London, 1981). *Armillae*, 89–91, figs. 9 and 10; also pls. 8c and 9c, and 253 for the extended eligibility for *dona*.

44 After 212 they were awarded only sporadically, but were known from both the mid-fourth and early fifth centuries, when given out by Julian (355–63) and Valentinian III (425–55).

45 Justin Martyr (ca. 100–ca. 165), *Apologia* I, 56, in *The Works Now Extant of St Justin the Martyr*, tr. 'E.B.P.' (Oxford, 1861), 42–3.

46 Multiple layers of meaning seem to have been common as educated viewers, both patrons and clerics, were not primarily interested in the superficial appearance of an image, but in the spiritual reality behind it. Liz James and Ruth Webb, 'To Understand Ultimate Things and Enter Secret Places: Ekphrasis and Art in Byzantium,' *Art History* 14 (1991), 1–17.

47 Daniélou, *Symbols*, 145.

48 Reggiori, *Basilica Ambrosiana*, 254.

49 J. Wilpert and W.N. Schumacher, *Die römischen Mosaiken der kirchlichen Bauten vom IV–XIII Jahrhundert* (Freiburg, Basel, and Vienna, 1976), 320, 'Beide Namen im Genitiv Panegiriae – Faustini nennen uns das Stifterpaar, das sich dem heiligen Victor empfiehlt.'

50 Reggiori, *Basilica Ambrosiana*, 193.

51 I thank Iva Matković for this suggestion.

52 Ambrose, *Epistola* 22, 'To His Sister Marcellina,' *PL* 16, col. 1063.

53 This legend is recorded for the first time in the eleventh-century *Historia Datiana*. See M. Caffi, *Storia di Milano*, 592, notes 1 and 2, for bibliography.

54 Ibid., 591.

55 Reggiori, *Basilica Ambrosiana*, 194.

56 Savio, 'De alcune chiese,' 163–73. Although a tradition exists that S Vittore in Ciel d'Oro is the Basilica Faustae, as believed in the fourteenth century

by Galvano Flamma, Savio identified it as S Vitalis on the basis of an inscription recorded by Puricelli that a certain Faustinus had built the chapel of S Vitalis in the time of Archbishop Mona. Mona's tomb was discovered there in 1018. See Picard, *Souvenir*, 28–9, for further information on S Vitalis, which he describes as 'un sanctuaire fort mal connu.'

57 For fragment, see Luigi Biraghi, *Ricognizione dei gloriosi corpi dei santi Vittore, Mauro, Satiro, Casto e Polemio, ecc.* (Milan, 1861). For Ferrario's drawings see G. Ferrario, *Monumenti sacri e profani dell'imperiale e reale basilica di Sant'Ambrogio in Milano* (Milan, 1824), plate facing p. 177. Ferrario's plates are also reproduced by Reggiori, *Basilica Ambrosiana*, 216.

58 Savio, *Vescovi: Milano*, on San Vittore, 100

59 Victor, *ActaSS*, May, II, 752 and 761. Savio, *Vescovi: Milano*, 101.

60 Savio, ibid., 100.

61 Dungalus Reclusus, *Liber adversus Claudium taurinensem*, PL, 105, cols. 447–530, esp. 527: 'Ambrosius suum fratrem Satyrum, quem nimium dilexerat, iuxta sanctum martyrem Victorem sepelevit, de quo tres libros edidit egregios, unum de eius planctu, alteros duos consolatorios de resurrectione et paradiso. Cuius epitaphium hoc dictatur tetrasticho.' The epigraph is also recorded in *ILCV*, I, ed. Ernest Diehl (Berlin, 1925), 424, no. 2165.

62 'Ambrose bestowed upon his brother Uranius Satyrus the supreme honour of being at the martyr's left hand – this the reward of merit – so that the fluid of the (martyr's) sacred blood by penetrating washes the adjacent remains.'

63 Tombs found by Reggiori, *Basilica Ambrosiana*, 216–38. See also Picard, *Souvenir*, 36, and, for bibliography, note 61.

64 See Y. Duval, *Auprès des saints corps et âme. L'inhumation 'ad sanctos' dans la chrétienté d'Orient et d'Occident du IIIe au VIIe siècle* (Tournholt, 1988), 100–2, and Diehl, *ILCV*, I, 2166.

65 The only three articles to deal specifically with the S Matrona chapel are: Giuseppe Bovini, 'Osservazioni sui mosaici paleocristiani della chiesa di S Prisco a S Prisco presso S Maria Capua Vetere,' *Capys* 2 (1967), 6–12 (lacks footnotes); idem, 'Mosaici paleocristiani scomparsi di S Prisco,' *CorsiCRB* 14 (1967), 43–62; and Raffaella Farioli, 'La decorazione musiva della cappella di S Matrona nella chiesa di S Prisco presso Capua,' *CorsiCRB* 14 (1967), 267–91.

66 'Signa ecclesiae, quae (primum) extabat (in area in qua S.Prisci corpus abditum erat) et a coemeterio circumdabatur, nuper observavit domnus Hieronymus meus gentilis ... Erat ecclesia vetus in planitie, quae nunc est ante ecclesiam; porta respiciebat ad orientem: hemiciclus [sic] in capite ab occidente, nunc prope viam.' Michael Monachus, manuscript prepared for the

second edition of *Sanctuarium Capuanum*, 1st ed. (Naples, 1630), Biblioteca Nazionale di Napoli, MS IX, G 32, fol. 45. Cited by G.B. De Rossi, 'Agostino vescovo e la sua madre Felicità, martiri sotto Decio e le loro memorie e monumenti in Capua,' *BAC*, ser. IV, 3 (1884), 104–13, esp. 111.

67 Bovini, 'Osservazione,' 7; Monachus, *Sanctuarium Capuanum*, 'SACELLUM ET SEPULCHRUM S MATRONAE IN ECCLESIA S PRISCI' (not 'apud S Prisci').

68 See Monachus, *Sanctuarium Capuanum*, for an account of the chapel's appearance in the seventeenth century.

69 A late inscription is recorded by Monachus, *Sanctuarium Capuanum*, 144. It attributes the building of the basilica to Matrona, in honour of St Priscus. Confusingly, it dated the construction to the year 506, and to the reigns of both Pope Gelasius (492–6), and the emperor Zeno (474–91). It also promised indulgences to those who visited the basilica in the year 1102.

70 Mission of the seventy disciples: Luke 10.1–16. Priscus is believed to have been the first bishop of Capua. His remains, translated from their resting place in Matrona's church, were discovered in the church of St Stephen, Capua, by Archbishop Nicolaus Caracciolus on 9 May 1712. There they had lain in wooden containers along with relics of other Campanian saints: Quartus, Quintus, Rufus, Carponius, and Decorosus. *ActaSS*, September, I, 99–108, esp. 104.

71 *ActaSS* (March 15), 392–8, esp. 392. Also, Monachus, *Sanctuarium Capuanum*, 143.

72 *ActaSS*, ibid., 392.

73 Émile Bertaux, *L'art dans l'Italie Méridionale*, vol. 1 (1903) (repr. Paris and Rome, 1968), 51.

74 Details of the saint's life in *ActaSS* (March 15), 392–8.

75 H.V. Livermore, *The Origin of Spain and Portugal* (London, 1971), 15–16. Also, E.A. Thompson, 'The Conversion of the Spanish Suevi to Catholicism,' in *Visigothic Spain: New Approaches*, ed. Edward James (Oxford, 1980), 77–92, esp. 78–9.

76 *ActaSS* (March 15), 392.

77 *Oxford Latin Dictionary* (Oxford, 1976), 1084. See also Kate Cooper, 'The Martyr, the *Matrona* and the Bishop: The Matron Lucina and the Politics of Martyr Cult in Fifth- and Sixth-Century Rome,' *Early Medieval Europe* 8 (1999), 297–317, for a discussion of the role of the *matrona* in the early legends of saints' lives.

78 *ActaSS* (March 15), 393.

79 Bertaux mistakenly places this medallion image among rinceaux of acanthus.

80 In the absence of information on the orientation of the church, it will be discussed as if it were conventionally orientated with its apse to the east.

81 Ejnar Dyggve, 'The Origin of the Urban Churchyard,' *Classica et Mediaevalia* 13 (1952), 147–58, and idem, 'L'origine del cimitero entro la cinta della città,' *Atti dello VIII Congresso di studi bizantini* (Palermo, 1951), repr. in *Rivista di Studi Bizantini e Neoellenici* (Rome, 1953), 137–41. Dyggve describes the rise of the funerary cult of martyrs as occurring in churches such as S Prisco that were built outside the city walls, conforming to Roman burial law.

82 Paulinus of Nola, *Epistola* 32, to Sulpicius Severus, dated 403. See Goldschmidt, *Paulinus' Churches*, 46–7, and C. Davis-Weyer, *Early Medieval Art, 300–1150*, Sources and Documents in the History of Art Series, ed. H.W. Janson (Englewood Cliffs, 1971), 20–3.

83 The Palestinian ampoules frequently show the triumphant cross between symbolic equivalents to the apostles: twelve stars (Ihm, *Programme*, fig. 22); or clipei containing apostle bust portraits (ibid., 87, fig 21) See also Grabar, *Ampoules*, ampoule 10, reverse, pl. X; ampoule 12, reverse, pl. XXIII.

84 Paulinus, *Epistola* 32: Goldschmidt, *Paulinus' Churches*: Nola, 38–9; Fundi, 46–7.

85 F. Wickhoff, 'Das Apsismosaik in der Basilika des hl. Felix zu Nola,' *Römische Quartalschrift* 3 (1889), 158–76, figs. p. 169, repr. Ihm, *Programme*, figs. 16 and 17, pp. 80–1. G. Rizza, 'Pitture e mosaichi nelle basiliche paoliniane di Nola e di Fondi,' *Siculorum Gymnasium* 1 (1948), 311–21.

86 'Crucem corona lucido cingit globo/ Cui coronae sunt corona apostoli/ Quorum figura est in columbarum choro.' This composition is also reminiscent of the mosaic at the early Christian baptistery of Albenga, where the altar niche features a chi-rho symbol surrounded by a wreath of twelve doves. Raffaella Farioli, 'Decorazione musiva,' has also drawn attention to similar compositions in Gaul, which are relevant in light of Paulinus's Gallic origin. A series of twelve doves also decorated the soffit of the apse arch at the sixth-century church of S Michele in Africisco, Ravenna, in an equivalent position to the portrait medallions of apostles and other saints found, for example, at Lythrankomi, Cyprus, as well as at the Archbishops' Chapel and at S Vitale, Ravenna.

87 Latin texts in note 18.

88 These motifs were popular in classical decorative schemes, as at Pompeii and at Hadrian's Villa at Tivoli.

89 Cabrol and Leclercq, *DACL*, 3/2, col. 2202.

90 The number twelve, too, may have a secondary meaning; legend tells that the number of maidens in Matrona's Capua congregation was also twelve:

though, of course, since the legend is late, the number of maidens may even have been suggested by this decoration.

91 Genesis 2.10.

92 These ideas are expressed by, among others, St Cyprian: 'Has arbores rigat quattor fluminibus id est Evangeliis quattor quibus baptismi.' Cyprian, *Epistola* LXXIII:10, CSEL, 3 (Vienna, 1866), 785.

93 See Gordana Babić, 'North Chapel of the Quatrefoil Church at Ohrid and Its Mosaic Floor,' *Zbornik Radova Vizantoloskog Instituta* 13 (1971), 271f.

94 Cyprian, *Epistola* LXXIII, tr. Rose Bernard Donna, 268–85, esp. 274: 'the Lord cries out that whoever thirsts should come and drink from the rivers of living water which have flowed from within him.' See also John 7.37–8.

95 As is shown in some of the Palestinian ampoules, where the cross is shown with its trunk jointed like a palm tree. See Grabar, *Ampoules*, for numerous illustrations.

96 See James Smith, 'The Garments That Honour the Cross in the "Dream of the Rood,"' *Anglo-Saxon England* 4 (1975), 29–37, for development of this idea.

97 The Walters Art Gallery cross is illustrated in Michael Gough, *The Origins of Christian Art* (London, 1973), 142, pl. 134.

98 Revelation 21.6, the words of the Nameless One upon the throne. See also Rev. 1.8, and Isaiah 44.6.

99 See Lehmann, 'Dome of Heaven,' 1–27, esp. 19.

100 Lehmann, 'Dome,' 3–12.

101 C. Leonardo, *Ampelos, il simbolo della vite nell'arte pagana e paleocristiana* (Rome, 1947), 216. See also Domenico Mallardo, 'La Vite negli antichi monumenti cristiani di Napoli e della Campania,' *RAC* 25 (1949), 73–103, esp. 98–9.

102 For example, the cross was featured at the Lateran Baptistery chapel of S Croce, and the chi-rho at the Naples baptistery, as well as at the Archbishops' Chapel in Ravenna. All were within wreaths.

103 A. Grabar, *Christian Iconography, A Study of Its Origins* (Princeton, 1968), 114–16.

104 Grabar compares the throne with the one at S Maria Maggiore, Rome, but there the dove is not present, making it inappropriate as a symbol of the Trinity.

105 John 1.32.

106 See F. van der Meer, *Maiestas Domini* (Vatican City, 1938), 236, citing Jerome, Hippolytus, and other Fathers.

107 Ibid., 231–6.

108 See the notes to this chapter of Revelation in the *NOAB*, 1493f., esp. 1497.

109 Rev. 4.6–8: 'and around the throne ... are four living creatures ... the first living creature like a lion, the second ... like an ox, the third ... with the face of a man, and the fourth ... like a flying eagle. And the four living creatures, each of them with six wings ... never cease to sing, "Holy, Holy, Holy."'

110 See Dale Kinney, 'The Apocalypse in Early Christian Monumental Decoration,' *The Apocalypse in the Middle Ages*, ed. R.K. Emerson and B. McGinn (Ithaca and London, 1992), 200–16, esp. 205–6, and Marjorie de Grooth and Paul van Moorsel, 'The Lion, the Calf, the Man and the Eagle in Early Christian and Coptic Art,' *BABESCH* 52–3 (1977–8), 233–41, esp. 235–9.

111 For illustrations of the Naples Baptistery, see Maier, *Baptistère*.

112 See Fasola, *Catacombe*, ch. 6 and colour plate XII.

113 This catacomb, which contains many fine stuccoes, was discovered in 1937 near the first mile of the Via Latina, and dates from the late third and the early fourth centuries. The vault is illustrated in Farioli, 'Decorazione musiva,' 273, fig. 3. See also G.P. Kirsch, *The Catacombs of Rome* (Rome, 1946), 120–1.

114 John 15.1–7.

115 'The divine and timeless vine has sprung from the grave, bearing as fruits the newly baptised, like bunches of grapes on the altar ... the vine has been harvested and the altar loaded with fruit like a winepress.' Asterius the Sophist (d. ca. 341), *Homilies on the Psalms*, tr. and ed. Marcel Richard (Oslo, 1956).

116 Zeno of Verona (d. ca. 375) *Tractatus* XXVIII, 'In Isaiam VII,' *PL*, 11, cols. 471–2. See also Daniélou, *Symbols*, 37–8.

117 Asterius the Sophist, *Homilies on the Psalms*, Homily 14, 1–2, 105. Tr. Daniélou, *Symbols*, 38.

118 Illustrated in Paola Pariset, 'I mosaici del battistero di S Giovanni in Fonte,' *CahArch* 20 (1970), 1–73.

119 A recently discovered example is the complex of rooms beside the pool at Poppeia's villa at Oplontis, wonderfully painted with olive trees, birds, and fountains on a golden yellow background.

120 H.N. and A.L. Moldenke, *Plants of the Bible* (Waltham, MA, 1952, repr. Mineola, NY, 1986), 185–6.

121 Other Campanian apse mosaics, known from brief mention in literary sources, will not be discussed here. See Ihm, *Programme*, 175, for apse decoration of the Basilica Severiana, Naples (between 366 and 412) and Bovini, 'Mosaici scomparsi di Napoli,' 21–34, for the lost mosaics of the

Basilica Stephania (S Restituta) (535–55), and the Ecclesia Salvatoris, both in Naples.

122 A hypothetical sketch of the apse mosaic appears in Ihm, *Programme*, 56, fig. 10.

123 E. Müntz, 'Notes sur les mosaïques chrétiennes de l'Italie,' IX, 'Les mosaïques de Siponte, de Capoue, de Verceil, d'Olona, et d'Albenga,' *RevArch*, ser. III, 17 (1891), 79.

124 Uranius Presbyter, *Epistola* 'De obitu S Paulini ad Pacatum,' *PL*, 53, cols. 859–66, describes the death of Paulinus, which Symmachus witnessed.

125 Monachus, *Sanctuarium Capuanum*, 104.

126 The saints approach from either side, led by Peter and Priscus and the child saints, Quintus and Quartus, and watched by Agnes and Felicitas in the wings. The saints are Campanian, except for Peter, Lawrence, and Agnes. See also Ihm, *Programme*, 178–9.

127 Von Simson, *Sacred Fortress*, 99, discusses *coronae* in the setting of S Prisco: 'The martyrs and virgins are shown offering crowns; the eucharistic bread offered at the altar by the men and women of the congregation was also shaped like a crown, and ... actually called *corona*.' This crown-shaped offering also expressed the fact that the saint accepted Christ as his crown. Refusal to wear a pagan crown of laurel was a distinguishing mark of a Christian among the military. See Tertullian, *Liber de Corona, PL*, 2, cols. 73–102.

128 See Bovini, 'Mosaici ... di San Prisco,' 43–62.

129 Müntz, 'Notes,' 74–5, identifies these figures: the names of the saints are inscribed beside them.

130 Lehmann, 'Dome,' figs. 5, Hadrian's Villa, and 17, S Prisco (my fig. 64). T. Mathews, in 'Cracks in Lehmann's "Dome of Heaven,"' *Source*, 1 (1982), 2–6, argues against Lehmann's theory, saying that astrological symbols were never taken into Christian vault decorations. Unlike Lehmann, who discussed the S Prisco symbol on p. 17 and illustrated it in fig. 17, Mathews seems to have been unaware of it, since it is not mentioned in his discussion.

131 Bovini, 'Mosaici ... di S Prisco,' 62.

132 Monachus, *Sanctuarium Capuanum*, 46–7: 'et Symmachus episcopus Capuae in S. Mariae Maioris ecclesia requiescit.'

133 Dating: dates from late fourth century (De Francovic) to fifth (Van Berchem and Clouzot; Bovini) to fifth to sixth (De Rossi), early sixth (Bertaux) and sixth (Ihm) have been proposed.

134 Farioli, 'Decorazione musiva,' 288.

135 Ibid., 284: 'qui, nella piccola cappella riscontriamo l'atmosfera di resurrezione dei cubicule cimeteriale.'

7 Mausolea of the Rulers in the West

1 *Liber Pontificalis*, I, 180–96.
2 Ammianus Marcellinus, *History*, XXI, tr. J.C. Rolfe (Loeb ed., 1937), 3 vols., vol. II, 92–3.
3 The excavation revealed a square room with apses on two adjacent walls: the third apse of the triconch is hypothetical since it lies under the pavement of S Costanza.
4 See David Stanley, 'New Discoveries at Santa Costanza,' *DOP* 48 (1994), 257–63, and 'An Excavation at Santa Costanza,' *Arte Medievale* 7 (1993), 103–12.
5 See F.W. Deichmann, 'Baptisterium,' in *Reallexicon für Antike und Christentum*, I, col. 1166, and also Henri Stern, 'Les mosaïques de l'église de Sainte-Constance à Rome,' *DOP* 12 (1958), 157–219, esp. 164, note 17: 'L'inhumation dans les baptistères n'était pas ... exceptionelle au IVe et au Ve siècle.'
6 See Stanley, 'New Discoveries,' 260.
7 This question is discussed in my 'A New Look at the Patronage of Santa Costanza, Rome,' *Byzantion* 67 (1997), 383–406.
8 Ammianus, *History*, II, 92–3.
9 Julian, *Collected Works* (Loeb ed., London, 1913–23), vol. III, 149, Letter 47, 'To the Alexandrians.'
10 See Stern, 'Mosaïques,' Appendix II, 216–18, and fig. 58. The design probably represents a lost antique pavement.
11 Ibid., 166.
12 For all known drawings of S Costanza up to the nineteenth century, see Adele Anna Amadio, *I mosaici di S Costanza, Disegni, incisioni e documenti dal XV al XIX secolo, Xenia Quaderni*, 7 (Rome, 1986).
13 These scenes are preserved in several versions. The watercolour of Francesco d'Ollanda (fig. 71) is the source for various copies, among them those of the Bartolis, father and son, and Ciampini's engraving (fig. 72). For various versions, see Stern, 'Mosaïques,' pls. 55–7 and 59–61, and also Appendix I, 215–16. An anonymous Italian, and Antonio da Sangallo, present somewhat different versions; Stern, pls. 2–3.
14 P. Ugonio, *Theatrum Urbis Romae*, partly transcribed by E. Müntz, 'Mosaïques chrétiennes d'Italie,' V, 'Sainte-Constance de Rome,' *RevArch* XXXV (1878), 355–67, esp. 365. Ugonio's text is largely indecipherable and divided between two libraries. The major part, in the Vatican, Vat.Barb.Lat. 1994, 1580, terminates on page 692. Continuing on page 693 is Ferrara, Biblioteca Comunale Ariostea, MS 161 NC6, fol. 1103–10, which contains Ugonio's text on S Costanza. Here Müntz was able to decipher 'circuit (?) autem

in gyrum pictura quaedam ad ornatum conflicta, ut videre est, fluvius enim argenteus excurrit. Et incipiendo supra arcum imminentem altari, in fluvio est cymbula in cujus prora duo quasi habitu sacro induti sedent, alius ad puppim cymbam impellit. Et haec forsitan aliqua est historia (?). See Müntz, 365.

15 Some versions, among them that of Ciampini (fig. 72), show this register of scenes as enclosed in rectangular frames: the version where a second level of 'paradise meadow' opens out above the first cross-piece of the *pergula*, the paired dolphins, seems preferable. For the Miracle of the Centurion's Servant, see Amadio, *Mosaici*, pl. 2 (Escorial 28–11–12, f. 4v) by an anonymous fifteenth-century Italian draughtsman.

16 A simple *pergula* of this type is seen at Hadrian's villa at Tivoli, beside Hadrian's imitation of the River Nile, the Canopus.

17 See Stern, 'Mosaïques,' 169–79, for Old Testament, and 180 for New Testament scenes; also 180–5 for discussion of the meaning of the program.

18 Stern, 'Mosaïques,' 182, note 118.

19 Damien Sicard, *La liturgie de la mort dans l'église latine dès origines à la réforme carolingienne* (Münster, 1978), 362f.

20 Ibid., 391–2.

21 Ibid., 362–6. See also Mackie, 'La Daurade,' 27, table 1.

22 'tribulationibus multis libera domine animam servi tui illi sicut liberasti ... Susannah – de falso testimonio; Hoenoch et Heliam – de communi mortem mundi; Moses – de manu pharaonis regis aegyptiorium; Noah – per diluvium; Abel – per sacrificium gratum.' Sicard, *Liturgie*, 362f.

23 Aimé Georges Martimort, 'L'iconographie des catacombes et la catéchèse antique,' *RAC* 25 (1949), 105–14. See also Sicard, *Liturgie*, 371.

24 Stern, 'Mosaïques,' 197.

25 Ugonio, in E. Müntz, ed., 'Mosaïques Chrétiennes d'Italie, V, Sainte-Constance,' 362: 'et in angulis oblongae mulieres alba veste stantes.' However, Müntz suggested they represented the Church of the Jews and the Church of the Gentiles: 362, note 3.

26 David Stanley, 'The Apse Mosaics at Santa Costanza. Observations on Restorations and Antique Mosaics,' *Mitteilungen des deutschen archäeologischen Instituts, Roemische Abteilung* 94 (1987), 29–42.

27 Theodor Hauschild, 'Die Grabungen in Centcelles,' *Archäeologischer Anzeiger* (1966), 86–92, esp. 91–2.

28 Athanasius, *Historia arianorum ad monachos*, PG, 25, 691–796, tr. Archibald Robertson, in *N&PNF*, ser. 2, vol. IV, *St Athanasius, Select Works and Letters, History of the Arians* (New York, 1903, repr. 1991), 266–302, esp. 296.

29 R. Delbrueck, *Antike Porphyrwerke* (Berlin and Leipzig, 1932), Catalogue,

pp. 164, 169. The connection with the burial of the emperor Constans was first suggested by Helmut Schlunk, 'Unterschungen im frühchristlichen Mausoleum von Centcelles,' *Neue deutsche Ausgrabungen im Mittelmeergegiet und im Vorderen Orient* (Berlin, 1959), 344–65, esp. 359.

30 See H. Schlunk and T. Hauschild, 'Der Denkmäler der frühchristlichen und westgotischen Zeit,' *Hispania Antiqua* 4 (1978).

31 Daniel 4.25.

32 Text from Book of Jonah 2.10: 'and [the fish] vomited out Jonah upon the dry land.'

33 Johnson, *Mausolea*, 105.

34 A. Calderini, 'La scoperta di un recinto fortificato romano presso la basilica milanese di S Vittore al Corpo,' *Palladio*, n.s. 2 (1952), 79. Also illustrated in M. Mirabella Roberti, 'Recinto di S Vittore al Corpo,' in *Milano. Capitale dell'impero romano, 286–402 d.c.* (Milan, 1990), cat. 2a17.

35 Johnson, *Mausolea*, 56–7.

36 Silvia Lusuardi Siena, 'Il mausoleo imperiale,' in M. Mirabella Roberti, ed., *Milano. Capitale*, cat. 2a19, 115.

37 Ambrose, *De Obitu Valentiniani consolatio*, PL, 16, l, cols. 1417–44, esp. 1413, 'Quam sepulcra vicina! ... inseperabiles in vita, et in morte non estis seperati.'

38 Johnson, *Mausolea*, 55–9, esp. 58–9, and for Maximian, 261–3. See also Dale Kinney, 'Le chiese paleocristiane di Mediolanum,' in *Il millenio ambrosiano. Milano, una capitale da Ambrogio ai carolingi*, ed. C. Bertelli (Milan, 1987), 59: 'l'ottogono di San Vittore, che molti ritengono essere stato una tomba costruita per il tetrarca Massiminiano.' Also, M. Mirabella Roberti, 'Il mausoleo romano di S Vittore a Milano,' *Atti del VI Congresso nazionale di archeologia cristiana, Pesaro/Ancona, 1983'* (Ancona, 1985), 777–83, esp. 778, and idem., ed., *Milano. Capitale*, esp. 114–15, with bibliography.

39 Lewis, 'San Lorenzo Revisited,' note 117, suggests the dwarf gallery is a vestige of the ambulatory that had served the funeral processions around the tomb in the pagan burial rite.

40 Bonaventura Castiglioni, d. 1555, cod. Ambr. N.153, f. 30v. See Savio, *Vescovi: Milano*, 774, for text: 'in cotesto tempio vi erano anche alcuni lavori di marmi finissimi di diversi colori tassillati, ossia alla mosaica, tavole di pietra segate con frisi varii componuti di vasi di fiori e di animali, or venuti al meno, e datovi il bianco levate l'opre magnifiche.' See also cod. Ambr. P.258, Besta, *Origine e meraviglie della città di Milano*: 'Questa chiesa dava segno dell'antichità sua per la materia di che era fatta, per haver io veduto certi pilloni longhi più di due oncie, quali per centinaia d'anni avanti non si sono usati nelle fabbriche, quanto ancora nel modo dell'architettura per

esser rotonda tanto di sopra come di sotto, tutta lavorata a musaico, et haveva otto altar dentro di sé e dall'una e dall'altra parte si passava per corridori.'

41 Johnson, *Mausolea*, 115, for texts dealing with the marbles.

42 Summary of arguments in Suzanne Lewis, 'San Lorenzo Revisited,' *JSAH* 32 (1973), 197–222.

43 Calderini, Cecchelli, and Chierici, *San Lorenzo*, 39, 182.

44 W. Kleinbauer, 'Towards a Dating of S Lorenzo in Milan: Masonry and Building Methods of Milanese, Roman and Early Christian Architecture,' *Arte Lombarda* 13 (1968), 1–22, esp. 3 and 18.

45 Ibid., 22, note 111.

46 Johnson, *Mausolea*, 117–18.

47 R. Krautheimer, *Three Christian Capitals* (Berkeley, 1983), 91.

48 M.J. Johnson, 'On the Burial Places of the Theodosian Dynasty,' *Byzantion* 61 (1991), 330–9, esp. 332.

49 C. Cecchelli, 'I mosaici e le pitture,' in Calderini et al., *San Lorenzo*, 229, and pl. XCI–XCIII. Cecchelli mentions these paintings in a preliminary way: my remarks are based on personal observations.

50 Rev. 4.4 and 5.11–14.

51 Victorinus (d. ca. 304), *Opera*, 'Commentarius in Apocalypsim,' recension of Jerome, in I. Haussleiter, ed., *CSEL*, 49 (Vienna, 1916), 50: 'XXIIII seniores ... sunt autem XXIIII patres XII apostoli et duodecim patriarchae.'

52 Ildefonso Schuster, *Sant'Ambrogio e le più antiche basiliche* (Milan, 1940), 75, was the first to identify these figures as representatives of the chosen.

53 Rev. 7.4–8.

54 Rev. 6.9–11.

55 John Chrysostom, Sermons: *De S. Pelagia Virg. ac Mart.*, *AASS*, Junii II, 154.

56 Ambrose, *De Virginibus ac Marcellinam sororem suam*, PL 16, cols. 241–4.

57 Ambrose, *De Virginitate*, PL, 16, ch. XIV, cols. 301–2.

58 Ambrose, *In Psalmum CXVIII*, PL 15, Sermo XVI, col. 1506, v. 22: 'Hos fontes habet Ecclesia, hoc est, in veteri Testamento duodecim Patriarchas, et in novo duodecim apostolos. Ideoque dictum est: 'in Ecclesia benedicamus Dominum Deum de fontibus Israel' (Psalm LXVII, 27).

59 See Schuster, *Più antiche basiliche*, 17–18, for other texts of Ambrose relating to the apocalyptic vision.

60 This iconography may derive from the scene on the façade of Old St Peter's. W. Oakeshott, *The Mosaics of Rome* (Greenwich, CT, 1967), 67. According to Oakeshott, 101, note 20, a fragment of a similar composition, once at S Maria Maggiore, and consisting of the horizontal arm of one elder, is

314 Notes to pages 161–7

shown by C. Cecchelli, *I mosaici della Basilica di Santa Maria Maggiore* (Turin, 1956), pl. LXXXVI. The earliest surviving example is in SS Cosma e Damiano, a sixth-century church in the Roman Forum.

61 Galvanei Flammae (Galvano Flamma), b. ca. 1283, *Chronicon Maius*, in *Miscellanea di storia italiana*, 7 (Turin, 1869), 506: 'mosaico opere miris figuris ornatum.'

62 A. Grabar, *Christian Iconography* (Princeton, 1968), 72.

63 2 Kings, 2.11–12.

64 Ambrose, *De Poenitentia*, I, *PL*, 16, ch. VIII, col. 497, v. 34.

65 Wilpert, *Die römischen Mosaiken*, I, 264–6, III, pl.41. Wilpert compared this figure to Christ as *Sol invictus*, seeing the chariot, just as in the biblical text, as a solar or fiery one. Unfortunately, not enough remains of the figure on the chariot to determine whether Christ or Elijah was portrayed.

66 Eusebius, *De Vita Constantini*, *PG* 20, IV, ch. LXXIII, cols. 909–1230.

67 This theme has been fully dealt with by Jo Anne D. Sieger in '"Pictor Ignotus": The Early Christian Pictorial Theme of Christ and the Church and Its Roots in Patristic Exegesis of Scripture,' PhD thesis (University of Pittsburgh, 1980). See also P. Testini, 'L'oratorio scoperto al "monte della Giustizia" presso la Porta Viminale a Roma,' *RAC* 44 (1968), 219–60, esp. 255f.

68 Ihm, *Programme*, pl. IV, 1. Apse program of S Agata dei Goti, after Ciampini.

69 See S. Waetzoldt, *Die Kopien des 17 Jahrhunderts nach Mosaiken und Wandmalerein in Rom* (Munich, 1964), Sant'Andrea dei Goti, pl. 1–13; Sant'Andrea Catabarbara, pl. 15.

70 Dom Chantelou, *Mémoire de l'église*, Paris, Bibl. nat. Lat. 1385 f. 47–99.

71 See my 'La Daurade: A Royal Mausoleum,' *CahArch* 42 (1994), 17–34.

72 For Lamotte's manuscript, see Paris, Bibl. nat. Lat 12680. Latin text edited by A.G. and J.H. (A. Grabar and J. Hubert) as 'Description des mosaïques de La Daurade à Toulouse,' *CahArch* 13 (1962), 261–6. English translation by Davis-Weyer, *Early Medieval Art*, 59–66.

73 Mackie, 'La Daurade,' 22.

74 Maximinus, *Diatriba ad Opus imperfectum in Matthaeum*, *PG*, 56, col. 601 f.

75 John 20.19.

76 Lamotte gives 'habetque ad caput sacrum istud verbum MA-RIA' in the Nativity scene; in the adoration of the Magi, 'habet ad caput verbum istud sacrum et sanum MA-RIA.' Of the figure beside Christ he writes, 'radiatum tamen gerit caput circa quod habet haec duo verba SANCTA MARIA.' Text from Grabar and Hubert, 'Description.'

77 Agnellus, *CPER*, 227–30.

78 Rev. 4.4 and 5.11–14.

79 See E.A. Thompson, 'The Visigoths from Fritigern to Euric,' *Historia* 12 (1963), 105–26, esp. 124–6.

80 See M.J. Johnson 'Toward a History of Theoderic's Building Programme,' *DOP* 42 (1988), 73–96, esp. 74.

81 Anonymous Valesianus, *RIS*, 24, ed. R. Cessi (Città di Castello, 1913), 21, lines 330–5: 'se autem vivo fecit sibi monumentum, ex lapide quadrato, mirae magnitudinis opus et saxum ingentem, quem superponeret, inquisivit.'

82 Ten was a perfect number, according to the Pythagoreans, a view also held by Theoderic's court, as expressed by Boethius, *De Institutione Arithmetica* II, 41, *PL* 63, col. 1146: 'At vero posteri propter denarii numeri perfectionem, quod erat Pythagorae complacitum.' See also Johnson, 'Theoderic,' 94, note 198, for translations and commentaries.

83 G. De Angelis d'Ossat, *Studi Ravennati. Problemi di architettura paleocristiana*, Parts II and III (Ravenna, 1962), 92–131.

84 De Angelis d'Ossat, *Studi Ravennati*, 104.

85 Johnson, 'Theoderic,' 92.

86 De Angelis d'Ossat, *Studi Ravennati*, 93–131, esp. 117–20, and figs. 5 and 6.

87 Agnellus, *LPER*, 304; *CPER*, 113.

88 Krautheimer, *ECBA*, 341, note 24, says De Angelis d'Ossat 'presents the latest and most reliable reconstruction' of the mausoleum.

89 Eusebius, *De Vita Constantini Imperatoris*, *PG*, 20, cols. 909–1232, Book IV, chap. LX, cols. 1210–11: 'Quod etiam in eo templo sepulcrum sibi aedificavit.' P. Grierson, 'The Tombs and Obits of the Byzantine Emperors, 337–1042,' *DOP* 16 (1962), 3–63, esp. 5, dismisses this as a fable, as nothing like this has survived in other descriptions of the Holy Apostles. Eusebius (ca. 260–ca. 340), though, may well have spoken from personal observation.

90 Krautheimer, *ECBA*, 47.

91 The possible presence of a church dedicated to St George nearby, and its relationship to the Mausoleum, await confirmation by archaeological excavation.

92 The brick format is unique, and so cannot be used for dating the building. Deichmann, *Ravenna*, II: I, 66.

93 Both revetments and alabaster window panes are replacements based on fragments found *in situ*: the marbles used are recycled *giallo antico*.

94 Details of the architecture also confirm the chapel's funerary function. For example, Deichmann, *Ravenna*, II: I, 64, cites the presence of the pine cone as finial on the central tower of the chapel. This is the traditional funerary acroterium, symbolizing immortality.

95 Eusebius, *Vita Constantini*, I, chaps. 28–30.

96 This church, too, owes its attribution to Galla Placidia to Agnellus, writing 500 years after the event. Agnellus, *LPER*, 306: 'Galla vero augusta haedificavit ecclesiam sanctae Crucis.' See Deichmann, *Ravenna*, II: I, 51f. S Croce's identification as Galla Placidia's palace church has been questioned by G. Cortesi, 'I principali edifici sacri ravennati in funzione sepolcrale nei secc. V e VI,' *CorsiCRB* 29 (1982), 63–107, esp. 103–4. He prefers to see it as a cemetery church.

97 Krautheimer, Corbett, and Frankl, *CBCR*, I, 168.

98 As was pointed out in this context by D.P. Pavirani, *Memorie istoriche della vita e governo di Galla Placidia, Madre e tutrice di Valentiniano III* (Ravenna, 1848, repr. 1977), 238, 'Placidia pure era si divota della S.Croce, che come si vede nelle sue medaglie la portava per distintivo nella spalla destra, come se ogni suo conforto si riponesse nella croce.' Galla Placidia's gold *solidus* with the chi-rho on the shoulder, dating ca. 430, is illustrated in J.P.C. Kent, *Roman Coins* (London, 1978), pl. 188.

99 See Suzanne Lewis, 'The Latin Iconography of the Single-Naved Cruciform Basilica Apostolorum in Milan,' *ArtBull.* 51 (1969), 205–19, esp. 206–8, for a discussion of the meaning of the cruciform basilica, with examples.

100 The cruciform plan in architecture may be seen as a by-product of the structural requirements of a square base crowned by a cupola: the outward forces generated by the weight of the cupola need counteracting forces, such as rooms or niches which open out symmetrically from the four sides of the square. This type of architecture, while not invented by the Christians, was adopted by them not only for its structural qualities but because it reproduced the symbol of their faith. J. Lassus, *Sanctuaires chrétiens de Syrie* (Paris, 1947), 116.

101 See Constantine Porphyrogenitus, *Book of Ceremonies*, II, 42. The list of imperial tombs is translated with commentary by G. Downey, 'The Tombs of the Byzantine Emperors at the Church of the Holy Apostles in Constantinople,' *Journal of Hellenic Studies* 79 (1959), 27–51, esp. 30–7.

102 Constantine Porphyrogenitus, *Ceremonies*, II, 45–8.

103 For the mausoleum's bibliography see Giuseppe Bovini, *Saggio di bibliografia su Ravenna antica* (Bologna, 1968); Rafaella Farioli, 'Principale bibliografia su Ravenna pre-romana, romana, bizantina ed altomedioevale,' *FR* 117 (1979), 117–28; Deichmann's multi-volume work, *Ravenna*, summarized all significant previous work, and so brought the bibliography up to the end of the eighties.

104 Agnellus wrote that many people claimed that the empress was buried before the altar of the *monasterium* of St Nazarius (i.e., the mausoleum). Agnellus, *LPER*, 307. For Latin text, see note 117 below.

105 Deichmann, *Ravenna*, II: I, 65.

106 Seston, 'Le Jugement Dernier au Mausolée de Galla Placidia,' *CahArch* 1 (1945), 37–50, esp. 37, note 2: 'L'attribution à Galla Placidia, contestée autrefois, est aujourd'hui universellement acceptée.' Despite his certainty in 1945, this acceptance is far from universal.

107 The main source for Galla Placidia's life was the *History* of Olympiodorus, which is lost except for excerpts which survived in Photius's library. See Photius, *Bibliothèque*, ed. and tr. R. Henry (Paris, 1959), and Warren Treadgold, *The Nature of the Bibliotheca of Photius* (Washington, 1980), 82. Sozomen's and Zosimus's histories both draw on Olympiodorus's work. For a summary of these sources see J.F. Matthews, 'Olympiodorus of Thebes and the History of the West (AD 407–425),' *Journal of Roman Studies* 60 (1970), 79–97. See also S.I. Oost, *Galla Placidia Augusta, A Biographical Essay* (Chicago, 1968).

108 See my 'New Light on the So-Called St Lawrence Panel at the Mausoleum of Galla Placidia in Ravenna,' *Gesta* 29 (1990), 54–60.

109 J.B. Bury, *History of the Later Roman Empire*, vol. 1 (London, 1923; repr. New York, 1958), 263.

110 Medieval sources are listed by Deichmann, *Ravenna*, I, 169–70. For Raynaldus (Rinaldo da Concareggio or di Concuretio, Archbishop of Ravenna in 1303, d. 1321), see *Tractatus*, ed. L.A. Muratori, *RIS*, 1/2 (Milan, 1725), 573f.

111 Giampietro Ferretti (d. 1577), *Galla Placidiae augustae vita*, Bibl. Classense, Mob. 3, 2, f. 2–5, as cited by C. Ricci, *Mausoleo*.

112 Raynaldus, *Tractatus*, 574. G. Rossi noted in his sixteenth-century history of Ravenna that he could not verify this because the hole had been plastered over.

113 Bury, *HLRE*, I, 263–4.

114 M. Lawrence, *The Sarcophagi of Ravenna* (New York, 1945), deals with these ideas about dating and matching the sarcophagi.

115 Ibid., 32.

116 See chapter 1 for a discussion of the chapels on the S Vitale site.

117 Agnellus, *LPER*, 307: 'sepulta est Galla Placidia in monasterio Sancti Nazarii, ut aiunt multi, ante altarium infra cancellos, quos fuerunt aerei, qui nunc lapidei esse videtur.'

118 Though Agnellus had quoted hearsay that she was buried there. Tommaso Tusco, *Gesta imperatorum et pontificum, MGH*, 22 (Hanover, 1872), 511: 'In hoc monasterio est quedam capella pulcerrima, quam hedificari fecit Galla Placidia, opere mosaici decorata, in qua de alabastro sunt tria sepulcra, in quorum uno imperatoris Theodosii corpus est positum, iuxta quem ensis

eius cum vexillo tale preferente insigne est positus. In alio est seu corpus uxoris cum suarum duarum corporibus filiarum.'

119 Raynaldus, *Tractatus*, 574: 'Construxit praeterea Placidia Ravennae juxta habitationem suam Ecclesiam in honorem Sanctae Crucis Domini, à qua habet nomen, & formam, in cujus Altari est lapis ex alabastro pernitidus, & in ipsa Ecclesia stans. orationibus vacabat prolixius. Secus eam Ecclesiam construxit Sacellum miro opere speciosum Beatis Martyribus Nazario et Celsio dicatum, in quo tria videntur Augusta mausolea. Horum in maximo corpus Placidiae per cavum inspicitur in sede Regali residens. In duobus reliquis elegantibus nimis requiescunt corpora Augustorum, altero Constantii Viri Placidiae, altero Placidi Valentiniani eorum filii ... Obiit autem Ravennae V. Calendas Decembris, & in sacello, quod construxerat secus Basilicam Sanctae Crucis, est sepulta.' Also see G. Gerola, 'Galla Placidia e il cosidetto suo mausoleo in Ravenna,' *Atti e Memorie della Ravenna deputazione di storia patria per la Romagna* (1912), 273–320, esp. 275–6.

120 For a fuller discussion of Galla Placidia's son Theodosius as the person for whom she built her mausoleum, see my 'The Mausoleum of Galla Placidia: A Possible Occupant,' *Byzantion* 65 (1995), 396–404.

121 Olympiodorus, frg. 27, in Photius, *Bibliothèque*, ed. R. Henry.

122 This was another borrowing from Rome, this time from imperial victory rites, which humiliated captives by making them walk in front of the riding ruler. McCormick, *Triumphal Rulership*, 86, note 27.

123 Rossi's 'NEP,' grandson, may well have been a misreading of 'NP, NOBILISSIMUS PUER,' 'Most Noble Boy,' a title given to young imperial children in infancy, and applied also to Galla Placidia's two infant brothers in the S Giovanni Evangelista mosaics.

124 The mosaics were pulled down in 1568, but votive inscription and subject matter were recorded by G. Rossi shortly before that date. See Davis Weyer, *Early Medieval Art*, 15–17. Also Ihm, *Programme*, fig. 2, for a possible reconstruction.

125 *Chronicle* of Prosper: 'Theodosius cum magna pompa a Placidia et Leone et omni senatu deductus et in mausoleo ad apostolum Petrum depositus est.' Prosper Tironis, *Chronicon*, Reichenau additions, *Chronica minora, saec. IV, V, VI, VII*, ed. T. Mommsen, *MGH, Auctores Antiquissimi*, 9 (Berlin, 1892), 489.

126 S.I. Oost, 'Some Problems in the History of Galla Placidia,' *Classical Philology* 60 (1965), 1–10, esp. 7.

127 M.J. Johnson, 'On the Burial Places of the Theodosian Dynasty,' *Byzantion* 61 (1991), 330–9, esp. 338.

128   For Tommaso Tusco, see note 118 above.

129   Riccobaldo, *Pomarium Ravennatis Ecclesiae*, RIS, 9 (Milan, 1726), col. 219: 'Vidi ego in Ecclesia Sancti Laurentii sacello, quod est apud Ravenna, sepulchrum nobile; iuxta id in pavimento erat petra scripta literis celatis, dicens sic TEODOSIUS IMPERATOR. Vidi et legi.' In col. 221, Riccobaldo states definitely that this S Lorenzo was the basilica at the palace of Honorius in Caesarea.

130   Nicolo della Tuccia, *Cronaca de'principali fatti d'Italia dell'anno 1417 al 1468 di Nicolo della Tuccia, Viterbese*, ed. Francesco Orioli (Rome, 1852), 283 (27 June 1458).

131   Ibid.: 'il Li 27 di Giugno si disse in Viterbo come alli 27 detto morì in san Pietro di Roma un penitentiero, e volendolo sepellire nella cappella di s. Petronilla, ove sta una tribuna a man dritta, nel qual luogo è pinta anticamente la storia di Constantino imperatore, cavandosi li fu trovato un avello di marmo bellissimo, e dentro una cassa grande et una piccola di cipresso coperta d'argento fino d'undici leghe che fa di peso libbre 832. Li corpi, che erano dentro, erano coperti di drappo d'oro fino tanto, che pesò l'oro libre 16. Dicevasi fosse il corpo di Constantino, et un suo figlietto: et altro segno non ci fu trovato, se non una croce intagliata fatta in questo modo +. Tutte queste robe hebbe il papa, e mandolle alla sua zecca.'

132   Either Calixtus III (1455–1458), who died 6 August 1458 or, possibly, his successor, Pius II, elected 3 September 1458.

133   See above, note 131: 'una croce intagliata fatta in questo modo +.'

134   Johnson, 'Burial Places,' 337–8, points out that only one child is known to have been buried in this mausoleum – Theodosius, son of Galla Placidia and Ataulf – and accepts the idea that the burial discovered in 1458 was probably that of Galla Placidia and her son.

135   For illustrations of this chapel see Deichmann, *Ravenna*, III, plates 1–31.

136   Jerome, *Commentaria in Ezechielem*, PL, 25, ch. 1, cols. 21–2. A good, brief summary of the history of this symbolism is found in J. Beckwith, *Early Christian and Byzantine Art* (Harmondsworth, 1970), 33–4. See also Marjorie de Grooth and Paul van Moorsel, 'The Lion, the Calf, the Man and the Eagle in Early Christian and Coptic Art,' *BABESCH* 52–3 (1977–8), 233–41; and Dale Kinney, 'The Apocalypse in Early Christian Monumental Decoration,' in R.K. Emmerson and B. McGinn, eds., *The Apocalypse in the Middle Ages* (Ithaca and London, 1992), 200–16, esp. 206–7.

137   See Julia Valeva, 'La Tombe aux Archanges de Sofia,' *CahArch* 34 (1986), 5–28, esp. 12, for a general discussion of this iconography. See also Tania Velmans, 'L'image de la Déisis dans les églises de Géorgie et dans le reste du monde byzantin,' *CahArch* 31 (1983), 129f., esp. 130–1.

138 See Erik Peterson, 'La croce e la preghiera verso oriente,' *Ephemerides Liturgicae* 59 (1945), 61f., esp. 62–3, for a discussion of the connection of the presence of the cross in the East with the direction of prayer. He comments: 'ma quand'è che la croce precede l'arrivo del signore? La risposta non più esitare un momento: il giorno del suo secondo arrivo nel mondo.'

139 Seston, 'Jugement,' 49: 'Elle précédera le Christ dans son triomphe comme la grande croix d'or qu'on portait dans les processions de Byzance devant l'empereur quand il se montrait à ses sujets à l'Hippodrome.' By the late sixth century, 'the army and the emperor marched behind the imperial battle standard, a gilded war cross containing a relic of the true cross.' McCormick, *Triumphal Rulership*, 247, and note 71. The origin of the cross as standard must lie in Constantine's victory by the cross at Milvian Bridge.

140 K. Lehmann, 'The Dome of Heaven,' *ArtBull.* 27 (1945), 1–27, esp. 13–19.

141 Christ himself taught his disciples that his return would be preceded by the cross: 'then will appear the sign of the Son of man in heaven ... and they will see the Son of man coming on the clouds of heaven with power and great glory' (Matt. 24.38).

142 Among the Fathers who commented on Christ's words from Matthew on his second coming (see previous note) was Eusebius, *Vita Constantini*, 1, 32, cols. 947–8. See also Peterson, 'La croce,' 61, citing the *Acta Hipparchi, Philothei et sociorum*, in *Acta sanctorum martyrum orientalium et occidentalium*, 2, ed. St. E. Assemani (Rome, 1748), 124–48: 'Christus veniens ex oriente praeceditur cruce.'

143 See A.H.S. Megaw and E.J.N. Hawkins, *The Church of the Panagia Kanakaria at Lythrankomi in Cyprus:Its Mosaics and Frescoes* (Washington, 1977), 107, for a discussion of the iconography of the apostles.

144 For Naples, see Jean-Louis Maier, *Le baptistère de Naples et ses mosaïques* (Fribourg 1969). Other precedents include a sarcophagus from Arles: Wilpert, *Sarcophagi*, I, pl. 34:3, where the twelve apostles, seated, include four who hold books or scrolls inscribed with the evangelists' names.

145 S Croce at the Lateran Baptistery is discussed in chapter 8.

146 Paulinus of Nola, *Epistola* 32, 15–16.

147 Lehmann, 'Dome of Heaven,' 13–14.

148 John 1.32.

149 John 15.1–7.

150 A symbolism current in the writings of the Fathers. See J. Daniélou, *Primitive Christian Symbols*, chapter 2, 'The Vine and the Tree of Life,' esp. 37–8. The vine here, as at the S Matrona chapel at S Prisco, Capua Vetere, is

stretched across the blue of the 'sky' as if it were tied to a trellis: in the words of Asterius the Sophist 'the divine and timeless vine has sprung from the grave, bearing as fruits the newly baptized, like bunches of grapes on the altar.' Asterius (ca. 350–410) *Homilies on the Psalms*, Marcel Richard, ed. (Oslo, 1956), esp. Hom. XIV, 1–2, 105.

151 Genesis 22.13.

152 John 3.5.

153 The Pula baptistery survived into the mid-nineteenth century, and is known in section and elevation from Seroux d'Agincourt, *Storia dell'Arte*, II (Milan, 1825).

154 Cyril, Archbishop of Jerusalem (ca. 315–386), *Catechetical Lectures*, tr. E.H.Gifford, *N&PNF*, 7, 14–18, Lecture III, 'On Baptism,' and Lecture XX, 'On the Mysteries, II. Of Baptism.'

155 E. Dyggve, *History of Salonitan Christianity* (Oslo, 1951), 55–6.

156 Romans 6.3–5. See also Cyril, *Catechetical*, 147–8, interpreting the text from Paul's Letter to the Romans: 'And at the self-same moment ye were both dying and being born; and that Water of Salvation was at once your grave and your mother.'

157 See Gordana Babić, 'North Chapel of the Quatrefoil Church at Ohrid and Its Mosaic Floor,' *Zbornik Radova* 13 (1971), 271f.

158 W.K.C. Guthrie, *The Greeks and Their Gods* (London, 1950), 230.

159 Ricci, *Mausoleo*, 84.

160 See Kitzinger, *Byzantine Art*, 53–4, for analysis of this scene, which he sees as an 'emblema.'

161 Grabar, *Christian Iconography*, 11.

162 L. de Bruyne, 'La décoration des baptistères paléochrétiens,' *Atti del V congresso internazionale di archeologia cristiana, Aix-en-Provence, 1954* (Paris, 1957), 345f., esp. 348–50.

163 A.G. Martimort, 'L'iconographie des catacombes et la catéchèse antique,' *RAC*, 25 (1949), 107, note 1: 'La constatation que la liturgie de la mort est en relation avec le souvenir de l'initiation: la mort du chrétien un second baptême.'

164 See Ricci, *Mausoleo*, 91.

165 See Seston, 'Jugement,' 37–50.

166 See Grabar, *Martyrium*, II, 35–6, note 1.

167 Exodus 27.1–8.

168 According to the Syrian exegete Ephrem, in his *Commentary on Exodus, Opera omnia*, V, Syr. lat. p. 43.

169 Ricci, *Mausoleo*, 85.

170 See P. Courcelle, 'Le Gril de Saint Laurent au Mausolée de Galla Placidia,'

CahArch 3 (1948), 29–40, esp. 36, and notes 7 and 8. Also Augustine, *Sermo* CCCIII, 1, *PL* 38, col. 1394, 'Craticula admota est, et tostus est,' and Pseudo-Fulgence, *Sermo* LX, *PL* 65, col. 931, 'Craticula habebat rotas.'

171 Though it appears from the writings of Tertullian that in Africa the penalty of fire was quite often used against the Christians. M.M. Barnay, *Some Reflections of Life in North Africa in the Writings of Tertullian*, PhD dissertation (Catholic University of America, 1968).

172 J. Lassus, 'Craticula habebat rotas,' *CahArch* 16 (1966), 5–8.

173 C. Diehl, *Ravenne* (Paris, 1903), 32.

174 Seston, 'Jugement,' 45.

175 Courcelle, 'Le Gril,' 29.

176 Ibid., 39: 'Le seul en Occident des grands martyrs par le feu.'

177 Deichmann, *Ravenna*, II: I, 77–8.

178 Prudentius, *Opera*, II, *Peristephanon Liber*, II: 'Hymnus in honorem passionis Laurentii beatissimi martyris,' tr. H.J. Thomson (Loeb ed., London and Cambridge, MA, 1961), 108–43, esp. 118–27.

179 Formerly in the collections of the Vatican Museums. G. de Rossi, 'Les médailles de dévotion des six ou sept premiers siècles de l'église,' *BAC* 7 (1869), 34–8, and fig. 8.

180 Illustrated in A. Pantoni, *San Vincenzo al Volturno e la cripta dell'abate Epifanio, 824–842.* (Montecassino, 1970), 38.

181 Mackie, 'New Light,' 54–60.

182 Augustine, Sermo CCLXXVI, *PL*, 38, col. 1257: 'Quae hodie regio, quaeve provincia ulla, quo usque vel romanum imperium vel cristianum nomen extenditur natalem non gaudet celebrare Vincentii?'

183 Prudentius, *Peristephanon Liber*, V: 'Passio Sancti Vincenti Martyris,' 168–203.

184 See H. Delehaye, *Les origines du culte des martyrs* (Brussels, 1933), 92, for sources and a discussion of his epic passion, and Pio Franchi de'Cavalieri, 'Della "Passio S Vincentii levitae,"' *Note Agiografiche*, 8, Studi e Testi, 65 (Vatican City, 1935), 117–25, esp. 117.

185 Augustine preached sermons on four successive feast days of St Vincent: Sermons 274–7, *In Natali (or festo) martyris Vincentii, PL*, 38, cols. 1252–68. Another sermon on Vincent's feast day is attributed to Leo I (440–61); see Sermon 13, *In natali S Vincentii martyris, PL*, 54, cols. 501–4.

186 Prudentius, *Peristephanon*, V, 180–4.

187 Ibid., 206–8.

188 Ibid., 217–20.

189 Ibid., 209–13.

190 As recorded on the lost mosaics of her church of S Giovanni Evangelista,

Ravenna. Agnellus, *CPER*, XXI, Iohn I, 128–9. This incident probably occurred in 424, when Placidia returned to Italy from Constantinople.

191 Agnellus, *CPER*, XXVII, Maximian, 191–2. The relics were among those of twenty important saints and apostles placed in St Stephen's church, built by Archbishop Maximinian and dedicated in 550.

192 Von Simson, *Sacred Fortress*, 84–5.

193 Hermann Vopel, *Die altchristlichen Goldgläser* (Freiburg, 1899), no. 401. 'VINCENTIUS AGNES POLTUS' [Hippolytus], from the catacomb of S Callisto, Rome.

194 Lesley Brubaker, 'Patterns in Byzantine Matronage: Aristocratic and Imperial Commissions, Fourth to Sixth Centuries,' *Byzantine Studies Conference Abstracts* 16 (1990), 27–8, and 'Memories of Helena: Patterns in Imperial Female Matronage in the Fourth and Fifth Centuries,' in *Women, Men and Eunuchs. Gender in Byzantium*, ed. Liz James (London and New York, 1997).

8 Papal Chapels

1 *LP*, I, 242–8, esp. 242–3, Hilarus: 'Hic fecit oraturia III in baptisterio basilicae Constantinianae, sancti Iohannis Baptistae et sancti Iohannis evangelistae et sanctae Crucis, omnia ex argento et lapidibus pretiosis.' A fourth chapel of Hilarus at the Lateran Baptistery, dedicated to St Stephen, is mentioned in alternate *LP* mss. BCDEG: 'Fecit autem oratorium sancti Stephani in baptisterio Lateranense.' Duchesne, *LP*, I, 247, note 11, identifies it with the ancient building adapted by Pope John IV (640–2) as a martyrium for the Dalmatian saints, the San Venanzio Chapel. It will not be discussed here, since almost nothing is known of its structure, decoration, or function.

2 See A. Nesselrath, *Das Fossombroner Skizzenbuch* (London, 1993), 159–62, for bibliography to that date of the S Croce drawings, and M.J. Johnson, 'The Fifth-Century Oratory of the Holy Cross at the Lateran in Rome,' *Architectura* (1995), 129–56.

3 The Damasan baptistery and all three chapels have failed to survive, though the Oratory of the Vatican Holy Cross and that of the Baptist were pulled down only in the mid-fifteenth century, in the site preparation for the choir of the new St Peter's.

4 *LP*, I, 261–2, Symmachus: 'Item ad fontem in basilica beati Petri apostoli: oratorium sanctae Crucis: ex argento confessionem et crucem ex auro cum gemmis, ubi includit lignum dominicum; ipsa crux aurea pens. lib. X. fecit autem oratoria II, sancti Iohannis Evangelistae et sancti Iohannis

Baptistae in quorum confessiones cum arcos argenters pens lib. XXX, quas cubicula omnes a fundamento perfecta construxit.' See also R. Davis, *Book of Pontiffs* (Liverpool, 1989), 43–6.

5 For the political significance of Symmachus's building program at St Peter's, see Joseph D. Alchermes, 'Petrine Politics: Pope Symmachus and the Rotunda of St Andrew at Old St Peter's,' *Catholic Historical Review* 81 (1995), 1–40, which, however, only touches briefly on the Vatican chapels.

6 Ibid., 16, note 41.

7 Hilarus was appointed papal legate to the Second Council of Ephesus of 449, the 'Robber council.' In his correspondence (Letters 28, 29, 33) Leo invariably refers to Hilarus as 'my son Hilarus, Deacon.'

8 *LP*, I, 242.

9 C.L. Feltoe, tr., *The Letters and Sermons of Leo the Great*, in *N&PNF*, XII (New York, 1895), 173, translating Leo the Great, Sermo LIX (alias LVII), 'De Passione Domini,' *PL* 54, ch. VIII, cols. 337–42, esp. 341: 'Traxisti, Domine, omnia ad te, quoniam scisso templi velo, sancta sanctorum ab indignis pontificibus recesserunt; ut figura in veritatem, prophetia in manifestationem, et lex in Evangelium verteretur. Traxisti, Domine, omnia ad te, ut quod in uno Judaeae templo obumbratis significationibus agebatur, pleno apertoque sacramento, universarum ubique nationum devotio celebraret. Nunc etenim et ordo clarior levitarum, et dignitas amplior seniorum, et sacratior est unctio sacerdotum: quia crux tua omnium fons benedictionum, omnium est causa gratiarum: per quam credentibus datur virtus de infirmitate, gloria de opprobio, vita de morte. Nunc etiam carnalium sacrificiorum varietate cessante, omnes differentias hostiarum, una corporis et sanguinis tui implet oblatio: quoniam tu es verus *Aguus* [sic] *Dei, qui tollis peccata mundi (Joan.I, 29).*

10 D. Johanne Mabillon, *Museum Italicum*, II: *Antiquos Libros Rituales Sanctae Romanae Ecclesiae* (Paris, 1687), 37f.

11 L. Duchesne, *Les origines du culte chrétien* (Paris, 1889).

12 Mabillon, *Museum Italicum*, II, 37f.: 'Deinde dicit sacerdos orationem & tunc vadunt ad sanctum Johannem f. ad vestem, canentes ant. Lapidem quem reprobaverunt, deinde All cum psalmo CXIII.' Note f: 'Deest in quibusdam ad vestem. Apud vulgatum Alcuinum "ad sanctum Johannem ad Fontes seu ad vestem." Exstat nunc quoque oratorium sancti Johannis Baptistae ad Fontes Lateranenses, a beato Hilaro papa constructum; quod quia fortasse baptizandi vestes ibi deponebant, easdemque jam baptizati ibidem resumebant, dictem est 'sancti Iohannis ad Vestem.'

13 L. Duchesne, *Les origines du culte chrétien*, tr. M. McClure (London, 1903) as *Christian Worship: Its Origin and Evolution. A Study of the Latin Liturgy up to the Time of Charlemagne.* See chapter 9, 'Ceremonies of Christian Initiation,'

and esp. 312–13, note 2: 'In the appendix to Mabillon's Ordo I, one of the lateral chapels of the (Lateran) Baptistery is called ad S Johannem ad vestem. It was probably there that the candidates divested themselves of their garments. As there were two similar chapels, it is possible that they were both used, one for the men, the other for the women.'

14 A. Khatchatrian, in *Les baptistères paléochrétiens* (Paris, 1962), shows annex chapels existed at Rome and Salona and nowhere else among his complete series of plans of all early Christian baptisteries known to that date.

15 E. Dyggve, *Salonitan*, 32.

16 J.-C. Picard, 'Les rites du baptême d'après les textes,' *Actes du XIe congrès d'archéologie chrétienne* (Vatican City, 1989), 1451–74, esp. 1457–8. See also Hippolytus of Rome, *The Apostolic Tradition*, ed. and tr. B. Botte as *Tradition Apostolique* (Paris, 1968), 21, 81–3, note 27: Children were baptized first, followed by the men and then the women, who totally removed all clothing as well as jewels and other adornments.

17 Although no specifically Roman source for this survives, segregation of the sexes for modesty's sake is described in the *Didascalia Apostolorum*, an early-third-century Syrian 'Church order' which was also known in the West. *Didascalia Apostolorum*, tr. M.D. Gibson (London, 1903), 76: 'It is not permitted to a woman to baptize' [on account of John, not Mary, baptizing Christ]; but see also 78, 'Of the appointment of Deacons and Deaconesses: but when there is a woman, and especially a deaconess, it is not fitting for the women that they be seen by the men ... let it be a Deaconess ... who anoints the woman ... and when she that is baptised arises from the water let the Deaconess receive her, and teach her and educate her, in order that the unbreakable seal of baptism be with purity and holiness.' But see also Charlotte Methuen, 'Widows, Bishops and the Struggle for Authority in the *Didescalia Apostolorum*,' *J.Eccl.Hist.* 46 (1995), 197–213, esp. 210. Methuen distinguishes between anointing, carried out by women for women candidates, and the actual baptism, which was the work of priests and deacons. Victor Saxer, in Picard, 'Rites du baptême,' discussion, 1473, suggests that the role of deaconesses as baptizers may have been limited to Syria only, and that in the West the curtains hung between the columns of the baldacchino at the font may have played a role in preserving women's modesty.

18 Picard, 'Rites,' 1457, note 24. M. Andrieu, *Les Ordines Romani du Haut Moyen Age* (Louvain, 1965–74), Ordo XV, 74.

19 Dyggve, *Salonitan*, 30: 'the group of rooms in a unique way illustrates the process of the early Christian Baptismal act.'

20 A.J. Wharton, 'Ritual and Reconstructed Meaning: The Neonian Baptistery

in Ravenna,' *ArtBull.* 69 (1987), 358–76, esp. 360, and note 8. See also Victor Saxer, *Les rites de l'initiation chrétienne du IIe au VIe siècle* (Spoleto, 1988), esp. 500–1, on the early-fourth-century baptismal complex at Aquileia.

21 P. Brown, *The Body and Society* (New York, 1988), 96, note 54.

22 *LP*, I, 174, Silvester (314–335), describing the gifts of Constantine to the Lateran Baptistery: 'cervos argenteos VII fundentes aquam, pens. sing. lib. LXXX.' The original seven were seized by the Vandals, and replaced by Pope Hilarus with three new ones, 'Item ad sanctum fontem: ... cervos argenteos III fundentes aquam, pens. sing. lib. XXX.' *Liber Pontificalis*, I, 243.

23 See note 17.

24 The most important baptism took place in the evening on Easter Saturday; a smaller ceremony occurred at Pentecost. By the 460s the other baptisteries built in Rome included one at the Basilica of Vestina (S Vitale) built by Pope Innocent (401–17), and one at S Maria Maggiore by Pope Sixtus (432–40); recent discoveries of Early Christian baptisteries include one at S Clemente. The Easter baptism at the Lateran undoubtedly still attracted large numbers of neophytes: see Picard, 'Rites,' 1454: 'Il faut donc se souvenir qu'au début de notre période, les rites ... sont accomplis pour les dizaines, peut-être même les centaines de personnes à la fois.'

25 *LP*, I, 245: 'Hic omnia in basilica constantiniana vel ad sanctam Mariam recondit. Hic fecit monasterium ad sanctum Laurentium et balneum et alium sub aere et praetorium. Fecit autem et bibliothecas II in eodem loco. Item monasterium intra urbe Roma ad Luna.' This version follows the text called 'A' by Duchesne, the most reliable of the 'second edition' texts in his opinion, and dated before 540. The 'first edition' is lost. See *LP*, I, ccix, and Davis, *Book of Pontiffs*, iii.

26 *LP*, I, 249, note 3.

27 G. Ferrari, *Early Roman Monasteries* (Vatican City, 1957), 182, and 184–5, note 3.

28 This was based on the alternate group of texts, discussed by Duchesne as *Liber Pontificalis* manuscripts BCDE, where after '*praetorium*' we find the words 'Fecit autem oratorium Sancti Stephani in Baptisterio. Fecit autem et Bib. II in eadem loco.'

29 P. Ugonio, *Historia delle stationi di Roma* (Rome, 1588), 46: 'Fece ancora Papa Hilaro in questo luogo, come scrive il Bibliothecario, due librarie per uso de Pontifici onde si vede quanto sia antico costume di tener le librarie nel palazzo pontificale, e quanto è da laudare la providenza del sommo Pontifice Sisto V. il quale rinuova hoggi di l'essempio di Hilaro, ornando il Vaticano della nuova Libraria.'

30 Smith, 'Side Chambers,' 195–7.

31 I have found no evidence that the chapels' walls (now reveted in marble) have been examined for evidence of facilities for storage of either books or clothes.

32 Although the short biography of Pope Felix (268–73), *LP*, I, 158, includes the sentence 'Hic constituit supra memorias martyrum missas celebrare' ('He decreed that Mass be celebrated over the memorials of the martyrs'), this does not imply that the martyrs' relics were moved from their *memoriae* to consecrate other churches in Felix's time: according to G.B. De Rossi, the entry probably applies to the situation in the sixth century. Apart from this, the earliest reference to actual consecration of altars by relics refers to Gaul, when Gregory I wrote to Bishop Palladius of Santenis about the need for relics for the thirteen altars of a church under construction there. Gregory I, *Epistola* XLIX, *PL* 77, col. 834.

33 S Giovanni Battista retains its original doors. For the portals, both of which survive, see M. Romano, 'Materiali di spoglio nel battisterio di San Giovanni in Laterano: un riesame e nuove considerazione,' *Bolletino d'Arte* 77 (1991), 31–70, esp. 56–61.

34 *LP*, I, 242, Hilarus: 'confessionem sancti Iohannis Baptistae ex argento, qui pens. lib. C, et crucem auream;/ confessionem sancti Iohannis evangelistae ex argento pens. lib. C, et crucem auream;/ in ambis oratoriis ianuas aereas argentoclusas. Oratorium sanctae Crucis:/ confessionem ubi lignum posuit dominicum;/ crucem auream cum gemmis, qui pens. lib. XX;/ ex argento in confessionem, ianuas pens. lib. L;/ supra confessionem arcum aureum qui pens. lib. IIII, quem portant columnae unychinae, ubi stat agnus aureus pens. lib. II;/ coronam auream ante confessionem, farus cum delfinos, pens. lib. V;/ lampadas IIII aureas, pens. sing. lib. II.' For Symmachus's chapels, see note 4.

35 Measured drawings made of S Croce in the fifteenth and sixteenth centuries give an average internal width of approximately 11.5 metres, with a range of just over 10 metres to about 12 metres.

36 P.A. Février, 'Baptistères, martyrs et reliques,' *RAC* 62 (1986), 109–38, esp. 121, comments that all three chapels must have contained relics, since they had *confessiones*, though he identifies only the fragment of the cross.

37 Gregory I, *Epistola* CXXII, *PL* 77, cols. 1052–6, 'Ad Recharedum visigothorum regem,' esp. col. 1055, 'Crucem quoque dedi latori praesentium vobis offerendam, in qua lignum dominicae crucis inest, et capilli beati Joannis Baptistae.'

38 Gregory I, *Epistola* XXX, *PL*, 77, col. 701, note f, citing Ripamonte, *Hist.Eccl.Mediol.*, VIII, 522–3: 'Theodelindae Langobard. reginae Gregorius

... concessit augustissimus reliquias ... quas inter visuntur ipsius Baptistae reliquias, liquidus in ampulla cruor, cineres cremato corpore, et cum dente modicum quid e calvaria ... sunt demum linteamenta quae martyrum sanguinem ebibere et ossium fragmina.'

39 For the reliquary, see R. Conti, ed., *Il Duomo di Monza* (Milan, 1989), 51–4, and colour plate facing 52. Recognition of the ashes, hair, and tooth is recorded on the new base plate made for the reliquary in 1680.

40 For relics of the Baptist present in the Lateran in the late twelfth century, see Giovanni Diacono (John the Deacon), *Descriptio Lateranensis Ecclesiae*, in R. Valentini and G. Zucchetti, eds., *Codice topografico della città di Roma*, III, *FSI*, 90 (Rome, 1946), 336–9: 'De arca et sanctis sanctorum, quae sunt in Basilica Salvatoris,' esp. 337: 'de sanguine sancti Iohannis Baptistae; de pulvere et cinere combusti corporis eiusdem praecursoris Christi; cilicium eius de pilis camelorum.'

41 Ibid., 338: 'De manna sepulturae sancti Iohannis Evangelistae ampulla plena. Tunica eiusdem apostoli et evangelistae, qua supposita corporibus trium iuvenum, surrexerunt; mortui enim fuerant propter venenum quod biberant.'

42 The inscription above the marble doorway of the chapel, reads 'LIBERATORI SUO BEATO IOANNI EVANGELISTAE HILARUS EPISCOPUS FAMULUS CHRISTI' ('To his liberator the blessed John the Evangelist from Hilarus bishop [and] servant of Christ.') Hilarus was in Ephesus in 449, as papal legate to the Council called by Dioscurus of Alexandria, and was obliged to take refuge in the Basilica of St John. See P. Martin, *Actes du brigandage d'Ephèse* (Paris, 1874), 10, quoted by Duchesne, *LP*, I, 245, note 3. Romano, 'Materiali di spoglio,' gives a further inscription from the lower moulding: the exhortation of Christ 'DILIGITE ALTERUTRUM' ('Love one another').

43 M.R. James, tr., *Acts of John*, in *The Apocryphal New Testament* (Oxford, 1924), 270: 'and forthwith manna issuing from the tomb was seen of all, which manna that place produceth even unto this day.' See also *Acta Apostolorum Apocrypha*, ed. C. Tischendorf (Leipzig, 1851), 276: 'Postea vero inventa est fovea illa plena, nihil aliud in se habens nissi manna; quam usque hodie gignit locus ipse et fiunt virtutes orationum ejus meritis, cum omnibus infirmitatibus et peniculis liberantur omnes et precum suarum consequantur effectum.'

44 Presumably the one at the Baptistery, though P. Lauer, 'Les fouilles du Sancta Sanctorum au Latran,' *Mélanges d'Archéologie et d'histoire* 20 (1900), 279–87, located it at the Lateran Basilica.

45 Gregory I, *Epistola* III, 'Ad Joannem abbatem,' *PL*, 77, cols. 605–6, to John,

abbot of Santa Lucia, later bishop of Syracuse, tr. James Barmby, *N&PNF*,
12 (New York, 1895), 123.

46 Krautheimer, *Three Christian Capitals*, 115.

47 In this case the building might possibly have been the original site of the
two bath chairs of *rosso antico* (one of which is in the Vatican Museum,
Gabinetto delle maschere, no. 434,130, the other in the Louvre), which
originated in the Lateran area and were later to be associated with papal
installation ceremonies. See J. Déer, *The Dynasyic Porphyry Tombs of the
Norman Period in Sicily* (Cambridge, MA, 1959), 142–6 and plate 188.

48 See V. Santa Maria Scrinari, 'Contributo all'urbanistica tardo-antica sul
campo Laterano,' *Actes du XI Congrès international d'archéologie chrétienne*, 3
(Rome, 1989), 2201–20, esp. 2210.

49 Johnson, 'Holy Cross Oratory,' 147–50.

50 See V. Santa Maria Scrinari, *Il Laterano imperiale*, II: *Dagli 'Horti Domitiae' alla
cappella cristiana* (Vatican City, 1995). See also her references to her previous
publications on the Campus Lateranus.

51 See Romano, 'Materiali di spoglio,' esp. 56–61.

52 Onuphrius Panvinius (O. Panvinio), *De sacrosancta Basilica, Baptisterio et
Patriarchio Lateranensi*, III, 7–9, in *Le Palais du Latran*, ed. P. Lauer (Paris,
1911), 466–7.

53 Panvinio, *De Basilica*, caput VII, 'De Duobus Oratorijs,' ed. Lauer, 467:
'absidulam stuccatam et elegantem.'

54 Occasional burials do seem to have taken place in the city before the sixth
century in special circumstances. For example, see Lesley Jessop, *Pictorial
Cycles of Non-Biblical Saints: TheEvidence of the Eighth Century Mural Cycles in
Rome*, PhD dissertation (University of Victoria, 1993), 54–61, for the burials
of martyrs at SS Giovanni e Paolo, Rome.

55 Liz James and Ruth Webb, 'To Understand Ultimate Things and Enter
Secret Places: Ekphrasis and Art in Byzantium,' *Art History* 14 (1991), 1–17.

56 These conflicts are discussed in my article, 'The Santa Croce Drawings:
A Re-Examination,' *RACAR* 24 (1997), 1–14, in which I suggest that the
drawings represent two different, though related, buildings: the Holy
Cross Oratories of Pope Hilarus and of Pope Symmachus.

57 O. Panvinio, *De Basilica*, 467–8.

58 P. Ugonio, *Theatrum urbis Romae* fol. 154 ed. Lauer, *Latran*, 580: 'La volta di
supra si vedono 4 angeli che tengono in mano forse una croce alta onde
venne detto di Santa Croce.' [Also,] 'et un (fogliame gentillisimo?) con
ucelli di varij colori contesto.' Ugonio's hand here was, as so often, virtually
impossible to decipher.

59 See K. Lehmann, 'Dome of Heaven,' *ArtBull.* 27 (1945), 1–27, esp. 2.

330   Notes to pages 203–6

60 Panvinio, *De Basilica*, 468: 'Fenestrarum interstitia e musivo omnia cum picturis SS Petri et Pauli, Joannis Evangelistae et Baptistae, Laurentij et Stephani, Jacobi et Philippi.'
61 Duchesne, *Christian Worship*, 314. Duchesne thought that the name of Santa Croce symbolized its role as the place of confirmation at the Lateran.
62 Picard, 'Rites,' 1465–6.
63 Ugonio, *Historia delle stationi di Roma*, 47: 'in questo loco soleva anticamente il Papa dar la chresima all i Neofiti dopo il battesimo nel Sabbato santo: il qual costume èstato ànostri tempi reintrodotto qui-vi per quelli che si battezano in quel giorno.'
64 Cabrol and Leclercq, *DACL*, 3/2, 'Confirmation,' cols. 2515–53, esp. 2521, suggest that the portico niche was the first confirmation site, and that according to Ordines X, XI, and XII the function was only later taken over by a chapel adjacent to the baptistery.
65 Picard's opinion is that S Croce would only have been used for confirmation if it were the most convenient place. He prefers the apse of either the baptistery or the basilica, both on the main route. Picard, 'Rites,' 1466 and notes 61 and 62.
66 A very similar example in ivory forms the central panel of the 'Five-Part Diptych' in the treasury of Milan Cathedral. See C. Bertelli, ed., *Il millenio ambrosiano. Milano, una capitale da Ambrogio ai Carolingi* (Milan, 1987), 120–1, pls. 139 and 141.
67 See H. Kessler, 'Through the Temple Veil: The Holy Image in Judaism and Christianity,' in *Studies in Pictorial Narrative* (London, 1994), for a discussion of the image of the tabernacle in Hebrew and Christian art, and its allegorical meanings.
68 For example, Psalm 27.6: 'I will offer in his tent sacrifices with shouts of joy,' tr. *NOAB*, see notes, 674.
69 'INTROIBO, DOMINE, IN DOMUM TUAM ET ADORABO AD TEMPLUM SANCTUM TUUM IN TIMORE TUO' (Psalm 5.7)
70 See Rev. 11.19: 'and the One who sits upon the throne will spread his tent over them,' and Bianca Kühnel, 'Jewish Symbolism of the Temple and the Tabernacle and Christian Symbolism of the Holy Sepulchre and the Heavenly Tabernacle,' *Journal of Jewish Art* 12/13 (1986–7), 147–68, esp. 149–53.
71 For a third- to fourth-century gold glass showing the Hebrew temple with its colonnade and two small tabernacles beyond in the desert, see Archer Sinclair, 'God's House of Peace in Paradise: The Feast of Tabernacles on a Jewish Gold Glass,' *Journal of Jewish Art* 11 (1984), 6–15.
72 Hebrews 10.22–3 (tr. *NOAB*).
73 Cross and Livingstone, *ODCC*, 2nd ed. (1983), 1288.

74 J.H. Bernard, *Odes of Solomon* (Cambridge, 1912), XX, 4, v. 7–8, which refers to Lactantius (ca. 240–ca. 310), who quoted the *Odes* before 310.

75 See D.H. VerKerk, 'Exodus and Easter Vigil in the Ashburnham Pentateuch,' *ArtBull.* 77 (1995), 94–105, esp. 103–4, developing the typological theme that 'the tabernacle was simultaneously the Jewish Tabernacle, the Christian Church and the Heavenly Jerusalem.'

76 See note 34 for Pope Hilarus's donations to his chapels.

77 Georges Rohault de Fleury, *Le Latran au Moyen Age* (Paris, 1877), 313–15.

78 See Stephan Steingräber, *Catalogo ragionato della pittura Etrusca* (Milan, 1985), Tomb 3700, no. 51, pl. 52–3, date 510–500 BC, and Maria Cataldi and Laura Ricciardi, *Tarquinia* (Rome, 1993), 44–5 and fig. 37.

79 Gauzes of this type were still being made in late Roman times: a fine sixth-century example in plain tabby weave ornamented with small black and coloured medallions of the hunt in tapestry weave hangs in the Royal Ontario Museum, Toronto (ROM acc. no. 910.125.32). See Veronika Gervers, 'An Early Christian Curtain in the Royal Ontario Museum,' in *Studies in Textile History in Memory of Harold B. Burnham*, ed. V. Gervers (Toronto, 1977), 56–81, esp. 57, fig. 1.

80 See Maier, *Baptistère de Naples*, figs. II and III.

81 See Demus, *Byzantine Mosaic Decoration.*

82 For development of this idea in the later middle-Byzantine period, see T.F. Mathews, 'The Transformation Symbolism in Byzantine Architecture and the Meaning of the Pantocrator in the Dome,' in *Church and People in Byzantium: 20th Spring Symposium of Byzantine Studies (Manchester, 1986)*, ed. Rosemary Morris (Birmingham, 1990), who sees the space under the dome beneath the central image of Christ as the area where the Christian could 'put on Christ' by standing under the 'shadow of his image, and thus be transformed into him.'

83 Very few exceptions to the rule of dedication of baptisteries to St John the Baptist are known. They include the second baptistery at Milan, which was dedicated to St Stephen, as were the Early Christian baptisteries at Lyon and Albenga. Février, 'Baptistères,' 126, suggests that any other dedication than to the Baptist must relate to the possession of specific relics.

84 Although Richard Krautheimer, *Aufsätze zur europäischen Kunstgeschichte* (Cologne, 1988), 193, has warned against reading meaning into a structure which was not part of the original intention, I feel that it is justified here in view of Pope Hilarus's new use for the building and his dedication of it to the Holy Cross.

85 'IN HONOREM BEATI JOANNIS BAPTISTAE/+HILARIUS EPISCOPUS D(E)I FAMULUS OFFERT.'

86 'BEATO IOHANNI BAPTISTAE HILARUS EPISCOPUS DEI FAMULUS FECIT.' G.B. De Rossi, *Inscr.christ.* II, 164 no. 46. In addition, 'ERUNT ASPERA IN VIAS PLANAS' is plainly inscribed on the inner trabeation.

87 '+HILARIUS EPISCOPUS+SANCTA PLEBI DEI+.'

88 'DOMINE DILEXI DECOREM DOMUS TUAE.' Psalm 26.8, tr. Davis-Weyer, *Early Medieval Art*, 35. It is interesting that many years later (in the thirteenth century), this verse from Psalm 26 was used as antiphon at vespers on the first night of the dedication of a new church. See C. Striker and Y. Dogan Kuban, *Kalenderhane in Istanbul* (Mainz, 1997), 138, and notes 11 and 12, for reference to R.-J. Hesbert, *Corpus antiphonalium officii* (Rome, 1965), II, 714, no. 127a, and for the possibly coincidental appearance of the text in the Franciscan chapel (ca. 1250) of the diaconicon at the church of the Virgin Kiriotissa (the Kalenderhane) in Istanbul, and in the diaconicon at Hosios Lukas in Phocis (ca. 1100).

89 'INTROIBO, DOMINE, IN DOMUM TUAM ET ADORABO AD TEMPLUM SANCTUM TUUM IN TIMORE TUO' (Psalm 5.7). See *LP*, Hilarus, 242–3, and O. Panvinio, tr. Davis-Weyer, *Early Medieval Art*, 36.

90 *NOAB*, Psalm 7, 659–60 and Psalm 26, 674.

91 Leo the Great, *Letters and Sermons*, tr. C.L. Feltoe, in *N&PNF*, XII (New York, 1895), Sermo III, esp. ch. 1: 'And finally, now that the mystery of this Divine priesthood has descended to human agency, it runs not by the line of birth, nor is it that which flesh & blood created, chosen, but without the privilege of paternity and succession by inheritance, those men are received by the Church as its rulers whom the Holy Ghost prepares: so that in the people of GOD's adoption, the whole body of which is priestly & royal, it is not the prerogative of earthly origin which obtains the unction, but the condescension of Divine grace which creates the bishop.'

92 Leo the Great, *PL*, LIV, 11, Sermo III: 'ipse ad Christi Domini gloriam consona voce cantavimus. Ipse est enim de quo prophetice scriptum est: *Tu es sacerdos in oetirnum secundem ordinem Melchisedech* (Psal., CIX,), hoc est, *non secundum ordinem Aaron*, cujus sacerdotium per propaginem sui seminis currens, temporalis ministerii fuit, et cum veteris Testamenti lege cessavit; sed *secundum ordinem Melchisedech*, in quo aeterni Pontificis forma precessit. Et dum quibus parentibus sit editus non refertur, in eo ille intelligitur ostendi, cujus generatio non potest enarrari. Denique cum hujus divini sacerdotii sacramentum etiam ad humanas pervenit functiones, non per generationum tramitem curritur, nec quod caro et sanguis creavit, eligitur; sed cessante privilegio patrum, et familiarum ordine praetermisso, eos rectores Ecclesia accipit, quos Spiritus sanctus preparavit; ut in populo adoptionis

Dei, cujus universitas sacerdotalis atque regalis est, non praerogativa terrenae originis obtineat unctionem, sed dignatio coelestis gratiae gignat antistitem.'
93 In the event, it was Symmachus who won out over his rival Laurence. See *LP*, I, Symmachus, 260–3.

9 A Collective Funerary *Martyrium*

1 The classic work on the *martyrium* is André Grabar's *Martyrium. Recherches sur le culte des reliques et l'art chrétien antique*, 3 vols. (Paris, 1946; repr. 2 vols., London, 1972). For Grabar's definition, see 47: 'les premiers *martyria* , monuments destinés à marquer l'emplacement des tombeaux des martyrs et à aménager l'espace autour de ces sépultures, en vue du culte et pour abriter les fidèles.'
2 R. Krautheimer, 'Review of André Grabar, *Martyrium. Recherches sur le culte des reliques et l'art chrétien antique*, 2 vols., Paris, 1943–1946,' *ArtBull*. 35 (1953), 57–61, repr. in Krautheimer, *Studies in Early Christian, Medieval and Renaissance Art* (New York, 1969), 151–9, esp. 159.
3 J.F. Niermeyer, *Mediae Latinitatis Lexicon Minus* (Leiden, 1976), records fifth- and sixth-century examples of churches called *martyria* purely because they were dedicated to a martyr or martyrs.
4 *LP*, I, 330: 'Iohannes, natione Dalmata, ex patre Venantio scolastico, sedit ann.1, mens. VIIII dies XVIIII. Hic temporibus suis misit per omnem Dalmatiam seu Histriam multas pecunias per sanctissimum et fidelissimum Martinum abbatem propter redemptiorem captivorum qui depraedati erant a gentibus. Eodem tempore fecit ecclesiam beatis martyribus Venantio, Anastasio, Mauro et aliorum multorum martyrum, quorum reliquias de Dalmatias et Histrias adduci praeceperat, et recondit eas in ecclesia suprascripta, iuxta fontem Lateranensem, iuxta oratorium beati Ioannis evangelistae, quam ornavit et diversa dona obtulit.'
5 'MARTYRIBUS XPI DNI PIA VOTA IOHANNES/ REDDIDIT ANTISTES SANCTIFICANTE DO/ AC SACRI FONTEIS SIMILI FULGENTE METALLO/ PROVIDUS INSTANTER HOC COPULAVIT OPUS/ QUO QUISQUIS GRADIENS ET XPM PRONUS ADORANS/ EFFUSAQUE PRECES MITTAT AD AETHRA SUAS.'
6 For summaries of earlier archaeological work, see especially Emerico Ceci (Mirko Čečić), *I monumenti cristiani di Salona* (Milan, 1963); and Dyggve, *Salonitan*.
7 J. Wilpert, 'La decorazione constantiniana della basilica lateranense,' *RAC* 6 (1929), 42–127. See also R. Giordani, 'Riflessioni sulla decorazione absidale

della basilica di san Giovanni in Laterano,' *RAC* 70 (1994), 271–313, esp. 272–3, note 4, for bibliography.

8 See Grabar, *Martyrium*, 54–5 for Kapljuć, 56 for Manastirine, 57 for Marusinac – all three sites at Salona.

9 Grabar, 'Martyria collectifs,' *Martyrium*, 54–63, where martyrs interred in
   shared graves at their deaths are discussed.

10 Anonymous, 'Restauri di mosaici fuori del Vaticano,' *RendPontAcc Rendi-
    conti* 23–4 (1947–9), 402–5.

11 *LP*, I, 245; also 247, note 11, manuscript variant #2: 'Fecit autem oratorium
    Sancti Stephani in baptisterio Lateranense.'

12 O. Panvinio, *De septem urbis ecclesiis* (Rome, 1570), 167, 'De Ecclesia Sancti
    Venantij,' repr. in P. Lauer, *Latran*, 468: 'habet ... parietes a tribus lateribus
    vetustissimus et non inelegantibus picturis praesertim a parte sinistra.'

13 See Grabar, *Martyrium*, esp. ch. V, 207, 'Les théophanies,' and 211–12 on the
    S Venanzio chapel.

14 Ceci, *Monumenti cristiani*, 69. F. Bulić, 'Kronotaska solinskih biskupa,'
    BASD, 35 (1912), 1–10, and 'Anno e giorno della morte, condizione e
    numero dei martiri Salonitani,' *BASD* 39 (1916), 126. Also, 'Mučenici Solin-
    ski, Broji stalis, godina i dan smrti mučenika solinskih,' *Dodatak k vjesniku
    za arheologiju i povjest dalmatinsku* (Zagreb, 1919), 1–31, esp. 9–10. J.J. Wilkes,
    Dalmatia (London, 1969), 427, disagrees on the ground of insufficient evi-
    dence. See also M. Ivanisević, 'Salonitanski Biskupi,' *VAHD* 86 (1993),
    223–53, esp. 226, note 5, for bibliography, and 250–3, for the argument that
    Venantius was a bishop, but not necessarily the first bishop of Salona.

15 For John's parentage, see *LP*, I, 330, text in note 4, above.

16 N. Duval and E. Marin, 'Encore les cinq martyrs de Salone. Un témoignage
    épigraphique désormais bien établi,' *Memoria Sanctorum Venerantes* (Vati-
    can City, 1992), 283–307, esp. 292.

17 Wilkes, *Dalmatia*, 429, for Domnio's origins, and Bulić, *Mučenici*, 8, for the
    date.

18 Dyggve, *Salonitan*, 73. Bulić, *Mućenici*, 7, records an inscription with the
    name Domnius.

19 Constantine Porphyrogenitos, *De Administrando Impero*, ed. Gy. Moravcsik,
    (Washington, 1967), I, 136–7, and II, *Commentary*, F. Dvornik et al., both
    vols. tr. R.J.H. Jenkins (London, 1962), 108–9.

20 Dyggve, *Salonitan*, 71f., 125f., with sources.

21 Diocletian's itineraries from Timothy D. Barnes, *The New Empire of Dio-
    cletian and Constantine* (Cambridge, MA, and London, 1982), 55–6.

22 Since construction of this enormous building, covering 9.5 acres, had
    started in 393, it must have neared completion by 304.

23 Ceci, *Monumenti cristiani*, 82.

24 Ceci, *Monumenti cristiani*, 81; Bulić, *Mučenici*, 12.

25 Grabar, *Martyrium*, I, 26.

26 For inscription, see *Ephemeris Salonitana* (Zadar, 1894), repr. in *Acta primi congressus internationalis archaeologiae christianae* (Vatican City, 1993), pl. 4, fig. 11.

27 Dyggve, *Salonitan*, 104.

28 *ActaSS*, 1863 ed., September, VII, 21–2; Dyggve, *History*, 73.

29 Antonio Nieri, 'Santi aquileiesi e veneti in Dalmazia,' *Antichità Altoadriatiche* 26 (1985), 261–88, esp. 269, finds that all sources that refer to Anastasius as an Aquilaean date from after 1000. Nieri, 273, also finds that Anastasius is not even described as a fuller in the early sources. For a summary of the archaeological evidence for his presence in Salona, see Dyggve, *Salonitan*, 83.

30 Dyggve, *Salonitan*, 83.

31 'HOC CUBILE SANCTUM CONFESSORIS MAUR(I) NIBEUM CONTE-NET CORPUS, /H/ AEC PRIMITIVA EIUS ORATIBUS REPARATA EST ECCLESIA. H/IC/ CONDIGNE TRANSLATUS EST UBI EPISCOPUS ET CONFESSOR EST FACTUS; IDEO IN HONORE DUPLICATUS EST LOCUS / ... / M S(U)BACTUS / ... / S.' See Ceci, *Monumenti cristiani*, 81–2, and note 104, for sources.

32 'I corpi santi erano stati sottrati a Parenzo da pagano Doria l'11 agosto 1354 durante la guerra con Venezia, e custoditi nella chiesa di San Matteo fino al 1934 quando vennero restituti alla cittadina istriana e l'urna vuota collocata nel chiostro.' The marble chest ordered in 1356 by Raffaello Doria for the bodies of the martyrs is illustrated in Carlo Ceschi and Leonard von Matt, *Chiese di Genova* (Genoa, n.d.), 60, pl. 31.

33 F. Bulić, 'Escavi dell'anfiteatro romano di Salona negli anni 1909–12 e 1913–14,' *BASD* 27 (1914), 22, and pl. 14.

34 Similar pagan shrines are known from the Colosseum, Rome, and from Dürres (Dyrrachium), Albania, where one was also converted into a Christian chapel. See Nicole Thierry, 'Une mosaïque à Dyrrachium,' *CahArch* 18 (1968), 227–9; Maria Andaloro, 'I mosaici parietali di Durazzo o dell'origine constantinopolitana del tema iconografico di Maria Regina,' in *Studien zur spätantiken und byzantinischen Kunst*, III, ed. O. Feld and V. Peschlow (Rome, 1986), 103–12; and, especially, Ivanka Nikolajević, 'Images votives de Salone et de Dyrrachium,' *Zbornik Radova Vizantoloskog Instituta* 19 (1980), 59–70, who suggests a sixth-century date and also discusses the Salona amphitheatre chapels, with line drawings of the paintings.

35 Bulić, 'Escavi dell'anfiteatro,' 31. The altar is now in the Split archaeological

museum; Ceci, *I Monumenti pagani di Salona* (Milan, 1962), 108. For bibliography on other gladiator shrines, see Ceci, *Monumenti cristiani*, 244, note 6.

36 See Dyggve, *Salonitan*, 49, fig. IV. The inscription read 'SCS (AST)ERIU(S) SCS T(E)LIU(S).'

37 Bulić, 'Escavi dell'anfiteatro,' 22 and pl. XII: 'vi sono avvanzi ... di una figura umana ... piuttosto di un fanciullo.'

38 Nikolajević, 'Images votives,' 70.

39 See Ceci, *Monumenti cristiani*, 243, for references.

40 See above, note 35.

41 E. Kitzinger, 'Some Reflections on Portraiture in Byzantine Art,' in *The Art of Byzantium and the Medieval West*, ed. W.E. Kleinbauer (Bloomington, 1976), 256–70, esp. note 19.

42 See C. Cecchelli, 'Le arti minori e il costume,' *La vita di Roma nel Medio Evo*, 1:2 (Rome, 1960), 1076.

43 The relics were found *in situ* in its *confessio* in 1736, identified by a silver tablet. R. Krautheimer et al., *Corpus Basilicarum Christianorum Romae*, vol. IV (Vatican City, 1937–77), 237.

44 See Brown, *Cult of Saints*, chapter 5.

45 Anxiety about the apparent presence of the martyrs' bodies in both Rome and Dalmatia gave rise to the duplication in legend of at least two of the saints: Domnus, as was discussed, and Anastasius, whose saintly alter ego was a legendary saint, Anastasius the *Cornicularius*, a soldier of that rank who was martyred under Aurelian; *ActaSS*, September, VII, 21–2; and H. Delehaye, 'Saints d'Istrie et de Dalmatie,' *Analecta Bollandiana* 18 (1899), 488–500.

46 John M. McCulloh, 'The Cult of Relics in the Letters and Dialogues of Pope Gregory the Great: A Lexicographical Study,' *Traditio* 32 (1976), 145–84, esp. 147; and Epistula 218, *Epistulae imperatorum pontificum*, in *CSEL*, 35, 679–80.

47 Gregory I, *Epistola XXX*, 'ad Constantinam Augustam,' *PL* 77, cols. 700–5, tr. James Barmby, *N&PNF*, 12 (1895), 154–6.

48 For the question of what is meant by Gregory's letter, see McCulloh, 'Cult of Relics,' 147–50. The sanctification of altars with martyr relics is first mentioned in the biography of Pope Felix (268–273), *LP*, I, 158: 'Hic constituit supra memorias martyrum missas celebrare'; Davis, tr., *Book of Pontiffs*, 11: 'He decreed that mass be celebrated over the memorials of the martyrs,' though this statement clearly does not proscribe its celebration in other locations, or at altars which were not sanctified in this way.

49 McCulloh, 'Cult of Relics,' 151–3.

50 For the translation of St Donatus's remains: Gregory I, *Epistola* VII, *PL*, 77, col. 1309. McCulloh, 'Cult of Relics,' 151.
51 Ambrose, *Epistola* XXII, 'To his sister Marcellina,' *PL*, 16, cols. 1062–9, esp. 1063.
52 The lead coffer and the inscription were provided for the remains after the building of a new altar in 1674.
53 The inscription reads in part 'CORPORA SS MM VENANTII DOMNUS-NIS' (the other names follow); Ceci, *Monumenti cristiani*, 91. See also Panvinio, 'De Ecclesia sancti Venantij,' 468: 'et sub eius altare corpora SS. Martyrum Venantij, Dominionis, Anastasij, Mauri, Asterij, Septimij, Sulpicianij, Telij, Anthiochiani, Pauliniani et Caiani ex Dalmatia et Istria Romam advecta recondidit.' Sulpicianus seems to be added in error.
54 Makso Peloža, 'Rekognicija relikvia Dalmatinskih i Istarskih mučenika, u oratoriju svetog Venancija kod Baptisterija Lateranske Bazilike u Rimu 1962–1964 godine,' *VAHD* 64 (1962), 163–80, with French summary.
55 Dyggve, *History*, 83: 'Among the extremely numerous sarcophagi, which in the course of years have been excavated there are scarcely ten, which have not been opened by violence.'
56 Wilkes, *Dalmatia*, 437. These communities retained their Roman character into the Middle Ages.
57 Ivan Marović, 'Reflexions about Year of the Destruction of Salona,' *VAHD* 77 (1984), 293–315.
58 F. Oreb, 'Archaeological Excavations in the Eastern Part of Ancient Salona in 1979,' *VAHD* 77 (1984), 25–35, esp. 28–9. See also Marović, 'Reflexions,' 293, coin 45, with facing portraits of Heraclius and Heraclius Constantine.
59 Nikola Jaksić, 'Constantine Porphyrogenitos as the Source for the Destruction of Salona,' *VAHD* 77 (1984), 315–26.
60 Primus, after 304; Gaianus, ca. 391; Symferius, 405; and Esychius, before 426. See Ivanisević, 'Salonitanski Biskupi,' for inscriptions and dating.
61 Patrick J. Geary, *Furta Sacra. The Theft of Relics in the Central Middle Ages* (Princeton, 1978).

10 The Chapel Revisited

1 See Davis, *Book of Pontiffs*, Introduction, ii–vii and xxxvi–xxxviii for a summary.
2 Antonio Ferrua, *The Unknown Catacomb. A Unique Discovery of Early Christian Art* (Florence, 1990; repr. New Lanark, 1991); the *transennae* and the strigillated sarcophagus fronts of *cubicula* N and O are shown in figs. 27 and 123.

3 All weights given in the *Liber Pontificalis* are in Roman pounds, weighing 327.45 g, as opposed to the 453.592 g of the English pound.

4 Leo I (440–61), *LP*, I, 239; tr. Davis, *Book of Pontiffs*, 38

5 Hilarus (461–8), *LP* I, 242–3; tr. Davis, *Pontiffs*, 39. The text is to be found in chapter 8, note 34.

6 Symmachus (498–514), *LP*, I, 261–2; for Latin text see chapter 8, note 4; tr. Davis, *Book of Pontiffs*, 45.

7 Boniface, *LP*, I, 227–8; tr. Davis, *Book of Pontiffs* 34.

8 Agnellus, *CPER*, Johannes II, 119. The chalice was inscribed 'OFFERO SANCTO ZACHARIA GALLA PLACIDIA AUGUSTA.'

9 Agnellus, *CPER*, 75.

10 See chapter 5 for the Archbishops' Chapel, and J.C. Smith, 'Side Chambers,' for S Vitale.

11 Silvester (314–35), *LP*, I, 182–3; tr. Davis, *Book of Pontiffs*, 23.

12 Terry, 'Sculpture,' 13–64, esp. 30–1 and fig. 56.

13 Psalm 26.8.

14 John 10.9–10.

15 John 10.11–14

16 Mark 10.14

17 Revelation 5.1–13.

18 The traveller was the 'Anonymous of Pola' ('Anonimo di Pola,' now identified as Pietro Degani), in his *Dialoghi due sulle antichità di Pola del 1600*, in *Cenni al forestiero che visita Pola*, ed. P. Kandler (Trieste, 1845), paraphrased in *L'Istra* 32 (1847), and reprinted in Kandler, *Notizie storiche di Pola* (Poreč, 1876), 174.

19 See M. Harrison, *A Temple for Byzantium* (Austin, TX, 1989), 117, for window frames at S Polyeuctos, Istanbul, and the size of the glass panes (3 × 9 cm) that would have been required to glaze them.

20 Ammianus, *History*, XVI.VIII.3–6.

21 Gregory I (590–604), *LP*, I, 312; tr. Davis, *Book of Pontiffs*, 61.

22 Leo III (795–816), *LP*, II, 28–31; tr. Davis, *Eighth-Century Popes*, 193–230 esp. 223: Lateran chapel of the Archangels, and 226: Oratories of the Virgin.

23 Gregory III, *LP*, I; tr. Davis, *Eighth-Century Popes*, 23: 'and the other things which are assigned for the *pergula*'s adornment and as altarcloths.' These cloths may well have been for adornment only, rather than serving to conceal the sanctuary, which was open to view at this period, at least in the East. See Mathews, *Early Churches*, 169–71.

24 John 8.12.

Bibliography

AAVV. *La Basilica di santi Felice e Fortunato in Vicenza*, 2 vols. Vicenza, 1979–80.

Acta Apostolorum Apocrypha, ed. C. Tischendorf. Leipzig, 1851.

Acta Sanctorum … collegit, digessit, notis illustravit Joannes Bollandus … Antwerp, 1643; new edition 1863.

Acta Sanctorum martyrum orientalium et occidentalium, ed. St E. Assemani. Rome, 1748.

Agnellus, Andreas. *Codex Pontificalis Ecclesiae Ravennatis*, ed. Alessandro Testi-Rasponi. *RIS*, n.s., II/3. Bologna, 1924.

– *Liber Pontificalis Ecclesiae Ravennatis*, ed. O. Holder-Egger. *Scr.Rer.Langob.*, *MGH*. Hanover, 1878.

Alchermes, Joseph D. 'Petrine Politics: Pope Symmachus and the Rotunda of St Andrew at Old St Peter's,' *The Catholic Historical Review* 81 (1995), 1–40.

Alpharanus, Tiberius. *De Basilicae Vaticanae, antiquissima et nova structura*, ed. D. Michele Cerrati. Studi e Testi, 26. Rome, 1914.

Amadio, Adele Anna. *I mosaici di S Costanza. Disegni, incisioni e documenti dal XV al XIX secolo*, Xenia Quaderni, 7. Rome, 1986.

Ambroise de Milan. Hymnes. Ed. Jacques Fontaine. Paris, 1992.

Ambrose. *Epistola XXII*, 'To His Sister Marcellina,' *PL*, 16, cols. 1062–9.

– *Epistola XXXVII*, 'To Simplicianus,' *PL*, 16, cols. 1129–42.

– *De Excessu Fratris sui Satyri*, *PL*, 16, cols.1345–1414.

– *Exhortatio Virginitatis*, I, *PL*, 16, cols. 351–80.

– *Expositio evangelii secundum Lucam*, *PL*, 15, col. 1746.

– Hymns to Sixtus and to Lawrence: LXXII, 'De S Sixto'; LXXIII, 'De S Laurentio,' *PL*, 17, cols. 1253–5.

– *De Obitu Valentiniani consolatio*, *PL*, 16, l, cols. 1417–44.

– *De Officiis ministrorum*, *PL*, 16, cols. 25–194.

- *De Poenitentia*, I, *PL*, 16, ch. VIII, col. 497.
- *In Psalmum CXVIII*, *PL*, 15, col. 1506.
- *De Virginibus ac Marcellinam sororem suam*, *PL*, 16, cols. 241–4.
- *De Virginitate*, *PL*, 16, ch. XIV, cols. 301–2.
- 'Victor, Nabor, Felix pii,' *Opera S Ambrosii*, V. Ed. Paolo Ballerini, 679. Milan, 1875–83.

Ammianus Marcellinus. *Rerum Gestarum libri qui supersunt*, ed. and tr. John C. Rolfe as *History*, 3 vols., vol. 2, Book XXI. London, 1937; repr. 1956.

Andaloro, Maria. 'Aggiornamento scientifico e bibliografia,' in G. Matthiae, *Pittura Romana del Medioevo, Secoli IV–X*. Rome, 1987.
- 'I mosaici parietali di Durazzo o dell'origine constantinopolitana del tema iconigrafico di Maria Regina,' in *Studien zur spätantiken und byzantinischen Kunst*, vol. 3, ed. O. Feld and V. Peschlow, 103–12. Bonn, 1986.

Andrieu, M. *Les ordines Romani du haut moyen age*. Louvain, 1965–74.

Anonimo di Pola (Pietro Degani). *Dialoghi due sulle antichità di Pola del 1600*, ed. P. Kandler under the title *Cenni al forestiero che visita Pola*, 59–158. Trieste, 1845.

Anonymous. 'Restauri di mosaici fuori del Vaticano,' *Atti della pontificia Accademia de archeologia. Rendiconti* vol. 23–4 (1947–9), 402–5.

Anonymous Valesianus. 'Excerpta Volesiana,' ed. and tr. J.C. Rolfe, in *Ammianus Marcellinus*, vol. III, 506–70. London, 1952.

Arnason, H.H. 'Early Christian Silver of North Italy and Gaul,' *ArtBull*. 20 (1938), 193–226.

Arslan, E. *Catalogo delle cose d'arte e di antichità d'Italia: Vicenza*. Rome, 1956.

Asterius the Sophist. *Homilies on the Psalms*, ed. and tr. Marcel Richard. Oslo, 1956.

Athanasius. *Apologia contra Arianos*, *PG*, 25, cols. 411–77, esp. 412.
- *Historia arianorum ad monachos*, *PG*, 25, cols. 691–796, tr. Archibald Robertson in *N&PNF*, ser. 2, vol. 4: *St Athanasius, Select Works and Letters: History of the Arians*, 266–302. New York, 1903; repr. 1991.

Augustine. *De Civitate Dei*, 7 vols., tr. G.E. McCracken and W. Green. London and Cambridge, MA, 1957–72.
- *Confessiones*, 2 vols., tr. William Watts. London and Cambridge, MA, 1960–1.
- Sermons: CCCIII, 'In natali martyris Laurentii,' *PL*, 38, cols. 1393–5; CCLXXIV–CCLXXVII, 'In festo martyris Vincentii,' I–IV, *PL*, 38, cols. 1252–68.

Babić, Gordana. *Les chapelles annexes des églises Byzantines: Fonction liturgique et programmes iconographiques*. Paris, 1969.
- 'North Chapel of the Quatrefoil Church at Ohrid and Its Mosaic Floor,' *Zbornik Radova Vizantoloskog Instituta* 13 (1971), 271–6.

Barbarano de Mironi, F. *Historia ecclesiastica della città, territorio, e diocesi di Vicenza*. Vicenza, 1649.

Barnay, M.M. 'Some Reflections of Life in North Africa in the Writings of Tertullian.' PhD dissertation. Catholic University of America, 1968.

Barnes, Timothy D. *The New Empire of Diocletian and Constantine*. Cambridge, MA, 1982.

Barnish, S.J.B. Review of M. McCormick, *Triumphal Rulership in Late Antiquity, Byzantium and the Early Medieval West* (Cambridge, 1986), in *Journal of Ecclesiastical History* 41 (1990), 79–81.

Bartoccini, Renato. 'Casaranello e i suoi mosaici,' *FR*, n.s., 45 (1934), 157–85.

Bartoli, Alfonso. *I monumenti antichi di Roma nei disegni degli Uffizi di Firenze*, 6 vols. Rome, 1914–22.

Bartoli, Pier Santi. *Gli antichi sepolcri*. Rome, 1699.

Baruffa, Antonio. *Le catacombe di San Callisto*. Turin, 1988.

Battisti, E. 'Per la datazione di alcuni mosaici di Ravenna e di Milano,' *Scritti di storia dell'arte in onore di M. Salmi*, vol. 1, 101–23. Rome, 1961.

Bauer, Franz Alto. 'La frammentazione liturgica nella chiesa romana del primo medioevo,' *RAC* 75 (1999), 385–446.

Beckwith, J. *Early Christian and Byzantine Art*. Harmondsworth, 1970.

Bernard, J.H. *The Odes of Solomon*, Texts and Studies. Contributions to Biblical and Patristic Literature, 8/3. Cambridge, 1912.

Bernardus Monachus Francus. *Itinerarium in Loca Sancta*, PL, 121, cols. 569–74.

Bertacchi, Luisa. 'La cappella con la tomba del vescovo Marciano nel duomo di Grado,' *Aquileia nostra* 37 (1966), 90–103.

Bertaux, Émile. *L'art dans l'Italie Méridionale*, 3 vols. 1903; repr. Paris and Rome, 1968.

Bertelli, Carlo, ed. 'Introduzione,' *Il millenio ambrosiano. Milano, una capitale da Ambrogio ai Carolingi*, 8–32. Milan, 1987.

– 'Mosaici a Milano,' *Atti del 10° congresso internazionale di studi sull'alto medio evo*, 333–51. Spoleto, 1986.

– 'I mosaici di S Vittore,' in *La basilica di S Ambrogio: Il tempio in interrotto*, 2 vols., ed. Maria Luisa Gatti, 342–5. Milan 1995.

Besta, J.F. *Origine e meraviglie della città de Milano*, cod. Ambr. P.258.

Bettini, S. *Monumenti paleocristiani delle Venezie e della Dalmazia*. Padua, 1942.

Bibliotheca Hagiographica Latina Antiquae et Mediae Aetatis. Brussels, 1898–1901.

Biraghi, Luigi. *Ricognizione dei gloriosi corpi dei santi Vittore, Mauro, Satiro, Casto e Polemio, ecc.* Milan, 1861.

Boethius. *De Institutione Arithmetica*, PL 63, II, 41, col. 1146.

Bognetti, G.P., B. Forlati Tamaro, and G. Lorenzon. *Vicenza nell'alto Medio Evo.* Venice, 1959.

Bosio, A. *Roma sotteranea.* Rome, 1632.

Bottari, Stefano. *Ravenna, mausoleo di Galla Placidia.* Bologna. 1966.

Bovini, Giuseppe. *Antichità cristiane di S Canzian d'Isonzo, S Giovanni al Timavo e Trieste.* Bologna, 1973.

– 'Gli edifici di culto milanesi d'età pre-ambrosiana,' *CorsiCRB* 8 (1961), 47–72.

– 'Le "imagines episcoporum Ravennae" ricordate nel *Liber Pontificalis* di Andrea Agnello,' *CorsiCRB* 21 (1974), 53–63.

– 'La "memoria antiqua S Stephani" e l'oratorio paleocristiano di Corso Garibaldi di Ancona,' *CorsiCRB* 13 (1966), 7–26.

– *Memorie cristiane scomparse dell'antica città di Classe.* Ravenna, 1965.

– 'Mosaici paleocristiani scomparsi di S Prisco,' *CorsiCRB* 14 (1967), 43–62.

– 'Mosaici parietali scomparsi: S Lorenzo in Cesarea e monasterium Gervasii e Protasii,' *FR* 55 (1951), 50–60.

– *I mosaici di Ravenna.* Milan, 1956.

– 'Osservazioni sui mosaici paleocristiani della chiesa di S Prisco a S Prisco presso S Maria Capua Vetere,' *Capys* 2 (1967), 6–12.

– *Saggio di bibliografia su Ravenna antica.* Bologna, 1968.

– 'Le "tovaglie d'altare" ricamate ricordate da Andrea Agnello nel *Liber Pontificalis Ecclesiae Ravennatis*,' *CorsiCRB* 21 (1974), 77–90.

Bratož, Rajko. 'The Development of the Early Christian Research in Slovenia and Istria between 1976 and 1986,' *Actes du XIe Congrès international d'archéologie chrétienne*, III, 2369–88.

Braun, Joseph. *Der christliche Altar in seiner historischen Entwicklung.* Munich, 1924.

Breviarius Hierosolyma (Itinera Hierosolymitana), ed. P. Geyer, *CSEL* 39. Vienna, 1898.

Brightman, F.E. *Liturgies Eastern and Western.* Oxford, 1896.

Broglio, A., and L. Cracco Ruggieri. *Storia di Vicenza*, I. Vicenza, 1987.

Brown, Peter. *The Body and Society: Men, Women and Sexual Renunciation in Early Christianity.* London, 1988.

– *The Cult of the Saints, Its Rise and Function in Latin Christianity.* Chicago, 1981.

Brubaker, Lesley. 'Patterns in Byzantine Matronage: Aristocratic and Imperial Commissions, Fourth to Sixth Centuries,' *Byzantine Studies Conference Absracts* 16 (1990), 27–8.

– 'Memories of Helena: Patterns in Imperial Female Matronage in the Fourth and Fifth Centuries,' in *Women, Men and Eunuchs. Gender in Byzantium*, ed. Liz James, 52–75. London and New York, 1997.

Brusin, Giovanni. *Aquileia e Grado*. Padua, 1959.

Brusin, Giovanni, and P.L. Zovetto, *Monumenti paleocristiani di Aquileia e di Grado*. Udine, 1957.

Bulić, Frane. 'Anno e giorno della morte, condizione e numero dei martiri Salonitani,' *Bulletino di archeologia e storia dalmata* 39 (1916), 126f.

- 'Escavi dell'anfiteatro romano di Salona negli anni 1909–1912 e 1913–1914,' *Bulletino di archeologia e storia dalmata* 37 (1914), 22.

- 'Kronotaska solinskih biskupa,' *Bulletino di archeologia e storia dalmata* 35 (1912).

- 'Mučenici Solinski, broji stalis, godina i dan smrti mučenika solinskih,' *Dodatak k Vjesniku za arheologiju i povijest Dalmatinsku 1917*, 1–31. Zagreb, 1919.

Bury, John B. *History of the Later Roman Empire*, 2 vols. London, 1923; rpr. New York, 1958.

Cabrol, F., and H. Leclercq. *Dictionnaire d'archéologie chrétienne et de liturgie* (*DACL*). Paris, 1914– .

Caffi, M. *Storia di Milano*. Milan, 1953–4.

Calderini, Aristide. 'Le basiliche dell'età ambrosiana in Milano,' *Ambrosiana*, 137–64. Milan, 1942.

- 'La scoperta di un recinto fortificato romano presso la basilica milanese di S.Vittore al Corpo,' *Palladio*, n.s., 2 (1952), 79f.

Calderini, Aristide, and F. Reggiori. 'Scavi alla ricerca della basilica dei SS Nabor e Felice,' *Ritrovamenti e scavi per la Forma Urbis Mediolani*, 2, 3–5. Milan, 1951.

Calderini, Aristide, G. Chierici, and C. Cecchelli. *La basilica di San Lorenzo Maggiore*. Milan, 1952.

Camprubi, F. 'I mosaici della cupola di Centcelles nella Spagna,' *RAC* 19 (1942), 87–110.

Canova dal Zio, Regina. *Le chiese delle tre Venezie anteriori al mille*. Padua, 1986.

Carile, Antonio, ed. *Storia di Ravenna*, II, 1: *Dall'età bizantina all'età ottoniana, Territorio, economia e società*. Ravenna, 1991; and II, 2: *Ecclesiologia, cultura e arte*. Ravenna, 1992.

Castagnoli, Ferdinando. 'Il circo di Nerone in Vaticano,' *RendPontAcc* 32 (1959–60), 97–121

Castiglioni, Bonaventura. Cod. Ambr. N.153, 30v, in F. Savio, *Gli Antichi vescovi d'Italia dalle origini al 1300*, I: *Milano*. Florence, 1913.

Cataldi, Maria, and Laura Ricciardi. *Tarquinia*. Rome, 1993.

Catalogus Archiepiscoporum Mediolanensium. MGH, Scriptores, VIII, ed. W. Wattenbach. Hanover, 1848.

Cecchelli, Carlo. *I mosaici della basilica di santa Maria Maggiore*. Turin, 1956.

- 'I mosaici e le pitture,' in *La basilica di San Lorenzo Maggiore*, ed. G. Chierici and C. Cecchelli. Milan, 1952.
- 'Le arti minori e il costume,' *La vita di Roma nel Medio Evo*, 1/2. Rome, 1960.

Ceci, Emerico (Mirko Čečić). *I monumenti pagani di Salona*. Milan, 1962.

- *I monumenti cristiani di Salona*. Milan, 1963.

Ceschi, Carlo. 'Santo Stefano Rotondo,' *Atti della pont.acc.rom.di arch.*, ser. III, *Memoriae* 15 (1982), 7–end of volume.

Ceschi, Carlo, and Leonard von Matt. *Chiese di Genova*. Genoa, n.d.

Chalkia, Eugenia. *Le mense paleocristiane. Tipologia e funzioni delle mense secondarie nel culto paleocristiano*. Studi di antichità cristiana, 46. Vatican City, 1991.

Chantelou, Dom. *Mémoire de l'église Notre Dame de La Daurade à Toulouse*, Paris, Bibl. nat. Lat. 13845, f. 47–99. Toulouse, 1621.

Chierici, G. 'Recenti lavori ... alle basiliche paoliniane di Cimitile,' *RAC* 16 (1939), 51–73.

Christe, Y. 'À propos du décor absidal de St Jean du Latran,' *CahArch* 20 (1970), 197–206.

Christie, Neil. 'The City Walls of Ravenna, The Defence of a Capital, AD 402–750,' *CorsiCRB* 36 (1989), 113–38.

Chrysostom, John. Sermons: *De S Pelagia Virg. Ac Mart. AASS*, Junii II, 154.

Ciampini, Giovanni. *Vetera Monimenta*, 2 vols. Rome, 1690–9.

- *De sacris aedeficiis a Constantino Magno constructis*. Rome, 1693.

Cirlot, J.E. *A Dictionary of Symbols*, tr. J. Sage. New York, 1962; 2nd ed., 1971.

Codice topografico della città di Roma, ed. Roberto Valentini and Giuseppe Zucchetti, Fonti per la Storia d'Italia, 4 vols. Rome, 1940–53.

Concise Oxford Dictionary, 5th ed. Oxford, 1964.

Constantine Porphyrogenitos. *De Administrando Impero*, vol. I: *Corpus Fontium Historiae Byzantinae*, ed. Gy. Moravcsik, tr. R.J.H.Jenkins. Washington, 1967; vol. II: *Commentary* by F. Dvornik, R.J.H. Jenkins, B. Lewis, et al., ed. R.J.H. Jenkins. London, 1962.

- *De cerimoniis aulae byzantinae*, ed. J. Reiske. Bonn, 1829–40; tr. Albert Vogt, *Le livre des cérémonies*. Paris, 1935–9.

Conti, R., ed. *Il Duomo di Monza*. Milan, 1989.

Cooper, Kate. 'The Martyr, the *Matrona* and the Bishop: The Matron Lucina and the Politics of Martyr Cult in Fifth- and Sixth-Century Rome,' *Early Medieval Europe* 8 (1999), 297–318.

Cortesi, Giuseppe. 'I principali edifici sacri ravennati in funzione sepolcrale nei secc. V e VI,' *CorsiCRB* 29 (1982), 63–107.

Courcelle, Pierre. 'Le Gril de Saint Laurent au Mausolée de Galla Placidia,' *CahArch* 3 (1948), 29–40.

Croquison, Jean. 'L'iconographie chrétienne à Rome d'après le *Liber Pontifica-lis,*' *Byzantion* 34 (1964), 535–606.

Cross, F.L., and E.A. Livingstone. *Oxford Dictionary of the Christian Church*, 2nd ed. Oxford, 1983.

Crostarosa, P. 'Le catacombe Romane,' *NBAC* 3 (1897), 113–30.

Cuscito, G. *Grado e le sue basiliche paleocristiane.* Bologna, 1979.

– 'Opilione e le origine del culto martiriale a Padova,' *Memoriam sanctorum venerantes, Miscellanea in onore di Monsignor Victor Saxer*, in *Studi di antichità cristiana*, 48, 163–81. Vatican City, 1992.

Cyprian. *Epistola LXXIII*, CSEL (Vienna, 1866); tr. Rose Bernard Donna, *Letters of Saint Cyprian, 1–81*, Letter 73, 'Cyprian to Jubaian,' The Fathers of the Church, 51, 265–85. Washington, 1964.

Cyril of Jerusalem. *Catechetical Lectures, N&PNF* (2nd series), 7, tr. E. Gifford, Lecture III, 'On Baptism, Romans VI, 3–4,' 14–18, and *On the Mysteries*, II: Lecture XX, 'Of Baptism, Romans, VI, 3–14,' 147–8. Oxford 1893; repr. 1996.

Da Lisca, A. 'Gli scavi nei pressi del sacello di S Tosca e di S Teuteria,' *Madonna Verona*, 1912, 20; 1913, 161–76; and 1914, 1–25.

Dandalus, Andrea. *Chronicon Venetum*, in Muratori, *RIS*, XII (1728), col. 102.

Daniélou, J. *Primitive Christian Symbols*, tr. D. Attwater. Baltimore, 1964.

Dassmann, E. 'Ambrosius und die Märtyrer,' *Jahrbuch für Antike und Christentum* 18 (1975), 49–68.

Davis, Raymond, ed. and tr. *The Book of Pontiffs (Liber Pontificalis).* Liverpool, 1989.

– ed. and tr. *The Lives of the Eighth-Century Popes (Liber Pontificalis).* Liverpool, 1992.

Davis-Weyer, Caecilia. *Early Medieval Art, 300–1150*, Sources and Documents in the History of Art Series, ed. H.W. Janson. Englewood Cliffs, 1971.

– 'S Stefano Rotondo in Rome and the Oratory of Theodore I,' in *Italian Church Decoration of the Middle Ages and Early Renaissance. Functions, Forms and Regional Traditions*, ed. W. Tronzo, Villa Spellman Colloquia, I, 61–80. Bologna, 1989.

De Angelis d'Ossat, G. *Studi Ravennati. Problemi di architettura paleocristiana*, Parts II and III. Ravenna, 1962.

De Blaauw, Sible. *Cultus et decor liturgia e architettura nella Roma tardoantica e medievale* (tr. from Dutch edition of 1987), 2 vols. Vatican City, 1994.

De Bruyne, L. 'La décoration des baptistères paléochrétiens,' *Atti del V congresso internazionale di archeologia cristiana, Aix-en-Provence, 1954*, 345–65. Paris, 1957.

De Capitani d'Arzago, Alberto. 'L'architettura cristiana in Milano,' in *Actes du VIe Congrès International d'Études Byzantines*, Paris, 1948, II (1951), 67f.

Déer, J., *The Dynastic Porphyry Tombs of the Norman Period in Sicily*. Cambridge, MA, 1959.

de Fabriczy, C. 'Vedute cinquecentistiche di alcuni monumenti milanesi,' *Rassegna d'Arte* 6 (1906), 87–90.

de Grooth, Marjorie, and Paul van Moorsel, 'The Lion, the Calf, the Man and the Eagle in Early Christian and Coptic Art,' *BABESCH* (*Bulletin Antieke Beschaving*) 52–3 (1977–8), 233–41.

Deichmann, F.W. 'Baptisterium,' in *Reallexicon für Antike und Christentum*, I, col. 1166.

– 'Cella Trichora' in *Reallexicon für Antike und Christentum*, II (1954), cols. 944–54.

– *Ravenna. Haupstadt des spätantiken Abendlandes*, 4 vols. Wiesbaden, 1969–89.

– Per la datazione dell'epigrafe dedicatoria di S Maria Mater Domini a Vicenza, *FR* 62 (1953), 48–50.

– 'Studi sulla Ravenna scomparsa,' *FR* 103 (1972), 61–112.

Deichmann, F.W., and Arnold Tschira. 'Das Mausoleum der Kaiserin Helena und die Basilika der heiligen Marcellinus und Petrus an der via Labicana von Rom,' *Jahrbuch des deutschen archäologischen Instituts* 72 (1957), 44–110.

Delbrueck, R. *Antike Porphyrwerke*. Berlin and Leipzig, 1932.

Delehaye, H. *Les origines du culte des martyrs*. Brussels, 1933.

– *Les passions des martyrs et les genres littéraires*. Brussels, 1921.

– *L'hagiographie ancienne de Ravenne*. Brussels, 1929.

– 'Saints d'Istrie et de Dalmatie,' *Analecta Bollandiana* 18 (1899).

Demus, Otto. *Byzantine Mosaic Decoration, Aspects of Monumental Art in Byzantium*. London, 1948; repr. Boston, 1955.

De Rossi, Giovanni B. 'Agostino vescovo e la sua madre Felicità, martiri sotto Decio e le loro memorie e monumenti in Capua,' *BAC*, ser. IV, 3 (1884), 104–13.

– 'Ancona, Cubicolo sepolcrale cristiano di diritto privato e musaico del suo pavimento,' *BAC* (1879), 128–32.

– *Inscriptiones Christianae Urbis Romae*. Rome, 1857–61, II, repr. 1888.

– 'Les médailles de dévotion des six où sept premiers siècles de l'Église,' *BAC* 7 (1869), 34–8.

– 'Il monumento d'un ignoto s Leone, vescovo e martire, nell'agro Verano,' *BAC* 2 (1864), 54–6.

– *Musaici Cristiani e saggi delle chiese di Roma anteriori al secolo XV*. Rome, 1899.

– 'D'un oratoire privé du quatrième siècle découvert sur le mont dit della Giustizia, près les Thermes de Diocletien,' *BAC* ser. III 1 (1876), 45–63.

– *Roma sotteranea cristiana descritta ed illustrata*, III. Rome, 1854.

- 'Scoperta d'una cripta storica nel cimitero di Massimo *ad sanctam Felicitatem* sulla via Salaria Nuova,' *BAC* 3–4 (1884–5), 149–84.
- 'Sepolcri antichi nell'Agro Verano,' *BAC* I (1863), 16.

Descoeudres, G. *Die Pastophorien in syro-byzantinischen Osten*. Doctoral thesis. Wiesbaden, 1983.

Didascalia Apostolorum. Tr. Margaret Dunlop Gibson. London, 1903.

Diehl, Charles. *Ravenne*. Paris, 1903.

Di Pietro, Filippo. 'Il prisco sacello di S Vitale,' *Bolletino d'Arte* ser. II, 5 (1926), 241–51.
- *La capella palatina di Palermo – i mosaici*. Palermo, 1954.

Dizionario patristico di antichità cristiana, 2 vols., ed. A. Bernardino. Rome, 1983.

Dondi Dall'Orologio, F.S. *Dissertazione sopra i riti, discipline, costumanze della chiesa di Padova*. Padua, 1816.

D'Onofrio, Cesare. *Gli Obelischi di Roma*, 2nd ed. Rome, 1967.

Downey, G. 'Nikolaos Mesarites: Description of the Church of the Holy Apostles at Constantinople,' *Transactions of the American Philosophical Society*, n.s., 47 (1957), 855–924.
- 'The Tombs of the Byzantine Emperors at the Church of the Holy Apostles in Constantinople,' *Journal of Hellenic Studies* 79 (1959), 27–51.

Duchesne, L., ed. *Liber Pontificalis*, 3 vols. Paris, 1886–92.
- *Les origines du culte chrétien*. Paris, 1889. Tr. as *Christian Worship: Its Origin and Evolution, A Study of the Latin Liturgy up to the Time of Charlemagne*, by M.L. McLure. London, 1912.

Dungulus Reclusus. 'Liber adversus Claudium taurinensem,' *PL*, 105, cols. 447–530.

Dupont-Sommer, A. *La doctrine gnostique du 'waw.'* Paris, 1946.

Duval, N., and E. Marin. 'Encore les cinq martyrs de Salone. Un témoignage épigraphique désormais bien établis,' in *Memoria Sanctorum Venerantes*, 283–307. Vatican City, 1992.

Duval, Yvette. *Auprès des saints corps et âme. L'inhumation 'ad sanctos' dans la chrétienté d'Orient et d'Occident du IIIe au VIIe siècle*. Tournholt, 1988.
- *Loca Sanctorum Africae. Le culte des martyrs en Afrique du IV au VII siécle*, 2 vols. Rome, 1982.

Dyggve, Ejnar. *A History of Salonitan Christianity*. Oslo, 1951.
- 'L'origine del cimitero entro la cinta della città,' *Atti dello VIII Congresso di studi bizantini*. Palermo, 1951; repr. in *Rivista di Studi Bizantini e Neoellenici*, 137–41. Rome, 1953.
- 'The Origin of the Urban Churchyard,' *Classica et Mediaevalia* 13 (1952), 147–58.

Engemann, J. 'Images parousiaques dans l'art palochrétien,' in *L'Apocalypse de Jean*, 91–4. Geneva, 1979.

Ennodius, Magnus Felix. *Opera Omnia*, ed. G. Hartel, *CSEL*, 6. Vienna, 1882; ed. F. Vogel, *MGH*, AA, 7. Berlin, 1885.

Ephemeris Salonitana (Zadar, Zara) 1894 repr. in *Acta primi congressus internationalis archaeologiae Cristianae*. Vatican City, 1993.

Ephraim. 'Hymn of the Baptised,' tr. A.E. Johnston, *N&PNF*, 13, 283. New York, 1898.

Ephrem (Ephraem Syrus). 'In Exodum,' *Sancti patris nostri Ephraem Syri Opera omnia quae exstant graece, syriace, latine* ... Rome, 1732–46.

Epistle of Barnabas, 9, 'Of Circumcision,' tr. Maxwell Stamforth, *Early Christian Writings, the Apostolic Fathers*. Harmondsworth, 1968.

Epistulae imperatorum pontificum, Epistola 218, *CSEL*, 35, 679–80.

Eusebius. *De Vita Constantini*, *PG*, 20, cols. 909–1232; tr. Ernest Cushing Richardson, *N&PNF*, 1. Oxford, 1890; repr. 1997.

– *The Ecclesiastical History*, 10, tr. J.E.L. Oulton. London and Cambridge, MA, 1926; repr. 1953–7.

Fabri, Gerolamo. *Le sagre memorie di Ravenna antica*. Venice, 1664.

Fagiolo, Marcello. *Roma e l'antico nell'arte e nella cultura del Cinquecento*. Rome, 1985.

– 'Theodericus-Christus-Sol: Nuove ipotesi sul mausoleo,' *Arheoloski Vestnik* 23 (1972), 83–117.

Fantuzzi, M. *Monumenti Ravennati*, 6 vols. Venice, 1801.

Farioli, Raffaella. 'La decorazione musiva della cappella di S Matrona nella chiesa di S Prisco presso Capua,' *CorsiCRB* 14 (1967), 267–91.

– *Pavimenti musivi di Ravenna paleocristiana*. Ravenna, 1975.

– 'Principale bibliografia su Ravenna pre-romana, romana, bizantina ed altomedioevale,' *FR* 117 (1979), 117–28.

– 'Ravenna paleocristiana scomparsa,' *FR* ser. 3, 31 (1960), and 32 (1961), 5–88.

Fasola, U.M. *Le catacombe di S Gennaro a Capodimonte*. Rome, 1975.

– 'Le ricerche di archeologia cristiana a Roma fuori le mura,' *Actes du XI congrès international d'archéologie chrétienne, 1986*, III (1989), 2149–76.

Feltoe, C.L. *The Letters and Sermons of Leo the Great*, in *N&PNF*, 12. New York, 1895.

Ferguson, G. *Signs & Symbols in Christian Art*. Oxford, 1954; repr. 1977.

Ferrari, G. *Early Roman Monasteries*. Vatican City, 1957.

Ferrari da Passano, C. 'Il restauro statico e conservativo della cappella di San Vittore in Ciel d'Oro, Basilica di Sant' Ambrogio,' *Notizario* (1989), 6–11.

Ferrario, Giulio. *Monumenti sacri e profani dell'imperiale e reale basilica di Sant'Ambrogio in Milano*. Milan, 1824.

Ferretti, Giampietro. *Galla Placidiae augustae vita*, Bibl.Classense, Mob. 3,2, f. 2–5.

Ferrua, Antonio. *Le pitture della nuova catacomba di Via Latina*. Vatican City, 1960.

– *The Unknown Catacomb. A Unique Discovery of Early Christian Art*. Florence, 1990; repr. New Lanark, 1991.

Février, P.A. 'Baptistères, martyrs et reliques,' *RAC* 62 (1986), 109–38.

Fiorelli, G. 'Notizie degli scavi di antichità,' *Atti dei Lincei*, ser. II, vol. III, parte III (1875–6), 127.

Forcella, V. *Seletti iscrizioni cristiane in Milano anteriori al IX secolo*. Cologne, 1897.

Franchi de'Cavalieri, P. 'Della "Passio S Vincentii levitae,"' *Note Agiografiche*, 8, Studi e Testi, 65, 117–25. Vatican City, 1935.

Frasson, G. 'Di un importantissimo monumento paleocristiano a Vicenza,' *Atti del R. Istituto Veneto di S.L.A.* 96, 2 (1936–7), 459–62.

Furlan, Italo. 'Architettura del complesso paleocristiano di Iulia Concordia: Revisione e proposte,' *Scritti storici in memoria di Paolo Lino Zovatto*, 79–95. Milan, 1972.

Gaborit-Chopin, D. 'Sedia di San Marco,' *The Treasury of San Marco, Venice*, 98–105. Milan, 1984.

Gabrielli, G.P. *L'oratorio e la basilica paleocristiana di Trieste (Via Madonna del Mare)*. Bologna, 1969.

Gagé, J. 'Le livre sacré et l'épreuve du feu. À propos d'une mosaïque du mausolée de Galla Placidia à Ravenne,' *Mullus. Festschrift Theodore Klauser. Jahrbuch für Antike und Christentum*, 1, 130–42. Münster, 1964.

Galvano Flamma (Galvanei Flammae). *Chronicon Maius*, in *Miscellanea di storia italiana*, 7. Turin, 1869.

Garrucci, Raffaele. *Storia dell'arte cristiana*. Prato, 1873–81.

Gatti, G. 'Notizie di recenti trovamenti di antichità in Roma e nel suburbio.' *Bullettino della commissione archaeologia comunale di Roma* XXIX (1901), 86–9.

Gattico, Johannes Baptista. *De Oratoriis Domesticis et de usu altario portatalis*. Rome, 1746; 2nd ed., 1770.

Geary, P.J. *Furta Sacra. The Theft of Relics in the Central Middle Ages*. Princeton, 1978.

Gerola, Giuseppe. 'Galla Placidia e il cosidetto suo mausoleo in Ravenna,' *Atti e Memorie della Ravenna deputazione di storia patria per la Romagna* (1912), 273–320.

– 'Il mosaico absidiale della Ursiana,' *FR* 1, (1912), 177–90.

– 'Il ripristino della cappella di S Andrea nel palazzo vescovile di Ravenna,' *FR*, n.s., 3 (1932), 71–132.

– 'Il sacello primitivo in San Vitale,' *FR* 2 (1913), 427–34, 459–71.

Gervers, Veronika. 'An Early Christian Curtain in the Royal Ontario Museum,' in *Studies in Textile History in Memory of Harold B. Burnham*, ed. V. Gervers, 56–81. Toronto, 1977.

Giordani, R. 'Riflessioni sulla decorazione absidale della basilica di san Giovanni in Laterano,' *RAC* 70 (1994), 271–313.

Giovanni Diacono. *Descriptio Lateranensis Ecclesiae*, in *Codice Topigrafico della Città di Roma*, ed. R. Valentini and G. Zuchhetti, III, *FSI*, 90, 336–9. Rome, 1946.

Giuliano da Sangallo. *Il Libro di Giuliano da Sangallo*, Codice Vaticano Barberiniano Latino 4424, intr. and ed. Christian Huelson, facs. Vatican City, 1984.

Gloria, A. 'Nuove esame della donazione di Opilione alla chiesa di S Giustina in Padova,' *Rassegna Padovana di Storia, Lettere ed Arti* 1 (1891), 97–106.

Gnirs, Anton. 'Forschungen in Istrien, III. Grabungen auf dem Scoglio S. Caterina bei Pola,' *Jahreshefte des Osterreichischen Archäologischen Institutes in Wien* 14 (1911), 188–96.

Goldschmidt, Richard C., ed. and tr. *Paulinus' Churches at Nola*. Amsterdam, 1940.

Gonin, H.L. *Excerpta Agnelliana. The Ravennate Liber Pontificalis as a Source for the History of Art*. Utrecht, 1933.

Gonosovà, A. 'The Formation and Sources of Early Byzantine Floral Semis and Floral Diaper Patterns Reexamined,' *DOP* 39 (1988), 227–37.

Gough, Michael. *The Origins of Christian Art*. London, 1973.

Grabar, André. *Ampoules de Terre Sainte (Monza-Bobbio)*. Paris, 1958.

– *Christian Iconography, A Study of Its Origins*. Princeton, 1968.

– 'Concordia Sagittaria,' *CahArch* 6 (1952), 157–62.

– *L'iconographie du Ciel dans l'art chrétien de l'Antiquité et du Haut Moyen Age,' *CahArch* 30 (1982), 5–25.

– *Martyrium, recherches sur le culte des reliques et l'art chrétien antique*, 3 vols. Paris, 1946; repr. 2 vols., London, 1972.

Grabar, André, and J. Hubert ('A.G. and J.H.'), eds. 'Description des mosaïques de La Daurade à Toulouse,' *CahArch* 13 (1962), 261–6.

Gregory I. *Dialogi*, cap. XL, lib. IV, 'De anima Paschasii diaconi,' *PL*, 77, cols. 396–7; tr. E.G. Gardner, *The Dialogues of Saint Gregory, Surnamed the Great, Pope of Rome and the First of That Name*, 234–5. London, 1911.

– *Epistola* III, 'Ad Joannem abbatem,' *PL*, 77, lib. III, ind. XI, cols. 605–6; tr. James Barmby, *N&PNF*, 12, 123. Oxford and New York, 1895.

– *Epistola* IX, 169, 'Gregorius Castorio notario nostro Ravenna,' *Registrum Epistolarum*, ed. Dag Norberg, Corpus chr. ser. Lat., CXL. Turnholt, 1982.

- *Epistola* XII, lib. II, 'De oratorio sanctae crucis consecrando,' to Castorius, Bishop of Ariminum, *PL*, 77, cols. 548–9;, tr. James Barmby, *N&PNF*, 12, 103. Oxford and New York, 1895.
- *Epistola* XXX, to Constantina Augusta, *PL*, 77, lib. IV, cols. 700–5; tr. James Barmby, *N&PNF*, 12, 154–6. Oxford and New York, 1895; repr. 1997.
- *Epistola* XLIX, 'Ad Palladium Episcopio,' *PL*, 77, lib. VI, col. 834; tr. James Barnby, *N&PNF*, 12, 202. Oxford and New York, 1895.
- *Epistola* CXXII, lib. IX, 'Ad Recharedum visigothorum regem,' *PL*, 77, cols. 1052–6; tr. James Barmby, *N&PNF*, 13, repr. 1997.
- *Homiliae in Evangelia, PL*, 76, *Homilia* XXXVII/9, cols. 1279–81.

Gregory of Nazianzus. *Oratio VII*, 'In Laudem Sororis suae Gorgoniae,' 8 (al. 11) 18; *PG*, 35, cols. 810–11; tr. C.G. Browne and J.E. Swallow, *N&PNF*, 7, 243, 'On His Sister Gorgonia.' 1894.

Gregory of Tours. *Historia Francorum, PL*, 71, cols. 161–576; tr. O.M. Doulton, *History of the Franks*, 2 vols. Oxford, 1927.

- *Liber Vitae Patrum, PL*, 71, cols. 1009–96.

Grierson, G. 'The Tombs and Obits of the Byzantine Emperors 337–1042,' *DOP* 16 (1962), 1–65.

Grimaldi, Giacomo. *Descrizione della basilica antica di S Pietro in Vaticano*, Cod.Vat.Barb.Lat.2733; facsimile, ed. Reto Niggl. Vatican City, 1972.

Guénon, René. *Man and His Becoming According to the Vedanta*, tr. R.C. Nicholson. London, 1945.

Guthrie, W.K.C. *The Greeks and Their Gods*. London, 1950; repr. 1968.

Guyon, Jean. *Le Cimetière aux Deux Lauriers*. Vatican City and Rome, 1987.

- 'Il complesso costantiniano presso la catacomba ad duas lauros. Bilancio di cinque anni di scavo (1975–1980),' *Archeologia laziale*, 4, Quaderni del Centro di studio per l'archeologia etrusco-italica, 5, 219–22. Rome, 1981.

Harrison, Martin. *A Temple for Byzantium*. Austin, TX, 1989.

Hauschild, Theodor. 'Die Grabungen in Centcelles,' *Archäologischer Anzeiger* (1966), 86–92.

Haussleiter, J. 'Les commentaires de Victorin, Tichonius et Jérôme sur l'Apocalypse,' *Zeitschrift für Kirchliche Wissenschaft* 7 (1886), 239–57.

Hefele, J. *Histoire des Conciles*, tr. H.Leclercq. Paris, 1907–38.

Heidenreich, R., and H. Johannes. *Das Grabmal Theoderichs zu Ravenna*. Wiesbaden, 1971.

Herbert, J.E. 'The Emblems of the Evangelists,' *Burlington Magazine* 13 (1908), 162–7.

Herodotus. *History*, tr. A.D. Godley. London and New York, 1926.

Hippolytus of Rome. *Sur les bénédictions d'Isaac, de Jacob et de Moïse*, ed. R. Graffin, tr. M.Brière, L. Mariès, and B. Ch. Mercier, *Patrologia Orientalis* 27 (1954).

– *Tradition Apostolique*, ed. and tr. B. Botte. Paris, 1968.

Hodgkin, Thomas. *Italy and Her Invaders*, I. Oxford, 1892.

Holweck, F.G. *A Biographical Dictionary of the Saints*. St Louis and London, 1924; repr. 1969.

Hoogewerff, G.J. 'Il mosaico di S Giovanni in Laterano,' *Rendiconti della Pont.Accad.Rom. d'Arch.* 27 (1952), 297–326.

Hunt, E.D. *Holy Land Pilgrimage in the Later Roman Empire, AD 312–460.* Oxford, 1982.

Huskisson, J.M. *Concordia Apostolorum. Christian Propaganda at Rome in the Fourth and Fifth Centuries. A Study in Early Christian Iconography and Iconology.* British Archaeological Reports, 148. Oxford, 1982.

Iacobini, Iacopo. 'Lancea domini. Nuove ipotesi sul mosaico absidale nell'atrio del battistero lateranense,' in *Arte d'Occidente, Temi e Metodi. Studi in onore di Angiola Maria Romanini*, 3 vols., II, 727–42. Rome, 1999.

Iannucci, A.M. 'Restauri ravennati: L'oratorio di S. Andrea nell'episcopio,' *CorsiCRB* 38 (1991), 229–33.

Ignatius of Antioch. *Ad Philadelphenses*, IV/I, ed. F.X. Funk, *Opera Patrum Apostolicorum*, I, 226–7. Tübingen, 1901.

Ihm, Christa. *Die Programme der christlicher Apsismalerei vom vierten Jahrhundert bis zur mitte des achten Jahrhunderts.* Wiesbaden, 1960.

Ivanisević, M. 'Salonitanski Biskupi,' *VAHD* 86 (1993), 223–53.

Jackson, T.G. *Dalmatia, the Quarnero and Istria*, 3 vols., III. Oxford, 1887.

Jaksić, Nikola. 'Constantine Porphyrogenitos as the Source for Destruction of Salona,' *VAHD* 77 (1984), 315–26.

James, Edward, ed. *Visigothic Spain: New Approaches.* Oxford, 1980.

James, Liz, and Ruth Webb. 'To Understand Ultimate Things and Enter Secret Places: Ekphrasis and Art in Byzantium,' *Art History* 14 (1991), 1–17.

James, Montague Rhodes. *The Apocryphal New Testament.* Oxford, 1924; 2nd ed. 1953.

Jerome. *Commentaria in Ezechielem, PL*, 25, cols. 15–512.

– *Epistola* CVIII, 'Ad Eustochium Virginem,' *PL*, 22, cols. 878–906.

– *Epistola* XLVIII, *PL*, 22, 211–34, cols. 493–511, 'To Pammachius'; tr. W.H. Fremantle, *N&PNF*, 6, 66–79.

Jessop, Lesley P. 'Pictorial Cycles of Non-Biblical Saints: The Evidence of the Eighth-Century Mural Cycles in Rome.' PhD dissertation. University of Victoria, 1993.

– 'Pictorial Cycles of Non-Biblical Saints: The Seventh- and Eighth-Century Mural Cycles of Rome and Contexts for Their Use,' *PBSR* 67 (1999), 233–79.

Johannes Diaconus (John the Deacon). *Chronicon Episcoporum S. Ecclesiae Neopolitanae*, ed. L.A. Muratori. *RIS*, 1/2, 293f.

- *Descriptio Lateranensis Ecclesiae*, in *Codice topografico della città di Roma*, III, ed. R. Valentini and G. Zucchetti, *FSI*, 90, 319–75. Rome, 1946.
- *Vita sancti Gregorii*, I/III, *PL*, 194, cols. 1545f.
Johnson, Mark J. 'The Fifth-Century Oratory of the Holy Cross at the Lateran in Rome,' *Architectura* (1995), 129–56.
- 'Late Antique Imperial Mausolea.' PhD dissertation. Princeton University, 1986.
- 'On the Burial Places of the Theodosian Dynasty,' *Byzantion* 61 (1991), 330–9.
- 'Toward a History of Theoderic's Building Programme,' *DOP* 42 (1988), 73–96.
Julian. Letter 47, 'To the Alexandrians,' in *Collected Works*, vol. III, ed. and tr. Wilmer C. Wright, 143–51. London, 1913–23.
Jung, C.G. *Collected Works*, 12: *Psychology and Alchemy*. London, 1932.
Jurlaro, R. 'Un martyrium a Brindisi,' *RAC* 45 (1969), 89–95.
Justin Martyr. *Apolologia prima pro Christianis*, PG 6 (1865), cols. 327–439; tr. Thomas B. Falls, *Writings of Saint Justin Martyr*, 'The First Apology,' *The Fathers of the Church*, 6. Washington, 1948; repr. 1963.
- *The First Apology of St Justin Martyr for the Christians*, in *The Works Now Extant of St Justin the Martyr*, tr. 'E.B.P.' Oxford, 1861.
Kandler, Pietro, ed. *Cenni al forestiero che visita Pola*. Trieste, 1845.
- 'Della basilica di S Maria Formosa in Pola,' *L'Istria* 32 (1847), 128–30; reprinted in *Notizie storiche di Pola*, 171–83. Poreč, 1876.
- Untitled excerpt, *Osservatore Triestino*, n.d., repr. in *Notizie Storiche di Pola*, 232. Poreč, 1876.
- 'S Andrea o scolgio grande di Pola,' *Conservatore*, N.517A (1871); reprinted in *Notizie storiche di Pola*, 187. Poreč, 1876.
Kazhdan, Alexander P., ed. *The Oxford Dictionary of Byzantium*, 3 vols. New York and Oxford, 1991.
Kent, J.P.C., *Roman Coins*. London, 1978.
Kessler, Herbert. 'Through the Temple Veil: The Holy Image in Judaism and Christianity,' in *Studies in Pictorial Narrative*. London, 1994.
Khatchatrian, A. *Les baptistères paléochrétiens*. Paris, 1962.
Kinney, Dale. 'The Apocalypse in Early Christian Monumental Decoration,' in *The Apocalypse in the Middle Ages*, ed. R.K. Emmerson and B. McGinn, 200–16. Ithaca and London, 1992.
- 'Cappella reginae: S Aquilino in Milan,' *Marsyas*, 15 (1970–1), 13–35.
- 'Le chiese paleocristiane di Mediolanum,' *Il millenio ambrosiano. Milano, una capitale da Ambrogio ai carolingi*, ed. C. Bertelli. Milan, 1987.
- 'The Evidence for the Dating of S Lorenzo in Milan,' *JSAH* 31 (1972), 92–107.
- 'A Fresh Look at the "Arian Baptistery" of Milan,' *JSAH* 28 (1969), 214.

Kirsch, G.P. *The Catacombs of Rome.* Rome, 1946.
- 'I santuari domestici di martiri nei titoli romani ed altri simili santuari nelle chiese cristiane e nelle case private di fedeli,' *Atti della Pontificia Accademia Romana di Archeologia,* ser. III, *Rendiconti,* II (1924), 27–43.
Kitzinger, Ernst. *Byzantine Art in the Making. Main Lines of Stylistic Development in Mediterranean Art.* London, 1977.
- 'The Cult of Images in the Age before Iconoclasm,' *DOP* 8 (1954), 83–150.
- 'Some Reflections on Portraiture in Byzantine Art,' in *The Art of Byzantium and the Medieval West,* ed. E. Kleinbauer. Bloomington and London, 1976.
Kleinbauer, W.E. 'Towards a Dating of S Lorenzo in Milan: Masonry and Building Methods of Milanese, Roman and Early Christian Architecture,' *Arte Lombarda* 13 (1968), 1–22.
Kostof, Spiro K. *The Orthodox Baptistery of Ravenna.* New Haven and London, 1965.
Krautheimer, Richard. *Aufsätze zur europäischen Kunstgeschisichte.* Cologne, 1988.
- *Early Christian and Byzantine Architecture,* Pelican History of Art. Harmondsworth, 1965; rev. paperback ed., 1975.
- 'Introduction to an "Iconography of Medieval Architecture,"' repr. in Krautheimer, *Studies in Early Christian, Medieval and Renaissance Art,* 115–50. New York, 1969.
- Review of André Grabar, 'Martryium. Recherches sur le cult des reliques et l'art chrétien antique,' *ArtBull.* 35 (1953), 57–61, repr. in Krautheimer, *Studies in Early Christian, Medieval and Renaissance Art,* 150–9. New York, 1969.
- *Rome: Profile of a City, 312–1308.* Princeton, 1981.
- 'Sancta Maria Rotunda,' in *Arte del primo millennio,* 21–7. Turin, 1950; repr. in Krautheimer, *Studies in Early Christian, Medieval and Renaissance Art,* 107–14. New York, 1969.
- *Three Christian Capitals.* Berkeley and London, 1983.
Krautheimer, R., S. Corbett, and W. Frankl. *Corpus Basilicarum Christianarum Romae, The Early Christian Basilicas of Rome IV–IX Centuries,* 5 vols. Vatican City, 1937–77.
Kühnel, Bianca. 'Jewish Symbolism of the Temple and the Tabernacle and Christian Symbolism of the Holy Sepulchre and the Heavenly Tabernacle,' *Journal of Jewish Art* 12/13 (1986–7), 147–68.
Ladner, Gerhart. 'The So-Called Square Nimbus,' *Medieval Studies* 3 (1941), 15–45; repr. in *Images and Ideas in the Middle Ages. Selected Studies in the History of Art,* 2 vols., 115–66. Rome, 1983.
Lafréry, A. *Speculum romanae magnificentiae.* Rome, 1575.
Lamotte, Odon. Paris, Bibl. nat. Lat 12680.

Lanciani, Rodolfo. *Pagan and Christian Rome*. London, 1892.

– 'Scoperte negli edifici cristiani di Ravenna, 7: 4, Mausoleo di Galla Placidia e chiesa di S Croce,' *BAC* 4 (1866), 74.

Lanzoni, F. *Le Diocesi d'Italia dalle origini al principio del secolo VII*, 2nd ed., 2 vols. Faenza, 1927.

Lassus, Jean. 'Craticula habebat rotas,' *CahArch* 16 (1966), 5–8.

– *Sanctuaires chrétiens de Syrie, Essai sur la genèse, la forme et l'usage des édifices de culte chrétien en Syrie*. Paris, 1947.

Latham, R.E. *Revised Medieval Latin Word-List*. Oxford, 1965.

Lauer, Philippe. 'Les fouilles du Sancta Sanctorum au Latran,' *Mélanges d'Archéologie et d'histoire* (1900), 279–87.

– *Le Palais du Latran*. Paris, 1911.

Lavin, Irving. 'The House of the Lord. Aspects of the Role of Palace Triclinia in the Architecture of Late Antiquity and the Early Middle Ages,' *ArtBull.* 44 (1962), 1–27.

Lawrence, M. *The Sarcophagi of Ravenna*. New York, 1945.

Leclercq, H., and F. Cabrol. *Dictionnaire d'archéologie chrétienne et de liturgie*. Paris, 1907–53.

Lehmann, Karl. 'The Dome of Heaven,' *ArtBull.* 27 (1945), 1–27.

Leo I, the Great. *Sermo* III (alias II), 'De Natali ipsius III,' *PL*, 54, cols. 144–8, tr. C.L. Feltoe, *N&PNF*, 12, 116–18.

– *Sermo* XIII, 'In Natali S.Vincentii Martyris,' *PL*, 54, cols. 501–4.

– *Sermo* LIX (alias LVII), 'De Passione Domini, VIII,' *PL*, 54, cols. 337–42.

Leonardo, C. *Ampelos. Il simbolo della vite nell'arte pagana e paleocristiana*. Rome, 1947.

Lewis, Suzanne. 'The Latin Iconography of the Single-Naved Cruciform Basilica Apostolorum in Milan,' *ArtBull.* 51 (1969), 205–19.

– 'San Lorenzo Revisited: A Theodosian Palace Church at Milan,' *JSAH* 32 (1973), 197–222.

Liber Pontificalis, I, ed. L. Duchesne. Paris, 1886–92.

Lipsmeyer, Elizabeth. 'The Donor and His Church Model in Medieval Art from Early Christian Times to the Late Romanesque Period.' PhD dissertation. Rutgers University, 1981.

Livermore, H.V. *The Origin of Spain and Portugal*. London, 1971.

Llewellyn, Peter. *Rome in the Dark Ages*. New York, 1971.

Loomis, Louise R. *The Book of the Popes (Liber Pontificalis), I: To the Pontificate of Gregory I*. New York, 1916.

Lorenzon, Giovanni. *La basilica dei santi Felice e Fortunato di Vicenza*. Vicenza, 1938.

– 'Il gruppo monumentale dei martiri Felice e Fortunato di Vicenza,' in G.P.

Bognetti, B. Forlati Tamaro, and G. Lorenzon, *Vicenza nell'alto Medio Evo*. Venice, 1959.

Mabillon, D. Johanne. *Museum Italicum*, II: *Antiquos Libros Rituales Sanctae Romanae Ecclesiae*. Paris, 1687.

Mackie, Gillian. 'La Daurade: A Royal Mausoleum,' *CahArch* 42 (1994), 17–34.

– 'The Iconographic Programme at the San Zeno Chapel at S Prassede, Rome,' *PBSR* 57 (1989), 172–99.

– 'The Mausoleum of Galla Placidia: A Possible Occupant,' *Byzantion* 65 (1995), 396–404.

– 'New Light on the So-Called St Lawrence Panel at the Mausoleum of Galla Placidia in Ravenna,' *Gesta* 29 (1990), 54–60.

– 'A New Look at the Patronage of Santa Costanza, Rome,' *Byzantion* 67 (1997), 383–406.

– 'The Santa Croce Drawings: A Re-Examination,' *RACAR* 24 (1997), 1–14.

– 'Symbolism and Purpose in an Early Christian Martyr Chapel: The Case of San Vittore in Ciel d'Oro,' *Gesta* 34 (1995), 91–101.

Maguire, Henry. *Earth and Ocean. The Terrestrial World in Early Byzantine Art*. University Park, PA, and London, 1987.

Maier, Jean-Louis. *Le baptistère de Naples et ses Mosaïques*. Fribourg, 1969.

Mallardo, Domenico. 'La vite negli antichi monumenti cristiani di Napoli e della Campania,' *RAC* 25 (1949), 73–103.

Mallius, Petrus. Vat.Lat. 3627, *Descriptio Basilicae Vaticanae*, in *Codice topografico della città di Roma*, III, *FSI*, 90, ed. R. Valentini and G. Zucchetti, 375–442. Rome, 1946.

Mango, Cyril A. *The Art of the Byzantine Empire, 312–1453: Sources and Documents*. Englewood Cliffs, NJ, 1972.

Mansi, J.D. *Concilium omnium amplissima collectio*, IX. Graz, 1960.

Marasović, J. and T. *Diocletian Palace*. Zagreb, 1970.

Marović, Ivan, 'Reflexions about Year of the Destruction of Salona,' *VAHD* 77 (1984), 293–315.

Martimort, Aimé Georges. 'L'iconographie des catacombes et la catéchèse antique,' *RAC* 25 (1949), 105–14.

Martin, Jacques. *La religion des Gaulois, tirée des plus pures sources de l'antiquité*. Paris, 1727.

Martin, P. *Actes du brigandage d'Ephèse*. Paris, 1874.

Martindale, John Robert. *The Prosopography of the Later Roman Empire*, vol. II: AD 395–527. Cambridge, 1980; and vol. III: AD 527–641. Cambridge, 1992.

Marucchi, O. 'La cella trichora detta di santa Sotere,' *NBAC* 14 (1908), 157–95.

– 'Le recenti scoperte nel duomo di Parenzo,' *NBAC* 2 (1896), 19f.

Marušić, Branko. *Kasnoantička i bizantinska Pula*. Pula, 1967; also published in German as *Das spätantike und bysantinische Pula*. Pula, 1967.

Mathews, Thomas F. *The Clash of the Gods*. Princeton, 1993.

– 'Cracks in Lehmann's "Dome of Heaven,"' *Source* 1 (1982), 2–6.

– *The Early Churches of Constantinople. Architecture and Liturgy*. University Park, PA, 1971.

– 'An Early Roman Chancel Arrangement and Its Liturgical Uses,' *RAC* 38 (1962), 73–95.

– '"Private" Liturgy in Byzantine Architecture: Toward a Re-Appraisal,' *CahArch* 30 (1982), 125–37.

– 'The Transformation Symbolism in Byzantine Architecture and the Meaning of the Pantocrator in the Dome,' in *Church and People in Byzantium: 20th Spring Symposium of Byzantine Studies, Manchester, 1986*, ed. Rosemary Morris. Birmingham, 1990.

Matthews, J.F. 'Olympiodorus of Thebes and the History of the West (AD 407–425),' *Journal of Roman Studies* 60 (1970), 79–97.

– Review of S.I. Oost, *Galla Placidia Augusta, A Biographical Essay* (Chicago, 1968), *Journal of Roman Studies* 60 (1970), 217–18.

Matthews, Jane T. 'The Byzantine Use of the Title Pantocrator,' *Orientalia Christiana Periodica* 44 (1978), 442–62.

Matthiae, G. *Pittura Romana del Medioevo, Secoli IV–X*. Rome, 1987.

Maxfield, Valerie A. *The Military Decorations of the Roman Army*. London, 1981.

Maximinus. *Diatriba ad Opus imperfectum in Matthaeum*, PG, 56, cols. 611–754.

Mazzolani, Lidia S. *Galla Placidia*. Milan, 1975.

Mazzotti, Marco. 'Chiese ravennati scomparse,' *Almanacco Ravennate* (1958), 365f.

– 'Nuovi problemi sul primitivo episcopio Ravennati,' *CorsiCRB* 17 (1970), 293–302.

McCormick, M. *Triumphal Rulership in Late Antiquity, Byzantium and the Early Medieval West*. Cambridge, 1986; also published under the title *Eternal Victory. Triumphal Rulership in Late Antiquity, Byzantium and the Early Medieval West*. Paris, 1986.

McCulloh, J.M.M. 'The Cult of Relics in the Letters and Dialogues of Pope Gregory the Great: A Lexicographical Study,' *Traditio* 32 (1975), 158–84.

– 'From Antiquity to the Middle Ages: Continuity and Change in Papal Relic Policy from the 6th to the 8th Century,' *Pietas Festschrift für Bernhard Kotting*, ed. E. Dassmann and K. Suso Frank, *Jahrbuch für Antike und Christentum*, Ergangzungsband 8 (1980), 312–24.

McVey, Kathleen E. 'The Domed Church as Microcosm; Literary Roots of an Architectural Symbol,' *DOP* 37 (1983), 91–123.

Megaw, A.H.S., and E.J.N. Hawkins. *The Church of the Panagia Kanakaria at Lythrankomi in Cyprus: Its Mosaics and Frescoes, Dumbarton Oaks Studies*, 14. Washington, 1977.

Menis, G.C. *I mosaici cristiani di Aquileia*. Udine, 1965.

Meslin, Michel. *Les Ariens d'Occident, 335–430*. Paris, 1967.

Methuen, Charlotte. 'Widows, Bishops and the Struggle for Authority in the *Didescalia Apostolorum*,' *J.Eccl.Hist.* 46 (1995), 195–213.

Metropolitan Museum of Art. *The Art of Medieval Spain, AD 500–1200*. New York, 1993.

Michelotto, L. 'L'oratorio paleocristiano di Opilione,' *Palladio*, n.s., 4 (1954), 179–84.

Mielsch, Harold. 'Zur stadtrömischen Malerei des 4. Jahrhunderts ...,' *Römische Mitteilungen* 85 (1978), 151–207.

Milenović, R.M. 'Der altchristliche Friedhof Marusinac,' *VAHD* 51 (1930–4), 237f.

Miles, Margaret R. *Image as Insight. Visual Understanding in Western Christianity and Secular Culture*. Boston, 1985.

Miller, Maureen C. 'The Development of the Archiepiscopal Residence in Ravenna, 300–1300,' *FR* 141–4 (1991–2; published 1997), 145–73.

Mirabella Roberti, M. 'Il mausoleo romano di S Vittore a Milano,' *Atti del VI congresso nazionale di archeologia cristiana*,' *Pesaro/Ancona, 1983*, 777–83. Ancona, 1985.

– ed., *Milano. Capitale dell'impero romano, 286–402 d.c.* Milan, 1990.

– *Milano romana*. Milan, 1984.

– 'I musaici di San Canzian d'Isonzo,' *Antichità altoadriatiche* 8 (1975), 235–44.

Moldenke, H.N., and A.L. Moldenke. *Plants of the Bible*. Waltham, MA, 1952; repr. Mineola, NY, 1986.

Monachus, Michael. *Sanctuarium Capuanum*. Naples, 1630.

Montano, G-B. *Scielta de varii Tempietti antichi*. Rome, 1624.

Moran, Neil K. 'The Skeuophylakion of the Hagia Sophia,' *CahArch* 34 (1987), 29–32.

Morassi, Antonio. 'La chiesa di S Maria Formosa o del canneto in Pola,' *Bolletino d'Arte*, ser. II, 4 (1924), 11–25.

Morin, D. Germain. 'Hieronymus de Monogrammate,' *Revue Bénédictine* 2 (1903), 225–36.

Müller-Wiener, Wolfgang. 'Riflessioni sulle charatteristiche dei palazzi episcopali,' *CorsiCRB* 17 (1970), 103–45.

Müntz, E. 'Mosaïques chrétiennes de l'Italie, II: Sainte Constance de Rome,' *RevArch*, n.s., 30 (1875), 224–30.

– 'Mosaïques chrétiennes de l'Italie, V: Sainte Constance de Rome,' *RevArch*, n.s., 35 (1878), 353–67.
– 'Notes sur les mosaïques chrétiennes de l'Italie, IX: Les mosaïques de Siponte, de Capoue, de Verceil, d'Olona, et d'Albenga,' *RevArch*, ser. III, 17 (1891), 70–86.

Nesselrath, A. *Das Fossombroner Skizzenbuch*. London, 1993.

New Oxford Annotated Bible, ed. H.G. May and B.M. Metzger. Oxford, 1973.

Nicolo della Tuccia. *Cronaca de'principali fatti d'Italia dell'anno 1417 al 1468*, ed. Francesco Orioli. Rome, 1852.

Niermeyer, J.F. *Mediae Latinitatis Lexicon Minus*. Leiden, 1976.

Niero, Antonio. 'Santi aquileiesi e veneti in Dalmazia,' *Antichità altoadriatiche* 26 (1985), 261–88.

Nikolajević, Ivanka. 'Images votives de Salone et de Dyrrachium,' *Zbornik Radova Vizantoloskog Instituta* 19 (1980), 59–70.

Nordhagen, P.J. 'Icons Designed for the Display of Sumptuous Votive Gifts,' *DOP* 41 (1987), 453–60.
– 'The Mosaics of John VII, 705–707,' *Acta ad Archaeologiam et Artium Historiam Pertinentia* 2 (1965), 121–66; repr. *Studies in Byzantine and Early Medieval Painting*, 58–104. London, 1990.
– 'Un problema di carattere iconografico e tecnico a S Prassede,' *Roma e l'età Carolingia*, 159f. Rome, 1976.

Oakeshott, W. *The Mosaics of Rome*. Greenwich, CT, 1967.

Olympiodorus. *Fragmenta*, in Photius, *Bibliothèque*, tr. R. Henry. Paris, 1959.

Oost, S.I. *Galla Placidia Augusta, A Biographical Essay*. Chicago, 1968.
– 'Some Problems in the History of Galla Placidia,' *Classical Philology* 60 (1965), 1–10.

Oreb, F. 'Archaeological Excavations in the Eastern Part of Ancient Salona in 1979,' *VAHD* 77 (1984), 25–35.

Orsi, P. 'Chiese byzantine del territorio di Siracusa,' *Byzantinische Zeitschrift* 7 (1898), 1–28.

Osborne, J. 'The Roman Catacombs in the Middle Ages,' *PBSR* 53 (1985), 278–328.

Ottolenghi, L. 'La capella arcivescovile di Ravenna,' *FR* 72 (1956), 9–31.

Oxford Latin Dictionary, 2 vols. Oxford, 1968–76.

Palladius. *Dialogus de Vita S. Ioannis Chrysostomi*, PG, 47, 5–82; tr. H. Moore, *Translations of Christian Literature*, series I, Greek Texts (1921).

Pantoni, Angelo. *Le chiese e gli edifici del monastero di san Vincenzo al Volturno*, Miscellanea Cassinense, 40. Montecassino, 1980.
– *San Vincenzo al Volturno e la cripta dell'abate Epifanio, 824–842*. Montecassino, 1970.

Panvinio, Onofrio. *De sacrosancta Basilica, Baptisterio et Patriarchio Lateranensi,* IV, *De Oratorio S Crucis,* in *Le Palais du Latran,* ed. P. Lauer, 467–8. Paris, 1911.
– *De septem urbis ecclesiis.* Rome, 1570; also appears as *Le sette chiese di Roma.* Rome, 1570.
Pariset, Paola. 'I mosaici del battistero di S Giovanni in Fonte,' *CahArch* 20 (1970), 1–73
Parker, J.H. *The Architecture of Rome,* XI: *Medieval Church and Altar Decorations in Rome and Mosaic Pictures in Chronological Order.* Oxford, 1876.
Passio sanctorum Vitalis, Valeriae, Gervasi, Protasi et Ursicini, in *Bibliotheca Hagiographica Latina.* Brussels, 1901.
Paulinus Diaconus. *Vita Ambrosii, PL,* 14, 10, col. 32; tr. John A. Lacy, 'Life of St Ambrose,' *Early Christian Biographies, A New Translation, The Fathers of the Church,* 15, 33–66. Washington, 1952.
Paulinus of Nola. *Epistolae: PL,* 61, *Epistola* 31, cols. 325–30, and *Epistola* 32, cols. 330–43; tr. P.G. Walsh, *The Letters of Paulinus of Nola, Ancient Christian Writers,* 35. Westminster, MD, and London, 1966.
– *Poemata, Carmen* 27, 'De S Felice natal.,' *PL,* 61, cols. 648–63; also, *Carmina, CSEL,* 30:2 (Vienna, 1894); tr. P.G. Walsh, *The Poems of Paulinus of Nola, Ancient Christian Writers,* 40. New York, 1975.
Pavirani, D.P. *Memorie storiche della vita e governo di Galla Placidia, Madre e tutrice di Valentiniano III.* Ravenna, 1848; repr. 1977.
Peloža, Makso. 'Rekognicija relikvija dalmatinskih i istarskih mučenika, u oratoriju svetog Venancija kod baptisterija Lateranske bazilike u Rimu 1962–1964 godine,' *VAHD* 64 (1962), 163f.
Percival, H.R., tr. *The Seven Ecumenical Councils of the Undivided Church, N&PNF,* 14. Oxford, 1900.
Perer, Maria Luisa Gatti, ed. *La basilica di S Ambrogio: Il tempio in interrotto,* 2 vols. Milan, 1995.
Perrotti, Raffaelle. 'Recenti ritrovamenti presso S Costanza,' *Palladio,* n.s., 6 (1956), 80–3.
Peterson, Erik. 'La croce e la preghiera verso oriente,' *Ephemerides Liturgicae* 59 (1945), 61f.
Pharr, Clyde, ed. *The Theodosian Code.* Princeton, 1952.
Photius. *Bibliothèque,* ed. and tr. R. Henry. Paris, 1959.
Picard, Jean-Charles. *Le souvenir des évêques: Sépultures, listes épiscopales et culte des évêques en Italie du Nord dès origines au Xe siècle.* Rome, 1988.
– 'Les rites du baptême d'après les textes,' in *Actes du XIe congrès d'archéologie chrétienne,* 1451–74. Vatican City, 1989.
Porta, Paola. 'Due sarcophagi nel tempo' in *7 colonne e 7 chiese. La vicenda ultramillenaria del complesso di santo Stefano,* 88–99. Bologna, 1986.
Prelog, M. *The Basilica of Euphrasius in Poreč.* Zagreb, 1986.

Previtali, Attilio. 'La basilica dei santi Felice e Fortunato in Vicenza,' in AAVV, *La basilica dei santi Felice e Fortunato in Vicenza*, 2 vols., 69–116. Vicenza, 1979–80.

– *San Felice: Una dimora dello spirito*. Vicenza, 1988.

Procopius of Caesarea. *Buildings*, 7 vols., tr. H.B. Ewing. Cambridge, MA, 1953–61.

Prosper Tironis. *Epitoma chronicon*, ed. T. Mommsen, *MGH, AA*, 9, 339–499. Berlin, 1892; Reichenau additions, *Chronica minora*, saec. IV, V, VI, VII, 489.

Prudentius. *Opera, II: Peristephanon Liber, II: Hymnus in honorem passionis Laurentii beatissimi martyris; V: Passio Sancti Vincenti Martyris; XI: Ad Valeriam Episcopum de Passione Hippolyti Beatissimae Martyris;* and *XII: Passio apostolorum Petri et Pauli*. tr. H.J. Thomson. London and Cambridge, MA, 1961.

Pseudo-Ambrose. *Epistola* III, alias LIV, and *Epistola* II, alias LIII, *PL*, 17, cols. 747–9 and 744.

Pseudo-Fulgence. *Sermo LX, PL* 65, col. 931.

Quasten, Johannes. *Patrology*, vols. I–III (Utrecht, 1950–60); vol. IV, ed. A. di Berardino. Westminster, MD, 1986.

Raby, F.J.E. *A History of Christian Latin Poetry from the Beginnings to the Close of the Middle Ages*, 2nd ed. Oxford, 1953.

Rampolla del Tindaro, M., ed. with commentary. *S.Melania giuniore, senatrice romana*. Rome, 1905.

Rasponi, Cesare. *De basilica et patriarchio Lateranensi*. Rome, 1656.

Ratti, A. 'Il più antico ritratto di S Ambrogio,' *Ambrosiana; scritti varii pubblicati nel XV centenario dalla morte di S Ambrogio*, 1–74. Milan, 1897.

Raynaldus (Rinaldi di Concuretio). *Tractatus, RIS*, I/2, ed. L.A. Muratori, 573ff. Milan, 1725.

Recio-Vegazones, A. 'Una posibile escena musiva paleocristiana vista por Bosio en el mausoleo de Sta. Helena,' *RAC* 53 (1977), 137–53.

Reggiori, Ferdinando. *La Basilica Ambrosiana. Ricerche e restauri, 1929–1940*. Milan, 1941.

Rhomiopoulou, K., A. Herrmann, and C. Vermeule. *The Search for Alexander, an Exhibition*. New York, 1980.

Ricci, Corrado, 'La cappella detta Sancta Sanctorum nella chiesa di S Vitale in Ravenna,' *Rassegna d'Arte* 4 (1904), 104–8.

– *Il mausoleo di Galla Placidia in Ravenna*. Rome, 1914.

– *Monumenti. Tavole storiche dei mosaici di Ravenna, V: Cappella Arcivescovile*. Rome, 1934.

– 'Il vivaio dell'arcivescovado di Ravenna,' *Bolletino d'arte* 13 (1919) 33–6.

Riccobaldo. *Pomarium Ravennatis Ecclesiae, RIS*, 9. Milan, 1726.

Rizza, G. 'Pitture e mosaichi nelle basiliche paoliniane di Nola e di Fondi,' *Siculorum Gymnasium* 1 (1948), 311–21.

Rizzardi, C. 'Note sull'antico episcopio di Ravenna: Formazione e sviluppo,' *Actes du XIe congrès international d'archéologie chrétienne*, I, 711–32. Rome, 1989.

Rizzardi, C., ed. *Il mausoleo di Galla Placidia a Ravenna*. Modena, 1966.

Rohault de Fleury, Georges. *Le Latran au Moyen Age*. Paris, 1877.

Romano, Marco. 'Materiali di spoglio nel battistero di San Giovanni in Laterano, un riesame e nuove considerazione,' *Bolletino d'Arte* 77 (1991), 31–70.

Rossi, Girolamo (Hieronymus Rubeus). *Historia Ravennatis libri decem*. Venice, 1689.

Rubeus, Hieronymus. *See* Rossi, Girolamo.

Ruffolo, Salvatore. 'Le struttore murarie degli edifici paleocristiani milanesi,' *Rivista dell'istituto nazionale d'archeologia e storia dell'arte*, n.s., 17 (1970), 5–85.

Ruinart, D. Thierri. *Acta Sincera*. 1711.

Salmi, M. 'Un problema storico-artistico medievale,' *Bolletino d'arte del ministero della PI* III (1958), 213–31.

Santa Maria Scrinari, V. 'Contributo all'urbanistica tardo-antica sul campo Laterano,' *Actes du XIe Congrès international d'archéologie chrétienne*, 3, 2201–20. Rome, 1989.

– *Il Laterano imperiale*, II: *Dagli 'Horti Domitiae' alla capella cristiana*. Vatican City, 1995.

Savio, Fedele. 'De alcune chiese di Milano anteriori a S Ambrogio,' *NBAC* 2 (1896), 169–72.

– 'Il culto di S.Vittore a Ravenna,' *NBAC* 7 (1901), 189f.

– 'Due lettere falsamente attribuite a S Ambrogio,' *NBAC* 3 (1897), 153–78.

– *Gli antichi vescovi d'Italia dalle origini al 1300*, I: *Milano*. Florence, 1913.

Saxer, Victor. *Les rites de l'initiation chrétienne du IIe au VIe siècle*. Spoleto, 1988.

– 'Victor, titre d'honneur ou nom propre?' *RAC* 44 (1968), 209–18

Schedel, Hartmann. *Das Buch der Chroniken (Nuremberg Chronicle)*. Nuremberg, 1493.

Schlunk, Helmut. 'Unterschungen im frühchristlichen Mausoleum von Centcelles,' *Neue deutsche Ausgrabungen im Mittelmeergegiet und im Vorderen Orient*, 344–65. Berlin, 1959.

Schlunk, H., and Hauschild, T. 'Der Denkmäler der frühchristlichen und westgotischen Zeit,' *Hispania Antiqua* 4 (1978).

Schumacher, Walter N. 'Das Baptisterium von Alt-St Peter und seine Probleme,' *Studien zur spätantiken und byzantinischen Kunst Friedrich Wilhelm Deichmann gewidmet*, ed. Otto Feld und Urs Peschlow, 3 vols., vol. I, 215–33. Bonn, 1986.

Schuster, I. *Sant'Ambrogio e le più antiche basiliche milanese. Note de archeologia cristiana*. Milan, 1940.

Scrinzi, Alessandro. 'Di un tempietto bizantino del VI secolo a Padova,' *L'Arte* 29 (1926), 75–84.

Semenzato, C. *Padua: Art and History*. Padua, n.d.

Seroux d'Agincourt, G.B.L.G. *Storia dell'Arte*, II. Milan, 1825.

Seston, W. 'Le Jugement Dernier au Mausolée de Galla Placidia,' *CahArch* 1 (1945), 37–50.

Sicard, Damien. *La liturgie de la mort dans l'église latine dès origines à la réforme carolingienne*. Munster, 1978.

Sieger, Jo Anne. '"Pictor Ignotus": The Early Christian Pictorial Theme of Christ and the Church and Its Roots in Patristic Exegesis of Scripture.' PhD dissertation. University of Pittsburgh, 1980.

Siena, Silvia Lusuardi. 'Committenza laica ed ecclesiastica in Italia setten-trionale nel regno goto,' *Settimane di studio del centro italiano di studi sull'alto medioevo* 39, 199–242. Spoleto, 1992.

– Il mausoleo imperiale,' cat. 2a19, in *Milano Capitale*, ed. M. Mirabella Roberti, 114–15. Milan, 1990.

Silloge epigraphica itinerario descrizione della mura di Roma del cod. Einsiedlense, Codice topografico della città di Roma, II, ed. R. Valentini and G. Zucchetti, *FSI*, 88, 163–207. Rome, 1940; repr. 1997.

Simioni, Attilio *Storia di Padova*. Padua, 1968.

Simson, Otto von. *Sacred Fortress*. Chicago, 1948.

Sinclair, Archer. 'God's House of Peace in Paradise: The Feast of Tabernacles on a Jewish Gold Glass,' *Journal of Jewish Art* 11 (1984), 6–15.

Smith, James. 'The Garments that Honour the Cross in the "Dream of the Rood,"' *Anglo-Saxon England* 4 (1975), 29–37.

Smith, Janet Charlotte. 'Form and Function of the Side Chambers of Fifth- and Sixth-Century Churches in Ravenna,' *JSAH* 49 (1990), 181–204.

– 'The Side-Chambers of San Giovanni Evangelista in Ravenna: Church Libraries of the Fifth Century,' *Gesta* 29 (1990), 86–97.

Socrates Scholasticus. *Historia ecclesiastica*, PG, 67, 29–842; tr. A.C. Zenos, *N&PNF*, 2, 1–178. Oxford, 1891.

Šonje, Ante. 'La chiesa paleocristiana nella insenatura marina di Šepen presso Castelmuschio (Omišalj) sull'isola di Veglia (Krk),' 1, FR 111 (1976), 137f.

Souter, A. *Glossary of Later Latin to 600 AD*. Oxford, 1949.

Sozomenus, Salaminius Hermias. *Historia ecclesiastica*, PG, 67, cols. 843–1630; tr. C.D. Hartranft, *N&PNF*, 2, 179–427. Oxford, 1891.

Stanley, David. 'The Apse Mosaics at Santa Costanza. Observations on Resto-rations and Antique Mosaics,' *Mitteilungen des deutschen archäeologischen Instituts, Roemische Abteilung* 94 (1987), 29–42.

– 'An Excavation at Santa Costanza,' *Arte Medievale* 7 (1993), 103–12.

- 'New Discoveries at Santa Costanza,' *DOP* 48 (1994), 257–63.

Steingräber, Stephan, *Catalogo ragionato della pittura etrusca*. Milan, 1985.

Stern, Henri. 'Les mosaïques de l'église de S Constance à Rome,' *DOP* 12 (1958), 157–219.

Stevenson, E. (Henri). 'Découverte de la basilique double de Ste Symphorose et de ses sept fils au neuvième mille de la voie tiburtine,' *BAC*, ser. III, 3 (1878), 80–7.

Stričević, Djordje. 'Djakonikon i protezie u ranohrišćanskim crkvama,' *Starinar*, ser. 4, 9 (1958), 59–66.

Striker, Cecil L., and Y. Dogan Kuban. *Kalenderhane in Istanbul. The Buildings, Their History, Architecture and Decoration*. Mainz, 1997.

Sulzberger, Max. 'Le symbole de la croix et les monogrammes de Jésus chez les premiers chrétiens,' *Byzantion* 2 (1925), 337–448.

Sunding Larson, Staale. 'Some Functional and Iconographical Aspects of the Centralised Church in the Italian Renaissance,' *Acta R.Norv.* 2 (1965), 203–53.

Surace, A. 'Milano, Basilica di S Ambrogio, Cappella di San Vittore in Ciel d'Oro. Restauro dei mosaici,' in *Notiziario*, Soprintendenza Archaeologica della Lombardia (1988–9), 322–3.

Taft, Robert F. 'The Great Entrance, A History of the Transfer of Gifts and Other Preanaphoral Rites of the Liturgy of St John Chrysostom,' *Orientalia Christiana Analecta*, 200. Rome, 1975.

Tavano, S. 'Le cattedre di Grado e le culture artistiche del Mediterraneo orientale,' *Antichità Altoadriatiche* 12 (1977), 445–89.

- 'Mosaici parietali in Istria,' *Antichità adriatiche* 8 (1975), 245–52.

Terry, Ann. 'Early Christian Cruciform Annexe Chapels in Northern Italy: A Family of Martyria-Mausolea.' Master's thesis. University of Illinois, 1979.

- 'The Sculpture at the Cathedral of Eufrasius in Poreč,' *DOP* 42 (1988), 13–64.

Tertullian. *Adversus Marcionem*, PL, 2, cols. 263–549, ed. and tr. Ernest Evans. Oxford, 1972.

- *De Fuga in persecutione*, PL, 2, cols. 123–42; tr. Edwin A. Quain, *Flight in Time of Persecution*, in *Tertullian. Disciplinary, Moral and Ascetical Works*, The Fathers of the Church, 40, 271–310. New York, 1959.

- *Liber de Corona*, PL, 2, cols. 93–122; tr. Edwin A. Quain, *The Chaplet*, in *Tertullian. Disciplinary, Moral and Ascetical Works*, The Fathers of the Church, 40, 225–70. New York, 1959.

Testini, Pasquale. 'Cimitile: L'antichità cristiana,' in *L'art dans l'Italie méridionale*, 4, 163–76. Rome, 1978.

- 'I due mausolei rotondi del vecchio S Pietro,' *RAC* 64 (1988), 287–315.

- 'L'oratorio scoperto al "Monte della Giustizia" presso la Porta Viminale a Roma,' *RAC* 44 (1968), 219–60.

- 'Osservazioni sull'iconografia del Cristo in trono fra gli apostoli,' *Rivista dell'istituto nazionale d'archeologia e storia dell'arte*, 20, n.s., 11 (1963), 230–301.

Testi-Rasponi, Alessandro. 'Note Agnelliane,' *FR* 18 (1915), 773–89.

Thierry, Nicole. 'Une mosaïque à Dyrrachium,' *CahArch* 18 (1968), 227–9.

Thomassin, L. *Ancienne et nouvelle discipline de l'église touchant les bénéfices et les bénéficiens*. Paris, 1725.

Thompson, E.A. 'The Conversion of the Spanish Suevi to Catholicism,' in *Visigothic Spain: New Approaches*, ed. Edward James. Oxford, 1980.

- *Romans and Barbarians. The Decline of the Western Empire*. Madison, 1982.
- 'The Visigoths from Fritigern to Euric,' *Historia* 12 (1963), 105–26.

Toesca, P. *Storia dell'arte italiana*, I: *Il medioevo*. Turin, 1927, repr. 1965.

Tolotti, Francesco. 'Le basiliche cimiteriali con deambulatorio del suburbio romano: Questione ancora aperta,' *Römische Mitteilungen* 89 (1982), 153–211.

- 'I due mausolei rotondi del vecchio S Pietro,' *RAC* 64 (1988), 287–315

Tomai, Tomasso. *Historia di Ravenna*. Ravenna, 1580.

Tonini, Luigi. 'La chiesa di S Andrea presso Rimini,' *Atti e memorie della R. Dep. Di Storia Patria per le provincie di Romagna* (1863), 76f.

Tonzig, Maria. *La basilica romanico-gotica di Santa Giustina in Padova*. Padua, 1932.

Toynbee, J.M.C. *Death and Burial in the Roman World*. London, 1971.

Traversi, Gino. *Architettura paleocristiana milanese*. Milan, 1964.

Treadgold, Warren T. *The Nature of the Bibliotheca of Photius, Dumbarton Oaks Studies*, 18. Washington, 1980.

Trinci Cecchelli, M.M. 'I mosaici di S Maria della Croce a Casaranello,' *Puglia paleocristiana*, III, 413–48. Bari, 1979.

Tronzo, William. 'Setting and Structure in Two Roman Wall Decorations of the Early Middle Ages,' *DOP* 41 (1987), 477–92.

- *The Via Latina Catacomb. Imitation and Discontinuity in Fourth Century Roman Painting*. University Park, PA, 1986.

Ugonio, Pompeio. – *Historia delle stationi di Roma*. Rome, 1588.

- *Theatrum Urbis Romae*, Bibl.Vat.ms.Barb.Lat. 1994, and Ferrara, Biblioteca Comunale Ariostea, MS 161 NC6 fol. 1103–10.

Uljčić, Željko. 'Pola paleocristiana alla luce del castato austriaco,' in *Acta XIII congressus internationalis archaeologiae christiana*, 3 vols., III, 743–60. Vatican City and Split, 1998.

Uranius. *Epistola* 'ad Pacatum,' *PL*, 53, cols. 859–66.

Valeva, Julia. 'La tombe aux archanges de Sofia,' *CahArch* 34 (1986), 5–28.

Van Berchem, M., and E. Clouzot. *Mosaïques chrétiennes*. Geneva, 1924.

Van der Meer, F. *Maiestas Domini*. Vatican City, 1938.

Van der Meer, F., and C. Mohrmann. *Atlas of the Early Christian World*, tr. M. Hedlund and H.H. Rowley. London, 1959.

van Dijk, A. 'Domus Sanctae Dei Genetricis: Art and Liturgy in the Oratory of Pope John VII, 705–707,' *Byzantine Studies Conference Abstracts* 21 (1995), 76.
– 'The Oratory of Pope John VII (705–707) in Old St Peter's.' PhD dissertation. Johns Hopkins University, 1997.
Velmans, Tania. 'L'image de la Déisis dans les églises de Géorgie et dans le reste du monde byzantin,' *CahArch* 31 (1983), 129f.
Venantius Fortunatus. *Carmina*, 8/3, *PL*, 88, *Miscellanea*, lib. VIII, cap. VI, cols 266–76.
– *Vita S Martini*, II, *MGH, AA*, IV, I; *PL*, 88, cols. 363–426.
VerKerk, D.H. 'Exodus and Easter Vigil in the Ashburnham Pentateuch,' *ArtBull*. 77 (1995), 94–105.
Verzone, Paolo. *L'architettura religiosa dell'alto medioevo nell'Italia settentrionale*. Milan, 1942.
– 'Il palazzo arcivescovile e l'oratorio di S Andrea di Ravenna,' *CorsiCRB* 13 (1966), 445–54.
– 'Ipotesi di topografia ravennate,' *CorsiCRB* 13 (1966), 433–44.
Victorinus. 'Commentarius in Apocalypsim,' *Victorini Episcopi Petavionensis Opera*, ed. J. Haussleiter, *CSEL*, 49. Vienna, 1926.
Vidulli Torlo, Marzia. 'Analisi spaziale della basilica di Santa Maria Formosa in Pola,' *Atti e memorie della società istriana di archeologia e storia patria*, n.s., 36, 4–21. Trieste, 1988.
– 'Valori spaziali proporzianali della basilica eufrasiana di Parenzo' in *Quaderno Giuliani di Storia* 1 (1985), 56f.
Vopel, Hermann. *Die altchristlichen Goldgläser*. Freiburg, 1899.
Waetzoldt, S. *Die Kopien des 17 Jahrhunderts nach Mosaiken und Wandmalereien in Rom*. Munich, 1964.
Ward-Perkins, Bryan. *From Classical Antiquity to the Middle Ages. Urban Public Building in Northern and Central Italy. AD 300–850*. Oxford, 1984.
Wharton, A.J. 'Ritual and Reconstructed Meaning: The Neonian Baptistery in Ravenna,' *ArtBull*. 69 (1987), 358–76.
Wickhoff, F. 'Das Apsismosaik in der Basilika des hl. Felix zu Nola,' *Römische Quartalschrift* 3 (1889), 158–76.
Wilkes, J.J. *Dalmatia*. London, 1969.
– *Diocletian's Palace, Split. Residence of a Retired Roman Emperor*. Sheffield, 1986; repr. 1993.
Wilpert, Joseph. 'Un battistero "Ad nymphas B.Petri,"' *Rend Pont. Acc. Rom. di Arch*. 2 (1923–4).
– 'La decorazione constantiniana della basilica lateranense,' *RAC* 6 (1929), 42–127.
– 'La nuova abside lateranense,' *Voce della Verità*, 1. 1886.

– *Die römischen Mosaiken und Malereien der kirchlichen Bauten vom IX–XIII Jahrhundert.* Freiburg, 1917.

– *I sarcofagi cristiani antichi.* Rome, 1929.

Wilpert, Joseph, and W.N. Schumacher. *Die römischen Mosaiken der kirchlichen Bauten vom IV–XIII Jahrhundert.* Freiburg, Basel & Vienna, 1976.

Woodruff, Helen. 'The Iconography and Date of the Mosaics of La Daurade,' *ArtBull.* 13 (1931), 80–107.

Zander, Giuseppe. 'Cenni sullo studio dell'architettura di Roma antica nella sua evoluzione nel Cinquecento,' in Marcello Fagiolo, *Roma e l'antico nell'arte e nella cultura del Cinquecento.* Rome, 1985.

Zeno of Verona. *Tractatus, PL* 2, XXVIII, 'In Isaiam VII,' cols. 471–2.

Zovatto, P.L. *Grado, antichi monumenti.* Bologna, 1971.

– L'oratorio paleocristiano di S Giustina a Padova,' in *La Basilica di Santa Giustina. Arte e storia,* 18–63. Castelfranco Veneto, 1970.

– 'La pergula paleocristiana del sacello di S. Prosdocimo di Padova e il ritratto del santo titolare,' *RAC* 34 (1958), 137–67.

– 'La prothesis ed il diaconicon della basilica di Santa Maria di Grado,' *Aquileia Nostra* 22 (1951), 74–95.

– 'Il sacello paleocristiano delle SS Tosca e Teuteria a Verona,' *FR* 33 (1961), 133–42.

– 'La trichora paleocristiana nel nuovo complesso monumentale di Concordia,' *FR* 36 (1962), 74–95.

Index